Goebbels and
National Socialist Propaganda
1925–1945

Goebbels and National Socialist Propaganda

1925-1945

by

Ernest K. Bramsted

MICHIGAN STATE UNIVERSITY PRESS

1965

★ ★
★
★ ★
★
★

To Dr. Margaret Lambert

in appreciation and friendship

"Indeed, to track down legend and to show up myth is the function that the professional historian today will look upon as his special contribution to society; a contribution making for sanity, for clarity of vision, for a heightened sense of individuality, for balance and moderation of judgment."

Pieter Geyl

"Historical truth may be discovered by professors of history later; we are serving historical necessity."

Dr. Goebbels at a mass meeting in Berlin, 5 December 1942.

Foreword

The aim of this book is to place the development of National Socialist propaganda and the role of Joseph Goebbels as its chief protagonist in a clearer and better proportioned perspective than has hitherto been possible. During the Second World War and immediately after it the opponents of Germany were probably inclined to underestimate the significance of the National Socialist propaganda system and the part it played in securing and maintaining the rule of the Third Reich. Recently, as more facts on the life and the deeds of Goebbels have come to light, the pendulum has swung to the other extreme. There is now a tendency to romanticise the man whom Robert Coulondre, the French Ambassador in Berlin, once called "ce petit diable boiteux," to concentrate on his personal traits and appetites, to exaggerate his importance as a policy-maker or to highlight his dramatic exit from the world stage as "a Roman death."

Although the astonishingly versatile talents of Goebbels, his tactical skill, his drive and efficiency and—though this is difficult to gauge—the impact of his efforts on the German people have to be fully recognized, there is little evidence to show that during the years of National Socialist control this indefatigable herald of the Führer had any substantial influence on Hitler's major political decisions. Goebbels' historical significance lies in his extraordinary fertility as a propagandist and political showman and in the commanding position which enabled him to display it to the full within a totalitarian system. It seems neither sufficient to "explain" the role of German propaganda by reference to the personal idiosyncrasies of the man who conducted it nor to interpret it as a mere by-product of the Führer State.

To understand the work and the functions of the "Reich Ministry of People's Enlightenment and Propaganda" during the twelve years of its existence one must not only comprehend the character and mentality of its Minister but also consider the concentration and handling of the modern mass media, the press, the radio, the cinema, the mammoth mass meeting, in a totalitarian state. The relationship between the insatiable drive for power of the National Socialists and their ideology has also to be kept in mind.

This book does not attempt to offer a biography of Joseph Goebbels or to cover all the aspects of the propaganda octopus he built up over the years. Instead I have endeavoured to throw new light on the development of the themes and the machinery of National Socialist propaganda, to analyse characteristic attitudes and methods employed by Goebbels and his subordinates in the changing circumstances of two decades and to examine the objectives and targets of their propaganda, sometimes publicly stated but often deliberately camouflaged.

The difficulty with a topic like this lies in the combination of the historical and the analytical approaches. Three out of the five parts of this book (I, II and IV) consider the development and the functions of Nazi propaganda in the days of opposition, during the pre-war years of the Third Reich and during the Second World War. Two further parts (III and V) concern themselves with an analysis of some significant overall aspects and strands in the fabric of that propaganda. Although the close connections between German propaganda and Nazi foreign policy has not been overlooked, an account of the content of propaganda directed to specific countries has been omitted. It is hoped to examine this aspect and also the question of the impact of Nazi propaganda on the German people in another context. However it has been possible to include two chapters tracing correlations between Nazi propaganda and one foreign country, Great Britain. National Socialist images and stereotypes of England and the English during the war have been examined in Chapter 17, while the counterattack of the B.B.C. propaganda broadcasts in German has been discussed in Chapter 13. Alas, not being a Government historian the present writer has not had access to directives issued during the war by PWE and the B.B.C. to the script writers of those broadcasts. These are still regarded in England as State secrets, *arcana imperii,* only to be released at an unknown distant date. Fortunately there exist sound reasons for thinking that the analysis of the scripts themselves can yield a good deal of information to the experienced eye.

Special attention has been paid to the press as a medium of propaganda and to the position of the journalists under the tutelage of the Propaganda Ministry. This is partly due to the fact that during a year of sabbatical leave spent in Europe in 1958 the author had the good fortune to be able to draw on some important and so far untapped collections of press directives of the Propaganda Ministry and on reports by journalists on its daily conferences for representatives of the home press. These are the Brammer collection (1933–1936), the Sänger collection (1936–1943), both of which are now with the Bundesarchiv in Koblenz, and the Oberheitmann collection (1939–1945) at the Institut für Publizistik of the University of Münster. I am greatly indebted to the staffs of these institutes for their kindness, and particularly to Oberarchivrat Dr. W. Mommsen in Koblenz and Professor W. Hagemann in Münster for putting these papers at my disposal. I also profited from the discussion of certain aspects of Goebbels' activities with Herr Werner Stephan, for many years a senior member of the staff of the Propaganda Ministry, and with Herr B. Reifenberg, a former editor of the *Frankfurter Zeitung.*

Use has been made of the text of the handwritten Goebbels' diaries for 1925–26 and of those for 1942–43 which are typewritten. The photocopies of these diaries drawn upon are those in the possession of the

Institut für Zeitgeschichte in Munich.[1] Only a fraction of the diaries has been published by Louis Lochner in his edition of 1949. Fragmentary as the war-time diaries are, they reveal much of the actual propaganda themes and techniques of the period and of Goebbels' daily routine and manner of working. It would be naive indeed to take them at their face value and to overlook the fact that Goebbels dictated his daily entries with a view to enhancing his reputation with posterity. Yet, after checking the text carefully, I am inclined to agree with the view expressed by an American political scientist that "the manuscript more or less faithfully reflects Goebbels' propaganda strategy and tactics" and that it can safely be regarded as "a convenient guide to his bulky propaganda materials."[2]

I should like to acknowledge my debt to the following institutes and libraries for making relevant material available to me: The Institut für Zeitgeschichte in Munich, the Foreign Office Library, the Wiener Library (Dr. A. Wiener, Mrs. I. Wolff) and the German Service of the British Broadcasting Corporation (the late Mr. Lindley Fraser and Mr. A. Earley) in London and the Netherlands State Institute for War Documentation (Dr. L. de Jong) in Amsterdam.

My thanks are also due to the Research Committee of the University of Sydney for several grants and for providing me with research assistance in 1956 and in 1959. I am grateful to Miss Elisabeth Wilson in London who helped in collecting material at an early stage of the work and to Mrs. Helga Tukk who devoted much time and energy to the revision of the manuscript.

While writing the book I have received constant encouragement from Dr. Margaret Lambert. My sincere thanks are due to her and to my colleagues, Professor R. N. Spann, Professor J. M. Ward, and Dr. L. McLashen, who read the manuscript and offered much useful criticism. I am also indebted to Sir John Wheeler-Bennett, for his very helpful comments on the text and for the kind and sustained interest he has taken in its publication. Last, but not least, the book owes much to my wife, as without her patience and generous assistance it could never have been completed. For all possible omissions and shortcomings I alone am responsible.

The manuscript was concluded early in 1962. It has therefore only been possible in a few cases to refer to material published since then.

Finally, I must beg the indulgence of my American readers, who will discover that the British rather than the American edition of secondary

1. The Munich Institute has since published an edition of the earlier of those diaries: *Das Tagebuch von Joseph Goebbels* 1925/26, ed. H. H. Heiber, Stuttgart, 1960. An English translation in *The Journal of Joseph Goebbels from 1925–1926* appeared in London in 1962.
2. Leonard W. Doob "Goebbels' Principles of Propaganda" in *Public Opinion and Propaganda*, edited by D. Katz, D. Cartwright, S. Eldersveld and A. McClunglee, New York 1954, p. 509.

works has been cited. The reason is that the book was written in Sydney and London and I did not anticipate its being published first in America. In this context I would like to acknowledge the valuable cooperation I received from Dr. Lyle Blair, the Director of the Michigan State University Press.

E. K. B.

University of Sydney,
Australia.

Contents

INTRODUCTION:

From Northcliffe To Hitler

1. NORTHCLIFFE HANDLES A NEW WEAPON

"There is little exaggeration in saying that the World War led to the discovery of propaganda by both the man in the street and the man in the study."

H. D. Lasswell in 1938.

A SUCCESSFUL twentieth century propagandist has to possess two different sets of qualities: he must have an intuitive grasp of the feelings and thoughts of the masses and must be able to convey messages to them which hold their attention and combine simplicity with attractiveness.

Only in this century has the professional propagandist become a specific type, a type different from the politician or the administrator. One could say that leading propagandists have earned their spurs in mass or popular rather than in refined or highbrow journalism; also they have not emerged from the old ruling class or bureaucracy but rather from more anonymous strata. Either the propagandist is a self-made man or he has made his way through his connection with a mass party. An expert in a new sense, he is a manipulator of words cum organizer, a man who thinks not in terms of individuals but of collectives such as the public, the movement, the Party. He is active, dynamic, aggressive rather than contemplative, objective and matter of fact.

Alfred Harmsworth in England and Joseph Goebbels in Germany can be regarded as leading figures of this type. There were, of course, great differences in their personalities and careers. Northcliffe's success was commercial rather than political, he was throughout a self-made man, whilst, in spite of the brilliance of his talents, Goebbels rose only with and through the Party. He owed much to the Führer to whose star he had hitched his wagon at an early date. Northcliffe owed little to others and least of all to politicians. But in different types of society both Northcliffe and Goebbels were unorthodox masters of mass appeal and mass manipulation. Their approach was intuitive rather than analytical, though Goebbels was much superior to Northcliffe in the art of argumentation. Both had their ears to the ground, to both the end justified the means, and the necessity of appealing constantly to the masses made them concentrate on tricks and stunts. Graphic and vivid in their writings, they were nationalists in outlook and full of contempt for their enemies. Living before the radio age and a poor orator, Northcliffe's strength lay exclusively in the written appeal; Goebbels excelled both as an orator and as a journalist.

While Goebbels was to be a political propagandist for twenty years, Northcliffe was one only during the first world war. Owning, as he then did, half of the London Press (including *The Times*), he had become a power and an influence which no politician could afford with safety to ignore. Though not by temperament of the breed of politicians—to quote Lord Beaverbrook—"he never attempted to understand them or to cultivate relations with them" [1]—he became during the war a maker and unmaker of Ministers, and a big factor in the replacement of Asquith by Lloyd George as Prime Minister. It was only in the fourth year of the War that Lord Northcliffe agreed to become Director of Propaganda to Enemy Countries, when Lord Beaverbrook was made Minister of Information in February 1918. This post, which gave him direct access to the Prime Minister, he held to the end of the war in November of that year.

Early in the war Northcliffe had realized that morale mattered a great deal and that warfare could not be confined to the military sphere. He had seen with misgivings that Germany was ahead in the field of home propaganda. "It is ourselves we have got to defend," he wrote in a letter to Asquith as early as November 1914. He wanted Ministers to stimulate the interest of the public in the war. "I find that whereas there is in Germany immense enthusiasm for the war, there exists in many parts of this country apathy, ignorance or ridiculous optimism, more especially in the provinces." [2]

He contrasted the position in Germany and in England. The German public were supplied with the work of photographers, artists, cinematograph operators and war correspondents, whereas the English people were offered "nothing but the casualty lists and the mutilated scraps with which it is quite impossible to arouse the interest or follow the war intelligently. The public cannot be roused by present methods." [3]

Northcliffe's instinct for propaganda, at play before he was given an official post in this field, can be traced in the impressions of neutral countries such as Switzerland and Spain which he gives in his book. Ardent partisan that he was, he deplored "the depressing air of neutrality" and criticized the weakness of British propaganda in Switzerland. He drew attention to the strong pro-German sympathies of the German-speaking Swiss and to the army of anti-Allied propagandists in Spain. He was by then well aware of the necessity for an energetic projection of the British and Allied point of view all over the globe. In August 1916 in a letter to General Charteris, of Haig's staff, Northcliffe urged that efforts should be made "to produce by propaganda a state of mind in the German army favourable to surrender." He believed that "this bombardment of

[1] Lord Beaverbrook, *Men and Power, 1917-1918,* London, 1956, p. 62.
[2] H.H. Fyfe, *Northcliffe, An Intimate Biography,* London, 1930, p. 205.
[3] H.H. Fyfe, op. cit., p. 174ff.

the German mind is almost as important as the bombardment effected by guns." [1]

One of the reasons for the relative success of the propaganda to enemy countries directed by Northcliffe from Crewe House in London was the composition of its personnel and its unbureaucratic character. Even a later German historian, sharply critical of Crewe House methods, regarded it as an advantage that the English were "neither systematizers nor bureaucrats." [2] It was indeed an advantage that, in contrast to the position in Germany, in England the execution of propaganda was not so much entrusted to professional civil servants as to writers, journalists and men experienced in politics. It was the strength of Northcliffe that he managed to gather a first-rate team of experts and journalists about him. In many ways ignorant of European conditions, he was quick and shrewd in deciding on a strategy for a country once he had consulted the experts. He directed a pragmatic band, an improvised outfit, in which different talents supplemented each other. [3]

It was only in the early days of 1918 that "political warfare," later to be renamed "psychological warfare," was born. Only then was it realized that propaganda to enemy troops and civilians would need a psychology superior to the one so far applied in the clumsy attempts to address an enemy public. Until then propaganda efforts reflected more the mentality of their English or French authors than that of their intended audience. Now the aim was to give them a truly native ring. In addition to right timing Northcliffe believed in the time-honoured combination of the stick and the carrot. Both the enemy's hopes and his fears should be raised.

Northcliffe was realistically aware of the auxiliary function of propaganda. He knew that it was only likely to bear fruit after military defeat had prepared the ground. Only when such defeat spread depression and despondency would there be a real chance to drive a wedge between the enemy's government and the masses. Only then would it be possible to appeal to the man in the street in Germany to overthrow the Hohenzollern regime and thus to put an end to the senseless slaughter.

Propaganda of fear could become effective at a moment when American troops were pouring into Western Europe. Northcliffe regarded their man-power, whereas the Allies had only just begun "to pump men out arrival in France in the spring of 1918 as "our biggest asset. . . . We must make the most of it. We must harp on it all the time." [4] The Germans were to be told that they were almost at the end of their resources in

[1] R. Pound and G. Harmsworth, *Northcliffe,* London, 1959, p. 657.

[2] Hans Thimme, *Weltkrieg ohne Waffen,* Stuttgart, 1932, pp. 13-14.

[3] According to one of his collaborators, the distinguished zoologist Sir Peter Chalmers Mitchell, "Northcliffe brought to the task a limitless faith in the possibility of controlling public opinion, a unique experience in the methods of publicity, and direct access to the Prime Minister and the War Cabinet." Sir Peter Chalmers Mitchell, *Encyclopedia Brittanica,* 12th ed., quoted in Sir Campbell Stuart, *Opportunity Knocks Once,* London, 1952, pp. 69-70.

[4] H.H. Fyfe, op. cit., p. 242.

of an enormous new reservoir of inexhaustible depth." It was thus in their own interest to give up the unequal struggle.[1]

Propaganda by evoking hope was more subtle. In an outstanding memorandum by H. G. Wells, then joint head of the German section in Crewe House, this appeal to hope is related to a concept of the specific German mentality.[2] With brilliant insight Wells perceived that German minds were particularly susceptible to systematic statements. They were used, he said, "to discuss and understand co-ordinated projects." Political ideas such as the phrases "Berlin-Baghdad" and "Mittel-Europa" had been impressed on them and now formed the bases of German political thought. To paraphrase Wells' approach, one could say that in his opinion good abstract concepts were required to drive out bad ones from the German mind. An attractive rival idea projected by British propaganda, he suggested, could be discussed by the German *and* the neutral press as a practical proposition.

The Wellsian rabbit to be produced out of the hat of Crewe House was the idea of a "League of Free Nations" which a reformed democratic Germany would be allowed to join. Though the memorandum did not refer to the last of President Wilson's Fourteen Points proclaimed a few months earlier, Wells' vision was not very different from the American concept, but relatively new was the Wellsian appeal from "Junker Germany to Germany Proper." Allied propaganda, Wells suggested, should draw a sharp distinction between the German government and the German masses. Wells saw further than the clichés of the Hun then so popular in English newspapers. He insisted on a dichotomy of Germans saying "We may be inclined to believe that every German is something of a Junker. We have to remember that he is also potentially a reasonable man." Northcliffe supported the main ideas of this proposal without perhaps realizing their full implication, and in a memorandum to the Prime Minister he stressed the suitability of the concept of a league of free nations.

And yet soon afterwards in July 1918 Northcliffe and Wells disagreed on points arising out of this very proposal, and Wells resigned in protest. A man of action and an impromptu journalist, Northcliffe was not a systematic planner or a thinker. "In private conversation," said Lord Beaverbrook of him, "he never conducted an argument; in journalism, he used the same method." [3] He was busy trying to solve the problem in hand

---

[1] Northcliffe stressed the appeal to self-interest also very much in the case of the dissatisfied nationalities of Austria-Hungary. "What we have to do then, is to make the oppressed nationalities realize that they are fighting against their own interests. Once we get that into their heads Austria will have to go out of the war" (H.H. Fyfe, op. cit., p. 240). A remarkable forecast of what did actually happen.

[2] See Sir Campbell Stuart, *Secrets of Crewe House, the Story of a Famous Campaign*, London, 1920, pp. 61-63, and H. G. Wells, *Experiment in Autobiography*, London, 1934, II, pp. 702-704.

[3] *Men and Power*, p. 60.

without reflecting on the situation the day after tomorrow. His patriotism was genuine, and he had thrown all his energy into persuading the enemy to give in. But the Government Director of Propaganda was at the same time a major newspaper proprietor, and his right hand did not bother about what his left hand was doing. It did not worry him that the tone of his newspapers differed greatly from the note of his propaganda which allowed for "another" Germany than that of the Junkers and the Hohenzollern. The *Daily Mail* ignored this line completely. For this paper the Germans remained Huns, it indulged in denouncing them and in doing so reflected a widespread hatred. Northcliffe the propagandist approved of the line of friendly counselling towards the Germans, but Northcliffe the newspaper owner still allowed some of his papers to depict the Germans as the lowest of criminals and to stimulate public hostility to them. These contradictory attitudes in Northcliffe irritated Wells and seem to have contributed to his resignation.[1]

Considered in the light of their immediate aim, to undermine German resistance and to make the enemy inclined to lay down their arms, the work of Crewe House, coming as it did at the right moment, was remarkably successful. It showed boldness, variety and originality. This was partly due to the novelty of much of the technique employed. The number of leaflets dropped by balloons or reaching the enemy by shells was intensified.[2] In August 1918, 4,000,000 leaflets were showered over Germany. As Hindenburg was to testify later: "This was a new weapon, or rather a weapon which in the past had never been employed on such a scale and so ruthlessly."[3] A trench newspaper in German was spread among the Kaiser's soldiers in the West, reaching a circulation of from 250,000-500,000 copies. The morale of the Navy too was affected for instance by a leaflet "The lost 150 German U-Boats" which gave details of the fate of 150 German submarine commanders and created great depression in German naval ports. To enlighten the enemy armies about the hopeless military situation was the one aim of Allied propaganda, to instill into them hope for a better post-war order was the other. "Its aim was to give the German people something to hope for in an early peace and much to fear from the prolongation of the war—that is to make it clear to them that the only way to escape complete ruin would be to break with the system that brought the war upon Europe, and to qualify for admission eventually into the League of Nations on Allied terms."[4]

[1] Wells does not mention his resignation in his *Experiment in Autobiography*, published in 1934, but discusses the power and deficiencies of Northcliffe's mind in general. "His soul held together in a delusive unity a score of flying fragments of purpose" (II, p. 700). He publishes extracts from his own Memorandum on propaganda in Germany and severely blames the Foreign Office which, he says, shelved the Memorandum and showed little interest in its constructive ideas.

[2] Sir Campbell Stuart, *Secrets of Crewe House*, p. 93.

[3] Marshal von Hindenburg, *Out of My Life*, London, 1920, p. 314.

[4] *Secrets of Crewe House*, p. 101.

In this way the propaganda from London acted as a parallel influence with that originating from the American Creel Bureau of Information which made the widest use in Central Europe of President Wilson's Fourteen Points. While these were not so greatly emphasized by Crewe House, Northcliffe too, drew a distinction between the German people and the German rulers. It seems that to some extent Crewe House and Northcliffe were able to reap where the Creel Bureau and Wilson had sown. For throughout the war the pronouncements of the American President "had won a substantial measure of confidence and respect in the minds of that minority of democratically-minded men who longed to transform the pre-war Germany of class discrimination and special privilege." [1]

The figure of Northcliffe remained semi-anonymous, while President Wilson impressed many Germans as a political Messiah. At least he appeared to them as the high-minded "mysterious figure in the White House, aloof from the ordinary passions of petty men, who spoke in elegiac prose of a better world when wars should be no more and a brotherhood of democratic peoples should bury their heritage of ancestral rancour and march toward a world of fellowship and reconciliation." [2]

Later German publicists denounced the utter perfidy of the Anglo-Saxon powers who, they said, made promises to the Germans which they had no intention of keeping. But this was too simple and stereotyped an interpretation. As one of Northcliffe's collaborators at Crewe House explained after the war, the discrepancy between words and deeds was by no means intended by the staff of Crewe House. Taking their cue from the Wells-Northcliffe memorandum they "addressed the Germans in the accents of comradeship; there was not one of the staff at Crewe House on whose lips those accents were false." [3] The propaganda issued in Crewe House emphasised that if the guilty Imperial Government were overturned by the German people "the German people would not be held responsible for its misdeeds." The tragedy was that once the armistice had been signed all that was quickly forgotten. "The sincerity of three and a half months was to curdle into the cynicism of a generation." [4]

Although Northcliffe was an opportunist in commercial as well as in national affairs, he cannot be called a hypocrite. How are we then to understand the fact—that was soon to be exploited by the Germans—that he and the British War Cabinet forgot the policy which had formed

[1] Harold D. Lasswell, *Propaganda Technique in the World War*, London, 1927, p. 216.

[2] Ibid. A full consideration of the impact of external propaganda on the German troops and civilians would also have to include the influence of Bolshevik propaganda which after the November revolution affected German soldiers and prisoners of war in Russia. However, a discussion of it falls outside the frame of this Introduction, as it was not Bolshevik, but British and American war-time propaganda which German nationalists later blamed for the collapse of their country in 1918.

[3] H.H. Fyfe, *Northcliffe*, p. 248.

[4] R. Pound and G. Harmsworth, op. cit., p. 659.

the contents of their propaganda? As Hamilton Fyfe stated, "He [North-cliffe] did not appear to recollect that such a policy had ever been laid down in documents signed by him. They had served their purpose. The German resistance had been weakened, they had been compelled to ask for peace. That created a totally different state of affairs." [1]

It is ironic and painful that Northcliffe apparently never realized the Germans had been deceived and that the promises given to them had been quietly dropped by the British Government after the end of hostilities. According to Fyfe there was "no dishonesty in this. He did not gloat over the deception practised; did not even perceive it. He simply passed on from one task to another, leaving behind him everything that had to do with the past." [2]

The dilemma was that Northcliffe never saw far ahead, that he was a propagandist but not a statesman. This can perhaps be regarded as one of the major reasons why his propaganda effort proved successful in the short run but a dangerous boomerang in the long run.

With the passing of time there developed among Germans a good deal of curiosity about the secret of the undeniable success of the Northcliffe machinery, but there was also a growing insistence that Germany must not fall a prey to such methods and techniques again. As it turned out, within an astonishingly short time they were not only imitated in the Reich by German nationalists, but surpassed both in skill and in lack of scruples.

2. Northcliffe: Four German post-war reactions

After the German collapse of 1918 there was a considerable measure of agreement in both camps on one important point. Both sides acknowledged that Allied, and particularly British, propaganda had contributed in some degree to the final outcome of the war. Few Germans, if any, were prepared to deny the effectiveness of anti-German propaganda from the West, however much they might condemn it from a moral point of view.

In this German generals and politicians shared the view of their hated and feared adversary, Lord Northcliffe. "If we have to some extent hastened the end," declared Northcliffe at a luncheon given in his honour in Paris on November 10th, 1918, "it is due to the fact that we are a company of experts and enthusiasts, and from the outset there has been a concentration of purpose born of complete unity." [3]

Before the Committee of Enquiry on the causes of the German collapse set up by the Reichstag of the Republic, the deputy Dr. Philipp stated that whilst it was difficult to measure the influence of enemy propaganda

[1] Fyfe, p. 249.
[2] Ibid.
[3] See G. Bruntz, *Allied Propaganda and the Collapse of the German Empire in 1918*, London, 1938, p. 221.

he did not "believe that without [its] successful help the German downfall could have succeeded as it did." [1] Apart from this, four different attitudes in German comments on the superiority of the former enemy in this new field can be distinguished during the years of the Weimar Republic: the attitudes of the liberals, the defeated war lords, the conservative nationalists, and last but not least, the new counter-propagandists, the mass-conscious totalitarians. Of the four, the last two are of special relevance to the theme of this book.

I

The liberal attitude of men who from conviction and rational judgment backed the Weimar Republic was less charged with emotion and more objective than the different nationalist reactions we shall discuss later. This attitude perceived the effectiveness of the Northcliffe propaganda and deplored its lack of scruple. But without distorting its significance the liberals regarded it as only one of the factors which had engineered the collapse of the German Empire. It must suffice to discuss here two voices from this quarter: one from the turbulent early days, and another from the time of the final agony of the Republic. Ernst Troeltsch, the dynamic Protestant theologian and philosopher of history, has been recently described as one of the "Elders" of the Republic, together with Max Weber, Meinecke, Friedrich Naumann and Rathenau.[2] Far from confining his wide range of interests to academic matters only, Troeltsch contributed regular articles under the pen-name of "Spectator" to the periodical *Der Kunstwart* from 1918 to the time of his death in 1922. In one of them he discussed dispassionately the reasons why Germany's former enemies believed in the legend of German war-guilt.[3] It was accepted, he pointed out, in the first instance, because the Germans had long become so odious abroad that people were prepared to believe even the most devastating reports about them. The crude realism with which Germans regarded all ethical elements in politics as but a cover for a brutal will to power appeared abhorrent, Troeltsch explained, to the moralizing Anglo-Saxons, whose approach to life was based on the self-righteousness of Calvinism. In addition, German war policy had proved most unfortunate. Tempted by successes at the beginning, it had revoked its original war aims which had been merely defensive. Under the harsh regimes of Falkenhayn and Ludendorff the militarists had, backed by the large economic associations and by the

---

[1] *Ibid.*

[2] See K. von Klemperer, *Germany's New Conservatism. Its History and its Dilemma in the Twentieth Century,* Princeton, 1957, pp. 91-92, 314-320. It seems, however, hardly justifiable to label the South German liberal Troeltsch "conservative" as the author ventures to do.

[3] "Das Schulddogma" in *Der Kunstwart,* 19 June, 1919; reprinted in Ernst Troeltsch, *Spektatorbriefe, Aufsätze aus der deutschen Revolution und Weltpolitik 1918-1922,* Tübingen, 1924, Appendix.

masses, demanded the acquisition of territories. The Kaiser had been unable to strike a balance between the military and the politicians. The nation had been divided between the champions of annexations and those of a moderate peace.

In such an unfortunate situation it was, Troeltsch felt, relatively easy "for the never-resting psychological warfare *(Suggestivkrieg)* of the Entente" to produce evidence of the German will to conquer the world, of their war-guilt, and of their bad behaviour during the war. Moreover the fact that the German *Herrenklasse* had shown no talent for a proper treatment of the people of the occupied territories had played into the hands of the new Allied technique of directing public opinion. In England and the U.S.A. this technique had long been tested in the peace-time election campaigns and had obtained astonishing successes. When the war came, the German replies to these techniques had proved poor and crude. Their failure had even helped the success of the enemies who had "managed the techniques of journalism incomparably better. We gave them inexhaustible raw material for their work, a fact no one should be allowed to forget, through our arrogance, our lack of spirit, our imprudent and reckless talking of all our secret wishes and ideas." In his inquest Troeltsch criticized his fellow-countrymen for ignoring the strength of moral forces in war and for playing into the hands of the Allies, "no matter if those hands were clean or not." [1]

Troeltsch was remarkably honest, seeking the causes of the success of enemy propaganda more in some fateful weaknesses of the German system itself than in the wickedness of the successful Allied propagandists. Ten years later, after the Republic had come to an ignominious end, another German liberal expressed much sharper criticism of the methods of Allied propaganda though he did so still in measured terms. Far from denying their success, this liberal deplored it as immoral and vulgar. It was a typical attitude shared by many of his political friends. In 1933 Dr. Edgar Stern-Rubarth, a cultured middle-of-the-road liberal and a friend of Stresemann who had once been director of Wolff's Telegraphen Bureau, expressed his views neatly before an American audience. He conceded that the Allies had been lucky enough to have had in Lord Northcliffe the very man for the exigencies of modern war, enormously energetic, a capable and unscrupulous organizer. Yet in Germany his work was still resented and rightly so, "for he and his helpers never abstained from utilizing even the most untrue and risky arguments for as long a time as they seemed useful for the purpose." [2]

In Stern-Rubarth's view "positive" propaganda was to be distinguished from "negative." Whereas the former was legitimate, the latter was not. To advertise one's own strength and accomplishments was "positive" propaganda, to exploit the weaknesses and shortcomings of the other side

[1] Ibid.
[2] E. Stern-Rubarth, "The Methods of Political Propaganda", in *Public Opinion and World Politics,* ed. Q. Wright, Chicago, 1933, p. 105.

was "negative." The magicians of Crewe House had used the black magic of "negative" propaganda. The English saying "Tell a lie and stick to it" had pointed to a deplorable cynicism characteristic of the inter-Allied propagandists during the world war. From the point of view of this scholarly liberal the Northcliffian type of propaganda was immoral and a disgrace that, he felt, must not be repeated because it was bound to poison the relations between nations and to form an obstacle to better international understanding and co-operation.

II

In the view of the men of the Supreme Command, of Fieldmarshal von Hindenburg and General Ludendorff, the success of the insidious but clever enemy propaganda spread among the tired German troops in the summer of 1918 had done much to undermine their morale and to increase their longing for an end of the war. In his reminiscences, published as early as 1920, Hindenburg admitted that in the last year of the war the German soldier's morale had been at a low ebb. Dangers and hardships in the field, the turmoil of war, the complaints from their families at home about some real and some imaginary privations had all played their part in weakening it. The combination of these factors had a demoralizing effect, especially as no end seemed in sight. "In the shower of pamphlets, which was scattered by enemy airmen our adversaries said and wrote that they did not think so badly of us, that we must only be reasonable and perhaps here and there renounce something we had conquered. Then everything would be right again and we could live together in peace, in perpetual international peace. As regards peace within our borders, new men and new governments would see to that. . . . There was therefore no point in continuing the struggle." The German Fieldmarshal provided an unsolicited testimonial for the Western propagandist by lamenting that the German soldier had "thought it could not be all enemy lies; he had allowed it to poison his mind and proceeded to poison the mind of others." [1]

Hindenburg, in some ways as simple a man as some of his privates, deplored that the policy of deliberate deception practised by an artful enemy had been so successful. The credulous Germans had been tricked. After the German armies had laid down their arms "nothing more was heard of all the promises which the enemy propaganda had announced. The vision of revenge appeared in all its nakedness. 'Woe to the vanquished!' A phrase which springs from fear as well as hatred." [2]

Equipped with a more powerful and more discerning mind General Ludendorff went much further than his senior colleague. Ludendorff's acknowledgement of the superiority of Allied propaganda was lavish. "We were hypnotized by the enemy propaganda," he admitted, "as a rabbit by

[1] Marshal von Hindenburg, *Out of my Life*, pp. 392-393.
[2] Op. cit., p. 438.

a snake. It was exceptionally clever and on a great scale. It worked by
mass suggestion, kept in the closest touch with the military situation and
was unscrupulous as to the means it used." [1] Ludendorff employed the
success of Crewe House as a trump card in proving that Germany had
not lost the war on the battlefield but "only" in the realm of political
warfare. There was the cause of Germany's disaster. Whereas on the
battlefield the Germans had retained the initiative almost to the very end,
in psychological warfare the enemy had attacked everywhere with a
united front—(a somewhat exaggerated picture)—and had found "auxil-
iaries in the many deserters in the neutral states and also, alas! support
in Germany." While he took for granted this connection between Allied
propaganda and unpatriotic subversive elements at home, Ludendorff
maintained at the same time that the lack of an effective counter-attack
of propaganda had been by no means the fault of the Army, but definitely that of the feeble civilian leadership, of the armchair bureaucracy.
Until August 1918 no special department for propaganda had been set
up on the German side. When it had been formed, it had proved totally
inadequate. In any case, it had then been too late.

Though Ludendorff, too, talked of the unscrupulous methods used by
enemy propagandists, he was much more concerned with and about their
undeniable efficiency. For this blunt and belligerent Machiavellian the
end justified the means, and he could only deplore the naivety and inep-
titude the German civilian authorities had shown in this new but vitally
important field.

III

Compared with the occasional utterances of the two war lords the reaction to the Northcliffe propaganda of a leading Conservative publicist
was much more systematic and intense. Whereas Hindenburg and Ludendorff had been soldiers and men of action, Paul Nikolaus Cossmann was
an idéologue in Napoleon's sense, a cultured and, in his way, sincere
Nationalist, whose monthly *Süddeutsche Monatshefte* became after 1918
a significant platform for the dispossessed and disgruntled South German
bourgeoisie. As editor of the journal for thirty years and as a leading
member of the publishing house which issued the largest Munich newspaper, Cossman was an important factor in the life of South German
conservativism and nationalism during the time of the Weimar Republic.
Though not a financial success, the *Süddeutsche Monatshefte* were instrumental in influencing the well-to-do and educated circles against the Republic, against Germany's former enemies, particularly France, and in
favour of a fervent nationalism which was a blend of Fichtean idealism
with Bismarckian *Realpolitik*. Seen today in historical perspective they
formed a bridge between the Wilhelminian and the totalitarian brands

[1] General Ludendorff, *My War Memoirs 1914-1918*, London, 1919, I, pp.
360 ff.

of nationalism. Cossmann and his circle of contributors helped to create an atmosphere from which the National Socialists were able to profit handsomely.

It is one of the grim ironies of German history between the wars that the man who did so much, in all sincerity, to alienate the upper classes in Bavaria from the existing regime and indirectly to pave the way for the triumph of National Socialism was eliminated from political life and journalism as soon as it had come to power. A Monarchist, a Jew by race and an early convert to Catholicism by conviction, this ardent apostle of German *Volkstum* ended his days in the concentration camp of Theresienstadt in 1942.[1]

Deeply shocked by the events of 1918, Cossmann never forgot Northcliffe's propaganda successes. He constantly tried a kind of shadow-boxing with what he regarded as the impact of Allied propaganda in the world war, though in doing so he proved more honest and clumsy than either the English press lord before him or Goebbels after him. Photographs of Cossman give the impression of stately fierceness; he looks like a member of the Hohenzollern family. A dreamer and a man of purpose at the same time, Cossmann was inclined to mould his periodical as a forum from which different voices could and should be heard. He often devoted his journal, which had a marked conservative and nationalist bias, to the discussion of specific issues and problems, political and cultural.

Immediately after the war the bitter controversial issues of the time, as for instance, "the Collapse," Bolshevism, and the war-guilt question were given prominence.[2] The last issue of 1919 was one long, resentful and acrimonious discussion of "Germany in the Dock." Other issues contained woeful reports of the experiences of German prisoners of war, or threw a glaring light on the role of propaganda during the war.[3]

Cossmann again and again insisted on exposing the machinations of Allied propaganda in the past and on preparing similar weapons for Germany in the future. One can only understand this properly by considering

[1] For the fate of Cossmann during the Third Reich see the article by the former co-editor of the *Süddeutsche Monatshefte*, K.A. von Müller, "Paul Nikolaus Cossmanns Ende" in *Hochland*, Munich, 1949-1950, vol. 42, pp. 368-379. There is also some information on Cossmann activities before 1933 and on his sufferings under the National Socialists in the memoirs of Erwein von Aretin, *Krone und Kerker. Erinnerungen eines bayrischen Edelmanns,* edited by Karl Buchheim and Karl Otmar von Aretin, Munich, 1955, particularly on pp. 19-31.

[2] See the issues of *Süddeutsche Monatshefte*, "Der Zusammenbruch" (December 1918), "Zur Wahrheit über den Krieg" (March 1919), "Der 'Friede' " (August 1919), "Bolschewismus" (January 1919), "Die Ausbreitung des Bolschewismus" (April 1919).

[3] See for instance "Was wir litten. Berichte von Kriegsgefangenen" (January 1920) and "Ein deutsches Gefangenenlager" (August 1920). The allegation that the Germans had been deliberately deceived by false promises of enemy propaganda was elaborated in the issue "Der grosse Betrug" (July 1920), which ran into three editions.

the overall platform of his monthly. It was neatly summed up in a statement by the publishers [1] which claimed: "The *Süddeutsche Monatshefte*
have fought since the day of mobilization *for* a German victory and
against the policy of [Chancellor] Bethmann which was detrimental to
victory. They have fought since the collapse (in 1918) *for* Germany's
honour and rise and *against* the November lies. They have fought since
the "peace" of Versailles *for* a peace of true rights and *against* the guilt
and atrocity lies."

In this framework Cossmann gave much space to a critical discussion
of the late *Meinungskrieg* or propaganda war and to the lessons to be
learned from it by patriotic and energetic Germans. Over a long period
the half-admired, half-abhorred name of Lord Northcliffe appeared in the
pages of the journal. The sinister but efficient role of the men of Crewe
House was frequently discussed by the editor and by some of his contributors. Their criticism was not always based on reality. In a lengthy
survey of Germany's unfortunate and unjustified position as loser of the
war, Count Ernst Reventlow, an extreme right wing politician, came much
closer to political metaphysics and occultism then to a dispassionate historical analysis.[2] He, too, deplored the ineffectiveness of his fellow-
countrymen in the field of propaganda. Too late in the war they had
realized the scope and significance of the British propaganda effort, of
that most terrible of all weapons to which neither the Government nor the
people had been able to provide a powerful enough antidote. Reventlow
shared the admiration of the shrewdness with which the British propagandists and their assistants, among them Poles and Frenchmen, had
exploited the national weaknesses of the Germans. As he saw it, their
skillful efforts had begun long before the war when they had caused a
rift inside the German nation. They had set the South Germans against
the North Germans and had fostered the economic and political growth
of the unpatriotic German Social Democrats. This was an operation with
far-reaching aims and ruthless tactics, the triumph of a perverted cunning.
To Reventlow it had been simply a fight of the fox against the lamb. "The
coalition of our enemies under its British leadership was aggressive and
thus belligerent, the attitude of the German Reich defensive and thus
peaceful."

A passionate nationalist, who was later in the mid-twenties to become
a member of the tiny National Socialist group of deputies in the Reichstag, Reventlow saw in British propaganda only a tool of a much wider
and more hidden conspiracy. Behind it, he claimed, was Freemasonry,
an anti-authoritarian movement prominent in Anglo-Saxon and Latin
countries. Bent on the overthrow of the Church and the Monarchy which

[1] In an advertisement in *Süddeutsche Monatshefte*, vol. 21, no. 7, April
1924.
[2] In the issue "Deutschland vor Gericht", *Süddeutsche Monatshefte*, vol. 17,
no. 3, December 1919. Reventlow's references to British propaganda are on
pp. 193-194.

were to be replaced by a World Republic and the rule of World Capitalism, it had determined that the German monarchies and the German Reich should disappear.[1]

Compared with such fanciful political metaphysics the comments on the success of the Northcliffe propaganda by another contributor to the monthly were empirical and factual. They came from a son of Admiral Tirpitz, who had spent nearly four years as a prisoner of war in England. A naval officer, too, Wolfgang von Tirpitz tried to analyze the undeniable success of Northcliffe's efforts more rationally by discussing his career and methods.[2] Prominence was given to Northcliffe's half Yorkshire, half Irish ancestry, to his flair for commercial propaganda, to his insight into human types and his skill in selecting personnel. Northcliffe combined Irish enterprise and persuasiveness with "English toughness, arrogance and art of hypocrisy." Even more than Hindenburg and Ludendorff, Tirpitz was impressed by the ruthlessly virile methods of Northcliffe, who employed sombre rather than rosy colours in painting the picture of the war for the masses. Nevertheless, Northcliffe had remained a deadly enemy of Germany and of truth, two concepts which were identical for Tirpitz as for other German nationalists. The practical lesson to be learnt from this was the futility of conceding German war guilt. It would, argued the author, only play straight into the hands of Northcliffe, and prove the correctness of his policy.

It was Cossman, himself, who put such opinions on to the wider canvas of contemporary history. Deeply convinced of the inadequacy of the German effort in war propaganda, he was inclined to blame the majority parties in the Reichstag of 1917-18 for it, the same parties who now backed the Republic. In a bitter article,[3] he maintained that to the Germans during the war "propaganda had not been an end in itself, but a mere instrument of tactics in domestic policy in order to gain the support of party politicians, newspaper publishers, journalists, and historians by way of commissions, fees and secret funds; in other words, it had served as a means for the formation of a majority in the Reichstag."

In Cossmann's view the German failure in this field was strikingly revealed by the contrast between the immense expenses incurred by Reuters during the war which, he alleged, brought this agency close to

[1] Op. cit., pp. 216-217. Reventlow's views on Freemasonry were also shared by Ludendorff and his fanatical second wife. The myth of a secret and international conspiracy of Freemasonry, said to be all the more sinister as it skilfully camouflaged its movements, was to remain a standby of extreme German nationalism for many years until it became an integral part of the official ideology of the Third Reich, though there the accent was more on international Jewry than on international Freemasonry. The National Socialist regime had all Freemason Lodges closed, and a special section of the Gestapo dealt with the activities and the property of Freemasons.

[2] W. von Tirpitz, "Northcliffe" in the issue "Lehren der Geschichte", *Süddeutsche Monatshefte*, vol. 17, no. 6, March 1920, pp. 433-441.

[3] "Der Meinungskrieg" in the issue "Hungersperre", *Süddeutsche Monatshefte*, vol. 17, no. 8, May 1920.

bankruptcy, and the parsimony of its German opposite number, the Wolff Telegraphen Bureau. The latter had then paid big dividends to its shareholders whilst its foreign correspondents had been instructed to send few despatches in order to economize. Even after the war the German news agency had failed. Whereas Havas and Reuter had flooded the world with reports of the alleged maltreatment of Allied prisoners of war in German prison camps, Cossmann argued that Wolff had never sent one single despatch abroad on the bad experiences of German prisoners of war. Heavy-footed and sincere, Cossmann admitted that the propaganda war had been lost all over the globe by Germany, but maintained stubbornly as part of "the convictions of us despised Germans" that "though truth can be delayed, it cannot be annihilated."

In their comments on enemy propaganda right-wing politicians like Cossmann and Reventlow, or for this purpose soldiers like Hindenburg and Ludendorff, were largely motivated by the desire to attribute the defeat of Germany to any cause rather than the true one, i.e. the defeat of the German armies in the field. By ascribing to British and American propaganda a deleterious effect on the German soldiers and civilians they established a parallel argument to that of the "stab in the back legend."

It is thus significant that the *Süddeutsche Monatshefte* became the ardent and continuous champion of this *Dolchstoss* legend. Five years after the war Cossmann devoted two entire numbers of his journal[1] to the propagation of the story that the German defeat had been the outcome of the stab in the back of the army by subversive and revolutionary elements at home. In putting forward this specious interpretation emphasis was laid on a close interaction between the "stab in the back" and the manoeuvres of Western propaganda. Cossmann declared it "one of the greatest achievements of Lord Northcliffe that he had brought the war behind the front under his control and that he had organised it in a manner suitable to the conditions of the people of the Central European powers whose morale had to be undermined."[2]

In Cossmann's eyes the men of Crewe House had at least worked for their nation's cause, however unclean and Machiavellian their methods, but the German Independent Socialists and other emigrés who had assisted them from neutral countries were nothing but traitors to the Fatherland.[3] Northcliffe's genius, Cossmann argued, lay in his sly exploitation of disgruntled German Leftists for foreign aims.[4]

---

[1] "Der Dolchstoss", *Süddeutsche Monatshefte*, vol. 21, no. 7, April 1924, and "Die Auswirkungen des Dolchstosses. Neue Dokumente", vol. 21, No. 8, May 1924.

[2] Op. cit., p. 1.

[3] Op. cit., p. 3.

[4] Quoting from *Secrets of Crewe House*, of which by then a German translation had appeared, and from Hansi and Tonnelat's *A Travers Les Lignes Ennemies* (Paris, 1922) which supplemented it on the French side, Cossmann discussed in detail the activities of men like Carl Minster, formerly a Social Democratic editor in Western Germany who had fled to Holland and pub-

It was only one step from such allegations to discrediting the concept of "democracy" as a foreign bogus article said to have been imported into Germany by the victors under false pretences. As Cossmann put it bluntly: "What the Germans had been told about democracy by the countries of the West had been part of their war propaganda." [1]

Cossmann's reaction to the success of the Northcliffe type of propaganda did not exhaust itself in a mere exposure of its tricks and subterfuges. Peace seemed to him only a continuation of war by other means. Deeply conscious of the permanent existence of the political propaganda of other nations, he tried to take a leaf out of the book of Germany's former and potentially future enemies. This he attempted negatively by refuting the tendentious propaganda spread abroad and positively by his indefatigable presentation of German nationalist and conservative ideas. He did not so much suggest the inferiority and perfidy of other nations as to proclaim proudly the strength, ability and superiority of the German people.

To give only one significant example of his techniques both of refutation and of assertion, in April 1925 the *Süddeutsche Monatshefte* came out with an issue on "The Czechs," [2] which, complaining bitterly of their Herrenvolk arrogance vis-à-vis their German minority, began with the translation of a nationalist Czech fairy-tale from a primer for Czech schools edited by two Czech secondary school teachers.[3] It was a crude black and white little story of the terrible hydra Germania with its hundred heads. The hero, young Tomas, had learnt as a travelling journeyman abroad of the misdeeds of the terrible dragon and of his repelling heads: hatred, lies, violence, servitude, cruelty and so on. Much later, as an old man, Tomas had occasion to remember this, for the dragon had set out to subject the entire world. He organized a big crusade against the arch-foe of his country and was backed in this by its shining knights. In the end Tomas managed to have the vicious dragon slain and became the hero of his fellow-countrymen who showed a touching gratitude to the man from whose forehead shone the stars of honesty and truth. Old Tomas returned home amid the enthusiasm of the people. They

---

lished a pacifist weekly *Kampf*. He had had contacts not only with associations of Germans in Holland who shared his outlook—Cossmann dubbed them "associations of deserters"—but also with English and American officials in the Hague. There had been similar subversive elements in Switzerland and Sweden. A factual account of the activities of Minster is to be found in Hans Thimme, *Weltkrieg ohne Waffen*, pp. 107-117.

[1] *Süddeutsche Monatshefte*, vol. 21, no. 8, May 1924, p. 9.

[2] *Süddeutsche Monatshefte*, vol. 22, no. 7, April 1925.

[3] "A Czech fairy tale of guilt." The text was taken from a Czech primer of model essays edited by Professor Wenzul Suk and Dr. Frantisek Simek. Publisher Jan Svatnek in Budweis.

waved white and red flags, applauding him like a king, and as the bravest man in the world. His name was Tomas Masaryk.

The naive nationalism of this story was manna from heaven for Cossmann. It served him as a convenient peg on which to hang his own nationalism. Did not this "fairy tale of German guilt" abuse and slander the German nation? Taking it very seriously Cossmann invited his readers to imagine [1] "what it meant for millions of Germans outside the German Reich to be subjected helplessly to such calumnies of their history and their civilization." They were Germans like themselves and their fight for truth should be shared by all Germans in the Reich.

Probably Cossmann did not realize that he was as much given to distorted thinking as was the Czech author of the "black and white" story. Both thought in sharp and extreme alternatives which ruled out any compromise. As Cossmann put it: "Either we are a community of honour and culture or manure for a foreign culture, a foreign economy and foreign armies." Thirteen years before Hitler ranted and raged on behalf of the Sudeten Germans, Cossmann had taken up their cause by publishing the bitter laments of Senator Franz Jasser: "The Czech aims," he alleged, "can be expressed in one sentence. The Czechs want to be not only the national and political Herrenvolk but also the economic, social and cultural Herrenvolk. They are the masters, we only the tolerated 'immigrants' who can only be treated as guests." [2]

Financed like the leading Munich newspaper *Münchner Neueste Nachrichten* by some tycoons of the Rhenish heavy industry, the *Süddeutsche Monatshefte* remained until 1933 an organ of the more educated section of the Conservative bourgeoisie.[3] Throughout the nineteen-twenties this section was divided in its loyalties between the German nationalists, fundamentally a North German party, and the Catholic "Bavarian People's Party," which inclined much more to the Right than did the related Centre Party in Prussia.[4] Throughout Cossmann's editorship his journal stood for such vague but emotionally charged concepts as *Volkstum*, "National Honour," and a "National Community transcending the existing frontiers of the Reich."

The reply to the continuing challenge which the success of Northcliffe's war propaganda meant to Cossmann was limited, mainly because the radius of appeal of the *Süddeutsche Monatshefte* was confined to the

---

[1] Op. cit., p. 2.

[2] Op. cit., p. 56. Actually the existing tension between the Czech majority and the German minority eased considerably in 1926 when the representatives of three German parties joined the Cabinet of Czechoslovakia.

[3] At a party to celebrate the 25th anniversary of the *Süddeutsche Monatshefte* in Munich in April 1929, at which the contributors and other supporters of the journal gathered, the élite of the Bavarian conservative intelligentsia was well represented. See the report "25 Jahr-Feier der *Süddeutsche Monatshefte*" by its co-editor K.A.v. Müller, vol. 26, no. 8, May 1929.

[4] On the origins of the "Bavarian People's Party" see Karl Schwend, *Bayern Zwischen Monarchie und Diktatur*, Munich, 1954, ch. 2, pp. 58-68.

educated middle classes. It never reached and affected the workers, a fact of which its editor seems to have been painfully aware. With characteristic honesty he said in his final statement during the Munich "stab in the back" trial of 1925 that he envied his Social Democratic opponent his proletarian reading public. Cossmann thought it very important and gratifying to have the possibility of reaching the ear of the German workers. Cossmann declared that he had striven to succeed in this, but he had to admit his failure.[1]

Like Charles Maurras and his *Action Française* in Paris, with whom he has many points of affinity—his dislike of the existing Republic, his ardent nationalism, his cultural interests, finally an endeavour to restore the former monarchy—Paul Nikolaus Cossmann never succeeded in impressing the masses. He was too refined, too dialectical, too magisterial. He lacked the catchwords and phrases of the demagogue, his crudity and astute political instinct. This lack of robustness and acumen restricted Cossmann's propaganda appeal. The man who was able to pull so many strings as controller of an influential newspaper and as editor of a prominent monthly was at a loss when trying to contact the man in the street, the unemployed, the hungry and dissatisfied masses. Cossmann ardently believed in the idea of the German nation as propounded first by Fichte and later implemented by Bismarck. In spite of his earnest Christian creed he was, as a friend of his has said, "always tempted to regard the nation as an absolute value." [2] Like his fellow-monarchist and companion Erwein von Aretin, he failed with his high-faluting romantic idealism and his cultured mind to understand the impact their nationalist policies were likely to have on the more primitive types in society.[3] Too late did these men realize how stereotypes like "national," "honour of the nation," "*Volkstum*" etc. could be misused and perverted in the hands of more unscrupulous people.

Such men as Cossmann, K. A. von Müller and their political friends did much to create the mental climate in which the demagogic tactics of Hitler and Goebbels were to prosper. The editors of the *Süddeutsche Monatshefte* never tired of emphasizing the necessity of imitating and surpassing the propaganda methods of Northcliffe. They raised the temperature in the Nationalist camp in Munich, they expressed themselves —and this is important—in favour of bridging the gap between the bourgeoisie and the workers, between the nationalists and the socialists, though they were ineffectual in providing this bridge themselves. During the Dolchstoss trial in 1925 Cossmann expressly rejected a division between

---

[1] See "Schlusswort unseres Herausbebers im Dolchstossprozess. Sitzung des Gerichts vom 19, November 1925." *Süddeutsche Monatshefte*, vol. 23, no. 4, January 1926, pp. 276-277.

[2] Erwein von Aretin, *Krone und Ketten, Erinnerungen eines bayrischen Edelmanns*. Edited by Karl Buchheim and Karl Otmar von Aretin, München, 1955, pp. 13-14.

[3] Ibid.

"bürgerlich" (bourgeois) and socialist. He felt, he said, close to all socialists who displayed a nationalist attitude, and deeply separated from
capitalists, who were internationally minded and anti-German.[1] Only
when the National Socialist movement had become a real threat, did
Cossmann and his aristocratic friend von Aretin openly propagate the
restoration of the monarchy.[2] But it is very interesting to observe that
even then, when Cossmann pleaded for a return of Crown Prince Rupprecht to the restored throne of Bavaria, he blamed once more his
favourite scapegoat, Allied propaganda in the World War. This time he
made it responsible for the overthrow of the German dynasties in November 1918. That propaganda, he maintained, had caused millions of
Germans to believe "that they would hear the angels sing in heaven if
all music at the courts were abolished." To him, he added frankly, "this
counsel from the enemies had been a strong argument to think that the
abolition of the monarchy would prove unfavourable to Germany." [3]

IV

Cossmann and his circle were the respected spokesmen of a conservative bourgeoisie, which looking back wanted to restore. Adolf Hitler, the
demon from the Viennese slums, systematically aimed at the overthrow
of the Republic and at the establishing of a one-party dictatorship. He,
too, admitted the great success of British propaganda in the last war. "For
what we failed to do in this direction," he wrote in *Mein Kampf*, "was
made up [for] by the enemy with really unheard-of skill and ingenious
deliberation." [4] In this field the Germans had been hopeless bunglers and
dilettantes, while the English had proved clever and adaptable in their
methods.

Ludendorff had blamed the failure of the German propaganda efforts
in the world war on the civilians and the bureaucrats, Cossmann on the
self-indulgent politicians of the Reichstag. Adolf Hitler, then still an
obscure political sectarian, took a wider view. To his resentful but penetrating mind a different explanation presented itself. Deeply convinced of
the essential role of propaganda for any movement set on obtaining

[1] "Schlusswort unseres Herausgebers," op. cit., pp. 276-277.

[2] See the issue of January 1933, "König Rupprecht", *Süddeutsche Monatshefte*, vol. 30, no. 4. The periodical had already earlier given space to a somewhat academic discussion of the ideology of monarchism. See the number "Die
Monarchie in Europa" vol. 26, no. 12, September 1929, with contributions by
Freiherr von Aretin and Professor Friedrich Lent of the University of Er-
langen. Lent expressed himself in favour of a restoration of the monarchy as
part of a forthcoming Third Reich in his article "Führung und Staatsaufbau"
(see particularly pp. 889-890).

[3] Op. cit., p. 193 on Bavarian Monarchism at the end of the Weimar period.
cf. Walter Kaufmann, *Monarchism in the Weimar Republic*, New York, 1953,
particularly pp. 216-19, and K. Schwend, op. cit., ch. 38, pp. 514-525.

[4] Adolf Hitler, *Mein Kampf*, Unabridged English Translation, New York,
1939, pp. 228.

power, he pointed out that the consumers of propaganda were the masses and *not* the intellectuals. It had proved a disaster that the German endeavour in the field during the last war had lost sight of this important consideration.

The self-educated agitator blamed its failure on the impractical intellectuals. He sneered at the professors who did not grasp the limitations of the masses and were therefore blind to the secrets of successful propaganda. The amateurs of the old ruling class in Germany had been unaware of the essentials of propaganda, the purpose of which was not "continually to produce interesting changes for a few blasé little masters, but to convince, that means to convince the masses." [1] To do this was only possible by a thousandfold repetition of a few slogans, he said. Here too, the propaganda of Germany's enemies had set an example. For it had been "limited to a few points of view, calculated exclusively for the masses" and " carried out with untiring persistency." [2]

Hitler was quite mistaken in his belief that the basic ideas of Allied propaganda and ways of implementing them had remained identical throughout the war and that no changes had been made. In fact, on both sides propaganda had gathered momentum during the last years of the war. The earlier attempt which had mainly concentrated on an effort to gain sympathy in neutral countries had then been replaced by a direct propaganda attack on the enemy. [3]

Hitler was scathing in his condemnation of the lamentable failure of German war propaganda. While in England it had been recognized as "a weapon of the first order," in Germany it had been an occupation for people with little talent, "the last bread of the politicians without office and a potboiler for the modest hero." Small wonder that its effect had been "just nil." [4] To Hitler one of the major deficiencies of German propaganda was the quite erroneous impression of the enemy it had created in the mind of the German soldier. Whereas German and Austrian propaganda had ridiculed their foe, British and American propaganda had taken their enemy seriously and depicted him as a barbarian. This approach had paid dividends while the German method had turned out to be futile and even harmful to their cause. It had created for the German soldier a bewildering discrepancy between the ludicrous image of the enemy and his actual behaviour in battle. From a psychological point of view enemy propaganda had proved correct. Experiencing the resistance of the enemy the German soldier (and Hitler says little about the German civilian) had felt deceived and disillusioned. He had despaired.

However, Allied propaganda had avoided this mistake. By depicting the Germans as barbarians and Huns, it had "prepared the individual soldier for the terrors of war and helped guard him against disappoint-

---

[1] A. Hitler, op. cit., p. 239.
[2] Op. cit., p. 240.
[3] H. Thimme, *Weltkrieg ohne Waffen*, p. 4.
[4] A. Hitler, op. cit., p. 240.

ment." [1] The German soldier had lost confidence because of the gulf between the real facts and the wrong image presented to him earlier and had "finally dismissed any information he received from his own side as 'swindle' and 'bunk' *(Krampf)*." [2]

Hitler's version was over-simplified and in some respects lopsided, for by 1917 English and French soldiers had often become sceptical of pep talks and of the accuracy of war reports in the press. The strength of the Allied propaganda effort had been less the hatred of the enemy it had spread among its own soldiers than its twofold approach to the adversary, which was both negative and positive. Not only had this propaganda attacked "Huns" and "Junkers" but, in addition, it had offered the German masses the blueprint of a better world, a League of Free Nations in which there might even be room for a de-Junkered and de-Hohenzollernized Germany.

In 1925 when *Mein Kampf* was first published, its pages on the success of British and the failure of German war propaganda met with as little general interest as the rest of this mixture of a crude *Weltanschauung* with a long-winded blue-print for totalitarian and nationalist action. But after 1933 Hitler's account of the German débâcle in 1918 became the "official" truth and was duly echoed by the younger generation of German historians and publicists. They eagerly spread the view, that, as one of them put it, "in the Wilhelminian age the [German] intelligentsia had lived without insight into the nature of propaganda." [3] It was to this state of affairs that they attributed the failure of German counter-propaganda in the first world war.

3. The Boomerang of the Atrocity Stories

Two distinct facets of Allied propaganda during that war were stressed by National Socialist writers after 1933, and particularly following the outbreak of the new conflict in 1939. The first was the proud assertion, justified in many ways, that National Socialist Germany had fully recognized the political importance of propaganda and would never display the weaknesses from which Imperial Germany had suffered in this respect. Owing to the feeble leadership during the last years of the régime Germany had become exposed to the tricks and subterfuges of Allied propaganda and had eventually succumbed to them. But having formed a special Ministry of People's Enlightenment and Propaganda, Germany had now made herself strong and fully a match for the wiles of her enemies. Again and again during the war Goebbels insisted that history did not repeat itself and that Germany was in an infinitely superior position. This, he claimed, was as much true of her political as of her

---

[1] Op. cit., p. 234.
[2] Op. cit., p. 235.
[3] See H. Wanderscheck, *Weltkrieg und Propaganda*, Berlin, 1936, p. 5.

military warfare.[1] As he explained at the time of the German attack on the West in 1940, German leadership in 1914 had been completely ignorant of how to influence public opinion and had not had the faintest idea of what Goebbels called "the dynamics of the people themselves." Then the enemy had known how to use cunning and slander effectively and how to put the German government in the wrong over any important issue. By 1940 the position had changed completely. In the field of propaganda Germany was now well prepared and on the offensive. She knew "how to handle the weapon of Truth with sovereign certainty. Her news policy was now quick, experienced, clear and effective." [2] Goebbels claimed that Germany had developed "a very detailed system of the highest perfection in the treatment of the opinion of the (German) people, and of the public opinion of the world." [3] He then confidently argued that all hopes of the enemy to destroy German morale were futile. What had happened in the First World War could never happen in the Second.

There was a second aspect of Allied propaganda in the world war as interpreted by the National Socialists. It could be called the boomerang of the atrocity stories. The National Socialist publicists claimed that by a general consensus of later world opinion much of Allied propaganda had been a tissue of lies and falsehoods and their atrocity stories had been freely invented. What had happened in the First World War was repeated in the Second. Again stories of unbelievable atrocities—this time alleged to have been committed in German concentration camps— were circulated by the enemy. They were declared by the National Socialists to be as little credible as their forerunners, to be deliberate fabrications.

Such is the uncanny irony of history. The admissions of the falsehood of atrocity stories circulated in the First World War, made unhesitatingly by British and American writers were to serve the machinery of National Socialist propaganda later to discredit reports of mass murder and mass atrocities committed by the SS in World War II. Since 1919 German commentators—Nationalists and Liberals alike—had been able to point to such flagrant falsehoods spread on the Allied side as the stories of the scientific exploitation of corpses of German soldiers, the *Kadaver-Verwertungsanstalten* (in fact the cadavers had been those of horses) or the tales of the cruel fate of Belgian children whose hands were said to have been cut off by German soldiers.[4]

In all these cases German commentators had some reason for explaining that what they described as the cynical English saying 'Tell a lie and

[1] See below chapter 19, "The Lure of Historical Parallels."

[2] J. Goebbels, article "Die Zeit ohne Beispiel", *Das Reich*, vol. 1, no. 1, 26 May 1940, reprinted in the collection of his articles and speeches under the same title, *Die Zeit ohne Beispiel*, Munich, 1941, p. 292.

[3] Ibid.

[4] For these stories see Arthur Ponsonby, M.P., *Falsehood in Wartime, containing an assortment of lies circulated throughout the nations during the Great War*, London, 1928.

it sticks' had been successfully applied by the Western enemies in the First World War.[1] But National Socialist propaganda went further. It realized that not only do lies stick in the mass mind, but once they have been unmasked so also does the unmasking. The grammar of the human mind is limited. Just as generals are often inclined to conceive of the next war in terms of the last one, so the German man in the street, when reminded of the use of falsehoods and atrocity stories by the enemies in the last war, was prepared to dismiss reports on atrocities committed in his own camp, if they originated again from the enemy side. Because the earlier stories had been unmasked as false, the later ones were easily believed to be false, and propaganda saw to it that this belief did not flag.

There existed a good many people in the West too, who were prepared during the earlier years of the Third Reich to discount reports of cruel treatment of Jews and of other inmates of German concentration camps as "mere propaganda" largely spread by resentful refugees. For obvious reasons this attitude was encouraged by the German authorities and was adopted by a great many people inside Germany. In fact, for many the memories of the false Allied atrocity stories from the First World War became a kind of protective curtain sheltering their minds from any close enquiry into the actual atrocities committed by the existing régime.

Wishful thinking on today's event was thus much aided by memories of yesterday's falsehoods. Before 1933 Hans Fritzsche was a journalist with conservative nationalist leanings and afterwards a high official in Goebbels' Ministry of Propaganda. Though he may not be deemed an entirely reliable witness, he probably told the truth when speaking, after the collapse of the Third Reich, of the deep impression the Allied atrocity stories of the earlier war had made on him. "Never did I forget the story of this lie" (of the hands of Belgian children severed by German soldiers), he wrote. "I thought always of it when news of the alleged atrocities was spread by the enemy and referred to in public" (in the Second World War).[2] The factual work by the English M. P. Arthur Ponsonby, *Falsehood in Wartime*, published in London in 1928, seems to have become a kind of Bible for him and his colleagues. During the rapid German advance in the West in May 1940 Fritzsche's Press Department not only gave instructions to the editors to expose the fresh "atrocity news" of the enemy, but at the same time also issued excerpts from Ponsonby's book to illustrate the traditional British methods. The printing of these quotations by the German papers was declared "particularly desirable."[3] To Fritzsche the Western propaganda methods employed between 1939-1945 were simply a gigantic extension of those used between 1914 and 1918. He seems to have regarded works such as *Propaganda in the Next War* by Sydney Rogerson (London, 1938) and the pamphlet by the Commu-

[1] See E. Stern-Rubarth, op. cit., pp. 105-106.
[2] *Hier spricht Hans Fritzsche*, Zürich, 1948, p. 237f.
[3] See the *Vertrauliche Informationen* (V.I.) nos. 116-40 (1.Erg.) of 21 May, and 121-40 of 27 May 1940. (Oberheitmann Collection).

nist W. Münzenberg, *Propaganda als Waffe* (Paris, 1938) as clear evidence of the intention of the Western Allies to employ hatred and fear as weapons of warfare. When later the Allied news reports of the mass murder of Jews by the SS and the Gestapo reached him, he was inclined to regard them as mere proof of the same propagandist attitude. Though one must be sceptical about Fritzsche's arguments, employed as they were for special pleading, in this case they were probably genuine.

Only during the Nuremberg trial (which ended with his acquittal) did Fritzsche acknowledge that he had been mistaken. Murder of the Jews by the SS had taken place on a large scale, by order of Hitler, and had been carefully hidden from the German public—and from him.[1] But again he blamed the enemy news services, this time not for their lies but for their apparent lack of efficiency in spreading the grim truth among the German people.[2] The small book by Sydney Rogerson,[3] cited by Fritzsche, is relevant in our context, for it illustrates the interrelation between past, present and future propaganda as it was viewed in England shortly before World War II. To Rogerson the building up of an effective propaganda machine by the Hitler régime was largely a reaction to the non-fulfilment of the promises made by Allied propagandists in the First World War. Coupled with the increasing pressure of the blockade and the growing hopelessness of the military situation Allied propaganda had then done its trick. But when the Germans had followed the Allied advice and had overthrown their princes and governments, the propaganda promises turned out to be worthless.

As a result of German disillusionment and of the powerful propaganda machine built up in the Third Reich, Rogerson predicted, shortly before the outbreak of the Second World War, that the Allies would find their task far more difficult next time. In a future war Germany would be "a difficult nut to crack." [4] For now the great majority of Germans were behind their masters. They would be difficult to reach by propaganda and to be converted, on account of the British failure to implement their promises in and after 1918.

Unlike many other English commentators during the interwar period Rogerson had, however, no guilt complex but merely viewed things from a pragmatic point of view. In spite of its strength, he thought, there were weak chinks in the totalitarian armour. One of them was the rigidity of propaganda control which compared unfavourably with the British gift for improvization. In 1938 this British author took a leaf out of Lord Northcliffe's book. What was required in the next war, he suggested, was

[1] *Hier spricht Hans Fritzsche,* p. 231.

[2] "In view of the information which I obtained from this Court I regard it as tragic that the enemy news service did not manage to secure a greater creditability for its news, provided they had then already had the information which they now claim to have." Ibid.

[3] Sydney Rogerson, *Propaganda in the Next War,* London, 1938. This is a volume in the series *The Next War,* edited by Captain Liddell Hart.

[4] Rogerson, op. cit., p. 59.

the efficient co-ordination of the military and the propaganda efforts, of which the simultaneous dropping of bombs and of pamphlets on German industrial towns would be a good example.

Such proposals were to prove to be too sanguine. As it turned out, several years of the Second World War had to pass before they could be implemented. Only in the later parts of it could Allied counter-propaganda wrest the lead from the German propaganda machine. But this is a development which will be discussed in another chapter.[1] Here it must suffice to have indicated the strange dialectic correlation that led from Northcliffe to Goebbels. The will to match and to surpass the effective Allied propaganda of the First World War was one of the major incentives for the making of National Socialist propaganda. As we shall see, there were others.

[1] See below, chapter 13.

PART I

Propaganda In Opposition

CHAPTER 1

The Rise Of An Agitator

1. BACKGROUND

To UNDERSTAND Goebbels the propagandist, one has to understand Goebbels the man. His youth and early history contain three features which are important for the interpretation of the later agitator. The first is Goebbels' physical deformity. As a result of infantile paralysis in early childhood he was lame in the left leg which was four inches shorter than the right. In later years Goebbels liked to give the impression that his deformity was the result of wounds received in the First World War; in fact he never served in it.[1] Rather small, swarthy, narrow-chested and limping he was a poor advertisement for the type of Nordic overlord or *Herrenmensch* eulogised in National Socialist writings. In his physique Goebbels had little in common with the vigorous rather simple types displayed on Nazi posters and postcards. Rivals and enemies inside the Party liked to ridicule him as a shrunken Teuton gone dark *(Nachgedunkelter Schrumpfgermane)*. Max Amann often called him "Mephistopheles" and Gregor Strasser, first his protector and later his bitter rival, cited Goebbels' clubfoot as "proof" that he was not free from Jewish blood. In spite of his lively and penetrating eyes he looked like "a living cartoon of all the racial theories sponsored by Hitler."[2] Much, perhaps too much, has been made of Goebbels' physical deformity by his rivals and critics. As with the crippled arm of William II, his limp was bound to affect his personality to some extent. Goebbels' malicious backbiting, his jealousy of better-looking rivals, can perhaps be partly explained by his physical deficiency, but his talents were little affected by it.

Goebbels' melodious Rhenish voice and manysided dialectical skill are as characteristic as his un-"Nordic" physique and his limp. The latter cannot "explain" the former, though it is true that his physical handicap sharpened his wit, his congenital restlessness and malice. "All his en-

---

[1] See Werner Stephan, *Joseph Goebbels*, Stuttgart, 1949, p. 17. An address by the young Party agitator to students in Frankfurt on Main during the winter of 1924-25 began "Wir Zerschossenen des Weltkriegs" (We shot-up men of the World War); A. Krebs, *Tendenzen und Gestalten der NSDAP*, Stuttgart, 1959, p. 158.

[2] W. Stephan, op. cit., p. 17.

3

ergies," observed a rival after his death, "had to be concentrated on one focal point; to show the others, who were healthy, cheerful and straight, that he too, could achieve something." [1]

The second relevant feature is his origin from the petty bourgeoisie of a small industrial town in the Rhineland. He was born in Rheydt in the Rhineland on 29 October 1897, the son of a *Werkmeister* or foreman. His ancestors came from the lower classes. The paternal grandfather Conrad Goebbels was a carpenter who married the daughter of a farmer, the maternal grandfather, a blacksmith, took as wife the daughter of a worker. Joseph Goebbels' father started at the bottom, was first an apprentice, later a clerk and foreman in a small gas-mantle factory of which in the end he became head clerk *(Prokurist)*. On his small salary he had to feed a family of seven, consisting of himself, his wife, three boys and two daughters, one of whom died early. For years this "black-coated worker" had to struggle to make ends meet. Later, as Reich Minister, Joseph Goebbels was inclined to overemphasize the frugality of his parental home. He told his assistants that as children they had to help their parents make lamp wicks to earn a few extra pennies. [2] Parsimony and lack of luxury had been a matter of course. It was impressed upon the children that their father had only advanced through strict economy and hard work. Having risen from the ranks father Goebbels entertained an ambition, so typical of his social milieu, to give his sons the solid secondary education he himself had missed.

Joseph's two elder brothers, Hans and Conrad, were like him undersized and shared his dark hair and Rhenish temperament. Their talents were not remarkable though by application and later through the influence of their then famous brother they both secured good positions without ever hitting the headlines. [3] The mother, Frau Katharina Goebbels, was a woman of little education but of "great strength of character." [4] With his physical handicap the youngest son was the special object of her tenderness and care. Frau Goebbels, for whom he seems always to have shown a certain regard, used to say with pride of the crippled schoolboy and student: *"Mein Josephchen hat ein Köpfchen!"* ("My little Joseph has brains!")

At the local Grammar School, the *Gymnasium,* with its emphasis on Latin and Greek, Joseph Goebbels was a good pupil and a voracious reader, but he was not popular. History and German literature were his favourite subjects. As a boy he had been rather lonely avoiding the company of other children who perhaps poked fun at him, of classmates

[1] Alfred Rosenberg, *Letzte Aufzeichnungen*, Göttingen, 1955, p. 195.

[2] See Goebbels' remarks to W. von Oven in April 1944, quoted in Wilfred von Oven, *Mit Goebbels bis zum Ende,* Buenos Aires, 1949, vol. I, pp. 239-241.

[3] Hans Goebbels became director of an insurance company in Düsseldorf, Conrad Goebbels director of the Party publishing office in Frankfurt/M. See W. von Oven, op. cit., I, p. 238.

[4] Roger Manvell and Heinrich Fraenkel, *Doctor Goebbels,* London, 1960, p. 2.

in whose games he could not participate.[1] He was reputed to be arrogant, quarrelsome and difficult.

In 1917 he matriculated with excellent results. Prompted by a strong urge for security his father would then have liked him to become a civil servant. Goebbels however preferred to study arts without, it seems, a fixed aim beyond the determination to rise in the world. To his chagrin, he had been rejected for military service in the war because of his deformity and was therefore able to pursue his university studies at once. It was a Catholic society, the *Albertus-Magnus Verein,* which between 1917 and 1920 granted the student a series of loans free from interest.[2] Although he received in addition a monthly allowance of 50 marks from his father, he still had to augment it by giving lessons and taking other odd jobs.

Resentment was an early feature in Joseph Goebbels' make-up. Poor himself, he seems to have looked with some envy and contempt on the rich *Korporations-Studenten,* carousing and dancing in Heidelberg. He could not afford to participate in their drinking parties and brawls. As he analysed his position twenty-five years later, probably not without some exaggeration: "It is true, as a son of the *alma mater* I belonged now to a higher social stratum. But yet I was a pariah, ostracised, only tolerated in it, not because I was less efficient or less clever than the others but only because I lacked the money which the others enjoyed so abundantly from the pockets of their fathers." [3]

It was then a time-honoured habit of German students to study at a number of universities, but young Goebbels did this to excess. He attended no less than eight of them, the universities of Bonn, Freiburg, Heidelberg, Würzburg, Cologne, Frankfurt, Berlin and Munich; he finally finished his studies in Heidelberg in 1921. There was a good deal of restlessness and desire for change in him. In Heidelberg he attended the lectures of the renowned Professor of German literature Friedrich Gundolf (who was of Jewish origin) and through him tried to get admission to the august circle of the poet Stefan George. Gundolf did not like Goebbels who therefore had to remain outside the poet's esoteric circle. It is one of the ironies of German history that, in this, a contemporary and later bitter adversary of Goebbels, Claus Schenk von Stauffenberg, succeeded where Goebbels failed. The man who was to attempt the assassination of Adolf Hitler in July 1944 enjoyed in his youth an intimate association with Stefan George.[4] One might add that after 1918 this

---

[1] Curt Riess, *Joseph Goebbels,* London, 1949, p. 11.

[2] Goebbels paid back the loans only many years afterwards when the Society had taken legal action against the then prominent National Socialist politician. See W. Stephan, op. cit., p. 24 and R. Manvell and H. Fraenkel, op. cit., p. 9 and pp. 299-300.

[3] W. von Oven, op. cit., I, p. 245.

[4] During the war Stauffenberg liked to cite George's powerful poem *Anti-Christ* as an expression of the hatred he felt for the Hitler tyranny, the contemptible brown flood. See J.W. Wheeler-Bennett, *The Nemesis of Power,* London, 1953, p. 582.

longing for a leader who would heal all the world's ills or provide a deeper vision of life was widespread among German youth. Though Goebbels never belonged to any of the many groups of the German Youth Movement he shared some of its vague hankering after a new style of living, its emphasis on community, its longing for a *Duce*.[1]

In Heidelberg Joseph Goebbels obtained his degree of doctor of Philosophy with a thesis on Wilhelm von Schütze, a minor playwright of the school of German Romanticism. Later as head of the Propaganda Ministry he insisted that in accounts of his life the title of the thesis should be changed to "The intellectual and political trends of Early Romanticism." This was significant. For whilst Goebbels had studied philosophy, history, history of art and German literature, he was then not yet aware of what he really wanted in life. His main talent was not one of scholarship but of politics, of political action and oratory. The university may have fed his restless intellect but it did not provide the platform for his specific talents and ambitions. Goebbels' marked *Geltungsdrang*, the desire to be someone, can be partly accounted for by his physical handicap and partly by his ambition to rise above the modest milieu from which he came. A first thwarting of Goebbels' journalistic ambitions may also have contributed to the growth of his anti-Semitism. Soon after he left the university he tried to gain a foothold with a leading German newspaper, the *Berliner Tageblatt*. The topics of many articles he submitted ranged from "Nationalisation" to "Christian Thought and Socialism."[2] They were all rejected by Theodor Wolff, the celebrated editor-in-chief of the paper, who, like its owner, was a Jew.

The third important aspect of his background and upbringing was Catholicism. Both his parents were devout Catholics. His mother prayed with her children regularly. When Joseph did well at the *Gymnasium* the parents had high hopes that the sickly child might one day become a priest, a career that was regarded as an honor by many German Catholics of their class. In Bonn he joined the *Unitas Verband*, a Catholic students' association. Its members were expected to attend church services regularly and lead an exemplary life. After the war Goebbels left the Unitas because it had excluded a friend of his for having disagreed with its strict moral principles.[3] By then, to the dismay of his father, Goebbels seems to have long discarded any belief in the Catholic creed.[4] Yet for some time he retained an ambiguous streak of religious idealism. When he

---

[1] The present writer remembers that in 1920 the German *Neupfadfinder* (New Boy Scouts), a section of the German Youth Movement, used to address their chosen head, a Protestant nationalist parson, as *"Der Herzog"*, a term corresponding to *Il Duce*.

[2] Curt Riess, op. cit., p. 18.

[3] W. Stephan, op. cit., p. 24.

[4] See the anxious admonitions of Goebbels' father contained in a letter to his son dated 7 November 1919. The text was published in a Catholic journal, the *Kirchenzeitung für das Bistum Aachen*, 27 October 1946. For an English translation see R. Manvell and H. Fraenkel, op. cit., pp. 14-16.

wrote his vague but significant autobiographical novel *Michael* [1] he made his hero say: "A people without religion is like a human being without breath." Michael, a twentieth century Faust, works on a play about Christ and is impressed by the Sermon on the Mount, "the simplest and greatest Sermon ever preached to mankind."

Like Goebbels' friend Richard Flisges—who introduced him to works by Marx, Engels and Walther Rathenau—his hero Michael loses his life in a mining accident. After Michael's death the Bible, Goethe's *Faust* and Nietzsche's *Zarathustra* are found among his belongings. [2] Michael [Goebbels] thought in terms of an antithesis between Christ and Marx. To him Christ was a principle of love, Karl Marx one of hatred. "The struggle which we shall fight to victory or to the bitter end is in the deepest sense a struggle between Christ and Marx." [3]

Soon the Führer was to take the place of Christ in Goebbels' attachments. Although a belief in the nation, in a Socialist Nationalism gradually became his creed, unlike Hitler and Himmler he was never able to discard his Catholic trappings entirely. He was no longer a practising Catholic yet he retained much understanding for the power and attraction of this religion; on the other hand he never had any sympathy for the liberal or Protestant point of view. In fact, his antiliberalism can be easily traced in the novel *Michael*. Its hero declares: "Liberalism, that means, I believe in mammon, Socialism, that means, I believe in work." [4] Like Nietzsche he insisted on the dictatorship of the Strong and the Bold. "Always a minority will be in control. The people have only the choice between living under the open dictatorship of the Bold or dying under the hypocritical democracy of the Cowards." [5] Long before Goebbels came in touch with Hitler and the National Socialist Party he was in favour of an authoritarian collectivism, a benevolent sort of dictatorship. Hitler became a man supreme to him, one who would speak *ex cathedra* with unchallengable authority. To this authority Goebbels was always ready to bring the *sacrificio del intelletto*. As one of his subordinates observed, Goebbels often subjected himself blindly to the Führer's wishes "as a monk is doing to his ecclesiastical superiors." [6] In later years, Goebbels, talking to members of his staff, expressed a certain admiration for the hierarchical structure and the organization of the Catholic Church. He was convinced that "human beings must be told what they have to

[1] Joseph Goebbels, *Michael, Ein Deutsches Schicksal in Tagebuchblättern*, Munich, 1929. The book was written in 1921 shortly after Goebbels had finished his university studies. Goebbels offered it to a number of publishers, including the Jewish firms of Ullstein and Mosse, without success until it was brought out much later by the National Socialist *Franz Eher Verlag*, possibly with interpolations. See Manvell and Fraenkel, op. cit., p. 19.

[2] See *Michael*, p. 158.

[3] Op. cit., p. 82.

[4] Op. cit., p. 139.

[5] Op. cit., p. 114.

[6] W. Stephan, op. cit., p. 25.

believe." He valued the uniformity in the church and found it "impressive" that "every Catholic priest in the whole world reads the same prayers on the same day, even at the same hour, in the same Latin language, from the same breviary." It attracted him that in the church "faith and order of service are clearly fixed once and for all and authoritatively."[1] He looked at the ritual, the clearly defined church festivals and processions as a model, as an exemplary frame which the Party should fill with its different doctrines and habits. At a course for war reporters he praised the rosary as "Rome's magnificent instrument of agitation." He was impressed by the professions which in an earlier type of society had held a privileged position, the priests and the officers. Like Charles Maurras in France, Goebbels still approved the forms, the ritual and the structure of the church into which he was born long after he had abandoned his religious faith.

It was for political and pragmatic reasons that this non-believer never formally left the church. He even had all his children baptised.[2] Goebbels was also opposed to the *Deutsche Glaubensbewegung* (German Faith Movement), the Nordic pagan religion sponsored by Alfred Rosenberg, Martin Bormann and Professor J. W. Hauer. As a tactician, he thought the time to boycott and abolish the Christian religion had not yet come. He once remarked to his officials: "Wait for the right time. Do not create any new clerical authorities! If we are to have a Pope, then I still prefer the Roman one to Mathilde Ludendorff," the wife of the general and fantastic champion of a non-Christian Germanic creed.[3]

Privately, Goebbels the realist praised the closeness of the Catholic clergy to the masses. He knew well that the priest was still an authority for the people in the village. It was true, he hoped for and visualised a day when the Party would take the place of the church, but he felt it would not happen for a long time. Goebbels maintained that "only when the Party was in a position to put into every village such well-trained and popular functionaries as the Church had there now, only then could it attract the simple folk permanently." [4]

During the war Goebbels talked contemptuously to his entourage of Christ's sacrifice for mankind: "Who still wants to hear of it to-day when hundreds of thousands of people are suffering a much more terrible fate on account of their political creed and nationality. The story of the crucifixion has lost its myth-appeal and power of persuasion!" [5] But traces of his former affinity, memories of his Catholic youth can still be found in a diary entry of April, 1943. He had then fallen ill and was treated in a Catholic hospital. Goebbels was impressed by the selfless

[1] Op. cit., p. 142.
[2] Op. cit., p. 138.
[3] Op. cit., p. 139. For the doctrines of Dr. Mathilde Ludendorff, the second wife of the famous soldier, see her book *Deutscher Gottglaube,* Munich, 1927.
[4] W. Stephan, op. cit., p. 140.
[5] Op. cit., p. 143.

care and devotion of the Catholic sisters whom he called "true bene-factresses of suffering mankind." [1]

It was his Machiavellian sense of political reality that caused him to avoid any open clash with the Churches. As much as he disliked the courageous resistance of Catholic Bishops like Count von Galen in Münster who in 1941 dared to criticise anti-clerical actions of the régime and to protest in his sermons against the putting to death of mentally defective persons and the confiscation of monasteries, Goebbels felt it in-opportune to suggest radical measures against the rebel. He knew how strong the hold of the Catholic Church on the masses still was. As he told his intimates during the war: "I have always been against provoking the Churches to a fight and wished in contradistinction from the Party Chancellery, to maintain the appearance of loyal co-operation. It will be easy after the war to deprive the Churches of their material basis and thus to break their back-bone." [2] Goebbels was never quite as radical and ruthless as his master, who disliked Christianity intensely, and its Pro-testant version even more than Catholicism. "I think I could have come to an understanding with the Popes of the Renascence" Hitler told Alfred Rosenberg, Philipp Bouhler [3] and Himmler in December, 1941,[4] "ob-viously, their Christianity was a danger on the practical level—and, on the propaganda level, it continued to be a lie. But a Pope, even a criminal one, who protects great artists and spreads beauty around him, is never-theless more sympathetic to me than the Protestant minister who drinks from the poisoned spring."

A fervid nationalism, a craving for power, contempt for the masses coupled with a belief in their manipulation were attitudes shared by Hitler and Goebbels. How did their intimate relationship begin? Why did it grow? These are questions we have to consider if we want to understand Goebbels' development from an immature student to a fanatic and self-seeking herald of National Socialism.

2. Changing Loyalties

Goebbels' diary for 1925-26 throws much interesting light on his out-look and habits as an obscure agitator in an equally obscure party.[5] During the fifteen months it covers—August, 1925 to October, 1926—its author was manager of the Gau Rhineland North of the National

[1] *Goebbels Tagebücher*, ed. L. Lochner, Zürich, 1948. Diary entry of 16 April 1943, p. 301.

[2] W. Stephan, op. cit., p. 146.

[3] Bouhler was a Reichsleiter and head of Hitler's Party Chancellery.

[4] *Hitler's Table Talk 1941-1944*, London, 1953, entry of 14 December, 1941, midday, pp. 145-146.

[5] The diary is in Goebbels' handwriting and sometimes difficult to decipher. All quotations from it here refer to the edition recently published by the "Institut für Zeitgeschichte" at Munich: *Das Tagebuch von Joseph Goebbels 1925/26,* ed. H.H. Heiber, Stuttgart, 1960. (abbreviated: *Tagebuch*)

Socialist Party which had its office in Elberfeld. At the beginning of that period he was also the private secretary of Gregor Strasser. This robust and fairly straightforward dispensing chemist from Landshut in Bavaria had been put by Hitler in charge of the Party's propaganda and was mainly concerned with pushing the Party forward in North Germany; together with his brother Otto he ran a publishing firm, the *Kampfverlag*, in Berlin. Impressed by Goebbels' oratorical talents, Gregor Strasser had persuaded him to give up his previous post of private secretary to Franz von Wiegershaus, a deputy of the Reichstag representing a small racialist group, the *Völkische Freiheitspartei*. Strasser was able to offer him a monthly salary of 250 Marks which compared favourably with the 100 Marks he had been receiving.

Goebbels threw himself with great energy into his new job and gave value for his salary. He edited a small journal, the fortnightly *National-sozialistische Briefe* on behalf of the Strasser brothers, he organized and addressed Party meetings, traveling indefatigably throughout the Rhine and Rhur area from Cologne to Krefeld and from Dortmund to Osnabrück. As his reputation grew, his territory extended, and Goebbels addressed audiences outside his region in Hamburg and Berlin, in Saxony and in South Germany. He could seldom stay long in one place, a fact which perhaps intensified the restless agility of his nature.[1] He was more often than not on the move, in trains, in the homes of Party comrades, frequently an irritable prisoner of his duties from which he found relaxation in the arms of a galaxy of girl friends. The Goebbels of this period was as little established and stable as the Party itself, restless, moody, contemptuous of the Party's enemies and suspicious of many of its leading men. The diary reveals an unbalanced *Stimmungsmensch*, half sentimental, half cynical, sometimes in the slough of despondency, sometimes on the heights, often sneeringly critical of his associates, whom at other times he professed to like, if only condescendingly, as good fellows.

In those days Goebbels was a "socialist" in so far as he disliked the bourgeois, the philistine, the self-satisfied and smug members of the middle class. It is significant that in the privacy of his diary he called his own father: "a good and well-meaning philistine, worthy and bourgeois."[2] At the same time he read the first volume of *Mein Kampf* with growing fascination. "Who is this man?" he asked, "half plebian, half God! Christ indeed, or only St. John?"[3]

In 1925 there was a marked difference of opinion and some tension inside the then rather weakened National Socialist camp. The bone of contention was the question of the restoration of their property to the various royal houses in Germany. Siding with the German National Party, Hitler was in favour of restoration, while the Strasser brothers were sharply against it. But much wider and more important issues were

[1] Goebbels claimed that he had addressed 189 meetings between 1 October 1924 and 1 October 1925.
[2] Diary entry, 6 October 1925. *Tagebuch*, p. 32.
[3] Diary entry, 14 October 1925. *Tagebuch*, p. 34.

involved. Hitler himself and the men around him in Munich, Esser, Feder, Streicher, had little sympathy with any form of socialism and regarded Russian Bolshevism as the main danger for Germany; on the other hand, the North German group led by the Strassers took non-Marxist socialism seriously and were unwilling to concentrate on Soviet Russia as the *bête noire*. At that time Goebbels was even inclined to put "socialism" before "nationalism." "National and Socialist—what comes first and what second?" he asked himself. "With us in the West the question must be ambiguous. At first the socialist salvation, then the national liberation will follow like a whirlwind." With his customary liking for dichotomy he added: "The whole thing is a question of generations: old or young! Evolution or revolution! Social or socialist! For us the choice is not difficult."[1]

In those days Goebbels was something of a National revolutionary or National Bolshevist, one who hated the capitalism of the victorious Western powers more than the Soviet Union. To him Locarno, an arrangement made by Germany with France, England and Belgium, was therefore as abhorrent as a red rag to a bull. Locarno meant that Germany was giving in and selling herself to Western capitalism. "Locarno and Security Pact: a horrible mixture of fraud, unfairness, perfidy and Pharisee-like attitude. Only one thing is true: money rules the world . . . We shall be the mercenaries fighting against Russia on the battlefields of Bolshevism." It was a grim alternative but Goebbels still preferred for Germany, if an ultimate decision had to be made, "to perish with Bolshevism rather than eternal slavery under [Western] capitalism." [2] At that time, in an oft repeated lecture on the theme "Lenin or Hitler," Goebbels presented Lenin as one of the greatest personalities in history who "had liberated the Russian people from the slave chains of Tsarism and of the medieval feudal system." [3] Alas, he asserted, this new freedom could not last, as it was based on decadent marxism, in itself a child of mechanical Western Enlightenment and the French Revolution.

Goebbels fully backed the "Socialist" angle at an important meeting of the Gauleiters from Western and Northern Germany convened by Gregor Strasser at Hanover on 25 January, 1926. Hitler was represented by the Party's financial "expert" Gottfried Feder. In the discussion of expropriation or restoration of the royal properties, Goebbels opposed Hitler's ideas on restoration strongly and successfully, putting the issue into a wider setting. "Russia, Germany, Western capitalism, Bolshevism—I talk for a half, for a full hour," he reported in his diary. "Everybody listens in breathless tension. And then came stormy applause . . . We have won . . . Strasser shakes me by the hand. Feder looks small and insignificant *(klein und hässlich)*." [4]

But there was a less comfortable sequel a few weeks later. At another

[1] Diary entry of 11 September 1925. *Tagebuch*, p. 27.
[2] Diary entry of 23 October 1925. *Tagebuch*, pp. 35-36.
[3] A. Krebs, *Tendenzen und Gestalten der NSDAP*, p. 159.
[4] Diary entry of 25 January 1926. *Tagebuch*, p. 56.

conference of Party leaders this time arranged by Hitler in Bamberg on 14 February, 1926, Goebbels found himself practically isolated. Apart from Gregor Strasser and Haake, a member of the Prussian Diet, no other representative of the North German opposition had been able to come. Hitler stuck to his anti-socialist line. Goebbels seems to have been horrified by his arguments and manner. "Hitler talks for two hours," he wrote in his diary, "I feel stunned. What sort of a Hitler? A reactionary? Astonishingly clumsy and unsure of himself. Russian question: he entirely misses the point. Italy and England our natural allies. Horrible! Our task is the smashing of Bolshevism. Bolshevism is a Jewish affair! We must inherit Russia. 80 million people!!!" [1] In the short discussion that followed Strasser spoke: "falteringly, tremblingly, clumsily, good honest Strasser." According to his own account, Goebbels did not dare to oppose the Master. "I cannot say one word. I am stunned," he wrote. On the other hand, Otto Strasser, who was not present at Bamberg, later alleged Goebbels did declare publicly that Hitler was right and there was no disgrace in admitting their mistakes and in rejoining him.[2]

In his diary Goebbels called Hitler's performance "one of the greatest disappointments of my life," lamenting, "I no longer believe unqualifiedly in Hitler. It is a terrible thing. I have lost my inner balance. I am only half myself."[3] Apart from shouting one or two slogans he kept silent during the Bamberg meeting, probably partly because he was, in spite of their different political views, fascinated by Hitler and partly because he was impressed by the relative wealth and display of Hitler's South German associates and lieutenants. Honesty to himself and to others was not often the *forte* of this restless agitator who wrote in his diary about events and his reactions to them with a mixture of candour, cynicism and make-believe. Although for a time as a "socialist" Goebbels continued to deplore Hitler's anti-Russian views, he realised too clearly the hopelessness of opposition to his leadership to persist long in this attitude. For to be with Hitler meant influence, status, promotion, to be against him disunity, ostracism, a split in the Party.

It is true for a while Goebbels seems to have been willing to continue to oppose Munich. There were lengthy discussions with Strasser and North German Party comrades in Hanover a week after the Bamberg débâcle. "Result: to become strong, not to begrudge to the Munichites their Pyrrhic victory: to work, to grow in strength and then to fight for socialism." [4] But Goebbels had begun to turn round. At first, it seems, he distinguished carefully between Hitler and some of his henchmen of whom at that time he hated Esser and Julius Streicher particularly. But when a month later Streicher contacted Goebbels at Nuremberg there was a long talk ending in reconciliation. Streicher, previously described

[1] Diary entry of 15 February 1926. *Tagebuch*, p. 60.
[2] Otto Strasser, *Hitler and I*, London, 1940, p. 100.
[3] *Tagebuch*, p. 60.
[4] Diary entry of 22 February 1926. *Tagebuch*, p. 62.

by Goebbels as "a swine" and "the most horrible man of them all," was now regarded in a milder light. "Julius is at least honest," runs a note in Goebbels' diary.[1]

Hitler, who had a shrewd assessment of Goebbels' talents, knew how to appeal to his vanity and thirst for prestige. In April, 1926 he invited him to Munich to address a Party meeting jointly with him. When Goebbels arrived he found Hitler's car waiting at the station to take him to a hotel. This was more impressive than the poorish milieu and the meagre finances of the Party office at Elberfeld. Behind the Munich headquarters there was money. "What a noble reception!" Goebbels jotted down in his diary, and, after he had met Hitler: "Tall, healthy, full of life. I like him. He shames us with his goodness . . . He puts his car at our disposal for the afternoon." [2] Both men addressed a large gathering in the *Bürgerbräu* hall, the traditional meeting place of the Party. There was a frantic welcome for them. Streicher opened the meeting, then Goebbels talked for two and a half hours. He fascinated the audience. "I give them everything I have. They rave, they shout. At the end Hitler embraces me. Tears are in his eyes. I am so to speak happy." Afterwards he was alone with Hitler in the hotel; they dined together. Here, too, Goebbels was impressed: "He is the host and how great he is in this too." [3]

Next day at the Party Office Hitler held forth to Hess and Goebbels on foreign affairs, on their policy in the East, on social questions. Goebbels was captivated. "He speaks for three hours. Brilliant. It could shake one's beliefs. Italy and England our allies. Russia will devour us. All this is in his pamphlet [4] and in the second volume of his *Kampf* to appear shortly. We are finding common ground. We ask questions. He answers brilliantly. I love him . . . social questions. Quite new insights. He has thought things out. He sets my mind at rest on all points. He is a man, in every way, in every respect. Such a firebrand *(Brausekopf)* can be my Führer. I bow before the greater man, the political genius!" [5] Though Goebbels now told himself that Hitler's ideas on foreign affairs in the East and the West were "convincing," he still felt the leader had not yet fully recognized the problem of Russia. However he (Goebbels) also must do some "re-thinking." [6] Obviously this was a rearguard action by Goebbels as he had been quite willing to toe the line. There is a revealing sentence in his diary: "Adolf Hitler, I love you, because you are great and uncomplicated *(einfach)* at the same time." [7]

Goebbels, moody, changeable and cynical, had long needed an anchor-

[1] Diary entry of 21 March 1926. *Tagebuch*, p. 66.
[2] Diary entry of 13 April 1926. *Tagebuch*, pp. 70-71.
[3] Ibid.
[4] Hitler's pamphlet *Die Südtiroler Frage und das deutsche Bündnisproblem* which Goebbels had read a few weeks previously. See his diary entry of 13 March 1926. *Tagebuch*, p. 73.
[5] Diary entry of 16 April 1926. *Tagebuch*, p. 72.
[6] Diary entry of 16 April 1926. *Tagebuch*, p. 73.
[7] Diary entry of 19 April 1926. *Tagebuch*, p. 74.

age, and he now found it in Hitler. Two months later, when the leader visited the Rhine and Ruhr area Goebbels was even more enthusiastic about him: "Hitler, the dear old comrade. One has to like him already as a human being. And in addition there is the outstanding intellectual personality. One never fails to learn from this independent mind. As an orator a wonderful trinity of gestures, mimic art and words. The born drummer *(Aufpeitscher)*. With this man you can conquer the world. Let him loose and he will make the corrupt Republic totter." [1] Goebbels was obviously under the spell of a man with a "charisma" who knew far better than he did himself what he wanted. "The spontaneously creative instrument of a divine fate," he commented, "I stand deeply moved before him . . . I feel something like happiness. Indeed, this life is worth while living. 'My head will not roll into the sand until our mission has been fulfilled.' There were his last words. That's like him! Yes, that is like him!" [2]

If the hero of his novel *Michael* commits suicide, Goebbels himself had no need for such ultimate despair. After a visit to Obersalzberg in July, 1926 he felt reassured and strengthened as never before, a convert to a new belief whose prophet was Adolf Hitler. "These days have shown me the direction and the way! In the midst of deep despair a star is shining! I feel drawn to it for ever. Now my last doubts have been shed. Germany will live! Heil Hitler!" [3]

What the dead Gretchen was to the repenting Faust, the living Hitler was to the Machiavellian radical from Elberfeld, a signpost to salvation. But salvation meant in his case also the road to success and power, both for himself and for the Movement. A fanatic who had often been violently torn between enthusiasm and despair, Goebbels had found a protective hold in a man who was equally fanatical, was fundamentally more sure of himself and was filled with a sense of mission to an extent which Goebbels had never felt. The leader personified a political mystique for which the disciple was to become the chief propagandist, a mystique which combined hatred of all opponents with faith in the dynamics of their Movement, a radical negation of the existing political system with emphatic but equivocal promises of a new authoritarian structure of state and society. In addition there was the hope of office and power should the Movement one day succeed.

Goebbels' attachment to Hitler was as much a fulfilment of a psychological need as it was a calculation. Nevertheless, the attachment was genuine and it endured, whereas Goebbels' relations with other prominent members of the party were largely dictated by opportunism. These were ambivalent with a quick change from friendship and co-operation to hostility and antagonism and vice versa. In Goebbels' eyes the "dear fellow" *(lieber Kerl)* of today could become "a blockhead," "an intriguer," "a swine," tomorrow. In those days Goebbels developed what he later used

---

[1] Diary entry of 16 June 1926. *Tagebuch*, p. 84.
[2] Diary entry of 24 July 1926. *Tagebuch*, pp. 92-93.
[3] Diary entry of 25 July 1926. *Tagebuch*, p. 94.

to call his *Schimpflexikon*, a systematic abuse of his opponents, rivals and enemies, in which sarcastic venom, Mephistophelian irony and the pleasure of persiflage were combined in a highly individualistic performance. That Goebbels' terms of reference to the political opponents of the Party were not exactly flattering is not surprising. In his diary Stresemann, then Germany's Foreign Minister, is called "this fat, old swine," and Severing, the Prussian Minister of the Interior, "this cowardly Social Democratic cad." Even the leader of the conservative German nationalists, Hergt, is spoken of as "a terrible mixture of cad, coward, *rentier* and swine." When Dr. Ley backed Hitler against the Strasser faction, Goebbels scoffed at him as "a blockhead, perhaps an intriguer." [1] Esser, who was later to become Under Secretary of State in Goebbels' Ministry, was referred to contemptuously as "a smart pocket-size Hitler" aping the mannerisms of his model.[2]

Although Goebbels was complicated, the sneering nihilism in him somehow did not impair his oratorical talents, his drive as an organizer and his skill in political demagogy. Goebbels' contempt for the masses never went so far as to make it impossible for the agitator to impress and to persuade them. If he had the unscrupulousness of a rabble-rouser, he had also the fanatacism of a missionary. His vulgarity went hand in hand with a German sentimentality which was curiously "modern" and rather removed from the stereotyped solemnities of the older type of nationalists, such as, for instance, were typical of the members of the "Pan-German League." When they made a pilgrimage to the Wagnerian shrine in Bayreuth in formal morning coats, Goebbels appeared in a proletarian blouse or in an equally undistinguished raincoat.

Unlike his later diaries, Goebbels did not write the earlier one with a view to possible publication, and there is therefore no reason to believe that he was deliberately posing. Even after he had become one of Hitler's disciples and was assured of his patronage, his moods still vacillated between depression and happiness, harmony with others and antagonism to them. On 26 October, 1925 he noted in his diary: "Else, my good and beautiful darling, Kaufmann, my loyal comrade. Who can still call me poor?" Six months later, after he had received some critical lines from Karl Kaufmann (by then Gauleiter of the Gau Rhineland-North) deploring Goebbels' lack of toughness, he wrote: "A nasty surprise before my departure. Kaufmann writes a rather insolent letter to me . . . I depart in a bad mood and depressed. Something in me is going to break. Poor Kaufmann . . . How dreadful is such a journey [by railway] during the night." [3]

In Goebbels a streak of romantic idealism mingled with little concealed aggressiveness. In those early years the linchpin between his genuine admiration for Hitler, for Bayreuth, for the ideas of Richard Wagner

[1] Diary entry of 30 September 1925. *Tagebuch*, p. 31.
[2] Diary entry of 6 November 1925. *Tagebuch*, p. 40.
[3] Diary entry of 8 May 1926. *Tagebuch*, p. 77.

and Houston Stewart Chamberlain, and his zest for denouncing enemies and rivals was cold ambition, a restless thirst for prestige and power. He liked to regard himself half as a restless whirlwind and half as an apostle and preacher; he observed with satisfaction that people were listening to him at mass meetings as if they were in church.

But there was nothing semi-religious in his deliberate attempts to shock and weaken the enemy, the men of the Republic, the Jews. To disturb the performance of a play like Zuckmayer's *Fröhlicher Weinberg* for political reasons [1] in the autumn of 1926 appealed to him as much as did the interference with the premiere of Remarque's pacifist film "All Quiet on the Western Front," which he organized in Berlin in 1931.[2] But in 1926 before Hitler appointed Goebbels Gauleiter of Berlin—a position which, in the economic trials of the late 'twenties, gave him an eagerly taken chance to push himself and his cause forward—a frequent note of pessimism, if not of nihilism, is struck in his diary notes. For example, at a mass meeting in Hamburg, after Goebbels had, as he put it, "preached for two hours to breathlessly listening people," who intensely applauded him, he jotted down: "In what can one still put one's trust? The system [of Weimar] is disintegrating of necessity. Good luck to those who are holding out until the last, the decisive moment. Will we not by then have spent our strength? Then we shall have lost, lost everything. What is then our task? To find the last form for a people doomed to perish? I believe I have found this form for myself." [3]

It is true, these pessimistic sentences were written before Goebbels had made his peace with Hitler and became one of his standard bearers. But even afterwards he lamented: "I am dead and was buried long ago. How heavy is my heart. I shall travel to Hanover and Brunswick. How much I dislike all this! I will then work. Work is my last consolation!" [4] He constantly dislikes people, places, arrangements. When in June, 1926 there was a struggle for power inside the Party Gau at Elberfeld, Goebbels comments acidly: "Today the personal struggle will begin. Kaufmann, Pfeffer or I. I find this rubbish horrible. I should like to shed the whole swindle. It makes one feel like vomiting . . . nonsense, intrigue, an urge to vomit!" [5]

When the leadership of the Gau Berlin was offered to Goebbels, he seems at first to have refused. An entry of 20 August, 1926 makes it clear that he did so because he did not want "to kneel in dirt." The agitator from the provinces was, moreover, half repelled and half attracted by the capital of Germany. After addressing a meeting there a fortnight later he commented in his diary: "Then we stroll through the streets. Berlin at night. A Babylon of sins! And into this I shall throw myself." [6]

[1] Diary entry of 10 September 1926, *Tagebuch*, pp. 102-103.
[2] See C. Reiss, *Joseph Goebbels*, pp. 91-92.
[3] Diary entry of 31 January 1926, *Tagebuch*, p. 57.
[4] Diary entry of 28 September 1926, *Tagebuch*, p. 105.
[5] Diary entry of 19 June 1926, *Tagebuch*, p. 84.
[6] Diary entry of 17 September 1926, *Tagebuch*, p. 104.

When he finally accepted the post as Gauleiter of Berlin, as Hitler urged him to do, he simply recorded: "On November 1 I am going definitely to Berlin. After all Berlin is the centre of things. For us, too." [1]

It was a shrewd move by Hitler who in this way transformed the private secretary of Gregor Strasser into the latter's most serious rival. Both men now had their headquarters in Berlin, but it was Gauleiter Goebbels and not Strasser who put the Party on the map there and who created new and striking techniques of propaganda.

[1] Diary entry of 18 October 1926, *Tagebuch*, p. 108.

CHAPTER 2

The Battle For Berlin

1. Techniques of a Gauleiter

EVEN FOR A hardworking and pushing young agitator Berlin was a tough assignment. The Party had not made any headway in the Reich Capital. There was a big Communist vote, the Social Democrats controlled the Town Hall, and apart from the right wing racialist *Deutsche Zeitung* which was not in the hands of the National Socialists the small band of Nazis was treated with indifference or hostility by the Berlin daily press.

In his lively propaganda account of the "Battle of Berlin" [1] Goebbels talked with characteristic contempt of the Party "sect" which he found on his arrival, split into factions that hated each other as much as they hated their common enemies. What existed in Berlin was not a party in the strictly disciplined manner aimed at by Hitler and Goebbels; "it was a widely chaotic crowd of a few hundred people thinking, it is true, on National Socialist lines, but everyone of whom had formed his own private views on National Socialism." Goebbels who then liked so much to decry the acts of terror said to have been committed by "the Reds" later admitted that at that time frequent brawls had occurred between the different sections of his Party. [2]

When he arrived the Party was in the doldrums and certainly no serious factor in the political life of the city. Moreover after 1925 the period of economic recovery and of the influx of much foreign capital into German economic life did not create a favourable climate for the spreading of extremist doctrines. Before Goebbels' appointment as Gauleiter the Party in Berlin had lacked drive and its finances were poor and disorganized. The Party Headquarters was in an obsolete and dirty cellar at the back of a house in the Potsdamer Strasse nicknamed "the Opium Den" by the comrades themselves.

Goebbels first endeavoured to reorganize the Party, to make it an effective instrument in the fight for power and, last but not least, to

[1] Joseph Goebbels, *Kampf um Berlin. Der Anfang,* 4th edition, Munich, 1932, pp. 22-24.
[2] Op. cit., p. 23.

18

establish his own authority. After some time he managed to eliminate all sorts of dissidents whom he labelled disdainfully "the anarchical elements." If we can believe his account, about one fifth of the total membership left the Party. Financially the Party had more debts than assets. There was no regular revenue, nor was there a serious will and capacity to get things done and to put the Party on the map. One of the first measures of the new Gauleiter was an appeal to the sense of sacrifice of the Party members he retained. They were asked to contribute a total of 1500 Marks (about £75) each month in order to put the organization on a sounder and more effective basis.

In those early days the Gauleiter seems to have been Jack of all trades. His natural versatility, reinforced by the modest position of the Party, became Goebbels' strength, for it helped him to avoid overspecialization, to keep in touch with the rank and file and to provide sufficient scope to advertise the Party through a calculated mixture of propaganda tricks and acts of terror. A year after he had begun his work in Berlin he made a revealing admission to his Party functionaries. The Nazi Movement, he explained, was "still so young and still so poor in really big and leading brains, of course not if you compare it with the other Parties." Making a virtue out of necessity he declared it good that things were so, "because the really big brains are now forced to deal with this or that specialized field, but the truly outstanding brain must be everything at one and the same time: propagandist, organizer, speaker and writer. He must be able to cope with people, to obtain funds, to write articles and to do many other things." [1]

Incidentally Goebbels claimed a similar unphilistine, adventurous versatility for the Berlin Storm Troopers (S.A.) in those early days. What Goebbels and his few fulltime collaborators did continuously, the SA-man did in his leisure time. He was on his feet for the Movement every evening and sometimes for entire nights and particularly during days of acute political tension. "Here he had to protect a meeting, there to stick up posters or distribute leaflets or to win new members, get subscriptions for his Party paper or to transport the speaker safely to or from a meeting." [2] In any case alertness and elasticity were indeed qualities indispensable for the leader of a Movement which had yet to make its mark.

Goebbels lost little time in building up a cadre of reliable Party members strongly imbued with the crude and aggressive *Weltanschauung* of National Socialism. As he frankly admitted, his aim was "to hammer it into the heads of the Party comrades so much that they could reiterate it, so to speak, in their sleep." [3] Although Goebbels managed to be on frank terms with many of the rather primitive members, he was contemptuous of anyone who dared to criticize him or his actions. "We established a

[1] J. Goebbels in his address "Erkenntnisse und Propaganda" of 9 January 1928, reprinted in *Signale der Neuen Zeit,* p. 42.
[2] *Kampf um Berlin,* p. 90.
[3] Op. cit., p. 33.

firm authority through a tough fight in an organization that was about to disintegrate in anarchy," he declared later. "Indifferent to the tittle-tattle of the all-too-many we planted the flag of the idea and set fanatical men marching for it, fighting unconditionally." [1] The nucleus of Party members was first consolidated by weekly meetings in small and unimpressive halls. Only after this internal consolidation had been established would larger mass meetings or *Kampfversammlungen* follow, intended to attract a wider audience. Goebbels seems to have found it immensely difficult to awaken Berlin, "that tough city monster of the pavements (*aus Stein und Asphalt*) from its lethargic sleep." [2]

He was astute enough to realize that some new and specific methods were needed to make the Movement felt in a big city where one sensation followed another, where millions of newspaper copies were issued daily, and where the amusement parks invited thousands to their ever changing products. "Berlin needs its sensations as a fish needs its water," the Gauleiter observed, "this city lives on it, and any political propaganda not recognizing this will miss its target." [3] There were two possibilities of attracting attention and furthering the aims of the Party. One was the ever new invention of stunts and tricks, the issuing of posters, addresses and slogans in a crisp, graphic and popular style, the other fights and brawls, provocative clashes with the Marxist enemies leading to "the conquest of the streets." Before Goebbels took over, the Berlin Storm Troopers, many of them proletarians and unemployed, had been mere fighters, rowdies who welcomed any altercation even among themselves. Later Goebbels claimed that one of the most difficult tasks of his early days in Berlin was to transform the SA-man into a *political* soldier.[4] What he wished to provide for these rather primitive *condottieri* and toughs was a new sense of purpose, a new orientation. Only a disciplined paramilitary organization would help towards the conquest of the streets. In the new mass-age the street was, as Goebbels put it, "the criterion of modern politics. He who can conquer the streets can also conquer the masses; and he who has conquered the masses has by it conquered the State." [5] Until Goebbels appeared in the capital the Party had confined its activities to the more respectable middle-class suburbs in the West and South of Berlin. Now determined efforts were made to obtain a foothold in the proletarian quarters of the North and East.

Part of Goebbels' routine was to challenge and to imitate the Communists by imitating their slogans and methods. To some extent the SA formed the opposite number to the Communist Red Fighters' League (*Rot Frontkämpfer Bund*). The new Gauleiter clearly realized that his Party needed many more members from the ranks of the workers and he

[1] Ibid.
[2] Op. cit., p. 27.
[3] *Kampf um Berlin*, p. 28.
[4] Op. cit., p. 30.
[5] Op. cit., p. 86. See also Goebbels' remark on p. 127 "We say it frankly: our aim was the conquest of the streets, by it we wanted to win over the masses and the people to us."

thought he might gain them by boldly marching into the lion's den, into the strongholds of the Communists.[1] In February 1927 glaring posters in red were put up by the National Socialists, screaming in Communist fashion "The Bourgeois State is Approaching its End." It was an invitation to a mass meeting in the Pharus Hall in the proletarian North of the town, a centre often used for Communist Party gatherings. Dr. Goebbels was to speak on the truly Marxist theme of "the Breakdown of the Bourgeois State." The Nazi posters were couched in the language of imperatives, proclaiming that "a new Germany must be forged, a Germany of Work and Discipline." There was the appeal of addressing the reader intimately as Thou *(Du)*: "For this task history is falling on thee!—Workers of brain and of brawn! The Fate of the German People is laid into thy hands!" [2]

What probably mattered as much as the meeting itself was the procession preceding it. The Party had called upon all its members to march through the streets of the Red North, displaying proudly its swastika banners and—hiding all kinds of weapons. In fact, by challenging the enemy in its own territory Goebbels and his toughs had asked for trouble. When the procession arrived at the Pharus Hall several members of the Communist "Red Front" organization were sitting inside. Tension ran high and a slanging match developed, words of abuse hurled against each of the hostile factions. There was much heckling by the Communists and when the Nazi stewards removed the most persistent of these from the hall a battle ensued, which was fought intensely with beer-mugs, glasses and chairs. It proved a stroke of luck for the cold-blooded and calculating Goebbels that some of the Storm Troopers protecting him were wounded in the scuffle. They were laid out on stretchers on the platform, and their screams could be heard before they were carried out of the hall at regular intervals. At last the Berlin Movement had its martyrs! Eventually the SA-men seem to have succeeded in driving their opponents into the street. And Goebbels, apparently more stimulated than cowed by the dramatic events, delivered his fervid address in the midst of bloodstains, broken stools and smashed beer glasses. He used every oratorical device: sadness, contempt, indignation and ridicule. He did his utmost to idolize the SA; at the end of his performance he talked for the first time of "the Unknown SA-Man"—the hero of Germany's forthcoming regeneration. It was a skilful variation of the "Unknown Soldier" theme, so popular in the nineteen-twenties.

As a result of the brawl which ended with the arrival of the police, thousands of Berliners who had been oblivious of the activities of the Hitler Party became aware of its existence. Next morning the Nazis made

[1] The Communist Party was for the National Socialists both a model and an enemy pursued with fanatical hatred. See M. Broszat "Die Anfänge der NSDAP in Berlin 1926/27", *Vierteljahrshefte für Zeitgeschichte*, vol. 8, no. 1, January 1960, p. 91 and pp. 92-117.

[2] The poster is reproduced in *Kampf um Berlin*, p. 67. In another poster the new mixture of Nationalism and Socialism offered by the Nazis became more evident. It was addressed to "Proletarians! Workers! German Slaves!"

headlines in the Berlin press, though none of them was friendly. But in the next few days 2600 applications for membership were reported to have been received at the Party's Headquarters and 500 of the applicants wanted also to join the SA.[1]

There was method in Goebbels' appeal to the masses. The language he used was graphic, direct, aggressive and charged with an emotional intensity bound to draw attention. He made a careful point of claiming that his Party was not a new edition of the traditional conservative or racialist elements of the Right. No, it was a modern phenomenon, employing an entirely novel approach. Indeed, none of the parties of the Right had ever attempted to win over the anonymous masses in such a deliberate way. There was a good deal of showmanship and of the American circus à la Barnum in Goebbels' techniques, but at the same time they were intended to provoke and incite the 'Marxists'—a convenient label for lumping together the governmental Social-Democrats and the oppositional Communists—to fool them and to expose their sham.

"Making noise," declared Goebbels, "is an effective means of opposition." It was to him a medium by which to impress the general public, to strengthen and intoxicate his followers and to intimidate opponents. Goebbels' methods had often entertainment as well as propaganda value. He shrewdly adapted them to the mentality of the man in the street. What he liked in the Berliners was their mobility and mental alertness. They had, he observed, "less feeling than intelligence and more wit than sense of humour. The Berliner is a busybody and full of vitality. He loves work and he loves amusements." [2] With his quick and fertile mind, his gift for coining hitting and cheeky remarks the new Gauleiter fitted well into the milieu of this large and vibrating town. Goebbels projected his own galling, fanatical attitude into the populace and then told himself with satisfaction that "a bitter fanaticism, particularly in political matters, was nowhere so much at home as in Berlin." [3]

Political entertainment with a purpose was Goebbels' own and in some ways inimitable line. It ranged from the drafting of mysterious aggressive posters heralding the publication of the Party newspaper Der Angriff [4] to the use of white mice and snakes which disturbed the elegant public in the Berlin West End at the premiere of E.M. Remarque's famous anti-war film Im Westen nichts Neues (All Quiet on the Western Front). There were well-defined slogans like those on the banner carried by fifty SA-men hiking from Berlin, where the Party was then forbidden, to the Party Reich Congress in Nuremberg of August 1927. One of them ran: "Fussmarsch Berlin—Nürnberg. Trotz Verbot nicht tot!" [5]

[1] Curt Riess, Joseph Goebbels, pp. 51-55. For Goebbels' own melodramatic account see his Kampf um Berlin, pp. 63-72.
[2] Kampf um Berlin, p. 27.
[3] Ibid.
[4] See below p. 53.
[5] "On foot from Berlin to Nuremberg—
Though forbidden, not dead."

Goebbels undoubtedly proved a pioneer in employing modern media in politics. His ingenuity had full play during the many election campaigns between 1930 and 1933. Electioneering for the Prussian Diet in April 1932 was particularly intense and bitter. During it Goebbels challenged Chancellor Brüning to appear with him on the same platform in a public debate, but well aware of Nazi tricks and sly methods Brüning refused. Whereupon Goebbels had a recording of a radio speech delivered recently by the Chancellor in Königsberg played back at a huge Nazi mass meeting in Berlin. Again and again Goebbels would stop and interrupt the recording to answer and challenge his invisible opponent, who of course could not defend himself. "The public was in a rage of enthusiasm," Goebbels noted in his diary, "it was an immense success. A few spirited supporters had been so impressed that they have given us 100,000 Marks for our election campaigns." [1] Unfortunately Goebbels did not disclose who these enthusiastic supporters were.

About the same time Goebbels organized Hitler's election air-trips under the adroit and ambiguous slogan "Hitler over Germany". Such flights for political purposes were then still a novelty in Germany and little employed by other parties. Hitler would fly from one region of Germany to another, from Cologne to Munich for instance, to address huge open air meetings. Sometimes he would appear on the same day in four widely separated towns. Once he covered 26 towns in a week, a considerable achievement in those days when regular air-services were still in their infancy. [2]

Travelling by car, train or aircraft during election campaigns, Goebbels, that totalitarian Mephistopheles, was ubiquitous and very short-tempered. His contempt for the masses he addressed day by day was unmistakable. In all his travels he had his main aim firmly in mind—the coming to Power of the Party—and he displayed everywhere the idiosyncrasies of the efficient mass-orator, who was at the same time a misanthrope. A sour diary entry of 1 July 1932 [3] is revealing: "Now the travelling season starts again. Work has to be done standing, walking, driving and flying. The most important conversations take place on the staircase, in the hall, at the door, whilst driving to the station. One has hardly time to think. One is carried zig-zag across Germany by rail, by car, and by plane. One arrives in a town half an hour before the meeting begins, sometimes even later, and then one steps on to the platform and speaks.

"Mostly the public has no idea of what the speaker has already gone through during the day before he delivers his address in the evening. Undoubtedly many imagine that he is doing nothing else but talk. They become unfair to him, if he is tired or not quite in form. They regret that he is not a master of wit and of the eloquent phrase. Meanwhile

---

[1] J. Goebbels, *Vom Kaiserhof zur Reichskanzlei*, Munich, 1935, p. 82.

[2] W. Stephan, *Joseph Goebbels*, pp. 54-55; also *Vom Kaiserhof zur Reichskanzlei*, p. 80.

[3] *Vom Kaiserhof zur Reichskanzlei*, pp. 120-122.

he struggles, with the heat, with words, with the logic of his thought, with a voice that is becoming more and more hoarse, with the tricks of bad acoustics, with the thick air which envelops him, coming up from the packed crowd of 10,000 human beings. And the next day a learned scribe, who at the meeting sat somewhere in a safe seat and took down a few keywords, raises his index finger and points out that unfortunately this time the speaker had been lacking in the vitality (*Frische*) otherwise so typical of him. In fact, he had never registered that vitality before, when it was present. He only registers its absence. . . ." [1]

There were very contradictory elements in Goebbels' techniques and attitudes. On the one hand he posed as a man of deep communal feeling, as he described the emotional egalitarianism inside the SA-"Elite"—"here we are all chums" (*Man verkehrt nur auf Du und Du*). "Here the new front of a national community (*Volksgemeinschaft*) is being formed which, we hope, will one day give guidance to and set an example for a new German nation, organized as a people's community." [2] "We sincerely regard the proletarian as an equal, man for man." [3] On the other hand a harsh authoritarianism with some Nietzschean undertones is unmistakable in everything Goebbels propagated. He claimed that "the first National Socialists had the courage to live dangerously," [4] a phrase obviously borrowed from Nietzsche. The same attitude of the *Herrenmenschen* is behind a remark of Goebbels such as: "To us the Party was a diamond which we cut in order to employ it later without mercy for the piercing of the enemy's front." [5] Activism, dynamic drive and ruthlessness were displayed with a strange mixture of idealism and cynicism. "The SA-man is destined," Goebbels pontificated, "to demonstrate the plastic strength and the popular force (*die volksverbundene Kraft*) of the National Socialist Movement in public before the whole world." [6] Goebbels was well aware of what he was doing and admitted it occasionally with refreshing candour. Looking back to the early years of the Battle for Berlin he remarked: "One should not hold it against us that we idolised this heroic struggle in our propaganda and that we gave the SA-man the aura of a valiant political soldier." [7]

To him the final aim of the Movement justified all means likely to lead to success. The worst evil was to be overlooked and martyrdom was welcome, provided it proved a good piece of propaganda. "No matter if they derided and slandered us, if they brutally knocked us down and threw us into prison, it was this very thing which seemed to us desirable. But to ignore us with an inciting indifference, that spurred us on to the last ounce of strength in us, drove us on to think out ever new means

[1] Ibid.
[2] *Kampf um Berlin*, p. 99.
[3] Op. cit., p. 48.
[4] Op. cit., p. 131.
[5] Op. cit., p. 32.
[6] Op. cit., p. 86.
[7] Op. cit., p. 94.

of public propaganda and not to miss any chance of intensifying the activities of the Party to such an extent that in the end it would take the breath of even this mammoth town away, if only for the time being: the enemy would laugh no longer." [1]

Activism, ruthless advance, half threatening imperatives, simple and crude, formed the appeal of the Party's posters and postcards. The passers-by could not ignore their dynamic language, which achieved considerable effect by comparatively simple means. Posters of invitation to a Nazi mass-meeting were never overloaded; neither their drawings nor their texts made heavy demands on the intelligence and the sensitiveness of the viewers. Slogans such as "Onward Berlin" (*Berlin Voran!*) or "Forward over Graves!" (*Über Gräber vorwärts!*) were bound to draw the attention of the crowds. Mjölnir's simplified Germanic heroes with marked chin, over life-size, with their hard fists and rather low forehead could create a mental image of strength, defiance and rebellion. Their appeal to brutal virility was accompanied by another one to the equally primitive feeling of *Schadenfreude*, the enjoyment of the discomfort suffered by those branded as enemies of the Movement. The Jew, said to try in vain to hide his true and ugly face behind a mask, is found out and exposed to the grinning contempt of the Teutonic Berliners.

Goebbels was a master of crude invective which showed his opponent in a ludicrous light. For instance in March 1930 he abused General Gröner, the Minister responsible for the *Reichswehr*, who did not favour the growing ties of sympathy between young *Reichswehr* officers and the Nazis. He was pictured as "the present confidential clerk of the Reichswehr, a General in a Jacobine cap" who had deserted his Imperial Master in November 1918. Praise for the Reichswehr was slyly mixed with denunciation of its Minister: "Here lies the legacy of Prussian Militarism —buried, one is inclined to say. Good Lord! A general with a peacock feather and a slouch hat, who thinks that too much wearing of uniforms is to be found in *this* Republic! Poor *Reichswehr*! How much longer is this going to last?" [2]

Goebbels himself called the vocabulary he used when he was inciting the Berliners against the "system" of the Republic: "a new and modern language which had nothing to do with antiquated expressions of so-called racialists." [3] It was the calculated use of uncomplicated metaphors and mental associations on which the style of his addresses and leaders relied. The harshness of force and obligation, the imperative of the Must ran through them. Phrases such as "to drive the Movement forward", "to push forward irresistibly", "human beings fighting fanatically and unconditionally are set on the march", or "Mass propaganda is the only

[1] Op. cit., p. 44.

[2] J. Goebbels' article "Gröner im Schlapphut", *Der Angriff*, 9 March 1930, reprinted in the book *Der Angriff, Aufsätze aus der Kampfzeit*, Munich, 1935, pp. 155-157. The quotation is on p. 157.

[3] *Kampf um Berlin*, p. 46.

main weapon" give an impression of continuous activity, of marching towards a goal, of a Movement bound to reach its target. It was a language which never allowed the reader or listener to rest. It incited him against the *status quo,* the existing social order and at the same time deliberately created the illusion of an all-embracing national community that had only to eliminate its hideous enemies in order to prosper and succeed.

2. Simplicity—Repetition—A Preference for the Spoken Word

How far did National Socialist propaganda borrow from the techniques of the two totalitarian regimes which were firmly established when Hitler and Goebbels were still obscure agitators of an insignificant party? This question is not an easy one, but it can be said that whilst Hitler's basic concept of propaganda was to some extent his own, his and Goebbels' insistence that in propaganda the spoken word is more effective than the written one, that it has, as we might say, a greater demagogic appeal was much influenced by both the Marxist and the Fascist patterns.

As we have seen,[1] it was the success of Allied propaganda which made Hitler realize that propaganda had to be primitive and to be attuned to the very limited understanding of the masses. It had to be confined to a few points and to be carried out with persistency.[2] Hitler was convinced that the Allies had looked at the masses with the same contempt that he himself felt for them. In *Mein Kampf* Hitler made much of the subjective character of the people, who, he declared, are "so feminine in their nature and attitude that their activities and thought are motivated less by sober consideration than by feeling and sentiment." [3] Their sentiment was uncomplicated, and very simple. It did not allow for differentiation; it was positive or negative, based on love and hatred, it only knew right or wrong, truth or lie, but no shades, no ability to see two sides of a question. English propaganda had "understood and considered all this in the most ingenious manner." [4] From these observations Hitler arrived at a basic tenet of all propaganda, "it has to confine itself to little and to repeat this eternally." [5]

In Hitler's view, the masses were slow and lazy, their memories were faulty, and they reacted only to "the thousandfold repetition of the most simple ideas." [6] Keeping perhaps in mind the traditional German indulgence in ideologies, Hitler made a good point by emphasizing that efficient leadership did not depend on extensive theoretical knowledge, that great theorists were rarely also great organizers, and that the organizer

---

[1] See above Introduction, pp. xxxi-ii.
[2] See A. Hitler, *Mein Kampf,* New York, 1939, p. 240.
[3] Op. cit., p. 237.
[4] Ibid.
[5] Op. cit., p. 238.
[6] Op. cit., p. 239.

must above all be a good practical psychologist. The talent of the leader consisted in his ability to move the masses and was quite different from the talents of the "ideologue", the man who developed and systematized ideas.

In examining the specific tasks of propaganda and of organization,[1] Hitler drew a fundamental distinction between followers and members. Whereas the followers were merely passive in their appreciation of the Party's main aims, the members took an active share in spreading and defending them. Hitler described the follower of a movement as "one who declares himself in agreement with its aims" whilst a member was a person "who fights for it." There should be a ratio of ten followers to one or two members. As only the most valuable of the followers were to be made members, it can be argued that Lenin's idea of the cadres influenced Hitler. But the difference is this: the concept of cadres had its roots in the clandestine nature of Communist organization under Tsarism, whereas in the tolerant Weimar Republic Hitler's movement could come out in the open and had no need to limit its membership for security reasons. The distinction between members and followers had psychological roots and was not motivated by considerations of security. In Hitler's view it was the task of propaganda "to force a doctrine upon an entire people", whereas the organization should only admit "those who for psychological reasons" did "not threaten to become a brake to a further spreading of ideas." [2]

The tasks of propaganda and of organization, each of them twofold, were thus distinctly different. Propaganda was to gain supporters and sympathizers for the Movement, the organization was to win members for the Party. To quote Hitler's own clumsy but significant formulations: "The first task of propaganda is to win over people for the later organization; the first task of the organization is to gain people for the continuation of propaganda. The second task of propaganda is the undermining of the existing order and the infiltration of the new doctrine into this order, whilst the second task of the organization must be the struggle for power in order to obtain the definitive success of the doctrine by it." [3]

As shown, Goebbels put this dichotomy into practice to a certain extent when building up the Gau Berlin of the Party between 1926 and 1930. But two other aspects of propaganda were to prove more important to him. The first emerged from Hitler's and his own mental attitudes, the second from foreign models; the first was the extremely pragmatic

---

[1] Op. cit., ch. XI.

[2] Op. cit., p. 850.

[3] A. Hitler, *Mein Kampf*, Munich, 1943, pp. 654-655. The difference between the relatively few members who actively pursue the implementation of the idea and the many followers won over to it implied for Hitler the contrast between the active and daring and the passive and cowardly types. The revolutionary force of the doctrine involved a risk likely to keep off "small and cowardly philistines" who though considering themselves followers would decline to manifest their attitude publicly by membership.

criterion by which to judge the "goodness" or "badness" of propaganda, the second was the preference to be given to the spoken rather than to the written word. Goebbels explained in a confidential address to the Party officials in Berlin in January 1928 that success was the only yard-stick by which to measure propaganda. He did not bother to conceal his opportunism or to wrap up the contents of propaganda in a moral cloak. "If a brand of propaganda has won over the circle of people which it wanted to persuade," he declared, "then I imagine it has been good; if not, then I imagine it has been bad." [1]

This Macchiavellism of the mass age rejected any moral criticism of the contents and methods of propaganda. Despising the respectable facade of the middle class parties and of the Social Democrats, Goebbels sneered at conventional ethics: "Nobody can say your propaganda is too crude, too low, too brutal, or it is not sufficiently decent, for all these attributes are not characteristic of its specific nature. By no means should propaganda be decent or mild or soft or humble, it should lead to success." [2] Although propaganda might employ moral arguments, ethics was not a criterion by which to judge it. We might say that to Goebbels propaganda was not conceived as a schoolmaster, but as a go-between. It was to form a tie between the idea that was to be spread and the people who were to be won over to it. As a medium between the individual and the multitude propaganda has to be "definitely flexible". The idea was "something unshakable, rigid and unchangeable", but the method used to sell it had to be pliable and adapted to a specific public. "If I talk in the provinces," Goebbels declared in 1928, "then I talk in a manner differ-ent from that in Berlin, and, if I address people in Bayreuth" (the Richard Wagner town) "then I talk of other things than in the Pharus Hall" (the slums of North Berlin). "It is all a matter of practice and not of theory." [3] Propaganda, Goebbels liked to assert, was an art and, like the playing of the violin, only teachable up to a point.

During his entire career Goebbels continued to stress that propaganda should be able to talk with different tongues in order to be able to per-suade the educated as much as the masses. But for practical reasons his technique largely concentrated on the level of the man in the street. In the early years of Goebbels' fight in Berlin against the hated "system" of the Republic he regarded it as the greatness of the Nazi Movement that it could spread its ideas in a way that made them "easily understood by the masses." [4] To succeed with propaganda meant to Goebbels a determination not to lose oneself "in the ivory tower of scientific en-quiry". "The rank and file are usually much more primitive than we imagine," he was to observe fourteen years later after a long talk with his mother. "The nature of propaganda lies essentially in its simplicity

[1] J. Goebbels, "Erkenntniss und Propaganda", *Signale der Neuen Zeit*, Munich, 1934, pp. 28-52.
[2] Op. cit., p. 29.
[3] Op. cit., pp. 46-47.
[4] Op. cit., p. 43.

and repetition. Only the man who is able to reduce the problems to the simplest terms and has the courage to repeat them indefinitely in this simplified form despite the objections of the intellectuals will in the long run achieve fundamental successes in influencing public opinion. If other methods are pursued he may influence a circle of unstable intellectuals here and there but will not even scratch the surface of the people." [1]

Off the record Goebbels did not claim that the National Socialists were the first effective propagandists in history. On the contrary, in 1928 he pointed to a motley historical gallery of forerunners, both sacred and profane; Christ, Buddha, Zarathustra, Robespiere, Danton, Mussolini and Lenin were included in it. What is more interesting, Goebbels mentioned Fascism and Bolshevism in the same breath as evidence for the primary importance of the great orators and organizers in modern revolutionary mass movements. Effective oratory was much more important than recourse to learning and erudition. What mattered was the living, the passionate speech rather than the calculated article. "Has Mussolini been a scribbler, or a great orator?" asked Goebbels. "Did Lenin, when arriving in St. Petersburg from Zürich, go from the railway to his study and write a book, or did he instead address thousands of people?" [2]

It is paradoxical that whereas Goebbels in mass meetings at the time heaped violent abuse on the "destructive" Marxist parties and their leaders, within the circle of his intimates he praised the skill and crude popular language of the Communist and Socialist agitators as exemplary. "Every leader in a Marxist newspaper," he remarked of the pre-1918 situation, "was a little propaganda address. These leaders had been written by agitators." They were "not full of esprit and finesse, but brutal and crude ideas which the man in the street understood." This was the reason why the Red press was eagerly read by the masses. And this was also the reason, Goebbels added emphatically, why the Nazis had to model themselves on that great example. Goebbels argued that although Marxism had no great prophets, it had succeeded because it was able to put agitators of the calibre of an August Bebel and a Lenin into "the service of its madness". Goebbels even went so far as to justify the negative approach in his own newspaper *Der Angriff*, which was sometimes criticized by more moderate and respectable nationalists, by pointing to the Marxist model. For sixty years, he maintained, Marxism had confined itself to the display of negative criticism. As a result it had conquered the State in the November revolution of 1918. A historical judgment, which, we might add, was more emphatic than correct.

3. GOEBBELS' NEWSPAPER *Der Angriff*

The birth of Goebbels' own newspaper can be traced to the decision of the Berlin police authorities to ban the Party in the capital until fur-

[1] Goebbels' Diary; entry of 29 January 1942.
[2] Address "Erkenntniss und Propaganda", op. cit., p. 49. See also *Kampf um Berlin*, 4th ed., Munich, 1934, pp. 18-19.

ther notice. When this happened on 5 May 1927, it became imperative for the Party to have at least a weekly newspaper of its own which would serve both as a rallying point for its members and as a spearhead of attack on the hated "system" of the Republic.

At a moment when even a moderate right-wing paper such as the *Deutsche Allgemeine Zeitung* expressed a sharp disapproval of the irresponsible methods of the Storm Troopers, branding them as criminal and outside the legitimate realm of politics, the ambitious Gauleiter required an organ for hitting back and for spurring the Movement on.

The beginnings were small and far from impressive. It was difficult to find suitable staff, particularly as the editor-designate, Dr. Julius Lippert, had to go to prison for a political offence before the first issue appeared. Most of the Party members concerned with the production of the paper had little experience in the technical and journalistic fields. Their work was, so to speak, additional to other and different tasks or functions allotted to them in the Movement.[1]

Its financial foundations were shaky and Goebbels himself seems to have felt obliged to invest 2,000 Marks in the new enterprise. The printer, a Party member named Schulze, allowed credit and the Gau organization, now underground, undertook to reimburse his expenses for paper and print. Members of the Party bought most of the 2,000 copies printed, while only one of the big wholesale firms in Berlin was prepared to act as distributor.[2]

From the start *Der Angriff* was designed as an "Either-Or" paper with the challenging motto on the front page "For the Suppressed Against the Exploiters!" To accomplish mass-appeal, to write in a popular vein was for Goebbels tantamount to renouncing any objective reporting. For, like Hitler, Goebbels was convinced of the simplicity of the mass-mind, of its desire to arrive at uncompromising solutions.[3]

Tiny as the new paper was, Goebbels used very modern advertising methods to acquaint the world with its appearance. To create public curiosity even before the publication of the first issue was the first requirement. A sequence of three posters appeared in the streets of Berlin. "THE ATTACK?" asked the first, "The Attack takes place on July 4th", proclaimed the second. The final poster explained that "The Attack" was to be "the German Monday paper", its motto "For the Suppressed! Against the Exploiters!", its editor-in-chief Dr. Joseph Goebbels. "The Attack" stands for a programme. Every German man, every German woman will read "The Attack" and subscribe to it."

[1] Some Party functionaries were simply transferred from administrative jobs in the Gau, officially no longer existing, to posts on the new paper. In this way the political manager of the Party, Dagobert Dürr, became an editor, and the head of the economic department of the Gau, Eberhard Assmann, managing director of the paper.

[2] Hans Georg Rahn, *Der nationalsozialistische Typ der Kampfzeitung*, Berlin, 1939, p. 129. (The account, written from a dogmatic Party point of view, has a foreword by Dr. Lippert, then Lord Mayor of Berlin).

[3] See, for instance, J. Goebbels, *Kampf um Berlin*, p. 191.

The new paper was simple and drastic in its language, almost limit-lessly aggressive, and pursued a "cockney" directness in its text and car-toons. It deliberately indulged in a vulgarity which reflected Goebbels' low opinion of the masses. "We were simple," he wrote later in retro-spect, "because the masses are simple. We thought primitively because the masses think primitively." [1] But when he added "We were aggressive because the masses are radical," he rationalized his own anti-bourgeois aggressiveness.

Like all National Socialist propaganda *Der Angriff* stressed two spe-cific lines of aggression, or anti-attitudes. Firstly it incited its readers against democracy, parliamentarianism, the Weimar Republic, in short against the existing "system", as the Nazi jargon put it. Secondly, it exploited and worked up anti-Semitic feelings by making the Jews respon-sible for most of the ills of "the system". It is true, both anti-parliamen-tarianism and anti-Semitism had deep roots in German history but never before had they been made so articulate and so welded together into a major aggressive force. Certainly anti-democrats and anti-Semitic agi-tation was by no means confined to Germany. For years the *Action française* movement had operated against the French Republic and its institutions and against the Jews and other minority groups branded as "foreign." But the *Action française* never became a major mass move-ment, as it did not succeed in gaining appreciable support from the workers.

Hitler and Goebbels, on the other hand, managed to employ anti-Semitism adroitly in order to secure sufficient numbers of active sup-porters required to put an end to the Weimar Republic. Their main slogan, repeated a hundred thousand times, was "*Deutschland erwache, Juda verrecke!*" (Germany awake, Judaism be damned!) It has been aptly remarked that "no one can say for certain" if Hitler would have come to power, had he confined himself only to the slogan: "Germany awake!" [2] But it is an historical fact that he succeeded with the help of both slogans. Hitler and Goebbels always regarded the anti-Semitic line as particularly powerful and effective, and it can be argued that its suc-cess proved their expectations to have been right.

Of the main features which gave the paper its stamp the most impor-tant was the leader on the front page, usually written by Goebbels him-self and signed at the end with a "Dr. G." He regarded the leaders as the very core of the paper, as "a written poster, or still better expressed, as a street corner address put on paper." [3] This was a paper for the street, the primitive mental food of those eager to march and to control the street. Leaders for a marching rather than a reading public had obviously to be brief, concise and effective from a propagandist point of view. As

[1] Op. cit., p. 200.
[2] See Professor Dr. F. Boehm, *Antisemitismus*. Address delivered at the con-gress of the German societies for co-operation between Gentiles and Jews in Munich on 12 March 1958, p. 2.
[3] *Kampf um Berlin*, p. 200.

with any product of popular journalism, the initial sentences had to attract the reader so much that he would have no alternative but to read it to the last word. But attraction meant in this case punch, ruthlessness, a passion to follow the swastika and to overthrow its enemies.

"Why attack?" asked Goebbels in no. 1, and gave the answer by painting a grim picture of a Germany impoverished as a colony of international Jewish finance, with three million unemployed as the grim result. A vigorous denunciation of the existing regime, of all other parties ("They make money out of the funeral of our nation and where is there a grave-digger who would not rejoice in a fat funeral?") was followed by the offer of a better future, a new totalitarian vision. True Germans need not despair, for the parties are not Germany, nor are the parliamentary cockroaches her true leaders. "Away then with these lamentable organizations and men," who brought Germany to ruin and disaster. "Put the German future into German hands"—a slogan of remarkable impertinence as it dismissed all non-Nazi politicians as bad Germans. Here was preached the radical determination of the dispossessed to change everything. "We take a total view!" shouted Goebbels. "We have nothing more to lose." And he attempted to hypnotize his readers into marching towards the goal: the German Workers' State. "Always the Aggressor has been stronger than the Defender. That is why we attack."[1]

Goebbels' leaders were the highlight, the only striking contribution in an otherwise often dull and largely vulgar publication. He alone managed to make destructiveness interesting and to explain the Party doctrine in his own inimitable way. His strength was the variety and the repetition of anti-arguments, intended to deride "the system" and to attack the Jews. Often Goebbels knew how to cover up a dearth of arguments by a self-confident, aggressive note: "All who have human faces are equal"— he said introducing an article on 'Democracy'—"that is very convenient for the blockheads, we for our part do not wish to be put on the same level with every blockhead and pimp." [2] But while the article began with impatient scorn and derision, it ended with a romantic appeal to the forcefulness of the great man. Had not Prussia been made great by one man, Bismarck? Only when everybody began to have a finger in the pie did Germany's glory and happiness fade. Therefore the call for one great man was once more imperative and forthcoming. That man was, of course, Hitler, though in the first two years of the paper he took a comparatively minor place in it. Compared with Goebbels' later eulogies of the Führer, an article by H.S. Chamberlain, Richard Wagner's then dying son-in-law, "The Image of the Führer" was feeble and lacking in vigour.[3]

As Der Angriff was Goebbels' own paper, it is not surprising that his

[1] Der Angriff, no. 1, 4 June 1927.
[2] Der Angriff, no. 10, 15 March 1928.
[3] Der Angriff, no. 8, 22 August 1938. H.S. Chamberlain saw in Hitler "einen grossen Vereinfacher", a great simplificateur, perhaps a particular virtue in the eyes of this complicated and introvert racial philosopher. He believed in Hitler's simple greatness as an expression of his veracity, courage, earnestness and love.

personality figured largely in it. He knew how to make himself interesting as the naughty Gauleiter in the bad books of the Prussian police. In an article published before the Reichstag elections of May 1928 he asked his readers with biting irony: "Do you really want to elect me?" [1] Hard-hitting as his leaders were, the impact of the paper was at first small. Years afterwards Goebbels admitted that the first issue had filled him with "shame, despondency and despair". Most of their supporters and readers had reacted similarly; after great expectations they found the actual achievement small.[2]

An attraction were the paper's political cartoons. Far from squeamish, they would expose and ridicule representatives of the hated "system" in a manner taboo to the old-established papers of the Right. For the Nazis cartoons were both safer and more popular than articles, safer because they were open to various interpretations and much less likely to bring down the hand of the Law on the editors. Too much impudence in articles might lead to police action against the paper, but as the political cartoons could be more ambiguous one could hide behind them. More-over, many would look at a cartoon who could not be bothered to read even short articles. Goebbels never thought the masses could be made to think, but they might be made to laugh. "And he who had laughter on his side, was always right." [3]

Without a stroke of good luck these practical considerations would, however, have remained academic. Luck came in the person of a talented cartoonist, whose work appeared under the Nordic pen-name of Mjölnir (The Hammer).[4] In his black and white drawings the heroic fighters for a new Germany were effectively though crudely contrasted with the ludicrous and ignominious figures of the odious Republic. The Party men appeared as strong, honest, idealistic youths and men, their opponents as pernicious parasites or as slimy little Jewish snakes whose chicanery would prove powerless to hinder the victory of the determined fighters for the nation. Mjölnir's giant holding the swastika banner seemed im-pervious to the brutality of the Republican police, and the intrigues of Jewish financiers. Though the Party had been forbidden, its vitality was shown to be unimpaired. A cartoon in three parts, revealed a worried little Jew, the Vice-President of the Berlin Police, Dr. Weiss, sitting on a box labelled NSDAP Berlin. Suddenly the box opens, a Storm Trooper in uniform emerges from it, and the little Jew is abruptly thrown into the air, dropping his precious horn-rimmed spectacles. In another carica-ture two ambulance men carry a badly wounded person into a police

[1] Article "Mich willst Du Wählen?", *Der Angriff*, no. 19, 7 May 1928. Goebbels described himself as a second class citizen with four sentences in the police records and eight others pending. Half outcast, half martyr, he teased his supporters on account of their odd enthusiasm for a man not very respectable in the eyes of the authorities.

[2] J. Goebbels, *Kampf um Berlin*, p. 203.

[3] Op. cit., p. 101.

[4] His real name was Hans Schweitzer. In the Third Reich he was given the title of Professor.

office. Three brutal policemen view him with crossed arms and a cynical expression. Caption: "Has the man fallen under a car? No, into the hands of the Berlin police."[1]

Goebbels frequently attempted to plug anti-Semitism by trying to expose the absurdity of pro-Semitic propaganda. This was a somewhat heavy-footed technique. The earlier issues of his journal had a supplement "Der Philosemit" which endeavoured to poke fun at the loyalty to Germany claimed by so many German Jews. It carried slogans such as "Subscribe to the Red Flag, the organ of the pro-Semitic terrorists", or "There can be no enslavement of the Jewish people before the elimination of all Germandom from the world," a parody, of course, on the Nazi demand for the removal of all Jews from the German nation.[2] A similar technique led to a regular column, "A life of beauty and dignity", which alleged that according to Dr. Stresemann, the German Foreign Minister, and the Jewish press, Germany was doing better and better. Unfortunately, many Germans did not appreciate the happiness of their existence, as was made evident by a long list of recent suicides, many of them due to unemployment.

The paper was filled with unscrupulous or sly headlines. For example, in one of them it was suggested that Fritz Ebert, a son of the first Reich President, had been involved in a big case of corruption in Brandenburg. In point of fact, it emerged from the story that Ebert had nothing to do with it at all, and Goebbels was unable to provide a scrap of evidence for it.[3]

As a student of Communist and Fascist techniques Goebbels was deeply conscious of the value of political mass symbols, both negative and positive. Totalitarian movements are always inclined to view society in terms of "polarity",[4] of a secularized God and a secularized devil, of extreme light and extreme darkness. In 1927 and 1928 Goebbels was convinced that in order to weaken the opponents of National Socialism, it was imperative to undermine and destroy their faith in their Heilslehre, their system of politico-social beliefs and doctrines. Soon they would regard the Nazis as champions of a new Heilslehre replacing the old one.[5]

[1] Der Angriff, no. 14, 3 October 1927.
[2] The same technique was also applied in later issues. The fourth special issue of Der Angriff, devoted to an an exposure of the large stores (Warenhäuser) contained an ironic leader by Goebbels, headed: "Germans, buy only in Jewish shops!" and asking "Why worry about the small German tradesman?" "He should go to Palestine and offer his goods there." The usual anti-Semitic arguments were turned upside down, in order to appear more effective. (Der Angriff, no. 50, 10 December 1928).
[3] Der Angriff, no. 48, 31 October 1929.
[4] For the concept of "polarity" see Henry M. Pachter, "National Socialist and Fascist Propaganda for the conquest of Power", in The Third Reich, London, 1955, p. 736.
[5] See Goebbels' Directives for the National Socialist Party Organization, written about 1928, in Dr. Goebbels. Nach Aufzeichnungen aus seiner Umgebung, Berlin, 1949, pp. 194-201.

One could give hundreds of examples of this deliberate dichotomy which converted the complex socio-political reality into the disquieting dream of a fight between Good and Evil, German and Alien, constructive and destructive forces. Take the following invitation to a Nazi mass meeting which appeared in *Der Angriff* in March 1928,[1] under the heading: "To the gallows with the spoilers of the people." In it leading questions bring everything down to the lowest and simplest dual common denominator. The black and white technique, the friend-enemy contrast is all-pervading. The superlatives abound. On the one side there was the heroic light: "Who once made Germany the proudest and happiest country of the world? Who sacrificed two million of our best far away on the battlefields? Who fought and starved and suffered during the war? It was us Germans." [2] On the other side was satanic darkness: "Who has besmirched [our] honour and made it a laughing stock of the enemies? Who has taken our free soil from us and stolen our money? Who owns our mines and railways today? Who has made a profit out of our misery while we starved and suffered? It was our enemies, Jews and serfs of Jews. The white Jews and the black Jews." [3] These destructive forces had split the German nation into two hostile halves: the bourgeois and the proletarians. The secret hand of a sinister intrigue had been at work. Such was the prelude to the forthcoming mass demonstrations of "the awakening Berliners" at which Goebbels would discuss the corresponding dual theme: "Freedom and Bread" (positive associations) and "To the gallows with the spoilers of the people" (negative association). It should be added that the entrance fee for the unemployed was only 10 Pfennig, while all other listeners paid 30 Pfennig.

4. Villains and Heroes

For the sake of effective publicity it was not sufficient to attack the doctrines, alleged or real, of the enemy, and to contrast them with those of the NSDAP; what was required were concrete symbols to personify, symbols to march against and to march for. Truth did not matter; what was imperative was to create images for striking denunciation or glorification. Goebbels developed great ingenuity in presenting living symbols for the polarity which signified the Nazi struggle for power.

He would debunk the leading men of the Republic by sly contrasts. For instance in April 1929, six months before the death of Stresemann, he attacked him in an article as an unheroic bogus statesman, as a petty bourgeois, confronting him with the magic spell of Prussia's greatest King, Frederick II. The German Foreign Minister was described maliciously as "a bit corpulent, a bit yellow, a bit artful, with an intolerable pro-

---

[1] *Der Angriff*, no. 13, 26 March 1928.
[2] Ibid.
[3] Ibid. Goebells understood by "black Jews" the Jews proper, and by "white Jews" gentiles who shared their "unpatriotic" methods.

vocative smile on his lips, with his small cunning eyes carefully bedded in a cushion of fat, a square forehead without any wrinkles and above it an immense baldness." Thus he was and thus he lived "amidst his dear Jews", a reference to the Jewish origin of Frau Stresemann. "That is" Goebbels fulminated, "how we imagine the German Minister of Foreign Affairs who one day will break Germany's chains." How small he was when measured against a truly great man: "and afterwards," Goebbels romanticised, "we stand a long time in front of a window; out of its darkness, from among a number of gimcracks, the worn features of the death-mask of Frederick the Great spread silence into the evening." [1]

But whereas Goebbels abused Dr. Stresemann only from time to time, he made the Jewish Vice-President of the Berlin Police, Dr. Weiss, the permanent target of his attacks and singled him out as a living symbol of the "Jewish" Republic, of the half-sinister, half-ludicrous Jewish power. He did this with the same intensity with which he was later to transform the murdered young Storm Troop Leader Horst Wessel into a twentieth century Baldur, symbolising the highest aspirations of the dynamic National Socialist Movement.

The selection of Weiss was, of course, calculated. [2] For the Berlin police authorities had, as we saw, forbidden the Party in the Reich capital and looked at its reappearance with disfavour. The President of the Berlin police, Zörgiebel, was a Social Democrat and Trade Unionist, and his deputy, Dr. Bernhard Weiss, was a member of the Democratic Party, which by then had become somewhat a party of officers without troops. A lawyer by profession, Dr. Weiss found himself much more hated than his chief by the National Socialists because he was a Jew. It may well have been that his physical appearance did not tally with the traditional German image of the strong man in charge of the police. In any case, it did not matter to Goebbels what Dr. Weiss was, but what he made him out to be. He bestowed on him the Jewish nickname "Isidor", he depicted him as the parasitic Jew *par excellence,* who, abusing his power over Germans, hobnobbed with the demi-monde, and belonged to the decadent "Society" of Republican Berlin.

In his innumerable cartoons of "Isidor" Mjölnir made the most of his victim's pointed nose and horn-rimmed spectacles, furnished him with cunning little eyes and presented him as a severe but ridiculous school-master or a boxer. [3] Or "Isidor" took the ludicrous shape of "the new Nero". Chained to a long stick, but with the mighty upper part of his

---

[1] J. Goebbels, "Der Fall Stresemann" in *Der Angriff,* 8 April 1929. The article is reprinted in *Der Angriff, Aufsätze aus der Kampfzeit,* 11th edition, Munich, 1942, pp. 150-152.

[2] It is true that the German Communist press often depicted capitalists as fat, self-indulgent monsters, extracting the last ounce of blood from the proletarians. But Goebbels' malignant pen, supported by Mjölnir's acid drawings, avoided such clichés and boldly concentrated on a definite functionary of the State.

[3] See *Der Angriff,* no. 7, 15 August 1927 and no. 10, 5 September 1927.

body free, was an SA man, symbolising the forbidden Party and smiling boldly down at Nero. The toga of this uncrowned Emperor of Berlin covered his paunch, clumsy feet stuck in sandals, and the laurel on his forehead took the shape of two horns. He held in his one hand a wretched little monkey with a balloon-shaped cap on its head, a personification of the "Jacobin" Zörgiebel.[1]

Years afterwards, when Goebbels was a Reich Minister, he admitted cynically to his staff: "How grand it was to transform Isidor, the 'Vipoprä', into the most brutal bailiff of the Weimar Republic, into the grinning mask of the eternal Jew—although this Deputy Commissioner of the Berlin Police and former Captain of the Royal Bavarian Army Reserve was actually only a harmless fool." [2]

Equally primitive and well calculated was a column in Berlin dialect entitled "Orje." This was a bright "cockney" boy with a dry sense of humour, always ready to crack jokes at the expense of the Party bosses of the Republic, the *Bonzen,* and to eulogise the exploits of the Berlin Storm Troopers. Orje became a standing figure of the paper, together with his mother, his fiancée, Grete, and his father-in-law, old Krüger, whom Orje gradually wins over from the Republican and the Socialist camp.

There is little evidence that during the first two years of its existence *Der Angriff* stirred the politically indifferent masses or the floating voters, but it did help Gauleiter Goebbels to keep in touch with his Party members at a time when its meetings could not take place. "Though forbidden not dead!" ran the defiant slogan, and the paper tried to make much of the heroism of persecuted Party members in the hands of the police. When in August 1927 a contingent of the disbanded Berlin branch of the Party returned by special train to Berlin territory from the Party Congress in Nuremberg, where it received many ovations, the police arrested all SA men and detained them for a few hours at Police Headquarters. The two standards which the Führer had handed over to the Berlin Storm Troopers at Nuremberg were confiscated. Goebbels was not slow in making a heroic drama out of this incident. He glorified the attitude of the SA men who "hid 'the sacred flag' under their shirts until the dirty hands of the police tore it in bits from them." He wove a halo round the youngsters who had refused to answer the questions of the Magistrate. He alleged that through the detention 74 Storm Troopers had lost their jobs. And he uttered sinister threats that one day the tables would be turned: "We wish to be accused, for we know: We shall sit in the dock

[1] *Der Angriff*, no. 23, 5 December 1927.
[2] W. Stephan, *Joseph Goebbels*, Stuttgart, 1949, p. 68. "Vipoprä" was a ludicrous abbreviation of "Vice President of the Police" coined by Goebbels. A number of Mjölnir's cartoons and Goebbels' articles attacking Weiss and other prominent figures of the Weimar Republic were published as a book in 1928 by the Party firm Franz Eher Nachf. in Munich under the title *Das Buch Isidor, Ein Zeitbild voll Lachen und Hass.* Weiss applied unsuccessfully to a court in Munich to have the book withdrawn as slanderous.

for only one hour. Plaintiffs will turn into defendants and defendants into plaintiffs . . ." [1]

When at the end of March 1928 the ban on the Party in Berlin was lifted by the police, its leaders threw themselves with renewed energy into the battle for the imminent Reichstag elections. Goebbels was then much in demand as a speaker at Party meetings, not only in Berlin but also in other big towns in Prussia, particularly as Hitler was still forbidden to make speeches there. In a special election issue of *Der Angriff* Goebbels felt obliged to take up the criticism of those Party members who argued that "he who joins Parliament will perish in it." [2] No, they would not become parliamentarians, Goebbels argued, but would remain revolutionaries. Theirs was the policy of infiltration in order to destroy from within. They would not come to the Reichstag as friends or even as neutrals. They would come as enemies "like the wolf who breaks into the flock of sheep". Yet the results of the Reichstag elections of 1928 were very modest from the Nazi point of view. The Party polled only 2.6% of the total votes and secured only 12 seats in the Reichstag. The tide was not yet running in its favour. It did not win a single seat in the constituencies of Berlin and Potsdam II which covered part of the capital. [3]

Gradually, with the increasing economic difficulties in which Germany found herself, the Party propaganda gathered momentum. In September 1928 it undertook a campaign against the Dawes plan. Neither Goebbels nor his colleagues from *Der Angriff* had any solid economic training, but they made up for it by simplifying the problems of Germany's reparations conveniently and by a play with slogans. "What does Dawes mean?" asked *Der Angriff*, and provided the diverting answer: *"Deutschlands Armut wird ewig sein"* (Germany's poverty will last for ever). [4] For this campaign a special Party emblem was reproduced, showing the German people as slaves under the Dawes cross, with a clenched fist as the symbol of resistance. During a special "Dawes week" Goebbels addressed Party meetings in the suburbs of Berlin, rousing his listeners against the overlords and exploiters of the "Dawes colony," Germany. On the Sunday following that week the Party managed to fill the huge Sport Palace for the first time, and *Der Angriff* commented triumphantly that National Socialism "had made its mark as a mass movement in Berlin." [5] Soon afterwards a second mass demonstration of the Party, this time with

[1] *Der Angriff*, no. 10, 5 September 1927.

[2] Article "Was wollen wir im Reichstag?" *Der Angriff*, 30 April 1928.

[3] However, a Jewish weekly summed up the position in Berlin with remarkable acumen: "They have not obtained a single seat, but that is no reason for rejoicing . . . Eighteen months ago the Hitler Movement in Greater Berlin consisted of a few dozen unorganized people. In a short time Dr. Goebbels has put into being a National Socialist organization which, it must be admitted, is remarkable." *C.V. Zeitung*, 25 May 1928.

[4] Special Dawes Plan issue of *Der Angriff*, no. 39, 24 September 1928.

[5] *Der Angriff*, no. 41, 8 October 1928.

Hitler as star speaker, was equally well attended. Goebbels employed all his indefatigable drive and skill in paving the way for the Führer, in building him up as a superman. "When Hitler speaks," Goebbels wrote the day after his address, "then all resistance collapses before the magic effect of his words. One can only be his friend or his enemy . . . this is the secret of his strength: his fanatical faith in the Movement, and with it in Germany." [1]

Semi-religious faith in the ultimate triumph of the saviour went hand in hand with the gloomiest predictions for the near future. There was much wishful thinking in *Der Angriff's* forecast at the end of 1928: "1929 will be a year of catastrophes for Germany in every field." [2] Goebbels was a radical, and at that time his anti-capitalist resentment may still have been genuine to some extent though it was entirely confined to Jewish and foreign capitalists. When a committee of allied experts on the vexed German reparations problem met in Paris, *Der Angriff* referred derisively to them as a mere "Bankers' Conference", and attacked J. Pierpont Morgan as "the embodiment of international finance", eager to extract as many reparations as possible from Germany, and in league with Dr. Hilferding, then the Reich Minister of France, "as tax-collector of international finance." [3]

Before and after the acceptance of the Young Plan for the settlement of the reparations question by the Government of Müller, Goebbels spoke constantly of the shadow cabinet of the Three Jews, Bernhard, Breitscheid, Goldschmidt, inside Germany. [4] It was this technique of exposing the hidden reality behind a feeble official facade which the Party in general and Goebbels in particular were to employ throughout. The searchlight was directed on to the glaring discrepancy between false pretence and reality, the nominal and the real. It was a myth of the hidden hand. "While the Social Democrat Workers' leaders have for ten years indulged in phrases of humanity and fraternity, finance capitalism has forged the chain by which it now wants to fetter German labour for ever." [5] To strike fear in, to evoke indignation from the masses was the aim. On one of the Party's posters of that time a powerful and sadistically clenched fist throws its menacing shadow over a child. The threat indicates sixty years of financial enslavement. In despair the child, being Germany's next generation, raises its tiny arms as a shield, a cry of fear

[1] Article by Goebbels: *"Adolf Hitler", Der Angriff*, no. 47, 19 November 1928.

[2] *Der Angriff*, no. 53, 31 December 1928.

[3] *Der Angriff*, no. 6, 11 February 1929.

[4] Georg Bernhard was the Editor-in-Chief of the *Vossische Zeitung* and a member of the Democratic Party in the Reichstag. Kurt Breitscheid, the chairman of the Social Democratic Party in the Reichstag, was its leading expert on foreign affairs. Jakob Goldschmidt, a prominent banker, was the head of the Darmstädter and National Bank. Goebbels had attacked him on posters and in assemblies as early as 1926.

[5] *Der Angriff*, no. 13, 1 April 1929.

distorts its mouth. By its side is its father, a German worker with bowed head, worn out. But a Brownshirt, upright and virile, shakes him and with an outstretched arm points to the threat, shouting into his ears: "Father! Rescue your child! Become a National Socialist!"

The pseudo-religious language of such propaganda borrowed largely from Christian symbols, from Christian concepts. For instance: "Young completes the circle of our misfortune and our shame. We are at the end of our Calvary. The German people has traversed the many stages of its Golgotha. And the henchman is just about to crucify it scoffingly." [1]

If this quasi-socialist movement had its Golgotha and its Saviour, it was also not without its martyrs. The National Socialist press made much of the alleged heroism of the SA men who were pictured as constantly involved in guerilla fights, in innumerable brawls with Communists and Socialists. They were always attacked by the other side and when they hit back they acted only in self-defence. Some of the SA men were actually killed in these clashes. Goebbels used all the graphic powers of his pen, his ability to evoke sentiments of grief, sympathy and anger to create mental images of martyred heroes which would stir and inspire the Movement. As one of the few shrewd contemporary analysts of the National Socialist Movement in the Republican camp observed in 1932, this combination of heroism and martyrdom was "a very important feature of their propaganda." [2]

The hero and martyr was the counterpoint to the fiend, and Horst Wessel the anti-pole to "Isidor" Weiss. The dramatic story of how Horst Wessel, a young Berlin SA leader, was wounded, fought for survival, and finally died in hospital offered rich material for creating a martyr's legend.[3] Whatever the motives of the shooting of Wessel may have been— and it appears difficult to establish them with certainty—there is as much discrepancy between the man as he was and Goebbels' idealized portrait of him as there is between the actual Dr. Weiss of the Berlin police and the Nazi cartoon of "Isidor".

Horst Wessel, a twenty-one year old student of law and son of a parson, was a familiar figure in the Berlin Party, both as a frequent speaker and as a leader of a section of Storm Troopers. He had quickly gained new members for it and had made it one of the most active sections, being constantly involved in street brawls with Communists. Wessel was also the author of a poem: *"Die Fahne hoch!"* which had been published in the supplement to *Der Angriff* entitled "The Unknown SA Man".[4] It was simple, crude and trenchant, an expression of the brutal activism, the

---

[1] Goebbels in a special issue of *Der Angriff* on the Young Plan, no. 38, 23 September 1929.

[2] Theodor Heuss, *Hitlers Weg*, Stuttgart, 1932, p. 125. Heuss showed remarkable insight into the techniques of National Socialism and the reasons for its appeal.

[3] Goebbels had used a similar technique on a smaller scale before in the case of the death of H. Kütemeyer, a minor employee in the Party offices, see *Der Angriff*, no. 48, 26 November 1928.

[4] *Der Angriff*, no. 38, 23 September 1929.

"marching" ideology of the Movement. It asked to "free the Street for the Brown Battalions", it immortalized the fallen Storm Troopers as "comrades, shot dead by Red Front and Reaction." The three verses quickly caught on throughout the Movement.

Soon after the publication of his poem Horst Wessel suddenly lost all interest in the Party and withdrew from its activities. He had become infatuated with a prostitute, Erna Jännicke, and had gone to live with her. Alas, there was also Ali Höhler, a former lover of the woman and her procurer, who had just finished a sentence of several years in prison. It seems that he was a member of the Communist organization *"Einheit"* in Berlin.[1] Even if he was a Communist—and the National Socialist press made much of this—his fateful clash with Wessel had not primarily a political motive but was the outcome of jealousy, the result of a somewhat sordid triangle. It did not please Höhler to find his "bride" in the arms of a National Socialist rival. He went to see Wessel. There was a scuffle. As Wessel made a movement to reach for his revolver Höhler anticipated him and shot him down. Severely wounded Wessel was taken to hospital.

Goebbels studiously ignored the questionable background of Wessel's fate. From the moment he learned of the shooting, he was determined to make political capital out of it.

There was widespread sympathy in the Party for the comrade in his extremity, and *Der Angriff* came out with daily bulletins on the state of Wessel's health. Goebbels gave a sentimental account of a visit to the suffering hero, propped up on pillows. Wessel spoke only a few words, emphasizing that they must hold out. The Gauleiter declared this to be one of the most pathetic moments of his life, one which he would never forget. Threatening the murderers with complete annihilation the Propaganda Minister quoted from Horst Wessel's song: "Comrades shot dead by Red Front and Reaction, march in spirit within our ranks!" [2]

A few days afterwards the dreaded event became a reality: Horst Wessel died. Goebbels wrote a leader filled with grimly realistic descriptions of the hero on his deathbed and with the call to action. But death had not the last word. Horst Wessel became the symbol of the Movement, the greatest of its martyrs. "His spirit has risen in order to live on in all of us. He himself has believed it and has known it: he has given it fascinating expression: he is 'marching within our ranks'." [3]

Horst Wessel was transformed into part of the vision of the future, and his song into a piece of the Movement's myth. "In ten years it will be sung by the children in the schools, the workers in the factories, the soldiers on wide roads. His song has made him immortal." Indeed Goebbels proved right up to a point, as in the Third Reich the Horst Wessel song was to become the second national anthem. Goebbels staged a tre-

---

[1] This is stated by Hans Otto Meissner and Harry Wilde in *Die Machtergreifung*, Munich, 1958, p. 356.

[2] *Der Angriff*, no. 7, 23 January 1930. Article "Horst Wessel".

[3] *Der Angriff*, no. 17, 27 February 1930. Article "Ein Toter ruft zur Tat".

mendous funeral with the Party and the Storm Troopers in attendance, and with himself giving a funeral oration, half sentimental, half fanatical. With a dramatic gesture he called into the crowd: "Horst Wessel!" and all the Storm Troopers would answer: "Present", in symbolic accordance with the words of the dead hero's song. Goebbels' cleverly calculated peroration combined religious language with a very pragmatic attitude. Horst Wessel was presented as a modern saviour, living and dying for his convictions: "A Christ and a Socialist! One who calls through his deeds: Come to me: I will redeem you . . . One man must set an example and sacrifice himself. Well then, I am ready for it." [1] The reality was very different. During the subsequent trial of Höhler, who was sentenced to six years' imprisonment for manslaughter, the truth of the case came to light with all its unsavoury details. Goebbels can have had no illusions about the real Horst Wessel. But as Hans Fritzsche explained after Goebbels' death: "That did not bother him in the least." [2] He realized the value of the legend of this "martyr" for the Party and simply stuck to it. Why bother about facts when the Horst Wessel song became the anthem of the Movement and his grave a Nazi shrine?

How Goebbels continued to build up the image of the martyr and hero becomes evident from one of his most brilliant articles. It was written on Wessel's twenty-third birthday, six months after his death and four weeks after the striking success of the Party, and it was simply headed "Horst".[3] "Those who went to his grave on September 15th, on the day after our triumph," wrote Goebbels, "saw there unemployed men and women who had returned from the market with children by the hand; they saw old grandmothers and neat young girls. Students and officials, petit-bourgeois and proletarians came and went. A mother raised her four-year-old boy in her arms, and showed him the grave which seemed to flourish anew under a wreath of flowers, and said, 'Here lies our Horst!' No other word. But this said everything. Our Horst! As if he had become the brother of all of us, as if he belonged to our family and had by his death risen in all of us."

The pseudo-religious language and the integrating force emanating from the dead hero were closely interrelated. Integration was one of the great attractions of the National Socialist Movement, which promised to give the little man, the anonymous shop-assistant, clerk, teacher, a new status, a higher prestige based on the reflected glory of the collective. The Movement was in the nineteen twenties and early thirties a *"Sammelpartei"* (Bracher), a party of integration which claimed to put an end to distinctions of class, caste, tax, and to replace parties and classes by a community, not without differentiations but embracing all "Aryan" Ger-

---

[1] Article "Bis zur Neige", by Dr. Goebbels, *Der Angriff*, no. 19, 6 March 1930.
[2] C. Reiss, *Joseph Goebbels*, p. 83.
[3] *Der Angriff*, no. 81, 9 October 1930, reprinted in *Wetterleuchten. Aufsätze aus der Kampfzeit*, Munich, 1939, pp. 29-30.

mans. With its ancient roots in German romantic thought this concept of "community" suggested integration as a positive counter to the negative forces of particularism and sectionalism. Its appeal strengthened by tradition was especially attractive in days of growing economic instability and political insecurity. Integration, led by a saviour, seemed a remedy for the "fear of freedom." [1] To the uneasy question of "Little Man What Now?" [2] reflected in the title of a popular contemporary novel, this drive for mass integration seemed to give a valid answer. [3]

It was the strength of Goebbels as a demogogue and a propagandist that he could be effectively sentimental as well as venomous. He was equally to appeal to the "higher emotions" as to their more negative instincts. "If we wish to keep the Party intact," he wrote a few days before the Reichstag elections of September, 1930, "we must once more appeal to the most primitive mass instincts." [4] Particularly on such occasions Goebbels liked to appeal to destructive aggressiveness, *Schadenfreude*, a feeling of grim revenge. In a special article written before that election Goebbels asked Party Members: "to fall upon the electors like a swarm of hornets. No one must be seen who does not carry in his pocket a leaflet, a brochure, a special issue of our newspapers. Say this loudly and distinctly, at home and in the circles of your acquaintances, at your places of work, in the streets in the Underground and in buses, wherever you are, walking or standing: Hitler is our man! The productive worker votes for list No. 9."

A good deal of Goebbels' contempt for the masses, whose votes were necessary for the Party, can be traced in this advice: "Do it jokingly, do it seriously! Treat your dear fellow-creatures as they are used to being treated. Stimulate their rage and their fury, direct them to the proper course. This time no one must be allowed to back the wrong horse. It must become a general reckoning with the system . . . We shall stop their lying mouths in a fashion never experienced before. This is our revenge which we want to enjoy ice-cold tomorrow." [5]

It was a cynic's very practical approach to electioneering, which combined the influence of Le Bon's mass psychology with a natural flair for Machiavellian tactics. [6] When it came to elections *Der Angriff* was keen

[1] See Erich Fromm, *The Fear of Freedom*, London, 1942.

[2] Hans Fallada, *Little Man What Now?* London, 1932.

[3] Writing on the role of the Storm Troopers at the Party Congress in Nuremberg in 1927, Goebbels observed that "today the one was not a clerk, the other a proletarian, the third one a farm labourer, and the fourth a small official. Today all of them were the last Germans who did not want to despair of the future of the nation." *Kampf um Berlin*, p. 229.

[4] J. Goebbels, *Vom Kaiserhof zur Reichskanzlei*, p. 157; diary entry of 7 September 1930.

[5] J. Goebbels, leader in *Der Angriff*, 14 September 1930, republished in his book *Der Angriff*, pp. 92-94.

[6] Goebbels had used a similar approach earlier before the municipal elections in Berlin of November 1929. See his article "Letzter Appell", *Der Angriff*, no. 53, 17 November 1929.

to be assured of assistance from women supporters too, although National Socialist leaders had a low opinion of woman's political capacity.[1]

What was the economic basis of *Der Angriff* in those earlier years? It has to be kept in mind that the commercial side of the paper was of secondary importance to its founder. For him it was primarily an instrument of politics. *Der Angriff* was financed through sales and advertisements, both of which proved poor in the beginning. During the first two years donations from friends of the Movement mattered, and even proceeds from carnival festivals of the Party in 1928 and 1929 helped to sustain the paper. Many Party members gave their week-ends to the packing and advertising of the current issue. Others exercised pressure on reluctant newsagents and street vendors to exhibit and sell *Der Angriff*. Their efforts seem to have been thorough as well as tough, for, as a reply to a reader's query indicated at the beginning of 1929, only a relatively small percentage of the sales came from subscriptions by Party members, whilst the great majority of copies went to indifferent "street customers." With the growing appeal of the Party some newsagents probably no longer regarded it safe to ignore the paper. As the official Party account of its history put it bluntly later: "*Der Angriff* was systematically imposed on the newsagents."[2] No opportunity was missed by Storm Troopers and other Party members to propagate their paper. Old issues were placed on the seats at sectional and mass meetings. Small labels drawing attention to *Der Angriff* were stuck on letters, shop-windows, advertising boards everywhere by fervent partisans. Every reader was admonished to bring along two new subscribers and to spread the journal in shops, pubs and waiting rooms. However, unorthodox as *Der Angriff* liked to be, it aped the "bourgeois" methods of some of its detested rivals by introducing a prize competition for gaining new subscribers. On one occasion a Christmas goose was promised to every housewife who managed to win over twelve new subscribers, while those who secured only six would at least enjoy a chicken. In the spring and summer of 1929 the paper promised a free return ticket by rail to the forthcoming Party Congress at Nuremberg to anyone who gained thirty subscribers, or a single ticket if he managed to mobilize only twenty. It was a somewhat ingenious way of killing two birds with one stone.

The revenue from advertisements was at first rather modest, as the bulk of Berlin shopowners and business people were then disinclined to identify themselves with the extremism of the Movement, particularly when their customers were workers. However, this attitude changed to some extent when *Der Angriff* came out with special issues attacking the big general stores, the *Warenhäuser*. Filled with anti-capitalist resentment

---

[1] On the negative attitude of the Movement to women in politics see the observations by Th. Heuss, *Hitlers Weg*, p. 135; for the positive tasks of National Socialist women in an election campaign, see *Der Angriff*, no. 43, 13 October 1929; also H.G. Rahn, op. cit., p. 143.

[2] Rahn, op. cit., p. 219.

gradually more owners of small and medium size shops began to patronise the paper. By the spring of 1929, two and a half out of the twelve pages of the paper were covered by advertisements. Not a striking figure, perhaps, but one which indicated considerable progress. By November, 1929 the paper not only paid its way, but its net income formed a substantial portion of the revenue of the Gau party organization.[1] The paper's income from advertisements helped to finance the Reichstag election campaign in the late summer of 1930, which in Berlin as elsewhere in Germany was to end in an avalanche-like triumph of the National Socialists. Their *Trommlerpresse,* papers like *Der Angriff,* which incessantly drummed in the cause, had proved their practical value, particularly at a time when radio was on the whole not available to the spokesman of an unscrupulous and resourceful opposition. The aim of *Der Angriff* was and remained written oratory.[2]

[1] See Rahn, op. cit., p. 233.
[2] In Goebbels' own words, "the reader should gain the impression that the writer of the leader was really an orator standing actually beside him and wanting to convert him to his opinion by simple and convincing arguments." *Kampf um Berlin,* p. 200.

PART II

Propaganda Ministry and Propaganda Campaigns

CHAPTER 3

Complex Channels of Control

"Das Volk ist als Masse weiblichen Geschlechts und
verlangt eine feste, sichere Hand."

Goebbels

IN THE Third Reich the system of propaganda, the attempt at a wholesale
indoctrination of the masses, was both simple and complicated. It was
simple because it was ultimately and visibly controlled by one man, talented as an orator and a journalist, elastic, fertile in inventing ever new
slogans, images and lies. It was complex because it worked simultaneously
through three different institutions and channels: the Reich Ministry of
People's Enlightenment and Propaganda, the Central Propaganda Office
of the Party and the Reich Chamber of Culture, each with its own sub-
divisions both on the central and on the regional levels. When the National Socialists came to power Goebbels continued to be head of the
Propaganda agency of the Party,[1] but he strengthened both the scope of
propaganda and his own position greatly by setting up a special State
Ministry of Propaganda, the first of its kind in Germany. It was this
Ministry which put him and his methods on the map. It became the vital
focal point of his work and the theme of much international discussion
and criticism. Though the Party Propaganda agency remained important,
it was less conspicuous to the general public and more limited in its scope.
The newly created Reich Chamber of Culture had the function of co-
ordinating the production and distribution of all cultural works and
activities on the lines of Nazi policy. It was more closely related to the
Propaganda Ministry than to the Central Office of the Party.

As the years passed by there developed a certain amount of over-
organization, something more or less bound to happen in any bureaucracy
not subject to the watchful eye of parliamentary control. Behind the
imposing edifice was Goebbels' belief that propaganda should be omnipresent and that public opinion could be manufactured and streamlined.
Such a "making" of the public mind required the invention of apt and
simple stereotypes and slogans like "Ein Volk, ein Reich, ein Führer,
(One People, one Nation, one Leader) or "The Jews are our Misfortune."

[1] He had been appointed Head of Party Propaganda (*Reichspropaganda-
leiter*) by Hitler in November 1928.

It also needed an all-comprehensive organization which would watch and direct the people as a whole or some specific sections of them.

A. STATE PROPAGANDA

1. BUILDING UP A NEW MINISTRY

When on 28 February, 1933, the Reichstag building was set on fire, the new Hitler cabinet submitted to President Hindenburg for his signature an emergency decree which in article one declared permissible restrictions on personal liberty, on the right of free speech, including that of a free press.[1] Thirteen days later, on 13 March, the Party's most skilful and aggressive expert of written and spoken propaganda became "Reich Minister for People's Enlightenment and Propaganda" and a member of the new cabinet.

The new Minister had arrived. Goebbels showed little of the timidity he claims in an entry in his published diary.[2] The thought that he was only 35 and had to carry "such a great burden of responsibility" elated rather than depressed him. He lost no time in setting to work in proclaiming the new total approach of the régime. Soon he proved an "émpire-builder" who firmly established his new Ministry and insisted on proper premises for it. On 25 March he moved into the building of the former press liaison office of the Prussian State at the *Wilhelmplatz*, which lay opposite the old Reich Chancery. Built in the classicist style of Schinkel, before 1914 it had served its owner, the rich Prince Friedrich Leopold, chief of the German Freemasons, for his luxurious receptions.[3] Goebbels had it refurnished and extended. He poked fun at the diehard bureaucrats who, afraid of changes, were unaware that a revolution had taken place. With the help of a few SA navvies he enlarged the Minister's room in which he would receive visitors; following Mussolini's example Goebbels' own room had to be three times the size of that of any Minister of the defunct Republic.[4]

Unlike the other members of the new cabinet, Goebbels started from

[1] Verordnung des Reichspräsidenten zum Schutz von Volk und Staat, 28 February 1933. *Der Nationalsozialismus: Dokumente 1933-1945*, ed. Walther Hofer, p. 53.

[2] J. Goebbels, *Vom Kaiserhof zur Reichskanzlei*, Munich, 1935, entry of 11 March, 1933, p. 280.

[3] W. Stephan, *Joseph Goebbels,* p. 74.

[4] The Palace of Prince Friedrich Leopold was soon to prove inadequate for the expanding staff of the Ministry. A new building was then erected in the traditional style, simple, practical and unimaginative. The ambitious Propaganda Minister had it pulled down instantly. Wilhelmplatz 7-9 was rebuilt according to his taste and the latest technical devices for press, radio and films were installed.

scratch with his Ministry. Even in his streamlined published diary he admits "some difficulties" in those early days, which arose from delineating the scope and the functions of his new Ministry. This meant a certain encroachment on those of the older Ministries.[1] In fact the new Ministry took over departments from some of the traditional Government agencies. The Prussian Press office and a number of its officials were incorporated. The Ministry of the Interior renounced its supervisory powers over press and radio, its right to fix national holidays and its censorship of immoral plays, books and films. The Ministry of Economics surrendered its commercial advertising activities and the control and management of exhibitions and fairs. The Reich Ministry of Transport (then still combined with the General Post Office) handed over its network of travelling agencies whilst its postal branch gave up the management of broadcasting. There was also a good deal of rivalry between Goebbels' Ministry and Rust's Reich Ministry for Science, Schools and Adult Education. Throughout the Third Reich Goebbels was eager to take over control of the universities which, however, remained under Rust. But the Propaganda Minister at least achieved that the teachers and the faculties of arts' schools were taken away from Rust's control and incorporated in the realm of the Chamber of Fine Arts [2] which as part of the Chamber of Culture was under Goebbels' supervision.

Goebbels was constantly involved in quarrels with ministerial colleagues. From the beginning there was some tension between the Propaganda Ministry and the Foreign Ministry over their respective competencies. At a conference of heads of departments on 24 May, 1933,[3] over which Chancellor Hitler presided Goebbels made a special plea that "the chief task of the Reich Ministry of Public Enlightenment and Propaganda must be to influence public opinion abroad. Hitler agreed and decided that in future the Press Department of the Foreign Ministry should "limit itself to its previous traditional activity" whilst "active propaganda abroad" was to be taken over by Goebbels' Ministry, which was then setting up a press office of its own.

However the relations between the officials of the old established Foreign Ministry and those of the bold and enterprising Propaganda Ministry remained cool and later, with Ribbentrop at the helm of the *Auswärtiges Amt* (Foreign Ministry), sometimes even became tense. Both Ministries continued to hold separate conferences and there was constant competition over the influence which each wished to exercise over the foreign journalists visiting Germany. When at the outbreak of the war

[1] *Vom Kaiserhof zur Reichskanzlei*, diary entry of 14 March 1933, p. 283.
[2] This was done through a law issued on 15 May 1934. Goebbels did not succeed in his further demand that curators of museums should also come under his control.
[3] Minutes of the Conference of the Heads of Departments, Wednesday, 24 May 1933, *Documents on German Foreign Policy 1918-1945*. Series C, vol. 1, doc. no. 261, pp. 483-485. The purpose of the conference was "the delimitation of duties between the Ministry of Propaganda and the Foreign Ministry."

the importance of propaganda to foreign countries increased still further Hitler had to issue a drastic order to co-ordinate the efforts of the rival ministers and to make sure that the German war effort would not suffer by their quarrels.[1]

In questions of culture Goebbels regarded Alfred Rosenberg as his rival, in those of art Göring, whilst the control of German literary production was disputed between Goebbels, Rosenberg and Bouhler.[2] When, early in 1934 Rosenberg obtained the majestic title of the "Führer's Commissioner for the control of the entire intellectual and ideological training and education of the Party and of all affiliated associations"[3] Goebbels became very jealous,[4] a feeling that was renewed after Rosenberg's appointment as Minister for the Eastern Territories in 1941. Often intriguing against rivals, to whom he felt superior, Goebbels was yet unable to displace them. However much Hitler appreciated the talents of the versatile little Doctor, he stuck to the line of "Divide and Rule" which could only strengthen his overriding authority.

In 1933 the Goebbels Ministry was a new formation without any precedent but with the dynamics of an uninhibited venture. This was perhaps a drawback from the viewpoint of traditional bureaucracy but an advantage for the building up of a new totalitarian institution which had to carry out tasks of indoctrination and of guidance.

2. ORGANIZED INDOCTRINATION

There are two important aspects of the institutional system of propaganda as it developed after the National Socialists had taken over on 30 January, 1933. The first was its total scope, the fact that it was not confined to the political sphere proper but that it extended to the whole range of cultural activities of the nation. In a sense previously unknown in Germany it was to penetrate every aspect of society. This system of indoctrination and mind control was as much concerned with Party rallies and Party demonstrations as with the control of press and radio, of art and literature, theatre and film. It was designed to propagate the ideas and

[1] By a special Command of the Führer (*Führerbefehl*) of 8 September 1939 the competencies of the Propaganda Ministry and the Foreign Ministry were redefined and Hitler expressed his unwillingness to be bothered by complaints of either of the Ministers. See *Documents on German Foreign Policy 1918-1945*, Series D, vol. VIII, doc. 31, pp. 30-31. At the time Hitler's decision meant "a substantial defeat for Goebbels". (Paul Seabury, *The Wilhelmstrasse*, Los Angeles, 1954, p. 77).

[2] See O. Dietrich, *The Hitler I Knew*, London, 1957, p. 117.

[3] Rosenberg was also head of the Office for Foreign Affairs of the Party.

[4] The reason was probably that Rosenberg's office had a special department for Fine Arts (*Hauptstelle Bildende Kunst*) which issued its own lavishly illustrated magazine under the caption *Die Kunst im Dritten Reich*. See H. Lehmann-Haupt, *Art under Dictatorship*, New York, 1954, p. 69. The rivalry between Goebbels and Rosenberg has also been ably discussed in an article by Hildegard Brenner, "Die Kunst im politischen Machtkampf 1933/34", *Vierteljahrshefte für Zeitgeschichte*, vol. X, no. 1, January 1962.

actions of the new regime both inside and outside the Third Reich
and to streamline and control the national output of the spoken and
printed word, of the arts, the theatre and the film accordingly. As Goebbels once expressed it: "The State which is governed by an authoritarian
régime will not allow itself to be diverted from its path if it is convinced
that this path is the right one. In a democratic state public opinion
largely determines the nation's political course. In the authoritarian state
the State guides public opinion towards its aims and determines its own
policy."[1]

It is true, the principles of National Socialist propaganda had been
laid down by Hitler and Goebbels long before 1933 and had been tested
while their Party was in opposition. But the Central Propaganda Office
of the Party was small fry compared with the new Ministry of People's
Enlightenment and Propaganda. Although both continued side by side,
it was the Ministry which became a nation-wide and all-embracing institution.

The second major aspect of the set-up of propaganda in the new State
was the concentration of its control in the hands of one man on a threefold level. Head of the Central Propaganda Office of the Party since 1932,
Goebbels continued in this position to supervise the Party's propaganda
activities. As Minister he was now able to mould his Ministry with a
jealous zest and a restless industry. Finally as President of the Reich
Chamber of Culture he was the ultimate arbiter deciding on the admission
or exclusion of anyone active in the cultural field and wishing to earn a
living in it. The three agencies were also interlinked because many of
their leading officials held positions in more than one of them. In order
to direct and control people's minds propaganda has to be in close contact with the feelings of the people, with their reactions to events and to
the measures decided upon by the Powers-that-be. If there cannot be an
independent "public opinion," there is still a "public mood" which has
to be ascertained, studied and tabulated. In order to be effective, the
totalitarian rulers have, so to speak, to carry out their own Gallup poll
on the reactions and attitudes of the masses.

One point which Goebbels impressed on all his officials again and
again was the necessity of constantly gauging public moods. It was imperative to keep a finger on the fluctuating pulse of the masses if propaganda
was not to be carried out in a void. To break outer resistance was child's
play, but to overcome inner resistance appeared less easy. It was one
thing for the propagandist, as Goebbels put it, "to introduce the people
to the insights which are to be put over for their understanding in such
a way that they submit willingly and without any inner resistance to the
tasks and aims of a superior state leadership which results from these
insights."[2] It was another to be close to the changing moods of the peo-

[1] Goebbels in an interview with the Editor-in-Chief of the *Berliner Tageblatt*,
Schwarzer, 5 December 1935.

[2] See Goebbels' address at the Party Congress in September 1934. *Der
Kongress zu Nürnberg,* 1934, 5-10 September, p. 131.

ple to understand them in order to be able to persuade and indoctrinate them. Goebbels was regularly informed from reports on their morale coming from the 32 Reichspropaganda offices and Himmler's *Sicher-heits-Dienst* (SD).[1]

Not only must the public be constantly watched, it must also be continuously occupied in a direction required and approved by the régime. Suppression of "evil" thought had to be accompanied by projection of "approved" thought. While the official policies and doctrines were regarded as beyond criticism, the methods and tricks by which they could be made more palatable had to be constantly reviewed and discussed in the Ministry.

Goebbels liked to ask his subordinates for precise statements and statistical data on how people reacted to policy measures, to books, plays and films sponsored by the Ministry. "I know then exactly," he remarked in an interview at the end of 1937, "if a film which we regard as inferior *(Schundfilm)* is better or worse received than a film which we have judged good."[2] He explained that everything that happened among the people culturally, politically and economically was registered and examined from a psychological point of view. This tabulated information would be used in the Ministry as a basis of propaganda for any new course that the Government might decide to pursue. However, Goebbels admitted that such information was not always sufficient to win the public. If it became evident that a line of policy had not been well received, the Propaganda Ministry would work out improved arguments to convince the people of its soundness.[3]

The reactions of the public were often telling. For instance if the Ministry had arranged a political mass meeting at the Sport Palace in Berlin they knew exactly from the sale of the tickets whether the people showed "a desire for a talk" *(ein Bedürfnis für eine Aussprache)*, whether or not they wanted to hear an address on a certain theme. The mood and atmosphere at the meetings themselves were for the propagandist a barometer that indicated how far the people were with the authorities and approved of their ideas and measures. Goebbels as probably not far from the mark when he claimed that they had developed a fine feeling for the people's reactions to arguments at such meetings.[4]

With undisguised vanity Goebbels regretted that, unlike Haroun al Rashid, he was unable to mix with the people without being recognised. But he consoled himself with the idea that he knew exactly the preferences of the people, what they liked better and what less. Yet Goebbels often

[1] During the war these reports on morale became particularly important. For Goebbels' attitude to them see below ch. 12, pp. 296-297.

[2] Goebbels' interview with Schwarzer, *Berliner Tageblatt*, 5 December 1937.

[3] Ibid. A case in point is a diary entry made by Goebbels on 26 November 1943. "The German people wavers between fear and hope. It underrates the danger of Bolshevism. People do not realize how bloody and terroristic Bolshevism really is." As a result of this information Goebbels decided that further efforts were required to enlighten the people on the Bolshevist danger.

[4] Ibid.

dismissed what he regarded as the opinion of the ignorant multitude with a simple wave of his hand. "On such occasions he insisted that it was the function of his Ministry not to discover public opinion but to create and mould it." [1]

3. PASSIVE PARTICIPATION OF THE PEOPLE

There were two preconditions which Goebbels thought necessary for the success of his Ministry. The Minister should not be drowned in paperwork but should control and guide a staff of efficient experts, able to prepare the ground for the decisions which he alone was entitled to make. The other was close contact with the people, a knowledge of where their shoe pinched.

If, as Goebbels maintained, in an authoritarian regime it is the State that directs public opinion towards given aims, then the authoritarian Government must be fully informed about the changing public moods. Goebbels claimed that every Gauleiter, every leader of a local Party branch knew what was going on at any moment and was not afraid to convey his opinion candidly, however unpleasant this might be. [2]

The fact that he thought it expedient to emphasize how much the work of his Ministry was carried out under the very eyes of the people throws a revealing light on the nature of a modern dictatorship. Goebbels admitted that the complex apparatus at his disposal was extraordinarily sensitive, he even conceded that it could not avoid mistakes and errors though "no serious damage" had ever occurred in the Ministry. With dexterous sophistry Goebbels identified the closeness of his Ministry to the masses with their control of its work, for the work was "subject to a daily and hourly control by the people." [3]

Goebbels never admitted that in the Third Reich politics was an affair of the few. On the contrary, he liked to contrast the esoteric character of politics in the past which had been only a matter of chancellors and diplomats, a *terra incognita* for the masses, with the different position in the National Socialist State where the masses actually participated in the shaping of events. Frequently Goebbels presented measures the Government were determined to implement as coming from the people, as the result of the spontaneous expression of their emotions and thoughts. [4]

Taking part in a mass meeting was claimed to be equal to having a say in the making of politics. As one of the scribes of the sophisticated *Frankfurter Zeitung* put it rather ambiguously in 1937: "The address as

[1] Fritzsche's statement to the American psychiatrist Dr. Douglas M. Kelley; see the latter's book *22 Cells in Nuremberg,* New York, 1947, p. 83.

[2] Goebbels' interview with Schwarzer, 5 December 1937.

[3] Ibid.

[4] A good example for this is his speech on 13 November 1938, in which he foreshadowed further sharp anti-Jewish measures in retaliation for the murder by a Polish Jew of a member of the German Embassy in Paris. "The people want it to happen so, and we execute their wishes." The speech is discussed more fully below, ch. 17, pp. 383f.

an instrument of politics, this is the egg of Columbus discovered by National Socialism. In a manner so far unknown, the masses have felt they have been participating in the political process by way of address and speech. The men who have led, have been able to make themselves understood. This is their secret." [1] Only the end, not the means of propaganda could be good or bad. "In this context even demagogy was not despised, provided it led to a good aim." That aim was "an educational task, to lead the people to the State, everybody to participate in it." [2]

If passive participation without any real influence in the making of political decisions was the role allotted to the masses, it was propaganda which largely conditioned them. In a system of mind control participation meant indoctrination. In order to make indoctrination effective propaganda had to be omnipresent. It must also be both uniform and varied. The technical development of modern mass media and the multiplicity of channels considerably facilitated the regimentation of minds. The "omnipresence" permeated both the regime and its publicity.[3] Propaganda worked with many different instruments, with daily newspapers, periodicals and books, with films and radio, but all of them were to be at play simultaneously everywhere, day and night, at the breakfast table, at the place of work, in pubs and restaurants and during leisure hours, until the last broadcast at midnight. Just as the political movement was to be total, must not stop at the private sphere of the individual, should organise his leisure time and holidays as much as his political attitude, so propaganda was to be universal too, by talking to him through a hundred different and yet co-ordinated voices. In an address on "Bolshevism as a world danger," delivered at the Party Congress in September, 1936, Goebbels observed that "Bolshevist propaganda was cleverly used to adapt itself to its specific audience in each case. It posed as radical or moderate according to the requirements of the matter," it was quite a different matter if the terrorist Dimitrov addressed the Komintern or the Jew Litvinov the League of Nations. This propaganda was "pious or godless as required." It knew no scruple, the end justified the means. Goebbels did not add that a similar pragmatism and expediency was true of National Socialist propaganda.

In 1928 Mussolini had compared Fascist journalism with an orchestra.[4] Goebbels took over a similar formula from Funk, his Under Secretary of State.[5] The press, he declared, was an orchestra which had to play the same melody on different instruments as directed by the conductor's baton. One could go further and maintain that in each campaign the various mass media were allotted different voices and tasks by the Propa-

[1] Article "Propagator", *Frankfurter Zeitung,* 29 October 1937.
[2] Ibid.
[3] This term was first coined by W. Hagemann, *Publizistik im Dritten Reich,* Hamburg, 1948, pp. 146-147.
[4] *Handbuch der Weltpresse,* 3rd edition, Leipzig, 1937, p. 228.
[5] W. Hagemann, op. cit., p. 151.

ganda Ministry. Not only was Goebbels well aware that the public varied according to intellectual level, education and interests; he also realized that the different mass media did not possess the same effect or the same degree of intensity in reaching the public.

As the Goebbels Ministry controlled all the mass media it could offer the food of indoctrination in different packages. There was a greater variety of levels in the Nazi-controlled German press than one might perhaps expect. It ranged from the pornographic crudities of Streicher's weekly *Der Stürmer* through the average local Party press to such clever wartime publications as the weekly *Das Reich*, destined for a more educated public, not to mention the *Frankfurter Zeitung*, that cultural Cinderella of the regime. In addition to this acknowledged variety, a clear distinction was drawn between the relative significance of various sectors of each mass medium. For the purpose of indoctrination some were more important than others. With radio transmissions news and commentaries counted most, then came entertainment items and finally those items which served an educational purpose. With films there existed a similar scale of significance: the newsreel mattered more than cultural films and these more than mere entertainment films, though some of them like "Jew Süss" or "The Great King," the epic of Frederick the Great, were clearly destined to promote indoctrination. In the printed output the daily press mattered most (and not only its political pages), then followed the weeklies, the periodicals, the books. To such degrees of propaganda effect corresponded the intensity of supervision, the greater or lesser bulk of directives to be followed and the demands of proved reliability. The personnel and the output of the dailies, of the newsreel, or the radio news, were subject to much sharper and more systematic supervision than art, plays, books and films for entertainment.

When running specific propaganda campaigns and appeals, each of the various mass media was often allotted special tasks and functions by the Propaganda Ministry. For instance individual media were to produce specific effects in the frequently planned anti-Semitic campaigns. The newspapers were obliged to devote space to day-to-day polemics on the basis of the last topical news item. Periodicals had to wrap the racial ideology in the garb of pseudo-scientific theories. The film producers assisted with such tendentious products as "Jew Süss" or the story of the House of Rothschild, in an effort to impress negative and positive images on the masses. Finally the radio was used to spread doubtful or false news of Jewish or anti-Semitic activities for which it would have been difficult if not impossible to produce documentary evidence.[1]

4. Who were the Propagandists?

A study of the Nazi élite in 1934 based on the data provided by the

[1] W. Hagemann, op. cit., p. 152.

official *Führerlexikon,* a "Who's Who of the Leaders," has thrown some interesting light on the Nazi propagandists as a type.[1] What is striking is the comparative youth of these propagandists, who were employed either by the Propaganda Ministry or by the Party. Their average age of 38.9 years was five years lower than that of the Nazi administrators and about 10 years less than that of the Nazi élite as a whole.[2] The majority of these propagandists had been only 18 at the outbreak of the First World War and had reached maturity during it or immediately afterwards.[3] They came from the upper middle class of Imperial (and Weimar) Germany. The percentage of their fathers in occupations enjoying a top prestige in Imperial Germany such as landowners and holders of military and ecclesiastic posts was higher than that of other Nazi groups analyzed. The educational level attained by the future propagandists was high too. More than half of them had attended a university as compared with only one quarter of the Nazi administrators.[4] And more than twice as many propagandists had reached the highest educational level at universities. One third of the propagandists had studied the humanities ("culture-oriented studies") as distinct from "skill-oriented" or "professional studies." Many of them had served as officers in the First World War and subsequently found it difficult to obtain employment in post-war Germany. A considerable percentage suffered temporary unemployment, a fact that made them inclined to become "alienated intellectuals," disaffected people shifting "their allegiance to the Nazi movement which offered them the promise of a brighter place in the sun." [5] One out of five of the propagandists with entries in the *Führerlexikon* declared that he had been without a job at some point of his career during the days of the Weimar Republic. The average span of unemployment reported was about 4 years.[6] One fourth of them had held only "Nazi jobs," employment in the Party or one of its agencies. This had saved them from starvation, but was, particularly in the earlier years of the Nazi movement, far from being remunerative.

The fact that most of the propagandists came from the upper middle strata of German society has to be set against the different origin of the administrators, the "plebeians on the make" (D. Lerner). There were exceptions such as Max Amann, Hitler's sergeant major in the First World War and later as a director of the Party's main publishing firm, an important manager of part of its propaganda machinery. Amann shared the "low" origin of the administrators and lacked the polish and education possessed by men like Walter Funk, Press Chief of the Reich Government

[1] Daniel Lerner, *The Nazi Elite,* Hoover Institute Studies, Stanford, 1951.
[2] Op. cit., p. 11. Lerner's categories of "Nazi propagandist" and "Nazi administrator" are useful. It must be kept in mind, however, that some of the propagandists also exercised administrative functions, for instance Goebbels as Gauleiter of Berlin.
[3] Op. cit., p. 14.
[4] Op. cit., p. 21.
[5] Op. cit., p. 32.
[6] Ibid.

and Under Secretary of State in the Propaganda Ministry, or Hans Fritzsche, a right-wing professional journalist who became a highly placed official in Goebbels' Ministry and later a prominent broadcaster.

But whereas most of these propagandists originated from higher social strata than the administrators, fewer of them reached eminence and top positions in the Party. Apart from Goebbels, only his rivals Dr. Dietrich and Max Amann held the high Party rank of *Reichsleiter*. Though the skilled propagandist, the master of the spoken and the written word, is important in any totalitarian regime, this importance has its limitations arising from the fact that "his skill is primarily as adviser and executor, but not as decision-maker and leader." [1] With rare exceptions, top honours in the Nazi élite went to the administrators and not to the propagandists. Few of the latter obtained any of the higher Party offices and positions, for instance, the post of *Gauleiter,* which enabled its holders to amass private fortunes. While the propagandist, too, enjoyed the institutionalized prestige bestowed on the totalitarian State as well as on the Party bureaucracy, there was a higher social premium on the administrator.

5. Goebbels and his Staff

Goebbels shared to the full the German bent for efficiency and *Leistung*. He was an indefatigable worker, punctual, intensive and, unlike Hitler, also interested in details in his field.[2] His misanthropy which grew with the years and which was only concealed by a certain charm in social intercourse made him inclined to regard others as indolent and as mere pleasure-seekers. In spite of his artistic pretensions, he liked strict discipline. If Goebbels discovered mistakes or failure in his subordinates he would heap abuse and threats on them in such a manner that the victims felt thrown into an abyss of humiliation and shame.[3] Yet, Goebbels was too practical, had too marked a sense of proportion, to overdo this procedure, as far as old Party members were concerned. Some time after an outburst Goebbels would try to humour his victims by way of invitations, decorations, promotion. These officials were never really dismissed, only transferred. For these old Party members were Goebbels' clique, his clientele. Nearly everyone of the top men of the Party had such a clan of his own. Its members were sometimes put down, but they were rarely dropped, at least not so long as they remained loyal to their clique leader.[4]

Some top rank leaders such as Himmler, Göring, and Bormann created specific types of underlings. The SS formed a type. Was this true of the higher officials in Goebbels' Ministry? According to Werner Stephan

[1] Op. cit., p. 82.

[2] W. Stephan, *Joseph Goebbels*, p. 81.

[3] On Goebbels' harshness to his subordinates, see also Fritzsche's remarks in Douglas M. Kelley: *22 Cells in Nuremburg,* p. 84.

[4] W. Stephan, op. cit., p. 99.

who held a senior position in the Ministry for 12 years, this was not the case. "Goebbels," he says, "could not be imitated. Under him you could learn a certain technique and method. But there was no standardized pattern of behaviour, no uniform type of thinking . . . He could not train a crew, because he was too much of an individualist himself, an individual who did not set himself up as an example." [1] His followers did not see in him a model, but most of them regarded him with "a mixture of amazement and instinctive dislike." In his Ministry, it seems, there were a variety of types: the old primitive, but often sincere Party member, the cold fanatic, the naive enthusiast working side by side with the ruthless careerist, the corrupt adventurer, the philistine official and the intellectual with an interest in *Kultur*. The departmental heads in the Ministry could be divided roughly into two categories, the professional civil servants and experts with many years of experience, such as Dr. Karl Ott, the head of the Budget department, and the career propagandists, like Alfred Ingmar Berndt, the questionable head of the German Press Department in 1938. Different from the procedure followed in ministries of democratic countries, it was quite impossible for heads of departments officially to consult each other. According to Goebbels' personal Press Officer, during the first half of the war, "it was generally known that the Minister was using them [the departmental heads] as tools and that when he did not need them any more he would throw them out." [2] The Minister was "full of distrust of the men around him, even of those closely connected with him." He always expected intrigues that might threaten his position. This distrust seems to have sharpened during the war.[3]

Soon after Goebbels joined the new Cabinet he put much emphasis on his social duties. The semi-proletarian Gauleiter of the late 1920's with his small case, lustre jacket and felt hat, gradually transformed himself into an elegantly clad man of the world. But though Goebbels seems to have enjoyed attending social functions as one of the more agreeable duties of a Reich Minister, it did not diminish his zest for hard work. Nor did he wish his subordinates to follow him into Society. What was proper for the son of a petit bourgeois family who had arrived, was not permissible for the heads of his departments, some of whom, like Fritzsche and Bömer, came from the upper middle class. The Minister warned them against the emptiness of social receptions in fashionable hotels, where always "the same smart well dressed people met who regarded themselves as politicians and diplomats, declared each other to be important, while they were in fact empty headed and without any real influence on the actual course of events." [4]

[1] W. Stephan, op. cit., p. 103.
[2] Statement by Moritz v. Schirmeister at the Nuremberg Trial, 28 July 1946, IMT, *The Trial of German War Criminals*, part 17, London, 1948, p. 303.
[3] See R. Semmler, *Goebbels—The Man next to Hitler*, London, 1947, p. 29, diary entry of 22 April 1941.
[4] W. Stephan, op. cit., p. 89.

6. THE MINISTRY AND ITS DEPARTMENTS

In 1938 there were three posts of *Staatssekretär* or Under Secretary of State in the Propaganda Ministry. With one exception they were held by men with long Party affiliations. Oddly enough, only the least important and talented of them, Hitler's old comrade in arms and protégé, Hermann Esser, who supervised the Department for Tourists *(Fremdenverkehr)* was in office throughout the lifetime of the Ministry (1933-1945). Under Secretary for matters of the Press was until 1937 Walter Funk, an economic journalist by profession and more a conservative bourgeois than a passionate Nazi before the days of the Third Reich. After Funk's promotion to Minister for Economic Affairs he was followed by Dr. Otto Dietrich, Reich Press Chief of the Party, who retained both posts until a few weeks before the end of the regime. The office of the third Under Secretary who, under the Minister, supervised all other departments, was first filled by Karl Henke (1937-1940) and then by Leopold Gutterer, the former head of the important Department II "Propaganda" who, like his predecessor, had a long Party record. In 1944, Gutterer had to give way to a younger and more ambitious man, Dr. Werner Naumann, who through hard work had risen from the post of head of the Office of the Minister *(Ministeramt)*.

Early Goebbels had declared that the staff of his Ministry should never exceed one thousand. Nevertheless during the twelve years of its existence the Ministry expanded considerably, though no exact figures of its strength are available. But Goebbels the anti-bureaucrat could not escape a process of departmental expansion and bureaucratisation. Originally he had only planned five departments, one each for the press, radio, active propaganda and film, and a fifth for theatre and adult education joined together.[1] But by the end of 1938 the number of departments had grown to eleven and by November, 1942 to fourteen. Over the years the work of some of them had become so extensive that new additional units had branched off. The Press Department, for instance, had soon developed separate sections, one each for the domestic and foreign press, and by 1942 its work was carried out by three different departments, for the home press, the foreign press and the periodicals respectively.[2] Similarly by 1938 the affairs of adult education had been separated from those of the theatres and entrusted to a special department for "folk culture" *(Volkskulturelle Arbeit)*. (XI).

In the context of this study we must confine ourselves to a survey of the more important departments. *Department I*, concerned with various aspects of administration, had by 1942 split into three different departments for Budget, Personnel and for Law and Organization respectively.

---

[1] See Goebbels' first address to the press after his appointment as Minister on 16 March 1933; reprinted in his *Revolution der Deutschen,* Oldenburg, 1933, p. 142.

[2] See the survey of the distribution of business in the Ministry *(Geschäftsverteilungsplan)* issued on 1 November 1942. The three departments were supervised by Dr. Dietrich as Under Secretary.

The work of each of them was comprehensive. In addition to administering the finances of the Ministry itself the Budget Department also looked after the financial affairs of the offices and organizations under the control of the Ministry, for instance, the 32 regional Propaganda Offices in the Reich. Similarly the scope of the Personnel Department extended beyond the staff of the Ministry to the salaries and wages of the many professional groups integrated in the Reich Chamber of Culture.[1] The Legal Department devised and drafted legislation for the entire sphere of the Ministry and was largely instrumental in transforming art and literature into tools of the regime.[2]

One of the main pillars of the Ministry was *Department II*, simply labelled "Propaganda," being more comprehensive and less specialized than the others.[3] Its overall task was to propagate and implement the policies of the Government and the programme of the Party, particularly during election campaigns.[4] The Department was above all a centre of campaigning for German *Volkstum*, for the racialists and anti-Semitic doctrines of the regime. It busied itself with the interests of Germans in frontier regions and neighbouring countries, the *Volksdeutsche*, and with other German national groups abroad. In fact many of the atrocity stories about the fate of the Sudeten Germans in 1938 and on the maltreatment of Germans in Poland on the eve of World War II emerged from this Department. Here much anti-Semitic propaganda for both home and foreign consumption was devised and the fight against other "enemies of the State" carried out. The department also propagated population policy—in other words it recommended that the Germans should have more children—and laid down economic policy, as in the Four Year Plan. Not only had its officials to make the propaganda stemming from their Ministry uniform, but they had also to suggest propaganda campaigns to other ministries. They designed plans for them, put various mass-media of propaganda at their disposal and finally supervised the implementation of the plans.

Sport was another field for the activities of *Department II*. Watch was

[1] See *Führer durch die Behörden und Organisationen*, ed. L. Münz, 4th ed. München, 1939, p. 103.

[2] In the official view "the professions and institutions of literature and art had to be changed from instruments of liberal individualism to fulfilling the public functions of indoctrination (*Einwirkung*) and leadership" (G.W. Müller, *Das Reichsministerium für Volksaufklärung und Propaganda*, Berlin, 1940, p. 12). This transformation was carried out partly through decrees issued by subordinated agencies such as the various divisions of the Reich Chamber of Culture and partly by over-all legislation originating from the Legal Department of the Ministry. The important decree on editors (*Schriftleitergesetz*) of 4 October 1933 and the decree on the showing of foreign films of 11 July 1936 are cases in point.

[3] G. W. Müller, op. cit., p. 14.

[4] For these reasons the Propaganda Department had also to maintain liaison with the Central Propaganda Office of the Party in Munich which had similar functions.

kept on the German sportsmen abroad and German sport relations with foreign countries were supervised jointly with the Reich Sport leader and the Foreign Ministry. With the immense emphasis on State occasions in the Third Reich, the Department constantly busied itself with preparing and supervising State festivals (for instance after the *Anschluss* in March, 1938) and public events such as pre-election meetings, historical anniversaries, the christening of ships and State funerals. It was its responsibility to draw up and carry out a detailed programme of all events in which the Führer took part. Another of its tasks was the planning of exhibitions,[1] many of them with aggressive political slants and with the intention of exposing Bolshevism or World Jewry.[2]

For some years there existed a special section (IIa) for the supervision of the very limited cultural life of the "Non-Aryans" in the Reich no longer allowed to share the normal cultural facilities for Germans. As the role of the *Press Department* (IV) is examined in another chapter [3] some consideration can be given here to the important *Department of Broadcasting* (III). Compared with the press, a medium that had a long and varied history, radio was somewhat of a newcomer in 1933, although its great propaganda potential had been recognised by Goebbels long before that year. In an address at the first Nazi radio exhibition in August, 1933 he declared that radio would be to the twentieth century what the press had been for the nineteenth. The invention of this "Eighth Big Power" and its application in the life of the community were of "a truly revolutionary significance." [4] The young Minister of Propaganda was determined to make the most of this new medium. He regarded mass listening, and in days still to come, mass viewing, as most suitable channels for bringing the people closer to the new State.[5] After the March elections of 1933 in which nearly half of the voters had still declared themselves against the new Government Goebbels told the heads of the German radio stations bluntly: "With this instrument you are making public opinion. If you do it well, we shall win over the people. If you do it badly, the people will in the end run away from us. Radio has to secure the missing 48% of votes for the Government. Once we have won them, radio must hold the 100% of our supporters, must defend them, must indoctrinate them so thoroughly that no one can break away any

[1] This also included German participation in exhibitions abroad.

[2] Attached to the Department was a "Propaganda Studio" which seems to have developed technical devices and gadgets.

[3] See below, chapter 4.

[4] J. Goebbels, "Der Rundfunk als achte Grossmacht", reprinted in *Signale der neuen Zeit*, Munich, 1934, pp. 18-19.

[5] In an address before the press in Berlin on 16 March 1933, Goebbels regarded it as imperative that in future the whole nation instead of a mere 15,000 people should listen to national events such as the opening of the new Reichstag or the Service of Thanksgiving in Potsdam. After the invention of television the entire nation would be able to view them. See *Revolution der Deutschen*, p. 144.

more." [1] Goebbels clearly saw in radio an instrument to create the indoctrinated type of obedient follower of the regime. It was to him, as he put it, "a means towards the uniformity *(Vereinheitlichung)* of the German people in the north and the west, in the south and the east, of Catholics and Protestants, of proletarians and bourgeois and peasants." [2]

In contrast to the decentralized state of German radio stations prior to 1933, the control of the German radio now became utterly concentrated. Official commentators talked of the Radio Department as the *Befehlszentrale,* a centre for issuing orders to the entire German radio world, or the "General Staff of the German Radio." [3] In fact, with Goebbels as overlord, a remarkable interlacing of offices took place, with the head of the Ministry's Department of Broadcasting also acting as chief of the corresponding department in the Central Propaganda Office of the Party and as President of the Reich Chamber of Radio. [4] The Ministry's Department laid down radio policy and supervised its implementatation through the RRG [5] or German Broadcasting Company. One of the three directors of the RRG, the *Reichssendeleiter,* joined the departmental heads of the Ministry at the Minister's daily conference. Here he received direct orders from Goebbels himself who, it should be noted, took a particular interest in radio programmes, which often extended to the most minute details. [6]

By 1940 the Department of Broadcasting of the Ministry comprised four sections, which dealt with (a) "cultural affairs and broadcasting to foreign countries;" (b) "special tasks;" (c) "production aspects, legal aspects of broadcasting and propaganda for it;" and (d) "technical aspects of radio," respectively. The hard core of the Department was formed by the section "Cultural Affairs and Broadcasting to Foreign Countries," responsible for the direction of political and cultural radio programmes. [7]

[1] *Mitteilungen der Reichs Rundfunk-Gesellschaft*, Sonderbeilage zu Nr. 334, 30 March 1933.

[2] Ibid.

[3] E. Hadamovsky, *Der Rundfunk im Dienste der Volksführung*, Leipzig, n.d. (1934) pp. 19-20.

[4] G. W. Müller, op. cit., p. 22 and Heinz Pohle, *Der Rundfunk als Instrument der Politik*, Hamburg, 1955, p. 77.

[5] From 1933-1937 these three positions were jointly held by H. Dressler-Andreas, from 1937-1939 by Hans Kriegler.

[6] According to his press officer, Moritz von Schirmeister, Goebbels did not scrutinize the activities of any other department in the Ministry as strictly as those of the Department of Broadcasting. See IMT, part 17, p. 305

[7] Its operations included: "Political radio transmission, radio programmes for national festivals, cultural exchanges with other countries, the establishing and feeding of German radio programmes abroad, scientific programmes, school programmes, cultural international radio matters, World Radio Union and the relations between radio and press. The section "Special Tasks" comprised "all radio tasks in case of mobilization, reorganization of radio in case of war and use of radio as a propaganda weapon" in such a situation. See G. W. Müller, op. cit., p. 22.

The *Department of Fine Arts* (IX) laid down the principles of what was officially regarded as desirable and undesirable in art. It was active in the official battle against modern decadent trends in painting and sculpture from expressionism to cubism which had to disappear. The Department arranged exhibitions in various parts of the Reich and *Gaukulturwochen*, and had to ensure that "the artistic level and the ideological contents" were in conformity with the spirit of the Third Reich.[1] It also encouraged and financed painters and sculptors to produce works of art of a National Socialist character. To achieve this, it placed remunerative State orders in the hands of those already sufficiently imbued with the Nazi ideology to proclaim the true Nordic gospel in marble, plaster or oil paint. In conjunction with the Chamber of Fine Arts controlled by the Department it promoted exhibitions of the works of "deserving artists" both in Germany and abroad, bought their works from State funds, arranged prize competitions and provided training courses for young artists.

The *Department of Music* (X) watched music activities in general and supervised the Reich Chamber of Music in particular. It controlled an office for the censorship for all musical production, the *Reichsmusikprüfstelle*, which could prohibit the publication or performance of any works deemed incompatible with the Nordic spirit of National Socialism.[2] At least in the earlier years of the regime there was some courageous opposition to the official policy of fostering Teutonic music, coming from such eminent men as the conductor Wilhelm Furtwängler and the national-minded composer Hans Pfitzner. In those early days Goebbels was prepared to make concessions to the independent spirit of men like Furtwängler in order to retain their high prestige for the new regime.[3]

In the official jargon, the *Film Department* (V) had the task "to direct from the centre the German film production in its artistic, economic and technical aspects as well as to ensure the harmonious co-operation of all forces engaged in the film industry." In fact the Department controlled or influenced both the production and distribution of general films and

[1] See G. W. Müller, op. cit., p. 28; also H. Lehmann-Haugt, *Art under Dictatorship*, ch. V, "The Organization of Total Control."

[2] In this field the term "Decadent Music" (*Entartete Musik*) corresponded to that of "Decadent Art" (*Entartete Kunst*) in the realm of fine arts. In consequence not only Jewish but also many "Aryan" musicians and composers were forbidden to carry out their profession.

[3] On 12 April 1933 Furtwängler wrote a letter to Goebbels, in which he maintained that a distinction could only be drawn between good and bad music but not between Jewish and non-Jewish music. Goebbels allowed the publication of this letter together with his reply in which he paid a sly tribute to the famous conductor, minimized the recent anti-Jewish boycott measures about which Furtwängler had complained and insisted on a sharp demarcation line between Aryan and non-Aryan music. E. Kroll, op. cit., p. 511; also Curt Riess, *Wilhelm Furtwängler*, London, 1955, pp. 102-104.

documentaries. It could also eliminate "undesirable films" and push "desirable" ones with all the authority at its disposal.

There is no doubt that Hitler looked upon the film as a major instrument of effective propaganda because of its four specific qualities: (1) subjective emotional appeal; (2) limitation of contents; (3) possibility of using it throughout to illustrate the fighting attitude and (4) continuous and uniform repetition.[1]

When the Nazis came to power the film industry was not nationalized. The organization of the big German film companies, such as Hugenberg's UFA and Terra was complicated and there were also many smaller firms. To nationalize them suddenly might have paralysed their contacts with foreign film distributors.[2] But by 1937 UFA was taken over by the Reich and Hugenberg sold out to Goebbels.[3] As with other departments of the Ministry the function was positive as well as negative. While it promoted and subsidised films regarded as valuable from the point of view of indoctrination or prestige, it kept a sharp watch on others which in parts or altogether were declared undesirable, damaging and anti-German.

Obviously the film companies could not afford to run counter to the wishes of the Propaganda Ministry. On the other hand, if they complied, they could reckon on financial and propaganda support from the Reich Film Chamber which, in its turn, was controlled by the Film Department of the Ministry. What the Law for Editors *(Schriftleitergesetz)* was for the press, the Reich Film Law *(Reichsfilmgesetz)* of 16 February, 1934 was for films. It established an office for the scrutiny of films *(Filmprüfstelle)*, to be supervised by the Propaganda Ministry, which evaluated all finished films.[3]

With the exception of broadcasting there was no other field in which the Propaganda Minister showed such keen and personal interest. To watch films, both German and foreign, was to him as much a pleasure as a duty. While only in a few cases was the film industry forced to make films on Goebbels' orders, in many cases he interfered a good deal with both the proposed scripts and the finished films. He made himself and his authority felt in all phases of production, often to the chagrin of the producers, requesting cuts here and additions there and even insisting on changes in the cast.[5]

There was a double control of film production. All scripts of proposed films had to be submitted for approval to a special censor, the *Reichs-*

---

[1] Cf. G. W. Klimsch, *Die Entwicklung des national-sozialistischen Film-Monopols von 1933-1940.* Munich, 1954.

[2] D. Sington and A. Weidenfeld, *The Goebbels Experiment*, p. 205.

[3] The nationalisation of the film industry was only completed in 1943.

[4] An elaborate scale of grades marking their relative value ran as follows: (i) particularly valuable politically and artistically; (ii) valuable politically and artistically; (iii) valuable politically; (iv) valuable artistically; (v) of cultural value; (vi) of educational value.

[5] R. Manvell and H. Fraenkel, op. cit., p. 147.

filmdramaturg, who also scrutinized the suitability of their authors. He provided the channel through which official recommendation of particular themes or political angles, even of entire stories and plots were passed on to the film industry. All finished films had to be passed by the *Filmprüfstelle* (Film Censorship Office). There was also a final authority for appeals, the *Oberprüfstelle*.

A major task of the Film Department, in co-operation with the Chamber of Films, was to initiate and supervise the production of propaganda films and of lengthy documentaries by the State.[1] The number of direct and full-length propaganda films made between 1933 and 1939 was relatively small, perhaps because Goebbels was aware that the masses wanted from the cinema entertainment and escape from reality.[2] These films were usually of inferior quality with the exception of Leni Riefenstahl's impressive works on the Nuremberg Party Congress in 1934 and on the Olympic Games of 1936.[3] Their artistic skill was remarkable and their persuasive propaganda value could be rated high at home and abroad.

German military victories were reflected in lengthy documentaries produced during the early years of the war.[4] Goebbels took a personal interest in the weekly newsreel, the *Wochenschau*, which all German cinemas were obliged to incorporate in their programmes. He viewed many before their release. The head of the Film Department in the Ministry was in charge of the newsreel centre (*Wochenschauzentrale*) and responsible to the Minister for its planning and production. In times of peace, and even more so in days of national crisis and war, the aim of the newsreel was obviously to create mass intoxication and to obtain mass approval for the projected deeds of the regime in both domestic and foreign affairs. Guiding the newsreel was the will to influence the people of today and the intention to produce "historical documentaries which would impress later generations." [5]

The firms producing newsreels had simply to accept the version of the big functions of the State, the Party and the armed forces, which was carefully prepared and executed by a special staff of the Propaganda

[1] G. W. Müller, op. cit., p. 23.

[2] Among them were films eulogizing the life of the storm troopers (*S. A. Mann Brandt*) and that of the Hitler Youth (*Hitler Junge Quex*); also *Hans Westmar*, recalling the heroic life of Horst Wessel.

[3] *Triumph des Willens* (1934) and *Die Olympiade* (1938).

[4] *Feuertaufe* (1939) and *Sieg im Westen* (1940) illustrated the lightning speed and devastating power of the German armed forces overrunning Poland and France. These films were shown by many German embassies in neutral countries with a view to intimidating the foreign viewers: they illustrated the point that resistance to the mighty German armies, up to date in their weapons, was equivalent to committing suicide.

[5] See Fritz Terveen, "Das Filmdokument der Nazis und sein Wahrheitsgehalt", *Das Parlament*, Bonn, No. 21-25, May 1955, p. 8. There were also the special newsreels for foreign countries, produced by the Propaganda Ministry in their own languages, particularly after 1938.

Ministry. These men were briefed before the events on their planned course and the desired angle and were given special facilities for effective filming.[1]

May 10, 1933, deserves to be remembered in the history of German literature. It was "the day of the burning of the books" when students and other National Socialists in Berlin threw books of twenty-four "undesirable and pernicious" authors into a bonfire on the immense Franz Joseph Platz, a square near the University. Freud and Marx, Heinrich Mann, Stephan Zweig and Erich Kästner (who watched this orgy of exorcism)[2] were among them. When the literary execution was at its height, the Propaganda Minister appeared and made a speech relayed by the German radio stations. "The age of extreme intellectualism has now ended, and the success of the German revolution has again given the right of way to the German spirit. . . ." he said. "You are doing the right thing in committing the evil spirit of the past to flames. It is a strong, great, and symbolic act . . . The past is lying in flames . . . The future will rise from the flames within our own hearts." [3]

In future the State was going to determine what was "good" and wholesome and what was "bad" and destructive literature, which type deserved execration and which official furtherance. As far as German writers were concerned, Goebbels regarded them as obliged to work for the nation rather than to follow their own whim and will. "Now the pen has been compelled to serve the nation like the sword and the plough," he declared three years later.[4]

Seen in this context, the purpose of the *Department of Literature* (VIII) (*Abteilung Schrifttum*) was described as providing "political leadership in culture" and assisting German literature, both inside the Reich and abroad. It had "to see to it that a broad strata of the German people were brought into contact with the achievements of German poets and writers." This task was to be performed in closest contact with the publishers, the booksellers and the libraries, for instance, by such large-scale propaganda actions as the "Week of the German Book" (every autumn) and propaganda for specialized literature (every spring).[5]

The Department also controlled a special agency, the *Werbe-und Berat-*

[1] All newsreel men had to be members of the *Reichs-Filmfachschaft,* a subdivision of the Reich Chamber of Culture. See the Third Decree on Film Reporters of 21 December 1934, published in *Völkischer Beobachter,* 27 March 1935.

[2] Erich Kästner, *Bei Durchsicht meiner Bücher,* Zürich, n.d. (1947?), p. 5.

[3] Quoted in L. Lochner's Introduction to *The Goebbels Diaries,* p. xxvii.

[4] Address by Dr. Goebbels at the opening of "Die Woche des deutschen Buches" in Weimer on 25 October 1936, quoted in *Es begann am 30. Januar,* Munich, 1958, p. 49.

5 G. W. Müller, op. cit., p. 25. According to an official statement issued in 1940, Department VIII controlled 2,500 publishers, 23,000 booksellers, 3,000 writers and 2,000 annual new publications. See D. Strothmann, *Nationalsozialistische Literaturpolitik,* Bonn, 1960, pp. 23-27.

ungsamt für das Deutsche Schrifttum, which dealt with the "systematic selection in all fields of literature." Employing a large staff of readers all over the Reich including university lecturers, literary editors, book-reviewers and librarians, this office issued regular lists of books to be recommended to lending libraries, many of which were run by party organizations. It also advised publishers and booksellers on what books they should boost and advertise on a large scale. In cooperation with the Chamber of Literature, which it supervised, and with various Party agencies [1] the Department had to promote "good" books and to ban "bad" ones or prevent their publication.[2]

The Department of Literature measured its importance by the number of publishers, booksellers, authors and new book titles involved in its work every year. According to an official statement issued in 1940, it had to deal with 20,000 annual new publications. It was also concerned with the bestowing of fifty important German prizes for literature and over a thousand meetings, conferences and congresses on literary questions.[3]

By 1938 the division had a number of senior officials whose qualifications lay more in their long Party membership than in any marked insight into literary matters. On the other hand some of the experts were not Nazi doctrinaires and often had a genuine sympathy with the plight of writers handicapped by the restrictive tendencies of the regime. Some of them showed on occasions a remarkably independent taste and judgment. Dr. Hugo Koch, for instance, guided and protected Jochen Klepper, a writer of conservative and Christian tendencies, after he had been excluded from membership of the Chamber of Literature on account of his Jewish wife. Koch defended Klepper against chicanery and growing pressure from Nazi doctrinaires and promised him, to quote Klepper's own words, "tolerance, loyalty, an assurance of quick examination [of his manuscripts], and in the case of enquiries, rejections of attacks on me." [4]

[1] Such agencies were the *Amt Schrifttumspflege* in Rosenberg's office supervising "the entire spiritual and philosophical education of the National Socialist Party" and the *Parteiamtliche Prüfungskommission zum Schutze des NS Schrifttums.* The latter supervised all publications on problems of National Socialism

[2] See below, p. 79.

[3] See G. W. Müller, op. cit., p. 26. There was further a foreign section dealing with the supervision of non-German literature to be imported, and with the export of German books. The division also organized exhibitions of approved German literature abroad and during the war in occupied, friendly and neutral countries, in co-operation with the *Reichskommissariat für Internationale Ausstellungen.*

[4] Jochen Klepper, *Unter dem Schatten Deiner Flügel. Aus den Tagebüchern der Jahre 1932-1942.* Stuttgart, 1955, pp. 578 and 1148. When during the war Koch joined the army, he was succeeded by a much more determined National Socialist, Dr. H. W. Hagen. In December 1942, Klepper, his wife and their stepdaughter committed suicide after the Security Service had granted exit permits for Sweden to him and his stepdaughter, but not to his wife. For Hagen's role during the events of July 20, 1944, in Berlin, see below ch. 15, p. 337ff.

The *Department of the Theatre* (VI) had similar functions to those of the Film Department. It supervised the Reich Theatre Chamber, decided on the scripts of new plays, kept a watch on the programmes of all German theatres and distributed the State subsidies without which many of them were unable to survive. The Department also controlled a number the State theatres and opera houses in Berlin, Wiesbaden and, since the *Anschluss,* in Vienna. It further supervised such annual events as the Wagner festivals in Bayreuth and in Zoppot, the Salzburg-Festspiele (which had become famous under Max Reinhardt, before he was expelled in 1933) and other festivals, all of which were classed as *reichswichtig* (important to the Reich).

Ministerialrat Dr. Schlösser, the head of the Department, who officiated at the same time as *Reichsdramaturg* (Reich Supervisor of the Drama) exercised decisive control over the repertoires of all German theatres. Schlösser, a personal friend of Goebbels, had begun as a dramatic critic of nationalist newspapers and afterwards had been for many years literary director of the Party paper *Völkischer Beobachter.* Authorised by the Theatre Law of 15 May, 1934 to ban or order the performance of any play, it was his task to watch its production "from the point of view of the conformity of its spiritual content with National Socialist ideology." [1] The theatre division, therefore, issued regular political directives to producers and managers. The Department particularly watched programmes on days of national importance such as 30 January, the day of the seizure of power, 1 May, the day of German labour, or the Harvest Thanksgiving Day. All theatre managers had to submit their programmes three weeks in advance and to wait for their approval or rejection by the Department.

In accordance with Nazi ideology, the Department saw to the elimination of plays by "non-Aryans" as well as to the promotion of playwrights who properly embraced the Nazi creed. Plays were more and more conditioned to fall in line with a limited and nationalist outlook. Any psychological experimenting on the stage was out of the question. During the war plays were favoured which illustrated such topics as British decadence, Bolshevik baseness [only after June, 1941], Prussian heroism, the supreme duty of procreation and the need for unquestioning obedience.[2] The German theatre did not neglect the great German authors of the past, but it tried to give their works a nationalist slant, and, in the case of Goethe and Schiller, to ignore their universal and humanist values. The German classics were regarded as a useful article for cultural export helping to increase the German prestige abroad.[3]

Political points of view also regulated the selections of the small number of new foreign plays admitted to the German stage by the Theatre

[1] See Sington and Weidenfeld, op. cit., p. 218.
[2] Sington and Weidenfeld, op. cit., p. 219.
[3] On August, 1940 Dr. Schlösser offered prizes for translations of Goethe's plays into Slovak, Bulgarian, Norwegian and Flemish.

Division. Before the war French plays and films ridiculing democracy were preferred, while Bernard Shaw remained a favourite even during the war as his plays were regarded as illustrating the vices of English hypocrisy and "plutocracy."

The Theatre Division controlled two further agencies, the *Auslandsstelle für Theater* which arranged the exchange of stage artists and guest performances with foreign countries, and the *Deutsche Tanzbühne— Deutsche Tanzschule,* serving the promotion of ballet dancing and the training of ballet dancers. Subordinate to the division was the *Reichsbühnenbildner,* the highest State authority on stage designing. The same official was responsible for the arrangement of ceremonial receptions given by the Reich Government, a clear indication of how closely State and stage were interrelated.

B. SOME ASPECTS OF PARTY PROPAGANDA

1. THE CENTRAL PROPAGANDA OFFICE OF THE PARTY

The Third Reich was based on the two pillars of the Party and the State. As a result of this a peculiar dualism of channels developed through which the people inside and outside the Party were to be influenced and indoctrinated.[1] Propaganda was primarily the business of the State, but its agencies were supported and reinforced by the Party, which had its own tasks, not suited to the State machinery. In the field of propaganda the Party was more an instrument than a pioneer, in many ways it followed a lead rather than gave it.[2]

The close co-ordination between the propaganda agencies of Party and State was symbolized by the concentration of their top functions in the versatile hands of Joseph Goebbels. As the Party's Director of Propaganda he was supposed "to show initiative and to concern himself with the permeation of the entire German people by the National Socialist ideology." [3] As Reich Propaganda Minister he had to put over the current

---

[1] In his final address at the Party Congress of September, 1935, Hitler described the different functions of the State and the Party as follows: "It is the job of the State to continue the historical development of the national administration within the framework, and with the help, of the law. The job of the Party is: 1) so to build its internal organization that there will develop a stable and self-perpetuating center of the National Socialist doctrine; 2) to inculcate in the whole people a natural taste for these ideas; 3) to transfer the indoctrinated to the State in order to become its leaders as well as its disciples. For the rest, these two powers must observe the rule of mutual respect and acknowledge their different competencies." L. Münz, *Führer durch die Behörden und Organisationen,* Berlin, 1939, p. 1.

[2] W. Schäfer, op. cit., p. 70.

[3] *Organisationsbuch der NSDP,* 3rd ed., Munich, 1937, p. 296.

policies and measures of the Government on the basis of the Nazi *Weltanschauung*. There was much interlocking of functions between the Party and State propaganda offices, on all levels.

For instance, one man, Horst Dressler-Andreas from 1933-1937 and Hans Kriegler from 1937-1939, combined the posts of head of the Department of Broadcasting in the Ministry, leader of the Office for Broadcasting in the RPL of the Party and President of Reich Chamber of Radio.[1] In 1938, one of Goebbels protégés, the demagogic Alfred Ingmar Berndt, was simultaneously in charge of the Department of the German Press in the Propaganda Ministry and of the Office for Press Propaganda in the Party's Central Propaganda Office (RPL). The Reich Propaganda Ministry as well as the Central Propaganda Office of the Party had regional sub-offices.[2]

What were the functions of the Central Propaganda Office of the Party, the Office of the Reichsparteileiter (RPL)? It had to determine the propaganda attitude for the whole Party movement and to enlighten the people "on the achievements of the leadership in Party and State."[3] This agency comprised two major groups of departments, one of them directly controlled by Goebbels himself, the other by his Chief of Staff.[4] To the first group belonged the Offices for Active Propaganda, Films, Broadcasting, Culture and Liaison. The second group was composed of the Management Office (*Geschäftsstelle*), the Reich League for NS Propaganda (*Reichsring*), the *Reichsautozug "Deutschland,"*[5] the Head Office for Press Propaganda and the Head Office for Exhibitions and Trade Fairs. The Central Propaganda Office had its headquarters in Munich and in Berlin. Departments mainly engaged in the execution of propaganda campaigns and actions were located in the Reich capital, where the closeness of the Propaganda Ministry facilitated their work, while others, particularly those concerned with the ideological aspects of propaganda, worked in Munich.

Here we can only consider those features of this complex set-up which throw a light on the focal points of propaganda organisation. Important was the *"Office for Active Propaganda"* with the task of "the organisational implementation of all due propaganda actions from the big functions on a mammoth scale with architectural features to the (mere) carrying out of functions of a local branch."[6] The planning and execution of the entire propaganda campaigns and activities of the Party

---

[1] They were the *Reichspropagandaämter* (State) and the *Gaupropagandaämter* (Party) but both were controlled by the same official.

[2] Hans Pohle *Der Rundfunk als Instrument der Politik*, Hamburg, 1955, p. 214.

[3] W. Schäfer, op. cit., p. 70.

[4] This office was held successively by Hugo Fischer, Eugen Hadamovsky, Wächter and Naumann.

[5] The *Reichsautozug "Deutschland"* was a motorised transport unit, which provided the technical equipment for carrying out big propaganda campaigns all over the country.

[6] *Organisationsbuch der NSDP*, p. 299.

originated from this Office. Of its two main sections, one, the *Haupt-stelle Grossveranstaltungen* looked after such organisational aspects of huge mass meetings and rallies as transport, accommodation, medical and sanitary services, food supply. It also concerned itself with technical questions of building and construction work in preparation for them. The other main section, the *Hauptstelle Rednerwesen,* which busied itself with the provision and control of Party Speakers, is of special interest as its work reflected the Party view that the spoken word mattered more than the written one.[1]

2. A GALAXY OF SPEAKERS

The vast hierarchy of speakers which sprang up is typical of both the authoritarian attitude and the bureaucratisation of the Third Reich. A Sub-section "Speakers' Training" had to select and train suitable Party orators and to provide refresher courses for the existing ones. It performed this duty with the help of a special Reich Speaker School (*Reichs-rednerschule*) to which only prominent Nazis were sent, i.e. people with many years of Party membership who held high ranks in the *Politische Leiter Korps* (Corps of Leading Party Functionaries). The big shots were the *Reichsredner,* the stars among the Party Speakers, only employed on major occasions and receiving much publicity. They formed the top-grade of a carefully worked out scale of oratorial talent, which included *Stosstruppredner* (Shock Troop Speakers), *Stosstruppredneranwärter* (Shock Troop Speaker Cadets), *Gauredner* (Regional Speakers), *Kreis-redner* (District Speakers), and *Fachredner* (Specialist Speakers).

Unlike the *Reichsredner* the Shock Troop Speakers, an appropriate term for a system in which oratory was married to violence, had had a shorter Party career than the Reich Speakers and were only used in specific and limited areas.[2] Many of them were recommended by and chosen from some of the affiliated organizations of the Party; they often addressed special audiences connected with them. The *Gauredner* were confined to one Party Gau and specialized in its affairs with which they were expected to be thoroughly familiar. They only operated part-time and often held other Party appointments. The District Speaker, in his turn, talked on local affairs of his district in a manner desired by the Party. All these categories were regarded as political speakers and were usually Party members of long standing (*Alte Kämpfer*).[3]

The specialists among the speakers, the *Fachredner,* presented quite

---

[1] Goebbels had declared in 1932 that "revolutionary movements are not made by great writers, but by great orators". *Kampf um Berlin,* p. 18. See above, ch. 2, p. 22.

[2] *Germany, Basic Handbook,* London, 1944, p. 313.

[3] There was at least one woman speaker with the imposing title of *Reichs-rednerin.* During the war when speakers were sent to address the troops the further category of *Frontredner* developed. It was the task of the sub-section for Speaker Supply (*Rednervermittlung*) to provide the appropriate type of speaker.

a different type. They were chosen from Party members according to their special knowledge of some field or theme, such as economic problems, Nazi foreign policy, the Jewish question, the English plutocracy, etc. Again there was an elaborate scale of grades for these specialists on different levels.

To make things even more complicated, some of the affiliated organizations like the German Labour Front (DAF) provided their own speakers, although these were subject to control by the Office of the Speakers of the RPL. All speakers were furnished with directive and authorised notes, supplied by the special sub-section *Redner Information*. There were also Party schools for speakers in every district. Potential orators had to work hard and to undergo a fairly solid ideological training.[1]

Compared with the comprehensive busybodiness of the *Office for Active Propaganda*, the activities of the *Office for Film* were of limited importance. After an early period of producing not too successful propaganda films, such as "SA-Mann Brandt" and "Hitlerjunge Quex," which upheld the heroism and martyrdom of early fighters for the Nazi cause, this office seems to have concentrated rather on routine matters such as the provision of cheap performances in the country, particularly in remote districts. In 1935 the Office produced 140 short films on topics closely connected with the Party and the State, which were exhibited by its 1500 mobile cinema vans all over the country.

Although the scope of the three sections of the *Office for Broadcasting* was limited and dealt with the receiving end of broadcasting rather than with its production, nevertheless its main tasks were significant. The first was to ensure a maximum number of people listening to the official German wireless. This was attempted in a double way: by suggesting the manufacture and by boosting the sales of cheap wireless sets and by organizing community listening through the local Party branches. "Already in 1933 the mass production of an inexpensive set, the VE 3031 was begun at a price of 76.-marks (about £6). Just before the war the cheapest set in the world, the *Deutscher Kleinempfänger* was produced at a price of only 35.-marks which enabled even poor Germans to acquire a set of their own. By the beginning of the war over 70% of all households had a wireless." [2] The number of owners of wireless sets increased from 4,177,000 on 1 May, 1932, to 12,503,000 on 1 May, 1939.[3] In 1939 a radio propagandist, Arthur Freudenberg, declared it impera-

---

[1] Musts were such books as the Party bible *Mein Kampf*, the prolix and longwinded *Myth of the Twentieth Century* by Alfred Rosenberg and his treatise *Nature, Principles and Aims of National Socialism*, also Goebbels' *Battle for Berlin*. Additional reading included the racialist works by Hans Günther, the *Handbook on the Jewish Question* by Th. Fritzsch, a pre-Nazi diehard anti-Semite, and last, but not least, H. von Treitschke's *German History of the Nineteenth Century*.

[2] Op. cit., p. 56 f.

[3] Op. cit., p. 50. However, the second figure includes the then annexed Austria and part of Czechoslovakia.

tive: "in the political interest of the State not only that the whole nation participates in broadcasting," but also that the entire nation was "ready to receive radio programmes at any moment." [1]

Such a goal made the second function of the Department necessary, that of listener-research, which had to sample and analyze the reactions of the public to the performances of the German radio stations. The work was carried out with the help of an elaborate network of Wireless Wardens *(Funkwarte)*. According to the official doctrine it was their task to direct the people's interest to radio, to popularize radio and to regard radio as a political and propaganda weapon of the regime. They also had to arrange facilities for community listening and to use other means to make listening to broadcasts a popular and recognized duty. [2]

In addition, the Wireless Wardens forwarded criticism of and requests for specific programmes. Their reports reached the regional broadcasting authorities and through them the Office for Broadcasting in Munich. When in the middle of the war (in 1942) Goebbels decided that a lighter type of programme should take the place of the more austere transmissions he was guided by reports from the Party Office for Broadcasting, which had pointed out that the existing type of programme bored the people. This illustrates the third task of the Office in Munich which was to put forward constructive suggestions for changes in the programme of the Reich Radio Company (RRG).

3. Culture Streamlined

Through the *Office of Culture* the Party imposed its will on the nation in all cultural activities, ranging from architecture of Party and national buildings to suitable music for the massed bands of the Party. As the official doctrine explained: the office "should stimulate artistic production on the lines of the formative expression of National Socialist *Weltanschauung*; it should further, supervise and employ it in the propaganda of the Party." [3] Of the five sections of this office, the first, concerned with architecture, determined the official style for all buildings and construction activities conducted by the Party and Movement. A second section, the *Hauptstelle künstlerische Formgebung*, laid down the Party line on artistic standards and supervised the style and design of all

---

[1] Op. cit. p. 122.

[2] The Party's Office for Broadcasting controlled 32 regional offices, one in each Gau. The wireless Wardens were attached to them or to one of the many branches of the affiliated organizations of the Party. For instance the "Strength through Joy" (KDF) organization had 31 regional radio wardens (*Gaufunkwalter*) of its own.

[3] *Organisationsbuch*, p. 301.

symbols of the Movement such as flags, badges, artistic documents.[1] It also devised standard programmes for all Party occasions. These were based on the work of two further sections, of which one selected suitable poetical and musical items for use by the Party, whilst the other provided a large variety of sample programmes.

The work of these sections, three and four, found significant expression in a periodical entirely devoted to proposals for the celebrations of National Socialist festivals [2] ranging from a name-giving celebration for children of true National Socialists to the funeral of a Party member conducted by a local branch complete with flags and small brass band. Much space was given to such important problems as how to celebrate the Führer's birthday suitably in a big town with the help of a symphony orchestra and the eulogy of a Shock Troop Speaker. In other words these proposals aimed at fixing the Party ritual on all possible occasions and at producing a conformity of the people regarded imperative for the continuity of a one party system.

Finally, section five, the *NS-Kulturwerk*, renamed in June 1942 *NS-Volkskulturwerk*, was supposed to stimulate and promote folk art in music and in the theatre on a local and regional basis.[3]

C. THE REICH CHAMBER OF CULTURE

Cultural policy or *Kulturpolitik* has always played an important part in German life but it was left to the National Socialists to try systematically to organize and control the entire cultural life of the nation. The task set for the Reich Chamber of Culture in Berlin, authorized by a special Government law on 22 September 1933, was certainly ambitious. As a subsequent decree explained, the Chamber of Culture had "the assignment—through the cooperation of all involved in its various fields of activity and under the direction of the Minister of Information and Propaganda—of furthering German culture with responsibility towards the people and the Reich; of regulating the economic and social aspects of cultural affairs; and of balancing all activities of its member groups." [4] In a double sense, this mammoth organization was "totalitarian" or all

---

[1] Op. cit., p. 303. The Nazi authorities themselves were sometimes alarmed by the deplorable lack of taste to be found in the Third Reich. Even during the war, in 1942, a report from Himmler's Security Service (SD) complained of "the mass invasion of inferior (art) products" and expressed "apprehension over a serious aberration of the taste among the population, which will interfere, for years to come, with all positive art education of state and party . . ." Quoted in H. Lehmann-Haupt, *Art under Dictatorship*, p. 120.

[2] Its title was *Vorschläge zur NS-Feiergestaltung*.

[3] See *Germany, Basic Handbook*, p. 288.

[4] "Erste Verordnung zur Durchführung des Reichskulturkemmergesetzes vom 1 November, 1933", paragraph 3. See *Presse in Fesseln*, Berlin, 1947 (Verlag Archiv und Kartei), Appendix IV. The text of the Reichskulturkammergesetz of 22 September, 1933, forms Appendix 3 of the same work. It was first published in *Reichsgesetzblatt* 1933, vol. 1, p. 661.

embracing. It endeavoured to supervise the entire realm of what the official jargon described as *Kulturgüter* (cultural goods) by setting up seven individual chambers for literature, the theatre, music, films, fine arts, the press and broadcasting. Further, only members of these chambers were allowed to take part in the production, distribution or public interpretation of these "cultural goods".

The field over which the Chamber was to exercise its power was defined in paragraph 5 of the decree as "all forms of artistic creation or activity which are made public" and all other "creation or activity if they are made public in print, in films or on the air". The wide range of membership to the various separate chambers becomes clear from paragraph 4 which lays down that "Anyone who takes part in the production, the reproduction, the artistic or technical elaboration, the publication, the presentation, the wholesale or retail selling, of Cultural Goods must be a member of the Chamber which is relevant to his activities." [1] In fact, this meant that in addition to creative workers such as writers, musicians, painters, sculptors, stage and film actors, broadcasters and journalists, many other categories of people employed in the industries, every single publisher, bookseller, librarian, manufacturer of radio sets or of musical instruments, press stenographer, even news agent, etc. had to belong to the relevant chamber if he wanted to continue his work or function. In this way the Reich Chamber of Culture and its affiliated organizations were able to encourage elements in conformity with the National Socialist ideology and to keep out others regarded as undesirable owing to their racial origin, their "non-German" or "decadent" outlook and their adherence to a type of art rejected by the Führer.

The close dependence of the Reich Chamber of Culture on the Propaganda Ministry is illustrated by the fact that in 1938 the two Vice-Presidents of the Chamber were holding or had held important posts in the Ministry, *Reichsminister* Walter Funk, a former Under Secretary of State under Goebbels, and Karl Hanke, his successor in that post.[2] It was of course Goebbels' prerogative to nominate the Vice-Presidents and the managers of the overall Chamber of Culture and the Presidents of its individual sub-Chambers. The latter formed an advisory body, the *Reichskulturrat*, to the meetings of which the Vice-Presidents and the manager had access. In addition there was also a special Senate (*Reichskultursenat*), to which distinguished personalities with outstanding service to the nation and national culture could be appointed by the President.[3]

[1] *Presse in Fesselin*, Appendix IV.

[2] The post of manager of the Chamber of Culture was reserved for well known Party people. It was held in 1938 by Franz Moraller, then heading the section Culture in the Central Propaganda Office of the Party, and in 1942 by Hans Hinkel, the head of the Ministry's Department for Entertainment of the Troops.

[3] It is telling that in 1942 such prominent high Party functionaries, without any cultural attainments as Hirl, Himmler, Lutze, Baldur von Schirach, Ruse and Ley were members together with men of real distinction like the composer Hans Pfitzner, the conductor Furtwängler, the producer Gründgens and the

Affiliated to each chamber were a number of professional or craft organizations associated with its activities. It was left to the president of each chamber to decide which bodies should be connected with it. With the Chamber of Theatre, for instance, no less than seventeen very diverse organizations were associated, including the German Community for Dancing (*Deutsche Tanzgemeinschaft*), the Old Age Homes for German Artists, the League of German Theatre Authors and Composers and the Goebbels Foundation for Creative Stage Artists. Particularly numerous were the organizations controlled by the Chamber of Literature. It was certainly a novelty for Germany to see her librarians, booksellers and book collectors united with authors and publishers under one roof. Similarly in the Chamber of Radio professional broadcasters and radio producers found themselves side by side with manufacturers and retailers of wireless sets, while a very odd collection of sub-organizations was attached to the Reich Press Chamber.[1]

In November 1933 a special decree gave the Chamber of Culture and its separate chambers power to regulate conditions of work and to decide on the opening and closing of business concerns in their particular fields. They could also determine the relations between different groups in each chamber.[2] Assisted by his advisers (*Präsidialräte*) the President of each Chamber had a wide measure of control over the members of his profession. His orders were equal to state laws and binding. He could exercise his power rather arbitrarily, being able to declare a person unsuited for membership, a taboo which spelt his professional ruin. Anyone could be refused membership of a Chamber or could lose it if facts came to light indicating "that the person in question does not possess the reliability and the qualifications required for exercising the activity in this field." [3] This meant that authors or artists who pursued a line disapproved of by the President could be forced to involuntary idleness and be forbidden any professional activity. Fines up to 100,000 Reich marks could be imposed on people who, without being members of the relevant Chamber, were exercising an occupation controlled by it or as members contravened its regulations.[4] An ominous paragraph in the decree of 1 November 1933 made it clear that on request the police authorities

---

actors Werner Krauss and Emil Jannings. According to a statement made by Hans Fritzsche in Nuremberg in November 1947, in fact the *Reichskultursenat* never met.

[1] They included the Reich League of German Correspondents and News Agencies, the Association of the Radio Press, the Reich League of German Press stenographers and that of German Railway Booksellers and, last but not least, the Reich Association of organizers of German Reading Circles (*Reichsverband der deutschen Lesezirkelbesitzer*).

[2] "Erste Verordnung", 1 November, 1933, article 25, see *Presse in Fesseln*, Berlin, 1947, Appendix IV.

[3] Op. cit., paragraph 10.

[4] Op. cit., paragraph 28.

were obliged to enforce the measures of the Reich Chamber of Culture or of its subordinated Chambers.[1]

Like the Propaganda Ministry, this Chamber octopus had tentacles spreading to the regions. In each Gau there existed a special sub-office, but its head, who enjoyed the pompous title of *Landeskulturwalter*, also presided over the regional office of the Ministry. Before turning to the individual chambers the point must be made that the enforced membership of this immense organisation was not disadvantageous to those in sympathy with the regime, or even to others for various reasons ready to toe the line. Through the ample financial means at the disposal of the chambers such painters, musicians, actors, etc. were assured of an easier economic existence and perhaps also of more public recognition than in pre-Nazi days.

1. The Reich Chamber of Literature

Under the successive presidencies of the prominent Nazi writers and *idéologues* Hans Friedrich Blunck and Hanns Johst this Chamber covered a wide field and conducted its work in six sections.[2] Section I was administrative, Section II was occupied with professional, legal and social welfare aspects in the life of the writers. Section III encompassed the book trade in all its various aspects, from publishing to the retailers. Lending libraries and commercial travellers for publishers also came under this category. Section IV dealt with literary associations and lecturing agencies. Section V was devoted to public and professional libraries, while the production of reference and handbooks was the concern of Section VI.

The difficult task of book censorship was not carried out by the Chamber of Literature but by the Reich Office for Literature (*Reichsschrifttumsstelle*), an agency under the direct control of the Propaganda Ministry. It was this office which decided on official approval and disapproval of books. On the other hand the Chamber issued regular black lists of forbidden books. By a decree of April 25, 1935, the Chamber was authorized to draw up an "Index" which included all books and authors considered in the Third Reich as un-German and detrimental to the true interests of the nation. The list extended to new publications, to reprints and to translations of foreign books, both old and new. Books on the black list could be confiscated by the Gestapo. The works of authors like Thomas Mann, Stephan Zweig, Franz Werfel, Carl Zuckmayer and Franz Kafka were completely banned from libraries and schools. The great bulk of non-political literature was less affected, provided the authors in question were not Jews or otherwise graded as enemies of the regime, and were at least prepared to pay lip service to it.

[1] Op. cit., paragraph 29.
[2] See Hans Schmidt-Leonhardt, *Die Reichskulturkammer*, Berlin, 1936, and D. Strothmann, op. cit., pp. 27-33.

2. The Reich Theatre Chamber

Its President, Ludwig Körner, and Vice-President, Eugen Klöpfer, were well known actors, who had sided with the Nazi regime in good time. This Chamber did not exercise direct censorship of stage productions, a task which had been assigned by the Reich Theatre Law of 15 May 1934 to the Office of the Reich Supervisor of Drama (*Reichsdramaturg*), Dr. Rainer Schlösser. Of the seven sections of this Chamber I and II concerned themselves with organization, legal matters and personnel. The opera was looked after by Section III which also selected new works in co-operation with the *Reichsdramaturg* and decided on the performance of foreign works. Section IV supervised all stage personnel and regulated their wages and working conditions. Section V covered variety theatre and protected the interests of artists in all sorts of variety shows, ranging from cabarets to circuses. While professional dancing formed the field of Section VI, Section VII was an organization for showmen (*Schausteller*), with sub-sections for promoters of showmen, for puppet shows and for circuses of all kinds.[1]

3. The Reich Chamber of Music

Dr. Peter Raabe, its President since 1935, and a former Director-General of Music, once claimed that this Chamber "was founded to encourage a study of music, to enhance the standing of the musicians, and to provide an agency through which the needs of the musicians shall be recognized, thus carrying out a task which neither individuals nor earlier organizations had been able to accomplish."[2] As with the other Chambers there was a heavy ideological slant. Folk music was declared to be particularly important; the Chamber was supposed to exercise a purifying influence and to keep out all "un-German" music.[3]

The structure of this Chamber, too, was thorough and comprehensive. In 1938 its work was done by four sections, of which the first was administrative and included an office collecting evidence of the proper "Aryan" origin of its members. Section II concerned itself with General Affairs, in particular looking after all matters of education, and established liaison with institutes for music and training colleges, both private and public. It also co-operated with the Hitler Youth, the Strength through Joy movement and with schools. More important, this section comprised a number of significant professional units. The Composers' Group dealt with pro-

---

[1] Attached to the Reich Theatre Chamber was further the Association of Theatre Publishers with a membership of about a hundred. The Chamber had offices at the Gau level and a number of philanthropic bodies, some of them dating from pre-Nazi days, were affiliated with it.

[2] *Germany, Basic Handbook*, pp. 310-311.

[3] The Chamber encouraged the wildly anti-semitic *Lexikon der Juden in der Musik* (Dictionary of Jews in Musical Life) which decried all composers of Jewish origin from Mendelssohn to Mahler and Schönberg.

fessional questions, the playing of contemporary music and the planning of programmes. A Performers' Group supervised the training of students, discouraged unsuitable performances and provided opportunities for young artists. The Orchestral Group dealt with the salaries and appointments of its musicians and was also concerned with raising the standards of musical performances at health resorts. By far the largest group was that of *Unterhaltungsmusiker,* providing music as an entertainment. It controlled the salaries and the work of 60,000 members in cabarets, hotels and so on. A number of professional organizations, of music publishers, owners of music shops and of manufacturers of musical instruments were affiliated with the Chamber. Choirs and folk music came under the third section which embraced a large number of traditional and popular associations.[1] Looking after the organization of concerts, Section IV had sub-sections for concert managers, concert impresarios and for secretaries of the musicians. There were also special offices arranging concerts for the blind and an agency STAGMA, an "approved society for musical copyrights".[2] All German musical publications were controlled by this Chamber. Altogether it seems that music, which has perhaps fewer political implications than other arts, suffered less under this system of control.[3]

4. THE REICH FILM CHAMBER

In the official jargon the Reich Film Chamber "had the task of furthering the realm of German films, of regulating economic and social affairs of the occupations concerned and of effecting a just balance between their members".[4] Again, Section I comprised administration, legal matters, finance and establishment. Political and cultural aspects were the concern of Section II, which ran a Press Information Service, maintained contacts with the foreign press and established a national film library. Artistic advice on creative films, on scenarios, casting and methods of presentation was provided by Section III, while Section IV dealt with economic matters, statistics, and provided liaison with the Film Credit Bank, which had been set up in July 1933 with a capital of one million Marks. Various technical aspects of film production were the

---

[1] For instance, the Association of German Singers, the Reich Association for Mixed German Choirs and the Association for Protestant Church Music and Trombone Orchestras.

[2] During the Nazi period STAGMA had no individual members, as it covered the corporate bodies of composers and publishers, and was for this reason connected with both the Chamber of Music and the Chamber of Literature.

[3] When in 1938 H. S. Ziegler, a friend of Goebbels, arranged an exhibition of "decadent music" (*Entartete Musik*) which was shown in Dusseldorf and Weimar, exposing the Jews, Bolshevism and *Atonalität* à la Schönberg, the President of the Chamber, Professor Peter Raabe, a music critic and biographer of some repute, refused to open it. See Erwin Kroll, "Verbotene Musik" in *Vierteljahrshefte für Zeitgeschichte,* vol. VII, no. 3, July 1959, pp. 510-517.

[4] L. Münz, *Führer durch die Behörden,* p. 206.

prerogative of Section V. Film producers were advised by Section VI on such questions as studios and export of films. Film distribution inside the Reich, the requirements of theatre owners, problems of film renting were covered by Section VII. Section VIII handled the elimination of unnecessary competition between theatre owners, the fixation of prices for seats, matters of entertainment tax etc., while film and photography, technical matters concerning patents and research arrangements for the distribution of raw materials were in the hands of Section IX. Finally the task of Section X was to make propaganda for cultural and educational films; it also busied itself with film lectures, travelling cinemas, documentaries, etc.

Two aspects of the Reich Film Chamber deserve mention. The one is the thoroughness of its regional organization. Each Gau had a representative of the President of the Film Chamber, who was supposed to co-operate with the regional representative of the overall Chamber of Culture,[1] and in particular had to boost cultural and propaganda films. The other interesting aspect is the close liaison between the Film Chamber and the Film Credit Bank, which was supposed to provide money on favourable terms for reliable film directors and talented artists to enable them to carry on their work without financial worries. The Chairman of the Bank was none other than the President of the Film Chamber.

5. The Reich Chamber of Fine Arts

The Reich Chamber of Fine Arts was a very comprehensive organization with sections for painting, sculpture and architecture, for interior decoration, landscape gardening, arts and crafts, the graphic arts, art and antique dealers, art publishers, etc. Under the supervision of the Ministry the Chamber exercised not only artistic control over the contents and type of art, but also commercial control over art exhibitions, sales and auctions with special reference to works of art, confiscated as Jewish property. Some of the professional groups were particularly favoured by the Chamber. Architects, a profession in which Hitler took a special interest, were regarded as important because of their work for public buildings, said to benefit the entire nation. Interior decorators were looked upon with approval as they made a contribution to the "cultural living plan" of the future. (One of their functions was to design special furniture for Germans receiving marriage loans and thus indirectly to further the upsurge of national fertility). As far as landscape gardeners were concerned, the Chamber was willing "to support this new profession, so that it may play its part in lending beauty to German daily life, to nature and landscape".[2] On the other hand a critical watch was kept on

---

[1] The former was called *Gaufilmstellenleiter* der NSDAP, the latter *Landeskulturwalter*.

[2] Landscape gardeners were organised as a profession by two decrees of the Chamber of September, 1922 and June, 1935.

the group of art dealers and auctioneers. Their task was defined by a special decree (of 30 July 1935) which fixed punishments for frauds and forgeries and insisted that only reliable auctioneers were permitted to join the Chamber, which had to be given advance information on every auction planned.[1]

Connected with this Chamber was a post of special Commissioner, the *Reichsbeauftragter für künstlerische Formgebung*, held by Professor Hans Schweitzer, who, earlier under the pen name of Mjölnir had designed effective but crude posters and picture cards to support Goebbels' Battle for Berlin.[2] Now it was his job to furnish ideas and suggestions for the designing of all symbols of the National Socialist State, ranging from statues to stamps.

But the independent artist was less fortunate. He could be forbidden by the Chamber to carry out work not only for others but even for himself in the privacy of his home. Under these circumstances it is not surprising that the membership of the Chamber of Fine Arts grew rapidly, and by the end of 1936 had reached the total of 42,000 men and women. Among them were 15,000 architects, 14,300 painters, 2,900 sculptors, 2,300 people working in arts and crafts, 4,200 graphic artists, 1,260 designers and 2,600 art publishers and art dealers.[3]

Severe restrictions on art criticism were introduced in 1936. By his decree of 29 November 1936, Goebbels condemned all real art and literary criticism. As he explained at a full meeting of the Reich Chamber of Culture in Berlin, only factual comments and straight reporting on works of art were now permitted. A month earlier the modern section of the National Gallery in Berlin, "the most representative German museum devoted to art" had been closed. It had taken the regime nearly four years to enforce "the official prohibitions of individual taste." [4]

It has recently been estimated that the actual influence of the Nazi ideology was highest in painting and sculpture and lowest in arts and crafts.[5]

6. THE REICH PRESS CHAMBER

This was a particularly important instrument of political control over everyone involved in producing, running and distributing newspapers and periodicals.[6]

Emphasis of control was perhaps less on the Chamber itself than on the professional organisations under its tutelage. As "regulation of compe-

---

[1] *Germany, Basic Handbook*, p. 311.

[2] See above Ch. 2, p. 21.

[3] Paul Ortwin Rave, *Kunst Diktatur im Dritten Reich*, Hamburg, 1949, p. 53.

[4] Op. cit., p. 74. See also the comments by R.K. "Der Kunstschriftleiter", in *Frankfurter Zeitung*, 29 November, 1936.

[5] H. Lehmann-Haupt, op. cit., p. 136.

[6] In the official view, it was the task of the Press Chamber "to put the members of its professional groups in a position to create a press answering the requirements of the political leadership." L. Münz, op. cit., p. 201.

tition" was regarded as a legitimate function of the Chamber, it served its ruthless President, Max Amann, who, as has been seen, controlled the Party Press, as a pretext for his policy of co-ordinating and eliminating as many non-Party papers as possible. With the help of the "First Decree" of 1 November 1933 [1] Amann was able to deprive 1,473 publishers of newspapers and periodicals of their publishing rights.[2] These operations of Amann and of his assistants Rolf Rienhardt and Wilhelm Baur were also greatly facilitated by a provision in the same decree which authorized them to lay down conditions for the running, the opening and closing down of firms and, moreover, to do so without admitting any claim to compensation by the persons affected. This provided most of the legal pretext for reducing the number of German newspapers from 4,703 in 1932 to 977 by the end of 1944.[3]

The channel through which this throttling process was carried out was "the Association of German Newspaper Publishers (*Reichsverband deutscher Zeitungsverleger*), affiliated to the Chamber.[4] According to its statutes of 1938 the Association would give advice and protection to its members in all professional matters. Everyone was entitled to use its facilities, but in fact members publishing newspapers not owned by the Party soon discovered with dismay that there was discrimination against them. They found out that "it was pointless to appeal to this mighty professional organization in Berlin against the taking away of innumerable subscribers by a Gau Party publishing firm. The Association always sided with the Party publishers." [5] To complain to the Press Chamber itself was equally futile for its president Amann had the same vested interest as his lieutenant Rienhardt, the moving spirit of the Association, in pressing the non-Party publishers to the wall.[6]

No less important was the Association of the German Press (*Reichsverband der deutschen Presse*) which, though affiliated with the Press Chamber, was in fact controlled by the Propaganda Ministry. It kept the official register of editors and journalists and acted as a kind of Labour Exchange for the profession. In 1937 it had 15,360 members and 18

---

[1] It declared in paragraph 10 that "membership in a Chamber may be refused, or a member ejected, if factual evidence shows that a person lacks the reliability and ability required to carry out its activities."

[2] *Presse in Fesseln*, p. 20.

[3] Two further decrees issued by Amann on 24 April, 1935 served the same purpose. The "Anordnung zur Beseitigung der Skandalpresse" eliminated newspaper firms "whose newspapers maintain their character and sale by reporting events in an unsuitable way, so as to create sensation and to reflect on the press in general" (*Presse in Fesseln*, Appendix VI). The "Anordnung über Schliessung von Zeitungsverlagen zwecks Beseitigung ungesunder Wettbewerbsverhältnisse" reserved the right to close down newspaper firms in places where a number of papers competed with each other "in order to create healthy economic conditions." (Op. cit., Appendix V)

[4] This was the successor to the much more independent *Verein deutscher Zeitungsverleger* which had existed during the Weimar Republic.

[5] *Presse in Fesseln*, p. 24.

[6] See below, ch. 4, pp. 111 f.

regional sub-organizations (*Landesverbände*). Its leader Captain Wilhelm Weiss, Editor-in-Chief of the main Party paper, the *Völkischer
Beobachter,* was determined to imbue all the members with a strong
National Socialist bias and to educate a new generation of young journalists on strict Party lines. A special training centre, the *Reichspresse-
schule,* served this purpose. At a Press conference in Cologne in
November 1935 Weiss emphasized that the true National Socialist editor
was never only and exclusively a journalist, but always and above all,
also a propagandist. Often he would be a journalist, a Party orator and
a Storm Trooper rolled into one. The aim was to train a type of journalist
who would "take a stand for the new Reich and its Führer, not because
they have to, but because they wish to do so".[1]

Publishers of periodicals were obliged to belong to the Reich Association of German Publishers of Periodicals (*Reichsverband deutscher
Zeitschriftenverleger*). With Teutonic thoroughness its 30 sections were
organized into six major groups (*Fachobergruppen*). These comprised
periodicals for specialists (*eigentliche Fachzeitschriften*), the illustrated
and entertainment journals, including those for the young, periodicals
for applied sciences, political and related periodicals, journals for the
export trade and periodicals carrying insurance for their subscribers.[2]

A special organization for religious papers and periodicals formed, by
order of the President of the Press Chamber, in December 1933 consisted
of separate branches for the Protestant and the Roman Catholic Church
press.[3] Its purpose was obviously to help the regime to keep a sharp eye
on church periodicals and to prevent them from discussing any political
and local events. They were rigidly forced to confine themselves to their
limited field and to indicate their aims clearly in the titles and headings.[4]
Another specialist group covered occupations concerned with all aspects
of the selling of newspapers and periodicals.[5] The motive for organizing
and supervising the last newsagent and lending library proprietor was to
keep watch on all transactions in this sphere. The right to sell and to
transport newspapers and periodicals became the prerogative of licensed
traders who were under constant surveillance by the Press Chamber and
its sub-organizations.[6]

7. THE REICH RADIO CHAMBER

In 1933 Goebbels and his lieutenants were eager to establish what they
dubbed *Rundfunkeinheit,* complete unity in all radio matters. This term

---

[1] W. Hagemann, *Publizistik im Dritten Reich,* p. 39.
[2] *Presse in Fesseln,* p. 186.
[3] They were the *Reichsverband der evangelischen Presse* and the *Fachschaft
der katholisch-kirchlichen Presse,* both seated in Berlin.
[4] *Presse in Fesseln,* p. 184 and p. 197.
[5] For details, see L. Münz, op. cit., pp. 201-202.
[6] *Presse in Fesseln,* p. 199. No Jew was allowed to sell newspapers or periodicals. Church influences in this field could also be easily detected and eliminated by the organizational octopus in Berlin.

meant the bringing together of all people connected in any way with broadcasting from radio speakers and producers to radio engineers, manufacturers and salesmen of wireless sets, and last but not least, the millions of radio listeners. The idea of a Radio Corporation after the model of Fascist Italy had been propagated even before Hitler's coming to power. In 1932 Eugen Hadamovsky who was to become the first National Socialist Reich Director of radio transmissions (*Reichsendeleiter*) was convinced that an integration of radio artists and listeners, radio industry, commerce and administration under a common head would represent "the strongest element in the forming and safeguarding of the national will".[1] A first step towards carrying out this idea was taken by Hadamovsky on 3 July 1933, with the formation of a National Socialist Radio Chamber. It was clearly intended to be a major instrument of propaganda.[2] This "voluntary" organization was six months later converted into the official Reich Radio Chamber. Membership now became compulsory for everyone occupationally connected with radio. But nevertheless the "radio unity", the dream of an all-in comprehensiveness soon proved illusionary. For the manufacturers and salesmen of wireless sets were removed from the control and membership of the new Chamber in the spring of 1934. On 19 March the Reich Government declared the representation of such economic interests to be a matter for the Reich Ministry of Economics and not for the Propaganda Ministry. In vain did the latter protest. The radio industry remained outside the Radio Chamber, though later in May 1935 some sort of co-operation was established through the formation of a voluntary working liaison between the Radio Chamber and the members of the radio industry. But by that time the Chamber was anything but all-comprehensive.[3] Attempts by the Ministry and the Legal Department of the Radio Chamber to draft a special "radio legislation" (*Reichsrundfunkrecht*) which would secure control of the whole field of broadcasting for the Propaganda Ministry were resented by the Reich Ministry of Justice as "interference" in its own sphere.

After 1937, even Goebbels himself realized the strength of practical difficulties and did not pursue the matter further. When afterwards the Radio Chamber in search of new fields of operation engaged in tasks which were regarded by the Broadcasting Department of the Propaganda

[1] Eugen Hadamovsky, *Propaganda und nationale Macht. Die Organisation der Öffentlichen Meinung für die Nationale Politik*, Oldenburg, 1933, p. 84. This brochure was written at the end of 1932.

[2] See Horst Dressler-Andreas, *Die Reichsrundfunkkammer*, Berlin, 1935, p. 12, quoted in H. Pohle, *Der Rundfunk als Instrument der Politik*, Hamburg, 1955, p. 203.

[3] Apart from the RRG, the *Reichsrundfunkgesellschaft* as the executive organ of the day to day broadcasting, only the Association of Radio Employees (*Fachschaft Rundfunk*) and a purely technical organization of owners of short-wave transmitting and receiving sets (*Deutscher Amateur-Sende-und Empfangsdienst*) made up the membership of the Chamber.

Ministry or by the RRG as part of their own spheres, the Radio Chamber seems to have lost its *raison d'etrê*, it was dissolved in October 1939, when the outbreak of war furnished a convenient excuse for this step.[1]

[1] See Pohle, op. cit., p. 206. The rights and duties of the Chamber were taken over by the Reichs-Rundfunk-Gesellschaft. In the last year of its existence the work of the Radio Chamber was carried out by four departments, which dealt with "administration and legal matters", "professional representation", "propaganda and press" and "economic and technical questions", respectively. See the survey in *Handbuch des Deutschen Rundfunks 1939/40*, pp. 233-234.

CHAPTER 4

Directing The Press

"You will not be hindered but furthered in doing
your own work. You will be protected from committing blunders that would be painful to both
sides."

(Hans Fritzsche at the Daily Press Conference
on 3 June 1939)

1. DAILY GUIDANCE

WHEN EARLY IN 1938, five years after the beginning of the Third Reich,
Dr. Otto Dietrich began his work as Under Secretary of State in the
Propaganda Ministry and Press Chief of the Reich Government, he summed up the practice of National Socialist press policy and control which
had by then been fully established.[1] It was the task of the newspapers, he
declared, to inform and to enlighten the people about events and developments, to support the activities of the Party Movement and of the State
and to "give impulses to the political thinking of the people." It is significant that to this positive task he added a number of restrictions. It could,
he warned, "never be the task of the press to lecture the Party and the
State and to give advice to them or to criticize public institutions and
personalities."[2] Dietrich's statement left no doubt that the press was
an instrument in the hands of Party and State, an instrument in every
respect for the propagation of official ideas and policies. It had to be
directed day by day and be prevented from indulging in any criticism or
advice regarded by the rulers as detrimental to the regime. The journals
and the journalists had therefore to be kept under constant supervision.
What the journalists needed was daily guidance to enable them to discharge their functions properly.

The press was not regulated by relatively free competition as in the
Western democracies, but by a system of official "do's and don'ts," by
constant criticism, frequent threats and occasional praise from the authoritarian rulers. The officials of the Ministry of Propaganda laid down
daily what had and what had not to be reported and published. At the

[1] Dietrich's statement was read to the journalists by W. Stephan at the
Daily Press Conference on 29 January, 1938. ZSg. 102/8.
[2] Ibid.

same time they furnished the journalists with a formidable barrage of criticism for inadequately carrying out the tasks allotted to them. The press people were so flooded with directives and so often convened to press conferences that the chances of spontaneous activity and performance gradually diminished. It is true, Goebbels and Dietrich often felt uneasy about the drab uniformity of the German press which, after all, was only the logical outcome of their policy, and allowed certain non-Party papers like the *Frankfurter Zeitung* and the *Deutsche Allgemeine Zeitung* a certain margin of freedom to preserve their traditional tone and lay-out, but this affected little the thorough overall control and direction of the press as a mass-medium.

In this chapter we shall consider some of the methods by which Goebbels' Ministry exercised this control. Special attention will be given to the system of conferences and directives and to the peculiar mixture of criticism, threats and occasional praise which made the life of the journalists, to say the least, uneasy. At the same time it has to be realized that the control of the press by the Propaganda Ministry could never be 100 per cent, not because there was any organized resistance in the ranks of the intimidated editors and journalists, but rather because of the frequent interference by some other Party offices and officials, in fact, if not nominally, beyond the control of the Propaganda Ministry.

The Press Conferences and the directives conveyed to journalists at them were important tools of control. Though conferences imposed on the journalists tended to multiply in the Third Reich, the daily Press Conference, which took place at noon and was later supplemented by a smaller one in the evening, remained of paramount importance. Unlike the Propaganda Ministry, it was not a novel feature introduced by the Hitler régime. It had existed before, but when the National Socialist rulers took it over from the Republic in 1933 they changed it gradually until it only faintly resembled the original. As so often in the course of history the shell of the institution remained, but its contents and spirit changed.

Since 1919 the editors of the leading Berlin dailies and representatives of the provincial press had met Government spokesmen every week-day at noon to obtain authoritative statements from senior officials on current policy and to ask for information. Before Hitler became Chancellor a journalist elected by his colleagues had presided at these conferences, and after the official part there followed a lengthy informal exchange of opinions between journalists and Government officials which often proved profitable to both sides. In 1933 the Press Department of the newly created Ministry of People's Enlightenment and Propaganda took the daily Press Conference under its wing. Several hundred journalists attended it. Each of the larger papers was allowed one representative and a number of substitutes. Admission was now severely controlled, Jewish journalists having been barred already in the previous March, a measure which was later reinforced by the Law of Editors *(Schriftleitergesetz)* of October,

1933. At first the old polite formula continued by which the Government authorities "directed the attention of the assembled press to certain points" and asked it to consider the point of view of the Government.[1] But the men of the press were soon to realize that even requests put forward politely by the new bureaucracy were in fact commands, neglect of which would have serious consequences. Gradually directives were issued which by way of "Confidential Information" (*Vertrauliche Informationen* (V.I.), also reached papers not represented at the conference.

By the autumn of 1933 journalists could have little doubt that the Government directives had to be regarded as binding even to the last detail. They were told by the head of the press conference, Jahnke, that the Government was determined to make editors, and particularly editors-in-chief, personally responsible for any infringement of the directives.[2] The journalists present were not there only as representatives of their papers, but also, conversely, as confidential agents of Minister Goebbels.[3] From then on the obligatory character of all directives and decrees of the Propaganda Ministry was stressed repeatedly.[4] Seasoned journalists soon realized that their relative independence had gone. When a leading radio official, who had found it difficult to readjust himself to the new régime, was sent on permanent leave, the journalists at the daily Press Conference were warned that "it was not a good thing to swim against the tide." [5]

As with the previous Government, information issued by the Press Department came within three categories:

1) News for immediate publication, to be released in full to the press.

2) Information and material to be used indirectly without indicating the source.

3) Strictly confidential directives which were only available to the journalists admitted to the press conference and to the editor-in-chief or the sub-editor responsible for a part of his paper (foreign affafirs, economics, etc.).[6]

[1] W. Stephan, *Joseph Goebbels*, p. 158.

[2] At that time journalists at the Press Conference were worried because of the severe measures taken against the chief editor and publisher of an Essen newspaper. They had been sent to a concentration camp because two photographs had been mixed up, with the result that the caption under a carnival picture had appeared under the photograph of a solemn SA procession.

[3] Letter by Dertinger, Berlin, to Dr. Heerdegen, *Chemnitzer Allgemeine Zeitung*, 20 October, 1933. (Brammer) Dertinger became frightened and told the recipient of his letter that he and his colleagues of the Berlin office wanted to safeguard themselves against any possible accusations. In future they would number all confidential information or technical instructions they sent to their head offices. They further asked for a written confirmation of the receipt of these instructions.

[4] For instance, at the press conference of 9 January, 1934 they were warned that in several cases directives had either been exceeded or not followed. (Brammer Anweisung No. 161, 9 January, 1934. There is a comment in handwriting in the margin "important" [*wichtig*]).

[5] "Bestellung" Press Conference 1 July, 1933 (Brammer).

[6] W. Hagemann, *Publizistik im Dritten Reich*, Hamburg, 1948, pp. 316-317.

There was a considerable security embargo. Both the reports sent to individual papers by their Berlin office and the *"Vertrauliche Informationen"* had to be treated as strictly confidential. Directives must not be dictated to unreliable typists, and when reaching the main editorial office must not circulate in any of the editorial sub-sections of the paper.[1]

A new feature after 1933 was that the directives and the reports on them had to be kept in safe places and to be destroyed at regular intervals, in the presence of a witness.[2] The officials of the Reich propaganda offices were entitled to control the security measures and the destruction of the directives of "Confidential Information," issued by the Ministry. Again and again the attention of the members of the daily Press Conference was drawn to their responsibility and that of their colleagues for any leakage which might occur through indiscretion or carelessness. During the twelve years of the régime a number of prison sentences and fines were imposed on journalists and editors for infringing these regulations.[3]

In addition to the spokesmen from the Propaganda Ministry at the two daily Press Conferences, of which the morning session was usually longer and more important than the one held in the evening, there were representatives of other ministries, particularly from the Foreign and Defence Ministries. Their task was to make requests, to explain a new law, to popularize a new measure, to express their wishes on how a specific theme should be treated. As time went on the chairmen became more authoritarian. Some of the earlier representatives of the Propaganda Ministry, such as Jahnke and Stephan, were fairly sensible civil servant types of the old school. Jahnke's successor, however, Alfred I. Berndt, head of the Deutsche Presse Department from 1935-1938, was a different man. A rabid National Socialist and a fertile inventor of half-truths and lies, he was often very rude to the journalists. Opposed to Dietrich, Berndt had the confidence of the Minister and worked very closely with him. Nevertheless after the Munich Conference Goebbels felt obliged to remove him from his post as Head of the Press Department because of his unscrupulous rewriting of reports on the Sudeten crisis. To quote a statement made during one of the Nuremberg trials by H. Sündermann, another member of the Press department: "Berndt took a whole series of reports, rewrote them and repeated them in such a manner that they could almost be called false reports. He took true reports and doctored them up in such a way that there was no longer a reliable information service." [4]

Another witness at Nuremberg, Berndt's successor as head of the Ger-

---

[1] Letter from the Berlin Office of *Frankfurter Zeitung* to Reifenberg, ZSg. 102/2, 10 June, 1936.

[2] See W. Hagemann, op. cit., p. 317.

[3] For instance, in July, 1938 punitive measures were taken against four persons connected with the periodical *Der Deutsche Volkswirt*. They received prison sentences ranging from nine months to two years for having made improper use of the confidential directives from the press conference. ZSg. 102/10 "Vertrauliche Ergänzung zur Pressekonferenz," 26 July, 1938.

[4] American Military Tribunal Case SI, p. 13660.

man Press Department at the end of 1938, Fritzsche, corroborated this evidence. During the months prior to the Munich Conference Berndt had sponsored the release of news on "incidents" said to have happened in the Sudeten region. "The latter were a very delicate theme." They were handled by Berndt himself and sent to the German News Agency (DNB). He exaggerated little events very greatly, and sometimes gave out old events as new. Complaints were even received from the Sudetenland itself that some news items published in the German press (on events there) were untrue. Berndt treated journalists like a sergeant-major with raw recruits.[1]

An experienced journalist and formerly a supporter of the German Nationalists, Fritzsche was more businesslike and diplomatic than Berndt.[2] Whereas Berndt had raved and threatened the journalists, Fritzsche often put forward skilful arguments, frequently explaining in a letter to the editor of a newspaper why there was cause for disapproval of a published article. When in 1942 Fritzsche resigned from his post after a disagreement on news policy and joined the armed forces, he was followed by Erich Fischer. Having earned his spurs in the Propaganda Office of the Party, this young fanatic lacked Fritzsche's superior intelligence and proclaimed the official line as if it were part of a secularised bible.

During the war the daily Press Conference was preceded by the more intimate Minister's Conference at which Goebbels determined the main lines and points of propaganda. Heads of Departments in the Ministry attended together with some men from the office of the Reich Press Chief such as Werner Stephan and Sündermann. (Dietrich himself was never present). When Goebbels arrived he had already digested all the foreign and home news, the material from the German News Agency (DNB) and from the radio. "He would come to the conference with comprehensive material and obviously knew in advance exactly what instructions he was going to give." [3] The Minister discussed particularly foreign press comments and the treatment that should be given to them. On the other hand, Goebbels rarely condescended to put in an appearance at the daily Press Conference though he always kept a close watch on it. Not trusting anyone, he studied its minutes carefully every day to make sure that his instructions had been carried out to the letter. Fritzsche, who admired Goebbels' versatile mind without agreeing with him on all points, developed a technique over the years for saying things at the conference which he could not say to Goebbels direct. At times he even ventured some mild criticism in answering a pre-arranged question by a journalist. On occasion the Minister used to make enquiries. If he saw through the game, he would come back to the topic after days, polemicizing against

---

[1] Documents Book 12H to Case XI, Fritzsche affidavit NG 3633.

[2] One of the journalists who had taken part in the daily Press Conference later described Fritzsche as "the most adroit and undoubtedly the most gifted man in the Ministry". See the anonymous article, "Wilhelmplatz Nr. 7-9", *Zeitungs-Verlag*, vol. 47, 1950, nos. 7-8, p. 7.

[3] Case XI, Affidavit, Werner Stephan, p. 13873.

Fritzsche or the journalist who had put forward the question which Goebbels thought was dangerous.[1]

There were soon additional press conferences. In 1937 it became the practice after the main conference for a small selected circle of journalists to gather in the room of its head. This was known as the *Glossenkonferenz* and it dealt with comments and interpretations of events rather than with hard news. The Ministry's spokesman showed greater frankness there. At the same time the directives and comments issued were to be treated with the strictest secrecy. Different from the directives dictated at the daily Press Conference which could at least be preserved for some time, those of the *Glossenkonferenz* had to be destroyed immediately after having reached the editorial offices in question.[2] Often some of the leading papers were allotted special tasks at this smaller conference. Thus in June, 1939 the *Völkischer Beobachter,* the *Börsenzeitung* and the *Hamburger Fremdenblatt* were asked to comment critically on the formation of the Ministry of Information in London. This step by the British Government was to be exposed as a crude attempt to counteract "the German encirclement propaganda." [3]

Occasionally at the *Glossenkonferenz* points of view were presented which differed greatly from the usual line. In June, 1937 a letter from the leading authorities of the Navy to the representatives of the biggest newspapers was read. It deplored certain tendentious reports on the Spanish Civil War published in the German press. It drew attention to the fact that the German newspapers had committed the same mistakes which they had criticized so vehemently in the foreign papers. "The German Press"—the letter suggested—"should give up any tendentious reporting in the interest of the strengthening of our position." A headline such as "British destroyer struck a Red mine" was no less an invention than the opposite report carried by a Berlin paper that this destroyer had struck a mine laid by the Spanish Nationalists. There was no evidence in official reports on which to base such deductions. In any case it was disagreeable that the German press did what it condemned in others—a remarkably honest comment which could never have originated in the Propaganda Ministry.[4]

At that more select conference changes in the political line were often foreshadowed which the authorities still felt it unwise to reveal to a wider circle. In November, 1937, for instance, members of the *Glossenkonferenz* were informed by Herr Stephan that in future far less space and attention were to be given to the colonial question. The reader must now realize that one had to be sceptical regarding Germany's chance of getting colonies.[5]

Gradually the press was forced to attend more and more confidential

[1] Article "Wilhelmplatz Nr. 7-9", op. cit., nos. 7-8, p. 7.
[2] ZSg. 102/12, letter to Dr. Welter from the Berlin office of the *Frankfurter Zeitung,* 3 September, 1938.
[3] ZSg. 102/17. "Aus der Glossenkonferenz", 13 June, 1939.
[4] ZSg. 102/5, 3 June 1937.
[5] ZSg. 104/7, 5 November 1937.

conferences. At the beginning of 1938 the Party started one in its headquarters in Munich, which seems to have been run by Sündermann, the
editor of the official National Socialist Press Correspondence (NSPK).
The idea was to make available "secret information" about the plans of
the Party to the editors of the Munich press and to correspondents of
some prominent German papers published elsewhere.

2. JOURNALISTS UNDER PRESSURE

Every new conference meant new intimidation of journalists. How
frightened they were by the ominous secrecy surrounding the press conferences becomes obvious from a letter written by the Munich correspondent of *Frankfurter Zeitung*, Kammerer, to its head office.[1] "We
have been put under an obligation"—it said—"by giving our word of
honour and by being told of possible heavy punishment (exclusion from
the [Press] Association) to treat the information as secret and to pass it
on to the Chief Editor only . . . We were informed that we have to post
the information we receive without indicating a sender. We also must
not use words like 'Information from the Information Conference' but
only phrases such as 'It is learned from well-informed circles.' Further
we have to ask the editor-in-chief to give a pledge that the information
items are not preserved in a folder but are completely destroyed immediately after being read. Secretaries and charwomen must not see them."
The anxious correspondent asked the recipient (Dr. Welter) for advice
on how to handle this delicate task. Frightened that the information
might go to unauthorized persons, he wanted to know "if I shall in future
despatch a 'bomb' to Frankfurt which will explode under me or if I can
rely on a quieter arrangement. Should I send these letters registered?
What sign shall I put on the envelope to make sure that the information
is being forwarded to you and to your authorized deputy but not to any
other person?"[2]

One of the main functions of these press conferences for the authorities
was to criticize and rebuke individual papers, both Party and non-Party,
and to do so with various degrees of vehemence. The tone of the criticism depended partly on the degree of offence the item in question had
given to Goebbels and Hitler, and partly on the personality of the spokesman who announced it. Though caustic at times, Fritzsche seldom became
abusive and preferred to convey his displeasure by official letters to the
editor rather than by citation at the press conference. His predecessor,
Berndt, on the other hand, had ruthlessly denounced the journal which,
in his opinion, had sinned. There was often sharp criticism for both omissions and commissions, the latter usually causing more concern and re-

---

[1] It was dated 28 January 1938 and addressed to Dr. Welter, one of the
leading members of the editorial staff. (ZSg. 102/8). There was no "Editor-
in-Chief" of the paper, but Dr. Welter was the editor responsible for the
contents.
[2] Ibid.

crimination than the former. For instance, after the remilitarization of the Rhineland in March, 1936 the *Frankfurter Zeitung* was criticized at the press conference for publishing a pessimistic article from London by their chief editor Rudolf Kircher.[1] Two days later Fackler from the Berlin office of the paper was told by Stephan that the foreign reports of the paper printed on the previous day had been contrary to the official directive not to publish anything which would result in international despondency. Kircher's article came as a bombshell to the highest quarters. Fackler tried to defend the *faux pas* by pointing out that the articles objected to had been written some hours before the official warning had reached him. But he had to inform his head office that Berndt, a determined opponent of the once liberal *Frankfurter Zeitung*, requested the political editor to telephone him, probably in order to be reprimanded. Fackler's advice sounds pathetic: "Do not forget that telephone call! Perhaps it is wise to inform the Paris office by 'phone that their reports must not strike any pessimistic note which means that they have to write with the greatest caution." [2]

The authorities were especially critical of and sensitive about headlines. Frequently editors were strongly advised to take the greatest care with them. This happened, for instance, in May, 1936, when an issue of the Berlin paper *8 Uhr Abendblatt* had been confiscated on account of its all too frank headline "An additional billion of taxation revenue required." [3] After the sudden German occupation of Prague in March, 1939 and the end of Czechoslovakia as a state, *Der Angriff* incurred official wrath for its large headline "France sees no reason for interference." At a specially arranged press conference Fritzsche deplored that even a leading Party paper had in this way indicated that a weight had been lifted from the German heart by the French attitude. And this came at the very moment when the Führer had ordered things peacefully by a gesture of his hand. It was much better to head an editorial "Hammer Blows" than to express fear of France. Fritzsche went on to lecture the journalists on the importance of headlines, over which they could never take too much trouble.[4]

If headlines evoked the ardent displeasure of Goebbels, let alone of the Führer himself, press officials at the Ministry naturally felt uneasy and branded the sinners in no uncertain terms. A rather amusing case in point occurred in June, 1939 when some papers were sharply criticized

[1] Referring to negotiations between England, France and Italy which had then taken place in London to consider their reactions to Hitler's *coup*, Berndt warned journalists "with the greatest intensity against publishing anything in the papers that could cause disquiet". "Aus der Pressekonferenz" ZSg. 102/2, 14 March 1936.

[2] ZSg. 102/2, 16 March 1936.

[3] Anweisung Nr. 424, Press Conference, 13 May 1936 (Brammer).

[4] ZIg. 102/15, "Aus der Pressekonferenz" 16 March 1939, 8:30 p.m. Fritzsche went on to tell the journalists that the moment had arrived for expressing the German people's profound gratitude to the Führer for what he had achieved in securing control of Czechoslovakia. But a headline "A Greater German World Reich" was still a bit premature.

for a headline "The Führer, Göring and Ribbentrop receive the Yugoslav Prince Regent." This was declared quite out of order, as only the Führer should have been mentioned as the Head of the State. The criticism could not be taken lightly for it had come from the Führer himself. It was established that the official German News Agency had in fact sent out the right headline. Fritzsche may have thought this *faux pas* was a reflection on himself, as he hinted darkly that he would have to think of proper means by which to discharge his responsibility in the future. More directives and proposals for the uniform leadership of the press were foreshadowed. In future semi-official and private information, too, would be released through the Press Department. Only in that way could he control the atmosphere of the press and know it.[1]

Through harsh experience journalists had to learn what they should and could say and what they must avoid. Frequently slogans and clichés must cover up the real reasons for decisions taken by the Führer. A good example are the important changes in some of the leading diplomatic and military posts at the beginning of February, 1938. The reshuffle marked the end of the last shred of independence of the *Wehrmacht* and also the beginning of a more aggressive course in foreign policy. Neurath, replaced by von Ribbentrop, had no idea that he was to be removed from his post, particularly as the Führer had personally congratulated him on his 65th birthday only the previous week.

Such facts were covered up by a propaganda of high-sounding and rather meaningless slogans. At the press conference of 4 February, 1938 [2] was coined the slogan of the "strongest concentration of capacity" as the leading idea behind the changes. Dietrich explained that National Socialism was a youthful movement. In order to prevent rigidity new blood had to be constantly pumped into the arteries of the Third Reich. He recommended his slogan "Increasing Strength Through Concentration" as the essence of National Socialism. The new arrangements under the guiding hand of the one and supreme Führer, now also Supreme Commander of the Armed Forces, meant Concentration, Unification and Rejuvenation. Dietrich thought it expedient to add that it would be quite wrong to look for any disharmonies in the régime as they simply did not exist. Yet journalists were expressly warned "not to emphasise details (for instance, on the enforced retirement of Fritzsche)", an oblique reference to the disgraceful dismissal of the Chief of the Army Command after a charge of homosexual misbehaviour trumped up by Himmler. On the other hand, Hitler's game of giving Neurath a high-sounding but in fact sterile new post was "explained" by arguing that the Führer did not want to be without the tested ability of Baron von Neurath whose great wealth of experience in foreign affairs could not easily be replaced.[3]

The frequent threat of elimination from the lists of journalists or

[1] ZSg. 102/10, "Ergänzung zur Pressekonferenz" 2 June 1939.
[2] ZSg. 102/8, 4 February 1938.
[3] Dietrich's post-war account of the changes in February 1938 is very different and sober. See O. Dietrich, *12 Jahre mit Hitler*, 1955, pp. 49-50.

editors hung forever like the sword of Damocles over the heads of members of the profession. Berndt often used this intimidation and even Fritzsche, his more reasonable successor as Head of the Department "German Press," employed it occasionally. When contrary to the official ruling a paper had, in October, 1936, published American agency reports on the Civil War in Spain that spoke of "Government troops" and "rebels" (instead of "Spanish Reds" and "Nationalists") Berndt remarked caustically that "he wished the gentlemen of these papers to continue to sleep well; they were unsuited for the profession of editor." [1] When during the time of the plebiscite in the Saar in January, 1935 the *Frankfurter Zeitung* had mentioned the name of the Socialist Max Braun who had declared himself in favour of the *status quo,* the member of the editorial staff responsible for this "crime" was, by order of the Propaganda Ministry, to be sacked at once.[2] The same thing happened to Dr. Fritz Klein, the Editor-in-Chief of the non-Party paper *Deutsche Allgemeine Zeitung,* after he had written in favour of an independent Austria in the autumn of 1933. His article had met with Hitler's personal wrath and disapproval.[3] Such dismissals were probably more frequent in the earlier years of the régime, for by 1939 the control of the press was so tight and the younger generation of journalists had, with relatively few exceptions, been so indoctrinated that drastic measures were less necessary.

There are no statistics available of the number of journalists dismissed by the regime; but it is interesting to note that the President of the "Reichsverband der deutschen Presse," Wilhelm Weiss, who was also editor-in-chief of the *Völkischer Beobachter,* remarked at a Press Congress in Cologne on 30 November, 1935 that by then 1300 Jewish and Marxist journalists had been dismissed. This number did not include journalists who did not fall into these categories but had been forced, or had desired, to give up the profession.[4] Forecasts and speculations on future events were particularly frowned on by the Propaganda Ministry, as they would have impaired Hitler's freedom of decision, his technique of staging surprises and blitz-like coups. When, for instance, in the summer of 1934, the aged President Von Hindenburg lay dying, Goebbels' Ministry resented any speculation about his successor. One paper, the *Deutsche Zeitung,* was confiscated for the comment that "the fate of the German people, and with it every decision lies in one single *hand,* that of the Führer." The controllers of the press saw in this obvious remark a lack of the required reserve. Reporting this *Verbot* the Berlin correspondent of a Hamburg paper urged on his editor "an avoidance of anything that could in any way give the impression that we are already racking our brains over the future decision on this." [5]

[1] ZSg. 102/3, 21 October 1936.
[2] *Die Gegenwart* Sonderheft. *Ein Jahrhundert Frankfurter Zeitung,* p. 49.
[3] See R. R. Koerner, *So haben sie es damals gemacht,* Vienna, pp. 33-36.
[4] W. Hagemann, *Publizistik im Dritten Reich,* p. 39.
[5] "Bestellung" by Dertinger to the *Hamburger Nachrichten,* Berlin, 31 July 1934 (Brammer).

In this as in other cases "propriety" was solely dictated by expediency. But often a too close probing into what happened and why—apart from reiterating the official propaganda "reasons"—was declared equally taboo. This applied particularly to unpleasant events likely to cause public uneasiness and a feeling of insecurity as did the murder of S.A. leaders and other "enemies" of the régime on 30 June, 1934.

The official explanation of this event was given in Hitler's famous Reichstag speech of 13 July. All other interpretations and rumours were condemned. Though there was no direct censorship there was an indirect one. A memorandum issued by the German News Agency to publishers and editors, dated 3 July, 1934, explained that because of the many abortive rumours circulating, the papers had before publication to submit their own news and all information concerning "the treasonable attempted coup and the persons involved in it" and to secure the consent of the Ministry of Propaganda or of one of its regional offices. This approval was required even for death notices and obituaries of persons shot, no matter whether they appeared in the news or in the advertisement columns.[1] There were good reasons why no light should fall on the foul murders of 30 June. A different type of *arcana imperii* or State Secrets to be safeguarded was the technique by which the National Socialists staged their foreign coups. There the aversion to reveal the know-how mentioned above is apparent. A month after the *Anschluss* Werner Stephan made a "particularly confidential" statement to journalists. He deplored that it had become the fashion for some participants of the action leading to the *Anschluss* to describe details of its technical, military and propaganda preparations. It had been necessary to confiscate one Party paper for revealing that some people had been given their mobilization orders on 10 March, two days before the German troops entered Austria. Any other paper lending itself to such a "false loquaciousness" would suffer the same fate. These things were definitely secrets. It was not possible to allow the entire world press to know the details of these preparations perhaps even under the motto "That is how they did it *this* time." [2] As the example shows, Party journals were by no means immune from confiscation. But when they were owned by influential Party cliques like *Das Schwarze Korps,* the organ of the S.S., or the *Stürmer,* Gauleiter Streicher's obscene anti-semitic weekly, the power of the Propaganda Ministry sometimes proved to be limited. In January, 1938 the *Stürmer* was forbidden to appear for an indefinite period for printing a confidential decree on foreign policy. The number containing the article was confiscated, but significantly enough other papers were not allowed to report the *Verbot* [3] and the ban was in fact of short duration. On the whole, the organ of a Party boss, who like Streicher enjoyed Hitler's confidence, was

[1] Anweisung Nr. 582, "Bestellung Pressekonferenz" 4 July 1934 (Brammer).
[2] ZSg. 102/10, "Schluss der Pressekonferenz", 12 April 1938. The confiscated paper, the *NS-Rheinfront* was owned by the Party.
[3] ZSg. 102/8, "Aus der Pressekonferenz", 21 January 1938.

not easily interfered with. Earlier, in July, 1935, the Ministry had banned the *Stürmer* for three months on account of a vicious attack on Staatssekretär Lammers. On that occasion also the press had been directed not to mention the ban. In actual fact the repressive measure was not really carried out. A week after the ban had been imposed it was lifted, and confiscated copies of the offending issue were even returned to the newsvendors. The cancellation, too, was not to be reported in the daily press.[1]

On the whole, the German Press Department was inclined to keep a jealous watch on contacts journalists made with press officers of other ministries. It insisted that all "hand-outs" from the Reich authorities must be released through it. Even journalists who required some specific piece of information from other ministries had to inform the Press Department of this later and to explain what use they proposed to make of the information. Any actions by the press officers of other ministries without the knowledge of the head of the Press Department was forbidden. This included distribution of material, commissioning of articles, the issuing of press directives and the request that journalists should mention this or that item.

All this tended to make the life of journalists uneasy and difficult. They were frequently blamed for mistakes committed by others, for instance by prominent Party officials whose statements had been reported by the press. This was the case with a speech made by Gauleiter Terboven to his political sub-leaders in June, 1936. He hinted in it at a forthcoming relaxation of the ban on admission of new members to the Party. Alas! the report of the speech in the press met with the displeasure of the Party pundits. At the next press conference Sündermann, the spokesman of the Party, singled out the *Berliner Tageblatt* for a heavy attack.[2] In fact, journalists were used as "whipping boys." They had to take the blame which, in this case, was, by implication, directed at Gauleiter Terboven.

To be a journalist in the Third Reich meant to be constantly reminded of heavy taboos imposed on activities. The statement by the Reich Press Chief of 29 January, 1938 mentioned above listed the various restraints which journalists had to keep constantly in mind. "Measures taken by Party or State, by the officials of the former and by the civil servants of the latter," were "*a priori* above any criticism by the press."

For such criticism would do more harm than good. If the press learnt of mistakes said to have been made in some offices of the Party or of the State, is was not allowed to inform the public about them. Instead it had to pass on the information to the authorities under the competency of

---

[1] Anweisung Nr. 1462 and letters from Dr. Kausch, not dated (20 July 1935) and Dertinger, 21 July 1935, (Brammer).

[2] See ZSg. 102/12, 9 June 1937.

which the elimination of such mistakes came.[1] A rather dubious device, for if S.S. men had mishandled Jews or other "enemies of the régime" it would have been very risky for a journalist to approach the Gestapo with the news.

Dietrich's summary of what journalists had to avoid ended with the customary threat that editors who infringed these rules would be ruthlessly taken to account. In particularly serious cases their names would be removed from the list of editors and their papers would be forbidden. If threats and other unpleasant pressures were frequent in the life of the journalists, there was also sometimes praise, however grudgingly it was often given. While the big stick prevailed, the carrot was not altogether missing.

Particularly in the early days of the régime, when the Ministry of Propaganda was still feeling its way, praise and encouragement from it meant much, especially to non-Party papers. For instance, in July, 1933 after a Conservative journal in Chemnitz had published an article by Lord Rothermere expressing strong sympathy for the new Germany, the Ministry of Propaganda conveyed its thanks for the careful and effective lay-out of the article. It used the opportunity to point out "that in the frame of the given possibilities the German press was able to do its work fruitfully and independently in the interest of the new Germany." The Berlin office of the newspaper added to its report optimistically that "the authorities shortly intended to lessen the ties of strict press control provided the press continued to follow the line of the Reich Government on foreign policy independently and with a sense of responsibility." [2] Pious hopes, never to be realized!

It was much commoner for the press as a whole to be complimented on a collective performance in carrying out one or another difficult directive than for an individual achievement in a single newspaper. Let us take as an example the press comments on the show trials against Catholic monks and priests at the end of April 1937. At a special press conference in the Propaganda Ministry on 28 April, Ministerialrat Berndt gave instructions on how to treat this topic. The State had to counterattack the Church—he declared—as the clergy tended to minimize the accusations put forward and to describe them as forgeries. The press was asked to give greater prominence to the trials and to discuss them in leaders. Points were to be made of the frivolous lusts of the monks, that they had not refrained from committing crimes before and after Communion, and that they had made the monasteries seminaries of

---

[1] Complaints in the economic field put forward to editors were not to be given space without their conscientious enquiry into the facts. Attacks on enterprises of vital significance to the State and the nation were not to be made without the prior consent of the relevant authorities. This was imperative, as in the past frivolous press attacks on firms "for alleged un-National Socialist behaviour" had done great damage to the national economy. The same applied to the sphere of culture.

[2] Letter from D. Kausch, Berlin, to the editor of *Allgemeine Zeitung*, Chemnitz, 11 July 1933 (Brammer).

homosexuality. The press should explain that it was not the State but the Church which bore the responsibility for such misdeeds, having neglected their duty of supervision. The fact that instead they had written and read aloud pastoral letters had to be stressed in every article. For the sake of true Christianity, ran the official line, the State had to take steps against these hotbeds of vice. Moreover, it was alleged that by carrying out such major actions of national solidarity as the Winter Help, National Socialism had done more for Christianity than the religious orders.[1] The journalists duly wrote on the dotted line and received a measure of praise. The next day Berndt conveyed to them a special acknowledgment from the Minister. The newspapers, he said, had discharged their task as it had been expected of them by avoiding any undesirable uniformity.[2]

After one of Hitler's big coups when the press had carried out official instructions efficiently and with fervour, it usually received a collective bouquet. In April 1936, when the plebiscite which followed the German remilitarization of the Rhineland had proved the expected success, Staatssekretär Funk expressed the cordial thanks of the Führer and of the Reich Minister of Propaganda to the press for its work during the election campaign. They appreciated its achievement, in which both editors and publishers had had their share.[3]

Hitler, who read a great many newspapers every day, was on the whole unfriendly, not to say hostile to the press and to journalists. He did little to conceal his resentment and complained that he was unable to forgive the press for its vehement attacks on him during the years when the Party had been in opposition.[4] He very seldom received journalists. Nevertheless it is wrong to say that Hitler had only addressed a wider circle of journalists once, on April 1935.[5] For a remarkable address has come to light which Hitler gave to four hundred representatives of the German press in Munich on 10 November, 1938. It was an official occasion at which Hess, Goebbels, Amann, Alfred Rosenberg and Staatssekretär Hanke were also present. Probably few journalists expected that the Führer would praise the press for its performance during the critical months before the Munich conference. However, on this occasion Hitler went so far as to describe the role of propaganda both

[1] ZSg. 102/5, Press Conference, 28 April 1937.

[2] There was, however, considerable uniformity, if not in the comments, at least in the reports on the Catholic Show trials. Whilst all the newspapers were free to comment on the lines set by the Propaganda Ministry, only local papers issued at places where the trials were held were allowed their own reporters. All others could carry only the official report from the German News Agency (DNB). ZSg. 102/5, 28 and 29 April 1937. As Stephan explained, the admission of local reporters should make sure that the people in the area in which "the dirty deeds" (*Schweinereien*) had occurred became properly enlightened about them.

[3] "Bestellung aus der Pressekonferenz" 1 April 1936, signed Dertinger. (Brammer).

[4] O. Dietrich, *12 Jahre mit Hitler*, p. 157.

[5] W. Hagemann, *Publizistik im Dritten Reich*, p. 320.

to foreign countries and to the German people as decisive in the development which had led to the acquisition of the Sudetenland by Germany.

"When this time the German people"—the Führer said clumsily—"had displayed an attitude different from that of other nations and also different from their own attitude until recently, this was to be attributed to the continuous work of enlightenment, in other words, to that propaganda by which they had impressed the German people. In this work the press had a large share." Talking proudly of the immense success of the German propaganda campaign on and against Czechoslovakia, Hitler said that he had become fully aware of the greatness of this success when he had first inspected the Czech bunkers. He had then realized what it meant to secure control of a line of nearly 2,000 kilometres of fortifications without having fired a single shot. "Gentlemen" —declared Hitler—"this time we have actually obtained 10 million men with over 100,000 square kilometres of territory through propaganda in the service of an idea. This is something gigantic." [1]

This speech off the record is a clear indication that Hitler was as much aware of the role of propaganda as an instrument of conquest in 1938 as he had been in 1924 when writing *Mein Kampf*. Obviously the docility of the men of the press in following changing instructions was no less marked than the fertility of mind and the ability to lie of those who had directed the anti-Czech and at times anti-Western campaign in the German press during the six months preceding the Munich Conference.

3. Directives for Special Appeals and Campaigns

The omnipresence of National Socialist propaganda was a matter of daily routine. But if this routine was not to become lifeless, it had to be supplemented by special appeals and special campaigns that were based on an ever new intensity and concentration. The appeals and campaigns undertaken were either negative or positive: either a stimulant to community action, to deeds for Führer and nation, based on "positive images and language associations", or an incitement against enemies of Germany, denounced as detrimental to the welfare and future of the nation. We can take the propaganda for the "Winter Help" with its "Day of National Solidarity" as an example of the first type, the anti-Semitic propaganda during the days of the November pogrom of 1938 as one of the second.

In order to obtain money from the public for the "Winter Help" Goebbels thought out the idea of the *"Eintopfgericht"*, the "one-pot meal" in homes and restaurants, and in 1933 two special Sundays were earmarked for it. The idea was that by spending less on their luncheons

[1] For the text of this recorded speech see "Rede Hitlers vor der deutschen Presse," *Vierteljahrshefte für Zeitgeschichte*, vol. 6, no. 2, April 1958, pp. 175-191.

on that day the masses would be able and ready to give for the national purposes of the "Winter Help." "A sacrifice for the community" was the obvious slogan. During the week preceding the "Sunday of the One-Pot Meal" the press was directed to carry out a systematic campaign. The event had to be given big publicity, which would then have to be gradually stepped up. For the five days prior to *the* Sunday the papers were supplied by the Propaganda Ministry with all the necessary material: headlines, articles, photographs, and, last but not least, special recipes for one-pot meals. On Saturday, 4 November, for instance, the proposed headlines ran:

1. Break the bread for the suffering brother!
2. Housewives—Mothers! Complete the work of the Führer!
3. Every household is a part of the national community.

There were three brief articles offered to the press for choice: a) The first one, headed "The invisible guest", sounded a strikingly Christian note; "In many German families the youngest member of the family prays from his childhood: 'Come, Lord Jesus, be you our guest!' There was a deep meaning in this prayer. To fulfill it they should use the opportunity given to them through the day of the one-pot-meal next Sunday." In other words, religion and patriotism were made to coincide. Every personal sacrifice on that Sunday would help a fellow-country-man and would assist in strengthening the foundation on which the united Third Reich was being built. b) The second of the articles "Table comrades of the Nation on November 5th" emphasized the glowing example set by the Führer who would eat his simple meal on the appointed day. It also stressed the deed of practical socialism which the success of that day would mean. c) And finally the searchlight was directed to the German *Hausfrau*: "The fifth November, the day of Honour of the German Housewife." Praised for her heroism and loyalty during the last war, the housewife was urged "to see to it that when the results come in the Führer will be filled with joy because sixty million hearts will rejoice with him in their readiness for sacrifices." [1]

The "Winter Help" developed into an annual event, and its impressive financial results were achieved by intensive propaganda, by cajoling and intimidating people. The success of the "Days of National Solidarity" was not regarded as only a financial matter, it was a sort of plebiscite for the régime. In 1937 the result was declared to be a record as it had increased by 35.2 per cent, compared with 1936. The press were asked to make the most of it and to call it "a people's vote on the largest scale, of a kind no other state has achieved so far." [2] Besides the "uniqueness" of the event the voluntary character of the donations had to be stressed. The fact that in the collection boxes 5 and 10 Pfennig pieces had predominated was proclaimed as clear "evidence" that it was the masses who backed the régime. As usual, propaganda did not stop at the facts, but constantly put them on to a wider

[1] Telegraphen-Union, 1 November 1933 (Brammer).
[2] ZSg. 102/7, "Kommentar-Anweisung," 5 December 1937.

canvas. Ingenious contrasts were drawn with the pre-Nazi days, with the time of the prospering Wilhelminian Empire, when several months had been required to collect six million Marks for the Zeppelin fund. And now the result, exceeding this figure by 1½ millions, had been obtained in a few hours!

The lay-out mattered a great deal. At a press conference in December 1937 journalists were advised that the results of the "Winter Help" collections had to appear in headlines on the front page, which should also carry a leader on them. The articles should be written with the greatest intensity (*Eindringlichkeit*), making the final point that "no government in the world would appeal to its nation with so much confidence and with such a good conscience as the Government of the German people." [1] A year later there were similar instructions on how to make the most of the result of this "Day of National Solidarity." This time Fritzsche told the journalists that only the largest print was adequate to splash the result.[2] Yet so parrot-like had the press become on these occasions that the commentators had to be expressly advised "to avoid clichés all too often used and to find formulae of their own." This difficult task for a press in fetters was made even more complicated by the demand that the opportunity should be used for a sharp reckoning with all the opponents of National Socialism at home and abroad. The dictatorships, Fritzsche suggested, had proved themselves to be true modern democracies, in which the people had become their own rulers. The papers should particularly stress the contributions made by the workers. Where else did Ministers go into the streets in order to serve the national community, where else did the masses form queues for hours in order to give a donation? Systematic efforts were being made to indoctrinate the readers with a collective superiority feeling based on a thinly disguised contempt for other political systems and races.

If we regard the campaigns before and after "the Day of National Solidarity" as a positive measure, the propaganda appeals against the Jews were negative. They, too, followed and foreshadowed action, and had very practical implications. After the pogrom of 9 and 10 November, 1938, for instance, with its trail of looting, burning and torture, there followed a conference at the Air Ministry on 12 November, summoned by Göring and attended by Goebbels, Funk, Schwerin-Krosigk and other leading Ministers. A number of important decisions were then taken, all directed against the Jews, such as the imposition of the heavy fine of 1,000 million Marks, the elimination of the Jews from business life, and the confiscation of all their insurance claims. These measures became law two days after the conference and others were soon to follow—the exclusion of Jews from German schools, public meeting places and places of entertainment, and the dissolution of all enter-

[1] Ibid.
[2] ZSg. 102/12, Press Conference 4 December 1938.

prises owned by them which would be transferred to German owners.[1] At that time the reaction abroad to the events of the "Night of the Broken Glass" was sharp. "No foreign propagandists bent upon blaspheming Germany before the world," declared *The Times*,[2] "could outdo the tale of burnings and beatings, of blackguardly assaults on innocent people, which disgraced the country yesterday."

The directives issued to the press in the middle of November had therefore, a double function: to answer the foreign criticism by counterattacks and to further indoctrinate the Germans in order to justify the forthcoming anti-Semitic measures.

At the press conference of 17 November Berndt alleged that Jewish refugees abroad had been treated badly and even taken to concentration camps. This should be used for an "exposure" of English colonial methods which had led to the death of 2000 Boers, women and children in concentration camps. Other dark chapters in English colonialism, the conquest of India, the unfairness to the Arabs in Palestine, should also be highlighted. The Germany of 1938 was not the Germany of 1918, and was not prepared to be scolded in a governess-like fashion. England had moreover not put one square mile at the disposal of the Jewish refugees. It was, however, the Jews who were to remain the target of the sharpest abuse. An all-out campaign was ordered to blacken their name, to show up the immense harm they had done to the nation. Every German paper had to publish a series of articles on the role of the Jews in Germany in the more distant past, in the pre-war days, at the Royal Court, during the war years, and in the Republic. A new note was struck in so far as Jews were declared even to be responsible for the chauvinism in Germany of the early war years (some poems of hatred by the Jewish writers, Ernst Lissauer and Alfred Kerr, were quoted) as well as for the destructive defeatism of November 1918. What was new was that in addition to the Jews, "the German philistines" who felt sorry for them were also to be attacked. These were the same elements, who before 1918 had declared themselves willing to die for the monarchy, who had later been grateful to Ebert, had welcomed the Young Plan, had revered Schleicher as a General with a social understanding, and finally had been frightened by the re-occupation of the Rhineland.[3] The statement that this campaign would be extended to radio [4] and film indicated the significance which the rulers attached to it.

[1] See Lionel Kochan, *Pogrom, November 10, 1938,* London, 1957, ch. 6 For an analysis of Goebbels' role in the November pogrom and in subsequent events see below ch. 17, pp. 383-87.

[2] *The Times* (London), 11 November 1938.

[3] ZSg. 102/12, Press Conference 17 November 1938.

[4] Berndt anticipated dialogues on the radio between the Editors-in-Chief of the *Frankfurter Zeitung* and the *Stürmer,* which probably meant that the entire range of the press from the most radical Party paper to the refined and formerly Jewish-owned *Frankfurter Zeitung* was put into the service of the campaign.

The omnipresence of anti-Semitic propaganda was also stressed in a further statement by Berndt during the press conference of 24 November.[1] He insisted that it "was necessary to take into account this principle in future under all circumstances and under all aspects of life (*bei jeder Lebensäusserung*)." Berndt proclaimed the necessity for a universal indoctrination of the readers with anti-Semitism. In terms of every-day journalism this meant that no news item and no article should be allowed to appear without that slant. But Berndt's statement contained a glaring contradiction. On the one hand he asserted that "the German people were anti-Semitic", but on the other hand that there was still a stratum of "pitiful philistines" who felt sorry for the poor Jews and stood up for them on every occasion. This, of course, was "an intolerable state of affairs" as it "must not be that only Party and State are anti-Semitic." The press had to carry out a big campaign of enlightening the people during the forthcoming winter. Every publication must be examined with a view to furthering it. If, for instance, English Marxists in the House of Commons championed the Jewish cause, the fundamental connection between Marxism and Jewry had to be revealed. If Jewish frauds were reported, then flashbacks to the misdeeds of Kutisker and Barmat during the days of the Weimar Republic should accompany them. If there should happen a Black Friday at the Stock Exchange anywhere in the world, earlier Black Fridays in Germany caused by the Jews or the crises of the Banks in 1931 should be referred to. Family journals and magazines for entertainment had to serve this campaign as well as periodicals for trades and professions. Foreign correspondents, too, should look out for anti-Semitic material. In France, for example, lately over a hundred trials of Jews for fraud had taken place without a single German correspondent reporting on them. Only the heads of foreign powers and their ministers in office (other than those of Soviet Russia) must be exempted from these attacks.

4. GOEBBELS—DIETRICH—AMANN

Although control of the press was from the beginning part of the task of the Propaganda Ministry, Goebbels' powers were to some extent restricted by the fact that inside the Party set-up there existed also a "Reich Leader for the Party Press", Max Amann, and a "Reich Press Chief of the Party", Otto Dietrich.[2]

Before discussing the complicated relationship and rivalry between

[1] ZSg. 102/12.
[2] Publicity was the concern of three different Party departments, the Propaganda Department under Goebbels (RPL), the Press Business Management under Amann and the Party Press Department under Dietrich. As all three men held the high rank of *Reichsleiter* they were at least nominally on an equal footing.

Goebbels and Dietrich, who early in 1938 joined the Propaganda Ministry as Under Secretary of State, we have to consider Dietrich's original post, that of "Reich Press Chief of the Party" which had been created for him by a Führer decree of 28 February, 1934. It declared that the Reich Press Chief was to determine the lines of policy for the entire editorial work of the Party press on behalf of the Führer. In addition he was "the supreme authority for all press publications of the Party and of all its offices." The editorial staff of the Party newspapers and the Party's regional Gau press officials were subordinated to him. He was to have a say in all questions of personnel.[1] While Dietrich had no jurisdiction over the administrative staff of the Party newspapers—this was controlled by Max Amann—he was obviously entitled to decide about the political reliability and professional qualifications of their journalists.

The office of the Reich Press Chief had two main divisions: the Division for Press Policy (*Pressepolitisches Amt*) in Berlin and the Division for Press Personnel (*Pressepersonalamt*) in Munich.[2] All chief editors of the Party papers had to be approved by the Office. At the same time these men served it as heads of the regional Press offices (*Gaupresseämter*).[3]

In fact Dietrich's Party Press office supervised two distinctly different groups of people involved in press matters: firstly, the editors and journalists of all Party papers accountable to it for their output. Secondly, the public relations officers or "press wardens" (*Pressewart*) of the Party Movement. Attached to formations like the Labour Front, the S.A., the Hitler Youth, they issued information to the press on their activities. They were responsible to the Reich Press Chief for the articles they would write for local papers or for journals with a nation-wide distribution, such as *Der Angriff* or the *Hitler-Jugend* etc. If any of the Party organizations wished to establish a press service or agency, it had to ask the Reich Press Chief for his consent.

When Dietrich entered the Propaganda Ministry he was there therefore in a relatively strong position. Dietrich and Goebbels were both Rhinelanders, were born in the same year (1897) and came from strictly Catholic families. But otherwise they differed profoundly. Dietrich regarded himself as a philosopher, Goebbels as a man of action. Dietrich had little sense for news-values, Goebbels lived for the hour and the day and changed his slogans according to their requirements. Goebbels was a born orator, Dietrich was never really able to establish

[1] *Organisationsbuch der NSDAP* 1937, pp. 303-306.
[2] The latter published the *Nationalsozialistische Korrespondenz*, which issued press material on the activities of the Party.
[3] There was an elaborate hierarchy of press officials. The Press officer of a local branch (*Pressebeauftragter*) was controlled by the official in charge of a district (*Kreispresseamtsleiter*). He in his turn was supervised by the regional official (*Gaupresseamtsleiter*) who received his instructions direct from the Party press headquarters.

contacts with his listeners. An officer in the First World War, Dietrich liked to appear in the uniform of the SS, while Goebbels always remained a civilian. Dietrich rarely contradicted himself, Goebbels quickly forgot his slogans of yesterday. "Dietrich was slow-moving and vindictive, Goebbels as ebullient and impulsive as he was quick to make peace. No collaboration between these two men, so fundamentally different, could ever succeed." [1]

Dietrich had little political, but some personal influence with Hitler, to whom he had rendered useful services in the late 1920's. A journalist by profession, he was then married to the daughter of the owner of the influential *Rheinisch-Westfälische Zeitung*, the organ of the heavy industry of the Ruhr. This enabled him to make valuable contacts for Hitler among such men as the industrialist Emil Kirdorf. Later Dietrich became Chief Editor of the Party paper *Essener National Zeitung* and managed to keep himself in Hitler's entourage. He organized publicity for the Führer from the election fights in 1932 to his entry into Austria.

When early in 1938 Otto Dietrich, essentially a "yes" man, succeeded Walter Funk as Press Chief of the Reich Government and as Under Secretary in the Propaganda Ministry, his appointment was not due to any wish of Goebbels. Dietrich later described how Hitler had casually informed him of the promotion in the Führer's living quarters in the Reich Chancellery. While Hitler was standing in front of a large table signing documents, he noticed Dietrich and told him that he had just been appointed *Staatssekretär*, adding that though Minister Goebbels had not yet signed the relevant document, Dietrich could rely on him, Hitler, that he would sign.[2] At that time relations between the Führer and Goebbels were strained, mainly owing to the discord between Goebbels and his wife, who had taken strong exception to his affair with the film actress Lyda Baarova, yet later when Hitler once more became friendly with the clever little Doctor, Dietrich still retained some influence with the Führer, however hard Goebbels tried to undermine and destroy it.

In the Ministry Dietrich was, of course, Goebbels' subordinate. All efforts by Dietrich to obtain the setting up of an independent Ministry of the Press failed, but on the other hand, it was only a few weeks before the collapse of the régime in 1945 that Goebbels was successful in persuading Hitler to dismiss his hated rival,[3] "the final result of long and determined efforts." [4] All the time in the weaker position, Dietrich

---

[1] Werner Stephan, *Joseph Goebbels,* pp. 166-167.
[2] O. Dietrich, op. cit., German edition, p. 251, English edition, pp. 237-238.
[3] See the article "Wilhelmplatz, Nr. 7-9", op. cit., p. 8.
[4] See the evidence given during the Nuremberg trial Case XI by Werner Stephan who was on Dietrich's staff in the Ministry: "Their personal relationship especially to the outside world was definitely good, and very often we *Referenten* were angry about the fact that we had to fight it out while our bosses were having tea together. But I myself am convinced that from the be-

found it difficult to compete with Goebbels, who, being so much more powerful and effective, had a strong influence on Hitler. "As soon as he went to Hitler one could assume he would get his way."[1] Yet it seems in some cases Hitler's decision went against Goebbels and in favour of Dietrich. If we can accept Stephan's statement, such events as the appointment of Sündermann as Deputy Reich Press Chief in 1942, the introduction of the *Tagesparole* or Daily Guide for journalists in 1940, the withdrawal of Fritzsche as Head of the Department "German Press" and his replacement by Fischer in 1942 were due to Dietrich's initiative. The explanation lies in the fact, that, in contrast with Goebbels, Dietrich was constantly in Hitler's entourage, either in Berlin or during the war at the Führer's headquarters, and was thus in a position to exploit a favourable mood of the Führer.[2]

It would appear that Hitler of intent let an ambiguous position continue. One reason for this was that while Hitler seldom interfered with the press directly, the constant presence of Dietrich as an obedient mouthpiece made it easier for him to do so. "I shall never be able to take the press from Dr. Dietrich" Goebbels complained to Fritzsche in November 1942, and "Hitler will never permit that the press will be completely eliminated from the Ministry of Propaganda."[3] At all events the leadership of the press was not homogeneous, for Dietrich and Goebbels thought of each other not as colleagues, but as rivals.[4] In his conferences Goebbels sometimes referred sneeringly to the fool who had ordered this or that to the press. Though he refrained from mentioning Dietrich's name, Goebbels' listeners knew who he meant. Dietrich, on the other hand, often did not follow a request from the Minister to see him, but instead sent a leading member of his staff (such as Ministerialrat Stephan). When Goebbels refused to receive him, Dietrich's subordinate handed the matter in question over to the managing Under-Secretary of State. The snag for Dietrich was that he and his press departments depended on the budget of the Ministry, a fact which may have prevented Dietrich from increasing his staff much. It is true that as Reichsleiter Dietrich had a fund from the Party at his disposal, but this was not sufficient to pay the salaries and

---

ginning Goebbels did not quite approve of the fact that Dr. Dietrich was appointed Press Chief and later on, I am sure, he tried everything to remove him from his position. And at the beginning of 1945 he was successful in that finally. This event was the final result of long and determined efforts." (Case XI, American Military Tribunal against Ernst Weizsäcker and alia, 1948, p. 8976).

[1] Case XI, p. 13978.
[2] This explanation is put forward by Stephan, Case XI, p. 13981. In his post-war memoirs *The Hitler I Knew*, 1957, Dietrich says very little about his own position and his relations with Goebbels. He preferred to throw light on Hitler rather than on himself. Dietrich died in November 1952.
[3] Case XI, Fritsche statement 16 June 1948, p. 8977.
[4] Article "Wilhelmplatz," Nr. 7-9, op. cit. nos. 9-10, p. 3.

wages of the Press Department. This situation was one more reason for Goebbels to claim that he was Master of that Department.[1]

Dietrich could never be completely ignored, however, as he often conveyed the Führer's instructions and orders to the press. Take the method of compilation of the daily *"Vertrauliche Informationen"*, the instructions read at the Daily Press Conference and transmitted to other papers through the regional offices of the Ministry. Many came from Goebbels direct through his Minister's Conference. Other ministries such as the Foreign Office, and later, during the war, the Supreme Command of the Armed Forces, also contributed to it. When Hitler's special wishes had to be incorporated they were usually conveyed through Dietrich. In his memoirs Dietrich later maintained that while his title as "Press Chief of the Reich Government" sounded impressive, he had not exercised any leading function. His work consisted rather in editorial duties and in keeping Hitler informed.[2] There is evidence that during the war Dietrich spent at least 90 per cent of his time away from Berlin, regarding himself in the first instance as Hitler's "press attaché." [3] In this function he selected news material for the Führer, drawing his attention to one or other article. When Hitler raved about some report or article in the press of which he strongly disapproved, his target was usually Dietrich, and only occasionally Goebbels. Such an outburst of displeasure by the All Highest in turn made Dietrich appear at the "Daily Press Conference" in his SS uniform, and even sometimes convene a special conference.[4]

The heads of the two Press Departments must have often felt as though they were dancing on a tight-rope. On the one hand, Goebbels took the view that only he had the right to give instructions, although, he conceded, Dietrich could express supplementary wishes. On the other hand, Dietrich, who could claim to be a mouthpiece of the Führer, was not to be regarded as a mere cipher, though few journalists seem to have always taken him seriously. Under the pressure of the impact of the war a significant compromise was found between the different pressures exercised on the press department by the two rivals. At the end of 1940 the *"Tagesparole* of the Reich Press Chief"* was introduced, a brief directive which gave the main binding points for the day. It was largely the work of Dietrich or his deputy, but Goebbels also contributed to it. Dietrich gave three reasons for its introduction of which the last is particularly significant: a) a clearer distinction between what were obligatory instructions and what were mere recommendations to the press; b) the prevention of the issuing of directives through non-competent authorities; and c) the concentration of that function upon himself.[5]

---

[1] Ibid.
[2] O. Dietrich, op. cit., pp. 130-131.
[3] Case XI, Affidavit by Werner Stephan, p. 13866.
[4] Article "Wilhelmplatz Nr. 7-9," op. cit., nos. 7-8, p. 7.
[5] Case XI, Fritzsche affidavit No. NG 3704, pp. 2-3.

As a result an additional conference was regarded as necessary to formulate the *Tagesparole*, with two representatives of the Foreign Ministry and the Supreme Command of the Armed Forces present. As Dietrich was nearly always at the Führer's Headquarters he had the *Tagesparole* read to him over the telephone and often made alterations. Though the evidence put forward by various witnesses at his trial in Nuremberg is conflicting, it seems that the introduction of the *Tagesparole* did in fact strengthen Dietrich's position.[1]

The realms of both Goebbels and Dietrich were curtailed by the third man in the field of press and propaganda. Reichsleiter Max Amann, Hitler's sergeant major in the first world war, was a more primitive type than his two university-trained rivals. A shrewd and ruthless organizer, with membership card No. 2 of the Party, Amann had believed in Hitler's rising star when it was still obscure. Hitler, in his turn, had already in *Mein Kampf* praised Amann's methodical skill as first head of the Party Office in Munich.[2] Subsequently in the Third Reich Amann became one of the most powerful and richest of Hitler's lieutenants, a man who knew how to make good use of his assistants' brains. As Reich leader of the Press of the Party he was responsible directly and only to Hitler, he controlled all the Party papers and was in 1939, on the eve of the war, the ultimate boss of about 3,000 editors, at least 600 managers, and about 8,000 employees.[3] He was also Director-General of the Party's publishing firm, the Zentralverlag der NSDAP. In addition to publishing such leading party newspapers as the *Völkischer Beobachter*, with its two editions, one appearing in Munich, the other in Berlin, it also brought out many lucrative best-sellers, among them Hitler's *Mein Kampf* and Rosenberg's *The Myth of the Twentieth Century*, and practically all the books of Goebbels. The firm controlled many well-known papers and periodicals like *Der Angriff* (after 1934), and the *Schwarze Korps*, the weekly of the S.S.[4]

Having no journalistic talents himself, Amann was well served by his Chief of Staff, Rolf Rienhardt, a hard worker who shared Amann's ambition to establish a press monopoly for the Party. The articles which appeared under Amann's signature in the *Völkischer Beobachter* and in the firm's weeklies were actually written by Rienhardt, who was eventually brutally dismissed in 1943. Both Amann and Rienhardt saw to it that the Propaganda Ministry had as little influence on their mammoth publishing firm as possible. The fact that Amann was Goebbels'

[1] Case XI, p. 13663-4. When the *Tagesparole* was introduced Schmidt, representing the Foreign Ministry, stayed away from the Press Conference for a few days as a token of protest, but had to give in eventually.

[2] *Mein Kampf*, Jubiläumsausgabe, Munich, 1939, p. 585.

[3] *Presse in Fesseln*, Berlin, 1947, p. 60.

[4] The *Hitlerjugend*, the *Arbeitsmann*, the organ of Dr. Ley's Reich Labour Service, the *S. A. Mann*, *Unser Wille und Weg* (the organ of the Party Propaganda Department), the *N. S. Monatshefte*, the monthly for the diehard Nazis, for Party members and Officials, etc. Sington and Weidenfeld, *The Goebbels Experiment*, p. 68.

publisher, that the latter is said to have received 2000 Marks alone for each of his stirring wartime articles in *Das Reich* [1] would indicate that Goebbels was not in a strong position to thwart Amann's empire-building. If for some reason or other Goebbels ordered an increase in the number of pages of the newspapers, the Propaganda Ministry had to approach Amann's Berlin representative to obtain the necessary amount of newsprint. Wishing to economize, Amann often decided that the granting of these additional paper supplies would have to be balanced by economies a week later, "decisions which neither Goebbels nor Dietrich tried to combat." [2]

Being only interested in the business and the Party aspects of the press, Amann was not prepared to spend money on any special features of the newspapers. "He never understood what foreign correspondents, leader-writers, feature-writers and modern methods of conveying news mean and are there for." [3]

Amann was much less concerned with the content of the paper, provided it followed the Party line, than with the banking account of his firms. For this reason he did his best to gain control over as many non-Party papers as possible by buying them up. For instance, he secured a leading share for the Zentralverlag in the famous Ullstein publishing firm, the Jewish owners of which had been forced to sell.[4] But Amann's empire-building did not stop there; on his behalf Dr. Winkler, a shrewd negotiator, bought up many formerly politically neutral papers of the *General-Anzeiger* type. For them the *Vera Konzern* was founded whilst small and medium-sized provincial papers, the so-called *Heimat-Zeitungen* and the former press of the Catholic Centre Party were combined in another of Amann's creations, the Phönix Company.[5] The relationship between Dietrich and Amann—said a witness at Dietrich's trial—was "cool at first, and tense subsequently." Their disagreements arose from the fact of their competing positions, though the two personalities, "by their entire sentiment and nature, were opposed to each other; they did not harmonize." [6] There was a marked divergency of views on the control of editors and journalists. Goebbels' *Schriftleitergesetz* of October 1933, with which Dietrich fully agreed, gave them no political freedom, but granted them more economic security than they had enjoyed before. Whereas under the Republic it had been the newspaper owner and his executives who had determined

---

[1] Ibid.
[2] Article "Wilhelmplatz Nr. 7-9", op. cit., Nos. 9-10, p. 4.
[3] Ibid.
[4] See *Presse in Fesseln,* pp. 73-82. It was renamed Deutscher Verlag and Amann promptly became chairman of its Board of Directors. Its own paper, the liberal *Vossische Zeitung,* ceased publication soon, but another leading non-Party paper, the *D.A.Z.* was transferred to this firm. It was the Deutscher Verlag which later, in 1940, issued Goebbels' quality weekly, *Das Reich.*
[5] Case XI, statement by Sündermann, p. 13634.
[6] Ibid.

the policy of the paper, under the new law the publisher was prevented from interfering with the text which was the exclusive responsibility of the editor. Special protection was also furnished to editors as regards dismissal from their posts. For reasons of both Party and self-interest, Amann endeavoured to restore the influence of the publishers. As Hitler's financial agent he looked after the Führer's immense royalties which accrued from the sales of *Mein Kampf*. When he appeared before Hitler once or twice a year to report on the Führer's financial position, Amann used the opportunity to make requests and to ask for additional powers within his own sphere. He was nearly always successful.[1] Early in 1934 Amann managed to secure a decree from Hitler which increased his own power considerably. It authorized him to hire and fire any member of the editorial staff of the Party Press. As its chief administrator he was to control appointments and dismissals, the conditions of payment, the increase or decrease of its editorial staff.[2] This decree amounted to an infringement of Dietrich's position as Reich Press Chief of the Party and was naturally resented by him. In his turn Dietrich probably used his influence with Hitler to obtain from him the decree of 28 February, 1934 mentioned above. It is not enough simply to suggest that whereas Amann was in charge of the business side of the Party press, the substance of the papers, their policy and contents were controlled by the Reich Press Chief of the Party, Dietrich.[3] While it is true to say that only Dietrich issued directives to editors and could reprimand journalists for infringements of the official lines, in fact the dividing line was by no means as neat and watertight. Frequently Amann proved stronger and tougher than the more ideologically minded and less forceful Dietrich. As Fritzsche has testified, whether or not Amann had the official authority to appoint editors for the newspapers, "he certainly had the power to do so and he used it." The Reich Press Chief could often nominate candidates for appointments to various positions, but "there were times when the expression of such a desire meant that this man would certainly not be chosen." [4] When in later years Amann managed to take over more and more of the non-Party papers, Dietrich resisted his encroachments and tried to place elsewhere journalists who had incurred Amann's animosity.

With the arrival of the Third Reich, Dr. Dietrich was appointed Chairman of the Reich Association of the Press. Until the end of 1933 the membership of this association was voluntary, but it then became compulsory for every professional journalist. When, therefore, the post of Chairman acquired greater importance, Goebbels, probably with the consent of Amann, removed Dietrich from it and appointed

[1] O. Dietrich, *12 Jahre mit Hitler*, p. 211.
[2] Case XI, pp. 13636-7.
[3] See Sington and Weidenfeld, *The Goebbels Experiment*, pp. 66-67.
[4] Case XI, p. 8980.

Captain Wilhelm Weiss, the editor-in-chief of the *Völkischer Beobachter*
in his place. It is true, Dietrich was given a consolation prize as
Vice-President of the Reich Press Chamber, but its President was
Amann. The Vice-President was only to be active should the President
fall ill or die, and neither of these contingencies ever applied to the
robust Max Amann.[1]

Perhaps Dietrich's weaker position vis-à-vis both Goebbels and Amann
has been best described by Werner Stephan who, as a witness at Dietrich's trial at Nuremberg, was asked if it would be possible to compare
the position of Dietrich with that of the American newspaper magnate
Hearst. "I would say," declared Stephan, "that it is an insult to Mr.
Hearst because, after all, Mr. Hearst existed for the purpose and was
able to carry out the purpose of getting his papers out and making
them into organs of world importance; while the work of the Press
Chief of the Reich Government, with the best will in the world, which
Dr. Dietrich undoubtedly had, only served, as is the way in a totalitarian state, to hamper the press by countless instructions, and to exclude it from fulfilling its normal functions, as well as to restrict its
effect on public opinion . . . His intentions were of the best, but his
functions and the effect of his position were undoubtedly of that kind.
. . . Hitler's desire for uniformity and Goebbels' propagandistic tendencies—Goebbels saw in the press only a function of propaganda—
prevented the possibility of achieving any positive aims." [2]

5. THE POSITION OF FOREIGN CORRESPONDENTS IN BERLIN

Foreign correspondents working in Germany were in a different
boat from that of their German colleagues. They could not be directed and coerced in the same manner. They were not subject to
the Editorial Law (*Schriftleitergesetz*) and they could not simply be
moved like figures on a chess board.

In the first year of its existence the Propaganda Ministry bothered
little about foreign correspondents. Goebbels then ignored the foreign
press as he resented the critical attitude of the majority of foreign
countries to the Third Reich.[3] Gradually the Propaganda Minister realized, however, that it was imperative to have some official contacts
with the representatives of the foreign press. "Even unfavourable publicity would be better than no publicity at all." A special section was
therefore built up in the Ministry to deal with the foreign press and
its correspondents in Germany. The Press Department was soon split
into two divisions, Home Press (IVa) and Foreign Press (IVb), each
with its own head who would preside over the daily conferences held
separately for German and for foreign journalists.

---

[1] Sündermann statement, Nuremberg, Case XI, p. 13641.
[2] Case XI, statement by W. Stephan, p. 13984.
[3] See *The Goebbels Diaries,* Introduction by L. Lochner, p. XXIX.

Among the heads of the foreign press division Professor Karl Bömer, who occupied the position from 1938-1941, was probably one of the ablest and most skilful of the officials in the Ministry. Bömer, who had studied and lectured at the Press Research Institut of the University of Berlin, had the experience of foreign countries which his master lacked. He had travelled in the United States and had issued hand-books on the world press.[1] A man with a good Party record, he had assisted Alfred Rosenberg in his Party Office for Foreign Affairs.[2] Versatile and suave, full of good stories, Bömer understood the needs of foreign correspondents. His approach to them was: plenty of information and as little censorship as possible.[3] Unlike some of his colleagues he did not explode over exaggerated or false reports on the events in Germany appearing in the foreign press, but tried to let the correspondents see things in the Reich for themselves. When on 4 February 1938 the dismissal of General von Blomberg as Minister of War and of General von Fritzsch as Chief of the Army Command caused a sensation, foreign newspapers published reports of a rebellion among garrisons in Pomerania. An officer of the Reserve himself, Bömer took some of the leading foreign correspondents by car to that province. They were given hospitality in officer clubs and barracks and saw something of the daily routine of the *Wehrmacht*. They were able to deny the truth of the earlier revolt story. Bömer was familiar with the importance of the "human interest" story in the Western press. At a time before the war when any mention of Eva Braun, Hitler's friend, was strictly taboo for the home press, Bömer talked about her to some prominent Anglo-Saxons, convinced that a Führer who had a girl friend would appear more natural and human in foreign eyes.[4]

When at the beginning of the Polish campaign Polish sources reported the destruction of the city of Czenstochau and of its famous miracle painting of the "Black Mother of our Lord", Bömer took American journalists to the place. They were then able to deny the truth of the story in their despatches.[5]

Bömer managed "to combine loyalty to his superiors with a sense of fair play to his subordinates". It seems he was well liked by his Minister and by the foreign correspondents who appreciated "his kindly manner and his efforts to give them something, at least, that was of value as news".[6] However, Bömer had one weakness which in the end brought

[1] See for instance, *Handbuch der Weltpresse, Eine Darstellung des Zeitungswesens aller Länder*, Herausgegeben in gemeinschaftlicher Arbeit vom Institut für Zeitungswissenschaft und dem Aussenpolitischen Amt der NSDAP unter Leitung von Univ. Professor Dr. Karl Bömer, 3rd ed., Leipzig, 1937.

[2] Sington and Weidenfeld, op. cit., p. 104.

[3] W. Stephan, op. cit., p. 194.

[4] W. Stephan, op. cit., p. 194-195.

[5] Ibid.

[6] A. Fredborg, *Behind the Steel Wall, A Swedish Journalist in Berlin 1941-1943*, New York, 1944, p. 3. See also W. Shirer, *Berlin Diary*, London, 1941, pp. 349-350.

about his downfall: he drank too much and then talked rather indiscreetly, a failing which, it has been alleged, was exploited by his rivals in the Foreign Ministry. When at a reception at the Bulgarian legation in the spring of 1941 the drunk Professor mentioned a top secret, the forthcoming attack on Soviet Russia, he was denounced and by order of the Führer put before the People's Court. The death sentence seemed a certainty, but for once Goebbels stood by his subordinate; he gave evidence in favour of him with the effect that Bömer was let off with only a prison sentence.[1] His successor, Dr. Ernst Brauweiler, a former provincial editor, was undistinguished. Under Bömer the daily press conferences for foreign correspondents at 10:30 a.m. and 5 p.m. had often been lively and not uninteresting; under Brauweiler they came dull and colourless. Where Bömer had made his comments with ease and a sense of humour, Brauweiler was stuffy. "When faced with a difficult question, he would become as obstinate as an army mule; sometimes he would answer with a direct insult." [2]

On the staff of the Foreign Press Division there were a number of *Referenten,* experts as a rule conversant with the languages and background of the country or countries concerned. Many of them were present at the conferences for the foreign pressmen, but only a few became popular with their foreign clientele.[3] The morning conference was usually attended by leading journalists only, that in the afternoon by a larger crowd. Eye-witnesses of important events and other men in the news such as war-aces made statements or were interviewed. In addition, there were two or three weekly propaganda lectures and once a week a preview of official newsreels.

A third daily conference in the Foreign Ministry took place from 1939 onwards. In theory this conference was to dwell more on the international aspects of current events, while it was the task of the officials in the Propaganda Ministry to give the foreign journalists a picture of Germany and German home affairs. In practice both conferences often covered the same ground. As long as von Neurath was Foreign Minister the two ministries ignored each other's conferences; only under Ribbentrop did they send representatives to the conferences of the rival ministry. Each

---

[1] Fredborg, op. cit., p. 4; W. Stephan, op. cit., p. 195. According to Stephan his sentence was one year in prison, according to Fredborg, two. Bömer was soon given a chance to rehabilitate himself by joining his old regiment in the East as a private. In 1942 he was wounded in battle and died in Cracow hospital to the regret of his Minister. Fredborg suggests that Bömer's downfall was engineered by his enemies in the Foreign Ministry, which seems uncertain. Stephan calls him "circumspect in his relations with the outside world, but careless in the struggle between the Ministries."

[2] Fredborg, op. cit., p. 5.

[3] Among the mere experts or Party fanatics there were a few who through their tact and friendliness made an impression on the foreign correspondents. Dr. Giese, in charge of passports, visas and other practical matters, "took everything in his stride, showed a keen sense of humour, and always did his best to straighten things out. He never forced his opinion on us as did the other Nazis." A. Fredborg, op. cit., p. 6.

ministry ran its own club for the foreign press and tried to outdo the other in the attractions provided. Goebbels' *Auslands Club* at the Leipziger Platz rivalled with the more sumptuous *Auslands Presse Club* in the Fasanenstrasse, off the Kurfürstendamm, organized by the Foreign Ministry. In September 1940, Goebbels appropriated several million marks to modernise his club.[1] After it was rebuilt it offered all the conveniences of an office and correspondents could work there as well as dine and converse.[2] Goebbels' club in the old Bleichroeder Palace was for the foreign correspondents "a place to chew the rag with the Nazis and see what was in their minds if anything," [3] but many of the foreign pressmen preferred the *Auslands Presse Club* in the former headquarters of the "German-English Society" which was "immeasurably more homelike" than its new and elegant rival.[4] Yet it was unwise to show any too marked preference, as this would immediately be registered by the other side, that means in this case the Propaganda Ministry. The acute rivalry between the Foreign and the Propaganda Ministries "proved the salvation of many correspondents." [5] If they were on bad terms with one Ministry they could expect sympathy from the other. This somewhat grotesque situation frequently saved the journalists from penalties which would have been inescapable otherwise.

In the Press division of the Foreign Ministry, too, there were in addition to career diplomats and trained experts on the countries with which they dealt in their work, mere Party men who owed quick promotion to their Party membership card and to their close contacts with von Ribbentrop. The head of this division, envoy Paul Schmidt, was only 28 when the Foreign Minister gave him this important job. Before 1933 a leader of the National Socialist Students League at Kiel University Schmidt had later joined the staff of the "Bureau Ribbentrop" which dealt with Foreign Affairs from the Party point of view at a time when most members of the *Auswärtiges Amt* showed little enthusiasm for it. Schmidt who conducted the daily press conference of his Ministry at 1 p.m. has been described by one foreign correspondent as "intelligent, quick-thinking and witty, biting in his replies, wholly without moral scruples." [6]

A cynic and a born actor he was able to lay on any emotion from mournfully shaking his head at the stupidity of the opponents of the régime to ranting at their infamy. Sometimes charming, but mostly ruth-

[1] W. Shirer, op. cit., p. 409.
[2] Howard K. Smith, *Last Train from Berlin,* p. 39.
[3] W. Shirer, op. cit., p. 409.
[4] Even during the first half of the war copies of the London *Times,* and the news services of Reuter in addition to the German news agency DNB and many lesser news services, were available there. H. Smith, op. cit., p. 39.
[5] Fredborg, op. cit., p. 18.
[6] Fredborg, op. cit., p. 7. However, another correspondent, the American, Joseph C. Harsh, had paid a tribute to his "straightforwardness, freedom from pompousness and a willingness to recognize honest differences in point of view." Joseph C. Harsh, *Pattern of Conquest,* London, 1942, p. 253.

less and arrogant and in addition a poor linguist Schmidt enjoyed little popularity among the foreign journalists. By contrast his deputy, Baron Gustav Braun von Stumm, was a scion of the South German aristocracy and a career diplomat with a thorough knowledge of most European countries. Unlike his chief, he was little of an orator and his speeches were regarded as "tedious and uninteresting".[1] It was more from a desire to prove his faithfulness to the Nazi creed than from any real inclination that the monocled Baron copied the brusque manners of his superiors. At the press conferences of the Foreign Ministry Schmidt or von Stumm invited questions, but during the war the first one was usually arranged and put forward by a pro-Axis journalist from an occupied country.

At the time of Germany's spectacular military successes both ministries provided diplomatic, military and economic spokesmen at their press conferences, who issued reports full of facts, though slanted from a propaganda angle. Criticism was out of the question but as one of the American correspondents present put it: "in those days of Nazi high summer there was seldom need of any criticism of the technical functioning of their propaganda machine."[2] In 1941 awkward questions were occasionally asked by some of the more enterprising Swiss and Swedish journalists, while their Italian and Japanese colleagues remained silent under instructions from their embassies. In 1942 these bold questions dried up. By then "almost any vital question was embarrassing to the Germans," and as a Swedish correspondent observed, "the tone of both Schmidt and Braun von Stumm became so insulting" that the journalists in question "could do only one of two things, either answer back and be told to leave the room or else leave voluntarily."[3]

The treatment of foreign journalists was quite naturally dependent on the course of foreign policy. Before the entry of the U.S. into the war the Nazi authorities still made an effort to impress American journalists in Berlin and to show them some consideration. According to Howard Smith they, more than any other national group of correspondents, were courted with a variety of favours. In 1940 Germany as represented by the Propaganda Ministry still hoped to keep America out of the war or even to turn her public opinion to favouring the Third Reich. At that time the Propaganda Ministry was "one great optometrist's shop which specialized in grinding rose-coloured lenses."[4] After Pearl Harbour and the subsequent state of war between the U.S.A. and Germany the remaining neutral correspondents in Berlin were treated more harshly and given less information to send home.

Wherever possible the Propaganda Ministry was willing to provide material on aspects of German life required by foreign pressmen for writing despatches and this was done with remarkable speed and thoroughness. Within 24 hours interviews with some people in the news were

---

[1] Fredborg, op. cit., p. 8.
[2] Howard K. Smith, *Last Train from Berlin*, p. 37.
[3] A. Fredborg, op. cit., p. 10.
[4] H. K. Smith, op. cit., p. 38.

arranged or data on economic developments furnished. The Ministry also organized excursions to the particular front then in the news, to bombed towns or to aeroplane factories and field hospitals. Though these excursions were naturally designed as propaganda, with some shrewdness the correspondents "could always glean good stuff out of what was offered." [1] Altogether, in spite of restrictions and some chicanery, "as late as 1941, a foreign correspondent could give his paper a fairly accurate picture of Germany and its politics." [2]

In addition to the hand-outs of the Propaganda Ministry and to news items culled from the German press, the correspondents had a special news service at their disposal, the *"Dienst aus Deutschland,"* which, although not strictly official, worked with the consent of the Wilhelmstrasse. It blundered frequently despite the considerable caution with which it was run. Often officials had later to request foreign correspondents to suppress news items gathered from this agency. The *DaD* was used by the officials in the Ministry as a channel "to circulate rumours without making themselves officially responsible." This placed the correspondents in a difficult dilemma, as they had to decide whether the news service was giving the truth or whether it intended to make use of the correspondents for the spreading of lies.[3]

Foreign correspondents in Germany needed a high degree of integrity, for they were subjected to much direct and indirect pressure from the authorities of the Propaganda Ministry and the Foreign Office. To quote one American correspondent at the time "they employed not only outright bribery but every form of cajolery, intimidation, blackmail, politeness and intrigue." [4] Favours and privileges bestowed on the journalists by the authorities could be withdrawn at a moment's notice. The Foreign Press Division of the Propaganda Ministry arranged leases for flats, secured visas for holiday trips and special passes for major events and provided them with opera and film tickets at reduced prices. In war time foreign journalists were allowed double food rations and also special permits for buying textile goods without restriction, while German civilians were strictly rationed. As William Shirer so neatly put it: "If the way to a correspondent's heart goes through his stomach, then Dr. Goebbels certainly tries hard." [5] Members of the Foreign Press Association, which included most of the authentic foreign journalists in Germany, were also privileged to buy marks at a cheaper rate than other foreigners. But these concessions also served as a means of exerting pressure. "Every attack against the Association was preceded by a 'shortage' of butter, or a rumor that the cheap mark would be withheld."

According to Fredborg, the Propaganda Ministry "had formulated a definite programme for bribing" foreign journalists. Although paid agents

---

[1] H. K. Smith, op. cit., p. 39.
[2] Fredborg, op. cit., p. 11.
[3] A. Fredborg, op. cit., p. 14.
[4] Joseph C. Harsh, *Pattern of Conquest*, London, 1942, pp. 242-243.
[5] W. Shirer, Berlin Diary, p. 408; entry of 25 September 1940.

of Goebbels' Ministry were excluded from membership of the Foreign Press Association which was run by the foreign correspondents themselves, nevertheless some members were suspected with good reason by their colleagues of being on the Nazi payroll.[1] In one case a Foreign Ministry official admitted freely to the American journalist Joseph C. Harsh that a certain Balkan correspondent who had asked what was obviously a "planted" question at a Press conference was in their pay. He added even casually that the Foreign Ministry paid this man one hundred marks a month, the Propaganda Ministry three hundred and the chemical trust I.G. Farben seven hundred.[2]

During the war years three types of foreign correspondent in Berlin can be distinguished. First there were those who subscribed fully to the policies of the Nazis. Most of these coming from Germany's allies and satellites and from the occupied countries, had to toe the official line regardless of their personal inclinations. Others representing non-belligerent and neutral nations had "literally sold out for cash or for other and subtler forms of privilege." [3] The second group consisted of correspondents who thought that it was in the best interest of their readers and employers if they avoided news items which might offend the German authorities or jeopardize their chances of remaining in Germany. By such an attitude they secured competitive advantages over their colleagues such as special interviews, special trips, advance information on important new developments and so on. Thirdly there were journalists who ventured to be as independent and critical of the régime as circumstances would allow. They often paid for it by expulsion from the Third Reich. During the German advance in the West in the spring of 1940 Dr. Bömer organized trips to the front for foreign journalists giving preferential treatment to certain correspondents from neutral countries including the U.S.A. He had these men earmarked for special favour to travel in his own car. When his guests thought they had collected valuable news "his car would leave the others and drive at top speed to the nearest telephone far behind the fighting lines. Other cars for the press would continue with the trip or follow at a slow speed." As a result Dr. Bömer's 'favoured sons' enjoyed a lead of two or three hours, which was an immense advantage to their papers and a serious handicap for their less fortunate competitors.[4]

It seems likely that some Gestapo agents and *agents provocateurs* were

[1] A. Fredborg, op. cit., p. 16.

[2] J. C. Harsh, op. cit., p. 241.

[3] J. C. Harsh, op. cit., p. 246-7.

[4] Among the correspondents forced to leave the country was the American Ralph Barnes, who had the courage to protest against this system of favouritism. By this he ran into opposition not only from the Propaganda Ministry, but also from those of his colleagues who were the beneficiaries of these methods. Barnes was excluded from any further trips, and while the Foreign Ministry protected him for a while "just to spite its rival ministry", when he dared to send home despatches about Russo-German relations the Foreign Ministry, too, dropped him and he was expelled. J. C. Harsh, op. cit., pp. 248-9.

planted among the journalists to spy on their colleagues. One of them, the Dutch journalist Max Blokzijl, was generally considered to have anti-Nazi leanings. He managed to conceal the fact that he was actually a Fascist. The truth came to light when after the German invasion of Holland he was promptly appointed Chief of Propaganda and radio announcer under Mussert, the leader of the Dutch National Socialist Party.[1] Foreign journalists were not only spied upon by some of their colleagues, but also their homes were sometimes watched and their telephones tapped. Like the staff of foreign embassies they had to reckon with the possibility that in Berlin telephones could be used as a dictograph, even with the receiver down. When talking freely many took the precaution of covering their telephone with a heavy cloth. There is evidence of secret recording gadgets and steel tape having been built into the walls of the flats of foreign journalists or in the homes of foreign embassies.[2] Not seldom foreign correspondents discovered that some of their private conversations had reached the long ears of the German authorities. It was a world of shadows, of twilight.

How did the German officials control the output of the foreign correspondents? Unlike England, Germany placed no censorship upon press cables, a fact appreciated by some American correspondents, who had earlier worked in London during the first months of the war. While the scripts of radio correspondents had to be submitted to the censorship of three different authorities, the Propaganda Ministry, the Foreign Ministry and the High Command of the *Wehrmacht*, "for newspapermen there prevailed a liberal policy regarding news transmission which was singular in a state where all else was so rigidly controlled." [3] Although this state of affairs could not be taken at its face value, it "made the job of routine reporting tremendously easier than it was in London." [4]

Apart from this there was little freedom of expression, and correspondents had to develop almost a sixth sense for what was permissible to report and what not. What the Nazi officials proudly called *die freie Berichterstattung* (unrestricted reporting) was in fact a very limited freedom. A correspondent from a neutral country ran constant risks. As one of them put it after having left Germany, "Outsiders sometimes asked us whether it was necessary to hew so close to the line, and take so many risks. We answered that it *was* necessary, partly because it was the only way to write anything of interest, and partly to keep the Nazis from imposing even tighter restrictions." [5] From our general knowledge of the restrictive attitude of the Nazi officials, one is inclined to agree with

[1] See A. Fredborg, op. cit., p. 4. Blokzijl was put on trial after the war by the Dutch Government, sentenced to death and executed at The Hague on 16 March 1946. See *Procession No. 1: Max Blokzijl*, Bronnenpublicaties, No. 1 ed. Rijksinstituut voor Oorlogsdocumentatie, Amsterdam, 1946, p. 95.

[2] See A. Fredborg, op. cit., pp. 21-22; also *Ambassador Dodds Diaries*, p. 364.

[3] Howard K. Smith, *Last Train from Berlin*, p. 37.

[4] Op. cit., p. 38. See also Joseph C. Harsh, op. cit., pp. 245-246.

[5] Fredborg, op. cit., p. 18-19.

Fredborg's argument that "had any great number of foreign correspondents set voluntary limits on what they wrote, the Germans would certainly have drawn the border tighter, following the lines of least resistance." [1]

There was sometimes an unpleasant *Nachspiel,* some punitive measure against the foreign offender following upon publication of his news items or articles. The German embassies and consulates abroad regularly reported on the despatches and articles which appeared in the countries to which they were accredited. They were often published in a condensed form and were not always free from errors. If the article or news report displeased the German authorities they had a whole range of penalties at their disposal, which were usually imposed by the Propaganda Ministry, though sometimes strictures were issued by the Press Division of the Foreign Ministry. The criticism could be conveyed to the journalist by an official over the telephone, or in more serious cases be uttered in the Ministry to which the culprit had been summoned. In still graver cases the offender had to appear before the head of the Press Division who would inform him of the imposition of a rather severe penalty. During the war there were five general categories of punishment:

1. A warning in writing;
2. Denial of telephone privileges for varying periods;
3. A strong suggestion that the correspondent in question would be well advised to leave Germany;
4. Expulsion from the country within 2 or 3 days;
5. Arrest for "high treason" and "espionage".

There was also the possibility of being banished from the press conferences and press clubs. The penalties varied a good deal according to the nationality of the offender and the importance of his newspaper. The correspondent's own political views and his personal relations with the officials censoring him also plays a part. [2]

According to V. McKenzie more than fifty resident foreign newsmen were ordered to leave Germany before the outbreak of the Second World War or had decided to go "for good and sufficient reasons". Some of them went "voluntarily" anticipating their expulsion. Thirteen of them left on account of their Jewish origin after they had been informed "that they were unwelcome and that they would not be given any access to normal news channels". [3]

An interesting case was the expulsion of Mr. Norman Ebbutt, the London *Times* special correspondent in Berlin. He was forced to return to England in August 1937 shortly after three German journalists had been expelled from England for alleged or suspected espionage activities. A violent campaign in the German press had preceded Ebbutt's expulsion. It was directed not only against him, but against "all foreign cor-

---

[1] Ibid.
[2] See A. Fredborg, op. cit., pp. 19-20.
[3] Vernon McKenzie, *Here Lies Goebbels! London,* 1940, p. 96.

respondents whose views on the regime were not entirely conformist." [1]
On 13 August the *Times* had published an article by Ebbutt on Göring's
organization of the German steel industry for armament production. "It
was not the sort of article that the Germans wished to see in the *Times*
or in any other British newspaper and was unlikely to be forgiven." [2]
In addition the German authorities were annoyed by Ebbutt's frequent
reports on the persecution of German Catholics and on the case of Pastor
Niemöller. They resented him "because he knew too much [that was]
detrimental to Nazi anti-religious activity." [3]

Another retaliatory measure by which to damage the interest of foreign newspapers was a *Verbot* of their circulation in Germany. This
applied particularly to Swiss newspapers in German, which were banned
partly in order to prevent "undesirable" news from reaching the German
public, and partly to make Swiss editors more amenable to the official
German views. When in December 1934 three leading Swiss newspapers,
Der Bund, Nationalzeitung and *Neue Zürcher Zeitung* were forbidden
in the Reich for an indefinite period without any explanation being given,
their editors in a joint statement refused "to adapt their reporting to the
unusual requirements", the fulfilment of which was obviously a condition
for the admission of their newspapers to Germany. The Swiss editors
felt that the German Government had "demonstrated in the last eighteen
months that no newspaper serving Swiss interests and opinions regardless
of its sale abroad could count on unrestricted circulation in Germany".
The three newspapers stubbornly refused to change their general attitude
and also declined "to publish for commercial considerations an especially
adapted edition for Germany".[4]

[1] See particularly the *Berliner Boersenzeitung* of 10, 11 and 12 August 1937;
the quotation is from McKenzie, op. cit., p. 96.
[2] *The History of the Times*, London, 1952, vol. IV, Part II, pp. 508-509.
[3] Ibid.
[4] *Der Bund, Berne*, 30 December 1934.

CHAPTER 5

The Strange Case of the Frankfurter Zeitung

1. A CAT AND MOUSE GAME

BEFORE Hitler came to power the *Frankfurter Zeitung* was the leading liberal German newspaper, a kind of German *Manchester Guardian*. Its three daily issues gave wide and usually accurate information. There was a big staff of competent and often brilliant correspondents both in Germany and abroad, and its editors lived up to C.P. Scott's famous demand for the separation of news and comment. The paper was also distinguished for its commercial pages and for a remarkable *feuilleton*, its parts and supplements devoted to literature, the arts and university life. Founded by Leopold Sonnemann, a Jewish banker, in 1856, it had always kept the flag of a rather broad and internationally-minded liberalism flying. It had dared to be critical of Bismarck's power politics after he had harshly annexed Frankfurt to Prussia in 1866. After 1871 the *Frankfurter Zeitung* had been equally opposed to Bismarck's *Kulturkampf* and to his severe anti-socialist measures. Permeated by a liberal rationalism based on belief in the power of enlightened self-interest, the paper had lost some important battles in Imperial Germany. In vain it had pleaded for a liberal treatment of the people in Alsace-Lorraine, ceded by France. The imperial regime had preferred a drastic *Machtpolitik* to its proposals of a more sensible policy. When in 1917 the *Frankfurter Zeitung* was opposed to the idea of unlimited U-boat warfare, the paper lost its fight against Admiral von Tirpitz and the Pan-German nationalists. These men had their way, with the result that the U.S.A. entered the war and eventually tipped the scales against Germany.

After the revolution of 1918 the *Frankfurter Zeitung* supported the platform of the Democrats, who, alas, soon turned out to be officers without soldiers. The paper was strongly opposed to the revival of German nationalism and to the "Stab in the Back" legend. At the same time the editors were critical of Versailles and pleaded for the revision of the German Peace Treaty. But there was a curious academic and detached quality in the *Frankfurter Zeitung* which made it inclined to underestimate the dangers from the powerful National Socialist movement in the Twenties and early Thirties. This was particularly so after the defeat

124

suffered by Hitler in the Putsch of 9 November 1923 in Munich. It is perhaps asking too much of one newspaper, however high its quality, that it should have proved an effective bulwark against the rising tide of nationalism during a period of intense economic crisis and mass unemployment. In vain did the editors after 1930 deplore the terror methods of the Nazis and the high price to be paid for the artificial unity they were to establish. It has recently been suggested by a member of the editorial staff that the battle against the tyrants was started too late.[1] In any case it was lost completely and irrevocably.

The *Frankfurter Zeitung,* owned by a Jew and with a number of Jews among its editors and correspondents, had often been described by German nationalists as a *"Judenblatt"*. In *Mein Kampf* Hitler had sneered at its spineless objectivity and cunning Jewish tactics.[2] To him the paper was a tool of the international Jewish conspiracy in which he seems to have believed, a hateful symbol of the *"Systemzeit"*. In a way the refined nationalism and somewhat academic liberalism of the paper was more obnoxious and sinister in Hitler's eyes than was the cruder and simpler manner of the Social Democratic press. Few people, therefore, expected that after the Nazis had come to power the *Frankfurter Zeitung* would be allowed to survive with many members of its old staff continuing in their posts. Yet while all the Social Democratic papers were closed down and their printing presses taken over by the Party papers, the *Frankfurter Zeitung* lasted for another ten years, until the end of August 1943.

The reasons for its survival in 1933 are obscure and there is no fully corroborated evidence available. In March 1933 it certainly looked as if the new powers-to-be would close down the paper. Some editors in Frankfurt were arrested and their homes searched. Police also appeared at the offices of the paper. On 11 March there was a threatening mob outside the building, and once S.A. men hoisted the swastika on its roof. But when the editors had it removed, the S.A. did not intervene. There was a strange reluctance on the part of the local Party authorities to take drastic action and to interfere with the activities of the paper. Probably the local Party officials regarded the fate of the paper as a major political matter, which could only be decided by higher authority in Berlin.[3]

Rudolf Diels, the head of the political police in Prussia in 1933-1934, claims that he saved the *Frankfurter Zeitung* from being closed down in June 1933.[4] At that time Goebbels had reminded him by telephone that "at last" the paper would have to be forbidden. Diels says he tried to reassure Goebbels, telling him of the negotiations he had had with the publisher of the paper, a representative of the Simon family, which had

---

[1] See B. Reifenberg, "Die zehn Jahre 1933-1943" in *Ein Jahrhundert Frankfurter Zeitung, 1856-1956. Gegenwart Sonderheft,* Frankfurt, 1956, p. 40.

[2] A. Hitler, *Mein Kampf,* Jubiläumsausgabe, Munich, 1939, pp. 242-244.

[3] B. Reifenberg, op. cit., p. 41.

[4] Rudolf Diels, *Luzifer Ante Portas. Zwischen Severing und Heydrich.* Zürich, n.d., pp. 48-50.

led to a new course being pursued by the paper in accordance with the new régime. No objections could be raised against the re-constituted editorial board. But Goebbels raised the matter with Hitler, and Diels had an interview about it with the Führer in the presence of Goebbels. Hitler wished to know why Diels was opposed to the closing down of this "Jew paper". Having fought against it for years as the symbol of Jewish journalism, no National Socialist would understand why it should be allowed to continue. After reporting on the changes among the editorial staff which he claimed to have effected, Diels told Hitler that he was convinced of the great political importance of the *Frankfurter Zeitung*. To forbid it would mean an irreplaceable loss for the Reich. "The *Frankfurter Zeitung*," he maintained, "was the most widely read German newspaper abroad, its news and views were quoted everywhere." Hitler was not impressed, and replied that in future other German papers with proved National Socialists as editors would have to be read abroad. Diels tried to gain ground by using one of the arguments then favoured by Hitler. He had repeatedly stressed that the Länder and big cities should preserve specific cultural features of their own; Munich should become the city of art, Nuremberg the city of culture, and Frankfurt had always been the city of German journalism. It was going to be deprived of its university,[1] it had lost much of its commercial character on account of the restrictions imposed on the Jews. If it was also to lose the *Frankfurter Zeitung* it "could only then rely on the reputation of the Frankfurter sausages". When Hitler protested against this cheap joke, Diels sang the praises of the cultural pages of the paper, which he described as "a great literary document of our age". Of all the dailies the *Frankfurter Zeitung* reflected the crisis of our time most faithfully: it was stupid to describe its approach as "destructive" (*zersetzend*). For a clarification of one's views and attitudes the paper seemed to be quite indispensable.

Hitler, who was not then entirely inaccessible to arguments adroitly put to him, gave in, telling Diels to do what he could not leave undone.[2] The *Frankfurter Zeitung* was allowed to continue, but it may be that Diels' claim to have obtained Hitler's consent for it is exaggerated. The editors, it seems, were not informed of any such decision. What is perhaps more surprising, "there was never any fundamental discussion between the men round Goebbels and the editorial staff of the *Frankfurter Zeitung*."[3] But it is remarkable that whilst other prominent non-Party papers were put under a National Socialist controller, this did not hap-

[1] The University was in fact preserved.

[2] Op. cit., p. 50. Diels' statement is indirectly corroborated by evidence that Hitler was critical of the poor performance of the Party press during the second half of 1933. At a conference of Party leaders in the autumn of that year Hitler is reported to have strongly criticized the National Socialist press. He warned it not to attack the non-Party papers as long as it could not reach the same standards. Based on tactical reasons Hitler's attitude was only transitory, but it did exist at the time. See the letter by Dertinger to Dr. Heerdegen, Chemnitz, 20 October 1933 (Brammer).

[3] B. Reifenberg, op. cit., p. 41.

pen in the case of the Frankfurt paper. By 1934 Goebbels no longer aimed at closing it down. He probably realized the value of it as a channel for a more subtle type of propaganda abroad and for the voicing of ideas destined to reach a foreign public which would be out of place in the harsher Party papers. Goebbels is said to have remarked in those early days of the régime that it would give him a special pleasure "to make the gentlemen in the Eschenheimer Gasse dance to his tune." [1] But as he believed in a certain variety of the press, at least in presentation and make-up, he wisely did not insist on its becoming another *Völkischer Beobachter*. This would have been pointless anyway. Thus for years a curious state of affairs prevailed. When the local Party authorities realized that drastic action against the paper had not been taken by the Propaganda Ministry, "the local Party authorities treated it as, so to speak, ex-territorial ground in the Gau of Hessen-Nassau: whilst the Party Headquarters, as well as the Party press, ignored its editors and their work as an odious but expatriated phenomenon." [2] Though the foreign and the social policies of the paper were largely readjusted to the Hitler regime, its language remained refined, unemotional and detached, and its celebrated cultural pages, the *Feuilleton*, made few concessions to the new course. Goebbels and his lieutenants undoubtedly realized that foreign statesmen and politicians who felt repelled by the shrill tones and bullying headlines of the German Party papers were more inclined to listen to the "sweet reasonableness" and detached near-objectivity of the Frankfurt paper.

The *Frankfurter Zeitung* was somewhat cautiously ambiguous in its references to any statements or speeches made by the Minister of Propaganda. It put on a show of belief in his good intentions, adding some guarded criticism of one or other of his remarks. It played the game of the mouse who declared that the cat was in fact not too bad. But at the same time the mouse had to remain constantly aware of the cat's existence. Take for instance the paper's treatment of an address Goebbels gave before the Reich Association of the German Press in Berlin on 19 April 1934.[3] In it he alternately praised and criticized the performance of the press. He expressed satisfaction that his appeal to the national responsibility of the press had not proved in vain. In the course of one year the face of the press had fundamentally changed, but—and Goebbels' praise usually turned out to be a back-handed compliment—its content now was by far too monotonous. "We have the doubtful honour," pronounced the Minister with some contempt, "of being praised most in papers that formerly attacked us. We would rather do without it and we would prefer them to show more reserve emanating from strength of character, just as we prefer those who remained outside the Party from strength of character to those who exploited the situation at once and saved their skin by a daring jump into the Party." Goebbels blamed the

1 Op. cit., p. 42.
2 B. Reifenberg, op. cit., p. 42.
3 *Frankfurter Zeitung*, 21 April 1934.

lack of variety in the press on the missing courage of the journalists, admitting that he was unable to "make the press more courageous than it was". He did not believe that he could educate people to a new mentality who were brought up with a different ideology. Only the young generation would be able to set its proper stamp on the twentieth century.

This speech was, incidentally, resented by some non-Nazi journalists. One of them, the Berlin correspondent of several provincial papers, refused to write the commentary which the Propaganda Ministry had suggested should appear in the press with the report on the speech. He felt that Goebbels had defined all non-National Socialist journalists alike, and that a proper self-respect forbade him to write it up, as he would not be able to express his true views.[1] Rudolf Kircher, the Berlin correspondent of the *Frankfurter Zeitung*, could not afford to ignore Goebbels' address to which he had listened. His commentary combined moderate praise for the Minister with cautious criticism of some of his *dicta*.[2] Kircher compared the hundreds of journalists who had listened to Goebbels from the benches of the former Prussian Diet to sixth-formers sitting before their headmaster, who allotted them marks. "To say it at once, none of them has passed. . . . The Minister of Propaganda made a long speech full of delightful formulations." He had given them a lesson on how to avoid becoming boring. Dr. Goebbels saw part of the evil in the lack of sureness of the journalists. This uncertainty, Kircher felt, had many causes. It was particularly rampant when the state erected barriers instead of leaving the duty of imposing a limitation on what he was writing to the journalist himself. We could say that in his speech Goebbels had offered the right of criticism to the journalists with the one hand and taken it back with the other. "It would have probably been more comforting to us," Kircher commented with some frankness, "if the Government had declared from the beginning: In such difficult times there can be no criticism. Instead, it came forward with the suggestion: 'Don't be shy, criticize, but in the right way'. This was almost a little cruel. Yet when the Minister left the platform he was strongly applauded." Obviously, criticism of the Minister could not have gone further without depriving the commentator of his permit to work.

It can be assumed, though solid evidence to prove it is lacking, that during the period 1933-1939 the more reasonable and moderate officials in the Propaganda Ministry and in some other Ministries, such as the Foreign Ministry and the Ministry of Economics, were in favour of the continued existence of the *Frankfurter Zeitung*. On the other hand, we know that such rabid Party members as Ministerialrat Berndt were opposed to it.

From 1937 onwards the paper lived in a state of permanent crisis and uncertainty. A certain group of Party fanatics, many of whom belonged

[1] Letter by Dertinger to the head offices of three papers in Hamburg, Breslau and Chemnitz, 20 April 1934 (Brammer).

[2] *Frankfurter Zeitung*, 21 April 1934. Article "Dr. Goebbels vor den Journalisten".

to the "Old Guard" and thus had the Führer's ear, constantly tried to bring about the end of the paper. These people endeavoured to incite the local Party authorities, the Ministries, and from time to time when they thought the moment opportune, Hitler's entourage against the paper.[1] In addition, the Party office in Frankfurt had compiled a list of members of the editorial staff, whose "political unreliability" had been established.

The brunt of the attacks was felt most strongly by the paper's Berlin office. Its members had to possess thick skins and great agility of mind at the daily press conference of the Propaganda Ministry and in private talks with leading civil servants. They had to put up with much sharp criticism and disapproval of news items or articles in their paper. The men on the spot, therefore, often felt more anxious than their colleagues in provincial Frankfurt. Reifenberg's claim that "the work in Frankfurt continued to remain independent of the Berlin office", however, seems exaggerated.[2] While there was no direct censorship, the official directives, which often changed from day to day, had to be kept in mind.

The editorial team of the paper—it had an editor-in-chief in name only to satisfy official requirements—exercised its own internal censorship, and everything to be published had to be read by a second member. This was done with two points in view: a) the danger of coming into conflict with the rulers in Berlin, and b) the chances of publishing material superimposed by the Propaganda Ministry "in a sufficiently detached manner." [3] The *Frankfurter Zeitung* still had a large staff of correspondents of its own, but their reports too had often to be tailored according to the Berlin orders and requirements. Though Dietrich and others in the ministry sometimes paid lip-service to the paper, acknowledging its individual tone, in fact any deviation from the prescribed conformity had to be justified by the editors; they even had constantly to explain why a certain news item appeared on the second page instead of the first, why not more or not less space had been given to it, why it had not appeared in larger or in smaller print.[4]

Often the paper was criticized at the press conference or after it. Sometimes a complaint came from the local Party offices in Frankfurt, but if the Berlin representatives of the paper were able to put forward counter-arguments the Ministry would often then drop the matter. A case in point was the obituary of Pope Pius XI published by the *Frankfurter Zeitung*. The Propaganda Office in Frankfurt objected that in it there was too much praise of the Concordat concluded by the new regime with the Vatican in 1933. The Berlin spokesman of the paper disagreed with this interpretation—after all, had not the Concordat been fully approved by the Führer? No action was taken in this matter.[5]

Frequently special Party organizations outside the realm of the Min-

[1] B. Reifenberg, op. cit., p. 50.
[2] Op. cit., p. 45.
[3] Ibid.
[4] Op. cit., p. 49.
[5] ZSg. 102/14, 11 February 1939.

istry launched complaints, some of which were quite ludicrous. On one occasion the *BdM* (Association of German Girls) took exception to a somewhat ironic report in the paper on a ceremony in Berlin at which women leaders of the organization had taken an oath. There had been a reply in the Reich Youth Press Service, and the speaker at the Daily Press Conference had also deplored the facetious tone of the report. But when the offensive report from the *Frankfurter Zeitung* was read aloud there was laughter among the journalists and the Berlin representative of the paper was able to reassure the editors in Frankfurt that they need not take the affair too seriously.[1]

Complaints which originated in the Propaganda Ministry itself were a more serious matter. Frequently the attention of the editors was drawn to articles or news reports written contrary to the official line. When, for instance, the paper had carried a news item "German artists decorated in Athens", Fritzsche sent an official complaint to the editor-in-chief, pointing out that this was an infringement of the repeated instruction that nothing should be written on the bestowing of decorations except when the news had come from the official agency or when special permission had been granted.[2]

Such disapproval was couched in much sharper terms if an item in the *Frankfurter Zeitung* caught the eye and caused the displeasure of a member of the upper hierarchy, of Dietrich, Goebbels, let alone the Führer. Any professional criticism of works of art, of plays, films, etc., had been expressly forbidden by a decree issued on 29 November 1936; only factual comment and straight reporting of artistic events were permissible. This was the reason why an independent appreciation of an advanced modern opera like Alban Berg's "Lulu" met with the sharpest censure. The premiere, which would never have been allowed in Germany, had taken place in Zürich. The critique published in the *Frankfurter Zeitung* was branded by the speaker, Werner Stephan, at a press conference as "quite unheard of", as it "was contrary to everything that had been said at the press conference in this respect." He even threatened

---

[1] Press Conference 10 June 1936 and letter from the Berlin Office to Herr Reifenberg 10 June 1936, ZSg. 102/2.

[2] Fritzsche letter to Hauptschriftleiter, *Frankfurter Zeitung*, 17 December 1938, ZSg. 102/13. Soon afterwards another news report in the paper on decorations evoked a sharper reprimand by the Ministry. This time it concerned decorations given to artists in the Soviet Union. Fritzsche acidly commented that there was no need for such news to be released to the German public. But if the reader was given that sort of news, he wanted definitely to know who the decorated people were. It would have been the paper's task in this context to draw attention to the large percentage of Jews in the film industry in Soviet Russia, and above all to characterize the producer Eisenstein as a Jew. This was an infringement of the relevant directive issued at the end of the previous year. "I disapprove of this"—Fritzsche declared—"and hope that your future reports will not fall short of the expectations expressed in that directive". (Fritzsche to Hauptschriftleiter, *Frankfurter Zeitung*, 22 February 1939, ZSg. 102/14.)

that the account would certainly have consequences for the author and the responsible editor. References to the twelve-tone system and to the remark that the premiere "was a great day for Zürich" were particularly resented. This type of opera was unacceptable in the Third Reich. It was for this reason that Dietrich had demanded that the sharpest steps should be taken against the responsible editor and the author too, if he lived in Germany. Reporting this the Berlin correspondent foreshadowed that the paper would receive an official warning, a more serious censure than a mere letter of disapproval,[1] which only expressed the expectation that the editor would in future conform precisely with the instructions given to the press.[2]

One of the main danger zones for the competent and cultured writers of the *Frankfurter Zeitung* was the sphere of painting and of architecture. For the Führer liked to pose as "Master-builder", and Goebbels referred to him publicly as "the Master-builder of the Reich". At the official Munich art exhibition of 1939 there was a large painting of Hitler as sculptor-architect. Doting admirers sent him books with the inscription "To the great Master-builder of the 'German Cathedral', Adolf Hitler." His indictment of "degenerate art" of which he arranged a special exhibition in Munich in the summer of 1937 was as telling as his inclination towards monumental buildings and sculptures giving an illusion of grandeur in the manner of Josef Thorak or of the architect Troost. Hitler regarded himself as an authority in this field no less than in others, and resented any deviations from his norms.[3]

It is significant that by 1939 the "sponsors" of the paper in the Propaganda Ministry admonished its editors not to give offence in their columns on art. On the occasion of a dinner at a conference of 400 sub-editors responsible for the cultural sections, the representative of the *Frankfurter Zeitung* was called to the table of Reich Press Chief Dr. Dietrich, who engaged him in a long conversation. Dietrich remarked that he "quite appreciated the paper and looked upon it as something special in the ranks of the press. In his opinion there were no dangers (threatening it) of any kind." But he once more asked the Frankfurter journalists most definitely to be very cautious with reports on art (architecture, exhibitions of paintings, etc.)" There were some people, who followed up in detail what the paper wrote, cut out some items and submitted them as evidence that the *Frankfurter Zeitung* was going its own way. "Espe-

---

[1] ZSg. 102/5, 7 June 1937.

[2] The same expectation was also expressed in a letter by Fritzsche to the *Frankfurter Zeitung* complaining that an article "The Czechs in the Sudeten area" had discussed the attitude of these Czechs with reference to the elections by the Sudeten Germans to the Reichstag. This had been an infringement of an instruction not to discuss this question, laid down in "Confidential Information" no. 258. Letter from Fritzsche to the *Frankfurter Zeitung,* 9 December 1938. ZSg. 102/13.

[3] Hellmuth Lehmann-Haupt, *Art under a Dictatorship,* New York, 1954, particularly pp. 45-61.

cially because of the interest of the Führer in art, the greatest caution in the manner of formulating (*in der Formulierung*) was imperative." [1]

Herr Bade, another official of the Ministry,[2] professed his special benevolent interest in the *Frankfurter Zeitung* on the same lines. Bade seems to have been more an experienced cynic rather than a pedantic tyrant, for he explained that "should something special occur" (obviously a euphemism for a serious violation of the press directives by the paper) he would, unfortunately, be forced to take drastic steps. But he added "that in the long run these punitive measures would not turn out to be so bad as they looked, for even if he had to strike off the name of an editor from the official list, he still had the power to restore him to it after a long interval. Such an elimination from the list had sometimes proved necessary in other cases in order to let the offender feel the official censure, and above all to carry out instructions received from above". Reporting these remarks which obviously hinted at the Führer, the journalist to whom they were made asked his office to regard them as particularly confidential and to exclude them from the records.[3]

Fortunately for the historian, this was not done, for the conversation reveals clearly that the authorities regarded the continuance of the former chief mouthpiece of German liberalism as still profitable for the régime. Some earlier evidence for this can be gained from the critical comment by Stephan on a brochure "The Liberal opposition in Germany under the new regime" by Wolff Heinrichsdorff.[4] This rather academic but highly critical account of the "odd" methods of the former liberal press is crowded with quotations from articles in the *Frankfurter Zeitung* since 1933. They were intended to illustrate the hypocritical subterfuges of an attitude that conformed to the new regime, but actually tried to undermine and weaken it. Though not aggressive in tone, the author obviously wanted to draw attention to the dangers of the survival of a paper that still used many of the old categories and ideas of liberalism while paying lip-service to the National Socialist regime. What this critic overlooked, or at least left undiscussed, was the political interest the Government had in allowing the paper to carry on a eunuch-like existence that combined some tame ideological opposition with the pursuing of the official line on economic and foreign policy. Even if the *Frankfurter Zeitung* was able to avoid any crude anti-Semitism, such a minus could be overlooked by the Propaganda Ministry because of the propaganda effect this "quality" paper was considered to have abroad.

[1] Letter by M.G. to Herr Stark, 21 April 1939, ZSg. 102/15; the initials M.G. probably stand for Max Geysenheyner, the editor of the *Frankfurter Illustrierte*.

[2] Ministerialrat Wilfried Bade was the head of the department "Periodicals" in the Propaganda Ministry from 1933 to 1945.

[3] Letter by M.G. Herr Stark, 21 April 1939.

[4] Wolff Heinrichsdorff, *Die liberale Opposition in Deutschland seit dem 30 January 1933, (dargestellt an der Entwicklung der "Frankfurter Zeitung")* Hamburg, 1937.

Stephan's comment on this pamphlet at a press conference is significant. Although admitting its scholarly manner, he asked the journalists to take no notice of the brochure, for its author had ignored the most elementary fundamentals of politics in pretending that there existed no Propaganda Ministry and no official control that kept a watch on obstruction and opposition in the press. The pamphlet gave the false impression that "we had looked on passively while a newspaper had been in opposition to the regime." Indeed, Heinrichsdorff had not mentioned Goebbels or his Ministry at all, confining his pages entirely to ideological issues and attitudes. By doing so he had hurt the professional *amour propre* of the supervisors of the press.[1]

There was an epilogue to Stephan's cryptic remarks. The author, who may have been a journalist, wrote a letter to the Ministry in which he expressed his concern that he had been criticized for his lack of political sense.[2] Claiming that he had shown political understanding in writing his pamphlet, Heinrichsdorff admitted, however, that he had been unable to document it. He quite realized the importance of the *Frankfurter Zeitung*, though he had not been in a position to say so in his foreword. In other words, one might paraphrase his remarks and say that he was aware of the ambiguous position of the Frankfurt paper but unsure of the line the Propaganda Ministry was taking toward it. Belatedly it seems to have dawned on him that there was a political motive in allowing the *Frankfurter Zeitung* to survive. He had now seen the red light, for commenting on Heinrichsdorff's letter a week later Stephan "wished to say without any irony that the author had indeed shown a full understanding of the situation of the *Frankfurter Zeitung*." [3]

2. AN INSTRUMENT OF FOREIGN POLICY

Though the readjustment of the *Frankfurter Zeitung* to the Third Reich, its "*Gleichschaltung*", was at first superficial and never really extended to a full adherence to the National Socialist *Weltanschauung*, it was bound to increase as the years passed by and to leave an imprint on the paper. It remained to some extent an organ of a subdued "opposition", as far as the cultural and religious policies of the regime were concerned, but it supported its foreign policy by and large from the beginning. Its value in doing so is probably one of the reasons for its prolonged survival. In this field too the language of the paper differed from that of the Party press; it was never aggressive, rude or even sly. Its tone corresponded more to the academic lecture hall, or the court, than to the boxing arena, let alone the gutter. As the *Frankfurter Zeitung* gradually became an organ of special pleading for the changing tactics of German foreign policy, it was all done with an air of polished

[1] "Aus der Pressekonferenz", 13 May 1937, ZSg. 102/5.
[2] "Aus der Pressekonferenz", 5 May 1937, ZSg. 102/5.
[3] Ibid.

bonhomie. The attitude of the Frankfurt writers to foreign affairs was that of considerate and plausible salesmen, to whom the ultimate aims and ambitions of their firm remained oddly unknown or obscure.

When during the first four or five years of the regime Hitler posed as a friend of peace in Europe, the Frankfurt editors accepted his pacifist professions, for these former liberals seemed to have a genuine desire for the maintenance of peace. At the same time they were better informed about public opinion and political moves abroad, about the attitude of the world to the new Germany than most of their colleagues. The special correspondents of the paper abroad continued to report fairly objectively and without too many concessions to the Third Reich.

The major error of judgment made by the editors in Frankfurt was that they did not realize the fateful correlation between Hitler's domestic and foreign policies. While sincerely, though mutely deploring the ruthlessness of the Party at home, they failed to grasp the ultimate aggressive consequence of the Nazi outlook in foreign affairs. As one of them confessed after the war, the *Frankfurter Zeitung* had

"argued in the realm of foreign policy as if it were, so to speak, a neutral field . . . as if there had existed a subject that, unimpaired by the National Socialist confusion of terms and corruption of the soul, was accessible to the reflections of Reason." [1]

The very fact that the editors were repelled by the crude potted Nazi philosophy made them more inclined

"to escape into the problems of foreign policy as into a genuine task with which they were familiar and that could only be dealt with by experts and so exclude all political dilettantism." [2]

It was a lack of vision and perhaps also of courage on the part of hard pressed men, who constantly refused to swallow the Party gospel of racialism and aggressive anti-Semitism. In the early years of the régime the editorial staff of the Frankfurt paper

"nearly stifled, nearly blinded by the sight of the 'inner enemies' (of the régime) being dragged through the streets, deprived of their hair, besmirched and covered with (abusive) posters, were incapable of the vision to realize that the same National Socialists who now made a mockery of the moral code without meeting with resistance, would one day cross the frontiers of the Reich with a shocking frivolity." [3]

Impressed and deceived by Hitler's bloodless victories in foreign affairs between 1934 and 1936, Rudolf Kircher, the former London correspondent of the paper and from 1934 onward its nominal editor-in-chief and his colleagues did not suspect Hitler of the sinister plans for armed conquest which he revealed to his top advisors at the famous secret meeting in the Chancellery on 5 November 1937.[4]

[1] B. Reifenberg in *Ein Jarhhundert Frankfurter Zeitung*, p. 46.
[2] Ibid.
[3] Ibid.
[4] See the Hossbach minutes, *Documents on German Foreign Policy, 1918-1945*, series D, vol. I, doc. no. 19.

Kircher had good contacts with the staff of the Foreign Ministry in Berlin and it is significant that the Foreign Minister granted the journalist an interview on his 65th birthday, incidentally a few days only before Neurath's appointment was suddenly terminated by Hitler and the post filled by the less gentlemanly Party parvenu Ribbentrop.[1]

The civilized tone of the *Frankfurter Zeitung,* its unemotional approach resented by Party diehards, sometimes proved expedient to officials concerned with foreign policy. That the paper seemed acceptable abroad had its obvious advantages for the rulers in Berlin. For instance, the fact that the *Frankfurter Zeitung* had continuously abstained from sharp attacks on the Austrian State between 1933 and 1937 made it unobjectionable to the Austrian Government. After the entire German press had been excluded from Austrian territory—a state of affairs which lasted from February 1934 to the conclusion of the "Gentlemen's Agreement" between the two countries on 11 July 1936— the *Frankfurter Zeitung* was the only paper to be admitted into Austria.[2]

Later the *Frankfurter Zeitung* was one of six leading German papers allowed into Austria and therefore of considerable propaganda value from the German Government's point of view. These newspapers had to abstain from any outspoken criticism of the conditions in Austria and had to rely on a more subtle ideological propaganda such as emphasis on the idea of Greater Germany.[3] Often they were allotted a special task, the writing of a special article for their Austrian edition, not to be carried by other German journals. On 15 January 1937, for instance, the Berlin representatives of these six newspapers were instructed by Herr Stephan to print a special comment for their Austrian readers on the exhibition in the House of German Art in Munich. They were to point out that this was to be a Greater German concern and that artists from Austria were included. This instruction originated in a special request from the Führer who had obviously in mind the usefulness of German cultural propaganda in Austria. However, no reference to the Führer's wishes must appear in these articles. But the editors had to realize that this special task allotted to them was, as Herr Fackler of the Berlin office put it, not only a request, but an order.[4]

The bigger and more reputable non-Party papers, including the *Frankfurter Zeitung,* were frequently given such special tasks for foreign consumption. They did not always originate in Goebbels' Ministry. For instance, in June 1936 Herr Stephan requested the representatives of a

[1] See *Frankfurter Zeitung,* 2 February 1938, article by R.K. "Der Reichsminister des Auswärtigen. Eine Würdigung zu Freiherr v. Neuraths 65. Geburtstag." Neurath who had attended the secret Hitler meeting of 5 November 1937, declared in the interview that the aims of German foreign policy could be achieved without a belligerent conflict.

[2] R.R. Koerner, *So haben sie es damals gemacht.* Die Propagandavorbereitungen zum Österreichanschluss durch das Hitlerregime 1933-1938, Vienna, 1958, pp. 91-92.

[3] Koerner, op. cit., pp. 103-104.

[4] ZSg. 102/4, "Eilige Ausrichtung. Politik." 15 January 1937.

dozen of such papers to refer frequently to the Soviet Russian-Czech Pact in articles, comments and news items. This could be done by their editorial staff, or by their Prague correspondents, or by their experts on problems of military policy. In this case it was the Reichswehr Ministry that was particularly interested in this request.[1]

In January 1937 a small number of journalists from leading papers, both Party and non-Party, were suddenly convened to a special conference and were handed an order from Minister Goebbels that their papers should discredit false reports on German domestic and foreign policy spread by the press abroad. The occasion for this counter-campaign was a report in the Paris newspaper *l'Oeuvre* that Germany was planning to establish herself in Morocco. The journalists were requested to take a stand against the "maddest statements and fantasies on Germany which was said to be guilty of everything possible and impossible."

It throws an interesting light on Goebbels' emphasis on variety that the papers were to discharge this task in different ways. "In order to guarantee variety," the *Völkischer Beobachter* should discuss the theme in a leader, the *Börsenzeitung* in a piece on the front page, the *Deutsche Allgemeine Zeitung* in its column "Our Views". The *Berliner Lokal-anzeiger* should tackle the issue in a comment on a topical item, the *Berliner Tageblatt* in its column "Pro and Con", the *Frankfurter Zeitung* in the form of a reflection (*Glosse*) and the *Essener Nationalzeitung* in a leader. What was required from all these papers was less a rejection of individual false news items than a polemic against their wanton frequency.[2]

But alas, it often proved easier to set such a task than to carry it out. In this case the *Frankfurter Zeitung* incurred the displeasure of Berndt, the influential and unscrupulous Head of the Ministry's Press Department. On the following day the Berlin office of the paper was told brusquely that the *Frankfurter Zeitung* had not given prominence to the false French reports on Morocco. The newspaper was threatened with punishment unless it would splash the item on the top of the front page on the following day, in thick print and big headlines. The hard taskmaster of the press found it particularly deplorable that the paper had not launched a counter-attack by exposing the plans of the French in Morocco. Whilst insisting that the *Frankfurter Zeitung* should refute the foreign lies, he wished that in doing so it should preserve its special character. It is true the Berlin correspondent of the paper managed to convince the suspicious Berndt that the relevant material from the news agency DNB had only reached his paper after the time for stop-press of the Reich edition. But he was nevertheless told that his paper should oblige by printing the relevant DNB material next day at the head of the issue.[3]

[1] ZSg. 102/2, letter to Reifenberg from the Berlin office of *Frankfurter Zeitung*, 3 June 1936.
[2] ZSg. 102/4, 9 January 1937.
[3] ZSg. 102/4, 11 January 1936.

Undoubtedly the Berlin office of the paper frequently felt itself placed between the devil and the deep blue sea. It had to convey the official instructions and directives to the editors in Frankfurt precisely, while the latter were obliged to read between the lines in order to find out how far they could venture to strike a note of their own. With the official material sent by teleprinter from the Press Conferences in Berlin, there were other channels by which to add interpretations and advice. The Berlin office tried to indicate the weak spots of the "enemy," i.e. the official propaganda bureaucracy, in telephone conversations on the directives, or through explanatory letters which were often carried by travellers to escape the official control. "And the enemy was always the Propaganda Ministry." [1]

But the fact of constant tension between the Propaganda Ministry and the Berlin representatives of the paper must not be exaggerated. For as long as the paper propounded the main official line, a certain limited margin of freedom could be conceded to it.

As early as the autumn of 1933 the paper can be compared with a flute on which soft and attractive melodies were played to the requirements of Berlin. Kircher maintained that the nation was convinced of the honesty of the German will to peace and understanding.[2] By April, 1934 Kircher had identified himself and the paper more closely with the official course of German foreign policy and asked the somewhat bitter question: "Those people on whose tongue there is always a malicious, ironic, biting, arrogant word—have these same people ever thought earnestly about our German position? By 'earnestly' I mean from this point of view: that in London, Paris, or Prague it is very easy to deny the new Germany, but that *inside Germany* we are faced with the overriding reality of the German community at grips with Fate." [3]

The editors did their best to make up for their reluctance to conform rigidly with the doctrines and attitudes of National Socialism in home affairs by giving ample and well reasoned support to Hitler's foreign policy. It was not only that the paper had to toe the line of the directives issued by the authorities in Berlin, but in the field of foreign affairs it did so with conviction, with the feeling of serving a worthy cause, the return of Germany to a respected position in Europe and in the world.

If on every occasion the paper underlined the peaceful intentions of Hitler's dynamic foreign policy, it tried to commit the regime to them. A passage from the paper's article to celebrate Hitler's 45th birthday in April, 1934 furnishes a good example:

"A whole people, without exception, stands behind those basic pronouncements in which Adolf Hitler defined Germany's position in Europe:

[1] Fritz Sänger, "Das schmale Seil" in *Ein Jahrhundert Frankfurter Zeitung 1856-1956*, pp. 23-24.

[2] Article "Zwei Tatsachen bleiben", *Frankfurter Zeitung*, 19 October 1933, nos. 763-764.

[3] Article "Zeitung und Ausland" by R.K. *Frankfurter Zeitung*, 19 April 1934, nos. 196-197.

there is no objective in Europe that would warrant a war; Germany and France could not find a better way to put an end to their common rivalry than in the spirit of the Front Generation; Germany can be counted on as a partner in any consolidation of Europe only if she has possession of its truth."

People abroad were advised not to forget
"that the spokesman for German foreign policy is supported by the convictions of a whole nation. As far as the outside world is concerned, there is only *one* Germany." [1]

Soon afterwards Kircher warmly welcomed the Anglo-German naval agreement of 1935, by which, he argued, the Führer had "destroyed the ghost of a new German Imperialism for good." [2] The Anglo-German agreement was hailed as "a powerful spur" and a "moral pressure"; it was "superimposing Reason on Europe." But unlike many of his colleagues this former London correspondent had a clear insight into the English national character, which in his opinion was far from being decadent. On the contrary, when revisiting the British Isles at the end of 1935, Kircher registered as his strongest impression the great increase in "the vitality and the self-assurance of that nation." Their prestige in the world, the British thought, had never been greater and never had England been more self-confident.[3]

Kircher acquired a special knack of developing extremely plausible arguments to suit the German foreign policy of the day. He hardly ever threatened or bullied, but instead reasoned and persuaded with a dexterity which was sometimes reminiscent of the skill of a Friedrich von Gentz. However, while Gentz had enjoyed the confidence of Chancellor Metternich, Kircher found himself restricted to contacts with officials of the Foreign Ministry in Berlin. He tried to be constructive and to hope and plead for European readjustment as Hitler desired it, because he told himself and his readers that this meant true co-operation and peace.

Kircher's snake-like but guarded plausibility was particularly evident after the world's sour reaction to Hitler's remilitarization of the Rhineland in March, 1936. He took a constructive line to make Hitler's *fait accompli* as palatable as possible to the Western powers:
"Thus it became an accomplished fact, and will remain so. The only person who can change things is the man who is willing to make war. No people wants war. Certainly not the English." [4]

The English, Kircher insisted, had realized to their surprise
"that, despite everything, Hitler has opened wide the door to good rela-

[1] Article "Adolf Hitler, zum 45. Geburtstag des Führers", *Frankfurter Zeitung*, 20 April 1935, no. 203.
[2] Article "Etappe England" by R.K., *Frankfurter Zeitung*, 23 June 1935, nos. 315-316.
[3] Article "England fühlt sich stark, ein Reisebericht", by R.K., *Frankfurter Zeitung*, 24 November 1935, nos. 600-601.
[4] Article "Die Aussichten. Zu den deutschen Vorschlägen", by R. K., *Frankfurter Zeitung*, 11 March 1936, nos. 130-131.

tions and to a tie between the peoples.—'The only hope,' says Baldwin, 'lies in the renewal of that three-sided friendship.'—For us too, that is spoken from the heart." [1]

Though there was probably a Goebbels directive behind this line, only Kircher could have presented it with so much sweet reasonableness and affability. These qualities seemed particularly suited to an argument with unemotional English politicians such as Lord Lothian, by no means an opponent of Germany. Quoting with approval Lothian's remark in an article in May 1937 that "the system of alliances was the murderous trap of the nations" and that "the question of the future of Germany was the most important world problem," Kircher then commented on Lothian's statement:

"The question that most occupies the English is whether a rearmed Germany will respect the national independence and autonomy of the new East European nations." [2]

Lothian pointed out that many English people felt suspicious of Germany's intentions. English public opinion on Germany was not yet fixed, but once it had stiffened into an anti-German attitude, it would spread to the Dominions and America and obtain the support of the "well-known persistent fighting power and the immense resources of the English speaking world." What was Kircher's reply? Simply a reference to Hitler's innumerable professions of his peaceful aims, which had made it quite clear firstly that he favoured genuine co-operation and secondly that the Reich did not deny recognition to any nationality and was determined to respect the right to live of other nations. [3]

Kircher tried his utmost to persuade the English to grant concessions to Germany and by doing so to assure the Reich's co-operative attitude. He suggested that the great powers of the West should find the path to each other. [4]

When at the same time a closer co-operation between the partners of the Berlin-Rome axis was emphasized by Mussolini's visit to Germany, Kircher headed his article dutifully "115 million people are united," and claimed that the official communiqué issued on that occasion, was accom-

[1] Ibid.
[2] Article "Europäische Zukunft. Ein Aufsatz Lord Lothians", by R.K. *Frankfurter Zeitung*, 6 May 1937, nos. 227-228. For Lord Lothian's views on Germany 1936-1939, see J.K.M. Butler, *Lord Lothian*, London, 1960, ch. XII.
[3] Ibid.
[4] As he put it neatly in an article on the European balance of power: "Especially, insofar as there really exists a readiness to settle unsatisfied claims, England can count on Germany's honest and very glad agreement and cooperation. For it is not Germany that wants to upset the European balance in Spain or anywhere else (a balance which, moreover, was never really in existence until Germany's rebirth). Germany is only concerned to see that the balance is not upset by the Soviet power. The Great Powers should, in the end, be able to find the way to each other in peace." Article "Debatte um das Gleichgewicht", by R.K., *Frankfurter Zeitung*, 17 September 1937, nos, 473-474.

panied "by a unique cry, such as the world had never heard before: Peace in Strength and Honour." [1]

With all its temperate language the *Frankfurter Zeitung* followed the official line. At the beginning of 1937 for instance the paper recommended courage and "the will to self-preservation." [2] Soon afterwards in a critical article on Beneš, Kircher talked of the change that had transformed a Germany weakly and painfully groping her way to "a strong Germany, a fully self-assured Reich which was looking after German interests with passionate zeal." Her intense confidence was bound to increase the courage of the Sudeten Germans.[3] Still Kircher's tunes did not sound too harsh. While proclaiming the interest of the Reich in the fate of the 3½ million Sudeten Germans Kircher argued with ambiguous dexterity: "No German government has questioned Czechoslovakia's right to exist. . . . Rather, Czechoslovakia stands before us as an accomplished fact. . . . *We* did not help to create it, *we* thus have no responsibility for the work of Versailles and Trianon." [4] In reviewing the plight of the Sudeten Germans Kircher, who had once written a book "Fair Play" on the English way of life, asked pointedly "But where, during all these years, were the Englishmen with their legendary 'fairness' . . . with their famous national spirit?" Was the request of the Sudeten Germans to be treated as "equals among equals" really unreasonable? [5]

Even when the language of the party papers had long become aggressive and bullying, the *Frankfurter Zeitung* stuck to an unemotional and moderate tone in its political comments and pronouncements. The world outside, it suggested, should regard Hitler's Germany as a strong and dynamic but not as a belligerent and aggressive power. To assert this persuasively became more difficult after the events of 1938. As Kircher and his colleagues genuinely wanted peace, their assurances of Germany's peaceful intentions were not so hypocritical as they may sound when contrasted with Hitler's determination at the time to risk a war of conquest. There was not only propaganda but also wishful thinking behind sentences like these:

"The power derives from the racial idea in the mind of Adolf Hitler, and his passion, his fanatical belief, drives Germany ahead. But this racial concept (*völkische Idee*) also defines at the same time the external goals, a fact which old-style imperialists cannot grasp. The course of history will, we hope, enlighten them." [6]

[1] Article "Einhundertfünfzehn Millionen sind einig", by R.K., *Frankfurter Zeitung,* 29 September 1937, nos. 495-496.

[2] Article "Masstab. Zum Jahresanfang", *Frankfurter Zeitung,* 3 January 1937, nos. 4-5.

[3] Article "Herr Benesch als Nachbar", by R.K., *Frankfurter Zeitung,* 7 March 1937, nos. 121-122.

[4] Ibid.

[5] Ibid.

[6] Article "Ins siebente Jahr", by R.K., *Frankfurter Zeitung,* 29 January 1939, nos. 53-54.

As Kircher was to realize when it was too late, the course of history gave the lie to this hopeful view. To the very day of the outbreak of the Second World War he seems to have clung to the fiction that peace would be preserved. On 1 September, 1939 he left Berlin and visited the paper's headquarters in Frankfurt. He and his colleagues reacted with "a kind of dull horror" to the fact that war had begun. Kircher, who collapsed and was shaken by a fit of hysterical sobbing, confessed to his closest associates: "I did not believe it." [1] Indeed this surprising admission throws light on the credibility of so outstanding a journalist, of whom a friend and former colleague had to say in retrospect: "Of course we cannot spare one of the best journalists in Germany the reproach that he failed to take seriously enough the increasing momentum of the crises brought on by Hitler's policy of expansion." [2] At the same time the episode reveals the Macchiavellian skill of Hitler, Goebbels and their lieutenants in veiling their true intentions. It was the tragic mistake of the men of the *Frankfurter Zeitung* that they believed Hitler because they wanted to believe him and that by doing so they contributed *nolens volens* their share to the creation of a state of foolery and confusion which in the end enabled Hitler to drag his nation and the world into a lengthy and bloody war.

By then the paper had long become a tool of the Propaganda Ministry which "planted" in it news items calculated to influence public opinion abroad. A significant example is the following urgent message sent to the Frankfurt paper from its Berlin office ten weeks before the outbreak of the Second World War:

"Important directive Politics 14th June.

Please publish the following news in the Reich edition on the second page. It should appear on the second page and without any special emphasis . . . The best way would be to print it for instance as second item in the column 'From the Reich,' if the column happens to be on page 2 . . . We alone are carrying this news item. The other papers will not take it over, with the exception of the *Börsenzeitung,* which will do so tomorrow as a quotation from the *Frankfurter Zeitung.* It should originate from Frankfurt in the manner in which we are used to print news from Frankfurt. The news item must not be changed, above all the introduction must run: "As we learn from Group Command 2 of the Army." The whole thing originates, of course, in the Press Department. Please confirm in the course of the day that the news will be published as desired."

Then followed the prescribed news item:

"Frankfurt, 14 June, 1939. As we learn from Group Command 2 of the Army, in the near future larger exercises will begin in the Western fortifications by the army formations destined for their occupation. The manoeuvres will take some time and will take place along the entire

[1] B. Reifenberg, op. cit. p. 52.
[2] Ibid.

Western frontier. They have the purpose of training the troops for fighting and living in fortifications." [1]

This news item formed part and parcel of Goebbels' propaganda designed to emphasize the invincibility of Germany's Western frontier, of the "impregnable *Westwall*." Destined for foreign consumption it had a political rather than a military motive. It was unimportant to Goebbels' Ministry whether the editors felt happy about the propaganda line or were chilled by it, whether they believed that there would or would not be another world war. What mattered to the regime was that it could conveniently use the paper as a first-rate channel for spreading news and views to reach readers abroad, who might still believe in its former liberal reputation.

During the war, too, the *Frankfurter Zeitung* was utilized by the Propaganda Ministry for the "planting" of stories and the misleading of the enemy. A year before Hitler was to give orders to an unwilling Goebbels to close the paper down, Goebbels used it to launch an "unauthorized" article, in which the economic and operational possibilities of an attack on Moscow were discussed. As Goebbels noted in his diary the article was an attempt to divert the enemy's attention to a sector different from the one in which the Germans actually were planning to attack.[2] After publication the issue in question was duly "officially suppressed" and to complete the pose, denounced at the Ministry's Daily Press Conference.[3]

When in May, 1943 the Führer insisted that the paper he had always loathed must disappear, it had long become only a shadow of its former proud self. One may sympathize with the plight of the few members of the original staff who carried on to the bitter end, but there can be little doubt that the survival of the *Frankfurter Zeitung* for ten years in the Third Reich paid dividends to the regime rather than to the defeated cause of German liberalism.[4]

[1] ZSg. 102/17. On the same day the Frankfurt office acknowledged receipt of this instruction: "Politics: we shall carry the news item as desired on p. 2 in the column: 'From the Reich'. We have thought out the following heading: 'Army exercises in the Western Fortifications'."

[2] *The Goebbels Diaries*, ed. Louis Lochner, London, 1948, Entry of May 15, 1942, p. 159.

[3] Op. cit., entry of May 20, 1942, p. 166.

[4] For Hitler's decision to close the *Frankfurter Zeitung* see Goebbels' diary entry of May 10th 1943, op. cit., p. 287. Goebbels claims that he was in favour of retaining the paper, but as the Führer was stubbornly of the opposite opinion it was doomed. See also the remarks by Otto Dietrich, *12 Jahre mit Hitler*, Munich, 1955, pp. 202-203. A factual but by no means flattering article in the *Frankfurter Zeitung* of 23 March 1943 on Hitler's early Party friend, Dietrich Eckhardt, on his 75th anniversary—Eckhardt died in 1923—had incurred the displeasure of the widow of Professor Troost, the Nazi architect, and then caused Bormann and Hitler to eliminate the paper. The offensive article has been reprinted in *Ein Jahrhundert Frankfurter Zeitung*, pp. 36-39. The last issue of the *Frankfurter Zeitung* appeared on 31 August 1943. For a number of reasons the paper was not revived after the collapse of the Nazi regime.

CHAPTER 6

Soft Pedalling For Foreign Consumption
(1933-36)

1. "A Typical German Phenomenon."

DURING the first two or three years of the Third Reich German propaganda to the West struck an unexpectedly peaceful note, avoiding on the whole the threatening language it employed later. Goebbels, in particular, was hard at work trying to pacify foreign suspicions, to dispel "misunderstandings" of the men and policies of the new Germany and to make the regime look as respectable and impressive as possible.

Early in April 1933, a few weeks after his appointment as Minister for Propaganda and People's Enlightenment, Goebbels addressed foreign press correspondents in Berlin. He took pains to explain and justify the restrictions now imposed upon the German press. It is true, he decried the idea of an absolute and irresponsible freedom of the press as the false ideal of a by-gone liberal age. But at the same time he assured his listeners that this new emphasis on national discipline of the press was imperative in order to remove a deficiency unknown in the countries of the West. Without any personal knowledge of those countries Dr. Goebbels asserted boldly that in England and France as a matter of course "in spite of all party political conflicts, public opinion is uniformly led and uniformly moulded as far as the great issues of national importance are concerned. The closer the concentrated national will of a nation, the more successful will be the effect of that national discipline." [1] In Germany freedom of the press had been badly abused during the previous regime. "Nowhere else in the world would it have been possible for the symbols of national honour and freedom, the foundation of the *Volkstum*, the most elementary moral laws of family, state and church to be trampled on and besmirched under the cover of an excessive intellectual freedom." Before this foreign audience Goebbels pursued a conservative rather than a radical line. The irresponsible attitudes of yesterday, he asserted, were being replaced by a strong sense of responsibility to the nation which was particularly marked in the new leaders. He adroitly mixed flattering remarks on the high office of the press with insistence on its responsi-

[1] Goebbels, *Signale der neuen Zeit*, Munich, 1934, p. 129.

143

bility to the collective. He argued that as the press was daily subject to the criticism of the entire nation, only the best men and writers were good enough for it. The profession of the journalist carried the highest national responsibility with it, and only people worthy of this responsibility and possessing sufficient moral maturity for it were entitled to join in and work with the press.[1]

In September, 1933 Goebbels paid a brief visit to Geneva. He was accompanied by a dozen SS men who shadowed him wherever he went. Though he appeared at sessions of the League of Nations Assembly, then in the thick of endless debates on disarmament, he studiously avoided addressing it. The largest table in the dining room of the hotel in which the German delegation stayed "was always reserved for Goebbels and he presided at it every evening and held forth to his admirers." [2] He had with him his old friend Julius Lippert, who had been recently appointed Lord Mayor of Berlin. They liked to indulge in loud anti-Semitic dialogues, gloating over the elimination of the Kurfürstendamm Jews from public life. Although on those occasions Goebbels seems to have "behaved like a complete cad," [3] he appeared as plausible and civilized as he could be when he addressed a packed gathering of foreign correspondents at a reception arranged by his delegation. Adapting his approach to this critical audience he succeeded in evoking some applause, which the Nazi propagandists promptly claimed to be spontaneous and "much stronger and more intense than international courtesy demanded." [4] An English correspondent reported that the tone of the Goebbels' plea "was extremely mild and it was clearly intended as a useful conciliatory gesture in the negotiations for disarmament, contrasting oddly with some former utterances from the same source." [5]

Goebbels eloquently presented National Socialism as a respectable though revolutionary movement, full of determination, but definitely a factor for the preservation of peace. Complaining bitterly of the mistrust and misunderstanding of the new regime by the outside world he made much of the fact that it had come to power by legal means. It was a complete misinterpretation of the principle of democracy, he suggested, to conclude from it that the people wanted to rule themselves.[6] The National Socialist regime was in fact a new type of democracy, governing by the will of the people (who wished to be governed with firmness and authority), but determined not to suffer any criticism or opposition. Goebbels indeed drew "a touching picture of a paternal State putting its opponents through a course of concentration camp (very pleasant places,

[1] Op. cit., p. 133.
[2] Wolfgang zu Putlitz, *The Putlitz Dossier*, London, 1957, p. 84.
[3] Op. cit., p. 83.
[4] See the foreword to this address in Geneva on 28 September 1933, "National Socialist Germany and her task for peace" in his book, *Signale der neuen Zeit*, p. 234.
[5] *The Times*, 29 September 1933.
[6] *Signale der neuen Zeit*, p. 240.

he assured his audience, and fully open to inspection), in the process of making them worthy citizens." [1]

National Socialism was made out to be the St. George who had liberated Germany from the two hydras of unemployment and Bolshevism. National Socialism had performed a miracle "by overcoming the feeling of despair which had seized very wide circles of the German nation with a new optimism of believers." There was above all the European aspect of the National Socialist victory. For the first time Goebbels introduced the theme of Germany as a European bulwark which subsequent National Socialist propaganda was to retain to the very end of the regime. "We believe," he declared, "the Europe of the future will be in our debt for our having erected a firm wall against anarchy and chaos. Should Germany become a prey to Bolshevism, it would be impossible to stop it and the entire civilization of the West would be buried under its flood." The possibility of this Bolshevist onslaught justified harsh measures and what was required was not so much democratic government, but good government.

Goebbels emphatically denied any intention of the regime to export National Socialism to other countries. "It is a typical German phenomenon," he remarked. The Germans were too much preoccupied with their own problems to have time or cause "for carrying out a more or less mystical world mission beyond the frontiers of our own country." The emphasis was on peace, not on conquest. Peace and the reconstruction of Europe were the great concern of the German Chancellor, who had witnessed the horrors of the last war as a simple corporal. "What Germany had to settle with the world was the question of its national existence," remarked Goebbels. "The distress from which Europe was suffering is too great to allow its causes to be overlooked . . . It has nothing to do with revenge or war, and it would be a good thing if these two words were eliminated from the discussion between the nations." [2]

As an anti-Bolshevist stronghold of order and authority the new Germany had much to offer to the world. "May all unite who are of good will," Goebbels concluded gently, "with the noble intention of mitigating the worries of the nations and of serving the general welfare." As far as Germany was concerned, she was "ready in all sincerity to co-operate for the peace of the world." [3] Dr. Stresemann could not have expressed the

---

[1] *The Times*, Geneva correspondent, 29 September 1933.
[2] *Signale der neuen Zeit*, p. 245.
[3] Op. cit., p. 249. In 1934 a Paris newspaper, the *Petit Parisien*, published a number of secret instructions said to have been issued by Goebbels to the press attachés of German diplomatic missions in the autumn 1933 after Germany had left the League of Nations. They appeared under the title *Les Instructions Secrètes de la Propaganda Allemande* and had allegedly been obtained by the French journal from a German newspaperman who had smuggled them out of his country. In the absence of the originals it seems uncertain if they can be regarded as authentic. However, their general tenor corresponds with the line taken by Goebbels in his speeches and directives to the German

German wish for co-operation with the West more neatly. A few weeks before the new Germany dramatically broke its connection with the League of Nations, Goebbels had persuasively voiced his nation's desire to live in peace and harmony with the world. Some of his listeners may have begun to wonder if this young Minister was really a wolf in sheep's clothing, or if the Nazis were as ruthless as they were depicted to be by German emigrés and Western supporters of the Left.

It is not surprising that the Propaganda Ministry wanted the newspapers to make much of the attention paid to Goebbels' Geneva speech by the foreign press. It even allowed the quoting of unfavourable foreign press comments: "since official circles consider it desirable to produce also a lasting echo in the German public." [1]

Six months later Goebbels still pursued the same cautious line. The old method had failed in international affairs, he told a gathering of foreign journalists at his Ministry on 18 February, 1934, there was "only one salvation for our sorely tried continent that had suffered so much: to seek new possible solutions with new methods." The youth who had gone through war was right to raise that demand which in Germany had been satisfied by National Socialism.

It all sounded very suave, sober and moderate. Germany wanted peace, she wished to work and to reconstruct in peace; she showed the same respect and the same sympathy for all the nations, but she also demanded from them that they viewed her gigantic fight against misery with respect and without bias. Germany had "given evidence of her love of peace." [2] She had to be listened to when she raised her claims for equal rights among the other nations. It was a seductive tune by which this master of political camouflage invited foreign journalists "to get to know the true, the eternal Germany" and thus "to render services of immeasurable value to the forthcoming better Europe." [3]

Goebbels' aggressive outburst after the massacres of 30 June 1934 was far removed from such sweet reasoning. The function of his radio ad-

---

press quoted in this chapter. The instructions declared it imperative that "to the outside world our propaganda must underline impressively that Germany does not wish for anything but a peaceful settlement of all pending problems." See C. Riess, *Joseph Goebbels*, p. 148.

[1] Dertinger to Neuhaus, Hamburg, 25 September 1933 (Brammer).

[2] Goebbels could have pointed to the Concordat with the Vatican of July 1933 and to the Non-aggression and Friendship Treaty between Germany and Poland, concluded in January 1934, as part of this "evidence".

[3] *Signale der neuen Zeit*, pp. 351-352. A similar tune could be heard in September 1934 when Goebbels addressed a delegation of Spanish and French publishers of technical and professional journals who had come to Berlin from an international congress in Warsaw. Goebbels emphasized the preservation of world peace, the need for truth and the necessity of trying to understand the different mentality of other nations. In order to understand another people, one should not judge it from the viewpoint of one's own nation, but try to understand it from its own premises.

dress, "The 30th June as mirrored abroad," [1] was obviously to reassure the German public and to blacken the foreign press. In Germany, he declared, there was true discipline of the editors, so often maligned by foreign critics, while some of the press abroad had reported the events of June 30 in Germany by way of "lies, calumnies and distortions almost without a parallel in journalism." "The 30th June" had occurred in Germany, Goebbels declared boldly, "without hitch *(reibungslos)* and without convulsion *(Erschütterung)*." By "his authority and admirable boldness" the Führer had simply overcome with blitz-like speed the revolt of a small clique of saboteurs and of abnormally ambitious pushers *(Ehrgeizlinge)*. There was peace and order all over Germany and everyday life proceeded as usual. If any change had taken place in Germany it was a growth of the people's love and loyalty to the Führer. The German press had never been permitted to insult the statesmen of other nations, to belittle them and to treat them with contempt. Foreign papers had, however, not reciprocated with the same tact and reserve.

The Propaganda Minister then produced a long list of alleged false rumours and reports on the events of 30 June. French and English papers had invented attempts on Hitler's life, while others had asserted that his dictatorship was now based on the Reichswehr (a suggestion close to the truth). Moscow radio had spread the story of the execution of prominent men still very much alive, such as Generals von Hammerstein and von Fritzsch. Goebbels obviously used the refutation of such lies as a convenient trick to distract attention from the enormity of the crimes committed on 30 June. By exposing false reports he threw doubt on foreign accounts which came only too close to the unpleasant truth. The Minister indulged in a bout of moral indignation, complaining that even papers such as *The Times* wrote that the revolt had been put down by gangster methods—a judgment with which the historian has little occasion to quarrel. Goebbels worked himself up into a violent frenzy over this "conscious and systematic poisoning of public opinion" abroad, threatening with expulsion foreign correspondents in the Reich responsible for such fabrications.

This outburst, obviously motivated by the conviction that "attack is the best means of defence" was not well received abroad. Even Alfred Rosenberg, the head of the "Party Office of Foreign Affairs," who was then favouring an Anglo-German rapprochement, condemned it severely— in the secret pages of his diary. He observed on 13 July: "As was to be expected, the 'address' of Dr. Goebbels on the evening of 30 June has created a truly catastrophic impression all over the world. Two phone calls from London: the Air Ministry was horrified: not since Bethmann's speech (in 1914) has any speech delivered in Germany had such a depressing effect. Our enemies (in England) declared: has our francophile

[1] Delivered on 10 July; for the text, see *Frankfurter Zeitung*, 11 July 1934.

attitude not been more than justified? . . . However well Hitler may now speak, he could not change the mood." [1]

If it was Goebbels' task to explain and to justify all measures taken by the Government, it was his trick to present the more important of them as contributions to a European peace. Though in many ways the Propaganda Minister echoed his master's voice, the ingenuity with which he backed up Hitler's dynamic military and foreign policy was his own. On 16 March 1935, Hitler stated that the German Government was re-introducing conscription, and would aim at the setting-up of an army consisting of 36 divisions with a total strength of 550,000 men. The Führer used the doubling of the period of service in the French army, announced by the French Government on 13 March, as a pretext to justify his measure which violated the stipulations of the Treaty of Versailles. Whereas Germany alone had disarmed, declared Hitler, the other nations had not followed suit, but were about to increase their armaments, a situation which forced Germany to do the same. [2]

There were notes of protest from the English and the French Governments, but the planned visit to Berlin of the British Foreign Secretary, Sir John Simon, and of Mr. Anthony Eden, was only postponed and not cancelled. On 19 March Goebbels published a very mild article under the caption "Clarity and Logic" obviously destined to dispel the clouds of anxiety felt in the capitals of the West over the challenging German step. He deplored the "highly dangerous war psychosis among the nations, the press of which had indulged during previous months in fantastic guesses on the intentions of the German government in this respect. Foreign circles had complained about the secretiveness surrounding German rearmament. What was needed was clarity. This has now been provided by the historical deed of the Führer on 16 March. The world now knows where it stands." [4] Goebbels skilfully twisted a speech by Mr. Winston Churchill delivered in the House of Commons on 28 November, 1934. With a singular clarity of vision Churchill had urged in it the vital necessity of increasing the strength of Britain's national defence and

---

[1] *Das politische Tagebuch Alfred Rosenbergs 1933/34 und 1939/40,* edited by Dr. Hans-Günther Seraphim, Quellensammlung zur Kulturgeschichte, vol. 8, Göttingen, 1956, p. 39, entry of 13 July 1934. Rosenberg had received a similar report on negative reactions in Warsaw official circles. There they attributed the responsibility for the many rumours circulating during the purge to the Berlin Propaganda Ministry which had not issued any information. In the United States the impression of Goebbels' speech had also been very unfavourable; Goebbels, Rosenberg felt, had "confused the position of a Reich Minister with that of a suburban agitator". He lacked "any sense of proportion; one cannot make foreign policy out of mere self-complacency."

[2] See the Proclamation of the Reich Government to the German people of 16 March 1935, *Dokumente der Deutschen Politik und Geschichte von 1848 bis zur Gegenwart,* vol. IV, pp. 216-218.

[3] Article "Klarheit und Logik", *Der Angriff,* 19 March 1935, reprinted in *Wetterleuchten, Aufsätze aus der Kampfzeit,* Munich, 1939, pp. 385-388.

[4] Ibid.

particularly that of her force. To do so, he had argued, was "not to assert the imminence of war. . . ." He did not believe, he had added, that war was imminent and that war was inevitable. The great new fact which rivetted the attention of every country in Europe and which threw almost all other issues into the background was the rearming of a nationalist and militarist Germany.[1]

In his very cautious reply to the speech for the British Government, Baldwin had remarked that "one of the foundations of the *malaise* today in Europe" was "not only fear, but ignorance outside Germany" of the extent of her rearmaments "and secrecy inside." [2] Referring to that exchange of views in the Commons Goebbels fully agreed with the words of Mr. Churchill which he in fact had never used—that there was "no reason to assume that Germany will attack." [3] Regarding Baldwin's uncomfortable *malaise,* Goebbels retorted smartly: "Can one blame the German government if it has removed the causes of this malaise four months later with a frank statement, putting an end to fear and ignorance!" [4] As usual, it was for Goebbels only one step from plausibility to sophistry. "Not the armed, but the disarmed Germany," he assured the world, "disquietened Europe." By the introduction of universal conscription, the balance had been restored, "necessary for arriving at fruitful discussions of the great unsolved problems of world politics." Germany wanted "to co-operate with others in peace; it needs it as much as other nations."

Goebbels here clearly followed his master's voice as the Führer's speech before the Reichstag on 21 May had contained "most of the tricks with which Hitler lulled the suspicions and raised the hopes of the gullible. His answer to the censure of the Powers was not defiance, but redoubled assurances of peace, an appeal to reason, justice and conscience. The new Germany, he protested, was misunderstood, and his own attitude misrepresented." [5]

On 19 March Goebbels had anticipated this emphasis on peace. All nations, he had written, were filled with a deep longing for it. "No one in Europe with a modicum of a sense of responsibility believes that the damages of a war which could not be eliminated in seventeen years of peace, could be removed by a new war." [6] Illusions and wishful dreams were to be discarded, clarity and a sense of logic to be encouraged. Let sweet reason and common sense prevail and a happier turn in European affairs will come.[7] "The often deplored secretiveness (*Geheimnistuerei*) is

[1] *The Times,* 29 November 1934.
[2] Ibid.
[3] As for Churchill's anticipation of the extent of German rearmament, this had not even been reached by the new law of 16 March 1935.
[4] *Wetterleuchten,* pp. 386-387.
[5] A. Bullock, *Hitler, A Study in Tyranny,* London, 1952, pp. 305-306.
[6] *Wetterleuchten,* p. 388.
[7] In an address Goebbels delivered in Karlsruhe on 1 April 1935 at the celebration of the tenth anniversary of the formation of the Gau Baden he took a similar line: "Germany does not contemplate war. We regard the eternal

now at an end; the atmosphere has been purified." If the visit of Sir John Simon and Mr. Anthony Eden to Berlin which did not take place after all at the end of March, was "a triumph for Hitler's diplomacy"[1] then Goebbels could justly claim some reflected glory from it.

2. A Piece of Window Dressing

In 1935 and 1936 many foreign visitors were greatly taken with the strength and the splendour of the Third Reich. In particular the Olympic Games held in Berlin in the summer of 1936 proved a windfall for the Hitler Government. That Berlin had been chosen was no merit of the National Socialist regime. This had been arranged by the Government of the Weimar Republic and by the Olympic Committee as far back as 1928 and 1932. Now it offered the National Socialists a splendid opportunity to indulge in clever window dressing. The leading sportsmen and sportswomen and their many fans from all over the globe soon praised the effective organization of the Games, the lavish hospitality, the thoughtful and varied entertainment provided for them. Moreover, the German authorities had banned all outward traces of rudeness and barbarism to make things as "nationally representative" as possible. The foreigners were to experience a kind of German "drawing room" behaviour. Signs such as "Jews not wanted here" had been carefully eliminated from restaurants, hotels and shops and Streicher's vulgar and pornographic weekly *Der Stürmer* was temporarily withdrawn from the newsagents.[2]

Before the Olympic Games very definite instructions were issued to the Press. By the end of January, 1936 the papers were warned that in future they must not publish any reports on clashes with foreigners or on any physical force used against Jews in Germany. Such items had to be kept out of all pages including those on local news, "in order not, at the last moment, to provide foreign propaganda with material against the Winter Olympics."[3] Though there was a half-Jewish member in the German hockey team at the Games, the editors were asked "despite a deep-rooted bad habit, to refer to him neither as a Jew nor as a half-

---

talking of war as a crime. It is not true that Germany has demanded the (Polish) Corridor, parts of Czechoslovakia, Austria and Alsace-Lorraine or any other territories. When foreign newspapers spread such lies it is they that upset Europe. We do not threaten anyone, but we also do not allow ourselves to be threatened. We are of the opinion that somewhat less talking and somewhat more reasoning would be very helpful for the world." (*Frankfurter Zeitung*, 2 April 1937).

[1] A. Bullock, op. cit., p. 305.
[2] Heinz Pohle, *Der Rundfunk als Instrument der Politik,* p. 415.
[3] Anweisung Nr. 82, Press Conference 27 January 1936 (Brammer): "With reference to the Winter Olympics it is expressly forbidden in the future to publish news stories about conflicts with foreigners and brawls with Jews."

Jew." On the sports page such a racial deficiency was suddenly declared to be irrelevant.[1]

While Goebbels put the anti-Jewish drive into cold storage for a time, having so many distinguished foreigners in Germany was an opportunity to be exploited to the full for propagating the regime. On 15 June editors were requested "to use the Olympic Games and the preparations for them for extensive propaganda in Germany."

For this the size of the issues was to be enlarged. As the main events of the Olympic Games took place a few months after the plebiscite for Hitler's Rhineland coup, editors were asked to select suitable items from the propaganda material sent to them at that time. The Ministry in Berlin and its regional branches could always assist them in this matter.[2]

The result was gratifying. As an American correspondent covering the Winter Olympic Games in Garmisch-Partenkirchen, observed: "They've greatly impressed most of the visiting foreigners with the lavish but smooth way in which they've run the games and with their kind manners that to us who came from Berlin of course seemed staged." [3] Businessmen and other foreigners were clearly taken in by these skilful and expensive efforts.[4] Seen in historical perspective, they formed a high-water mark in the successful technique of Nazi persuasion by effective mass communications, pageantry and showmanship.

Obviously technical progress in the development of radio played right into the hands of the National Socialist regime. For the first time in the history of the Olympic Games it enabled millions of people in many countries to take part in the events. The German Reichs-Rundfunk-Gesellschaft (RRG) provided facilities for sixty-seven radio reporters from nineteen European and thirteen overseas countries to broadcast their commentaries from Berlin. Altogether 2,500 reports in twenty-eight foreign languages were transmitted in addition to 500 reports in German. As the foreign radio commentators put it in their telegram of thanks to the Reich Minister of People's Enlightenment and Propaganda after the games had ended: "We leave Berlin filled with admiration for the magnificent achievements of the German radio in the technical no less than

[1] Anweisung Nr. 89, Press Conference 28 January 1936 (Brammer): On the other hand only certain local papers were allowed to mention that Helene Mayer, "the well known fencer", who had earlier emigrated to USA, had now returned to play for Germany in the Olympic Games. Comments on her non-Aryan origin and her chances of obtaining a gold medal at the Games were declared "undesirable". Anweisung Nr. 182. Press Conference, 19 February 1936 (Brammer).

[2] Anweisung Nr. 577, Press Conference 15 June 1936 (Brammer).

[3] William L. Shirer, *Berlin Diary, The Journal of a Foreign Correspondent 1934-41,* London, 1941, pp. 46-47.

[4] However, the U.S.A. Ambassador in Berlin, the historian William E. Dodd was sceptical: "The propaganda of it all may have pleased the Germans. It had a bad influence on foreigners, as reported to me, in spite of the fine entertainment of all concerned." (*Ambassador Dodd's Diary, 1933-38,* London, 1941, p. 349).

in the organizational fields." [1] Designed for the peaceful competition between the nations the Olympic Games were sometimes used by the
German authorities for a display of the growing martial strength of the
regime. For instance, the indoor horse jumping contest with German,
Polish, Italian and Japanese horses in the show in Berlin on 1 February
was followed by "an amazing army demonstration: a cavalry parade
(not bad), Black Shirt soldiers marching, then cannon wagons . . . with
tank and machine gun operations. It was intended as a sham battle, the
machine guns being fired by soldiers prostrate on the ground. The vast
audience, 20,000 perhaps, applauded, and Hitler and Göring gave
salutes." [2]

On the evening before, Goebbels had given a lavish reception for
several thousand people at the *Pfaueninsel*, an attractive island in the
Havel that had until 1918 formed part of the private property of Emperor William II. The festival took place in the wide grounds of the island
park. For the occasion a special pontoon bridge had been built to connect
the island with the mainland. Under it thirty soldiers from a pioneer
regiment were posted in boats during the entire night in order to prevent
any vibrations of the bridge. Distinguished visitors from many lands,
ambassadors, generals and admirals, German princes, leading singers,
actors, writers and journalists rubbed shoulders with the stars of sport,
and last but not least, with some tough old Party members. On arrival
they all passed through "a guard of honour formed by young dancers
dressed smartly as pages in rococo style and with burning torches in their
hands. The island was beautifully illuminated. Thousands of lights strung
everywhere, some of them in ancient trees, had the shape of gigantic
butterflies." [3] There was an impressive array of excellent food and cham-
pagne. Several dance bands played incessantly and dancing went on all
through the night "imitating Greek and Victorian performances." Fire-
works were let off and, significantly, even some sort of exercise in warfare
(though not with live shells) was staged which, according to the irate
U.S. Ambassador, annoyed a great many of the guests.[4] As the night
proceeded, some of the tougher Nazi types and a number of the less
reputable girl pages seem to have got out of control and their uninhibited behaviour displeased the more refined among the visitors.

Dodd calculated that the display at which Frau Goebbels "in a white
organdie evening gown" and her smiling husband "clad in a white,
double-breasted gaberdine suit" presided, must have cost the Government
40,000 Marks.[5] But however vulgar the festival may have appeared to
some cultured guests, however cynically Goebbels may have commented
on the doubtful behaviour of some others, the event could prove to the

[1] H. Pohle, op. cit., pp. 417-478.
[2] *Ambassador Dodd's Diary*, pp. 313-314.
[3] See Erich Ebermayer und Hans Roose, *Gefährtin des Teufels*, Hamburg,
1952, pp. 210-211.
[4] *Ambassador Dodd's Diary*, p. 349.
[5] Ibid., see also Curt Riess, *Joseph Goebbels*, p. 166.

world that both he and the regime were firmly entrenched and were determined to stay.

3. How to Comment on Foreign Rulers and Statesmen

Compared with the diatribes against foreign statesmen and politicians which the German press was often obliged to publish in later years, the tendency in the early period was rather to warn the press against such excesses and to admonish it to speak of them cautiously and politely. It is true at times such warnings were a reaction to some aggressive remarks made in one or the other Party papers or by Party speakers, yet by and large the official course of treading warily and of not giving offense to leading foreign politicians unnecessarily was unmistakable during the years 1933-1936. The impression to be created abroad was one of a strong but peaceful nation. Particularly to be avoided was anything which might create fear of German rearmament abroad. In September 1934 the press were advised not to quote Göring's remark that "the German nation must become a nation of flyers." [1]

The newspapers were frequently advised to display a correct attitude to the Heads of foreign States and Prime Ministers. This applied to countries with which Hitler still hoped to come to terms as well as others of which the German press was critical. An endeavour not to offend the English was naturally strongest at the time of the conclusion of the Anglo-German Naval Pact of June, 1935. Hitler then seems to have entertained some hopes of an Anglo-German entente. When early in 1936 King George V was dying, the editors were asked to picture him in their obituaries as "a good and venerable man" and to avoid any reminiscences of the last war in connection with him. The Prince of Wales was to be given a friendly welcome as King. After the death of King George journalists were requested to remember that he had been the ruler of the entire British Commonwealth. The German sympathy did not only extend to the English, but to the whole British nation. [2]

Heads of State were in a different class from responsible politicians. When Foreign Minister Beneš succeeded Thomas Masaryk as President of Czechoslovakia the Propaganda Ministry declared: "The attitude toward the former Foreign Minister and present Prime Minister [sic] of Czechoslovakia must be changed, in accordance with the general policy of not attacking foreign heads of state in the German press. Even though the Czechoslovakian political outlook can be as seriously criticized as before, direct personal attacks on Beneš must without exception be stopped." [3]

This insistence is all the more ironic as it was precisely President

[1] Anweisung Nr. 704, Press Conference 1 September 1934 (Brammer): "Prime Minister Göring's remark that 'The German people must become a nation of aviators' must, for reasons of foreign policy, cease to be quoted in the German press."

[2] Anweisung Nr. 63, Press Conference 21 January 1936 (Brammer).

[3] Anweisung Nr. 1970, Press Conference 18 December 1935 (Brammer).

Beneš who in the summer of 1938 became the *bête noir*, the target of unlimited and calculated abuse by Hitler, Goebbels and the full choir of the German press.[1]

Cabinet ministers of any country with whom Hitler still hoped to come to an arrangement, let alone form an alliance, had to be nursed carefully and possible insults to them strictly avoided. Before the visit of British Cabinet Ministers John Simon and Eden to Berlin in March 1935 the German editors were warned that "the question, of whether the English Foreign Minister Simon is or is not a Jew, must not be discussed under any circumstances. In fact he is not a Jew, but even to raise this question was bound to offend the British Government." [2]

Tact was also recommended when Simon's successor as British Foreign Secretary, Sir Samuel Hoare, ran into stormy weather at the end of the year. Through a leakage the Hoare-Laval Plan became known and British public opinion reacted sharply against it. There is little reason for believing that Hitler could have wished it to succeed. There was indeed relief in Berlin when the agreement was repudiated.[3]

The fact that Hitler had not yet written England off may account for the press directive issued on 15 December, which warned the press not to display any *Schadenfreude* over the failure of the League and the difficulties in which the English Foreign Secretary found himself. On the other hand the critical foreign press, particularly that in England and America, could be fully quoted.[6]

During these early years of the Third Reich the number of taboos imposed on the press was striking: the aim behind them was not to alarm and excite public opinion abroad or to provide it with material for attacks on Germany. Sometimes the reasons for these taboos were quite obvious. There was no point in advertising candid utterances, such as that made by Göring quoted above.

The enforced omission of the names of foreign politicians was more

[1] See below, pp. 174-75.

[2] Anweisung Nr. 1150, Press Conference 1 March 1935 (Brammer). For the visit of the two English statesmen see A. Bullock, *Hitler*, pp. 304-305, also Viscount Simon's memoirs, *Retrospect*, London, 1952, Chapter X, and *The Eden Memoirs, Facing The Dictators*, London, 1962, Chapter VIII.

Equally significant for the efforts of the Nazi rulers at that time to avoid offending English susceptibilities was the advice given to editors in October 1934 not to describe the British Labour Party as Marxist, as many non-Marxists belonged to it. (Anweisung Nr. 865, Press Conference 29 October 1934, Brammer).

[3] See Viscount Templewood (Sir Samuel Hoare), *Nine Troubled Years*, London, 1954, p. 190.

[4] Anweisung Nr. 1948, Press Conference 15 December 1935 (Brammer). On the following day the papers were advised "not to overestimate the English opposition to the Laval-Hoare Plan . . . The English people are so disciplined that even in the present situation the Government is in full control of affairs." Anweisung Nr. 1959, 16 December 1935 (Brammer). After Hoare's fall the editors were ordered to avoid any show of *Schadenfreude*. (Anweisung Nr. 1985, 21(?) December 1935).

far-fetched and seemingly Macchiavellian. In November 1935 orders were given "to drop the name of Churchill definitely from the German press." Apparently the Nazi leaders feared that violent abuse of Churchill in Germany might increase his prestige at home and tempt the Tories to offer him a seat in the Cabinet. Churchill in the wilderness, Churchill in opposition was for the men of the Wilhelmstrasse a lesser evil than Churchill in the Cabinet. In any case, as the Propaganda Ministry saw it: "A German debate over him could be used by the British government to make his entry into the cabinet a question of prestige." [1] To the officials in the Propaganda Ministry the press was like a tap which could be turned on and off at will according to the changing requirements of the political situation. When in 1934 Italo-German relations were at a low ebb and Mussolini, displeased with the vain attempts of the Nazis to obtain a foothold in Austria through the murder of Chancellor Dollfuss, allowed the Italian press to make slighting references to and even to attack National Socialists, Goebbels requested the press to comment "on the curious attacks by the Italian papers on our policy in a superior and cynical fashion, without making a big political issue of it." [2]

It was probably from a wish not to annoy the fellow dictator and not to endanger the intense preparations for German conscription that six months later "for reasons of foreign policy" the press were warned to avoid "any *irridenta* propaganda (South Tyrol, Eupen-Malmedy, etc.)" for the time being including maps which illustrated "Germany's bleeding frontiers." [3]

At the beginning of the Abyssinian conflict the press was told to treat the clash between that country and Italy "with a brutal disinterestedness and with complete objectivity." [4] But when Hitler quickly realized the widening of the rift between Italy and the Western Powers over this issue and the chances for Germany to hitch Italy to her wagon, very different instructions were issued and labelled "particularly important":

"High government authority asks that in the handling of the Abyssinian-Italian question nothing be said that would reflect on the Italians. Avoid anything which would mean a belittling of the Italian army. The Abyssinian affair cannot give Germany the right to judge Italy harshly. Special attention is drawn to this directive, since in the last few days several German newspapers have offended against it." [5]

Any traditional slogans which did not fit into the requirements of Hitler's current policy were quickly discarded. An interesting case in point is the slogan of the "yellow peril" which had been widespread among Germans during World War I, when Japan was an adversary of

[1] Anweisung Nr. 1857, Press Conference 22 November 1935.

[2] Anweisung Nr. 698, Press Conference 24 August 1935 (Brammer).

[3] Anweisung Nr. 1049, Press Conference 21 January 1935, which added: "It is sufficient for the Germans outside the Reich to increase this propaganda campaign because of the vote taken in the Saar."

[4] Anweisung Nr. 1101, Press Conference 12 February 1935 (Brammer).

[5] Anweisung Nr. 1141, Press Conference 27 February 1935 (Brammer).

the Reich. Hitler who had never been anti-Japanese saw no reason for offending that nation by the continued use of outmoded clichés. As early as December, 1933 it was pointed out that expressions such as "yellow peril" and "the drive to the East" *(Drang nach Osten)* should be avoided in articles on Far Eastern problems. A year afterwards another press directive made the reasons for this unambiguously clear: "The Yellow Peril must no longer be made out as a picture of horror, for Germany's attitude toward other races leaves completely open the question of the worth of other races—especially when these races must not, for political reasons, be offended." [1] When it suited the aims of the moment the regime was prepared to decry complexes of thought that were clearly in line with its basic ideology. The fact that a few weeks after the Rhineland coup Hitler thought it expedient rather to soothe and pacify than to alarm foreign public opinion, seems to motivate the following press directive: "Various Pan-Germanic tendencies have lately been observed in the German press. It is pointed out by the highest authority that such articles seriously hamper German foreign policy. The government of the Reich has always emphasized the cultural unity of all Germans in the world, but it has never demanded their political union." [2]—a subtle distinction which Hitler and his lieutenants were the last men to maintain and respect.

When expedient a marked note of caution and restraint was insisted upon, an attitude often required in those early years. There was, for instance, the propaganda drive for the return of the Saar to Germany which began with a big demonstration in the Saar and throughout the Reich many months before the actual plebiscite. Though by April 1934 the German press in the Reich had been instructed to prepare special supplements or issues on this theme, it was at the same time also asked to show restraint in polemics on the Saar question.[3]

Similarly, when a year later the issue of Danzig and of Poland's attitude to this Free City was discussed in Geneva before the League of Nations, the German press was admonished "to show the greatest reserve in its own reports and its quotations from the foreign press on this issue and not to incite its readers." [4]

[1] Anweisung Nr. 1079, Press Conference 4 February 1935 (Brammer). Soon afterwards the Ministry complained that a West German paper had come out with a series of articles full of attacks on Japan. Such attacks had to be avoided at all cost and the problems of the yellow race could no longer be discussed. Anweisung Nr. 1874, Press Conference, 27 November 1935 (Brammer).

[2] Anweisung Nr. 360, Press Conference 21 April 1936 (Brammer).

[3] Anweisung Nr. 420, Press Conference 7 April 1934 (Brammer). As a directive expressed it: "Under no circumstances must the press attack the French people on the grounds of racial inferiority. Similar polemics against the governing commission of the Saarland are to be avoided. . . . In all, the attack must be factual and determined, but its form diplomatic and restrained."

[4] Anweisung Nr. 1486, Press Conference 25 July 1935 (Brammer).

Yet the hoof of Mephistopheles could already be discerned. It only needed the success of the daring Rhineland occupation in March 1936, which Hitler had carried out against the advice of his generals and the criticism of many people abroad, to make him ever more adventurous. Goebbels and his staff then duly followed suit by issuing daring and aggressive propaganda policies. But the contours of things to come can already be traced earlier, in two directives issued at the end of July 1935. The first was a reply to anti-German demonstrations against a German liner in the port of New York. These events were to be splashed "with big headlines" and to be supported by commentaries: "which point out the monstrosity of what had happened and emphasize especially what the Americans would say if an American ship were similarly treated in a German port. In this connection, intensive attention can be focussed again on the whole foreign pack of hounds that have for the last few weeks been in full cry." [1]

Two days later Goebbels or possibly Hitler, went a step further by informing editors of the very great dissatisfaction in authoritative quarters with the inadequate manner in which the press had dealt with unrest abroad. It had not pointed out the discrepancy between the sensational exaggeration of German events in the foreign papers and actual events that had happened abroad. The German journalists were now to comment on the factual news of events abroad in a skilful, effective and sensational manner. [2] These were clear pointers that the pose of "peaceful co-existence" was about to end and that from now on the tone of the German press would become harsher and more belligerent than during this early period of camouflage and soft pedalling.

[1] Anweisung Nr. 1494, Press Conference 27 July 1935 (Brammer).
[2] Anweisung Nr. 1494, DNB-Rundsprüche vom 29 July 1935 (Brammer).

CHAPTER 7

The Stormy Propaganda of Crisis
(1936-1939)

THROUGHOUT the period 1933-1939 National Socialist propaganda on foreign affairs emphasized two lines which were in fact often in contradiction, but were presented as two facets of the same young, constructive, and aspiring regime. On the one hand, the Reich and Hitler were presented as guardians and guarantors of peace; on the other the necessity for action, dynamic expansion to fulfil just claims for more living space was stressed, particularly when the drama of Hitler's successful coups unfolded itself. "To provoke a war," Goebbels told a mass meeting of the Gau Berlin in January 1936, "would be much more dangerous for the National Socialist Government, which foreigners like so much to dub an autocracy, than for any of the so-called democratic states. With them a majority can provoke a war, but this majority will not exist at the end of the war and therefore cannot be made responsible for it." [1]

At the same time German propaganda emphasized more and more the growing military strength of the Reich. As Goebbels put it succinctly, "Germany is not only an island of peace—she is an armed island of peace," she enjoys peace "because she is in a position to defend her freedom." However, at first Germany's need for living space was only played up mildly. Having no colonies and no raw materials the German people had tried to manage somehow. An over-populated Germany needed "the necessary space for her population and her economy." Goebbels assured his audience that "no sensible person in the world was today opposed to such a demand."

1. A SUCCESSFUL GAMBLE AND AN APPEAL TO REASON

Hitler's surprise action of March 1936 in sending German troops into the demilitarized zone of the Rhineland was one of the boldest and most successful ventures of his career. There can be little doubt that it was Hitler alone who decided on taking this daring course. Whereas the lead-

[1] Speech in Berlin on 18 January 1936, see *Frankfurter Zeitung*, 19 January 1936.

158

ing German generals were worried about the possible military repercussions abroad, there is evidence to assume that his measures "met with the absolute approval of the Party members who enjoyed his confidence and who filled important Government posts. Men like Göring and Goebbels certainly encouraged more than warned him. Ribbentrop still claimed at Nuremberg he had advised the Führer that in England they would acquiesce in the restoration of Germany's military sovereignty in the Rhineland." [1]

It was Hitler himself who laid down the German propaganda line explaining and defending his drastic step, in a lengthy memorandum to the signatory powers of the Locarno Pact on 7 March 1936, published by the German News Agency on the same day.[2] Hitler put the blame on France for having signed a Pact with the Soviet Union on 2 May 1935. The obligations which France had undertaken under it were declared incompatible with her earlier obligations under the Locarno Pact. France, Hitler declared, had "answered the friendly offers and peaceful assurances given her by Germany by a military block with the Soviet Union violating the Rhine pact (of Locarno) and exclusively directed against Germany." Through this the Locarno Pact had lost its meaning and Germany was no longer bound by it. "In the interest of the elementary right of a people to secure its frontiers and to preserve its chances of defence, the German Reich Government has therefore restored the full and unrestricted sovereignty of the Reich in the demilitarized zone of the Rhineland as from today."

But to declare old agreements invalid was not enough. The German Government was willing to come to new agreements "in order to forestall any misinterpretations of its intentions and to put the merely defensive character of the measures beyond any doubt and to give expression to her eternal longing (*ihrer ewig gleichbleibenden Sehnsucht*) for a real pacification of Europe between states with equal rights and equally respected." [3] A whole galaxy of new treaties was proposed. Hitler was ready to negotiate with France and Belgium about the establishing of a mutually demilitarized zone, and to conclude a non-aggression pact with these powers guaranteeing the inviolability of the frontiers in the West for twenty-five years. He would also agree to an air pact which would eliminate the danger of any sudden air attacks on the signatory powers. The Führer also expressed his willingness to conclude non-aggression pacts with Germany's Eastern neighbours after the model of the German-Polish pact of 1934. Moreover, Germany was even willing to re-enter the League of Nations, provided that the question of her colonial equality

---

[1] Max Braubach, "Vor zwanzig Jahren. Der Einmarsch der Truppen in die entmilitarisierte Zone am Rhein im März 1936". *Aus Politik und Zeitgeschichte*. Beilage zur Wochenzeitung *Das Parlament*. Vol. ix, 14, March 1936, p. 183.
[2] For the text, see *Dokumente der deutschen Politik und Geschichte*, vol. IV, 1933-1938, pp. 266-270.
[3] Ibid.

and the separation of the League's Covenant from the Treaty of Versailles were clarified.

It was a daring gamble with the German generals shivering uncomfortably in their shoes. By an intuitive recognition of the weakness of the French military and political authorities and of the unwillingness of the British public to enter into a war Hitler had not miscalculated. Though their newspapers were suspicious of Hitler's motives, a large section of British public opinion echoed Lord Lothian's confident words, "after all they are only going into their own back garden." [1]

The sterile Maginot-line mentality of the French Government was hardly a secret to Hitler. The reason for the ultimate decision of the French Government not to take military action was later neatly expressed in the words of the French Minister of War, Maurin, to Reynaud: "When France has spent billions to build the Maginot Line, we should not show ourselves mad enough to advance in front of its protection on Heaven knows what adventure." [2] Hitler knew well how to lay his bait, and how to exploit the French confidence in its eastern belt of fortifications. In the Peace Plan of the Reich Government of 31 March, he again claimed that Germany had no intentions of attacking Belgium or France: "It is known," he added unctuously, "that owing to the gigantic armaments of France and the enormous fortifications on the French eastern frontier, such an attack would be pointless from a military point of view." [3] Hitler continued to use pretty words which read like a page from a liberal tract on the League of Nations.[4]

At the same time Hitler and German propagandists took great pains in demonstrating the unanimous support the new measures were declared to have from the German people. In his address before the Reichstag on the day of the Rhineland coup, Hitler solemnly talked of their "two sacred inner vows"; "Firstly, the pledge not to yield before any power and before any coercion when the restoration of the honour of the German people was at stake, but rather to succumb to the deepest misery honourably than ever to capitulate before it. Secondly, the pledge to work now for an understanding between the nations of Europe and particularly with those in the West." [5] The heroic line of sacrifice and the pacifist line of the Germans as good Europeans were coupled. In the same speech Hitler dissolved the Reichstag as new elections were to serve as a plebiscite of

[1] D.C. Watt, "The Reoccupation of the Rhineland," *History Today*, April 1956, p. 250.

[2] Op. cit., p. 251.

[3] *Dokumente der deutschen Politik und Geschichte*, IV, p. 284.

[4] "In order to give the forthcoming agreements the security of a European peace, the character of holy treaties, all nations in question participate only as members with equal rights and respected equally. The one compulsion for signing these treaties must lie in the visible expediency of these agreements for European peace and thus for the social happiness and the economic prosperity of the nations." Op. cit., p. 285.

[5] Op. cit., p. 276.

the people on the leadership of the Führer and his collaborators—a plebiscite the result of which was a foregone conclusion.

During this election campaign Goebbels indulged in soft suavity. In his opening address at a mass meeting in the huge new Deutschlandhalle in Berlin, which was also relayed to the audiences of two hundred other simultaneous meetings, he struck a conciliatory note. Far from wishing to burn their bridges with France, the German authorities wanted the Führer's recent measures to become "the first steps towards a real new order in Europe." He assured other powers that it was quite safe to conclude treaties with Germany. "One can see from the German-Polish agreement [of 1934] how we keep our treaties. We keep that treaty because it is based on reason." Goebbels went on to explain and to paraphrase Hitler's proposals glibly: Germany was now again sovereign mistress of her entire territory, and possessed full military equality. There was thus the possibility of a German return to the League.[1]

Once more the Führer's path was presented in apodictic fashion as the only one leading to salvation. Goebbels was all sweet reasoning and in favour of rational business-like agreements. A Germany of strength, honour, freedom and complete sovereignty over her territory could again conclude pacts "for she feels herself now an equal partner and is thus able to re-enter the circle of other nations as a nation of the first rank." [2] The Minister ended on a "prophetic" note, using his favourite parallel. The Führer was now doing the same for the world that he had done earlier in Germany: seeing reality as it was and speaking the truth. "His efforts for the peace of the world will one day be as much crowned by success as they were crowned in Germany." Goebbels' final appeal to the masses to approve Hitler's bold steps by their vote was a plea, not for adventure, but for the voice of reason. The Germans had always known, he remarked in another election speech, "how to fight bravely and to die heroically, but only seldom how to act reasonably. Here was an opportunity for doing so, perhaps the last." [3]

The main line recommended in the press directives was one of restraint. On 14 March Berndt, the spokesman of the Propaganda Ministry, issued a warning to the press that it must not publish anything which could give cause for alarm. As such reports would only serve the interests of the other side, sharp measures were threatened against any paper causing disquiet.[4] By the end of 1936 Goebbels was still busy lulling suspicions abroad that Mars was in the ascendant in Germany. "We have

[1] *Frankfurter Zeitung,* 12 March 1936.

[2] Ibid.

[3] For Goebbels' address at Frankfurt on 23 March 1936, see *Frankfurter Zeitung,* 25 March 1936.

[4] ZSg. 102/2, 14 March 1936. It is interesting that the same line was taken in another crisis two years later. After the *Anschluss* the Propaganda Ministry told a representative of the *Frankfurter Zeitung*: "In no case must a note of panic be struck in any fashion. The word 'war' must not appear, either positively or negatively." ZSg. 102/19, 13 March 1938.

not done wrong to anyone," he told a Belgian journalist on 18 November.
"We have 'reconquered' a province (the Rhineland) which belonged to
us and we have restored our army which is our good right to do, a right
which every other country has too. We have no reason to take something
which belongs to another country that has not offended us. *We are the
realists of peace.*" [1] A neat phrase, clearly destined to reassure the Belgian neighbour at a moment when Belgium had loosened her ties with
France and had embarked upon a policy of unambiguous neutrality.[2]

By the Locarno Treaty of 1925 Britain, France, Italy and Germany had
guaranteed the frontiers of Belgium as they had been laid down at Versailles. But the remilitarization of the Rhineland destroyed Locarno and
with it the basis of Belgian post-war policy. 1936 saw "a revolution in
Belgian policy, designed to reverse the developments of 1914 and to recover a guaranteed status." [3] With some subtlety Goebbels professed to
be well aware that the re-orientation of Belgian foreign policy had not
been carried out "for the sake of our pretty eyes," adding, however, "that
he had observed with great joy that little Belgium representing a great
nation has not hesitated to withdraw from all the complications that involve the danger of serving the intrigues of the Bolshevists."

National Socialism, the Belgians were told, did not pursue any international mission with aggressive intentions. Different from Communism,
which imposed "its ideology on all peoples and nations to prepare an
international revolution," National Socialism respected "the specific character of any nation, visualising a permanent European co-operation on
the basis of a mutual understanding." Such golden words might help to
strengthen the position of the pro-German and fascist (Rex) movement
in Belgium, on which Goebbels diplomatically refused to comment as he
had "no right to interfere with the domestic policy of another country." [4]

In January 1936 Goebbels had for the first time talked "of the great
task of making our nation a world people (*ein Weltvolk*) with a share in
the goods of this continent." [5] A year later, when German troops inter-
vened in the Spanish civil war, he coined the phrase of "Great Power
Germany as a guarantor of peace." His soft pedalling had not disappeared
entirely. "We only wish to pursue our work with honour and in peace!"

[1] Interview with a representative of the Brussels paper *Le XXe Siècle*. See
Völkischer Beobachter, 19 November 1936.

[2] On October 14 the Belgian Government under Prime Minister van Zee-
land had given up the Belgian alliance with France, after the German Government in a note of October 13 had guaranteed the inviolability of Belgium.

[3] *The World in March 1939*, edited by Arnold Toynbee and Frank T. Ashton-Gwatkin, London 1952, p. 156.

[4] Declining to comment on the Rexist movement of Leon Degrelle, Goebbels
merely hinted at his sympathy for it: "When a young man of 30 is able to
develop such a strong movement, then this is an element worth noticing".
See *Survey of International Affairs, 1936*, by Arnold J. Toynbee, London
1957, pp. 36-37 on the Rexist Party.

[5] Speech to members of the Gau Gross Berlin, 18 January 1936, see *Frankfurter Zeitung*, 19 January 1936.

Goebbels declared in Berlin on 13 February, 1937.[1] They had peaceful relations with a number of nations. The Axis Rome-Berlin had proved its mettle. A tolerable *modus vivendi* had been arrived at with Austria. There were good relations with Poland and on the German side the hope that the Danzig question would be eliminated once and for all. All this was underlined as evidence of a peaceful and constructive policy. Yet there was also a note of challenge. Whether the world likes it or not, declared Goebbels, it had gradually to resign itself to Germany as a Great Power.[2]

Six months later he expressed himself somewhat more ambiguously. Addressing Germans living abroad who had visited Germany, Goebbels still rejected the idea that the National Socialists were imperialists, but the German desire for peace was now more conditional: In their own way the Germans wanted to be good Germans, and if no one prevented them from doing this, they were gladly prepared "to make a great and valuable contribution to universal world peace."[3] The European mission of the Reich was now put into the foreground, the Germans being depicted as the spearhead of opposition to world Bolshevism, self-appointed guardians of European culture against its subversive forces, at work to achieve a world-wide revolution.[4] At that time the Führer had not yet given the signal for the process which was to lead to "Operation Otto" and "Operation Green," the destruction of Austria and Czechoslovakia as independent states with a calculated risk of a war against Great Britain and France. Goebbels now made much of the dichotomy of the world being split into Bolshevist and anti-Bolshevist camps. But while he ridiculed the naivety and ignorance of Western liberal politicians, he did not yet decry the democracies as hypocritical satellites of Bolshevism. In fact, the farce of the Western non-intervention policy in Spain suited the Axis pretty well. A parallel with the pre-1933 days in the Reich seemed expedient. The old Nazi slogan "Germany awake!" was now modified fittingly into "Europe awake!" with National Socialism as the white knight leading the crusade against the Bolshevik dragon.

At the Party Congress in Nuremberg in September 1937 Goebbels chose as his theme the contest between Bolshevist-Jewish imperialism and the positive forces of Europe and tackled it with all his skill and plausibility. The Party was the herald of truth which unmasked "the dark plans of Bolshevism." Behind them was the Bolshevist Jewish Satan himself as the events in Spain proved clearly. He was behind all the unspeakable atrocities and miseries committed by the Reds in Spain, the torture of nuns and hostages, the killing of children, the plunder and destruction of churches, convents and schools. The master-plan of the Bolsheviks was unmistakable. For them Spain was a springboard, a military and

[1] See *Völkischer Beobachter,* 14 February 1937.
[2] Ibid.
[3] *Frankfurter Zeitung,* 7 September 1937.
[4] *Völkischer Beobachter,* 14 February 1937.

naval base for an attack on Western Europe and the Western Mediterranean. The Western liberals were as usual blind to danger; they remained unaware of the catastrophe until it struck the nations "like terrible scourges of God." [1]

Quite obviously the motive behind that line of propaganda was the wish to transform the international triangle over the Spanish civil war—the two conflicting parties and the "neutral" non-interventionist powers—into the desired polarity. A clear-cut division was proposed: the evil forces of Jewish Bolshevism on the one hand, the resisting champions of Western civilization on the other. There is something of the language of apocalypse in this diatribe, of a semi-religious crusade against the wicked plots of Satan. Metaphorically speaking, one might paraphrase Goebbels' arguments, this was another stage in the heroic struggle against Lucifer. The fight became clearer and more hopeful because it was the same in a wider setting as the earlier struggle of National Socialism against the Jewish "system" of the Weimar Republic. As it happened then in Germany, it was now happening in the wider world: Truth would prevail in the end. It could not be stopped by anything or anybody in the long run. The fight, still in the balance, was by no means confined to Spain alone, it extended to Italy, Japan, Austria, Hungary, Poland, Brazil, Turkey and Portugal.[2] Having before 1933 overcome this evil enemy at home, the new Germany was now proud to head the international front of defence.

For the first time the image of a rejuvenated and German-sponsored Europe was projected, as the vision of a better world to come.[3] Goebbels contrasted the wicked deeds of the archfiend of mankind in Spain with the *fata morgana* of a better Europe—a technique which he was to employ again and again in days of war to the very end of the Hitler regime.

2. AGGRESSIVE EXHILARATION: THE ANSCHLUSS.

It belongs to the very nature of a totalitarian system of the Fascist type that it is restless, dynamic, wanting action for its own sake, and constantly devising imperatives. The situations produced by Hitler's foreign policy since 1936 made for a kind of permanency of crisis, of constant alert, of ever new challenges. As a demagogue who had to "expose" the "plots" of the opponents and to find telling phrases for the Nazi policy which would appeal to the masses and persuade them, Goebbels was at his best in days of political success and in hours of extreme crisis,

[1] "Die Wahrheit über Spanien", report on Goebbels' speech on 9 September 1937, at Nuremberg, *Völkischer Beobachter,* 10 September 1937.
[2] Ibid.
[3] "It will be a Europe based on self-respect, on generosity (*Grosszügigkeit*) decency, honour, freedom, on the will to reach an understanding (between its states), the granting of the right of existence to each nation, of social reconstruction, economic progress and a new flourishing of art and science." Ibid.

genuine or manufactured. The Chief Propagandist shone in the peak hours of national achievement after a Hitler coup, as well as in the tense moments of attack leading up to it. At such moments he knew how to play on the emotions of the masses, on the German sense of romanticism, of national integration, on the majesty of "the historic hour" in the one case, on aggressiveness, intolerance, the urge to crush the weaker and "inferior" nation or race in the other. It was comparatively easy to voice gratitude to the cause, the Fatherland, the Führer, when one of Hitler's adventurous coups had bloodlessly succeeded. To justify tension, crisis, possible war was more difficult and tricky than to be the *laudator victoriae* after all was over. Nevertheless, Goebbels seldom excelled more than when he deployed his specific talents after the triumphs of Hitler's surprise strategy.

The enforced *Anschluss* of Austria was of itself popular among the rank and file in Germany, yet it needed a Goebbels to celebrate it as an unheard of event, with a characteristic blend of sentimentality and ice-cold calculation which gave a final kick to the defeated opponents. On 30 March 1938, Dr. Goebbels addressed a mass meeting in "liberated" Vienna jointly with Seyss-Inquart, the new Governor (*Reichstatthalter*) of Austria. Goebbels offered the official version of the recent events: ridicule for the former Chancellor Schuschnigg, historical reminiscences and parallels, apotheosis of the Führer, simple imperatives for work in the future; all these elements were contained in Goebbels' speech. Schuschnigg had foolishly regarded Hitler as a great orator and a bad military leader. "His slumber," Goebbels sneered, "had been abruptly disturbed by the 'jackboots of Prussian militarism' to quote the jargon of the world press." Its picture of a country longing for national independence under the tyranny of the Reich was quite absurd. "In fact it had been the German armed forces who had secured her national life for Austria."[1] Schuschnigg was depicted as a third-rate intriguer, constitutionally unable to understand the refreshing frankness of the Führer during their famous meeting at the Obersalzberg on 12 February of that year.

More original were Goebbels' historical parallels, the skill with which he connected what had just occurred with earlier events and traditions. The *Anschluss*, he declared, had been nothing but a revolution. The people had made the decision. It always happened with revolutions that the men of the sinking system were not aware of the oncoming revolution. "This was so in 1789 when they stormed the Paris Bastille. This was so in 1848 and also in November 1918. What had to come always came."[2] Racialism was the key, it explained everything. The voice of the

[1] Report "Kundgebung der Hunderttausend in Wien," *Völkischer Beobachter*, 31 March 1938. Goebbels gave an extremely twisted account of German-Austrian relations after the Agreement of July 1936, which, he alleged, had only been used by Schuschnigg "to suppress and to persecute the Austrian people all the more brutally."
[2] Ibid.

blood was stronger than the voice of the paragraphs. "Austria has been taken back to the Reich by right of her racial foundation *(Volkstum)*."

Goebbels recalled an earlier event which usually counted little with the Nazis and was rather despised by them, the revolution of 1848.[1] He claimed, perhaps with some justification, that the liberators of Vienna in 1938 were the heirs of the "Greater Germany" ideology of 1848. To prove his point, he produced a manifesto from three Viennese citizens in 1848, Hoflich, Klopf and Eurich, which he alleged had been discovered in the Reich archives in Potsdam: "The Ten Commandments of the Age." [2] This half romantic, half ethical appeal to create a better and more dignified life in a new Germany, including Austria, reads indeed like a prophetic anticipation of the Nazi platform of 1938, though there is a streak of naivety, of honesty lacking in the Nazi leaders. The First Commandment in it ran:

"Germans everywhere! Only under the wings of a united powerful land can freedom be strengthened, order prevail that springs from respect of Law permeated with the spirit of freedom. Virginal Austria! Only in a Reich of your own can you live in the unshakeable permanence to which your people is destined in eternity." [3]

All other commandments followed this line. "A united Germany . . . would be more beautiful than all other countries, better in her foundations and greater in her success. The citizens demand preservation of their customs and *mores*. They will be better preserved in a united Germany than in a disunited people, split into two states." This sounded like the voice of a forerunner of the twentieth century National Socialist doctrine, of the gospel of National Integration: "There is only one single nation, with only one class, no matter if they are peasants, tradespeople, officials, clergy, teachers, scholars, artists, soldiers. And the poorer anyone of them is, the more he should be assured of protective welfare." In foreign affairs, too, there were apparently striking parallels between 1848 and 1938. The great work of unification, declared the alleged manifesto, must not fail at a moment "when all of us are threatened by our enemy, by the hordes of Russia." [4]

[1] For the Nazis' interpretation of the revolution of 1848, see Theodore S. Hamerow, "History and the German Revolution of 1848", *American Historical Review,* vol. LX, No. 1, October 1954, p. 35.

[2] The present writer has been unable to trace this document.

[3] *Völkischer Beobachter,* 31 March 1938.

[4] Ibid. There can be little doubt that most of the Greater Germans of 1848, were passionate nationalists. If the Nazis generally despised the men of 1848, Goebbels knew when to use material from those turbulent days to the advantage of his *ad hoc* propaganda. In any case on this point he was better informed than other Nazi leaders, of whom Professor Namier has said: "Had not Hitler and his associates blindly accepted the legend which latter-day liberals, German and foreign, had spun round 1848, they might well have found a great deal to extol in the *deutsche Männer und Freunde* of the Frankfurt Assembly". L.B. Namier, *1848: The Revolution of the Intellectuals,* London, 1944, p. 124.

From these mystical reminiscences of 1848 Goebbels soon returned to the practical tasks of 1938. As usual his addresses abounded with slogans and imperatives. For the next weeks, months and years, reconstruction was the task in Austria as a new part of Greater Germany. "Work! Take a hand! Don't talk! Act!" he advised his audience, "Don't bother about theoretical problems, but set about working! Take a hand in it! I am convinced, things will turn out all right." [1] Everyone should play his proper part in the forthcoming plebiscite which was to confirm Hitler's liberation of Austria. A very proper thing when ordered by the Führer but a wicked affair so long as the "traitor" Schuschnigg had demanded it. The main slogan was now time-honoured, though new for most Austrians: "Führer command, we will follow!" [2]

3. The Road to Munich: Concentrated Attack

A study of the press directives on the Sudeten question issued by the Propaganda Ministry, and in some cases, by the Foreign Ministry, reveals a considerable elasticity and adaptability to changing situations from day to day.[3] The orders to the press laid as much emphasis on omission as on commission; what was to be treated as taboo and what had to be stressed changed frequently; it was all a matter of expediency and of the Führer's tactics.

Immediately after the *Anschluss* of Austria the Czechoslovak Minister in Berlin, Mastny, received assurances from Field Marshal Göring and from Foreign Minister von Neurath that the action of German troops in Austria was "nothing but a family affair," (Göring) and that Germany was willing to continue the present policy of improving the relations with

[1] *Völkischer Beobachter* 31 March 1938.

[2] When a few months later Goebbels addressed Party meetings in Austrian provincial towns, at Klagenfurt and Graz, he received lively ovations. His speeches breathed both sentimentality and aggressiveness. He now revealed that at the last Party Congress at Nuremberg in September 1937 he "had had one of the most touching experiences" of his life, meeting somewhat reluctantly, a gathering of several hundreds of Austrian Party Comrades. "In a few minutes such a fanaticism, national enthusiasm (*Besessenheit*) and strength of faith had been displayed that from then on I was convinced the hour of decision in Austria would come in the foreseeable future." Therefore, it was easy for him to make short shrift of "the evil forces abroad" which now spread the lie that the Nazi movement in Austria had experienced a severe crisis since the *Anschluss* and Austria's integration in the Reich was seriously threatened. He had come to Graz to find out the truth, and he had been received most cordially. The false reports abroad were only endangering European peace. *Reichspost,* Vienna, 22 July 1938.

[3] Where not stated otherwise, the quotations from press directives on the Sudeten question and on the crisis arising from it are taken from the book by Walter Hagemann, *Publizistik im Dritten Reich,* pp. 348–377. In addition the Sänger collection at the Bundesarchiv in Koblenz has been used (abbreviated here "ZSg.").

Czechoslovakia.[1] It is true, von Neurath declared it as the view of the Führer that a further improvement of the relations would depend on a greater understanding to be shown by the Czech Government to the three and a half million Germans in Czechoslovakia,[2] but Hitler was still determined to go slow. When at a demonstration after his return from Vienna a banner appeared in Berlin, "The Sudeten Germans await the Führer," the press was told on 16 March 1938 not to publish such or similar slogans or photographs. On 18 March journalists were expressly advised at the Press Conference against "encouraging efforts on behalf of Pan-Germanism in foreign countries where the tendency toward demonstrations and public clamor is great. Even if we had reports of this kind of thing from Eupen, we should not help them from Germany. Although there were thirteen areas on our border where German minorities lived, it would not be to our advantage to egg them on, for we should only succeed in arousing fear and dislike in other nations, many of which would turn against us." [3]

But such an attitude of caution based on fear of a possible conflict with other powers soon receded before the looming contours of the Führer's further ambitions. As Werner Stephan put it with remarkable candour to journalists on 21 March: "It is of course not possible to picture Germany as satisfied forever after the Anschluss with Austria, or to call the greater Reich of today the Great Reich (Grossdeutschland) which we must work for. All our national dreams are not yet realized. A significant step has already been made in this direction, but a full realization has yet to be achieved." [4] Yet on the same day the papers were asked to treat "the Czechoslovak affairs, including their internal problems, with great detachment and a cool reserve." When on 25 March the leader of the now united Sudeten German Parties pressed for new elections "of all legislative and administrative bodies" the German press was asked to give prominence to this item but to avoid any bitterness. Even after Konrad Henlein had issued his eight point programme at the conference of the Sudeten German Party at Karlsbad on 24 April, demanding political equality for the German minority and territorial autonomy inside the frame of the Czech State, journalists were told to avoid any sensation but to emphasize the demands in a serious and dignified manner. On 27 April the papers were requested to send special correspondents into the Sudeten area; "the serious type of newspapers should continue to discuss the intolerable social and cultural situation of the Sudeten Germans, in order to show the world how things there really are." In the campaign for the communal elections in Czechoslovakia a number of serious incidents

---

[1] See Documents on German Foreign Policy, 1918-1945, Series D, Vol. II, Docs. Nos. 72, 74 and 78.
[2] Ibid., Doc. 78.
[3] ZSg. 102/9, Press Conference, 18 March 1938.
[4] ZSg. 102/9, Press Conference, 21 March 1939.

occurred, often provoked by Nazi agents.[1] At the same time Berndt of the Propaganda Ministry conveyed special instructions to the correspondents of seven leading German dailies including the *Frankfurter Zeitung* which he said had a certain impact on the public in Czechoslovakia and England. These papers were asked to refute certain Czech assertions, particularly those contained in an interview the Czech Clementis had given to English newspapers. While the tone of the articles should be sharp, they should be based on factual material of Czech deeds of terror against the Sudeten Germans.[2]

When on 20 May serious election incidents occurred in Prague and Brünn, Goebbels commented: "We must talk in somewhat sharper terms, at least it must be made clear that we feel for the Sudeten Germans." The next day, on the eve of the elections, two people were killed at Eger; there were movements of Czech troops near the frontier and a class of reservists was called up. The Czech Government was under the impression that German troops might march into their country. The German press was now ordered to write very outspoken commentaries on the Czech measures, but to avoid the creation of a panic. On 30 May Hitler issued the directive for "Operation Green" to the commanders of the German army, the navy and the air force, in which he stressed his firm decision to smash Czechoslovakia in the foreseeable future by military action.[3] Soon afterwards the comments of the press became more hostile though in the directives a note of caution was struck. Thus on 28 May the Propaganda Ministry asked the press not to treat frontier incidents prominently any longer, as otherwise Germany would have to support strong words by deeds. The military measures of Czechoslovakia could be published "on the line that Czechoslovakia was waging war against phantoms."

It is interesting in this respect that when Goebbels gave an address at a ceremony in Dessau on 29 May, celebrating the inauguration of the first theatre in the Third Reich, an aggressive passage in it was omitted in the German press. What was reported was his praise of the German Government's love of peace and his warning to the democracies that the German peace must be an honourable peace.[4] However, according to the correspondent of *The Manchester Guardian* (30 May 1938), Goebbels

---

[1] On 19 May German editors were advised that each of them should have on his staff a specialist on Sudeten German questions, "who masters the subject and has good archives. What has been written so far, was too thin. Real material is required, not generalities, figures of German schools in proportion to the number of children, etc." ZSg 102/10. Press Conference, 19 May 1938.

[2] ZSg. 102/10, "Vertrauliche Austrichtung Politik", 18 May 1938.

[3] See *Documents on German Foreign Policy, 1918-1945*, Series D, Vol. II, Doc. No. 221.

[4] According to the German press Goebbels had declared, "They say: 'The world's peace is in danger'. What world's peace? We are also for peace. But we want our vital rights and have no mind to let ourselves be continually attacked by the great democracies." See the report in *Völkischer Beobachter*, 30 May 1938, under the caption *"Abrechnung mit den Friedensstörern."*

had denounced the Czechs for their provocative violations of the German frontier, adding: "Should this not exhaust our patience? We are 75,000,-000 and they are twelve or thirteen million people, and they act as if it were the other way about. In making such statements I well know that I am not using the language of diplomacy. But I believe that the right word in a critical hour is the right thing." This significant passage did not appear in the German press. As *The Times* correspondent pointed out, the versions of the speech in the German press "bore traces of ex-purgation." [1] But a week later, on 3 June when the Sudeten Germans had asked for propaganda support in Berlin for their negotiations with the Government in Prague the press was told to be more outspoken.

It is noteworthy that in a telegram to the German Foreign Ministry on June 19th the German Minister in Prague, Eisenlohr, regretted the continuation of sharply worded attacks in the German press and radio; while during certain periods it had been a useful reaction to the news of Czechoslovak mobilization, it would now be regarded internationally as a sign of aggressive German intentions. He warned that the Czechs would thus regain sympathies even in foreign circles which until then had condemned their actions.[2] But this well informed advice was apparently ignored in Berlin.

A week before, on 10 June German editors were warned that under no circumstances must the impression be created that Germany was now disinterested in the Sudeten German question. The latest news had to be "featured as large and sensational items and be extremely sharply commented upon under shrill headlines such as 'orgies of thrashing' and 'acts of terror.' " [3]

The anti-Bolshevist line was equally stressed on the occasion of an exhibition in Prague 'Our ally—the Soviet Union.' The press was to point out "that like Red Spain" Czechoslovakia regards herself as an outpost of the Soviet Union and that it is a glacis for the advance of Bolshevism. The question should be put to the English what they would say if three and a half million Englishmen in Germany were forced to support an anti-British policy. In Czechoslovakia the Germans were actually involved in an anti-German Bolshevist current.[4] Goebbels himself alluded to Czechoslovakia only indirectly in his address before 120,000 people on 21 June at the Nazi festival of the Solstice in the Olympic stadium of Berlin. He chiefly attacked the Jews, but he also asked the "Marxist-Jewish foreign press" which showed so much concern for the fate of the Jews in Germany, to busy itself with the terrorization and the brutal persecution of three and a half million Germans in another country.[5]

[1] *Survey of International Affairs, 1938,* Vol. II, *The Crisis over Czechoslovakia, January to September 1938* by R.G.D. Laffan, London, 1951, p. 61.

[2] *Documents on German Foreign Policy,* Series D, Vol. II, Doc. No. 246.

[3] ZSg. 102/10. Instructions from the Press Department of the Propaganda Ministry to the Berlin Office of *Frankfurter Zeitung,* not dated. (10 June 1938).

[4] ZSg 102/10. Press Conference, 10 June 1938.

[5] *Völkischer Beobachter,* 23 June 1938, translated in *Documents on International Affairs, 1938,* II, p. 163.

While the Czechs were not attacked violently during most of June and July, the Sudeten question was not allowed to slip into the background. The German press "maintained a continuous, if not shattering barrage of criticism of the Czechs." [1] But on 15 July the editors were informed that the treatment of the Sudeten German question "had to be intensified again, as the fabulous minority statute is said to have been submitted to the Parliament in Prague. The English already say that the Sudeten Germans should be content if 60 to 70 per cent of their demands are granted. Czech public opinion has by no means been prepared for such concessions; on the contrary, during the last few days, the administrative measures have again become rigorous." [2]

Like the magician's apprentice in Goethe's poem "Der Zauberlehrling," the Propaganda Ministry sometimes found it difficult to restrain the malignant spirits it had released and goaded. During the period of relative official restraint the papers were even sometimes criticized for too much zest in abusing the Czechs. To call the Czech people a nation of deserters or to deride their character, as some German journalists had done,—a directive of 22 July remarked—might be "objectively correct but imprudent," for the unity of the Czechs would grow the more the German papers insulted it. The attacks should be directed against their leading men, but should refrain from insulting the nation as a whole or the Czech army. On 26 July caution was recommended in comments on the mission of Lord Runciman sent by the British Prime Minister to advise and mediate between the Prague Government and the Sudeten Germans. The mission was neither to be welcomed nor to be rejected.

The unscrupulous character of Goebbels' methods is well illustrated by his directive of 9 August which advised a drastic "treatment of the facts" concerning the murder of the Sudeten German labourer Wenzel Paierle in Grünerwald by German Social Democrats.[3] "Special care should be devoted to comments on this new bloody deed. What matters is to show that the murder has been committed by a Czech. From our point of view, not only the instigators, but also the murderers are Czechs. It is emphasized that Social Democrats are not to be mentioned in this context. It is an unconfirmed allegation to say that Social Democrats were standing close to the murderer. The comments should explain the special circumstances of the deed, perhaps like this: it was unknown how the group close to the murderer was constituted; undoubtedly thugs and a Czech official belonged to it, the crime had been committed before his eyes, it was unknown how far he was its instigator. In that frontier area all sorts of dubious characters turned up; there were paid creatures *(Subjekte)* of a doubtful background; Prague had unlimited funds at its disposal and there were sometimes traitors whom one could buy. Amongst

[1] *Survey of International Affairs, 1938,* II, p. 188.

[2] At that time the *Berliner Börsenzeitung* of 15 July sharply stressed the danger which might arise from the reckless attitudes of the Czechs to Anglo-German relations. See *Survey of International Affairs, 1938,* II, p. 191.

[3] W. Hagemann, op. cit., pp. 356-357.

the emigrés there were persons who had fled from Germany because they had committed crimes. These were the fruits of Czech propaganda, the Sudeten Germans were outlawed. The comments should end by saying that those deeds could only occur because, so far, murderers and assassins had hardly been punished by the Czechs."

By the end of August Hitler's intention under no circumstances to allow a compromise between the Sudeten Germans and the Government in Prague became clearly reflected in the directives to the German press. On 20 August the press was asked during the next few days to denounce Prague's proposal of offering a few postmasterships to the Sudeten Germans, in leaders and commentaries in the sharpest terms. They should point out that after all the provocations and acts of violence Prague showed again nothing but a scandalous scorn. The alleged Runciman plan on the partition of Czechoslovakia should not be mentioned in any way. A directive of 27 August recommended both restraint and aggressiveness. "The appeal of the Sudeten leaders to Party members to make use of the right of self defence in an emergency should not be given too much display." [1] The appeal had been forbidden and the Czech radio had sharply attacked the emergency measure with the argument that the state was maintaining peace and order through the police, and that no one had the right to an illegal self defence. "This argument should again be confronted with lists of attacks, acts of violence and murders. It should be said that this was the sort of peace and order safeguarded by the (Czech) state." [2]

The German press promptly followed this command. On 30 August the Berlin paper *Der Angriff* gave, under the headlines, "Bloody terror of the Czech bands," "The unleashed mob rages through the tortured land," an alarming but carefully vague account of Czech workmen organized into "storm troops" and "engaged in massacre and loot." [3] By this time the German press abounded with such reports on alleged Czech atrocities. They now extended their attacks to the Czech army, after Goebbels had advised it accordingly on 27 August in complete contrast to his earlier instructions. "The insults to the German armed forces in the Czech press," he ordered, "have to be given pride of place in four columns on the front page and refuted most sharply." In reply the Czech soldiers who had committed atrocities should be castigated.[4] The mixture of caution and aggressiveness in the propaganda line continued well into September. On the 8th the newspapers were expressly told "to avoid most

---

[1] For the text of the proclamation by the Sudeten German Party and the reply by the Government in Prague, see *Survey of International Affairs, 1938*, Vol. II, pp. 228-250.

[2] W. Hagemann, op. cit., p. 557.

[3] See *Daily Telegraph* (London), 31 August, 1938 and *Survey of International Affairs 1938*, Vol. II, pp. 228-230.

[4] Three books by Tschakoff, Dwinger and Erich von Ludendorff dealing with the exploits of the Czech Legion in the First World War were recommended for this purpose.

carefully any unnecessary attack on another country, and also belittling
and insulting it. Excepted from this is the state which at the moment
allows terror to break out against the Germans who are not allowed the
right of existence (*Lebensrechte*)." [1]

But in his speech before the Party Congress in Nuremberg on 10
September Goebbels did not confine his attacks to Czechoslovakia. On
the contrary, speaking on "National Socialism, Bolshevism and Democracy" he lumped the last two systems together.[2] Like the ardent French
nationalist, Charles Maurras,[3] he declared that the differences between
liberalism and Bolshevism were largely fictitious. Bolshevism had its
roots in the liberal tradition and was the grandchild of 1789, "with democracy the very political chaos began that has found its finality in
Bolshevism." Despite their pretensions to the contrary, the democracies
were not opposed to Bolshevism, in fact they were operating as its political, economic and intellectual champions. Bolshevism was "the naughty
boy of democracy. Democracy gave it birth, brought it up, and alone
keeps it alive." Goebbels' technique of "unmasking" a conspiracy was
here fully displayed.[4] "Prague represented the organizing centre of Bolshevist plots against Europe," he proclaimed, "it harbours the 'Central
European bureau' of the Comintern."

On 14 September the surprising news was announced that the British
Prime Minister would visit the Führer in Berchtesgaden. At 11 p.m.
the Propaganda Ministry issued orders to the press by telephone that:
"the news of the journey of Chamberlain to Berchtesgaden was to be
given a big splash. Incidents (in Sudetenland) were still to be treated as
front-page news; the press should continue to use the sharpest language,
it must not become 'soft.' Fresh news items of serious incidents and
arrest of Sudeten German leaders had to be featured very prominently
and be very sharply commented upon. They should not talk of a relaxation of tension, but of dreadful persecution, of terror, etc." [5]

On the following day (15 September) Chamberlain's visit was described at the German press conference as "a world sensation." It had
given the Führer the greatest satisfaction of his political career. But the
press should not become over enthusiastic. Chamberlain must not appear
as an Angel of Peace, and the position was not as though everything was
already settled. This success would not have been achieved without the
hard and intransigent policy of the last few months. Final success would

[1] ZSg. 102/11 *Dnb. Rundruf*, 8 September 1938.

[2] See *Völkischer Beobachter*, 11 September 1938.

[3] For the views of Charles Maurras on this theme, see the Chapter "Les
Partis" in *Mes idées politiques*, Paris, 1937, particularly pp. 206-210.

[4] Ibid. To prove his allegations of a Democratic-Bolshevist plot, Goebbels
quoted from such heterogeneous sources as the French pro-Fascist paper *La
Renaissance, The Wall Street Journal, Pravda* and the official *Gazette of the
Czechoslovak Republic*.

[5] ZSg. 102/12. Instructions by telephone from an official of the Propaganda
Ministry to the Berlin office of *Frankfurter Zeitung*, 14 September 1938.

not be secured if they gave up that attitude too early.[1] The press was advised to feature the news of military operations in Czechoslovakia in a sensational manner with slogans such as "A last warning to Prague," "Insolent provocations," etc. Four days later the press had to intensify its attack. "The newspapers, which have so far shot with 7.5 centimeter guns should remember that there are also 21 centimeter guns. The numerous DNB news items on new atrocities, murders, maltreatments, should be published in a brief and dramatic manner without additions." The task was to show what a barbarous nation the Czechs were and that their's was an impossible State . . . Important was also the theme that Moscow assisted Prague. For once the hardpressed German journalists received a bouquet. The German press had "done brilliant work. The Führer was extraordinarily pleased with it." [2]

One of the basic tactics of totalitarian propaganda is the preference for concentration in attacks on the leaders of a "hostile" nation rather than on the nation itself. *Pars pro toto*—to hit opposing forces by singling out their representatives had always been a device popular with the Nazis. Hitler and Goebbels therefore deliberately heaped abuse on the head of the President of Czechoslovakia, Dr. Beneš, picturing him as a half sinister and half ridiculous figure.

In Hitler's important speech on the Sudeten German question at the Berlin Sport Palace of 26 September Beneš appeared as a brutal oppressor of minorities. "Herr Beneš," shouted Hitler, "demands of Sudeten Germans: If I wage war against Germany, you will have to fire at Germans. And if you do not want to do so, you are a traitor to the State and I will then have you shot . . . He who opposes Herr Beneš, is above all finished economically. This fact the democratic world apostles cannot lie away. In this state of Mr. Beneš the consequences for the (non-Czech) nationalities have been appalling. I speak only of the Germans. It is they who have the highest death-rate of all the German tribes, their poverty in children is the highest, their unemployment is the most frightful." [3]

Using a favoured Nazi technique of polarity Hitler pointedly set himself up as a positive figure against the negative one of Beneš: "Now two men stand arrayed one against the other: there is Mr. Beneš and here stand I. We are two men of a different make-up. In the great struggle of the peoples while Mr. Beneš was sneaking through the world, I as a decent soldier did my duty. And now today I stand over this man as the soldier of my people!" [4]

Hitler's personal attack on Beneš was intended to set a pattern. At a special press conference on 26 September it was pointed out that "the entire weight of the arguments had to be concentrated as in the Führer's

[1] Hagemann, op. cit., p. 363.

[2] W. Hagemann, op. cit., pp. 366-367.

[3] *The Speeches of Adolf Hitler, April 1922-August 1939,* ed. by Norman H. Baynes, Oxford 1942, Vol. II, p. 1519-1523.

[4] Op. cit., Vol. II, pp. 1525-1526.

speech not so much against Czechoslovakia but against Herr Beneš personally—analogous to the approach of allied propaganda between 1914 and 1918 which was directed not against the German people but against the Kaiser." [1] Beneš was to be exposed by the German press as "one of the fathers of Versailles, a witness of a bygone age, a modern Nero." The German people wished to live in peace with the Czechs. Not one of the states so ready on paper to assist Czechoslovakia would be able to give bread to the Czech workers. It was by way of a clear dividing line between the two nations that reconciliation and co-operation were "most likely to emerge." [2]

On 28 September, the day when the dramatic news of the Munich Conference was released, Goebbels continued the line of concentrated attack on President Beneš. In a speech in Berlin he compared him with the manipulator of a puppet show (*Puppenspieler*), moving others, i.e. England and France, on his strings.[3] A directive on this speech and on the news of the Munich meeting issued on 28 September at 10 p.m. ordered the journalists to write "that it was hoped the Western statesmen would now realize that they had been deceived by Herr Beneš during the last few days." [4] The main theme of next morning's papers was not to be the Munich talks (the term "Conference" was definitely to be avoided), but the terror in the Sudetenland or Goebbels' speech. The greatest prominence and the largest headlines had to be given to the mammoth demonstrations arranged by the Party all over the Reich, for the rights of the Sudeten Germans. But as in fact the news of the Munich Conference came as a great relief to many Germans, some papers reflected this mood and consciously or unconsciously ignored the last directive. Next day at the press conference of 29 September these editors were severely scolded.[5]

[1] It had to be emphasized that Beneš was "personally responsible" that he wanted war and was "from vanity and vindictiveness prepared to wade through streams of blood and to expose the German *Volksgruppe* to annihilation". Beneš was said to have secured a fortune in mysterious circumstances which he had put safely in French banks. "At any moment a three-engined plane was ready to take him to Moscow while his people bleed to death." W. Hagemann, op. cit., p. 371.

[2] Ibid.

[3] See *Völkischer Beobachter*, 30 September 1938.

[4] Hagemann, op. cit., p. 373.

[5] W. Hagemann, op. cit., pp. 373–374. "Last night," the speaker declared, "some chief editors had" apparently lost their nerve or some publishers put their profits above the fatherland. "In spite of all directives to the contrary the Munich talks had been given much prominence and the news had also been sold by way of special editions. But abroad all German moods were watched. During the last fortnight the German press had worked so splendidly, that it would not do now suddenly to take a different attitude. The Propaganda Ministry was not prepared to acquiesce in a deviation from the official line. At the same press conference the "defeatism" of some of the financial editors was branded and they were threatened with a charge of treason. Some of them were declared to be a relic from the liberal age; they were thinking only "of vacillations on the Stock Exchange instead of Germany."

Goebbels was never slow in sailing with the wind. After the Munich conference had ended with a bloodless victory for Germany, the tune of the directives quickly changed from venom and unscrupulous attack to cautious satisfaction and thanks to the Führer, who had "once more succeeded in preserving world peace" (directive of 1 October). A cordial welcome was to be extended to the Sudeten Germans who were now joining the Reich. "No howl of triumph over the Munich results in order not to annoy other powers," dictated the directive of 30 September. The impression was to be avoided that "a weight has been lifted from our hearts . . . Kind words should be used when referring to the statesmen of the three other powers, particularly cordial words for Mussolini, Germany's most loyal friend. But the acknowledging of the initiative of the Western statesmen should not be overdone to avoid the opposition in their countries pointing a finger at them and declaring that Chamberlain and Daladier had allowed themselves to be duped." [1] The alleged Czech "atrocities" were now to be played down: only factual news items should be reported but without splashing them.[2] On 3 October the press and radio were "urgently requested to write no longer of Czech licentious soldiery (*Soldateska*) and also not to suggest that the Czech army was in a state of disintegration." It was not in the German interest at this moment to write disparagingly of the Czech army.[3] The fabrication of fictitious atrocity stories was no longer permissible, an omission of facts which did not fit in with the latest line was imperative. Committed acts of destruction could be published, however, "not on the line that through them 'a brutal nation showed its true character,' but as an effect of a political error now righted." [4]

Some editors were obviously slow in adapting themselves to the new post-atrocity course. "Unfortunately there is still an attitude towards the Czechs to be found which is no longer opportune," complained the Ministry on 12 October. "In previous days which had a different leitmotiv all the heavy guns of propaganda had to be used in the struggle." But this attitude now belonged to the past. The press was urgently ordered to avoid, under all circumstances, expressions such as 'licentious soldiers,' 'Czech pig sty' and to treat the Czechs in a gentlemanly fashion . . .[5]

On the whole the controllers of the German press seem to have been

[1] ZSg. 102/12. "Aus der Presskonferenz", 30 September 1938 and "Ausrichtung Politik", 30 September 1938.
[2] Ibid.
[3] W. Hagemann, op. cit., pp. 374-375.
[4] Op. cit., p. 375. Directive of 7 October 1938.
[5] ZSg. 102/12, not dated (12 October 1938). It is interesting that similar official advice to the German press not to hurt the feelings of the Czechs, was given after Hitler had put an end to the rump state of Czechoslovakia. At the end of March 1939 Fritzsche told the journalists: "It is imperative that we do not make the mistake of claiming that the Czechs are celebrating the entry of the German troops. The assumption that the Czechs are now breathing freely is completely mistaken: this would be too close to a slur on the Czech people's honor." ZSg. 102/15, Press Conference, 31 March 1939.

pleased with its labours. Reich Press Chief Dr. Dietrich, most likely acting on instructions from Hitler, sent a letter of thanks to the chief editors of all German dailies, not to be published. For once the Führer himself praised the performance of the press at a confidential meeting with its representatives.[1]

4. "THE SUPERIOR HAND OF A MASTER OF STATECRAFT"

Public relief over the war avoided at Munich was one thing, the Führer's disappointment was another. "The fellow has spoilt my entry into Prague," said Hitler to Dr. Schacht on his return to Berlin, referring to the British Prime Minister.[2] As Hitler put it a year later at a conference with his Commanders-in-Chief: "It was clear to me from the first that I could not be satisfied with the Sudeten-German territory." [3] In any case, three weeks after Munich Hitler issued a new directive to the Armed Forces urging their commanders to prepare for the possibility of liquidating what the Führer now contemptuously described as "Czechia." Meanwhile a more docile and submissive Government in Prague tried hard to pacify the powerful German neighbour. Dr. Emil Hacha, a non-political judge had succeeded Dr. Beneš as President; the new Prime Minister was Dr. Beran and the Foreign Minister Dr. Frantisek Chvalkovsky, a former Minister in Berlin and Rome, well known for his pro-Axis sympathies.

For several months the German press and radio paid comparatively little attention to the affairs of Czechoslovakia. However, the planned German attack on the unfortunate rump state was preceded by deliberate subversive disintegration from within. While the Government had to grant far-reaching concessions of autonomy to the Eastern provinces of Slovakia and Ruthenia, Berlin expressed dissatisfaction and pressed a long series of further demands on the hapless Prague government.[4] "It was through a national *Auflösung* that the destruction of Czechoslovakia was designed." [5] The non-German national minorities, the Slovaks, the Ruthenes and the Hungarians were now greatly encouraged by Berlin to voice their grievances. Though the Reich Government did much to stimulate the disintegration of Czechoslovakia by agents, funds and diplo-

[1] See above, Ch. 4, p. 177.
[2] Statement in evidence by Schacht before the International Tribunal at Nuremberg on 2 May 1946, quoted in J.W. Wheeler-Bennett, *Munich. Prologue to Tragedy*, London, 1948, p. 331.
[3] International Military Tribunal, Nuremberg, XXVI, 329 (789-PS), translation in *Documents on International Affairs 1939-1946* (R.I.I.A.), Vol. I, p. 529; see also the Führer's Directive on the liquidation of the remainder of the Czech State, of 21 October 1938. *Documents on German Foreign Policy, 1919-1945*, Series D, Vol. IV, Nr. 81.
[4] See e.g. Chvalkovsky's interview in Berlin with Hitler and Ribbentrop on 21 January 1939. *Documents on German Foreign Policy*, Series D, Vol. IV, Documents Nos. 158 and 159 Ed. Arnold Toynbee and Frank T. Ashton-Gwatkin, London 1952.
[5] *The World in March 1939*, p. 286.

matic pressure, it was, of course, not in the German interest to reveal
the Führer's intentions openly. This time the position was quite different
from that in the summer of 1938. While then a racial issue—the sufferings of an allegedly suppressed German minority in Czechoslovakia—
could be exploited, the number of Germans in the Czech rump state was
now negligible and no sympathy for them could be expected in the West.

For some months the German press and radio were directed to treat
the developments in this region solely by way of news and news reports
without committing Germany in its political comments. Only in March,
1939, shortly before Hitler began to carry out his well planned moves,
did the German press again indulge in sharp arguments and fiery denunciation.[1] In February the agitation of the Slovak extremists for Slovak
autonomy had reached a peak. On 6 March President Hacha dismissed
the Ruthenian Government and three days later the Slovak Government.
On 7 March a new Slovak Cabinet, more acceptable to Prague, was
formed in Bratislava (Pressburg). On the following day the former
Slovak Prime Minister, Monseigneur Tiso and some of his ministers were
arrested. The acts "were the last attempts of a government in Prague
to assert its authority throughout the territories of the Czechoslovak
Republic." [2]

At first Goebbels advised the German press to maintain reserve.[3] Yet
at another conference on the same day tendentious headlines were recommended such as "the Czechs are returning to their old methods." An appeal by the deposed Tiso Government to the Führer on 10 March was to
be treated as a main news item but without giving it a sensational splash.[4]

On the next day (11 March) the press was bluntly informed that the
authorities "were not interested in news that claims that things are quiet
and orderly everywhere. Of course, it is quiet when Czech soldiers interfere in Pressburg. The term to be used should no longer be Czechoslovakian Government, but only the Czech Government in Prague. The fact
that the Slovaks have had their first dead should be duly emphasized. . . .
No comments but the headlines should clearly express German sympathy with the fate of the Slovaks suppressed by Prague." [5] On 14 March,
under strong Nazi pressure, the Slovak Diet expressed itself in favour

---

[1] "The exact moment when Hitler decided to march on Prague cannot be
decided from our present evidence". W.H.C. Frend, "Hitler and His Foreign
Ministry 1937-1939", *History*, XLII, No. 145, June 1957, p. 126.

[2] *The World in March 1939*, p. 287.

[3] W. Hagemann, op. cit., p. 380. At the Press Conference of 10 March it
was decreed that "news from Pressburg may be published in two columns, but
by no means in a sensational fashion". For the time being a manifesto by
President Hacha on these events should not be printed. "In no case do we
make the cause of Prague our own, but we might hint at a certain sympathy
for the Slovak rights of existence. But only to a limited extent in order that
foreign circles (*das Ausland*) should not be able to blame us for having furthered this development in any way."

[4] This was done accordingly in the German morning papers on 11 March.

[5] ZSg. 102/15 Press Conference, 11 March 1939.

of independence; after Tiso, who had managed to escape to Berlin, had received orders from the Führer to that effect.[1]

Now the heat in the German press was deliberately intensified. At a conference on 12 March editors were informed that the front pages of the papers next day were to be filled with news from Czechoslovakia. "What was desired was the biggest possible splash, the largest letters, headlines over the entire page couched in the sharpest tone, but no comments."[2] However next morning comments were allowed on the following lines: (1) A new revival of the Beneš trend of the worst kind had to be observed. (2) The Czechs had not learned anything since Munich. (3) Nobody denied that some Czechs were men of good will. (4) But these few were powerless in comparison with the collective overall mentality of the Czechs who were full of hatred of the Germans. The autonomy of the Slovaks or of the Carpatho-Ruthenians promised in Munich by the Prague Government had not materialised. The *Volk* Germans were completely denied their rights. This was in contrast to the splendid position of the Czechs now living on German territory, who were free from victimisation. On the other hand, masses of the *Volk* Germans had lost their jobs; they were not granted unemployment benefits; they remained at the mercy of Czech policemen and judges; the Czechs had undermined their existence in order to remain exclusive. At the same time journalists were asked never to couple a demand or a threat with an exposure of the Czech mentality or reports on the most recent events in that ill-starred country. The attempt made in Munich to pacify the motley crowd of nations it comprised had proved a failure; as Fritzsche explained with a mixture of cynicism and professional pride, this imposed an obligation on the journalists to write their comments with care and with such professional ambition that they could become "*the* leaders of their lives."[3]

At noon on 14 March the German News-Agency released to editors the news of the Slovak declaration of independence and of Tiso's telegraphic request to the Führer that he should undertake the protection of the Slovak Republic. Tiso's telegram was, however, only published on 16 March.[4]

Even more telling was a further telephonic instruction to the newspapers issued two hours later. From now on the German press was only to refer to the parts and not to the whole of the dying republic. It should

[1] J.W. Wheeler-Bennett, op. cit., p. 342. See also *Documents on German Foreign Policy*, Series D Vol. IV, No. 22.

[2] W. Hagemann, op. cit., p. 381.

[3] ZSg. 102/15. Press Conferences of 13 March 1939; the first took place at 9:15 a.m., the second in the afternoon.

[4] For the text of Tiso's telegram see *Documents on German Foreign Policy*, Series D, Vol. IV, no. 209 (draft), p. 250 and Vol. VI, no. 10, pp. 10-11. The marching of Hungarian troops into Carpatho-Ruthenia was announced at the same time. A directive of the Propaganda Ministry issued by 'phone on that day shortly before 2 p.m. insisted that Tiso's telegram to the Führer and his manifesto to the Slovaks should not be published until German troops had entered Slovakia. Meanwhile headlines such as "disintegration of a State", "autonomy for Slovakia" were desirable.

only talk of the lands of Bohemia, Slovakia and the Carpatho-Ukraine, a clear indication that the Czechoslovak state was regarded in Berlin as a thing of the past.[1] On the evening of 14 March Hitler summoned President Hacha and Foreign Minister Chvalkovsky to Berlin for an "interview" which, extending to dawn next day, became "the most notorious and brutal as well as the best attested to which Hitler ever subjected a foreign statesman." [2] The anxious visitors were curtly told by the Führer that "he no longer had confidence in the Czech Government . . . This very morning at 6 a.m. the German Army would invade Czechoslovakia at all points and the German Air Force would occupy all Czech airports." [3]

Bullied into submission by the threat of immediate annihilation of Prague by German bombers, Hacha and Chvalkovsky signed a communiqué at 4 a.m. which gave the impression of an amicable arrangement by stating that the Führer had received the two Czech visitors at their request. They had had a frank discussion about the serious situation "in the present Czechoslovak state territory." Both sides had been in agreement in expressing the view "that it must be the aim of all efforts to secure calm, order and peace in that part of Central Europe." To serve this purpose the Czechoslovak President had "confidently placed the fate of the Czech people and country in the hands of the Führer." The Führer had accepted this declaration and had "expressed his intention of taking the Czech people under the protection of the German Reich and of guaranteeing them an autonomous development of their ethnic life, as suited to their character." [4] Two hours later, at 6 a.m. Goebbels read over the wireless a proclamation of the Führer to the German people telling them that he had decided to let German troops march into Bohemia and Moravia. "By disarming the terrorist bands and the Czechoslovak forces they will protect the lives of all who are threatened and thus secure the basis for a fundamental settlement which does justice to the meaning of a thousand years of history and to the practical needs of the German and the Czech people." What was to appear to most people outside the Axis orbit as a flagrant violation of the Munich Agreement was presented by Goebbels as a protective measure eminently suited to further "the practical needs of the German and the Czech people."

The instructions to the press issued at the Press Conference on 16 March speak for themselves.[5] Now it was the right moment, the journalists were advised, "to thank the Führer for his peaceful achievement. A headline such as Greater German World Empire was very much premature as a slogan, things should not be exaggerated." On the other

[1] W. Hagemann, op. cit., p. 383.

[2] The World in March 1939, p. 287.

[3] Minute by Hewel, Documents on German Foreign Policy, IV, No. 228.

[4] Völkischer Beobachter, 16 March 1938. See also Documents on German Foreign Policy, Vol. IV, doc. No. 229.

[5] W. Hagemann, op. cit., p. 384.

hand, a caption in the Party paper *Der Angriff,* "France Sees No Reason for Interference" was severely criticized as it might suggest that "this news had lifted a weight from the German breast, and this at a moment when the Führer had ordered things peacefully by a gesture of his hand." The point of view that Hitler had come to Prague "not as a tyrant but as guardian of a New Order" was duly stressed in the German press. "History does not know of another event of that kind" wrote the *Frankfurter Zeitung.* "In these days above all the superior hand of a master of statecraft has become visible." [1]

Reactions from the foreign press were not to be put on the front page. If some smaller countries were worried about their fate, German comments should reassure them and tell them they had been led astray by panicky news reports. The Propaganda Minister was quick in providing a counter attack at a press conference a few days afterwards. The English, Goebbels declared, were the last people who had a right to talk in terms of race, "for England has all the races in her Empire from Aryans [sic] to Australnegroes [sic]. For six years the English have been indignant because Germany talked of race and they have almost let loose a crusade against this, but now they pose as guardians of the race theory. A climax of hypocrisy!" The German leaders had "scrupulously preserved the rights of the Czechs, who will have their own citizenship." [2]

After the journalists had written accordingly, they received praise from the Ministry. At another Press Conference they were asked to continue their attacks on England, and the searchlight was then turned on the history of the British Empire. [3] "Basic idea: like an old spinster England sits smugly on her seat and through a spy hole in her window watches every young girl in the street with much jealousy and moralising, forgetful of her own past." German papers should point out that it was very easy for the rich to be moral, for they were not expected to steal their bread. [4] What was required from the journalists was not dry historical reflections, but lively reporting. The most important themes from the history of the British Empire were then divided between individual Ger-

---

[1] *Frankfurter Zeitung,* Nos. 140-141, 17 March 1939. Article "Auf dem Hradschin. Von der Prager Burg wehen die deutschen Fahnen."

[2] ZSg. 102/15, Press Conference 19 March 1939. Before Hitler returned to Berlin after a short visit to conquered Prague, Goebbels issued an appeal to the Berliners to give him a rousing welcome. On 17 March Fritzsche asked the Berlin papers to print Goebbels' appeal on the front page and support it through articles of their own. "The task of enticing hundreds of thousands into the streets was of great political significance. It was always said abroad, the German people acquiesced in the events without inward participation. A mass reception for the Führer would prove that this was not so and might also have a quietening effect abroad." (Ibid.)

[3] ZSg. 102/15, Press Conference 21 March 1939. The speaker was Hans Fritzsche.

[4] The same argument was also put forward by Goebbels in an article "Die Moral der Reichen." *Völkischer Beobachter* 25 March 1939, reprinted in *Die Zeit ohne Beispiel,* pp. 84-96.

man papers and to each of them was allotted one country which was said to have suffered from British misrule, such as India, Palestine, Cyprus, Malta, Egypt, Gibraltar and Ireland.

It was simply the method of the thief trying to divert attention from his exploits by shouting "catch the thief." This sort of argument was probably impressive to many German readers, but it was unlikely to cut much ice abroad. On the following day a sharp counter attack on foreign critics of Germany's latest move, particularly on Mr. Duff Cooper, was suggested to the newspapers. The journalists were to explain that Munich was not outdated but had been further developed.[1]

As we know, the final drastic elimination of the Czech state had farreaching repercussions on English political opinion. Even Chamberlain now felt badly let down and sadly disillusioned. On 17 March in his speech at Birmingham he complained that Hitler had taken the law into his own hands.[2] The British Prime Minister repudiated "any attempt to dominate the world by force" as "one which the democracies must resist." Though not inspiring, this speech contained a definite warning: "No greater mistake could be made," Chamberlain said bitterly, "than to suppose that, because it believes war to be a senseless and cruel thing, this nation has so lost its fibre that it will not take part to the utmost of its power in resisting such a challenge if it ever were made." [3]

The reply to Chamberlain's speech by the Propaganda Ministry, issued at a special press conference on 18 March at 7 p.m., followed the old Goebbels tactics that attack is the best means of defence. Chamberlain's speech was not to be treated in the same (rude) manner as those by Duff Cooper, "After all the man is 70 and Prime Minister. But he was 30 when Germany showed sympathy for the Boers. Then his father indicated to the Germans that the Boer question was no concern of Germany. England had then no geographical and historical arguments, she was motivated by mere greed for money. Chamberlain was 50 at the time of the 'Black and Tans.' England easily overcame her feeling of shame when blacks were sent to the Rhineland. And were the Canadians ever asked if they wanted to become an English colony?" [4] Chamberlain, the directive insisted, had himself admitted that the Czech problems had been neglected and that the patient could only be saved through an operation. It was in the nature of things that the Munich operation could only succeed for a short while, and that the patient had finally died from it. The secession of Slovakia had preceded the journey of Hacha to Berlin, it had created a new situation which invalidated Munich. The precondition for consultation of the other signatories of the Munich Agreement had been lacking, i.e. discord between Germany and the Czech

[1] ZSg. 102/15, Press Conference 17 March 1939.
[2] *The Times*, 18 March 1938. See also *The Eve of War 1939,* ed. Arnold Toynbee and Veronica M. Toynbee, London, 1958, pp. 36-37.
[3] Ibid.
[4] W. Hagemann, op. cit., pp. 385-386.

people. For "Hacha had declared that he had undertaken his visit to Berlin voluntarily and at his own request."

In answering Chamberlain's arguments the German press should stress that Bohemia-Moravia [sic] was a purely German affair. Did not England regard Palestine as a purely English concern, though it was under a mandate? Chamberlain's threats of encirclement, the rapprochement with the Soviet Union and the anti-German attitude of the United States were forcing Germany to develop her security with all possible means. The totality of their threats was being countered by a totality of defence. Yet one of the most pertinent points in foreign criticism of Hitler's ruthless action against Prague, the allegation that Hitler had thrown his racial ideology overboard, remained unanswered. Hitler could justify with some plausibility the *Anschluss* of Austria and of the Sudeten Germans, but he could not overnight transform Czechs and Slovaks into *Volksdeutsche*.[1]

5. THE "HAVES" AND THE "HAVE-NOTS"

In the interval between Munich and the outbreak of the Second World War, National Socialist propaganda employed a double line to depict the attitudes of the leading political circles in the Western democracies. It continued to expose and "reveal" their sinister machinations in the wake of Bolshevism. Indeed, as is shown in another context below, the theme of *Einkreisung*, of the deliberate encirclement of Germany and Italy, reached a crescendo in the spring and summer of 1939.[2] But simultaneously Goebbels pursued another and more obvious line by emphasizing the weakness and slow motion of the Western politicians, their faulty thinking and fear-psychosis, their inability to match their words with deeds. Hitler and Goebbels were well aware of the weakness of their opponents who found it difficult to readjust themselves to the Axis dynamics. With a good deal of truth Goebbels pointed out that the democracies were limping behind the course of events, that they allowed themselves to be pushed around and outwitted by it. A long register of their recent ineptitudes was cited.[3] In every case before Italy and Germany had taken action the West had raised a hue and cry, but afterwards they had quickly resigned themselves to the *fait accompli*.[4] In looking back on the fateful year between Munich and the outbreak of the war Goebbels was indeed in a strong position with his argument that the democracies had constantly underestimated the strength and power of the authoritarian states. In February 1939 he could deride their "lack

[1] Few people were so shocked by Hitler's cynical indifference to his own ideology than the British Ambassador in Berlin. See Sir Nevile Henderson's comments to the British Foreign Secretary on 16 March 1939, *Documents on British Foreign Policy*, Third Series, Vol. IV, No. 288, pp. 278-279.

[2] See below chapter 17, p. 383.

[3] See particularly the article "Krieg in Sicht," *Völkischer Beobachter*, 25 February 1939, reprinted in *Die Zeit ohne Beispiel*, Munich, 1941, pp. 39-47.

[4] Op. cit., p. 40.

of the necessary instinct for a proper judgment of the international situation" or claim that "the problems were never solved with them but partly without them and partly against them." [1]

The National Socialists believed in the effectiveness of brute force and noticed with gleeful contempt, to use the words of Arnold Toynbee, that the Western Liberals (a term which included Conservatives and Socialists) "were horrified by the brutal world which had now suddenly and unexpectedly closed in around them." The West found it repugnant to admit the possibility that "they might have to conform to the jungle's violent ways if they and their countrymen were to survive in it." [2] Though the Nazis did not hesitate to express hearty contempt for what they looked upon as spineless behaviour, in fact this behaviour suited them excellently and they wished it to continue. Goebbels therefore questioned the wisdom of the West to strike a more virile and pugnacious note. Later he acknowledged that the Western states were rearming and demanding great sacrifices from their people. This was rather pointless, Goebbels asserted, for Germany had no demands on, or quarrels with, the Western states. They were not interested in imposing National Socialism or Fascism on other nations. Goebbels maintained that there was no reason for them "to convert other states by force, cunning or intrigue to a political system," which they knew would strengthen "the substance of the nations and make them fit for their struggle for existence." [3] National Socialism was not an article for export to France, England and America. It was all very puzzling to think that the Western nations felt threatened by Germany and were demanding a gesture of friendship or of international co-operation from the Reich. Goebbels saw the Western tactics as part of a war of nerves. "They wish to make us nervous and yet they become only nervous themselves through their own shouting." Germany still desired peace, but peace at her price. It had to be a peace with a difference, a peace "compatible with the German right of existence" (Lebensrechte), as the Reich no longer wanted to belong to the "Have-Nots." [4] The democracies so much maligned at the beginning of Goebbels' twisted but forceful argumentation were at its end gently asked to "consider how the pressing problems of Europe could be brought closer to a reasonable solution."

Three weeks after the publication of Goebbels' article, Hitler by the occupation of Czechoslovakia "solved" one of these "pressing problems" without bothering to consult the Western powers beforehand. The Nazis lived up to their "peace plus" doctrine. It was expansionism for the sake of national security. As Goebbels had formulated it in the article with smooth plausibility: the German people wanted peace, but they also

[1] Ibid.
[2] *The Eve of War 1939*, p. 40.
[3] Article "Krieg in Sicht", op. cit., p. 41.
[4] Op. cit., p. 47.

wanted "something in addition that other nations have had for a long time: security for their national life and justice." [1]

While the German propagandists continued to talk of "peace plus" for the first time the English Prime Minister seriously considered the alternative of a "bad" peace, "peace minus" so to speak. This time Chamberlain acted quickly. On 30 March Britain issued a guarantee of her independence to Poland. And in the weeks and months to follow the division of public opinion in Britain over the German issue disappeared. Even the former "appeasers" shed their illusions over the ultimate aims of Hitler's drive for world dominance.[2] France, on the other hand, was rent by internal feuds and showed "signs of the debility underlying her brave words and vigorous gestures" which were astutely recognized in Berlin.

For the time being the leaders of the Third Reich had good reason for riding on the crest of the wave. As an official of the Propaganda Ministry remarked to a Frenchman a few days after Prague: "We have before us so many open doors, so many possibilities that we no longer know which way to turn or what direction to take." [3] It has been said of Neville Chamberlain and his Cabinet that they followed a dual policy of wielding truncheon and carrot simultaneously from mid-March, 1939 to the outbreak of the war.[4] In a speech delivered at Chatham House on 29 June 1939 Lord Halifax, the Foreign Secretary, pointed to the 'twin foundations' on which that policy rested. One, he declared "is determination to resist force. The other is our recognition of the world's desire to get on with the constructive work of building peace." [5] It lies outside the task of this book to determine how far the British Government succeeded in combining these two aims or whether or not it managed to present them to the outside world clearly and convincingly.[6] But it should be noted that in a way German propaganda, though not necessarily German policy, also followed a double line during those fateful months. Whilst it denounced the Western war-mongers and "encirclers" with increasing venom, it still played melodies of peace, in case, as it hoped, sense and reason should prevail on the other side and Germany's demand for a "peace plus" be granted.

[1] Ibid.

[2] "Those who had been prepared to seek an agreement with Hitler joined hands . . . with those who had cried "Hitler means war" and the country was united in the thought that "Hitler must be stopped." J.W. Wheeler-Bennett, *Munich*, pp. 349-350.

[3] Report by the French Ambassador in Berlin, Coulondre, 19 March 1939, *Le Livre jaune Français: documents diplomatiques 1938-1939*, Paris, 1939, p. 80.

[4] *The Eve of War 1939*, p. 41, also pp. 204-224.

[5] Op. cit., p. 204.

[6] As a member of Chamberlain's Cabinet remarked after the war: "The double policy of peace and rearmament needed not only very skilful handling, but also a very subtle presentation. In a sense, the two aims were contradictory, often difficult and sometimes also impossible to reconcile." Viscount Templewood, *Nine Troubled Years*, p. 383.

In an article on 1 April under the caption "Who wants war?" Goebbels poked fun at the "war psychosis" which he claimed had developed in London, Paris and Washington, but he also repeated his earlier arguments that there was no real reason for waging war in Europe.[1] With one of his most ingenious arguments, obviously more destined for home than for foreign consumption, Goebbels used the alleged ignorance of European affairs of the man in the street in London and Paris for concluding that the British and French people had no reason to fear war from Germany: "For what can it really matter to the average Englishman or Frenchman that Austria consummates her *Anschluss*, that the Sudetenland returns to the Reich, or that Germany, with Prague's agreement, sets up a protectorate over Bohemia and Moravia? The man in the street in Paris and London usually doesn't even know where these countries are on the map." [2] For the people of good will in all nations there was still one alternative to war, i.e. "peace plus," which in Goebbels' language meant "to face facts squarely, to grant, without argument, the legitimate aspirations of young and struggling peoples, and in this way to follow a practical path to a *real* peace." [3]

Two months later Goebbels declared peace was still possible, "a true peace," which would redress the balance of power and possessions between the "Haves" and the "Have-Nots" among the nations. For the Axis Powers peace could not simply mean the preservation of the *status quo*. It had to be a constructive peace, "that will bring to the chaos of Europe a clear order," a peace "to resolve the class-struggle of the peoples—a struggle which menaces us all; a peace which will achieve a new order among nations, based on justice and having as its goal the welfare and happiness of all." [4]

This forceful dualism which underlined the new military strength of the Berlin-Rome Axis but which also made play of offering the chance of a "peace plus," of a new and better order for all nations, was the final note struck by the Propaganda of Stormy Crisis. By posing the question: "Will this development bring about another war, as the fathers of the Versailles Treaty wished, or, as Germany and Italy wish, a true peace?" [5] It put the onus of making the fateful decision on the shoulders of the troubled statesmen in London and Paris.

[1] Article "Wer will den Krieg?" 1 April 1939, *Die Zeit ohne Beispiel*, p. 92.
[2] Op. cit., p. 93.
[3] Op. cit., p. 96.
[4] Article "Klassenkampf der Völker? *Völkischer Beobachter*, 3 June 1939, reprinted in *Die Zeit ohne Beispiel*, pp. 157-163. The quotation is on p. 163.
[5] Ibid.

PART III

Goebbels and the Creation of the Führer Myth

CHAPTER 8

A Machiavellian Radical

DURING the twenty years of his life as a propagandist and manipulator of public opinion Goebbels sponsored many ideas. But one idea he never touched, though it was pushed by most of his colleagues in the top layer of the Party. Why did Goebbels not care for the idea of the master race? Partly, it seems, because he realized that the concept of *Herrenvolk* did not particularly appeal to the masses and partly, no doubt, on account of his physical disability, his club-foot. As we know from Hans Fritzsche, Goebbels rejected this idea and ridiculed it in front of subordinates.[1] We have seen that Goebbels' showmanship and his insistence on hard work and *Leistung* came to some extent from an urge to compensate for his physical deficiency. He may also have realized that he had to apologize or to compensate, for being an intellectual in a party where aversion to the intelligentsia was a standard pattern. It is just possible that with a normal gait Goebbels' dynamic nature might have been more Faustian and less Mephistophelian, that he might have felt less at home at mass meetings and less contemptuous of the intellectuals, to whom he fundamentally belonged.

Early in his political career Goebbels discovered that he could sway audiences, raise them to peaks of fury and enthusiasm. With his histrionic performances he was even able to impress Hitler, who only appreciated "people who could sway an audience." He admired the cleverness of the little doctor, but even more his oratorical skill. "I have heard them all," Hanfstaengl reports him as saying, "but the only speaker I can listen to without going to sleep is Goebbels. He can really put it over."[2] Both Hitler and Goebbels established contacts with the masses easily and intensively, they knew how to appeal to their instincts, their foibles and prejudices. They were both first-rate actors, but there was this difference. Hitler often not only played a role, but identified himself completely with it and embodied the personality he played, whereas Goebbels usually calculated every word in advance, knowing all the time that he was playing

[1] See Fritzsche's statement at Nuremberg, IMT, Nuremberg, Vol. XVII, p. 253.
[2] P. Hanfstaengl, *Hitler, the Missing Years*, London 1957, p. 182.

a role.[1] With Hitler sometimes his fanaticism carried away his calcula-tion, while Goebbels manufactured frenzy, contempt, rage, but seldom identified himself with them.

Yet basically Goebbels was a restless radical. He was not made for times of comparative peace and stabilization. On the contrary, he throve on crises and was on the top of his form in periods of fights for power, of internal party feuds and of reverses in times of war. He built up the Gau Berlin at a time when a challenge to Communists and Social Demo-crats in the capital seemed to be hopeless, he was "on the bridge" during the pogrom action in November 1938, he managed to reassure innumer-able badly shaken Germans after Stalingrad and again after the attempt on Hitler's life in July 1944.

With his quick detection of changing currents Goebbels was as much an opportunist as a radical. He was ready to put his radicalism into cold storage when it seemed advisable, but even then there remained his in-stinctive dissatisfaction with the world, his contempt of the masses, his constant irritation over the mistakes and follies of colleagues and sub-ordinates. These features were part of the nature of a radical *manqué*. According to Schwerin von Krosigk, his conservative colleague in Hit-ler's Cabinet, Goebbels regretted that National Socialism had not come to power by way of a fully-fledged and "bloody" revolution. However much his intellect may have shown him the advantage of the facade of legality behind which Hitler achieved power, his temperament would have preferred a more drastic and direct revolutionary change. "To issue Jacobin proclamations in a Convention of Terror would have been a role in which his diabolical temperament would have had full scope."[2] In times of internal and external crises of the Party and later of the régime Goebbels was in his very element. Though first a "left-winger," he knew how to detach himself from more genuine "Socialists" inside the Party like the Strasser brothers and from the leader of a Party faction like Röhm. Goebbels was both a political bohemian and an opportunist. As an opportunist he was careful enough never to antagonize the Führer or to go too far in his hostility to any rival, provided he still had the confi-dence of Hitler. But as a political bohemian Goebbels had "a horror of the quiet enjoyment of orderly times."[3] When as after the Röhm "Putsch" it seemed highly inopportune to stress the revolutionary line in domestic affairs, he transferred his political dynamics largely to the realm of for-

[1] See Schwerin von Krosigk, *Es geshah in Deutschland*, Tübingen 1951, p. 233.

[2] Op. cit., p. 231. Franz von Papen, Hitler's Vice-Chancellor in 1933, takes a similar view when he describes in retrospect Göring and Goebbels as men "who can only be compared with the great figures of the French Revolution. They attacked (in the Cabinet) every problem and encountered all criticism with the furious élan of the rabble rouser." But unlike Göring, Goebbels was more than a rabble rouser, he was, in von Papen's eyes, also a masterly dialectician. See von Papen's *Memoirs*, London 1952, p. 291.

[3] Schwerin von Krosigk, op. cit., p. 251.

eign affairs, making himself the spokesman of the "Have-Nots," of the exploited victims of the Western "plutocracies."

There is some truth in Hanfstaengl's comment on the Goebbels of the Nineteen Twenties that "with his right foot he gave the Communist salute and with his left the Nazi *Gruss*." [1] Though the simply clad Gauleiter of 1926 had by 1934 turned into a Minister whose personal style of living did not shun parvenu luxury, he remained at heart an anti-bourgeois. He never had much sympathy for the bourgeoisie, the "Philistines," the middle-of-the-road people, the solemn figures of a pre-1914 drawing-room world. Frequently he was worried that the Party movement might lose its dynamic anti-philistine impetus.

While this impetus was genuine, by and large his anti-intellectualism was mainly a pose and remained ambiguous. In the days of his obscurity and "Storm and Stress," the young Doctor of Heidelberg University liked to strike a half romantic, half Machiavellian attitude averse to any *jeu d'esprit* beyond the grasp of the masses. "Intellect is a danger to the formation of character," declares the hero of Goebbels' immature and lyrical novel *Michael*.[2] It was the same suspicion of a rational world with its accent on technological progress and political decisions made in terms of rational majority votes which lurked behind the bulky tome *Der Geist als Widersacher der Seele* by Ludwig Klages, a figure from the circle of Stefan George to which young Goebbels had sought admission in vain.[3]

"Michael," alias Goebbels, despised the specializing study of academic scholars as pedantic and sterile, while he praised the thinkers of an all-embracing *Weltanschauung*, Dostoevsky and Goethe, Wagner and Nietzsche. His outlook was dynamic and therefore not so stereotyped and "closed" as that of other leading figures in the Führer's entourage. Provided one recognized Goebbels' authority and did not challenge some basic tenets of the regime such as its will to power and its fundamental anti-Semitism, it was possible for his subordinates to argue with him, to talk to him *sachlich*, as the German term has it. Hans Fritzsche declared at the Nuremberg Trial that he "valued Goebbels' intelligence and his ability, at least sometimes, to change his own opinion in favour of a better argument." [4] Other former members of the Ministry of Propaganda have confirmed this view.[5]

Goebbels was able to justify practically any position and idea, though to few of them was he attached wholeheartedly. Every politician has to readjust his opinions and arguments from time to time, but Goebbels often did this with a demagogic skill and a cynical sophistry which re-

[1] F. Hanfstaengl, op. cit., p. 224.

[2] J. Goebbels, *Michael, Ein deutsches Schicksal in Tagebuchblättern*, Munich 1929, p. 14.

[3] L. Klages, *Der Geist als Widersacher der Seele*, Leipzig 1929, 2 volumes.

[4] I.M.T., vol. XVII, p. 142.

[5] For instance, Ministerialrat W. Stephan, to whom the author is indebted for his views on Goebbels' personality and working habits.

mained unsurpassed in the ruling clique of the regime. A complete volte face in the official political line and policy such as the Russo-German Non-Aggression Pact of August 1939 was facilitated by Goebbels' skill, his ability to think out and to "put over" arguments that would satisfy the masses and make them forget the complete break with the anti-Soviet attitude hitherto maintained and propagated by the regime.[1] It is true, Goebbels sometimes allowed discussion of specific issues behind closed doors among the senior officials of his ministry and he was always prepared to learn from the *Stimmungsberichte*, the secret soundings of public feeling taken by the SD or his own officials.[2] But this did not diminish the sharp demarcation line between the rulers and the ruled, characteristic of the Third Reich as of any totalitarian regime. The intellectuals, the writers and scholars were not allowed to indulge in objectivity or criticism. Truth, like action, had to remain the monopoly of the Party. Propaganda and free enquiry—outside the field of natural science—were incompatible, as the latter might become a serious danger to the requirements of the State.

This was the paradox of Goebbels' existence. His mental agility, his interest in and understanding of theatre and music, of the ballet and the film made him an embodiment of the very type of the intellectual which he so often attacked,[3] largely for reasons of political expediency. In Goebbels the sense of power and of self-glorification was much stronger than his love of truth and of objectivity. Fairness was not a working concept in his dictionary. Any injustice, any twisting of facts and arguments were permissible—*ad majorem gloriam patriae*—a term identical first with the Party Movement and later with the established régime, but coinciding at all times with Goebbels' own self-interest. Goebbels liked to regard objectivity and fairness as chronic weaknesses in the German national character, and repeatedly quoted a warning to the Germans uttered by the poet Klopstock at the beginning of the nineteenth century: "Don't be too just, they are not sufficiently noble to realize how beautiful are your faults." [4]

Some one-time members of the National Socialist oligarchy who for one reason or another were no longer in favour, stressed Goebbels' propensity to lie. Otto Strasser characterized him as "ambitious, an opportunist and a liar," [5] while "Putzi" Hanfstaengl, who felt bitter because Goebbels, for whom he was no match, had recently ousted him, described him as "not only schizophrenic but schizopedic, and that was

[1] For details see below pp. 244–45.
[2] See below, ch. 12, pp. 271–79.
[3] See O. Meissner, *Staatssekretär unter Ebert-Hindenburg-Hitler*, Hamburg, 1950, p. 623.
[4] See for instance the conclusion of Goebbels' first address as Minister of Propaganda before German journalists on 16 March 1933, printed in J. Goebbels, *Revolution der Deutschen, 14 Jahre Nationalsozialismus*, Oldenburg, 1933, p. 151.
[5] O. Strasser, *Hitler and I*, London 1940, p. 94.

what made him so sinister." [1] Perhaps the most revealing lies told by Goebbels were those about himself. As has been shown, the young Party agitator used to explain that his physical disability was the result of an injury he had suffered in the First World War. Later he posed as a martyr of the French occupation of the Ruhr in 1923, claiming to have been imprisoned by the French and to have been flogged daily in his cell. When the Strasser brothers instigated enquiries a few years afterwards the fact was established that Goebbels had never spent a day in prison in his life and that his story was a complete fabrication.[2]

His ice-cold intellect, his caustic wit and sarcasm did not prevent him from playing on the sentimentality of the people, if this suited his purpose. What enabled him to do so and to establish many contacts with crowds and masses was his oratorical talent, his gift of graphic description, his often felicitous phrases, the coining of new words. Though Goebbels often repeated himself, his articles and speeches were seldom boring. He had the happy knack of inventing or applying expressions which were lucid, precise, and would stick in people's minds. This is particularly true of his speeches after 1933. Expressions like "penetrant" (penetrating), "schizophrenic," "Experten," "Kritikaster" (pocket-size critic), "moralinsauer" (sour through moralizing) took on a new emphasis or meaning in his contexts. He was a master of persiflage and liked to "expose" his personal opponents or those of the régime either as incompetent blockheads—stupidity was contemptible in his eyes—or as hypocrites and men of false bonhomie. "I can reckon with the wickedness of men, but their stupidity is often incomprehensible," he once remarked to his press secretary.[3] His phrases sounded new and concise and never went over the heads of the masses. "We know what we want but what is still more important we also want what we know" is one of his *jeu de mots,* while another from a wartime speech in the packed Sport Palace in Berlin runs: "We pursue by no means hypocritical aims. After the war we shal gladly live up to the pjrinciple: Live and let live. But during the war the maxim is valid: Fight and let fight." [4]

Totalitarian regimes cannot exist without proclaiming norms of proper and improper behaviour. They may be changed from time to time, they may even differ in different years, but they are an intrinsic and inevitable ideological part of the system. Goebbels had a special flair for finding the *mot juste* of the moment, clear and attractive slogans, never dull and often original. He was a master in giving new meanings to old concepts, in readjusting them to the new requirements of official policy. The term "freedom," for instance, in his hands lost any reference to the individual and was applied only to the fate of the nation. "Nothing is too precious

[1] P. Hanfstaengl, op. cit., p. 224.
[2] O. Strasser, *Hitler and I,* London, 1940, p. 95.
[3] Friedrich Christian zu Schaumburg-Lippe, *Zwischen Krone und Kerker,* Wiesbaden, 1952, pp. 159-160.
[4] Joseph Goebbels, *Der steile Aufstieg,* Munich, 1943, p. 186.

to be sacrificed for Freedom"—a typical wartime sentence of Goebbels ran—"It is better for a nation to come out of a war very poor but free than to be apparently in full control of its possessions and unfree." [1] To him Freedom meant "a national Freedom," liberty of the German nation vis-à-vis other nations, not freedom of the individual from the bonds of the state in the sense of John Locke or Wilhelm von Humboldt.

Another example of the transfer of meaning can be found in Goebbels' usage of the term "class struggle" on the eve of the Second World War. For years National Socialist propaganda had denounced the concept of "class struggle" inside the nation as a diabolical invention of Jewish conspirators, a disintegrating instrument of international Marxism. But this time-honoured denunciation of the Marxist concept did not prevent him from coining the formula of *Völkerklassenkampf* (class struggle between the nations), when he wanted to press the revisionist claims of the Fascist "Have Not" nations against the *'beati possidentes'* or conservative "Have" powers of the West.[2]

Goebbels seldom told complete lies, but with a consummate skill he knew how to twist ideas and how to conceal facts. In most cases there was a grain or a nucleus of truth in his arguments and explanations. As Schwerin von Krosigk put it: "he hid this nucleus of truth with all the veils of interpretation. He always had a channel of escape ready when one wanted to prove that he had told lies." [3] With his talent for "double-talk" Goebbels did not find it difficult to spurn what he had previously worshipped and to worship what he had previously spurned. The sudden denunciation of the leader of the SA, Röhm, and of his associates after the bloody events of June 30th, 1934, the new line of friendship with the Soviet Union after the conclusion of the German-Soviet Non-Agression Pact of August 1939 ending years of bitter abuse of the Stalin regime, the denunciation of the Italian King and his generals after Mussolini's fall in August 1943, are classical examples of a re-direction of propaganda which, though drastic, was always carried out with an awareness of the mood and temper of the public. While Goebbels was convinced that the memories of the masses were short, he was obliged to reckon with them. Wherever possible he avoided a sudden and complete reversal of the line of propaganda. A good example is the confidential instructions to the German press issued before the news of the German-Russian Pact was released. As this volte face of Hitler's policy had to be explained, a historical note was struck: "The decision presents a sensational turning-point in the relations between the two nations and is a

---

[1] Article 25 of "Thirty Articles of War for the German People", Joseph Goebbels, *Das Reich*, 26 September 1943; reprinted in *Der steile Aufstieg*, pp. 464-474.

[2] See Goebbels' article "Klassenkampf der Völker?" published on 3 June 1939 and reprinted in his book *Die Zeit ohne Beispiel*, Munchen, 1941, pp. 157-163.

[3] Schwerin von Krosigk, op. cit., p. 233.

return to the traditional co-operation (*traditionelle Gemeinsamkeit*) in German-Russian policies. This aspect particularly of the historical preconditions for such a political line must be emphasized in commentaries and leaders, as it has been all-decisive for the overall European situation." [1] Before the news had been made known to the people the journalists were advised to stress "that the announcement had met with a profound echo among the people." As it could be expected that many Germans would feel embarrassed by this sudden change from a rabid anti-Bolshevism to co-operation with the Bolshevists, the directive emphasized that "no reference, either positive or negative, must be made to the ideological differences (*weltanschauliche Verschiedenheiten*) between the two states." [2] In order not to make the reversal too marked the journalists were advised that "the tone of the comments must be matter of fact and sober. The reader must get neither a feeling of triumph nor of *Schadenfreude* from it." [3] As the news was likely to cause a shock to many Germans it had to be made more palatable by putting it into a traditional framework.

As a master of subtle lies, re-interpretations and innuendoes, Goebbels was unrivalled in the top layer of the Party. While such men as Göring, Himmler and, later, Bormann were hardly less unscrupulous and were equally convinced that the cause justified its means, they proved less subtle and skilful in the use of words than was the Minister of Propaganda. They were, it seems, lesser masters too in the gentle art of blackening the character of rivals. The very fact that in a dictatorship the struggle for power cannot be revealed to the public (or only after it has ended with the decisive overthrow of a faction) could make a man with Goebbels' restless push, caustic wit and sharp critical faculty powerful and feared. Goebbels knew how to ridicule others effectively and was well aware that Hitler soon dropped people from his entourage who had appeared in a ridiculous light. With his malicious tongue and his brilliant *aperçus* Goebbels was the Voltaire among the Nazis, a Voltaire with a dagger. From Goebbels' sharp tongue only the Führer was immune. At Hitler's table the Minister of Propaganda often amused himself and his master by making one of the persons present the target of his cynical ridicule. He had the knack of ridiculing people by imitating their gestures and manners of speech or by telling sharp-edged anecdotes about them, so much so that no one would take the victim seriously any longer.[4]

Goebbels undermined the position of others, working "with an equip-

[1] Vertrauliche Informationen, Nr.188/39, 22 August 1939 (Oberheitmann).
[2] Ibid.
[3] Ibid.
[4] A. Zoller, *Hitler Privat, Erlebnisse seiner Privatsekretärin*, Düsseldorf, 1949, p. 212; see also H. Hoffmann, *Hitler was my Friend*, London, 1955, p. 199; P. Hanfstaengl, op. cit., p. 220, and A. Rosenberg, *Letzte Aufzeichnungen*, p. 195.

ment of superficial smiles and false bonhomie, getting his enemy in the web of ridiculousness and then suddenly exposing him in some discreditable light." [1] He did this partly from sheer malice, and partly with the purpose of improving his own position or that of his Ministry at the expense of others. By applying this method he lowered the prestige of Gürtner, the Reich Minister of Justice, and obtained control of the press division of the Ministry of Justice. He was not able to oust Rust, the Reich Minister of Education, though he spoke badly enough of him, wishing to deprive his Ministry of the control of the universities. Only in February 1945, a few weeks before the end of the Third Reich, did Goebbels succeed in persuading Hitler to dismiss his rival Dr. Dietrich. But such setbacks did not make Goebbels a less dreaded adversary, an adversary always willing to employ any suitable means likely to damage the position and the prestige of others. This may explain why, to a less versatile rival such as Rosenberg, he appeared in retrospect as "the Mephistopheles of our Movement once so straight." [2]

[1] P. Hanfstaengl, op. cit., p. 225.
[2] A. Rosenberg, op. cit., p. 188.

CHAPTER 9

The Projection of the Hitler Image

THERE WERE only two constant factors in Goebbels' political evolution: his adamant and uncompromising hatred of the Jews and his admiration of and his *Gefolgschaftstreue* (feudal loyalty) to the Führer.

As we have seen, after an early rebellion Goebbels had remained under Hitler's spell from the time he had first been invited by the Party boss to address a mass meeting in Munich in April 1926. Emotional needs, the admiration of an intellectual for a man who instinctively knew what he wanted, went together with the sober calculation of a careerist who realized that he could only rise with and through but never against Hitler. It is true that Hitler's relations with the "Little Doctor" underwent some modifications over the years. They were at their lowest ebb in 1938-39 when Goebbels' sensational love affair with the Czech film star Lyda Barova caused a serious estrangement from his wife and Frau Goebbels wanted a divorce, which the Führer, for reasons of the prestige of the régime, was unwilling to allow. Yet Goebbels himself, even when less in favour with Hitler, continued to remain attached to the Führer. With all his versatility and cleverness Goebbels, acutely conscious of his physical handicap, lacked Hitler's self-assurance and intuitive handling of people and situations. Therefore he was not insincere in proclaiming his faith in the Führer. But his personal adherence was one thing, his calculated building up of the Führer myth over the years another. It is the purpose of this chapter to examine how Goebbels propagated and developed this myth in the context of the National Socialist movement and of the Third Reich between 1925 and 1945.

Any totalitarian system is bound to aim at a maximum identification between the directing leader and the directed masses. To achieve this the leader has to appear at one and the same time as a charismatic superman *and* as a fellow human being. He must be made to seem both distant and near, cunning and simple, lonely under the weight of national decisions, but approachable and open-minded towards the masses. All his successes are shown in a light that reveals his exceptional infallibility whilst any failure or mistake is explained away as a mere hallucination of ignorant onlookers or as a malevolent invention of plotting but frustrated enemies. In an age of mass media, the press, radio, films, etc., can be skilfully employed to project this complex but highly uniform image.

1. BEFORE 1933

In December 1941, when the Swastika was hoisted over most of Europe and Germans could take a German victory for granted, Goebbels talked to some of his officials in the Propaganda Ministry about the services he had rendered over the years to the rise and triumph of the National Socialist Party. "In four decisive ways," he said, "he had virtually strengthened the movement." [1] First, in the early days he had introduced the Socialist element into a Party that had begun as a purely middle class affair; secondly, "he had won Berlin and thereby prepared the way for seizing power in the Reich"; thirdly, "he had worked out the style and technique of the Party's public ceremonies. The ceremonial of the mass demonstrations, the ritual of the great Party occasions had their roots in his experiences and achievements as leader of the Gau Berlin." Finally—and this is the point relevant to this chapter—there was "his creation of the Führer myth. Hitler had been given the halo of infallibility, with the result that many people who looked askance at the Party after 1933 had now complete confidence in Hitler." This was the reason "why even now millions of Germans drew distinction between the Führer and the Party, refusing their support to the latter while believing in Hitler."

Although these claims reveal an exaggerated self-projection calculated to strengthen Goebbels' position in the Party, they contained a core of truth. There were other factors which contributed to the widespread belief among Germans in the genius and infallibility of the Führer during the period from the coming to power of the National Socialists in 1933 to the shattering defeat at Stalingrad exactly ten years later, but Goebbels could assert with truth that without his tireless activities the Hitler-myth would not have been so effective and so firmly ensconced during the first decade of the regime.

How did he present Hitler to the public when the Party was still an insignificant racialist splinter group? At a time when Goebbels was an obscure and often dissatisfied small official of that group in the Rhineland, and when his admiration for Hitler was by no means unqualified, he published an impassioned booklet, *The Second Revolution*. It contained all the ingredients of the half-autocratic, half-romantic ideology which he was to employ for the next twenty years. One of its chapters took the form of an Open Letter to Hitler on "the question of leadership." [2] Addressing him still only as "Esteemed Herr Hitler," Goebbels made a fervent confession of faith in the principle of leadership and in Hitler as the charismatic figure embodying it. Aversion to the political system of Weimar and a romantic mysticism formed the background of the pic-

---

[1] R. Semmler, *Goebbels, the Man next to Hitler*, London 1947. Diary entry of 12 December 1941, pp. 56-57.

[2] Joseph Goebbels, "Die Führerfrage", *Die Zweite Revolution—Briefe an Zeitgenossen*, Zwickau, n.d. (1926), pp. 5-8.

ture Goebbels painted of his political Messiah. The true leader, he explained, was *not* elected, he was *not* subject to the whims of the masses, he was *not* a parliamentarian, but a liberator of the masses. He exposed the shameless perversion and corruption of a system in which leaders were chosen according to party colour and the gift of empty oratory. Hitler was all the more dangerous to the moribund old system as he believed absolutely in what he preached. Goebbels borrowed from the language of German romanticism, from the ideology of the Youth Movement, when describing the Führer as "the fulfilment of a mysterious longing," as a man who showed them in their deepest despair the way to a faith. "You are like a meteor before our astonished eyes, and you have worked a miracle of enlightenment and belief in a world of scepticism and despair."

Hitler appeared only as the foremost pioneer and not yet as the Führer of all. "You personify the faith"—Goebbels remarked, addressing himself to Hitler—"and it suffices to your true modesty to be its first servant in the struggle for the mastery of the future." Was Hitler to become "the first servant of his people" on the lines of Frederick the Great? In any case in 1925 the scope of the "Führer" was not yet defined as universal. It was, Goebbels, insisted, "not the task of the Führer to do everything." With a cheeky aside, probably aimed at Hitler's sycophantic entourage in Munich, Goebbels explained that the Master did "not tolerate the flatteries of vain fools and dreamers." He was looking for real men, he-men (*Kerle*), and knew how to find them whenever he required them.

At this stage in the history of the National Socialist Movement—obscure and rent by internal feuds—the Leader was still pictured as the head of a limited minority. Goebbels was emphatic in praising "these small but determined minorities" who, "inspired by the faith of a unique personality, at the turning point of history put a spoke into the wheel of a development making for the abyss." It was they who preached faith to the despairing and roamed the country as preachers, "as apostles of the new idea performing the miracle of redeeming liberation." In his pseudo-missionary jargon Goebbels contrasted two types of political orators, the parliamentarian and the preacher. The first was depicted as being entirely negative, was said to shout, rave, grumble only in order to corrupt, whereas the preacher destroyed solely in order to build up. As a political Ezekiel he desired more than to draw a parliamentary salary, or to become a President. He worked genuinely (though somewhat obscurely) for "the final fulfilment of a mysteriously recognized idea."

Had not Hitler in his defence before the People's Court in Munich, in March 1924, contrasted the ministers, the high civil servants and the barons with Richard Wagner, a truly romantic racialist?[1] "Before the

[1] See the text of Hitler's final speech before the People's Court on 27 March 1924, printed in *Adolf Hitler's Reden*, ed. by Dr. Ernst Boepple, Munich, 1933, pp. 110-122. The reference to Richard Wagner is on p. 118.

court in Munich you grew before our eyes into the full stature of a Führer. What you said there were the greatest words spoken in Germany since the days of Bismarck." Nevertheless, Hitler was not yet introduced to the few readers of this eulogy as a demigod or superman, but only as the spokesman of a hard-pressed generation, as a champion of irresistible fanaticism. Religious expressions like "miracle" and "mission" abound in the pamphlet.[1] Man was not in this world—Goebbels explained—"in order to suffer, to enjoy life and to die" but rather in order "to fulfil a mission." This mission-complex was, of course, not new in German history, it went back to Fichte, to Arndt, to Heinrich von Treitschke.[2]

The contempt for the soft-hearted and small-minded man in the street, the belief in the magic power of political passions, the cult of the strong man—these were formulae handed on from the past to the turbulent minority round Hitler. In this early catechism of National Socialist *Weltanschauung* Goebbels professed that Hitler had become to him both leader and friend.

When four years later the Brüning Government was faced with the ills of mass unemployment, Goebbels, who had by then created a strong position for himself as head of the Party Gau of Berlin, continued to propagate the myth of the Führer in similar terms; with the difference, however, that he now felt that the rising tide of economic disaster was playing into the hands of the self-confident National Socialist opposition.

On Hitler's birthday in April 1929, Goebbels explained to the readers of the Berlin Party paper that four qualities were required to make a Führer: character, will-power, ability and good luck.[3] The Führer had to combine the gifts of the philosopher (*Erkenner*) with those of the orator and organizer.[4] But luck, too, was an indispensable ingredient. The Führer had to be lucky. The masses must gain the impression that what he did, or omitted to do, was under the protection of a higher force. Goebbels declared with his tongue in his cheek: "The Führer can be forgiven everything by the masses except lack of good fortune. On this point alone they are merciless." [5]

Goebbels was still relatively modest in his claims, as he did not yet

---

[1] A typical example of the continuous use of the term "miracle" as a form of *Ersatz* for religion is the following passage: "You started from below as every great leader does. But like all great leaders you have grown with your task. You became greater with it. You have become a miracle as it became a political miracle." For the pseudo-religious use of Christian language by early National Socialists, see also the article by Werner Betz "The National-Socialist Vocabulary" in *The Third Reich*, London 1955, pp. 784-796.

[2] Goebbels quoted Treitschke's dictum that "great political passions are an invaluable treasure."

[3] Article "Der Führer" in *Der Angriff*, 22 April 1929: reproduced in the collection of Goebbels' articles *Der Angriff*, 11th edition, Munich 1942, pp. 214-216.

[4] Article "Adolf Hitler," *Der Angriff*, 19 November 1928: reprinted under the title "Wenn Hitler spricht", op. cit., pp. 217-218.

[5] Article "Der Führer", op. cit., p. 215.

expressly assert that Hitler possessed all these four qualities. His lucky star had still to prove itself. Goebbels merely pointed out to his Party comrades that the Führer was in control of a political organization, the machinery of which had to function in every detail. He expressed his belief in Adolf Hitler's rising star, but could not boast yet of his overwhelming success or of his magic luck. "Today we are celebrating solemnly Adolf Hitler's fortieth birthday. We believe that Fate has chosen him to show the way to the German people. Therefore we salute him in devotion and reverence, and can only wish that he may be preserved for us until his work is completed." [1]

Within a short time the historic tide began to turn in favour of the National Socialist Party. With the elections to the Reichstag in September 1930 it emerged as the second largest party and the claim to be admitted to power was pressed incessantly by it. By March 1932 Hitler had become a serious rival to the aged Field Marshal von Hindenburg as candidate for the Presidency. There were two national ballots in this election. Before each of them Goebbels naturally made an immense effort to boost Hitler. On the eve of the first he wrote a fervent article "We vote for Adolf Hitler!" [2] in which he heralded his master as "Hitler—the Greater German—the Führer—the Prophet—the Fighter."

"Hitler, the Greater German", it was explained, meant the man who had himself experienced German "racial misery", a man, "born as an Austrian, whose entire life had been filled with a longing for the "Greater German Reich". It meant too, the former navvy, familiar with the people and the workers, sharing their plight; and the ex-soldier, determined as a statesman to realize the justified claims of his comrades. "Hitler, the Führer" had enabled a "laughed-at and derided small sect to become the most imposing mass movement in Europe." It was his aim, Goebbels wrote—"to unite the German people and to weld them together into a show of strength never seen before." "Hitler, the Prophet", was able to create a new political faith in the midst of the post-war misery. He had instilled into millions of National Socialists a new meaning and content of life, had saved them from despair and anarchy.[3] Finally there was "Hitler, the Fighter" challenging the policy of decay of the Republican system. He now wanted to tear the German people away from blind resignation, to put a new ideal before them. He was presented as the last hope of the masses, the shining symbol of the German will to freedom. "Hitler must become Reich President as the representative of the German idealism of the young, as the spokesman of the national activists and the pioneer of an impending economic and social revival." [4] For everyone and from every point of view his election was imperative.

[1] *Der Angriff*, p. 216.
[2] *Der Angriff*, 5 March 1932; reprinted in the collection under this title, pp. 269-270.
[3] Ibid.
[4] Ibid.

At the first ballot none of the candidates received an absolute majority; the second ballot developed into a close fight between Hindenburg and Hitler. Goebbels wrote a couple of powerful articles boosting "Adolf Hitler as a Statesman" and "Adolf Hitler as a Human Being".[1] He applied to Hitler the double approach sketched above, depicting him on the one hand as an infallible guide equipped with an uncanny instinct for essentials, and on the other hand as surprisingly humane and kind. The first of them was largely defensive, trying to prove that Hitler was not the demagogue inciting the masses and only effective in opposition, but the farsighted planner of reconstruction, whose first task in Germany would be to create a united nation. Hitler was declared a statesman *sui generis*. To the true statesman, Goebbels explained, the people were the raw material on which he exercised his political art. The true politician looked at the people as the sculptor looks at unhewn marble. Just as the sculptor created a work of art, so the statesman shaped the mass of people into a nation. In a decadent age Hitler "had managed to reimbue the masses with a new faith and the will to a new joy in the State (*Staatsfreudigkeit*)." [2]

Though this sort of argument was also put forward by other National Socialist writers and speakers, Goebbels struck a specific propaganda note of his own in recommending "Adolf Hitler as a human being". He cleverly contrasted caricatures of Hitler circulated by his opponents with the "real" Hitler. Goebbels alleged that his unscrupulous enemies liked to present Hitler as "lacking in any esprit and culture, without any insight or experience, an unintelligent rowdy, with the rubber-truncheon as his only argument, a tyrant in his own milieu and to his sub-leaders a posturing actor, who rehearses his speeches and addresses before the mirror in order to give them a maximum effect, a glutton and a rake, a friend of the capitalists and an enemy of the toiling masses." In reality, Hitler was quite different. He was fundamentally an artist, an architect and painter, whom only the misery of the German people, which began on 9 November, 1918, had called into politics.[3] In addition, Hitler was kindness itself. "That for innocent German children a new life in their fatherland had to be created and that they should have it better than their fathers and mothers, probably proved the main stimulus for his entry into politics."

To anyone doubting this highly sentimental argument and pointing to the *Machtmensch* Hitler, Goebbels replied that, like every statesman, Adolf Hitler "had to claim power for himself in order to implement his political ideas," but he did not want civil war and anarchy, on the contrary, he wished to ban these dangers permanently by establishing a strong authority. Hitler was presented as being averse to all pose, giving

---

[1] "Adolf Hitler als Staatsmann", *Der Angriff*, 1 April 1932, and "Adolf Hitler als Mensch", *Der Angriff*, 4 April 1932; reproduced in the book *Wetterleuchten*, pp. 272-274 and pp. 274-276.

[2] Op. cit., p. 273.

[3] Op. cit., p. 275.

himself as he was, "natural and without embellishment." He never uttered a word in which he did not believe. And as regards his alleged excesses in eating and drinking, the fact was that he neither took alcohol nor smoked, and was also a vegetarian. There was, incidentally, telling proof against the slander that Hitler was a tyrant, for he did "not want others to follow his personal abstinence." [1]

On the contrary, this good comrade and loyal friend of his subordinates showed his humanity and companionship unmistakably when travelling for his mass meetings by car through the country. Then he filled his pockets with cigarette packets, but instead of cigarettes they contained two and three mark pieces. He made a habit of stopping groups of hikers passing by. A brief conversation followed, and the astounded hikers, finding themselves presented with a small gift, realized only at the last minute that "they had spoken to their Führer." This very touching story served to show that Adolf Hitler was "a man who enjoys the greatest love and veneration of all who know him, not only as a politician but also as a human being." [2] Goebbels wanted to make it easy for the non-political masses to find in Hitler not only the Führer but also a father's image.

It has been aptly said that the relationship between the leader and those he leads can be "that of a father, of a comrade, of a despot and of a demi-god." [3] In the modern type of Caesarian or plebiscitarian dictatorship the despot is played down while prominence is given to the father, the comrade and the demi-god. Total identification of the led with their leader was for the next twelve years to be the main motive behind Goebbels' agile manipulation of the Führer cult.

2. BETWEEN 1933-1939

After the Nazis had come to power Goebbels' efforts to establish the Führer as the great national symbol were intensified. The process of *Gleichschaltung* (co-ordination) which put an end to all other parties and trade unions made it imperative to win over the still indifferent or hostile elements. When Goebbels published his so-called diary notes for the fifteen months from January 1932 to April 1933, he wanted to indicate the "clarity of instinct" and "the sureness of a sleepwalker" with which the Führer had gone his way and had led the Movement on the road to power, through all perils and threats, unperturbed and tenacious. "He alone," Goebbels emphasized, "was never mistaken." The new Chancellor never allowed himself "to be deceived or tempted by the favour or disfavour of the moment." This servant of God "had done justice to his historical mission in the highest and best sense of the word." [4]

---

[1] Ibid.
[2] Op. cit., p. 276.
[3] W. Hagemann, *Vom Mythos der Masse*, Heidelberg, 1951, p. 63.
[4] J. Goebbels, *Vom Kaiserhof zur Reichskanzlei*, 35th edition, Munich 1942, p. 14.

During the next ten years the Führer's infallibility, his imperturbability, his living-up to his historical mission, were underlined by Goebbels with suitable variations. It is significant that the address on Hitler's first birthday as a chancellor by the newly-styled "Reich Minister of Propaganda and People's Enlightenment" again emphasized both the *charisma* and the humanity of the Führer. With a somewhat cynical naivety, Goebbels observed: "Today the newspapers are filled with congratulations for Reich Chancellor Adolf Hitler. According to the tone, character and attitude of the papers, the nuances differ. On one point, however, all accounts are agreed: that Hitler is a man of calibre, that he has already solved a great historic task, and that a still greater one is awaiting solution by him. A statesman of a type found only rarely in Germany, he has already in his life enjoyed the good fortune of being respected, beloved, and, what is still more important, of being understood by the overwhelming majority of his people." Still thinking it inexpedient to claim the affection of the entire nation for his leader, Goebbels exploited the traditional veneration of Bismarck by the conservatives. "It need not be emphasized at this moment," he said, "when already definite facts give practical proof to the malevolents and the sceptics that he [Hitler] took up Bismarck's work and is about to complete it." [1]

Once the National Socialist regime was established, there was a great rush of people to join the Party.[2] Therefore Goebbels, who viewed these converts with a mixture of satisfaction and contempt,[3] made a point of asserting the right of the thousands of old Party members to claim the Führer as their man. "We leave it to others," he declared sardonically, "who a few months ago were still in the camp of our opponents and perhaps excelled themselves in calumny and slander against the Führer, to glorify him now with a false eloquence and glibness of tongue." They knew how little Adolf Hitler valued this and "how much more the devoted loyalty and the never-wavering faithfulness of his friends and fellow-fighters" appealed to him.[4]

The newcomers, of course, did not know Hitler intimately. The millions who had faith in him—Goebbels reflected—saw him only from afar as a symbol of a better future. All the more the necessity to point to the great man's essential humanity, to show him as a "human being amongst other human beings, a friend to his comrades, a helpful promoter of every ability and of all talents." In building up the Hitler myth, in offering a "close-up" of the Führer, Goebbels took pains to explain that his idol was

[1] "Unser Hitler!" Broadcast on 20 April 1933, cf. J. Goebbels' *Signale der neuen Zeit, 25 ausgewählte Reden*, p. 141.

[2] See the article "Die Zehn Jahre 1933-1943" by Benno Reifenberg in *Hundert Jahre Frankfurter Zeitung 1856-1956*" (Frankfurt, 1956), pp. 41-42.

[3] Goebbels' animosity against the countless opportunists who were now joining the victorious camp also found expression in a characteristic note in his diaries. See the entry of 8 April 1933 in *Vom Kaiserhof zur Reichskanzlei*, p. 296.

[4] *Signale der neuen Zeit*, p. 142.

different from all other outstanding men. "Usually," he said, "great men who had been revered from a distance, lost charm and impressiveness when one came closer to them. With Hitler it was the reverse. The longer one knew him the more one learned to appreciate and love him, and the more unreservedly did one identify oneself entirely with his cause." [1]

A carefully calculated image of the Führer emerged. There was the "fine and noble feature" of his stubborn loyalty to his friends. ("He never dropped anyone who had once gained his confidence.") There was his astonishing tolerance towards his lieutenants. He was not one of those unable to tolerate strong characters near them. The harder and more distinct the personality, the more he liked the man. "And if antagonism among the men around him should lead to clashes, his reconciling hand would immediately iron things out." [2] A euphemistic picture of a man who successfully exploited the principle of "divide and rule"!

The Führer's simplicity, Goebbels went on, revealed true greatness, showing itself as much after defeat as after victories. In bad days he never lost courage or faith and filled hundreds with new hope. Less than fifteen years ago he had been a lonely figure among millions. What distinguished him from them was his great faith and the fanatical determination to translate this faith into deeds. To him Nietzsche's aphorism (so popular with educated Germans) could be applied: "What does not kill me, can only strengthen me." Again much was made of the Führer's kindness, even to strangers. For every mother he had a friendly word and for every child a warm handshake. Once when the Führer had passed through the cheering crowds at Traunstein in Upper Bavaria a leader of the local SA had reported that in the local hospital there lay dying an old Party comrade whose last wish was to see his Führer once more. In spite of masses of work waiting for him, the Führer at once complied with the request and spent half an hour at the deathbed of his loyal supporter.

Again and again Goebbels was to repeat this technique of an appeal to the "Father Image," to the complete identification of Hitler with his followers. The Führer, we learn, shared both the good and the bad fortunes of those who worked with him. And how modest he was! On his birthday he fled the noise of the Reich Capital to avoid laurels and hymns of praise. He withdrew to some place in his beloved Bavaria to look back and to look forward in solitude. But it might well be that someone would switch on the wireless in the room next to his. Then Hitler would hear glowing tributes and thanks in the name of "millions and millions of the best Germans," and Goebbels addressing him before all the world with the intimate *"du."* [3] The peroration would conclude by offering the then

[1] Op. cit., p. 143.
[2] Op. cit., p. 144.
[3] Op. cit., p. 149. "Thou hast led Germany from the deep humiliation upward to honour and prestige; today thou shouldst know that behind thee, and if necessary also in front of thee is a united and determined troop of fighters always ready to give their last for thee and thine idea."

customary wishes. "We wish you and us on your birthday that fate may preserve you for the fatherland for many decades to come and that you may remain our best friend and comrade for ever . . . We give you our hands and vow that you will ever be for us what you are today: 'Our Hitler!' " [1]

It would be an exaggeration to assert that Goebbels invented the belief of the masses in Hitler's personal modesty and even in his kindness. He did not so much create this belief as strengthen and exploit it. Hitler, whose personal habits were frugal, gave himself in public and outside the field of power politics an air of kindness, of love of children, of benevolence for old Party comrades or their families—at least in the pre-war years of the regime. Few were in a position to realize how quickly this seeming kindness could be replaced by an outburst of wrath, by unfeelingly harsh calculation, by contempt for men. The masses, by no means uncritical of lesser Party bosses, saw in Hitler the man who had risen from their midst, who had kept his sympathies for "the little man" and who burnt himself out in the service of the nation.[2] The avoidance of pomp and luxury in his private life was contrasted with the greedy attitude of other Party leaders. Hitler "appeared as the unpretentious fighter for the highest aims," [3] and Goebbels, of course, knew how to make the most of this impression.

Two years later,[4] Goebbels still concentrated on Hitler *als Mensch,* as a human being, wanting to convey to the entire nation an impression of the charm and the strength of the Führer's personality. In 1933 he had only claimed that Hitler was revered "by the overwhelming majority of the people," but by 1935 he pronounced that a miracle had happened. Only Hitler's few intimates, privileged to know him from close daily experience, comprehended the miracle of how and why it was possible that a man who not three years before had been still opposed by half of the nation, could now stand "above all doubt and criticism in the eyes of the entire people." This new unshakable unity of the nation was interpreted as meaning that Hitler was a Man of Destiny, a man with a mission. At that time, a few weeks after Hitler had suddenly reintroduced conscription, openly flouting certain clauses of the Versailles Treaty, Goebbels began to stress the miraculous role of the Führer in foreign affairs. He celebrated Hitler as the man with "the calling to lead the nation upward to the desired freedom from the most terrible cleavages and most shameful humiliation in the sphere of foreign policy." [5]

Yet the theme that Hitler was the man to restore Germany to her rightful place as a great Power was not pursued further. In that year Goebbels

[1] Ibid.
[2] Schwerin von Krosigk, *Es geschah in Deutschland,* pp. 219-220.
[3] Ibid.
[4] In 1934 Goebbels did not deliver a radio address on Hitler's birthday.
[5] Goebbels, Radio address, 20 April 1935, *Frankfurter Zeitung,* 21 April 1935.

still concentrated on projecting the strong personality of the Führer and on his aversion to the mere seeking of effects. He claimed that the simple clarity which shaped his political outlook was the dominating principle in his life. To him the words of Schlieffen should be applied, "to be more than to seem." Again the propagandist's searchlight was thrown on the personal habits of the Führer, on his diligence, his toughness in pursuing his aims, all of which were said greatly to transcend the capacity of the man in the street. Behind his simple habits there was his genius. Hitler was a universalist *and* an expert, "the most widely skilled military expert." He understood any gun or machine-gun like a specialist, and his subordinates had to be familiar with the most minute details when they reported to him.

This was a significant new angle: Hitler as a military expert and as a statesman on the international chessboard. Yet he had come from the people and remained with the people. The man "who negotiated for two days at a fifteen hour conference with the statesmen of world dominating England (*des weltbeherrschenden England*) on the fateful questions of Europe, in polished dialogue and with a masterly control of arguments and figures," yet spoke in an informal and natural way to the man in the street. Goebbels again stressed the sentimental aspect. He recalled two touching photographs of Hitler which had appeared in the German press in the summer of 1934. The first had illustrated "his tragic loneliness" following the events of 30th June. Then the smashing of the SA group around Röhm had led to the murder of scores of real or suspected adversaries of the regime. The 30th June as interpreted by Hitler's chief propagandist meant that the Führer like another Siegfried "had to clean up treachery and insurrection by shedding blood." On the following day, when Hitler took the salute of the Reichswehr passing under the windows of the Reich Chancellery, to quote Goebbels, "his face was almost rigid as a result of the stark bitterness of the grave hour through which he had just passed." Taken six weeks later, the second photograph showed the Chancellor leaving the manor house of the dying President von Hindenburg, a figure so dear to millions of non-Nazis. As Goebbels saw it, Hitler's face reflected "grief and sadness over the merciless death about to take away his fatherly friend in a few hours".[1] In fact this event had strengthened Hitler's position, enabling him to style himself "Führer und Reichskanzler" and to increase the number of functions united in his person.

Hitler was even presented by Goebbels as something of a clairvoyant. "With the almost prophetic gift of the seer," Goebbels confided, he had predicted the serious dangers of 1934 to his most intimate circle on New Year's Eve, and also the likely death of Hindenburg during that year. It seems that Goebbels now wanted to create a mother rather than a father image in the masses. "The simplest people approach him with a

[1] Ibid.

friendly confidence, because they feel that he is their friend and protector. The whole nation loves him, because it feels safe in his hands like a child in the arms of his mother."

Obedience towards such a genius was declared to be a matter of course, and Goebbels tried to propagate this attitude, the basic virtue in any authoritarian state and traditionally strong in Germany, by vowing that he and other lieutenants closest to the Führer wanted to be "nothing but his most obedient followers". They were setting the example for the masses to follow in a total identification with Hitler, which was neatly underlined in the final sentence of Goebbels' 1935 birthday peroration: "And as we say it, who are standing close to him, so the last man in the most distant village says it in this hour: 'What he was, that he is, and what he is, he shall remain to us: Our Hitler!' " [1]

In subsequent years (1936-1939) which saw aggressive National Socialist dynamics becoming a key-factor in international affairs, Goebbels' birthday addresses were able to dwell on the Führer's remarkable contribution to the revival of a strong Germany as a world power.

The 20 April 1936 came only a few weeks after the dramatic remilitarization of the Rhineland. When that daring coup was carried out it had filled even the Führer with marked uneasiness, while his War Minister, Field Marshal von Blomberg, had lost his nerve at a critical moment. But Hitler's assessment of the position had turned out to be right. France was not prepared to act on her own, "Britain was in no position to support her, and British opinion neither understood nor sympathized with France's Rhenish anxieties." [2]

In a speech in Munich at the end of the crisis Hitler made his famous pronouncement: "I go with the assurance of a sleep-walker on the path Providence dictates." The German masses, including many people still critical of the Party, were in fact deeply impressed. It is against this background of a triumphantly asserted German self-confidence that Goebbels' birthday address of 1936 has to be viewed. The Propaganda Minister did not greatly exaggerate when he claimed that the nation was thinking "with a rare unanimity and a unity never displayed before" of the man who had become "the image of the German resurrection and the symbol of a strengthened and revived Reich." The new and surprising successes of the Führer seemed to underline Goebbels' boast that "never before in the history of all times" had "a man concentrated in his person the confidence and collective feeling (*Zusammengehörigkeitsgefühl*) of an entire nation." [3]

[1] The remarkable skill of Goebbels' method of building up Hitler and bringing him close to the man in the street becomes evident by a comparison with an article written on the same occasion, by Goebbels' rival, Reich Press Chief Dr. Dietrich. (*Nat. Soz. Korrespondenz*, 19 April 1935). This was just an ordinary newspaper leader praising Adolf Hitler as a fighter and as builder of the new Reich and stressing his recent political and military achievements.
[2] See the article "The Reoccupation of the Rhineland", by D.C. Watt in *History Today*, vol. vi, No. 4, April 1956, p. 251.
[3] *Völkischer Beobachter*, 20 April 1936.

Hitler now became a rock in the sea of everyday life, or an Atlas stoically carrying the ever-increasing burden of work, worry and responsibility on his back. At a moment when the Führer was declared to have raised the Germans to the level of a world power (*ein Weltvolk*), Goebbels discerned in him a combination of qualities otherwise seldom found together. Simplicity of demeanour was significantly linked with the monumental character of his historic deeds. Generosity towards things and people deserving it, was coupled with firmness towards things and people who require it. As Goebbels puts it: "He is not only called the Führer, he *is* the Führer." In this birthday speech a new and more explicit religious note was struck, a note which evidently served Goebbels' purpose to underline and sanctify the total integration of the people with the aims and methods of the Führer.

After the Rhineland crisis the Government had arranged the usual plebiscite for the people to demonstrate their approval of the Führer's bold action. On its eve, on 27 March, Hitler had given an address over all German radio stations from Cologne. In his birthday oration Goebbels alleged that the speech had made an immense impression on the people and referred to it in pseudo-religious terms: "One had the feeling as though Germany had been transformed into one big church embracing all classes and creeds, in which its spokesman appeared before the high chair of the Almighty in order to render an account of his aims and work and to implore His mercy and His protection for a future still uncertain and impenetrable. We saw in Cologne hard and strong men who had overcome many a danger burst into tears during the last words of the Führer." [1] Goebbels presented this mass infatuation as a religious phenomenon: "This was religion in the deepest and most mysterious sense of the word. There a nation professed its belief in God through its spokesman and put its fate and life trustingly into his hands." [2]

When after Hitler's address Goebbels had travelled back with him by train through the Ruhr to Berlin, thousands of people had acclaimed the Führer at the stations. "The Führer," said Goebbels with a romantic touch, "sat silently at the window of his compartment, and travelled through his country, through his nation, probably with the happy feeling of resting in this hour deeply and safely in the heart of his nation". The identity of Führer and nation was now implied to be complete.

A year later no special dramatic events helped the propagandist to highlight the Hitler myth. In April 1937 there were no clouds on the horizon, no impending lightning actions or other surprises. In April 1937 Goebbels had, therefore, to fall back on generalities, on some "unforgettable words" uttered by the Führer at the previous traditional gathering of the Old Party Guard in Munich on 8 November 1936. There Hitler had described the great difficulties he had been forced to overcome to regain German freedom and security, adding that "his work had now so far advanced that for the first time in his life he could face the

[1] Ibid.
[2] Ibid.

future without great worries." Goebbels applied to this episode his customary technique of a literary 'close-up' of bringing the remote Führer
closer to the masses. They had experienced "one of those rare hours,
when the Führer opened his heart in public, in order to afford the nation
a glimpse into his inner life." Thus suddenly every German had "a very
personal share in the great historic task which the Führer was fulfilling
solitarily, drawing only on his own resources." [1] At home in every sphere
of public life, the Führer was a man with a keen sense for essentials
and with a phenomenal memory, who, for example, knew Berlin better
than the Berliners themselves. He was that miracle, a universal expert,
an expert in every specialized field, one who, moreover, knew well how
to use his knowledge for action.

By the next birthday in April 1938, the *Anschluss* of Austria had
just been completed and the ease with which it had been achieved had
greatly increased the Führer's prestige at home and abroad. Goebbels,
jubilant and excited, made his radio address of 19 April 1938 one of
his most dramatic performances.[2] It was a huge "success" story couched
in superlatives. "The unhappiest nation on which God's sun shone," he
declared, had become "the happiest on this wide globe." A strong superiority feeling was in the air. "In our wide fatherland there is no German,"
proclaimed Goebbels, "who would like to be a member of another nation
or a member of another state. Under the blessed hand of the Führer
the dream of all good Germans has materialized: A united people in a
great, free, strong Empire." The key struck in this address was indicated
by the cry of some Austrians after the *Anschluss*; "We thank the
Führer".

Goebbels did his best to throw a sentimental light on the Austrian-
born Führer who had at last brought his own country into the Greater
Reich. He recounted how when he had been with the Führer at Obersalzberg some time previously, Germans from all *Gaue* of the Reich
had frequently come to pay homage to Hitler. It had been a moving
experience to see these Germans from the then independent Austria.
Little had been said, they had simply filed past the Führer in deep silence.
When he had asked one or other of them to come up to him, they had
rarely been able to answer his questions, because tears had choked them.
Again the aim of Goebbels' efforts was clearly the maximum of identification of Führer and *Volk*. "In these touching moments we realized from
the face of the Führer that the grief of his people was his own grief,
that he suffered its worries and torments very deeply and that no one
could suffer more for his home-country (*Heimat*) than he did himself." [3]

Goebbels then recalled some glimpses of the Führer during the days
of the "Austrian crisis". There had been Hitler's sharp reaction to the
former Herr Schuschnigg's "treacherous speech at Innsbruck" in which

[1] *Frankfurter Zeitung*, 20 April 1937.
[2] See *Völkischer Beobachter*, 20 April 1938.
[3] Ibid.

he had announced a plebiscite—a case of extreme disloyalty. The Führer's face had reflected "divine wrath and holy indignation". He had been "struck and wounded to the depth of his soul by cowardly treachery". To Hitler and his entourage it was, Goebbels explained, simply a question of two alternatives: "either Schuschnigg would succeed once more in legalizing his system of terror in the eyes of the world by a cowardly election swindle, or the people themselves would rise and, to secure their rights, reach for the stars." Then came the request for help from the Nazis in Austria and the order to march. In a few hours the swastika was hoisted over Vienna. Once more Goebbels indulged in religious language. "None of us was ashamed of his tears when at midnight we heard the Horst Wessel Song from the Radio Vienna for the first time. The Hour of Salvation had come," a happy end, presented in convenient superlatives, with "the hour of the greatest danger" also becoming "the hour of his greatest triumph".

But this exploitation of Hitler's undeniable success over the *Anschluss* was not enough. Goebbels went further by inventing a martyrdom of young Hitler in Austria. "What must his feelings have been in liberated Vienna: he who already as a boy had demonstrated in the streets of his home town for the Greater German Reich and had been persecuted, maltreated and arrested for it by the henchmen of the Habsburg regime" —an allegation by no means based on any evidence. Goebbels now fervently applied Treitschke's saying that "men make history" to Hitler, the man, able "to make the impossible possible". He drew a picture of the lonely Führer weighed down by the tremendous burden of the decisions he had to take.[1] Goebbels, who, as we saw, constantly aimed at a maximum identification between the Führer and the people, seems to have been acutely aware of the danger of over-emphasizing Hitler as a superman. It is true that in this birthday oration he had made the point that the man in the street was hardly in a position to analyse and examine a political situation as a whole, lacking, as he did, the training, the experience and the necessary information to arrive at a clear and unambiguous judgment. But with his slick sophistry Hitler's chief propagandist reasoned the problem away. This deficiency of insight of the man in the street, he declared, would not matter provided that at the helm was a man of truly historic calibre wishing to lead and able to do so. Then the people would back this leader to the hilt, would put all their love and blind confidence at his disposal. In this way a oneness of identification could be achieved which National Socialist propaganda couched in the terms of a secularized Trinity: 'One people, one Reich, one Führer.'

---

[1] Whilst he wrestled with Fate, the people had been oblivious of the historic moment. "Through the Wilhelmstrasse the people walked as if nothing had happened, only casting shy and reverent glances at the Reich Chancellery: here (they thought) lives the Führer; here he works, here he carries the burden and responsibility for us all." Ibid.

Two aspects of the Führer's successes were emphasized; paraphrasing Goebbels' jargon, one could call them "pragmatic" and "religious". Extreme shrewdness, high courage and a virile readiness to go to the utmost had conditioned the pragmatism which had achieved this miracle, "the result of ceaseless labour blessed by the hand of the Almighty". Here the "religious" aspect became evident. The concern for one's nation was declared a religious act. "Perhaps this, too, is some sort of religion," sermonized the little Doctor, "to put one's entire life into the service of one's nation, and to work and act for the happiness of the people. A religion, verily, without empty phrases and dogmas, but nevertheless springing from the very depth of our soul. That is how our people look at it." In religion also the Germans had proved superior to other nations who paid lip-service to God, but whose hearts remained cold and empty. Prayer, national resurrection, religious symbolism more intense than ever filled Goebbels' peroration, which lacked the aggressive tone of the later birthday speeches.

A few weeks before his next birthday in 1939 Hitler had ruthlessly destroyed Czechoslovakia as an independent state and had established a German Protector in the Hradshin in Prague. On the eve of the 50th birthday Goebbels' radio address could "register the felicitous fact" that again the map of Europe had been altered in favour of the Reich in a far-reaching manner; a change which had been "carried out without any bloodshed, an event unique in history." [1] Hitler was now presented as a realistic pacifist and, for the first time, as the creator of a New Order for Europe. His pacification of the Czechoslovakian area was described not as "a peace of pale, moralizing theory" but as "a peace of practical realism", founded on the instinctive insight "that only power gives a nation the opportunity to bring about a final solution of immediate problems". [2]

Against this new international background Goebbels painted a glowing picture of a great statesman and leader. Two qualities, as he saw it, were required for success in politics—imagination and realism. The Führer possessed both "in a unique harmony, rare in history". Imagination helped him fix his aim, realism suggested the methods for achieving it. He was clear and uncompromising in his principles, but extremely elastic in his political means—it was this combination "that had led to the great and unimaginable success of Germany's position". [3]

There was the usual flashback to the past, the analogy to the days of the Party in opposition. The political methods of the Führer were the same then as today, but earlier they had only been applied to smaller and apparently less important aims and problems. Goebbels liked to stress this continuity in Hitler's work. In the course of time only the dimen-

[1] "Führergeburstag 1939" reprinted in *Die Zeit ohne Beispiel*, Munich 1941, p. 98, a radio address delivered on 19 April, 1939.
[2] Ibid.
[3] Op. cit., p. 99.

sions of the political actions of the Führer had changed whilst his ways and aims had remained the same. Goebbels was now eager to rationalize and justify recent acts of conquest *post festum*, explaining how the emotional plight of the "outer" Germans, first in Austria, later in Czechoslovakia had made the integration of these countries in the Reich imperative. When the suffering *Volksdeutsche* had pointed to their problem, the Führer quickly recognized and solved it. This technique becomes evident through a flashback in his speech of 1939 to an episode of 1938. "We saw the Führer on a burning hot Sunday at noon stand again on a tribune in the Castle Square in Breslau. In front of him German *Turnerschaften* (gymnastic unions) filed by. When the national comrades (*Volksgenossen*) from the Sudetenland passed him a wall suddenly built itself in front of him without command or order. The people who had hurried from the Sudeten areas to Breslau only to look into the beloved face of this man could not be prodded to march on. Weeping women came up to the Führer to touch his hand. One could hardly understand what they said to him, for their voices were stifled by their tears."[1] According to Goebbels, as in the earlier case of the delegation from Austria, the Führer had reacted quickly to the moving sight of the suffering Sudeten Germans. Within a few months he had solved their problems, at Munich. Goebbels conveniently omitted to add in this speech in November 1937 that some months before that Sport Congress in Breslau Hitler had already decided to break up and take over the entire state of Czechoslovakia.[2]

As well as Hitler himself Goebbels constantly realized the need for the demagogic leader to give the impression that he was part of the masses, the mouthpiece and executor of their demands and wishes. In a totalitarian state, as Professor Hagemann has put it, "it not seldom appears as though the led acted before the leader and as if they superimposed the law of action on him, whereas in reality they are only the executors of his will." [3] Yet Goebbels' apotheosis of the Führer of 1939 had not only the usual sentimental overtones, it was also blatantly polemical. "Though the Führer had restored peace in *Mitteleuropa* (Central Europe)," [4] Goebbels declared in April, the Western democracies disliked his move. Their hysterical shouts deserved contempt. Today Germany was strong and fully conscious of the strength to which it had been restored by the Führer. Once sunk into deepest impotence, the country had risen to new grandeur.

There was a new feature in this last pre-war birthday speech. Hitler was now presented as a good European. Congratulations to the Führer

[1] Op. cit., p. 101.
[2] See the well-known Hossbach minute of 10 November 1937. *Documents on German Foreign Policy, 1918-1945*, Series D, vol. I, document 19.
[3] W. Hagemann, *Vom Mythos der Masse*, p. 63.
[4] On the *Mitteleuropa* ideology see H.C. Meyer, *Mitteleuropa in German Thought and Action 1815-1945*, The Hague, 1955.

did not only come from Germans inside and outside the Reich. Goebbels said dramatically that the "choir of a hundred million" (Germans) was "joined by all people outside our *Volkstum* who want a true peace and who love the order of Europe, her history and her culture." [1] As in 1938, the address of 1939 ended with a fervent prayer of the German people to the Almighty to preserve the Führer for them in vigour and health for many years and decades to come.[2]

The image of Hitler built up by Goebbels over the years with such skill did not, of course, rely only on articles and radio addresses. To appreciate its full extent one has to keep in mind the regular Party and State events during the years before the war at which the Führer and Chancellor formed the centre of attention, the apex of a pyramid. There was an astonishing amount of stage-management concentrated on his person. He was the focal point in carefully planned and organized mass-shows, which were a characteristic feature of the entire National Socialist regime.[3]

From the arrival of the various Party formations, the SA, the SS, the Hitler Youth, the Labour Service, to the often organized shouts of "Heil" by the onlookers, everything was calculated to create a specific effect. This whole pageant and ritual would have been pointless without the Führer, whose very existence gave it direction and meaning. His exalted position was, for instance, emphasized by the building of a special avenue in Berlin, the "East-West Axis", along which formations of the *Wehrmacht* marched past the Führer on his fiftieth birthday in 1939. There were also the squares near the Reich Chancellery in Berlin and the Brown House in Munich suitably arranged for "spontaneous" ovations of the people. The peak event in this context however remained the annual Party Congress at Nuremberg lasting at first four, later seven, and finally, in 1939, eight days.[4]

It was a remarkable effort of mass integration and mass intoxication in which the participants and onlookers were equally conditioned for worship of the Führer. Everything was on a gigantic scale. The huge Zeppelin field completed in 1938 allowed 100,000 people seated on the tribunes to watch 140,000 members of the Labour Service and of the corps of political functionaries march into the grounds. Even more ambitious were the plans for the German Stadium destined to hold 200,000 spectators, the foundations of which were laid in 1937, whilst

[1] *Die Zeit ohne Beispiel,* p. 102.

[2] Op. cit., p. 103.

[3] In the planning of the programme of the Party Congresses Goebbels, as head of the Party Office for Propaganda and the members of its section "Active Propaganda" took an important share. But the Führer, whose word was final, was also much concerned with it and even busied himself with details concerning the choirs.

[4] The stage-management of the Party Congresses has been well analysed in the study by Karlheinz Schmeer, *Die Regie des öffentlichen Lebens im Dritten Reich,* Munich, 1956, pp. 105-116.

the March Fields enabled half a million people to view the exercises
and parades of the Armed Forces.

In this gigantic show, half semi-religious pageant, half threatening
mass demonstration, every move had its special note, its specific function. With its brilliant festival dress of garlands and colours Nuremberg
"for eight days was filled by exciting colourful events which almost every
hour offered new peaks like a kaleidoscope. Carefully planning the producer provided each act of the great play with a special propaganda
note." [1] In all these performances the Führer was the high light, the
hero and the secularized saint of a many-scened revue. Here we can
only refer to a few events in the pageantry of the Party Congress week.
On the first day attention was focused on Hitler's arrival in the town,
on the warm welcome given to him by a jubilant crowd waving little
swastika flags. A few hours later fanfares greeted him as he entered the
richly decorated main room of the Town Hall. In the presence of an
élite of representatives of State and Party and of the Diplomatic Corps
he was welcomed by the Lord Mayor and offered a special gift in the
name of the city of Nuremberg. After the Anschluss the golden shrine
with the Insignia of the First German Empire (*Reichskleinodien*) which
had been preserved in Vienna since the Napoleonic Wars was displayed
for this occasion. The insignia were to symbolize the continuity of the
Reich and to provide Hitler's realm with something of the mystical aura
of the ancient "Holy Roman Empire of the German Nation".

On the second day a much larger crowd witnessed the opening of the
Party Congress. Its ceremonial "was intended to imitate the solemn
atmosphere of a religious festival service".[2] The walls of the Luitpold
Hall were draped in white silk. A huge golden swastika hung behind the
platform on which the entire corps of leading functionaries of the Party
was assembled. Fanfares sounded and bands played Hitler's favourite
Badenweiler March as the Führer entered amid the immense applause
of the assembled crowd. On the eve of the fourth day there was a torch-
light procession of the political officers, ending with a march past the
Führer in front of his hotel, the Deutscher Hof. This was the prelude
to the following day also given over to men of the Party bureaucracy,
of whom there were no less than 110,000. When Hitler's arrival had
been signalled, they stood rigidly to attention in their brown uniforms
while the public greeted the Führer with the customary waves of *"Heil."*
It was then that 150 searchlights converged in the sky forming a gigantic
cupola of light. Again fanfares greeted the Führer who approached the
main tribune as his standard was hoisted. At a command 30,000 flags
unfurled from the platforms opposite were dipped in salute, the searchlights bringing them into strong relief. The entire spectacle concentrated
on the Führer's podium in the centre of the main tribune. The main
stream of the flags pointed to it, the symmetry of the whole show con-

[1] Op. cit., p. 108.
[2] Op. cit., p. 109.

verged on it. Silence in honour of the dead Party members fell over the crowd, a solemn song of dedication was heard, and then Hitler briefly addressed the assembly in the language of National Socialist theology. When he had ended with a "Hail Germany" the flags were lowered once more into the glaring searchlights. Half a million people sang the two national anthems, the traditional *"Deutschland über alles"* and the Party's own Horst Wessel Song. The Führer's unique position was even more highlighted on the seventh day when over 100,000 members of the SA (in brown) and of the SS (in black) filled the wide Luitpold arena. After the usual ceremony at the Führer's entry his standard was hoisted over his platform and all the assembled flags and standards were raised. To Hitler's possessive shout: "Hail My Men!" the thousands roared back "Hail My Führer!" It was significant that at this exchange the pronoun "my" and not "our" was employed, thus giving each man the feeling that it was "his" Führer to whom he belonged. The men and the flags took position before the shrine of honour. While solemn tunes of mourning were played Hitler moved forward along a special "Road of the Führer", followed at some distance by the Chief of Staff of the Storm Troopers, Lutze, and the Reich Leader of the SS, Himmler. With the flags dipped as a tribute to the dead, Hitler stood in silence in front of the *Blutfahne*, the Party banner said to be stained with the blood of men who had lost their lives in the abortive Putsch of November 1923.

On such occasions Hitler appeared as a Caesar and as a comrade, as a link with the national past and as an arrow pointing to Germany's future. He was there "amidst the formations of his loyal men, founded on strict military obedience; at the same time he was surrounded by an unbridgable distance marking a Caesarean loneliness, as well as by the dead heroes who had sacrificed themselves because they had believed in him and in his mission." [1] Hitler was made to appear close and yet far away. In the afternoon of the same day the endless columns of the SA and SS men filed past the Führer who was standing erect in his car in the square in front of the Frauenkirche, the surrounding gaily decorated houses of the old patrician families forming a background. Hitler is alleged to have tried to catch the eye of every individual Party warrior as he went by. The impression to be created was that the Führer had noted him personally—an experience never to be forgotten. In past centuries, too, the public appearance of an Emperor like Charles V, or of an outstandingly successful general such as Prince Eugène, not to mention a soldier-dictator like Napoleon, attracted great crowds and was a spectacle surrounded with glamour and sometimes with enthusiasm. But never had hundreds of thousands been so deliberately conditioned and

[1] Op. cit., p. 113.
The "religious" function of the Führer became evident in the act of "touching" as part of the ceremony. Through touching the sacred *Blutfahne* the Führer dedicated new standards of the two Party organizations. Each time he touched the sacred banner a salute was fired.

the roles of the one and of the many so thoroughly planned and streamlined as at these annual Party Congresses. They completely lacked the lighter touch, the informal note that is characteristic of the big Party Conventions in the United States, for example. There was, however, a streak of American showmanship, of gigantic advertising in the Nuremberg performance that went oddly with the heavy para-militarism which cast its spell over participants and spectators alike.

The propaganda effect of the huge parades of Party members, or of troops paying homage to their Führer, could be intensified through their projection by radio and film. A case in point is the film specially arranged to convey an impressive picture of the festivities in Berlin in honour of Hitler's fiftieth birthday, one month after his troops had occupied Prague and only four months before they were to invade Poland. For this purpose a special edition of the UFA newsreel was planned and carried out by selected cameramen under the supervision of the Propaganda Ministry. The survey of the official events on April 19th and 20th was to be as manysided and effective as possible. No less than 10,000 meters of film were shot, out of which in the end one twentieth was cut to form the special edition of the *Wochenschau*.[1]

Its most interesting part is the great parade of detachments of the *Wehrmacht* before the Führer, who took the salute from a tribune of honour. The technique behind this film was revealed in a report written later for the benefit of film specialists under the telling title *Parade als Paradestück* (Model of a Parade). It throws much light both on the cult of the Führer and on the possibilities of the film as an instrument of calculated propaganda under a dictatorship.

"The Führer's fiftieth birthday. Berlin put on its finery, made the last preparations for this twentieth of April, 1939, which was to become a unique day of thanksgiving.

"The *Filmwochenschau* had a specific assignment in this. Transcending the present, it was to create a historic document for the future, to capture in pictures the greatness of this day for all the future to see. This parade had to become a paradigm of film reporting. It was not simply a matter of outward form—the spirit of the hour must be captured, too, the whole atmosphere of discipline and of concentrated power. Every second of the action must be captured as it occurred. If something was missed, it could not be repeated and was forever lost.

"The program begins. The Führer drives between the line of troops from the park (*Lustgarten*) to the parade ground. Immediately on his arrival the march past begins. But in the meantime, unseen by most of the people despite the variety of events, the formation of the units of the parade took place. Each unit, after first lining the street, is wheeled into a marching column; men on foot and men in vehicles were skilfully in-

[1] See Fritz Terveen, "Der Filmbericht über Hitlers 50. Geburtstag. Ein Beispiel nationalsozialistischer Selbstdarstellung und Propaganda". *Vierteljahrshefte für Zeitgeschichte*, vol. 7, no. 1, January 1959, pp. 75-84.

terspersed in a colorful order. A broad street, many kilometers long, was completely filled by soldiers of all the armed forces, which now had to be ordered into a precise flow for the great moment when they would march past Adolf Hitler. The twelve pairs of eyes of the twelve cameramen had to see more than all the hundreds of thousands of onlookers. And so they did, as the success of this *Wochenschau* demonstrates." [1]

The film itself features the preparations on 19 April and the events on the birthday itself:

"Under a bright, shining sky the birthday itself begins. Merry marching tunes resound: the SS *Leibstandarte* gives Hitler a birthday serenade. Surrounded by some of his co-workers, among whom Himmler stands out, Hitler receives the homage. The camera lingers lovingly on the Goebbels children, all clothed in white, who stand, curious but well-behaved, next to Hitler, thus strengthening his reputation as a true lover of children —a special shot for the women in the audience. Now the picture turns to the crowd. A gigantic chorus before the Reich Chancellery swells in a song of jubilation for Hitler. Now Hitler appears on the balcony before the crowd, which breaks out into ovations.

"In the second half of the film the scene shifts finally from the preparations to familiar close-ups, to mass demonstrations, and then at last to the realm of the official, political, and military. With screaming engines the great automobiles leave the Wilhelmstrasse: Hitler and his entourage depart for the parade. Military orders and marching tunes introduce the second act of the spectacle. Jubilation breaks out: the film is focussed, sight and sound, on the exact moment when Hitler passes the Brandenburg Gate between the troops. The Hitler who now, erect and poised, climbs the steps to the canopied platform and takes his place on a 'throne' (already significantly picked out by the camera) to await the parade—this Hitler is not only a 'statesman' but also clearly a field-commander-to-be, who intends to review his armed forces. This is the way the film has it." [2]

It is not difficult to discern the political aims behind this film. Hitler wanted to impress the people, who since the Munich crisis had displayed little enthusiasm for war, with the concentrated might of his armed forces, including the Luftwaffe. But this display of might was also addressed to the representatives of foreign countries present on this occasion. Among the guests of honour whose arrival in Berlin was filmed were Dr. Hacha, the former President of the now defunct state of Czechoslovakia, the Slovak President Dr. Tiso and the Rumanian Foreign Minister Gafencu.[3]

[1] Op. cit., pp. 76-77.
[2] Op. cit., pp. 81-82.
[3] Hitler had previously issued this order to his Foreign Minister: "For the celebration of my fiftieth birthday I should like you to invite a group of foreign guests, among them as many cowardly civilians and democrats as possible. For them I will produce a parade of the most modern armed forces in the world." The Parade was obviously intended to intimidate these foreign observers. Op. cit., pp. 82-83.

3. DURING THE WAR OF 1940-1945

It is a truism that to nations involved in war leadership matters more than in times of peace. What is perhaps less obvious is that this applies also to totalitarian societies in which the leader has from the outset a greater prestige and a greater social significance. Usually in Western democracies national integration only begins to become important when the nation is threatened by a rival power and the continuance of its ways of life and of its status is questioned. When individuals are called upon to make great sacrifices, not only of their goods, but even of their lives, the need both for national integration and for a leader as its visible symbol becomes imperative. The strong man who knows how to act swiftly and effectively and at the same time how to exhort and to inspire the nation is listened to and revered as never in times of peace. Clemenceau in France, Lloyd George in England fulfilled such functions as symbols of national unity in the First, Mr. Churchill in England in the Second World War. In both states it became evident that in times of peace and in times of war different qualities are required in a Prime Minister.

In the Fascist states there was no change in leadership. There the war did not demand a different type of leader as it did in England and France. In Germany, as in Italy, the image of the leader had been carefully built up through many years. When war came, by no means as a surprise, propaganda had only to elaborate and to modify the image of the infallible leader, which it had already developed. The propagandist could draw on the store of confidence and loyalty that the dictator had or was said to have acquired through his successful political manipulation during times of "peace." It was therefore easy for Goebbels to continue the line that he had pursued for so long. His suggestion that the Führer had frustrated all the vile plots of his enemies, that he had carried out all his plans, could now be extended to mean that he would continue to do so in the more difficult conditions of war. His uncanny insight into the political intrigues of his enemies and his capacity for quick and decisive action would make him the strongest shield of the nation. Goebbels' wartime addresses emphasized both the Führer's role as supreme protector and shield of the nation and his uncanny ability in military campaigns. Hitler was now shown as a military genius, as the friend of his people, and later as the constructive planner of a New Europe. Compared with the earlier years of the Third Reich, Goebbels' wartime image of the Führer was less fanciful and more realistic, particularly so during its later phase. Hitler was depicted as the principal Saviour of the nation rather than as the infallible superman. He appeared now less like a figure from a fairy-tale and more like one in a heroic epic.

On the whole Goebbels' wartime birthday addresses were much more polemical than those drafted in days of peace. The first of them, delivered on 19 April 1940, made no reference to the earlier phase of Hitler's Western offensive, which had begun on 9 April with the occupation of Denmark and of vast parts of Norway. Goebbels simply used it for an attack on Neville Chamberlain and the stupid plutocratic English ruling class, an answer to English propaganda said to speculate on divisions inside Germany. In a broadcast to the German people on 3 September 1939, two hours after the outbreak of the war, the English Prime Minister had suggested that England was not waging war against the German people, but only against the Führer and Hitlerism.[1] Once the German people had discarded the latter, they would be granted a fair peace. Six months later Goebbels alleged that English publicists had declared it the goal of British plutocracy to annihilate Germany as an Empire and a nation and to reduce it to the status of 1648. Their speculation on disunity inside the Reich was scoffed at as entirely futile. For democratic countries did not understand the deep confidence which existed between the Führer and the people. "There is nothing which could cause any difference between Germans as regards their love of, obedience to and trust in the Führer. And we all realize that this is the strongest protection for the German nation in its fateful struggle." [2]

Through the educating influence of the Führer the German people were now immune to the impact of such destructive foreign propaganda.

Less dramatic or emotional than usual, the address underlined the strong ties between front and home front, the quiet, almost sovereign confidence in the outcome of the war prevailing among the German people. The 51st birthday of the Führer was to be celebrated not by loud festivities and striking parades, but by a nation fighting and working." [3]

Applying his usual technique of bringing the personality of the Führer into focus by a vivid flashback, Goebbels this time took his sample from the newsreel of the campaign in Poland, later incorporated in the frightening propaganda film *Feuertaufe*. In the train which takes the military leaders to the Polish front the German generals are seen assembled round a map, debating serious problems of warfare. "Then the camera slowly turns from the group of the deliberating generals and shows at one side of the room the Führer sitting; and with deep emotion the eye of the viewer discovers the man, to whom all of us look up, his face filled with worry, under the shadow of the burden of his thoughts, a historic personality, utterly great and utterly lonely." [4] As in previous birthday orations stress is laid on the reaction of the people as much as on the Führer himself.[5] It was the identity of feeling, this identification with and subordination

[1] See *The Times*, 4 September 1939.
[2] Article "Führergeburstag 1940" *Die Zeit ohne Beispiel*, p. 284.
[3] Op. cit., p. 287.
[4] Op. cit., p. 286.
[5] Ibid. Goebbels described the attitude of the usually sceptical Berlin public at the premiere of the film of the Luftwaffe *"Feuertaufe"*. "When the face of the Führer suddenly appeared on the screen, a deep silent and noiseless movement went through the large room crowded with people. No one said a word and yet all felt the same at this moment."

to the Führer which Goebbels wished to suggest now, even more emphatically than before.

In the serious and perilous hours of war again "the German miracle" was evoked. The determination to trust and obediently to follow the Führer "gives us as a people and as a nation that immense strength which foreign nations call and probably feel to be the German miracle. An enigma for the world, but for us a matter of course! We can hardly visualize that this could one day be different or even that it had ever been different." [1]

Maximum identification between the people and the Führer was naturally a major motive in Goebbels' propaganda on the eve of the big German push to the West. A year later, when Germany had achieved astonishing military successes and controlled most of Europe, either directly or indirectly, the miracle theme still prevailed. "It has been one man," proclaimed Goebbels, "who, as a pioneer, has given meaning, content and direction to the overall trend of this age." "We experience the greatest miracle existing in history: a genius is building a new world." [2] Another and new leitmotif can also be detected in these war-time birthday speeches. Reverence for the Führer was utilized to strengthen war morale, to spur the masses on to an ever greater war effort. "The German nation pays homage to the Führer on his birthday"—Goebbels suggested —"by the vow of a doubled devotion to his work. Love and veneration of him urge on our fight and our work for victory." [3]

The 1941 address was again one long controversy with England, spiced with the strong and seemingly reasonable confidence that Germany would win, integrated and led as she was by the Führer. Again Hitler was contrasted with the English Prime Minister. "When Mr. Churchill recently talked on the chances in this war, he declared England would win, he merely did not yet know how. We can give him only this answer: The Führer will win, because he also knows how he will win. He has filled the nation with his spirit. It is oriented towards his will. . . . A nation led by *one* will and dominated by *one* fanaticism—means victory!" [4] The man who achieved all this was declared to be "above praise and glorification. Before him the nation can only bow." But if the Führer was great, his heralds and propagandists knew how to sun themselves in reflected glory.[5] In their youth they had had the supreme good fortune to be with him when he won a revolution, and now they were again enjoying the same privileged position when he was about to win this great war for Ger-

[1] Op. cit., p. 287.

[2] "Führergeburstag 1941", a radio address on the occasion of the birthday of the Führer, 19 April 1941, *Die Zeit ohne Beispiel*, p. 464.

[3] Op. cit., p. 465.

[4] Op. cit., pp. 468-469.

[5] Ibid. "We, his old co-fighters . . . thank fate that it gave us so early and in such young years the strength and the insight to recognize his greatness and to accompany him from his beginnings on his path full of vicissitudes but always leading to victory and triumph at the end."

many's life and freedom. This old companionship engendered confidence in prediction. "We have fought so long side by side with him, that we have the right to say from our experience, but also from our knowledge of things, that victory is as good as certain, that we only need to remain strong, faithful, brave and upright in order to march with our heads high to the hour of our proudest victory." [1]

As the spokesman for the reverent gratitude of the entire nation Goebbels named the various sections of the nation, all of which he claimed carried his name on their lips. The soldiers and workers, those who defended the safety of the Reich in the South East or in North Africa, the man of the Luftwaffe who carried death and destruction to the British Isles, the sailors of the German Navy who laid an iron ring round Great Britain, they all saluted their Supreme Commander, and the peasants, the women, the German youth, they all thanked him. In all their variety these sections of the nations were united in their trust and belief in the Führer. The eulogy ended with the traditional prayer to God for the Führer's preservation and for the blessing of his liberation of the nation.[2]

A year later the war had still not ended in a victory, but had been widely extended. In April 1942 the old German nightmare of fighting in the West and in the East lay heavily on the hearts of many Germans. Churchill had not given in. No longer did the Propaganda Minister think it opportune to contrast British "mediocre and bluffing" statesmen with the great Führer. As final victory seemed to be rather elusive, propaganda struck a new note of heroic resistance and stoicism took the place of the earlier superior enthusiasm. It was in these circumstances that a new figure to compare the Führer with made his bow from the shades of history. In the spring of 1942 a new film on Frederick the Great was shown all over Germany. "The Great King" illustrated the heroic attitude of Frederick II during the crititcal phases of the Seven Years' War and brought out his disappointments, difficulties and sufferings. The parallels were obvious.[3]

Speaking of the film in the first part of his Führer birthday oration in April, 1942 Goebbels declared it a fallacy to believe that great victories in history were primarily the outcome of a sustained military and political superiority and of a permanently smiling Fortune. It was, he insisted, equally wrong to believe that an apparent danger or an occasional threat to success could impair the reputation of the leading personality.[4] Goebbels praised the deeply moving qualities of this film and the astonishing parallels with the present age to be found in the Great King's sayings and in the psychological crises which he had experienced

[1] Ibid.

[2] Op. cit., p. 470.

[3] See the entry in Goebbels' Diary of 19 February 1942, quoted below ch. 12, pp. 278-79.

[4] "Führergeburtsagsrede 1942", radio address, 19 April 1942; reprinted in J. Goebbels, *Das eherne Herz,* Munich, 1943, p. 287.

fighting and suffering with his people. What was the main lesson to be learned from the film? At all times it was not the greater economic or military potential, the more fortunate geographical situation, the greater toughness of the soldiers or civilians, but superior leadership that decided wars. "The leadership turns the scales," proclaimed Goebbels at a moment when millions of German soldiers faced the miseries of a Russian winter. "If in addition it has also the better material chances at its disposal, then no power on earth can snatch victory from it." [1] *Quod erat demonstrandum.*

To the propagandist it seemed only a small step from 1761 to 1942. Another Frederick the Great, Hitler was presented as a tower of strength, a magic fountain of reassurance for the hard fighting nation. It was the solidarity of all in a harsh struggle which had to be emphasized. Goebbels therefore suggested that during the hard weeks and months the minds of the nation had constantly turned to the Führer. They had never felt so close to him as in the present time which spared no one. The more rarely Hitler now showed himself to the masses, the more Goebbels realized the necessity of pointing to his symbolic image. "One felt everywhere the need to see him, even if only his photograph, in order to gain strength just from glancing at him, for the mastering of the heavy task which every day has brought for everyone. All of us have felt under an obligation to him particularly in these last months. All have been with him, even without any word spoken without any request!" [2]

Goebbels drew attention to the enormous burden borne by the Führer day and night by comparison with which the daily problems of the masses were relatively insignificant. They had only to follow but he had to pave the way. "He stands alone facing his and our fate in order to fight out to a victorious end the titanic struggle imposed on us for the life of our nation." [3] It was now the stoic attitude of holding out that Goebbels stressed as the common tie between the Führer and the nation.

By April 1943 the need to appeal to this line of sombre perseverance had become more pressing. The calamity of Stalingrad had shaken the easygoing optimism of the Party hierarchy and the masses. Total war was imminent. The need to continue a costly struggle, the end of which was still not in sight, had to be explained and defended. Goebbels' radio peroration of 19 April, 1943 had largely this apologetic function.[4] Apart from the introductory statement that the German people were this year celebrating the birthday of the Führer "with particular seriousness of conduct and mood," the name of the Führer was hardly mentioned in the first part. Goebbels admitted that the fourth year of the war had brought its hardest phase and that for the time being a way out of the burdens and sufferings could not be discerned. In times of peace—Goebbels explained

---

[1] Op. cit., p. 290.
[2] Op. cit., p. 291.
[3] Op. cit., pp. 293-294.
[4] "Führergeburtstag 1943", reprinted in *Der Steile Aufstieg*, pp. 252-262.

—naive people might imagine that it was easy to govern and to lead; in times of danger even they had an obscure feeling "that he fares best who stands on the lowest rung of the ladder," while the man "who stands on its very top and has to give orders, must carry the heaviest burden."

We could say that in a military crisis Hitler, as projected by Goebbels, had the appearance of a figure from a painting by Goya: "Endless days of work and endless wakeful nights, beset by worry, write their indelible furrows on his face." In him "the suffering and grief of the individual human beings tower like a mountain to become the suffering and grief of a whole nation." [1] Goebbels now put forward a new aspect of his favourite image-theory identifying the Führer and the people. "Could one draw the face of our people," he asserted, "it would, during the course of this war, probably reveal the same deep changes which we observe with earnest pride in the face of the Führer. In him are seen not only the features of hardness, of determination, but also unmistakably those of a deep suffering for the nation and in a wider sense for mankind who, quite against his will and intention, have to bear and suffer so much bitterness and hardship."

Such an attempt at close identification must have seemed all the more necessary to Goebbels as by then the Führer had made himself less and less visible to the German public. During the winter 1942-43 he had spoken in public only once, on the traditional date of 8 November, to deliver an address to the old Party Guard. Between Stalingrad and the end of the war he made only two more public speeches, excluding two funeral addresses.[2] The Minister of Propaganda was very uneasy about this reluctance of the Führer to exercise his oratorical gifts and tried to "explain" it by Hitler's restless absorption in war-work. As the war went on Goebbels thought it wise to admit that there were often voices among the German people regretting "that the Führer has almost completely disappeared behind his work, though he is the determining factor of the entire political and military development. In this he stands in very marked contrast to the practice of the commonplace figures on the other side who miss no opportunity of showing themselves before the full footlights of the world stage." [3] Men of true historic calibre did not need the unstable approval of publicity. Their strength "sprang from the demon of their historic mission which they fulfil according to a higher law." [4] Of the unwillingness of the Führer to appear in public Goebbels made, from necessity, a virtue. As much as they might sometimes regret this fact, it was "just by this entirely unobtrusive manner of living and working

[1] *Der Steile Aufstieg*, p. 256. By the end of 1942 Hitler accepted the fact that the war could not be won. He knew "that the balance of power was such that without some *deus ex machina* in the shape of a new weapon, defeat was unavoidable." F. H. Hinsley, *Hitler's Strategy*, Cambridge, 1951, p. 236.

[2] Alan Bullock, *Hitler, A Study in Tyranny*, p. 662.

[3] *Der Steile Aufstieg*, p. 257.

[4] Op. cit., p. 258.

that he has come closer to our hearts." Hitler's simplicity and directness were contrasted with the grandiloquence and boastfulness of the enemy.

By Hitler's 54th birthday in April 1944 the German armies were in full retreat on the Eastern front and the Allied invasion in the West was imminent. Goebbels was forced to use the Führer myth to the full to bolster the imperilled German morale and to combat what he called "the evil of doubt and discord." He asserted that the German people approached the Führer "with a feeling of particularly faithful confidence." [1]

Confidence, he argued, was the best moral weapon in wartime. "Only if it should begin to fail, then would the beginning of the end have come." [2] The beginning of the end! An ominous phrase coming from Goebbels and one which he hastened to explain away. There was not the slightest reason, he explained, for fearing that they might lose, such a possibility was nothing but a propaganda wish-dream of the enemies.

Identification of the people with the Führer—a theme, as we have seen, so often pursued by the Minister of Propaganda—was now to mean identification with victory. "We believe in the great German victory because we believe in him. . . . A people that can call such a Führer its own and adheres to him with unconditional loyalty, is chosen for greatness. It only has to will this greatness incessantly." [3] By April 1944 devastating air raids and reverses in the East had made the war position more critical for Germany than ever before. Goebbels recommended the taking of a detached and historical view of things, of looking at the present hard days *sub specie historiae*. In other words, he escaped to some extent into history, into analogies with the past, in order to sweeten the pill of a merciless and all-destructive present. "The war," he proclaimed in his birthday address at the State Opera House in Berlin on 19 April 1944, "can only be assessed as a whole. Besides its actual it has also an historic development. One has to view it (the war) with a thoroughly trained and practiced eye in order to recognize this even while it is taking place." [4] Not before the end of a war and usually only a considerable time afterwards, Goebbels maintained, was it possible to arrive at an objective assessment of its individual factors or events. These oratorical explanations in a birthday speech were obviously made in order to substantiate Goebbels' major point that "in times of war not only *fortuna* but also fame vacillates continuously to and fro between the great men and the nations."

The German public saw or heard hardly anything of Hitler after his short broadcast on 9 November 1943 in Munich to the Old Party Guard. Then Goebbels felt relieved: "I am very glad that the Führer has spoken again after such a long interval," he commented in his diary. "It was high

[1] Op. cit., p. 260.
[2] Ibid.
[3] Op. cit., p. 261. There was also the usual eulogy of the old Party Guard as a model of unwavering faith and mental fortitude for all.
[4] *Völkischer Beobachter* (Viennese edition) no. 111, 20 April 1944.

time. It was, so to speak, a case of his speaking the redeeming words." [1]
Yet no further "redeeming words" from the mouth of the Führer were
heard. There was a growing discord among Hitler's top sub-leaders. As
a result Goebbels sent a long memorandum to the Führer a week before
his birthday in 1944, in which he recommended an attempt to come to
terms with Stalin. At the same time Ribbentrop was attacked as "the man
responsible for our isolation abroad and for the violation of numerous
treaties." [2] But Goebbels was far from revolting against the Führer himself, and remained deeply emotionally tied to him. According to von
Oven he continued to show him "a child's love and reverence." [3] Each
time Goebbels visited Hitler at his H.Q. he was "full of distrust of the
Führer's genius, full of irritation, criticism and hard words," and "determined to tell Hitler just what he thinks." And yet each time he returned from those visits "full of admiration for the Führer" and exuding
an infectious optimism. [4]

While his own loyalty remained unimpaired under the pressure of adverse circumstances, he had to fall back on laboured historical perspectives for the benefit of the hard-pressed public. In his 1944 birthday speech
Goebbels once more drew a comparison with Frederick the Great to make
the image of Hitler's greatness palatable for the masses. This time from a
different angle. Cleverly he tried to parry criticism of the Führer's re-
moteness by an analogy with the changing judgments on Frederick the
Great. What his contemporaries thought about the Prussian King between
1760 and 1763, he explained, was entirely different from the present
views. "The contemporary judgment about the historic significance of his
personality and of his deeds was distorted and disfigured by partisanship;
our present assessment of him is arrived at by historic perspective, that
means, it is objective and just." [5] The historian Goebbels led the way to
the crystal gazer. What event of this war, he asked, would still be regarded as of historic significance a hundred years hence? Not so much
the impact of the air raids on German towns, the traces of which presumably would have disappeared in ten years' time. The great issue would
be, whether Europe went Bolshevist or whether this deadly peril could be
avoided. "The man who is able to liberate Europe from Bolshevist

[1] *The Goebbels Diaries,* entry of 9 November 1943, p. 411.

[2] R. Semmler, *Goebbels, the Man next to Hitler,* 10 April 1944, p. 120.

[3] W. von Oven, *Mit Goebbels bis zum Ende,* II, entry of 20 April 1944,
p. 235.

[4] See R. Semmler, op. cit., 6 June 1944, p. 128. Goebbels conveyed his personal congratulations on Hitler's birthday in 1944 by a midnight conversation
with the Führer over the telephone and by a birthday letter which was kept
secret. Von Oven, who saw it, noted in his diary that "it has made a deep
impression on me to read a sentence like this, as coming from the pen of a
man whom we know as a raging despot: . . . 'When I am with you, my
Führer, then you tower before me in such overwhelming greatness that I
mostly lack the courage to address a personal word to you'. " W. von Oven,
op. cit., II, entry of 20 April 1944, p. 235.

[5] *Völkischer Beobachter* (Viennese edition) no. 111, 20 April 1944.

encirclement will—seen in historical perspective—be the man of this war." In future history books Hitler would therefore appear as "a radiant phenomenon of human greatness and of farsighted vision," whilst his opponents would only form "the dark background" for it.[1]

The Führer had always remained the same during the ups and downs of the war. In contrast to other statesmen he recognized dangers in time and then faced them bravely. His leadership was the safest pledge of the forthcoming victory. Goebbels now felt obliged to modify his "identification" line. "Never were we so close to him as in the moments of danger, never did we feel so much identified with him as when we had the feeling that he needed us as much as we needed him."[2] Again the Minister of Propaganda made himself the speaker for millions of Germans. Hitler was declared to be "everything to us, in the grievous present as well as in the brighter future. We wish him good health and strength and a blessed hand. He should know that he can rely on his people."[3] Though as usual the identification between Führer and nation was declared absolute, the closing formula of the 1944 address had a different emphasis: "In this fight between life and death too he is and remains to us what he always was: Our Hitler!"[4]

It is interesting that during the last few months of the war, with the "Twilight of the Gods" approaching, Goebbels made an even greater effort than in the previous war-years to build up the Führer. In 1944 Hitler only twice addressed the German public on questions of national significance over the air: on New Year's Eve and again eight months later after his lucky escape from assassination on the 20th July. For the first time in the history of the Third Reich Hitler did not appear in November at the traditional gathering of the old Party Guard. Instead, Himmler merely read a proclamation of the Führer on the formation of the *Volkssturm,* the frantic attempt to form a people's militia. Western propaganda was not slow in exploiting Hitler's non-appearance and asked searching questions: "Had his health failed? Had he been seriously injured on July 20th? Had he felt that he could not face the Germans because he knew the outlook was hopeless?"[5] Such enquiries did not fail to make some impact, particularly as the war situation on both the Eastern and Western fronts was deteriorating rapidly. Negative rumours about the Führer circulated suggesting that he was ill or no longer alive. As Goebbels' press secretary observed, these rumours were "believed by the German people who have waited a long time in vain for this speech of the Führer. The rumours are not altogether unfounded for the Führer not only suffers from deep fits of depression, but is weakly and delicate like an old man."[6]

[1] Ibid.
[2] Ibid.
[3] Ibid.
[4] Ibid.
[5] W. Carroll, *Persuade or Perish,* Boston, 1948, p. 344.
[6] W. von Oven, op. cit., Diary entry of 12 November 1944, p. 176.

Small wonder that Goebbels thought it necessary to propagate once more the image of Hitler as a strong personality enjoying good health. "The Führer," he wrote in a special article under the same caption for the New Year issue of *Das Reich,* had "not more aged through the war than all other people who have felt its burden resting on their shoulders. If his head is now slightly bowed, this is the result of his continuous study of maps, for he takes the war more seriously than others." [1] This time Goebbels' favourite analogy between Hitler and Frederick the Great was drawn at the expense of the Prussian King. The Führer, described as "the German miracle," was "now as old as Frederick had been at the end of the Seven Years' War when his people and his soldiers nicknamed him "the old Fritz." In contrast Hitler gave almost the impression of being young. "His eyes shine with unimpaired radiance, the features of his face are tranquil and harmonious, his high forehead is bold and noble, and only his hair reveals a light silver touch, the sign of countless days of work and worry and of nights in which he was awake and lonely." Once more Hitler appeared as a St. George, slaying the dragon of the enemies of Germany and Europe for the salvation of mankind. The nobility of his character was said to be as marked as his genius: "Never does one word of falsehood or of baseness pass his lips." But Goebbels' talk of him as "the chosen leader of a chosen people," as the "transformer of mankind leading it into a better future" had by now a hollow ring. The further the enemy armies advanced into Germany, the more Germans began to doubt Hitler's military skill and acumen, the more intense and glowing became Goebbels' projection of his hero and of "the Hitler age of mankind" to be realized after the tempests of war had passed.

At the time of Goebbels' very last peroration on the eve of Hitler's 56th birthday,[2] less than a fortnight before the Führer and after him Goebbels with his whole family marked the final collapse of the Third Reich by committing suicide, the chief propagandist of the regime had long given up all hope of a compromise peace or of avoiding the defeat which, with the Russians at the gates of Berlin, was now inevitable. But the desperate eulogist still went on reproducing the old clichés and playing the same gramophone record. The Führer was still the "man of the century." He would follow his path to the end, and then experience "not the death of his nation, but a happy beginning of an unparalleled golden age of *Deutschtum.*"

The *Nibelungentreue,* the Germanic faithfulness of the followers was pronounced for the last time and the identification between the Führer and people still stood, even in the final calamity. "We feel him in us and around us," this last birthday address ends with religious undertones: "May God give him strength and health and protect him from every

[1] *Das Reich,* 29 December 1944.
[2] Radio address of Reich Minister Dr. Goebbels on the occasion of the Führer's birthday 1945, Grossdeutscher Rundfunk, 19 April 1945 (BBC Monitoring).

danger. The rest we will do ourselves. Our misfortune has made us mature, but not spineless. Germany is still the country of faithfulness. It shall again celebrate its finest triumph while the country is in danger." History would never be able to record of this time that a nation had deserted its Führer or that its Führer had deserted his people. And this meant victory. "What we so often requested from the Führer on this evening in times of good fortune, has today in days of suffering and of great danger become a deeper and more inward appeal to him *(eine tiefere und innigere Bitte)*. He shall remain what he is and always was to us: Our Hitler!" [1]

Although by then there was in Goebbels' mind no hope of victory, there glimmered the lesser hope of survival in history as a heroic figure, for ever devoted to his Führer. At one of their last conferences the Minister implored his staff to stick it out to the very end and thus to cut worthy figures in the historical films of times to come. "Gentlemen," he warned his officials on 17 April 1945, with reference to the new colour film *Kolberg*, depicting the heroic resistance of that fortress against the troops of Napoleon, "in a hundred years' time they will be showing another fine colour film describing the terrible days we are living through. Don't you want to play a part in this film, to be brought back to life in a hundred years' time? Everybody now has the chance to choose the part which he will play in the film a hundred years hence. I can assure you it will be a fine and elevating picture. And for the sake of this prospect it is worth standing fast. Hold out now, so that a hundred years hence the audience does not hoot and whistle when you appear on the screen." [2]

Such were the last despairing words of a showman who, as his role in the grim setting of the present was so clearly coming to an end, wished at least to preserve a niche for himself in history by the Führer's side.

[1] Ibid.
[2] R. Semmler, op. cit., entry of 17 April 1945, p. 194.

PART IV

Propaganda At War

CHAPTER 10

Confident of Victory (1940)

IT IS IN the nature of things that propaganda cannot be a substitute for military success, but it can prepare, accompany and exploit it. The propagandist can support military campaigns by whipping up an aggressive and self-confident spirit and by heaping deliberate abuse on the enemy nation, or its leaders, to be challenged in a major combat. In any state involved in war, propaganda has to readjust itself constantly to the changing military situation. This is, to some extent, easier in a society under totalitarian control, as there the volume and intensity of propaganda can be switched on and off with unrivalled facility. Nothing succeeds like success. The lightning German victories in Poland, and later in Scandinavia, had created a marked confidence in the German public mind, a confidence both in the superb skill of Hitler's military planning and in the efficiency of the *Wehrmacht* under him. This confidence had been strengthened and amplified by radio reports and feature articles, by newsreels and films like *Feuertaufe,* which depicted the grim fate of Poland in an eighteen days' campaign. After the quick occupation of the Netherlands and the early capitulation of Belgium, the fall of France seemed to the German public a matter of course. When it had indeed happened, and the daily *Wehrmacht* bulletin could, on July 3rd, 1940, speak of Britain as "the only enemy left," the propagandists and the man in the street alike in Germany were confident of a speedy victory over England and of an early termination of the war. But when this final blow did not materialize, a major readjustment of German propaganda was required. It was comparatively easy for the Goebbels machinery to lay on and later to abandon a fierce campaign of hatred against France. It was, as we shall see, more difficult to pour some sobering water into the wine of high expectancy when by December 1940 England had not given in and no end of the war could be visualized in the near future.

National Socialist propaganda had always indulged in unmasking perfidious enemy plots. By alleging sinister Allied schemes of military aggression it had found a device to explain and to justify Germany's military coups, even if they meant the violation of the neutrality of the invaded countries. In this way the successive German expeditions into Denmark,

Norway, Holland and Belgium were made to appear as preventive measures indispensable to forestall unscrupulous action by England and France
who were using these neutral states as pawns in their game.

Before the German invasion of Norway the Western enemies were denounced as blackmailers about to invade that helpless country. When on
9 April 1940 the German Supreme Command announced that German
troops had landed on the shores of Norway, a directive from the Propaganda Ministry to editors insisted that their headlines should present the
action as "a blitz-like German answer to the British attempts to make
Scandinavia a theatre of war against Germany." [1] In fact, this line of a
"preventive coup" was not entirely fictitious, as Britain and France had
planned to carry out some naval action in Norway at that time. There
had been rival plans for action in Norwegian waters and for the occupation of Norwegian territory, the "Operation Wilfred" on the Allied side,
Hitler's *Weserübung* on that of Germany.[2] "Operation Wilfred" provided
mainly for the laying of mines in Norwegian waters and for the occupation of Narvik, Bergen and Stavanger.

Both sides looked for reasons to justify their action in the eyes of the
world, but "the Germans had the enormous advantage that the carrying
out of their plans did not depend on Norwegian goodwill." The British
plan, accepted by the Supreme War Council on 28 March, was to come
into effect with minelaying on 5 April as a sequel to the despatch of jus-
tificatory Notes to the Scandinavian Powers. For certain reasons the
Notes were, however, not delivered in Stockholm and Oslo until the evening of the 7th, and the actual minelaying followed on the 8th. By then
the newspapers in these capitals had become agitated about the Allied
intentions. It seems that Hitler had finally decided on 3 March that the
attack on Scandinavia was to be given precedence over the attack upon
the Low Countries. Action *Weserübung* began in the early hours of 9
April. It so happened that the naval forces of both sides were in motion
simultaneously for the execution of their respective plans. Hitler knew
probably less of Allied plans than vice versa, but he was anxious that
Germany should be able to strike first.[3]

German propaganda insisted that evidence of enemy intrigues in Scandinavia had been in the possession of the German Government for many
months. The quick German reply to the intended piece of British piracy
was said to be justified by the alleged English slogan. "neutrality no
longer exists." The only possible German answer could be "to put Denmark and Norway under the protection of the Reich," a familiar phrase
ever since German troops had occupied Prague and dissolved the state of
Czechoslovakia. The "peaceful character" of the German measures in

[1] Vertrauliche Informationen Nr. 83/40, 9 April 1940.
[2] See T. K. Derry, *The Campaign in Norway*, London, 1952, ch. II.
[3] Derry, op. cit., and Paul Reynaud, *In the Thick of the Fight 1930-1945*,
London, 1955, pp. 226-271.

Denmark and Norway was to be duly emphasized. Germany, the world was to be told, had no intention of making these countries bases for attacks on England, and their independence was declared secure.

In a further directive the editors were warned not to write under any circumstances that "Germany had taken these measures in order to safeguard her ore supplies or to obtain bases for future war operations." [1] Editors had also to realize that no expression of exultation or triumph over the occupation of Denmark and Norway was permissible.[2] But this did not preclude an exposure of the humiliation England and France had suffered and of the impotence of their rulers it had revealed when compared with the speedy German action. A fortnight later this line was reinforced by the convenient discovery of documents in Norway said to provide clear proof of sinister intrigues by England and France in that country. The discovery of the documents served the double purpose of proving once more the legitimacy of Germany's preventive measures and of indicating the loss of prestige England had suffered in the eyes of the world by the exposure of her evil machinations in Northern Europe.[3]

When, immediately after the German coup in Scandinavia, voices in the enemy camp predicted that Holland and Belgium were about to suffer a similar fate, the German press received express instructions not to mention these countries in any way.[4] As late as two days before their actual invasion, propaganda denied any German intention of attacking Belgium and Holland. The whole idea was to be ridiculed as a manoeuvre of diversion and camouflage by Britain whose aggressive plans were once more exposed. It was Germany who protected the world while the enemy was bent on aggression and on "enlarging the theatre of war." [5]

This "catch-the-thief" line was promptly repeated by Goebbels, even after the German invasion of Holland and Belgium had begun. Following up the cue contained in a statement by Ribbentrop, German press and radio were asked to emphasize "the unequivocal proof" that England and France had been about to occupy these two countries when they were forestalled once more by the Führer. The Governments of Holland and Belgium had sided with the enemy for a long time.[6] The victims of the latest extension of the war by the plutocratic powers were by no means free of guilt, the Dutch and Belgian General Staffs having long regarded themselves as branches of the General Staffs of England and France.[7]

---

1 Vertrauliche Informationen Nr. 83/40, 1. Erg., 9 April 1940.
2 Vertrauliche Informationen Nr. 84/40, 10 April 1940.
3 Vertrauliche Informationen Nr. 100/40, 29 April 1940.
4 Vertrauliche Informationen Nr. 85-40, 11 April 1940.
5 Vertrauliche Informationen Nr. 106/40, 8 May 1940 and 1. Erg. 9 May 1940.
6 Vertrauliche Informationen Nr. 108/40—1 Erg. 10 May 1940.
7 S. I. Nr. 9/40, 10 May 1940.

There followed the usual "discovery" of suitable documents which implicated the governments of the states now occupied by the Third Reich.[1]

The idea of a "preventive action" was now supplemented by the propaganda order to drive a wedge between the Allies, between the Belgians, French and English. Such an effort, it was explained, had to be carried out "in an extremely skilful manner." The theme was only to be discussed casually. It was desirable to throw into the debate the notions of military disunity among the Allies and of a lack of power of decision in military matters. Neither the Belgians nor the French could have any interest in the continuation of the fighting in Belgium, the former because they could not want the possible annihilation of Brussels, whilst the French would have to think now about the defence of their own capital.[2] This argument was further pursued after the capitulation of the Belgian Army on May 28th. The French Prime Minister Reynaud was to be sharply attacked by the press as he had deplored that event. A high moral tone of indignation prevailed in this as in other German directives. The lamentable attitude of the French Government of warmongers, who had first seduced Belgium and involved her "in their criminal plan against Germany" was decried. Now when the Belgian King had drawn the necessary conclusion from the hopelessness of the military situation they attacked him and accused him of treachery.[3]

A double attempt to divide the enemy camp is discernible in German propaganda of that period. To drive a wedge between the Allies was the first one, to cause division between different sections in an enemy nation was the second. In the case of Belgium it was a matter of playing off the King against the Government in exile, whereas with England the Government was presented as being opposed to the real interests of its people. The various emigré Governments who assembled in London in the course of the summer were an obvious target for attack. They were described as mere emigrés who for selfish reasons had deserted their nations.

The line of playing off the masses against their government began with the case of Norway. A few days before the German invasion of that country the Norwegian Government had protested in London against the violation of Norwegian territorial waters by British ships. This protest was called "very timid" *(lendenlahm)* and the German press was asked to contrast it with the very different attitude of the Norwegian people, who were depicted as being "deeply indignant about the unheard of event" and "inclined to panic." [4]

[1] Vertrauliche Informationen 109/40, 4. Erg., 13 May 1940. A directive on 13 May quoted a report from a German war correspondent alleging that a German Officer had found 32,000 General Staff maps of Greater Germany in Holland, "documentary evidence that an invasion of Germany had been planned". The Belgians and French were to be told that they had been dragged into the war only in the interests of England.

[2] Vertrauliche Informationen Nr. 119/40, 24 May 1940.

[3] Vertrauliche Informationen Nr. 122/40, 28 May 1940.

[4] Vertrauliche Informationen Nr. 82/40, 8 April 1940. Secret!

The next opportunity for harping on contrasting attitudes came for German propaganda with the capitulation of Belgium. The King had behaved in the true interests of his nation, whilst the Pierlot Government fleeing to London had not. Against Reynaud's allegation that King Leopold had decided on the capitulation against the will of the Belgian Government,[1] the German papers were to make it clear that one could not talk of a Belgian Government, but only of emigrés who had deserted their people and their troops and had fled.[2] There was the significant addition, however, that "the Belgian King was not to be portrayed with a halo."

A similar technique was applied to England during the summer and autumn of that fateful year. To give one example of many: on July 5th German editors were asked not to include any attacks on the English people in their polemics against England. "Our policy"—the directive ran —"aims at the separation of the people and the Government." [3] After the British attack on the French Fleet at Oran the question had to be asked, what the English people were saying to this perfidious act. "If there are still some decent elements in England, Churchill must not remain Prime Minister any longer." [4]

When after the fall of France Lord Halifax rejected Hitler's final plea to Britain to lay down her arms, German propaganda regarded this as evidence that the plutocratic English warmongers wanted war instead of peace, whilst the helpless English people were not considered or consulted.[5] The intention was obviously to make a careful distinction between the "real" masses and the "unreal" but selfish ruling class which used them with haughty indifference to their fate.[6]

Some of the old Germanic sagas tell us that when the warriors lined up ready to do battle they flung mockery and abuse at one another that served to incite them to the highest pitch of fury. This ancient example

[1] See Paul Reynaud's account of his attitude to the capitulation of the Belgian King, *In the Thick of the Fight 1930-1945*, pp. 418-441.
[2] Vertrauliche Informationen Nr. 122/40, 28 May 1940.
[3] Vertrauliche Informationen Nr. 154/40, 4 July 1940.
[4] Vertrauliche Informationen Nr. 155/40, 5 July 1940.
[5] Vertrauliche Informationen Nr. 68/40, 24 July 1940.
[6] Vertrauliche Informationen Nr. 185/40, 8 August 1940. To try to drive a wedge between "the Government" and "the people" is of course a device by no means confined to National Socialist propaganda. It was also used on the Allied side. See for instance Neville Chamberlain's broadcast to the German people of 4 September 1939. For the definition of the enemy compare also P. M. A. Linebarger, *Psychological Warfare,* Second edition, Washington, 1954, pp. 50-52.

Early in August 1940 the German press was advised that in England human rights were proclaimed in order to tie the workers closer to the Government. The impact of dropped German leaflets on the English workers had been so immense that the alarmed trade union leaders had to make special efforts to counter this influence. The German press should therefore attack these trade union bosses who were by no means representative of the British people.

was given modified new lease of life on a more systematic scale by Goebbels' propaganda machine.

During the period of the "phoney" war, German propaganda had not concentrated on France and the French, except to tell them that England would fight to the last Frenchman. This changed as soon as France became a theatre of war. At the end of May 1940 editors were requested to concentrate on France with the same ruthlessness they had previously employed for the unmasking of Britain. Time-honoured anti-French clichés were reassembled. There was the old accusation against the traditional French anti-German policy which, from the days of Richelieu and Napoleon, had aimed at the dismemberment and disunity of Germany. There was the slogan of decadent France which had already been popular with Treitschke and the German nationalists before 1914. And there was the new Nazi criticism of France, that she had lowered herself by mixing with inferior races. After 1918 these self-styled champions of culture had committed the greatest *Kulturschande* by putting the Germans, "the racially highest developed nation," under the control of negroes in the occupied Rhineland. Now the day of reckoning had come. The task of the press for the next two weeks was "to raise the fury against France and the detestation of her in the German people to a peak." [1]

Attention had to be focused drastically on France's role as a *Blutknecht*, a serf bleeding for England, and it was this theme that had to be dealt with every day by every newspaper in one form or another. During the next fortnight "all the detestable features of the Rhine and Ruhr occupation after 1918" had "continuously to be hammered into the minds of their readers." [2] The sensational German military advance into France was accompanied by an all-out press and radio campaign on these lines. By the beginning of June it had reached a crescendo with the journalists being admonished to continue their large-scale polemics against France and "her sadistic and negroid methods." [3]

Perhaps it was the fact that Nationalist propaganda in Germany had traditionally regarded the French as *the* enemy, the *Erbfeind*, that caused some newspapers in carrying out this order to go to extremes. This was disapproved of by the Propaganda Ministry. A week later the Ministry insisted that the anti-French campaign must not be pursued "by mere phrases or insults," but should be strictly based on facts. Recent French atrocities were perfectly suitable "to evoke hatred and contempt" among Germans, it was unnecessary to try to create hatred by artificial declamations. It would be inexpedient to attack concepts and symbols sacred to the entire French nation, such as the Tricolore, as this would evoke very inopportune reactions. [4]

Obviously the authorities were not interested in the strengthening of

[1] Vertrauliche Informationen Nr. 124/40, 30 May 1940. Geheim!
[2] Vertrauliche Informationen Nr. 125/40, 31 May 1940.
[3] Verrauliche Informationen Nr. 126/40, 1 June 1940.
[4] Vertrauliche Informationen Nr. 131/40, 7 June 1940.

French morale by too crude insults to France in the German press, which would act as a boomerang. The earlier directives had been followed with such religious zeal that now a warning had to be issued "not to attack France so to speak with a big stick." [1]

The striking victories of the German *Wehrmacht* meant that the former German inferiority feeling towards France was now a thing of the past. As the directive for the treatment of the German occupation of Paris put it unmistakably: "It should and must also be pointed out for some definite reasons that the German troops had (now) achieved in a few weeks what could not be secured during the (entire) war of 1914-1918." They had done so because this time they had "better weapons, a better leadership and a better home front," an argument which at the time seemed plausible and based on facts. [2]

Whilst any ideas "leading to sentimental reflections" had to be avoided [3] Marshal Pétain was not to be attacked. They should leave such inglorious behaviour to the French who in the past had badly abused Marshal von Hindenburg, when he had protected the undefeated Germans in 1918. [4]

With the German armies heading for Paris, German journalists must have found it difficult to distinguish, as instructed, between the idea of revenge, which had to be avoided, and the "sharp retaliation" suggested "for the reckoning with France."

Once the fury of battle and of the German Stukas had died away and the Armistice had been signed at Compiegne, the editors were advised to modify "the propaganda of hatred," though "any false sentimentality" towards France was still out of the question. [5] "The big account of French guilt from 1648 to the present age" which had been stressed in a previous directive [6] could now be put into cold storage. There was to be a switch-over from France to England as Enemy No. 1. [7]

"Without making ourselves the speakers of France," the press was advised on 26 June to expose "the bottomless perfidy shown by Churchill to his former ally." Not only had England never sent the number of troops promised to France, but at a time when thousands of Frenchmen were

1 Vertrauliche Informationen Nr. 159/40, 10 July 1940.
2 Vertrauliche Informationen Nr. 137/40, 14 June 1940.
3 Op. cit., Nr. 141/40, 19 June 1940.
4 Op. cit., Nr. 141/40, 19 June 1940.
5 Op. cit., Nr. 146/40, 25 June 1940. This point was also emphasized in a directive of the following day which dealt with the German comment on a speech by Pétain in which he gave an account of the causes of the French military defeat. Vertrauliche Informationen Nr. 147/40, 26 June 1940.
6 Vertrauliche Informationen Nr. 141/40, 19 June 1940. Geheim!
7 Vertrauliche Informationen Nr. 153/40, 3 July 1940. For the switchover from concentrated attacks on France to England Churchill's speech of 18 June 1940 was recommended as a suitable target, as in it the English Prime Minister had revealed his lack of scruples by appealing to all the French wherever they might be to fight for and with England. See also W. S. Churchill, *The Second World War*, Vol. II, *Their Finest Hour*, Reprint Society ed. pp. 180-184.

shedding their blood, 30,000 Englishmen had gone to the Derby to amuse themselves.[1] The plight of the French refugees was to be "explained" as the result of the curse which England had brought on France.[2]

Whereas German propaganda against France simmered down after the end of the Third Republic, propaganda against Britain reached a new crescendo during the summer and autumn of 1940, when the overwhelming majority of Germans from the Minister of Propaganda to the last Party Comrade took England's imminent fall for granted.[3] Gradually there came a change from superb confidence that Mr. Churchill's perfidious game was lost, to a more cautious note trying to bring to the reader an awareness that the English did not regard themselves as beaten, and that therefore no early end of the war was in sight.

When Goebbels' new attractive weekly for the more educated, *Das Reich*, made its bow on 26 May the editors took it as a matter of course that England was losing the war. A month later, after Dunkirk and the fall of Paris, England's fate could with some probability be described as sealed. On 14 July a leader-writer assured his readers that in England "the man in the street realizes gradually that the war cannot be won." [4] At the end of August *Das Reich* posed the question: "Why is England losing?" [5] and at the end of September it still declared it as only a question of when and in what form England's collapse was going to take place.[6] But already during the second half of July, after the British Government had shown no interest in the advice Hitler gave to England in his speech before the Reichstag, to end the war and to conclude peace, the press was warned not to create the impression by its commentaries that the attack against England was imminent.[7] A fortnight later it was again ordered not to splash possible forthcoming special bulletins (*Sondermeldungen*) in a manner likely to create the impression that the big blow against England had begun.[8] The timing of the knock-out-blow, Germans were told, could be confidently left to the genius of the Führer whose perspicacity and flair had been proved beyond measure.[9]

When in September 1940 the German newspapers published hair-raising accounts of the bombed and burning English capital, and of the plight of its inhabitants, they were repeatedly warned by the Propaganda Ministry not to overdo it. The press was not to print any reports on panic

[1] Vertrauliche Informationen Nr. 145/40, 24 June 1940.

[2] Op. cit., Nr. 142/40, 20 June 1940.

[3] See for instance the observations by William L. Shirer, *Berlin Diary*, p. 375, and by Ruth Andreas-Friedrich, *Der Schattenmann*, Berlin 1947, pp. 73-74.

[4] *Das Reich* Nr. 8, article "Festung England", 14 July 1940.

[5] *Das Reich* Nr. 14, 25 August 1940.

[6] *Das Reich* Nr. 19, 29 September 1940.

[7] Vertrauliche Informationen, Nr. 168/40, 20 July 1940.

[8] Vertrauliche Informationen, Nr. 184/40, 6 August 1940. This warning was repeated on 11 August, Vertrauliche Informationen, Nr. 187/40.

[9] See the directive Vertrauliche Informationen, Nr. 199/40, 24 August 1940.

in London, and its news should not cause the readers to think that the morale of the Londoner was already broken.[1] However grim the situation was in London, however lurid the colours in which it was depicted, the journalists had definitely to avoid any prophecies or speculations on future events. They must realize that England's spine had not yet been broken, and that she still had the will and the capacity to continue the fight.[2]

After the Battle of Britain had turned out to be a failure for the *Luftwaffe*, it was even more realized in the *Wilhelmsplatz* that the often highly dramatized accounts in German papers of burning streets and houses, of overcrowded underground stations and of inadequate air-raid shelters in London created a false picture. Early in December a directive for German periodicals said that drastic descriptions of the situation in England might be published as long as no wrong conclusions could be drawn from them about the morale and power of resistance of the enemy. The German people must not gain the impression that English resistance was only a question of weeks.[3]

German propaganda was, however, not prepared to admit a victory of British defence in the air. For it "the Battle of Britain" simply did not exist. It countered the British claim that the preparations for a German invasion of England had been spotted and frustrated and a German landing thereby become impossible, by saying that English propaganda tactics were similar to those employed in October and November 1939. Then the British press had alleged that Germany had given up the attempt to involve Holland and Belgium in the war. Subsequent events in these countries had shown that Germany acted when it suited the Führer. There was a close parallel in the present situation. The newspapers had only to quote a recent remark made by the Führer in a speech at the Sport Palace: "And when people in England are very curious today and ask: Why does he not come?, the answer is: Take it easy. He will come." [4]

These directives with their emphasis on suitable analogies with previous developments were faithfully implemented by *Das Reich*. "Time would help Churchill"—remarked a front-page article—"as little as it had helped his French ally. They too had waited many months—until the Führer had fixed the date for the final attack. For this Churchill was now waiting; he could do no more." [5] The impression created by these analogies was firstly that the entire situation was decided by the Führer, and secondly that England was like the squirrel which waited spellbound for the deadly attack of the snake.

By the end of September the thesis that the collapse of England was

[1] Vertrauliche Informationen, Nr. 216/40, 12 September 1940.

[2] Vertrauliche Informationen, Nr. 223/40. Geheim. 20 September 1940.

[3] Presse-Rundschreiben Nr. 11, 507/40, Berlin 9 December 1940. This directive was issued by the Reichspressestelle of the Party (NSDAP).

[4] Vertrauliche Informationen Nr. 225, 1. Erg. 23 September 1940.

[5] Article "Die Insel ist Kriegsbiet", *Das Reich*, Nr. 14, 1 September 1940.

only a matter of time was still maintained, but an early end of the war was no longer visualized. A note of apology had crept into German propaganda. Again the Führer was quoted. Five years, he had said recently, was the only date-line by which he felt bound. "This did not mean," an article in *Das Reich* explained, "that we believe that the war would last so long. That sentence only emphasized the German determination not to make the date a matter of prestige, but to prepare thoroughly for the conclusion of the war." [1]

Two months later the final destruction of London seemed a matter of course. As one of Goebbels' lieutenants in the Propaganda Ministry explained to the readers of *Das Reich*, the superiority of the *Luftwaffe* made it inevitable that London would be destroyed from the air. All that Churchill's stubbornness could achieve was that one day the capital would be eradicated from the map.[2] All hopes of Churchill that the enemy might be diverted, that the Mediterranean could become a major theatre of war were to be declared futile. "The island which is no island" would remain the central theatre of war. There the decision would fall in due course.[3]

By the beginning of 1941 the accent of German propaganda was less and less on an immediate conquest of England, and more and more on the false hopes of the English. In vain did Churchill put his trust in the sea which surrounded England. This sea-wall could only protect England so long as it suited the Germans.[4] Gradually the fact that the English could "take it," that the heavy air-raids had not shaken their will to resist could not be entirely concealed from the German public. When Ernest Bevin was appointed Minister of Labour and National Service, *Das Reich* discussed the "new whips in England" whose appeal was not to be underrated.[5] They were able to raise the morale of the English, to strengthen their courage and to retard the psychological crisis that had been threatening them repeatedly. But such pep talk could not alter the hard facts. The island remained the main theatre of war and there the decision would come—against England and for the liberation of Europe from British control. Whilst others talked Germany was working all the more vigorously "for the victory which no power on earth could wrest from her."

[1] Article "Die überfällige Landung", *Das Reich*, Nr. 19, 29 September 1940.
[2] Lieutenant Eugen Hadamowsky, "Warum London fallen muss. Stationen des deutschen Luftsieges", *Das Reich*, Nr. 27, 24 November 1940.
[3] Article "Der kritische Zeitpunkt", *Das Reich*, Nr. 30, 15 December 1940. In another article a parallel was drawn with the First World War. Then the German victories in Russia, in the Balkans and in the Orient had been of no avail, for the war was not decided at the periphery but in the main theatre, in the West. The same applied this time. The Mediterranean was only a sideshow and the decision would be enforced from above the English Isles and on the sea round them. Article "Der Krieg und die fernen Fronten", *Das Reich*, Nr. 31, 22 October 1940.
[4] Article "Unbeirrbare Achse", *Das Reich*, Nr. 1, 5 January 1941.
[5] Article "Neue Einpeitscher in England", *Das Reich*, Nr. 2, 12 January 1941.

By the time the German military might had turned East and invaded Russia, the German press and radio had become much more cautious in their reports on the precarious situation in England. The plight of the English masses was still featured, but much less so than in July or September 1940. Perhaps one can regard a cunning manoeuvre of diversion which Goebbels attempted in an article in March 1941 as the terminal point of the propagated line that the invasion of England and her collapse were imminent. There was little hope and much fear, Goebbels suggested, behind the efforts of English propagandists who tried to console their fellow-countrymen. In the forthcoming spring, German facts would take the place of English lies. Soon England would have other worries. The contours of forthcoming events could already be seen on the horizon. "In our radio studios the fanfares for proclaiming Special Announcements *(Sondermeldungen)* are already being polished. Front and Homefront are awaiting the command of the Führer." [1]

But the momentous event to come three months later was not the final blow against England, Operation "Sea Lion," which had long been cancelled, but the German attack on the Soviet Union. It brought relief to England and gradually let the German image of a final victory over Great Britain disappear like smoke in the air.

[1] Joseph Goebbels, "Wenn der Frühling auf die Berge steigt," *Das Reich,* Nr. 10, 9 March 1941.

CHAPTER 11

The Russian Campaign: Before and After
Stalingrad (1941-1943)

1. THE FIRST EIGHTEEN MONTHS

22 JUNE 1941 came as a surprise to the German masses. The preparations for the invasion of Russia had been carried out in the greatest secrecy. It is true, in mid-June many rumours had circulated in Berlin. Ribbentrop's office planted the "news" that Stalin was coming to Berlin in a special armoured car. Diplomatic circles expected some big event and there were even a few leakages.[1] But the man in the street had no idea of what was to come.

When the blow fell the propaganda machine gathered momentum. There had to be arguments to "explain" Hitler's *volte face vis à vis* Germany's erstwhile friend. Two main lines of argument were used to justify the decision that had brought war again on two fronts for Germany, in the East and the West, a situation which the German generals had dreaded for so long. The one harped on the necessity for self-defence to parry Russia's imminent attack. The Communist ogre had been concentrating troops on Germany's Eastern frontier in ever increasing numbers. Germany was seriously threatened and attack was therefore the best line of defence. There was a strong appeal to the fear motive. "Human imagination cannot visualize", said Goebbels of the Russians, "what it would mean, had their beastly hordes flooded Germany and the West of this Continent." Fear and salvation motives were interlinked in the idea of a German crusade against the Bolshevist "sub-human beings" *(Untermenschentum)*, which was the second argument put forward. The German soldiers who willingly followed Hitler's order to

---

[1] The most sensational was an indiscretion by Professor Karl Bömer, the Head of the Foreign Press Section in the Propaganda Ministry, who talked freely when he had drunk much. At a reception at the Bulgarian Legation in the spring of 1941 Bömer had revealed the exact date of the planned attack on Russia, much to the satisfaction of his rivals in the Foreign Ministry. Accused of high treason he escaped the death sentence only through Goebbels' energetic appeals to the Führer. It is doubtful if this indiscretion was taken seriously by foreign journalists. See W. Hagemann, *Publizistik im Dritten Reich*, p. 327; for another leakage see Ruth Andreas-Friedrich, *Berlin Underground 1939-1945*, London, 1948, pp. 63-64.

march into Russia were. in Goebbels' dramatic phrase, "the true saviours of European culture and civilization from the threat of the political underworld." [1] They held in their raised hands a torch "that the light of mankind might not be extinguished".[2]

Though the declaration of war against Russia was not greeted with enthusiasm, the German masses "accepted the decision as inevitable".[3] Fortified by the *Blitzkrieg* successes of 1940, many soldiers and civilians alike were not averse to the idea of a new crusade. A feeling of superiority over the Slavs had been strong in Germany long before the name of Hitler had become a household word. What was anticipated was another lightning victory in a few months. "Most people expected a short campaign, anything from two to six months, after which the Russians would be out of the picture." [4] These expectations were probably not very different from those in the British War Office or in some Chancelleries of neutral states. As a Pole predicted to the present writer in London at the end of June 1941: "The German armies will thrust themselves into Russia like a knife into butter."

The technique of releasing the crop of German victories in the early days of the Russian campaign was adroit. During its first week the Supreme Command of the *Wehrmacht* remained silent. But on Sunday, 29 June, the German masses were compensated by no less than twelve Special Victory Announcements read over the radio with intervals of music every quarter of an hour. In this manner, the fall of Brest-Litovsk, Byalistok, Grodno and Minsk were highlighted. In the following weeks, too, conquests and victories were not made public at once, news was often withheld for days, and tension rose to find release in another special Victory Bulletin. German home morale was high, and of course, press and radio sounded very confident; yet from an early date a note of caution was struck by some newspapers. Fighting in Russia was different from the earlier campaigns in the West. The enemy in the East, explained the *Frankfurter Zeitung* soberly on 6 July, reacted to the German tactics of wedges and extensions in a way very different from that of the French. There was not the same mental paralysis which had usually followed the blitz-like German breakthrough. "In most cases the enemy did not lose his capacity for action, but instead tried to turn to encircle the German pincers." Whilst press and radio painted a grim picture of the murderous practices of Russian political commissars and soldiers, of a veritable hell on earth, even the *Völkischer Beobachter* admitted a week after the beginning of the campaign that the Soviet Russian soldier surpassed Germany's other opponents in his contempt for death. His tenacity and fatalism persisted till he was blown sky-high with his bunker or lost his life in close man-to-man fighting.

[1] J. Goebbels' article "Der Schleier fällt", *Das Reich,* 6 July 1941; reprinted in *Die Zeit ohne Beispiel,* p. 524.
[2] Op. cit., p. 525.
[3] A. Fredborg, *Behind the Steel Wall,* New York, 1944, p. 27.
[4] Ibid.

A note of realism was particularly struck in the reporting by war correspondents and camera men, all members of the Propaganda Companies (PKs). Attached to fighting units of the Armed Forces and supervised by the Propaganda Ministry, they accompanied the troops into battle and were able to give a dramatic, though slanted, picture of the fighting. Their "Front Reports" featured small groups or individuals and built up the image of the German soldier.[1] As German soldiers also listened in, there was little point in telling lies about military life or in painting too rosy a picture of the conditions under which they fought. These reporters referred early to the hardships suffered by the German Army under Russian conditions. "The story of the Front Reports remained success, great success, for the Germans who, despite the snipers, the burning sun, the terrible dust—not white as in France, but grey, yellow and black—despite sore feet, moved with 'the precision and calm of the parade ground.' "[2]

Yet in Russia there were factors with which Hitler had not fully reckoned: the vastness of the space, the hazards of the seasons and the immense manpower potential at the disposal of a centralized government. By the beginning of October the threefold German thrust towards Leningrad, Moscow and Rostov had so far advanced and had overcome so much Russian resistance that Hitler felt safe to declare: "The enemy already lies defeated and cannot rise again." But it was Otto Dietrich, Hitler's Press Chief who, in a famous statement to German and foreign journalists at a conference in the Propaganda Ministry on 9 October, announced: "The campaign in the East has been decided by the smashing of the Timoshenko Army Group. Further developments will take place as we wish them to happen. Through these last immense blows inflicted by us on the Soviet Union she is finished militarily. The English dream of a war on two fronts has definitely come to an end."[3] Once Otto Dietrich had committed himself (Goebbels never allowed him to forget that colossal blunder), the German press splashed his forecast the next day in large red or black banner headlines.

The *Völkischer Beobachter* carried the Dietrich sensation in big red letters as front page headlines on 10 October:

"The Great Hour has Struck"

"CAMPAIGN IN THE EAST DECIDED!"

This was followed in black letters on 11 October by:

"EASTERN BREAKTHROUGH DEEPENS"

On 12 October the headlines shouted:

"ANNIHILATION OF SOVIET ARMIES ALMOST CONCLUDED"

Yet there came a curious anti-climax on 14 October:

[1] Ernst Kris and Hans Speyer, *German Radio Propaganda, Report on Home Broadcasts during the War*, New York, 1944, p. 68.

[2] Op. cit., p. 356.

[3] W. Hagemann, *Publizistik im Dritten Reich*, p. 253; see also R. Semmler, *Goebbels: The Man Next to Hitler*, London, 1948, p. 54.

"Operations in East Proceed According to Plan"
and on 15 October:
"Operations in East Proceed as Foreseen"

On 16 October an editorial on the front page of that same paper carried the heading: "Three Millions" (of Russian prisoners of war in German hands), which pin-pointed the main theme: that the Bolshevist Army was crushed. What the Soviets might have in the way of questionable reserves could be no obstacle . . . The war in the East had "achieved its objective: the annihilation of the enemy." Stalin's armies had "simply disappeared from the face of the earth." [1] Though Goebbels had in the first months of the campaign been even more optimistic than Hitler, he now took great exception to Dietrich's blunder, for he feared that the people would say: "That's the end of our difficulties and efforts." [2] After Dietrich's gaffe Goebbels' prestige seems to have grown, and he became more independent in his propaganda planning.[3] In spite of further German advances, from the beginning of December Russian troops were counter-attacking on the entire northern and central fronts, and this, together with the severity of the Russian winter, created a completely new situation. With the German armies ill-equipped for the winter and facing a determined enemy, Goebbels gave the signal for a more realistic approach to the situation in an article "When or How?" published in *Das Reich* on 9 November 1941. One of Goebbels' assistants was to describe it later, with much truth, as "a lead in the turning away from any illusionary idea of the war during the decisive weeks at the beginning of the winter of 1941." [4] There was nothing of Dietrich's sanguine optimism in that grim article which stressed three major points:

1. The necessity for a gigantic exertion of strength by the German people in order to win the war.
2. The grimness of the war which was "anything but a pastime for the soldiers".
3. The absurdity of speculating on the date of victory. ("Do not let us ask when it comes, but let us see to it that it comes").[5]

Goebbels had anticipated the reverse in Russia by several weeks. On 28 November Captain Sommerfeldt, the spokesman of the General Staff, still told foreign correspondents confidently that "German troops had

[1] Quoted in Howard K. Smith, *Last Train from Berlin,* p. 84.

[2] R. Semmler, op. cit., p. 55.

[3] According to Werner Stephan, then a senior official in the Propaganda Ministry, after 9 October 1941 "Goebbels no longer waited for the directives of the Führer for his propaganda but now issued his own without any previous enquiry (at Hitler's Headquarters). They originated in his instinct as an agitator, not in the Hitlerian dream world." W. Stephan, *Joseph Goebbels, Dämon einer Diktatur,* pp. 229-230.

[4] M. A. von Schirmeister, foreword to *Joseph Goebbels, Das eherne Herz,* Munich, 1943, p. 15.

[5] Article: "Wann oder Wie?" *Das Reich,* 9 November 1941, see *Das eherne Herz,* pp. 82-84.

reached the Greater Moscow region, in other words, that they were between 25 and 30 miles from the city." But ten days later, on 8 December, the Daily Bulletin of the Supreme Command of the Armed Forces had to admit drily that "From now on operations in the East would be dicated by the winter." Many Germans began to feel disappointed that the expected quick end of the Eastern war was no longer in sight. The war began to get on people's nerves, it began to become real, though the mass of the people "did not believe that the Russians—whose defensive strength was pretty generally admitted—would be able to take the offensive against the German Army. The *Wehrmacht* was still considered invincible." [1]

The serious reverses in Russia were soon described by German propaganda as solely due to "General Winter", to the unforeseen impact of a severe winter which, in fact, had taken German authorities by surprise.[2] The violent counter-attacks by the Red Army in December 1941 and January 1942 had also been unexpected. But German propaganda only admitted the severity of the winter and "explained" all reverses persuasively by it. Hitler, in his anniversary address on 30 January 1942, struck this note. "It was not Russia that forced us into defence, but only 38, 40, 42 and sometimes 45 degrees below zero that did it." [3]

When during these months the Russian climate was declared Enemy No. 1, Goebbels devised a special propaganda campaign to help the German soldiers fight its horrors. This was the famous *Winterhilfsspende*, a collection of all kinds of winter-clothing for the frost-bitten soldiers in the East. It served as an effective method of reinforcing the ties between the fighting front and the home front; moreover, it would occupy the minds of the people and make them less inclined to ask awkward questions. It would be both useful and diverting and strengthen the flagging community spirit. Goebbels' arguments were skilful, both in what he stressed and in what he omitted. These were his major points:

[1] Arvid Fredborg, *Behind the Steel Wall, A Swedish Journalist in Berlin 1941-1943*, New York, 1944, p. 55.

[2] On November 8th it has been claimed that, though the weather had recently been bad on the central front, the Russian climate had shown a tendency in the past three years to approach that of Central Europe, thus making the temperature in Moscow approximately the same as that in Berlin. Consequently the "Russian Winter" was not to be expected before January (A. Fredborg, op. cit., p. 42). At that time the official view stressed "that it was by no means certain the winter would prove advantageous to the Russians".

[3] *Der grossdeutsche Freiheitskampf*, vol. III, *Reden Adolf Hitlers vom 16. März 1941 bis 15 März 1942*, Munich, 1943, p. 203. Hitler's degrees of temperature follow the Celsius system. A German Home Broadcast of 2 February 1942 embroidered the theme: "Never was the Bolshevik Army the main adversary of the German soldier, although from the beginning of the campaign they were over-powerful in numbers. The main adversary was always the tremendous expanse, the lack of roads and the climate: we struggled with dust, thirst, water, mud; today we are fighting against the ice, snow, the Siberian cold, and the storms from the East. These are hard enemies, we do not deny it." (Kris and Speyer, op. cit., p. 408).

a) *An appeal to gratitude*: To give for the Army was presented as a way of showing gratitude to the Saviours of the Nation.
b) *The abnormal winter*: It had come early and with an unusual intensity.
c) *Justification of the blameless High Command*: The authorities of the Armed Forces had done everything to equip the front line soldiers adequately. But in spite of their preparations, carried out with the highest amount of material and of energy, the German soldiers still needed many additional things.
d) *A task for the people*: The people at home did not deserve a moment's peace of mind, so long as one single German soldier, particularly in the East, the South-East, in Norway or in Finland, remained exposed to the hardships of the weather.[1]

Goebbels concluded with a long list of items of clothing needed at the front, ranging from pullovers to thick winter gloves, from pants to ear-covers. In a later radio appeal on 22 December, even single gloves, old rags and torn blankets were included.[2] Everything with fur was particularly badly needed and thus doubly welcome. During the last week of December the Party carried out a house to house collection of such items, which were to be sent to the fighting soldiers as quickly as possible. It was clearly implied, though never stated in so many words, that the position in the East had become critical and perilous. As a Swedish journalist in Berlin observed at the time, this Goebbels' speech "hit the people like a bomb". They felt that there had been an unwarranted delay in preparing for the winter, but above all it made them aware that "fate had touched the German nation in a way that it had heretofore escaped during this war, and that a catastrophe was to be feared." But people were so frightened of a Russian invasion of Europe—undoubtedly a success of the official propaganda line—that "even the most violent anti-Nazis became willing to sacrifice something".[3]

[1] The text of Goebbels' appeal for the collection of winter clothing for the front of 21 December 1941 is to be found in *Das eherne Herz*, pp. 131-137; for the text of Hitler's appeal in the same matter of 21 December 1941, see *Der grossdeutsche Freiheitskampf*, vol. III, p. 153.

[2] British propaganda made much play with the oddities of this appeal. "We had a lot of fun with the single gloves," says a leading English propagandist looking back; "were these for men who had already lost one hand from the frost-bite? The old rags, were these to stuff into worn-out boots? And the torn blankets, were these for the dying in the field hospitals?" J. Baker White, *The Big Lie*, London, 1955, p. 98.

[3] A. Fredborg, op. cit., p. 62. In his address on 30 January Hitler referred to the collection campaign as to "a plebiscite", adding: "While the others talk of democracy, this *is* true democracy." The pressure put on the people to achieve the purpose of the appeal was by no means confined to persuasion. On 23 December Hitler issued an order valid for the Reich and all countries occupied by the German armies, to the effect that anyone who "enriches himself by means of articles collected or intended for collection, or otherwise withdraws such articles from their destined use," could be executed. See John Baker White, op. cit., p. 98.

For several weeks Goebbels' propaganda machine gave first place to the collection. As usual, film stars and athletes were put into its service. Their photographs in the press showed them setting a good example by donating all sorts of clothing. On 4 January the press and radio announced preliminary results, saying "the people have responded to the Führer's appeal to help our soldiers in the cold lands of the East by donations of winter garments with an enthusiasm which could hardly be surpassed." [1] There was such a rush to give on the final Sunday that Goebbels decreed the extension of the collection by one week (to 11 January) "to give all who had not had time to get their gifts ready a chance to contribute." Naturally, propaganda made the most of the satisfactory outcome.[2] By 14 January, when Goebbels rendered a final account over the radio of the collection, the total number of items of clothing received had reached over 67,232,000, and the Reich Minister expressed his "warmest appreciation" and "most cordial thanks". He singled out several categories of people for his eulogy, and particularly praised the two million helpers who had collected the goods, and the million German women who had followed the call of the Führer and were indefatigably busy in 24,000 sewing offices to repair or alter the pieces of warm clothing for the benefit of the soldiers. Goebbels hailed the result as "convincing evidence of the determination with which the German nation is ready to carry this war through to victory".[3] He seems to have had reason for satisfaction, for as a sober Swedish observer in Berlin noted at the time, "the collection had brought about a definite improvement in morale." [4]

"This War has become harder."

By the spring of 1942 two new features can be observed in German

[1] Quoted in Kris and Speyer, op. cit., p. 416.

[2] "The provisional results of over 56,000,000 collected articles," declared the speaker in the radio "Political Review" on 12 January, "is so overwhelming that nothing need be added to it. The final result will probably surpass this gigantic figure when the counting is completed." Kris and Speyer, op. cit., p. 416.

[3] See the text of Goebbel's radio address, 14 January 1942, under the heading "Ein Volk hilft sich selbst", in *Das eherne Herz*, pp. 176-179.

[4] A. Fredborg, op. cit., pp. 67-68: Goebbels reacted to the ironic statements by British propaganda on the truth behind the wool collection with a sharp counter-attack. In his article "Qualm aus London" (*Das Reich*, 18 January 1942) he complained that Churchill's press had falsified the result by alleging "that only over 4 million articles had been collected, whilst there were actually more than 60 million". He ridiculed with heavy sarcasm claims by the London propagandists that the collection had taken place under duress, that the women of Berlin had demonstrated against the brutality of the police "who had literally torn them from the back of the pedestrians in the street, leaving them exposed to the maximum winter cold, naked there and bare, swearing and trembling in the cold." *Das eherne Herz*, p. 182. See also the address by Goebbels at the Hamburg Town Hall, 15 January 1942.

propaganda, a more "realistic" and harder touch regarding the future, and, correlated to it, a certain gloom admitting the ordeals of a winter that had passed. The greater realism extended to both the fighting and the home fronts. Goebbels admitted in an article at the beginning of 1942 that the war in its third year had "thrown up an immense number of problems of which we would have never thought in normal times." [1] "The winter," Goebbels suggested with calculating skill, "had been an eye-opener to many." With what erroneous ideas of the war had some people entered this winter, and how realistically and soberly did all view the position now that it was coming to its close. "The German people had undergone a great inner change in the last few months." [2]

Goebbels indulged in a particular kind of *post festum* gloom. He sketched the tremendous dangers and handicaps of the Russian campaign after they had passed. On 22 March he referred to the statement in an unnamed prominent neutral newspaper that the Germans had managed to avoid the mistakes made by Napolean during his winter campaign in Russia, and had been able to hold the essence of what they had intended to hold during these hard months and to obtain more. Goebbels added: "It need not be at all concealed what immense difficulties had to be overcome for it." [3]

The narrow and heroic escape from danger during that grim winter remained a propaganda theme for some months. Again the parallel with Napoleon at the Beresina was drawn. Hitler proudly declared on 26 April "We have mastered a fate which crushed another man 130 years ago." [4]

When in May the second German summer offensive began Goebbels devoted an entire article to the heroism of the German soldiers on the Eastern Front during the previous winter. Though it was, he declared, still too early to give details of their "nearly mythical achievement". This "gigantic battle of defence" had had no parallel in the First World War or during the Napoleonic campaign. The German troops had succeeded in preventing the planned big Russian operations. The Russians had been (the reader might add, still were) a formidable enemy who "had carried out the proclaimed system of the scorched earth almost to perfection". There were hardly any quarters in the Western sense for the troops. Villages which had escaped destruction consisted in the best case of wretched, unheated and unheatable huts.[5] Difficulties of transport were

[1] Article "Das Neue Jahr", *Das Reich*, 4 January 1942, see *Das eherne Herz*, p. 163.
[2] Article "Neue Perspektiven", *Das Reich*, 22 March 1941, see *Das eherne Herz*, pp. 251-252.
[3] Op. cit., p. 250.
[4] Quoted in Goebbels' article "Die Ostfront", 17 May 1942, *Das eherne Herz*, p. 317. Hitler had insisted that Napoleon's troops had fought in a less grim winter, the worst cold then had been minus 25 degrees, while the German soldiers had sometimes to cope last winter with a cold of minus 50 and more degrees.
[5] Article "Die Ostfront", *Das Reich*, 17 May 1942, *Des eherne Herz*, p. 317.

beyond imagination. Motors were frozen, cars could not be started. German horses succumbed to the climate, trains did not arrive.

In describing the heroic sense of duty of the German soldier, Goebbels used romantic and semi-poetical language. "Who was not struck by the change in the faces of our soldiers during this winter in the East? You can notice it in the newsreels, in photographs or when talking to them. Their eyes have a peculiar glance. They have seen more than human eyes usually see. Their features have hardened and become more stony. A smile on their faces impresses one like kindness. Our soldiers do not talk as much as they did after the Polish campaign or after the offensive in the West, but what they say has more weight. . . ." [1] If Goebbels was often cynical and belligerent, he could on occasions forcefully appeal to romantic sentiment, create a myth of stoicism, transcend the everyday routine of words and thoughts. As he put it in the epic conclusion of this remarkable article: "What could happen to us after all this that we would not be able to master? The big test has been passed. No matter if we quarreled with Fate or willingly responded to it and overcame it bravely, no matter, it is ours. No one can in future speak of German heroism without giving pride of place to this barbarous winter at the river Volckov and near Demjansk, near Juchov and Rshev, at the Donetz and near Kertsh. And through the century the name will shine by which it proved its mettle: the Eastern Front." [2]

When the German offensive was resumed German propaganda pursued a cautious line. Neither the conquest of the Kertsh peninsula at the end of May nor the fighting in Kharkov were presented as the beginning of the new summer offensive promised by Hitler. After an attack by the army of Marshal Timoshenko south of Kharkov had failed, in spite of initial successes, the Germans counter-attacked and encircled Timoshenko's army. By the end of May 1942, a considerable German success could be claimed. Although the difficult siege of Sevastopol ended in victory only after a month of hard fighting, it is significant that during the siege German propaganda did not predict its fall.[3]

The change in the tone of propaganda is reflected in a telling entry in Goebbels' Diary on 24 February 1942: "We shall have to change our propaganda and our policies in the East as already arranged with the Führer. These were hitherto based on the assumption that we would take possession of the East very quickly. This hope, however, has *not* been realized. We must, therefore, envisage operations of longer duration

[1] *Das eherne Herz*, p. 319.

[2] Op. cit., p. 322. In a speech on the Hero Memorial Day of 15 March 1942 Hitler assured the Germans that "whatever fate holds for us, it can only be easier than what is behind us." He also predicted that the Bolshevist masses would be beaten in every direction in the coming summer. However, he did not promise an end of the war in the current year. A month later, in his speech before the Reichstag on 26 April, he talked at length about the next winter, declaring that he was taking measures to save the country from a repetition of the hard experiences of German soldiers during the last winter.

[3] Kris and Speyer, op. cit., p. 378.

and are accordingly compelled to change our slogans and our policies fundamentally." [1]

German press and radio reports on the actual fighting were now confined to local events, while the Russian soldiers continued to be pictured as collective animals, fighting with great toughness and a remarkable contempt for death. Goebbels was at pains to point out that their toughness was not identical with valour. [2] But he admitted that the "blunted human material of the East without a will of its own" was Germany's most dangerous enemy. This admission was made to evoke fear in the German public, fear of Russian victory, by which "the nation would be the prey of the blunted beastliness of a primitive race". However, Goebbels was confident that once more the superior race would triumph, provided the war effort at home was intensified. [3]

Fortunately for Goebbels, positive events in another theatre of war occurred during the early summer of 1942, to exhilarate the German masses. Rommel's advance in North Africa, culminating on 21 June in the unexpected fall of Tobruk, raised the highest hopes in the war-weary German populace. [4] Some Germans formerly critical of the Nazi régime, who had maintained earlier that Germany ought to make peace and be satisfied with a compromise result instead of an unattainable full victory, now saw in imagination England already conquered and a link up of the German and Japanese forces through India as a definite possibility. Once more they identified themselves with the regime as "triumphant members of the master race." [5] But later, when Rommel's victories proved to be as transitory as those of the German troops in Russia, the end of the war seemed as far off as ever.

Propagandists make neither defeats nor victories. They have to cover up and apologize for the one, and exploit to the full the other. But in all circumstances they have to reckon with the changing moods of the people at home and to provide them with safety-valves. As we have seen, in February 1942 Goebbels and his officials started on a new propaganda line; painting the war picture in sombre colours, they struck a note of psychological realism. In the later years of the war, Goebbels was to denounce grumblers, defeatists, pessimists in the sharpest terms; but in 1942 he still tended to overlook annoyance, war-weariness and bad temper up to a point. One is inclined to agree with a Swedish observer

[1] *The Goebbels Diaries*, entry of 24 February 1942, p. 61.
[2] "Die sogenannte russische Seele", *Das Reich*, 19 July 1942; *Das eherne Herz*, pp. 398-405.
[3] Op. cit., p. 404.
[4] "Instantly the general feeling throughout the country rose to a pitch that had not been reached since the end of the Battle of France in 1940. Rommel was the man of the hour, the General for whom nothing seemed impossible. Perhaps we can win the war after all, everybody said, and the Germans joyfully congratulated themselves over something they felt was real victory, not so far away or so hard to judge as the successes in Russia." A. Fredborg, *Behind the Steel Wall*, p. 100.
[5] A. Fredborg, op. cit., p. 103.

in Berlin who felt in the spring of that year that Goebbels' "new" and "realistic" policy regarding domestic affairs was among his greatest achievements. Essentially it consisted of discussing the general atmosphere and the varying public reactions, point by point, and assuming that everything was rather natural and of no great significance.[1]

For instance, Goebbels made realistic allowances for the bad temper and irritability of some Germans.[2] There was no danger to the steady, reliable attitude of the populace from "the urge to grumble fully from time to time according to all the rules of this art". The reasons for it varied. Some became abusive about the cold weather, others about the lack of coal or of potatoes, or on account of the overcrowded trains, over the Eastern Front, or over the war in North Africa. This was not so bad, for all of them were overworked and therefore somewhat irritable. Goebbels brushed this dissatisfaction lightly off as of no consequence, as not affecting the positive basic attitude of the people. "Ask a thousand Germans if they prefer peace to war and they will answer you unanimously: Peace! Ask them further if they prefer to wage war or to give in, and they will answer with the same unanimity: Waging war for so long as it may last." [3]

In the summer campaign of 1942 the German troops advanced quickly on a wide front and achieved considerable gains of territory in a relatively short time. The combat for the Kharkov salient in the last days of June developed into an attack on a front of 185 miles. On 5 July the Don was reached, and soon a bridgehead on its further bank was established. By the end of July the German armies were divided, with considerable forces pushing eastwards, and other no less formidable units moving towards the South. On 24 July the Germans announced the fall of Rostov, the entire Russian front was shaken, and the lower Don was now crossed by German units on a wide front. With lightning speed German troops advanced southwards. On 9 August Krasnodar and Maikop with its important oil fields were claimed by the German High Command, and German troops poured into the northern plains of the Caucasus. By 7 August the High Command declared that German troops had reached its first mountain ranges on a front of 250 miles. The aim was obviously Baku. There were similarly startling advances in the bend of the Don, and at the end of August it was announced in Berlin that German troops had penetrated Russian positions South-West of Stalingrad.

Nevertheless, in the summer of 1942 there was no longer any talk of finishing the war in a few months' time. Now instead of strategic victories economic conquests were declared to be decisive. It was not the number of prisoners that was said to matter, but the extent of economic resources under German control. The *Blitzkrieg* had long changed into a

[1] A. Fredborg, op. cit., p. 82.
[2] Joseph Goebbels, "Über das Vertrauen in die eigene Stärke", *Das Reich*, 8 February 1942; reprinted in *Das eherne Herz*, pp. 202-208.
[3] Op. cit., pp. 206-207.

war of attrition which, German propaganda claimed, would be won by the superior economic resources now in German hands.

In an article in *Das Reich* at the end of May, Goebbels resuscitated his pre-war theme of the "Have-Nots" who had lived so long under the shadow of the "Haves".[1] He alleged with much exaggeration that since 1914 the Germans had been unable to sit down to meals of plenty, but had existed by living from hand to mouth on too narrow a food basis. They had constantly run the risk of facing catastrophic famine should there be two or three bad harvests. And this while in other countries, such as the Ukraine, land and resources had remained unused. By then Goebbels had discarded the idea of a German mission and had come down to popular economic war aims. This was no war for throne and altar; it was a war for grain and bread, a plentiful breakfast, lunch and dinner table. It was a war to secure raw materials, to obtain rubber, iron and ore, in other words a war "for a more dignified national existence" from which you Germans, "as the deserving poor, have so far been barred."

The Utopia round the corner had become very concrete. Prosperity, not idealism was now declared to be the motive of the gigantic German war effort. This critic of the Western "plutocrats", accused of saying Christ and meaning cotton, preferred a robust cynicism to such hypocrisy; the Germans could not, he asserted, go on fighting for ideals for ever. They were definitely tired of the role of the cultural fertilizer of the world. They wished at last to cash in as a nation.

The "grain and oil" theme was kept up throughout the summer, not only in the popular press, but even in the technical and commercial magazines such as *Öl und Kohle* which declared that the Russians were unworthy to have oil because they wasted it.[2] Fritzsche, then at the Eastern Front, described Russia in a broadcast of 13 August as a "country the fields of which could with good care feed a continent". A redistribution of the earth was—Goebbels declared on 13 August—"only a question of power, not of ethics." It was Living Space that mattered. Germany's enemies possessed everything and she nothing.[3]

At this time decrees were published to assure German soldiers that they would be the first to be given land and also business opportunities in the fruitful territories of the East. In July 1942 a Berlin newspaper office received a number of letters "from enthusiastic apostles of final victory among our readers, enquiring about the possibilities of settling in the Crimea and the Caucasus." [4] In his speech at the opening of a

[1] Article "Wofür?", *Das Reich,* 31 May 1942, see *Das eherne Herz,* pp. 330-336.

[2] Kris and Speyer, op. cit., p. 183.

[3] Article "Vom Sinn des Krieges", *Das Reich,* 23 August 1941, see *Das eherne Herz,* pp. 439-440.

[4] R. Andreas-Friedrich, *Berlin Underground 1939-1945,* diary entry Saturday 1 August 1942, p. 72.

further Winter Help Campaign on 30 September, the Führer too stressed this idea of economic conquest. He listed as the major aims of the Summer Offensive of 1942: "firstly, to take from the enemy his last big wheat areas; secondly, to deprive him of the last remnant of his coal supplies; thirdly, to come close to the sources of his oil to take them from him or at least to cut him off from them." [1]

From the point of view of the German citizen at home the practical results of the conquests in Russia were perhaps more relevant. On 6 October, in an address to the German farmers on the supply of food and other vital commodities, Göring employed the same *post festum* gloom in which German propaganda had abounded earlier, by contrasting the grim situation of the past with the more attractive picture of the present improved position. "We have conquered the most fertile district in Europe," said Göring (obviously referring to the Kuban region), "and we are extracting the maximum from the occupied countries. The enemy is advised that if there is to be hunger anywhere, it will not be in Germany." [2]

Yet in spite of this speech and an increase in rations, more and more clouds gathered on the horizon for the German masses: the increasingly heavy air raids on West German towns, the stopping of Rommel's offensive, above all, the prospect of another grim winter in Russia, with no end of the war in sight darkened the scene. There was now a special "Song of the Eastern Campaign" (just as there had been the *England Lied* before) and its rhythm was solemn:

> "Wir standen für Deutschland auf Posten
> und hielten die grosse Wacht. —
> Nun hebt sich die Sonne im Osten
> un ruft die Millionen zur Schlacht." [3]

But the great *Schlacht,* the big battle, seemed endless and was never fully won . . . . . .

2. Goebbels' Problems of one Day

During 1942 and 1943 Goebbels realized more and more clearly that the war would be a long drawn-out affair and that the serious setbacks in

[1] *Dokumente der Deutschen Politik und Geschichte,* vol. V, ii, No. 159, p. 385.

[2] A. Fredborg, op. cit., p. 130. These promises were no mere rhetoric. Earlier an increase in bread and meat rations for the Reich had been announced, to begin on 19 October. Like a benevolent Father Christmas Göring was now able to promise that there would be an additional increase in the meat ration in districts under air attack, and that every German soldier on leave, when reaching the border of Germany proper, would receive a package of provisions for the benefit of his family.

[3] "We have been standing guard for Germany, keeping the eternal watch. Now the sun is rising in the East, calling millions into battle." Quoted in A. Fredborg, op. cit., p. 129.

the East and the growing might of Allied air raids on German towns were severely testing the people's morale. Diaries for this period, incomplete as they are, allow us a clear insight into the ambitious versatility and alertness of the Propaganda Minister, into his ways of dealing with rivals and rival organizations and his methods of manipulating people. Goebbels' diary notes on one day, usually dictated on the next, included a report on the military situation, comments on his meetings with the Führer (which had by then become rather infrequent) and with other high Party functionaries or Ministers, reflections on discussions with or reports by his immediate subordinates in the Ministry and on the decisions he made arising out of them. Film production being a favourite interest of the Minister, he seldom let a week pass without some remarks on the latest *Wochenschau* or weekly newsreel. Short summaries of the reports on the morale of the people were included; these were the so-called *Stimmungsberichte,* furnished by Himmler's *Sicherheitsdienst* (SD) or by the regional propaganda offices of the Party and also derived from an analysis of the letters received from the public by Goebbels himself.

The diary entry for 7 February 1942 [1] (Saturday) can be taken as typical for it illustrates both the wide scope and the varied problems which impressed themselves on his mind at that time. It began with a review of the military events on the various fronts which emphasized Wavell's manifesto to the garrison of besieged Singapore, the Japanese communiqué on the battle in the Java Sea, and the situation in North Africa which continued to be unfavourable to Britain. In spite of this Goebbels had instructed the press to refrain from excessive prognoses, advising it to be content with describing what *was* rather than indulging in speculation of what presumably would be. As so often Goebbels discussed the mood of the English, which was reported to be "extraordinarily depressed".

There was fear in Britain of the forthcoming German offensive in the East too. Goebbels interpreted this English pessimism with some caution, maintaining that "it cannot be argued that it has a defeatist tinge; however, the English seem gradually to awake from their illusions and to face facts". On the English attitude regarding the Wafd Party which had lately come into power in Egypt, Goebbels commented: "We behave with reserve in order not to create difficulties for its leader, Nahad Pasha". After brief references to American leaflets dropped over Occupied France with the message "the Yanks are coming", and the strained relations said to exist between Nanking and Chungking, Goebbels turned to the domestic front. There the situation "can be regarded as consolidated", an assessment based on the innumerable letters Goebbels had received from the public, the great majority of which he found "absolutely positive and extraordinarily enjoyable". Being vain by nature,

[1] Photocopy of Goebbels diary, Munich (00223-231).

Goebbels registered the applause for his articles with great satisfaction. However, seen in retrospect, his belief that they had "essentially contributed to the hardening of the German power of resistance" was not entirely unfounded. Goebbels then turned to his own Ministry. Administrative changes had become imperative as some male personnel had to be released to the armed forces and the armament industry and would be replaced by women. Goebbels would see to it that their political reliability was thoroughly examined. A very acute problem presented itself with the need for an increase of production, particularly so in war industry. A campaign to increase output was now being planned and Goebbels noted with a sigh of relief that the Führer wished to occupy himself with this topic and would perhaps take part in a big conference on it. This had been sufficient reason for the Propaganda Minister to ban a speech by Ley on the proposed campaign. Goebbels wanted to wait until the Führer had spoken for "only then will the intensification of output become a topic for public debate and a propaganda drive will have a corresponding big chance of success".

There were also a few *Kleinigkeiten aus dem innerpolitischen Leben,* small items on the home front which caused Goebbels some worry, but which he settled *en passant (mit der linken Hand),* for instance, some irresponsible statements on the war effort by a Party member, Herbert Volk. Bormann's Party Chancellery had seen to it that the man was sent to a concentration camp. Goebbels' sense of power as a top executive of the State can be traced from his comments on the extraordinarily difficult problem of the merger of the two State news agencies *Transocean* and DNB and of their cooperation with the *Büro Graf Reischach,* the news agency of the Party, and the *Eher Verlag,* the Party's publishing firm.[1] An indefatigable empire builder, Goebbels was apparently worried that such a concentration might lead to an increase of the power of men who regarded themselves as outside his control. He was aware that he had to tread very warily "in order to prevent the news agencies not owned by the Reich from having a more authoritative influence." Arguing that "news policy is a function of the sovereignty of the State, which can neither be exercised by private persons nor by the Party," Goebbels realized that his view was "contrary to that of a number of influential *Reichsleiter*" (of the Party). But this did not disturb him. "If the State is renouncing this function of its sovereignty," he commented, "then it has to give up the whole field. But as long as it is a true State, the news policy must be under its control". But in addition to being a very prestige-ridden Reich Minister, Goebbels was also Gauleiter of Berlin. That meant he had not only to concern himself with the control of the media of mass communication, but also with that of the luggage rooms at the

---

[1] Count Reischach was a Party official attached to the Reich Press Executive of the Party. See *Who's Who in Germany and Austria,* n.d., London, (April 1945), Part II, p. 129. Reischach had the rank of *Reichshauptstellenleiter* in the Party.

main Berlin railway stations where some minor bomb explosions had taken place lately. Goebbels regarded this as a source of potential danger and brooded over the probelm of a more effective supervision of passengers' luggage.

A more cheerful topic was a reception Goebbels had given to the representatives of the organization for Germans abroad, the *Auslands-Organisation* (AO). They had come from all the European States and from overseas to Berlin. Goebbels allowed himself full marks for his address to them. "I was in excellent form and used striking and well formulated arguments." The AO men, who had applauded him strongly, "were certainly returning uplifted to face their difficult task." The entry for this day ended in praise of Lanke, his country estate, where he had spent the afternoon. There "one can deal with issues of a more complex nature which require a more intensive study. In Berlin, on the other hand, one no longer finds time for work which requires real thought." Goebbels deplored the nervous routine, the mere *Betrieb* in Berlin, which, lasting for seven or eight hours daily, he felt stifled his brain. Yet he would have been the last man to give it up. In the evening the last news items came in. There was little news of Singapore. Would the Japanese— Goebbels asked himself—manage to take the town in four days' time, on the day of their national festival? Often, previously, they had surprised the world by their deeds—would they do it again this time? Certainly they were following a plan which no one in the outside world comprehended at his moment. "Let us hope," added Goebbels, "that their action will lead to another devastating blow against the British Empire."

3. A Saga instead of Truth

The surrender of the Sixth Army at Stalingrad at the beginning of 1943 shook even the most sanguine members of the Nazi hierarchy as much as the ignorant masses, and made them realize that the character of the war had fundamentally changed. "Now, for the first time, there was doubt and despondency among the civilian population, as well as in high military or official circles." [1] The German troops in the East found themselves in a very precarious situation. The fall of Stalingrad was a greater disaster for Germany than the fall of Dunkirk had been for the British. The Sixth Army was lost, while the bulk of the B.E.F. had been saved. Moreover, for months German official statements on the events on the Stalingrad front had been optimistic. "The capture of Stalingrad will be completed, and you may be sure that no one will ever drive us out of this place again," Hitler had declared in his speech on 30 September 1942.[2] He had stressed the great strategic importance of Stalingrad, lying as it did on the most important traffic artery of the Soviet Union and

---

[1] J. W. Wheeler-Bennett, *The Nemesis of Power*, London, 1953, p. 539.
[2] *Dokumente der Deutschen Politik und Geschichte von 1848 bis zur Gegenwart*, vol. V, ii, Berlin, n.d., p. 385.

covering the rear of all operations in the Caucasus area. On 8 November Hitler said of Stalingrad: "The fact is that we have got it." A military spokesman declared on the radio on 16 November: "The real objective of our offensive from its very beginning was to gain this point (Stalingrad); to have gained it—for it has been gained—crowned the operations of this summer and autumn." [1]

Inexperienced in military strategy and far from the front, Goebbels had "no conception of the bitterness of fighting" at Stalingrad, one of his assistants discovered when he returned from the Eastern front to the Ministry in December 1942. To his question "whether Stalingrad was to be held at all costs", Goebbels replied that the Führer's reputation as a strategist was at stake. "We would not dare to wreck his handiwork." [2]

But soon afterwards the Russians were able to wreck the Führer's handiwork completely. What remained of the Sixth Army surrendered to the Russians, and its commander, Paulus, only recently promoted to Field Marshal and General von Seydlitz became prisoners of war. Hitler was duly infuriated by the attitude of these generals, whose "ingratitude and disloyalty" he declared to be "beyond his comprehension". [3] On 22 January Hitler had refused a suggestion from Paulus, backed by his superior, Field Marshal von Manstein, that he should be allowed to enter into surrender negotiations. Hitler's grounds for rejecting the request by the two generals were "that every day the enemy's Stalingrad divisions were prevented from being committed elsewhere represented a vital saving." [4] After the struggle of the Sixth Army had come to a close Hitler admitted on 5 February to von Manstein " *I alone* bear the responsibility for Stalingrad." It is hard to agree with Manstein's post-war view that "it was certainly to Hitler's credit that he accepted responsibility unreservedly in this instance and made no attempt whatever to find a scapegoat." [5] For there is little reason to believe that Hitler's admission of his momentous blunder went beyond the ears of a few frightened and submissive generals.

Goebbels on his part felt depressed over the ominous turn of events

[1] See Kris and Speyer, *German Radio Propaganda*, p. 113. As early as 18 September the newspapers had received an article from the official press service—"Stalingrad has fallen. Stalin's command to hold the city at any price did not avert fate. When Adolf Hitler, the Captain, and German soldierhood set themselves a goal that goal is achieved. Even if death and the devil are in league against it." Newspapers were advised to hold this prepared article "for an official special bulletin on the fall of Stalingrad." Ruth Andreas-Friedrich, *Berlin Underground 1939-1945*, p. 77.

[2] R. Semmler, *Goebbels: The Man Next to Hitler*, p. 59, diary entry of 16 December 1942.

[3] A. Bullock, *Hitler, A Study in Tyranny*, p. 632.

[4] Field Marshal Erich von Manstein, *Lost Victories*, edited and translated by Anthony G. Powell, London, 1958, p. 360. Manstein did not resign after Hitler had refused to listen to his advice that the Sixth Army should be allowed to surrender. His assertions that he stood up to the Führer are not convincing.

[5] Op. cit., p. 365.

and in private abused "Field Marshal Paulus for not having committed suicide".[1] He did not doubt the correctness of the Russian claims that Paulus and other high-ranking German officers were in their hands.[2] Goebbels realized correctly that the Soviet Government was making use of these top-rank prisoners for purposes of propaganda. He would have liked to do the same with Allied prisoners. When later post-cards from Stalingrad prisoners arrived in Germany, Goebbels tried to withhold them from their destination. But he could not prevent the Soviet Radio from broadcasting in their German Service the names and addresses of many of the 90,000 or so prisoners who had surrendered.[3]

Officially, all suggestions that some of the 300,000 Stalingrad fighters might be still alive, were taboo. They all had to be dead, heroic figures in Valhalla, blessing and inspiring the determined resistance of their nation. German propaganda tried to create the impression that the Sixth Army had fallen nobly to the last man. Goebbels told a mass meeting in Berlin on 18 February that shortly before the end the heroes of Stalingrad had listened at their radio sets to the Führer's proclamation which Goebbels had read on 30 January, the tenth anniversary of the régime. They had then "sung the national anthems with raised arms together with us, perhaps for the last time in their lives . . . What an attitude for German soldiers in this great time. . . . Stalingrad was and is Fate's great call of alarm to the German nation." [4] This propaganda line of heroic death was fairly consistently pursued after the release of the first news of the débâcle. On 1 February the official *Wehrmacht* communiqué announced that the southern group of the Sixth Army under Paulus had been "overwhelmed in battle by the superiority of the enemy, after more than two months of heroic defence". On 2 February the German Home Service described how "during the heroic fighting every man, up to the General fought in the most advanced line with fixed bayonets." A Special Announcement on the following day, admitting the end of the struggle, transformed a highly unpleasant fact into heroic fiction, explaining that the sacrifice of the Sixth Army was not in vain. As the bulwark of a historic mission it had broken the assault of six Soviet armies for several weeks.

The reading of the Special Announcement over the radio was preceded by slow marches and followed by muffled drum rolls and by three verses of *"Ich hatt' einen Kameraden"*. After the playing of the German, Roumanian and Croatian national anthems a radio silence of three minutes followed. Preceded and followed by martial music and Beethoven's Fifth Symphony, an order was read to the effect that all theatres, cinemas,

[1] R. Semmler, op. cit., diary entry of 2 February 1943, p. 68.

[2] W. Stephan, op. cit., p. 258. This was all the more remarkable as Hans Fritzsche, the head of the Radio Division in the Ministry, who had served six months as a war reporter with the Sixth Army, regarded them as false and their photographs showing the Field Marshal talking to foreign correspondents as faked.

[3] J. W. Wheeler-Bennett, op. cit., pp. 538-539.

[4] J. Goebbels, *Der steile Aufstieg*, p. 167.

and variety halls in the Reich were to close for three days. In subsequent broadcasts these clichés of heroism and of a mission continued. Expressions like "triumph of fortitude over bestiality . . . a condition imposed by fate . . . town of destiny . . . fighters in fact for Western civilization and culture" were typical. As two American analysts put it at the time: "Goebbels thus managed to organize Germany's mourning of the defeat at Stalingrad into a Wagnerian celebration, comparable only to the victory celebrations of June 1940, hoping in this way to evade a realistic appraisal of the defeat." [1]

Glibly Goebbels promised a sober examination of the causes of the catastrophe at a later date. This account—which was in fact never rendered—was to be a grand justification of what had happened. "It will be given," Goebbels promised solemnly on 18 February, "with full frankness and will make clear to the German people and the world that the disaster of the last few weeks has a deep, fateful meaning. The great heroic sacrifice made by the German soldiers at Stalingrad has been of decisive historical importance for the entire Eastern front. It has not been in vain. Why, the future will show".[2] The uglier the facts, the greater their hidden and beneficial meaning. It was all part of a well-calculated technique, intended to evoke greater efforts from the people at home by bestowing a higher significance on stark facts which it was inexpedient to reveal. In his apotheosis of the perished Sixth Army Goebbels turned moralist, making much of the obligation the heroic attitude of the soldiers of Stalingrad placed on the masses at home. Their fate gave impetus to the radical ideas he had proposed for some time, for the proclamation of "total war". Already in December 1942 he had suggested drastic readjustments on the home front to the Führer. Owing to the disquieting crisis at Stalingrad Hitler had, it seems, been ready to accept his proposals, though they were subsequently implemented not by him but by the "Big Three", Bormann, Lammers and Keitel.[3] "Total War" on the home front was imminent. On 27 January 1943 Sauckel, the General Plenipotentiary for Employment of Labour, issued a decree by which men, not in the armed forces, between 16 and 65, and women between 17 and 45, were conscripted for war-work. This measure was justified by the necessity of "directing all forces towards one goal, i.e., the quickest possible gaining of victory in the total war we are waging." [4]

Total war meant also a considerable switch-over of the propaganda line. "I regard it as my task to train the people in the coming months to be tough," Goebbels told German journalists in confidence early in

---

[1] Kris and Speyer, *German Radio Propaganda*, pp. 431-432.

[2] J. Goebbels, *Der steile Aufstieg*, p. 168.

[3] R. Semmler, op. cit., pp. 62-63, diary entry 26 December 1942. Goebbels had then pressed for "a substantial cutting down of the standards of life, in many places still little different from that of peace-time". "The upper ten-thousands," he had said to Semmler, "must make special sacrifices. By these measures it is hoped to release much manpower and material for the war."

[4] *Dokumente der Deutschen Politik und Geschichte*, Vol. V, ii, No. 166, pp. 397-398.

March 1943. "To applaud a *blitz* campaign needs no toughness. But I have the feeling that this war will not come to an end quickly. So we must prepare our minds and hearts for bitter experiences." [1] The official propaganda line now became an admonition to a grim steadfastness rather than an expectation of dynamic victory. "We will hold what we have and we have many pawns of victory," was the note struck in contrast to the former confident suggestion that the German armies were unbeatable and irresistible in their attack and expansion. Even to refute the idea of capitulation had been out of the question before Stalingrad. Now Goebbels saw fit to declare: ". . . the word 'capitulation' does not exist in our vocabulary." [2] At the same time the expression 'pawns' *(Faustpfänder)* for the European territories under German control became one of Goebbels' favourite concepts.

The changed situation at the front and at home, the necessary readjustment in the outlook of the masses caused him to display some show of frankness. As usual, he admitted some difficulties and even errors, but only when they had lost their significance. Goebbels preferred to talk of the "changed outlook on the war" and to demand a new attitude, based on greater detachment and on a viewing of things in a proper historical perspective. Only now was the struggle to be a true "people's war", to be borne by the entire nation. The idea of making war total was hammered in incessantly and almost became an obsession with Goebbels. "The enemy wants to destroy us totally; thus let us wage war totally, in order to bring about total victory." [3]

Total war, he suggested, required a "broader" outlook on the part of the hard-pressed Germans in the towns, who saw shops and bars being closed, their personnel conscripted for war-work, their lives seriously threatened by an endless chain of air-raids. In these circumstances the little doctor, proud of his close contacts with the masses, adopted a pose of frankness. In fact, he admitted little, but made the most of his "admissions": "The width of our warfare," he remarked in a message to the soldiers at the front, "has led to a longer duration of the war than many had expected and believed in 1939. With such width the problems we have to solve in this war have developed infinite proportions." [4] The language of "admissions" became more drastic, when further setbacks and even disasters had to be acknowledged.[5] In times of war it is obviously inadvisable for any leading figure of any regime to tell the masses the full truth, if only for the reason that the enemy may deduce valuable information from it. What Goebbels did, however, was to pretend to

[1] R. Semmler, op. cit., Diary entry 3 March 1943, p. 73.
[2] Address on the Tenth Anniversary of the Nazi regime, 30 January 1943, under the caption, "Führer befiehl, wir folgen!", *Der steile Aufstieg*, p. 139.
[3] Article "Der totale Krieg", 17 January 1943, *Der steile Aufstieg*, p. 121 and p. 128.
[4] Article "Neujahrsgruss an unsere Soldaten", *Das Reich*, 1 January 1943, See also *Der steile Aufstieg*, p. 105.
[5] After the end of the Fascist regime and the fall of Mussolini in Italy, events which profoundly upset the Nazi leadership, Goebbels wrote grimly in

give his listeners the full, harsh facts, whilst actually offering them a saga. "The German people, educated, indoctrinated and disciplined by National Socialism," he declared, "can stand the full truth." [1]

With his ear to the ground Goebbels realized the necessity of staging some big demonstrations of national resistance after the catastrophe of Stalingrad. He was well aware that to his public and audience of millions "the name 'Stalingrad' had become a symbol of the first real crisis of war." [2] The huge rally at the Sport Palace in Berlin on 18 February 1943 was one of the dramatic highlights in Goebbels' career, and one of his masterpieces in organized mass propaganda. It had been very thoroughly prepared. The old Party Guard in Berlin had been joined by a few thousand reliable old Party functionaries from other regions, brought to Berlin for this special occasion. These men and women had been briefed by Party officials on the aims of the mass meeting. [3] Goebbels' performance and the so-called "spontaneous" frenzied reactions of his representative audience were broadcast and listened to by many community meetings all over the Reich. The Minister wanted to impress foreign countries, Allied, enemy and neutral alike. The official reports of the meeting carefully registered the frantic applause and the fanatic, half-hysterical interruptions of Goebbels' speech by the audience, which had all the trappings of being stage-produced. [4] On the way to the monster meeting Goebbels had told his personal entourage coldly: "Today we shall have a demonstration compared with which that of 30 January [1933] will look like a gathering of the *Wirtschaftspartei*". [5]

Admitting in his peroration the existence of "a severe military crisis" (*Belastung*) in the East, Goebbels as usual blamed the wicked satanic forces of Jewry for it and appealed for fanatical devotion to total war. He explained the precarious military situation in order to organize a 20th century *levée en masse*, which would mean a transfer of many men from the civilian sector to the army and a strengthening of the industrial war effort. He announced a number of far-reaching measures because "only the supreme effort, the most total war, can and will meet this peril".

---

an article on 7 August 1943: "In these weeks we pass through a decisive phase of the war. With an onslaught of weapons that never existed before and with moral means of pressure the enemy tries to wrest the position from us which we gained in the first half of this gigantic struggle and which forms the pre-condition of our victory." Article "Die Moral als kriegsentscheidender Faktor", reprinted in *Der steile Aufstieg*, p. 406. The article appeared in the German press on 7 August 1943.

[1] *Der steile Aufstieg*, p. 168.

[2] J. W. Wheeler-Bennett, *The Nemesis of Power*, p. 537.

[3] See W. Hagemann, *Publizistik im Dritten Reich*, pp. 464-465.

[4] The report appeared in the press under a caption taken from a poem by Theodor Körner, the poet of the War of Liberation: *"Nun, Volk, steh' auf und Sturm brich' los!"* ("Arise my people, now and storm unleash!") For the text, see *Der steile Aufstieg*, pp. 138-204.

[5] This was the name of one of the minor parties in the Reichstag during the Weimar Republic. See W. Stephan, *Joseph Goebbels*, p. 260.

With that aim in view and with the propagandist's instinctive desire to simplify things, he proclaimed three theses of which only the third can be regarded as being new and significant. They ran:

1. If the German Armed Forces were not in a position to break the danger from the East, the Reich and soon afterwards the whole of Europe would be the prey of Bolshevism. ("Germany, the Saviour").

2. Only the German Armed Forces and the German People, with their Allies, have the strength to carry out a fundamental rescue of Europe from this menace. ("Germany, the only Saviour").

3. There is danger in delay. Quick and thorough action has to be taken, otherwise it will be too late. ("Allons enfants de la Patrie!").[1]

At the Sport Palace there was above the Speaker's platform an immense ribbon with the words *TOTALER KRIEG*. The audience was intended to represent all sections of the community. On the platform and in the first two rows of the audience sat high Party officials, Reichsleiter and Gauleiter, Generals, Reich Ministers, scholars and artists, teachers, civil servants, engineers and white-collar workers, many soldiers in uniform including wounded men from the Eastern front, some of them without a limb or blind. Goebbels made much of this "representative" cross section of the nation as indicating full national integration.

The official report on the meeting duly registered the mass intoxication which magician Goebbels was able to produce. To quote only one instance, it said: "At this question the Sport Palace experiences a demonstration the like of which even this old scene of the fight of National Socialism has only seen on special peak events of our national life. The masses jump from their seats as if electrified. A 'Yes' from thousands of voices rages like a hurricane through the wide round hall. What the participants of this demonstration experience is a national vote and an expression of will power, which could not be expressed more spontaneously." [2]

Goebbels helped that "spontaneity" along by a shrewd technique of question and answer, which it seems had a double function: first, it allowed him to use to the full his suggestive powers for instilling suitable images and ideas into the masses, and secondly it helped him to "prove" to the world that there was full accord between the rulers and the ruled, who gave their full approval to the measures of total warfare to come. At a major crisis of the war a show of identification of all sections of the people with the leadership was imperative and, if successfully staged, might well prove invaluable.

The people selected to attend this meeting were all more or less ardent supporters of the German war effort and of the régime. Goebbels could therefore take the desired answers for granted, and by having the performance relayed by the radio, hoped that it might raise the morale of

[1] *Der steile Aufstieg*, pp. 173-174.
[2] See also below ch. 18, p. 422. The passage is to be found in *Der steile Aufstieg*, p. 199.

unseen millions. By proclaiming his audience as "representative" of the German people, he undoubtedly hoped to reassure the doubters and waverers among them and to give to both Germans and foreigners the impression of a nation united in the war effort. In this sense Goebbels' play with question and answer, as adroit as it was determined, will indeed "remain memorable as an example of National Socialist technique in public meetings and propaganda." [1]

It is useful therefore to list both the arguments Goebbels was anxious to refute and the slogans he wanted to instil into the public mind at that juncture of the war. The first five questions aimed at a ruthless exposure of English lies on the situation in Germany, whilst questions six to ten were obviously intended not only to evoke a vote of confidence in the Führer but also to demonstrate that identification of the ruled with their rulers, which Goebbels had, as we have seen, always regarded as indispensable. There was very little talk of Stalingrad and the Russians in Goebbels' questions and very much of British propaganda lies, perhaps because Goebbels found it easier to cope with propaganda arguments than with hard military facts. The English, being regarded at the time as the lesser danger for the Reich and its armed forces, were used as a sort of catalyst or whipping boy to divert attention from the primary evil, the enormous catastrophe in Russia. Here are the ten questions and the reactions of the fanatical audience as registered in the official press report issued afterwards by DNB: [2]

"Thus you, my listeners, are representing the nation at this moment. And to you I should like to direct ten questions which you should answer me with the German people before the whole world, particularly before our enemies who are listening in at their radio sets too." [3]
"First: The English allege that the German people have lost their belief in victory.
I ask you: Do you believe with the Führer and with us in the final total victory of the German people? I ask you: Are you determined to follow the Führer through thick and thin in the struggle for victory and to put up even with the heaviest personal burdens?
Second: The English allege that the German people are tired of fighting. I ask you: Are you ready with the Führer and as a phalanx of the home front standing behind the fighting armed forces to continue this struggle, with a wild determination and impervious to all ordeals of Fate, until victory is in our hands?

[1] R. Semmler, op. cit., p. 69. The diary entry is, however, erroneously given as "15 February 1943"; in fact, the meeting took place on the 18th.
[2] See *Der steile Aufstieg*, pp. 199-202.
[3] Comment in the official report: "Only with difficulty can the Minister make himself heard with his questions to follow. The crowd is in a state of extremely high spirits. The single questions cut with the sharpness of a knife. Every individual feels they are addressed to himself. With utmost participation and enthusiasm the masses give their answer to each individual question. The Sport Palace echoes a single cry of approval."

Third: The English allege that the German people are no longer in a mood to take upon themselves the ever increasing war work demanded by the Government.

I ask you: Are you and are the German people determined, when the Führer orders it, to work ten, twelve, and if necessary fourteen and sixteen hours a day and to give your utmost for victory?

Fourth: The English allege that the German people resist the total war measures of the Government. (Cries: Never! Never! Never!)

I ask you: Do you want total war? Do you want it, if necessary more total and more radical than we can even imagine it today?

Fifth: The English allege that the German people have lost their confidence in the Führer.

I ask you: Is your confidence in the Führer, greater, more faithful and unshakable than ever before? Is your readiness to follow him in all his ways and to do everything necessary to bring the war to a victorious end, absolute and unqualified?" [1] Response as explained in the official report: "As if by command, the flags and standards are now raised, a supreme expression of the solemn moment when the masses pay homage to the Leader."

With questions six to ten Goebbels continued this well-staged game of challenge and response. Were they ready to exert their full strength and to put all the men and arms at the disposal of the Eastern Front required to give the fatal blow to Bolshevism? Would German women be willing to play a major role in war work and thus free men for the Fighting Front? Did the audience agree that the most radical measures were required against selfish shirkers and war profiteers? All in all, did they wish that in solidarity the home front would take the heavy tax burden of war on its shoulders and would see it equally distributed between rich and poor?

Tremendous applause followed which Goebbels, of course, triumphantly interpreted as manifesting the full identification of Government and people. In his short rhythmical sentences he insisted that both were one in their determination to see the war through in its new total phase: "I asked you—you gave me your answers. You are part of the German people and from your mouth the attitude of the German people has become manifest. . . . Thus we are firmly and fraternally united with the German people, as has been the case from the first hour of our being in power and through all the ten years." Goebbels played the part of the go-between, the middleman. He was standing before them, "not only as the spokesman of the Government, but also as the spokesman of the people." [2] There was something of a patriotic revivalist in Goebbels. Although he had revealed little of the pathetic truth of Stalingrad, he

[1] Official comment: "The crowd rises like one man. The enthusiasm of the masses explodes in a demonstration never seen before. With many thousands of voices *Sprechchöre* thunder through the Hall: "Leader, command, we follow." An endless wave of shouts of "Hail, the Führer", resounds.

[2] *Der steil Aufstieg*, p. 197.

had used semi-religious language by expressing his "deep conviction" that the German people had been "inwardly purified very profoundly by the tragic blow of fate at Stalingrad". They looked into "the hard and pitiless face of war." They knew now "the cruel truth" and were determined to go forward with the Führer through thick and thin".[1]

It is significant that German comments on this frenzied mass meeting have since varied a good deal. Looking back later, a sensible official in the Propaganda Ministry thought the secret of Goebbels' strength lay in "his ability to calculate the effect of every single word in advance. He really succeeded in intoxicating millions of Germans." [2] On the other hand, it has been pointed out by Walter Hagemann, that, at later enquiries showed, "even to sympathizers who had not been present in person and had therefore felt this mass intoxication only by ear, the hysterical shouting and screaming was odd, even repellent." In any case, this analyst claims, "the address made a permanent impression on the German people, because it showed to anyone who was not blind or deaf, how seriously the regime itself judged the position and what one had to expect for oneself from this total war now finally proclaimed".[3]

A distinction might be made between the short and the long term effects of that extraordinary mass meeting. Its immediate effect was impressive and served to strengthen morale, but when the intoxication had worn off "the German people began to reflect upon Goebbels' urgent tone and the sharpness of his words. People also began to ask themselves if a catastrophe was not threatening in the East".[4] For the time being Goebbels' peroration served its purpose well, but eventually it may well have proved a boomerang.

[1] Ibid.

[2] W. Stephan, op. cit., p. 260. See also the diary entry for 18th February 1943, in *Berliner Aufzeichnungen. Aus den Jahren 1942-1945* by U. von Kardorff, Munich, 1962, p. 32. An anti-Nazi fellow journalist who had attended the mass meeting remarked to the author: "If Goebbels had put the further question: 'Do yuo wish to die?' they would have shouted the same 'yes.' "

[3] W. Hagemann, *Publizistik im Dritten Reich,* p. 472f. A comment by a determined anti-Nazi in Berlin made the day after Goebbels' speech is worth quoting: "Goebbels is running a 'demonstration of fanatical will' in the *Sportpalast*. 'For the salvation of Germany and civilization.' 'Only the supreme effort, the most total war', he adjures his listeners, 'can and will meet this peril'.

Total, totaller, totallest. I didn't know that even ultimates could have superlatives, probably people who are unsure of themselves have to fall back on such things. They have to struggle from one exaggeration to the next. After all, what would still pull in the 'Greater German Reich' if not the superlative of all superlatives? The best people in the world . . . the wisest people in the world . . . the most chivalrous people in the world. Breker's sculptures, Speer's buildings, Goebbels' propaganda speeches, the thundering pathos of George. 'People that boast have need of it', says the proverb. Things don't look good on the Russian front." Ruth Andreas-Friedrich, *Berlin Underground 1939-1945,* Diary entry 19 February 1943, p. 81.

[4] Fredborg, *Behind the Steel Wall,* p. 173.

CHAPTER 12

Hardened Realism: Keeping up Morale (1942-1943)

"It is my task to provide the naively credulous with the arguments for what they think and wish, but which they are unable to formulate and verify themselves".

Goebbels to Werner Stephan in 1943.

1. THE CHALLENGE OF ENEMY "TERROR RAIDS".

DURING the second half of the war Goebbels' position in the eyes of the people gathered strength. Perhaps the reason for this was that he was in touch with them. His calculated fanaticism proved effective as it seemed to be supported by a first hand knowledge of the plight of the masses. He was well aware of the serious effects of the heavy British and American air raids which gathered momentum in the course of 1943. In March of that year he admitted to himself that the English were justified in making so much of their air offensive, for it was gradually becoming very vexatious to the German people. "Nearly every night massive air attacks on some German town," he commented in his diary.[1] "The cost to us in terms of material and also of moral values is heavy."

In a speech in Berlin on 5 June Goebbels conceded the "sometimes very harsh results of the British and American air war terror". In the privacy of his diary he asked himself searching questions. "The English wrested air supremacy from us," he told himself on 28 March, "not only as result of tremendous energy on the part of the Royal Air Force and the British aircraft industry, but also thanks to several unfortunate circumstances and to our own negligence. Why cannot we in time wrest it back from the English, if once we abandon the thesis that the war in the East must be ended first?"[2]

Two months later after a very powerful air raid on Duisburg Goebbels registered the somewhat depressing feeling that the Germans were in an inferior position in the whole field of air warfare. "We have," he admitted,

---

[1] Diary entry of 6 March, 1943.
[2] *The Goebbels Diaries*, ed. L. Lochner, p. 317.

269

"allowed too many calamities to happen and we have now to pay dearly for past omissions." [1] By the end of the year Goebbels even conceded that "the enemy air terror and its consequences for the German homeland" had "become the most burning of all problems". In an address before leaders of the Hitler Youth and their parents in Berlin he used his oratorical talents to whip up hatred of the ruthless foe and to expose his inhumanity.[2] German propaganda did not try to deny the heavy damage done by these raids on German towns. Apart from threats of an early and most complete retaliation it attempted to offset its effect by claiming that these raids were a futile piece of terrorism and would merely serve to strengthen the morale of the civilians.[3]

Though cynical, Goebbels was brave. He did not shirk the unpleasant issues. Very different from the ever absent Führer, he travelled frequently through the heavily bombed areas encouraging and inspiring the unfortunate people. When after a major air raid on Cologne in July 1943 he visited the Rhenish town, a companion observed to his surprise "that Goebbels was everywhere cordially greeted in the Rhineland dialect. One notices, even in Cologne, that he is, at the moment, the most popular of the nation's leaders. These suffering men and women feel that at least one of them is interested in their fate." [4] Goebbels had a knack of underlining his close and specific regional ties, and he did so equally in the Rhineland, his first, and in Berlin, his second *Heimat*. Addressing a commemoration meeting for the victims of air warfare in Elberfeld in June 1943, the Minister introduced himself "as a son of this land, blessed in times of peace and praised in songs, a son who has never cut the close ties that connect him with his home country." [5]

With the Berliners Goebbels took a similar line. He told them in January 1943 that he was happy "to be in charge of the political leadership of the largest German community, i.e. the capital of the Reich. This prevents us from making the mistake of judging and deciding things from an arm chair." [6] After the devastating air raids on Hamburg in July 1943 the Minister had reason to fear that Berlin would be the next target for the Anglo-American bombers, and therefore insisted on the evacuation of women and children.[7] Aware of the Berliners' fear that

---

[1] Diary entry of 14 May 1943. See also his lament in the diary notes on 18 May 1943: "The air force has rested too long on its laurels and the German people now have to foot the bill for it."

[2] See the report in *The Times*, London, 29 November 1943.

[3] See the article "Through German Eyes" in *The Times*, 18 December 1943.

[4] R. Semmler, *Goebbels: The Man Next to Hitler*, Diary entry of 10 July 1945, p. 88.

[5] "In vorderster Reihe, Rede auf der Trauerkundgebung in der Elbefelder Stadthalle", 18 June 1943, reprinted in *Der steile Aufstieg*, pp. 323-324.

[6] Article "Die Heimat im Kriege", *Das Reich*, 3 January 1943; see *Der steile Aufstieg*, p. 117.

[7] R. Semmler, op. cit., pp. 94-95, entry of 26 July 1943; W. von Oven, op. cit., I, pp. 88-89, entry of 2 August 1943; *The Goebbels Diaries*, p. 320, entry of 26 July.

should there be more serious raids on Berlin "the Government would be the first to run away",[1] he took pains to underline his solidarity with the inhabitants who remained in Berlin. In an article published early in August [2] he declared that as Gauleiter of Berlin he would not leave the Reich capital, because like many hundreds of thousands of his fellow-citizens his place of work was there. Moreover, he believed that in case of air raid attacks he could and should do something for the population. By then, Goebbels' connection with Berlin had lasted seven years. "I acquired," said the Minister, "the honorary title of Conqueror of Berlin in seven years (1926-1933). I am determined to deserve that of Defender of Berlin after just as many weeks." [3] The gap between the authoritarian leaders and the still docile masses had to be narrowed as much as possible.[4]

In Berlin Goebbels became more rather than less popular, perhaps because he did not shirk the issue. In November 1943 Semmler noted: "Goebbels drives round the whole city—everywhere desolation. At several points he takes charge of the fire fighting. Amid all this misery his gleaming black armoured car looks strangely conspicuous. Someone who did not recognize him shouted "plutocrat!" into the car. Wherever he is recognized he gets a friendly greeting in spite of everything. Even bombed-out people come and shake him by the hand. He is always ready for a jest . . ." [5] Goebbels constantly claimed personal credit for the disciplined and unrevolutionary attitude of the Berliners.[6]

2. GOEBBELS AND THE PUBLIC: FOUR ASPECTS

It is interesting enough to see how Goebbels reacted to the changing moods of the public during this second period of the war which tested the morale of the people so much more than the first. Four distinct aspects of Goebbels' relations with the public can be distinguished. First, there was his eagerness for and his insistence on obtaining as much exact information as possible about the mood, the thoughts and feelings of the people. He looked upon the various types of reports he regularly studied and commented on from a very pragmatic point of view. It would be false to maintain that Goebbels only appreciated those sections which

---

[1] See *The Goebbels Diaries,* entry of 29 July 1943, p. 335.

[2] *Völkischer Beobachter* (Berlin edition), 4 August 1943.

[3] See W. von Oven, op. cit., I, p. 89.

[4] It was from that time onward that Goebbels preferred in his addresses and writings to talk of *"Führung"* (leadership) rather than of *"der Führer"*. Implicitly he included himself in this collective term. On the other hand, off the record Semmler noted the frequency of Goebbels' uttering with a sigh: "If I were the Führer." R. Semmler, op. cit., diary entry of 7 August 1943, p. 96.

[5] R. Semmler, op. cit., diary entry of 24 November, 1943, pp. 110-111.

[6] Goebbels regarded it as "a personal success for himself that the Berliners did not gather in crowds on the *Wilhelmplatz* (the seat of the Government bureaucracy) and demand an end to the war". As Semmler observed on 24 November 1943 "75 per cent of the workers were at their jobs this morning. For this high morale Goebbels also takes the credit". Op. cit., p. 111.

agreed with his own views; he was often able to learn and to readjust his own position accordingly. At the same time he was acutely conscious of the danger of too much candour, of the unvarnished truth. When in May 1943 he found that an SD report was too realistic, Goebbels made the charge of "defeatism" and Himmler agreed to discontinue the reports.[1] A different type of report took its place, the distribution of which was restricted to Goebbels and his staff and would not include the personnel of other ministries.

As long as the public were appreciative of Goebbels' own efforts, all seemed well or at least not too bad to him. "Of course, people grumble a lot and over various subjects," he wrote in his diary on 18 April 1942. "Personal vulgar attacks are also not lacking in anonymous letters which, as can be asserted rather unequivocally from their style, originate from Jews." This is a typical indication of his bias, for few Jews would have cared to be found out and to increase their chances of being deported to the East by writing to Goebbels; there existed also no "Jewish" style of writing in German. But the vast majority of the letters Goebbels found "moving and enjoyable". He felt proud that his journalistic work evoked "the strongest interest" and contributed "so much to brighten the mood *(die innere Stimmung)* and to clarify the most important problems of our domestic policy." If there was any unmistakable public discontent Goebbels never hesitated to put the blame for it on others, on the Jews, or more frequently on his own rivals and on rival organizations. On 14 December 1942, for instance, he registered with obvious glee the criticism of the daily *Wehrmacht* bulletin by the people. He noted that after the Allied victory at El Alamein various confidential reports on the people's mood had severely criticised the dishonest official German news policy on the deteriorating situation in North Africa. "I feel free from any guilt concerning this failure," Goebbels wrote smugly, "one should not hesitate to point out the seriousness of the position. I feel also that concerning the front the German people can take quite a lot. They are only becoming uneasy when they feel that there is the intention to spare them excessively. And," he added soberly without perhaps realizing the irony of his words, "the people think for themselves and master absolutely the art of reading between the lines (of the official bulletin)."

According to intelligence reports the German people by then had written Tunisia more or less off before the authorities admitted its loss, a fact which evoked the somewhat naive remark from Goebbels: "On the whole the people are more clever than it is thought." [2] When the populace were kept in the dark on the fate of Tunisia, their meat rations cut and they had to face continuous severe air raids in many towns, the reports registered a marked deterioration of the people's mood. This time people did not lay the blame on the *Wehrmacht*, but on Goebbels' own

---

[1] Diary entry of 12 May 1943; see also *Goebbels Tagebücher,* ed. L. Lochner, Zurich, 1948, pp. 340-341.
[2] Diary entry of 9 April 1943 (01983).

instruments, the mass media. "As usual, the scapegoat is the radio and the press," Goebbels commented sadly, "we are severly criticized for the smallest tactical mistakes that occur in our press and radio." [1]

The people felt uneasy—he observed—because they had no clear conception of the future course of the war. They wanted him to give them an authentic picture of the war situation. This was not possible, but Goebbels admitted to himself that the press was at the moment much handicapped by the whole series of *Verbote* and restrictions as the result of the present situation. However, there was a redeeming feature, the letters he had received from the public were more positive than one would have expected from reading the intelligence reports. There was unanimous praise of his journalistic work in these letters, a fact, he claimed, "of decisive value in the present situation".

The second aspect of Goebbels' relations with the public was his insistence on taking the people into his confidence. What did he mean by this phrase? All he wanted, it seems, was to create the impression of doing so and to provide the public from time to time, if not with reliable news, at least with strong guidance talks and articles. Goebbels achieved this more by his regular contribution to *Das Reich* than through any other channel of mass communications at his disposal.

When at the end of July 1943 Mussolini was quite unexpectedly removed from office and the Badoglio régime established in Rome, there was at first much confusion at the Führer's Headquarters and in Berlin. Goebbels thought it opportune to wait for further development before commenting on the momentous events in Rome.[2] For some weeks, therefore, his regular weekly article in *Das Reich* remained unwritten.[3] Only in mid-September when the German troops were in control of Rome and of Northern Italy did the Reich Minister of Propaganda come out into the open with his remarkable article "Das Schulbeispiel," [4] in which he branded the treacherous attitude of the Italians as an object lesson on how not to behave. By then the liberation of Mussolini through the bold action of Colonel Otto Skorzeny and his men greatly improved German home morale and had created a world-wide sensation.

To boost morale, Goebbels also managed to persuade the Führer to give a radio address on German relations with Italy, an exceedingly rare event as Hitler had remained silent for the previous six months.[5] Public opinion, he claimed, was uplifted by the Führer's speech. Reports showed

[1] Diary entry of 22 May 1943 (02458).

[2] See below, pp. 282-283.

[3] However, it seems that during this period Goebbels contributed anonymously to the periodical. See *Goebbels Tagebücher*, p. 513.

[4] *Das Reich*, 19 September 1943; reprinted in *Der steile Aufstieg*, pp. 456-463. See also below pp. 282-283.

[5] Hitler spoke over the air on 10 September 1943. (For the text see *The Times*, 11 September 1943). On the following day Goebbels wrote in his diary: "Thus I had at last managed to put the Führer before the microphone for the first time since the Heroes Commemoration Day. Now I can return to Berlin with my mind at ease", *Goebbels Tagebücher*, p. 409.

that its impact was immense. "The authority of the Führer," Goebbels observed, "was now once more entirely undisputed." Hitler's remark on the principle of loyalty in the life of the State had made a particularly deep impression. When, two months afterwards, in November 1943, the war position in the East and in Italy had deteriorated, Goebbels again was eager that Hitler should address the masses. An opportunity for this presented itself with the twentieth anniversary of the Hiter *Putsch* of 1923. On this occasion the Führer spoke to the old Party Guard assembled at Munich. Goebbels was elated. Hitler's words, he noted in his diary, had made "an immense impression".[1] The simple fact that the Führer had spoken at all had been a tonic to the people. In addition "a number of phrases in the speech" had "blown away the worries and the anguish of the masses to a considerable extent. Especially the passage that the German people could be reassured, victory would be with the German side, had had the effect of balm on open wounds". Hitler's promises of a forthcoming retaliation against England and of rebuilding the destroyed German towns had evoked the enthusiasm of the people very quickly. The wise "father" of the nation had shown his children the promised land. As a report from the Reich Propaganda offices was to express it succinctly soon afterwards: "Hitler had convinced the people that everything would turn out all right in the end".[2]

The less the people were able to see or to listen to the Führer, the more important it was in Goebbels' eyes to remove false ideas from their minds. With a clever and sustained pose Goebbels took them into his confidence, in order that their faith in the leadership should be restored or strengthened. Nevertheless, there was by now little left of the former arrogance of infallibility; instead a marked undertone of self-defence can be discerned. Most people, Goebbels lamented, had quite wrong ideas of what leadership in wartime really meant. In fact, it was "a continuous sequence of work, worry and responsibility throughout the days and usually the nights also." [3] With subtle casuistry Goebbels deplored the unfairness of all criticism of the Government's deeds or omissions. Confronted with these facts, who had the courage to ask if the Government knew this or that, or what it proposed to do to remedy it? "It knows so much and does so much that it would only be just to cover what perhaps remains undone for once with the mantle of love and understanding." [4] Obviously, the leadership emerged from such "frank"

---

[1] Diary entry of 11 November 1943 (03145).

[2] Diary entry of 19 November 1943 (03240-41).

[3] *Der steile Aufstieg*, p. 383.

[4] In an article written a few weeks earlier Goebbels had played down the idea that the Government made real mistakes by drawing a fine distinction between "real" and faked mistakes. He had argued that "not everything regarded today by the public as a mistake of the leadership is a genuine error". Much of it was in fact a deliberate ruse to mislead the enemy. Its true motives could only be accounted for after the war and would then be properly appreciated: See "Vom Reden und Schweigen", *Das Reich*, 20 June 1943, reprinted in *Der steile Aufstieg*, p. 336.

reflections with flying colours. But they clearly reveal that for the first time Goebbels was worried about a possible alienation of the masses from the régime. It was a new line for him to have to prove that the leadership *(Leitung)* deserved the confidence and the unqualified loyal support of the entire nation, on which it depended in making history.

Goebbels believed in mass campaigns to indoctrinate the people, such as the wave of mass meetings *(Versammlungswellen)* which were organized in the autumn of 1943. This can be regarded as the third aspect of his relations with the public. People were not allowed to be left alone to brood over their hardships and the ugly face of Mars. They were to be imbued with hatred against their enemies, a hatred which was particularly whipped up after intensive air raids. These mass meetings were designed to make people more fanatical and fill them with an intense hatred of the Anglo-American "terrorists." As Goebbels had shrewdly observed in his diary in May 1943, "an interesting transformation is taking place among the German people. Those who are confident of victory have become even more fanatical in their belief, while the defeatists, especially the intellectuals, are outdoing each other with pessimistic utterances. These positive elements should have their backs stiffened by a great speech, and the doubtful elements should be restrained. The citizens who are faithful to the State must be given the arguments necessary to combat defeatism during discussions at their places of work and at street corners." [1] "Our series of meetings has proved a tremendous success," Goebbels observed six months later, "thousands of them were held and they were overcrowded almost everywhere." But also more and more defeatists were denounced, arrested and executed. The announcements that death sentences had been promulgated and carried out served as a calculated deterrent.[2] "The everlasting grumbling has also diminished considerably since death sentences against

[1] Diary entry of 28 May 1943. *The Goebbels Diaries,* p. 318.

[2] For some of the death sentences promulgated by the People's Courts against opponents of the regime and their execution in 1943, see *Der lautlose Widerstand,* ed. by G. Weisenborn, Hamburg, 1953, Anhang I, *Dokumente zur Widerstandsbewegung.* The case of *Regierungsrat* Theodor Korselt in Rostock is typical. After the fall of Mussolini in Italy and heavy air raids on Rostock, Korselt was alleged to have said in a tram to a National Socialist town councillor that the Italian example would have to be followed in Germany. The Führer would have to resign, for there was no longer any chance of German victory, and they would not like all to be burned alive. Korselt was declared to have forfeited his honour for ever and was sentenced to death because "as a man in a responsible position and with a special responsibility he had broken his oath of loyalty (to Hitler), he impaired our National Socialist readiness for a manly defence and had thus helped our enemy in the war." Op. cit., p. 26. One of the two signatures under this judgment was that of the President of the People's Court in Berlin Dr. Freisler, the "Judge Jeffreys" of the Nazi regime. The similar case of Frau Elfriede Scholz, the sister of E. M. Remarque, author of *All Quiet on the Western Front,* then living in the United States, was also heard before Dr. Freisler. Korselt was sentenced to death on 23 August and Frau Scholz on 29 October 1943. For the Scholz case, see op. cit., pp. 262-264.

defeatists have been pronounced, executed and published," wrote Goebbels with grim satisfaction, "that had a very sobering and deterrent effect on the defeatists. Our Reich propaganda office claims that one single victory on any front would completely change morale at home." [1]

Goebbels was acutely interested in the reaction of the people to propaganda themes. At the end of November 1943, for instance, he noted with some alarm that the masses veering between fears and hopes, were still underestimating the Bolshevist danger. As intelligence reports showed, they "did not regard Bolshevism as bloodthirsty and terroristic as it actually is". In the circles of intellectuals the view was often voiced that "Germany's plutocratic enemies would meet us half way *(Entgegenkommen beweisen würden)*; whilst in fact this could not happen at all." [2] In the reports from the Propaganda offices an important distinction was drawn between *Stimmung* and *Haltung*. The mood of the people might fluctuate, they might get depressed, but this was of lesser importance as long as their morale, their active support of the war effort remained unimpaired.

In May 1943, for instance, the reports on morale *(Stimmungsberichte)* from the Reich Propaganda Offices all registered a *Stimmungseinbruch*, a lowering of the mood of the people throughout Germany. This was explained by Goebbels as the outcome of the loss of Tunisia, the increasing severity of air-raids, the temporary failure of the U-boat warfare and the reduction in the meat ration.[3] He regarded it as "quite natural that the people look for a scapegoat, since the facts themselves cannot be altered." But the position became more serious with the following *Stimmungsbericht*, again furnished by the Reich Propaganda Offices. This time the report talked "of a general severe depression to be observed in the entire people. It was now possible to say that not only their mood but also their *Haltung* or morale was impaired *(Es könne nicht nur von einem Stimmungs-sondern von einem Haltungseinbruch gesprochen werden)."* The people were not seeing any way out of the dilemma, and were greatly puzzled by it. This was a serious state of affairs. It is surprising, though perhaps a clear indication of Goebbels' sober realism which was often stronger than his fits of wishful thinking, that he found "this understandable, as our news policy is now so restrained, that no one can see rhyme or reason in it." [4] In fact, there is scant evidence that the morale of the people was greatly changed; they had little alternative but to continue the war effort though their faith in victory had been shaken.[5]

---

[1] Diary entry of 12 November 1943, *The Goebbels Diaries*, p. 415.

[2] Diary entry of 26 November 1943 (03325).

[3] Diary entry of 23 May 1943, *Goebbels Tagebücher*, pp. 355-356.

[4] Diary entry of 28 May 1943 (02531).

[5] In a totalitarian state a drop in morale need not, and often cannot, lead to a change in behavior. In this respect, the observation is relevant that "long-term propaganda such as that transmitted in Germany by the BBC probably

As far as the devastating impact of the growing Allied air raids was concerned, Goebbels thought it inexpedient to hush things up too much. For in this case rumours would exaggerate what had happened. "We cannot manage this with the tactics of concealment. The damage created [by enemy air raids] is so immense, that we have to supply the people with additional moral strength. But this can only be done by a frank discussion of the problems *("durch ein offenes Aussprechen der Probleme")*.[1] Goebbels realized the astonishing discrepancy between the official news policy and the actual mood of the people. He thought of giving the German press "a quite different face." In future it should "concern itself with the questions which are being discussed by the people, and less with those that are only debated in editorial and government offices. . . . I believe that by this the press will be closer to the people than is unfortunately the case at the moment."[2]

While Goebbels was always prepared to measure the pulse of public mood, naturally he was happiest when this mood coincided with his own preferences and policies. After his great appeal for total warfare after Stalingrad in February 1943, he had invited the people to send in suggestions on the total war effort through the newspapers or radio. As a result, he received a lot of letters. The suggestions they contained he found partly useless, even idiotic, and partly very useful. "One can see from them," he remarked in his diary, "that the people occupy themselves very much with the problems of total war and that they regard the measures so far taken for it by no means as adequate. The people are today much more radical than their leadership."[3] The people claimed that a month after Goebbels' appeal not much had been done about the intensification of the war effort. They were partly right, though Goebbels told himself, that this was not his fault, but that of the bureaucrats. "Wherever I turn, the bureaucrats are standing in my way."[4]

If it was rarely expedient to keep the people adequately informed about the war effort, it was at least possible to provide some entertainment and relaxation for them. The mixture of propaganda and entertainment favoured by Goebbels in publicity forms the fourth aspect of his relations with the public. In this respect, Goebbels was more far-sighted than many of his colleagues or subordinates. He realized that, apart from their function of propaganda, radio and film could also act as escape valves and offer a diversion to the weary and hard-working masses. There was no point in pursuing them with heavy radio talks à la

---

did much to affect the mood of the average German listener, but relatively little to affect his behaviour—there was as good as no translation of the induced emotions into the sphere of action"; Lindley Fraser, *Propaganda*, London, 1959, p. 100.
[1] Diary entry of 10 April 1943.
[2] Ibid.
[3] Diary entry of 18 March 1943.
[4] Ibid.

Rosenberg. With its huge mass audience the radio had to cater for the many rather than for the select few. It was better that its programmes should be based on the lowest common denominator of the masses than on the taste of a few pretentious intellectuals.[1] Goebbels complained that his subordinates in charge of the German radio did not fully realize that "radio speakers and radio producers had always to think of the entire people as their public".

The Minister was prepared to readjust the tactics of radio policy according to the wishes of the public, provided this would help and did not hinder the war effort. He liked to think of himself as a mind reader who intuitively knew what the public required. "The public desires an objective and unsensational news service, that conceals its tendency in its formulations rather than makes it explicit after them," he told himself in December 1942 with self-satisfaction, adding; "On the whole the taste of the public corresponds with my intentions. I can observe here once more that as far as the emotions and feelings of the broad masses are concerned I feel them very sensitively in my finger tips." [2] If this was a boast, it was one largely justified. In Goebbels' view, broadcasters appeared before the microphone "in order to inform the masses or to provide relaxation and enjoyment for them." [3] It was possible as well as desirable to combine indoctrination and entertainment. In 1942 Goebbels believed as much in the role of symbols as he had done in 1928. He still wished to give the public symbols which would attract them and would personify the spirit of hard realism which was now required.

When things went badly on the front and the heavy Allied air raids were apt to convince the people of the strength of an enemy once so much derided by Goebbels' propaganda, it seemed imperative to find a symbol of stoic resistance, of fearless heroism in trials and tribulations. Such a symbolic figure had to be both familiar and remote and it had to be brought close to the masses not through patriotic sermons but by way of entertainment, by way of a film. As is shown in another chapter of this book, Frederick the Great became the great traditional symbol of persistence when things went wrong for the rulers of the Third Reich.[4] The idea of producing a new version of an old theme, of retelling the story of Frederick the Great, was therefore attractive. Though the film "Der grosse König" had been planned in times when fortune had smiled on the German armies, its message was particularly suited to days of distress and of national misfortune. "With this film we can make politics, too," Goebbels told himself. "It is a good expedient *(Hilfsmittel)* in the struggle for the soul of our people and in the process of a permanent

[1] See Goebbels' diary entry of 4 February 1942.
[2] Diary entry of 18 December 1942.
[3] Diary entry of 4 February, 1942.
[4] See below chapter 19, pp. 444-449.

hardening of the German power of resistance which we need in order to pass successfully through this war." [1]

Goebbels did his utmost to boost the film. At its premiere on 4 March before an audience mainly composed of holders of the Knight's Cross, of wounded soldiers and armament workers, he bestowed the title "Film of the Nation" on it and by permission of the Führer announced the promotion of the actor Otto Gebühr, who played the role of the great King, to "Actor of the State" (*Staatsschauspieler*). "The film is a sensational success," Goebbels remarked after the premiere, "it has exactly the effect I predicted." Undoubtedly it would do much to educate the German people, particularly in the present situation.[2] Goebbels was also pleased with the timing of its release. It had appeared "just in time to justify and initiate a harsher type of warfare also through this medium." [3] That such sanguine hopes should be pinned to the morale-raising effect of one historical film seems somewhat ludicrous.

3. WHEN TO ADMIT MISTAKES

Like any other propagandist and politician, Goebbels was reluctant to admit mistakes. Nevertheless, he realized that sometimes admission of miscalculations and errors was unavoidable and might even be expedient, provided it could be sufficiently adulterated and counterbalanced by positive statements or promises. After the fall of Stalingrad, Goebbels described it as understandable that, "owing to the large-scale machinations of camouflage and bluff by the Bolshevik régime", they had not properly estimated the war potential of the Soviet Union.[4] Three months later he conceded in an article that the Government were not clairvoyants. "They knew exactly what they could do and wanted to do", Goebbels declared; but as far as the chances and intentions of their enemies were concerned, they depended essentially on guesswork. The Government—Goebbels had to admit—were subject to error in this field, and one could not really blame them for it. The general war situation changed constantly and these changes were brought about not only by them, but also by the enemy.[5]

Goebbels clearly recognized that much of the confident propaganda put out by the Ministry during the first half of the war had misfired. It was somewhat grotesque for the chief propagandist to be obliged to admit publicly in August 1943 that "our judgment on the war has been somewhat biased on account of the great victories in the past. They led

[1] Diary entry of 19 February 1942.

[2] Diary entry of 4 March 1942.

[3] Hitler had given his approval to the film after some of his generals had expressed doubts of its value. Diary entry of 20 March 1942.

[4] In his address on 18 February 1943, see *Der steile Aufstieg*, p. 171.

[5] Article "Das ewige Gesetz", *Das Reich,* 18 April 1943; reprinted in *Der steile Aufstieg,* p. 245.

us to a view of things which has been often greatly dimmed by false images". Many of them had imagined for a time that so gigantic a world struggle could be mastered without crises.[1] The events of Stalingrad had seriously shaken the belief of the man in the street in the infallibility, omniscience and omnipresence of the Government. Goebbels thought it opportune, therefore, to tell the people that it was "demanding too much of a Government that it should prove always right".[2]

From 1943 onwards Goebbels was eager to take note of reasonable criticism of individual measures of the Government and to bear it in mind when making an apology for the Government. On 25 July 1943, the Propaganda Minister observed in his diary: "The letters addressed to me are disturbing; they contain an unusual amount of criticism. Above all, they keep asking why the Führer does not visit the bombed areas, why Göring is nowhere to be seen, and especially why the Führer does not talk to the people and explain the present situation. I consider it very necessary for the Führer to do this, despite his heavy military burdens. One cannot neglect the people too long; in the last analysis they are the very kernel of our war effort. If the people ever lost their will to resist and their faith in German leadership, the most serious crisis we have ever faced would result." [3] Goebbels smugly alleged that the letters were full of praise for his work, and that his work as a writer and speaker was specially appreciated "and was contrasted with the activities of a number of prominent people who hardly ever face the public".[4] There is evidence that he conveniently ignored the growing number of anonymous letter-writers who then threatened and abused him.[5]

This awareness of the more critical mood of many people, harassed as they were by an endless chain of enemy air raids which often compelled mass evacuation from the attacked towns, can be detected between the lines of one of Goebbels' articles with the significant caption: "Does the Government really know this?" [6]

Goebbels' arguments moved on to a double line of defence:
(a) the Government knew more than was generally believed, and
(b) there could be no question of the Government "being sparing with itself" or "being treated sparingly by its surroundings".

The position was somewhat ironical: a totalitarian regime taking trouble

---

[1] Article "Die Realitäten des Krieges", *Das Reich*, 22 August, 1943, and *Der steile Aufstieg*, p. 424.

[2] Article "Das ewige Gesetz", Das Reich, 18 April 1943; See *Der steile Aufstieg*, p. 247.

[3] *The Goebbels Diaries*, p. 320.

[4] Ibid.

[5] See W. von Oven, op. cit., I, p. 94, entry of 27 August 1943, on the type of letters received by the Ministry, and also R. Semmler, op. cit., p. 98 f., 16 August 1943. In his diary Goebbels also keeps silent on letters deploring the eternal harping of the propaganda machine on the wicked Jews.

[6] "Weiss die Regierung das eigentlich?", *Das Reich*, 11 July 1943; see *Der steile Aufstieg*, pp. 376-383.

to convince its subjects and supporters that it was close to them and was incessantly concerned with keeping in touch with the people. Goebbels declared "as a mere fancy, the antediluvian idea that the Government was surrounded by a Chinese wall composed of entirely malicious people who in their turn were only interested in keeping the Government away from all things and events which it has not only to know but has also to tackle dutifully." [1] The Minister took great pains to explain that the National Socialist dictatorship was not to be confused with the bygone autocracy of "arbitrary and moody kings and princes, surrounded by courtiers who had to conceal any annoying and unpleasant news from them." [2] He claimed that it was a twentieth century highly effective and well-informed régime. In this totalitarian system, without any safety-valves of public opinion, where the public were asked to make considerable sacrifices every day, Goebbels thought it imperative to present the Government as well-informed and always ready to consider suggestions from the public. He was anxious to explain that the information obtained by the Government came from a thousand different sources, including the daily letters from the public which were carefully studied and analysed by experts. If a matter raised in them really seemed of importance to the State, it was "not thrown into the sausage machine of bureaucracy", but was manfully tackled. [3]

There was a distinct feeling among the masses that the Government was not willing to face unpleasant facts; hence Goebbels' somewhat laboured explanation that the stream of daily news reaching the Government included both "good news" and "bad news", and that it was submitted to the leaders "in an unexpurgated version". The Minister was so anxious to assure his public that the leaders were "not brass-hats", but always acted in close contact with the people, that he declared it even "essential that the measures coming from above" were "always subjected to scrutiny from below". The concept "below" did not refer to the average citizen, but meant "the Party which has its fingers on the pulse of the people". [4] With the critical situation on the Eastern front and the growing impact of Allied air raids, Goebbels was eager to convey an impression of the utmost effectiveness of his Ministry and of the utmost care being taken before important decisions were taken. Orders were only given after everything had been fully examined and discussed. If there was no public debate, there were at least discussions among the ministerial bureaucracy.

Without telling a lie, but not without exaggeration, Goebbels could claim that he received much additional information through his many visitors, particularly from soldiers on leave. Between 1942-1944 he did

[1] Op. cit., p. 376.
[2] Op. cit., pp. 376-377.
[3] Op. cit., p. 377.
[4] Op. cit., pp. 378-379.

make a point of talking to them.[1] Goebbels undoubtedly obtained some information about the morale at the front and the views of the fighting soldiers in this way, but he made much of it for the sake of publicity and *réclame*. Extracts from his informal talks with wounded soldiers or with holders of the *Ritterkreuz*, the German equivalent to the V.C., were frequently relayed by radio. In these conversations Goebbels alleged that suggestions were given and received. A frank word counted for much there. "One can learn many details from them that one would hardly obtain through official channels." [2]

4. THE ITALIAN SHADOW

The sudden overthrow of the Mussolini régime in Italy two months later was likely to increase the peril of defeatism. This drastic move by "the treacherous clique" round Marshall Badoglio and King Victor Emmanuel took the agile Doctor by surprise and made him reflect on a possible growth of opposition in his own country. "Knowledge of these events," he jotted down in his diary on 27 July 1943, "might conceivably encourage some subversive elements in Germany. The Führer ordered Himmler to see that the most severe police measures were applied if any such danger seems imminent here. He does not believe, however, that much of the kind is to be expected. The German people are much too hostile to the Italians to regard the crisis as a precedent." [3] Nevertheless the Propaganda Minister was not prepared to take any chances. On the same day he had instructed the press to follow a line of "wait and see", though he felt that this would by no means improve the mood of the people. But it was wiser to keep silent than to talk and expose oneself to the criticism that they had given a false picture of the situation.[4]

When after an interval of several weeks Goebbels resumed his weekly articles in *Das Reich* he boldly alleged that "the Italian example" had had on "us Germans not an encouraging but a deterring effect. We regard it as a typical example of how things must not be done. None of us has the ambition to tread in the steps of the Badoglio clique." [5] Yet though many Germans had indeed never shown much respect for the military

[1] See W. von Oven, I, op. cit., p. 141 and II, p. 143, and W. Stephan, *Goebbels*, pp. 273-274.

[2] *Der steile Aufstieg*, p. 380.

[3] On 28 July 1943 Goebbels wrote in his diary: "I am sending immediate instructions to Berlin on how the *coup d'état* against Fascism is to be handled publicly. All we can do is keep on waiting, even if that will by no means improve public sentiment. In any case, we have a whole bunch of news items in hand that will serve to pacify the people's hunger for news. When new events arise initiated by our side it is better to keep our peace than to be reproached with misrepresentation of the situation." (02595).

[4] *The Goebbels Diaries*, p. 326.

[5] Goebbels' article "Das Schulbeispiel", *Das Reich*, 19 September 1943; see *Der steile Aufstieg*, p. 461.

valour of their Italian ally, Goebbels' "make believe" propaganda was not borne out by the facts. A Swiss observer in the Reich noticed that "the departure of Mussolini had an even worse impact on public opinion in Germany than the fall of Stalingrad. Even the German leaders needed time to recover from their shock. Their day-long silence resulted in a flood of uncontrollable rumours which only made worse the declining morale of the Germans, already badly weakened by the British air offensive." [1] People had now serious misgivings, which although not openly expressed weighed heavily on their minds. The accumulation of bad news was shaking even the firmest believers in the Führer. Faith in the régime had waned, particularly as the long promised reprisals against air-raids had not come, while "the destruction of German cities has attained unimaginable proportions". More than ever the question was "heard from people: 'Do we deserve this?' " [2] With amazement the people were beginning to realize that they had been systematically misled by the Nazis. "German hopes of victory," the observer discovered, had been "replaced by a deep anxiety, as the people are convinced that the Party will not give in, even if more towns like Hamburg are erased." The people felt they were faced with a terrible dilemma. "Either they must fall with the Government—which has no more links with the people—or they must bear the consequences of total defeat. This dilemma explains the indecision of the German people." [3] It could be said that the overwhelming mass of the German people—outside the Party bosses and the small groups of the anti-Nazi resistance movement—had by then acquired a quasi-defeatist outlook without—and this is important—transforming it into defeatist behaviour. They were anxious, yet they remained passive and just carried on.

Small wonder that Goebbels thought it expedient in another article to attack bitterly "certain outsiders in our nation", who indulged in the dangerous habit of reacting to world events and also to the problems and interests of their own country "in a merely objective and critically observant manner." [4] These fools, he said, hardly realized that not the life of a régime, but their own lives and that of the nation were at stake. It was "this extremely thin layer of the nation" which the enemy regarded as a favourable target for his war of nerves, and which Goebbels therefore abused with a calculated vehemence. These defeatists and opportunists were an easy prey for enemy propaganda. Apparently they

[1] *Neue Zürcher Zeitung,* 10 August 1943.

[2] Goebbels exploited this sort of self-pity in an article in *Das Reich,* a year later when the situation had become much worse. See "Warum wird es uns so schwer gemacht." *Das Reich,* No. 15, 9 April 1944. In this article Goebbels presents a picture of German history as one of continuous heroic suffering, "one great *via dolorosa*".

[3] *Neue Zürcher Zeitung,* 10 August 1943.

[4] Article "Von den nationalen Pflichten im Kriege", *Das Reich,* 12 September 1943; *Der steile Aufstieg,* p. 448.

were particularly impressed by the British attitude in the war, for the very reason, Goebbels suggested, that they lacked the qualities they admired in the English.[1]

Goebbels eagerly asserted that the Germans, too, possessed the qualities of determination, vigour and absolute belief in the righteousness of their cause. "Of course, these noble virtues exist also in the German people to an abundant extent. How could we survive otherwise against a world of envy and revengefulness?" Whereas Bismarck had deplored the lack of moral courage (Zivilkourage) in so many Germans, Goebbels now made propaganda for it without perhaps being aware of the paradox of this attempt within the framework of a totalitarian régime. The good citizen—he insisted—countered "the temptations of the enemy with a virtue which we Germans are learning to comprehend and understand properly in this war: 'moral courage'." [2]

Goebbels could have few illusions about the steadily deteriorating war situation. In the East, he explained in the article, a battle of armaments was raging on a gigantic scale and a relentless enemy was battering against the German lines of defence. But he must have known, though he did not say so, that the July offensive of the German army near Kursk had failed. His Press Secretary, von Oven, made a gloomy entry in his diary at the end of August: "In the East our movements of disengagement have not come to a standstill since Stalingrad. It is increasingly difficult to believe that they are going according to plan. The argument that our shortening of the front is 'advantageous' is losing its persuasiveness more and more. The failure of the German offensive near Kursk has had an effect on our soldiers in the East still more demoralizing than Stalingrad. . . . At Kursk the confidence in victory of the German fighter in the East suffered a heavy, I am almost inclined to say, a fatal blow. . . . From now on, he doubted his strength and irresistibility." [3]

It was at the end of August 1943 that the Propaganda Minister mentioned for the first time to von Oven the possibility that the Germans might lose the war. The situation in the East and in Italy, together with the impact of the uninterrupted air war, caused him to reflect that a German defeat was not impossible. For this contingency he declared his decision had been made. "I would gladly throw away a life under the domination of our enemies. Either we shall master the crisis—and I

---

[1] "The offensive and astonishing feature is that this type regards just as admirable in the enemy what he completely lacks himself, the rigid sticking to a goal, even under doubtful and risky circumstances, the strength not only to give, but above all to take, the nationalist passion, a nation's sense of sacrifice in time of war which goes beyond parties and their views, the hatred of the enemy, the absolute conviction that only their own cause can win, and above all the readiness to devote oneself to one's country even if it means giving up one's life." Op. cit., p. 450.

[2] Op. cit., p. 453.

[3] W. von Oven, I, op. cit., pp. 91-92, entry of 27 August 1943.

shall use all my strength for it—or I shall bow once more before the English spirit and then shoot a bullet through my head." [1]

A month earlier, Dr. Goerdeler, the Chancellor-designate of the German opposition, was probably carried away by his sanguine temperament when he pressed Field Marshal von Kluge to take steps to end the war and to overthrow Hitler. He had assured von Kluge: "I can also, if you so desire, make Herr Goebbels or Herr Himmler your ally; for even those two men have long realized that with Hitler they are doomed." [2] The fact remains that by then Goebbels had fewer illusions than some other top-ranking Nazis. On 7 November 1943 he confided in his diary: "I have the impression that we sometimes take the war altogether too lightly. It has become a bitter life and death struggle. The sooner the German people, and especially our leadership realize this, the better it will be for all of us. It would be tragic if at a certain point in this war we should have to say 'too little and too late'." [3]

5. THE THIRTY ARTICLES OF WAR

By the end of September 1943 the situation looked grim, much grimmer than it had after Stalingrad. During that month British planes had dropped 14,000 tons of bombs and made ten major attacks on Germany and the territories occupied by her in the West, including several raids on Berlin, Mannheim-Ludwigshafen, Munich and Bochum. In addition, American planes released 5,400 tons of bombs on targets in Western Europe. On 3 September Allied troops landed on the Italian mainland and on the same day the Badoglio Government signed an armistice with them, a measure answered by Hitler with the swift occupation of Rome and of the whole of Northern and Central Italy. On the Eastern front the Russian counter-offensive in the central sector gathered momentum and succeeded in retaking the Donetz Basin and in recapturing Smolensk on 25 September. It is true, the Germans gained a considerable prestige success by the unexpected liberation of Mussolini who became the head of a neo-Fascist Republic. But though German propaganda made much of this bold deed of German SS paratroopers, Goebbels lamented privately that the military propaganda to foreign countries outside his control had "completely failed". Despite his earnest warnings it had claimed Salerno, where American troops had landed on 9 September, as a German victory. "I have always held that victories must be announced only after they have actually been achieved and that the skin of the bear must not be distributed until the bear has been killed.

---

[1] W. von Oven, I, op. cit., pp. 92-96.

[2] See J. W. Wheeler-Bennett, *The Nemesis of Power*, p. 573. Goerdeler's letter was dated 25 July 1943.

[3] *The Goebbels Diaries*, entry of 7 November 1943, pp. 406-407.

Our military public relations officers have again sinned grievously against the elementary principle of war-news policy." [1]

But such a criticism of a rival propaganda service was a minor matter compared with the continuing bad news from the Russian front. "It gives one the creeps," Goebbels confided to his diary on 21 September, "to look at the map and compare what we had under our dominion about this time last year with the distance we have now been thrown back. Certainly the Soviet Union is in a much better position now than it was a year ago. At that time the Soviet Union was actually struggling with military and economic death. Now there can be no talk of that." [2] But if Goebbels, scorning illusions, looked at the situation very soberly, he was too much steeped in totalitarian methods to want high-ranking members of the Nazi Party to share in his disillusionment. When, a day later, Dr. Ley asked him for information on the latest developments in the theatres of war, Goebbels discovered that the chief of the German Labour Front had "rather odd ideas" regarding the German intentions in the East and in the South. "One can see that much of the information at my disposal is being withheld from him, otherwise he would judge the situation more realistically and not let his imagination run wild. But," Goebbels added with his tongue in his cheek, "it is a good thing that the men who frequently address the masses should be free from any knowledge of unpleasant news. This gives them much more self-assurance when they talk to people." [3]

It was against this background that the Minister of Propaganda decided on a gigantic propaganda campaign for the Party at the end of September. He called a meeting of all the Reichsredner, the heads of the Reich propaganda offices and the local Nazi sub-leaders of Berlin, gave them a survey of the situation and supplied them with material. He found their "morale" excellent. Here were first-rate people trained in politics who would never fail in a crisis.[4] Goebbels' propaganda line at that time is clearly discernible from his "Thirty Articles of War for the German People".[5] With its outspoken "do's" and "don'ts" this masterly manifesto reveals both Goebbels' worries about the morale of the masses and his line in guiding and directing them. A diary entry of 9 September shows that Goebbels took particular trouble with this leader which was to be

[1] *The Goebbels Diaries*, entry of 18 September 1943, p. 367. Soon afterwards Goebbels complained to Hitler about the deficiencies of the public relations section of the *Wehrmacht*. The Führer seems to have promised him that both the propaganda of the Supreme Command of the Armed Forces and in the occupied areas would be subordinated to his Ministry, but these hopes were not fulfilled. See *The Goebbels Diaries*, entry of 23 September 1943, pp. 384-385.

[2] Op. cit., entry of 21 September 1943, p. 371.

[3] Op. cit., entry of 19 September 1943, p. 369.

[4] Op. cit., entry of 25 September 1943, p. 392.

[5] "Die 30 Kriegsartikel für das deutsche Volk", *Das Reich*, 26 September 1943; reprinted in *Der steile Aufstieg*, pp. 464-474.

also issued as a pamphlet with a circulation to reach millions. The text was to contain "everything which, so to speak, has to be regarded as the basis of our warfare and our leadership". Goebbels was confident that the mass circulation of this manifesto would have a very good effect.[1]

The negative imperative of "we must not give in!" has now largely taken the place of the more positive version "we must win!", and the image of victory is only just touched upon in the last Article. The keynote of the appeal is struck in Article 1: "Everything may be possible in this war except one thing: that we should ever capitulate or bow to the force of the enemy." Those who spoke or even only thought of it were traitors and "must be expelled from the fighting and working German community in utter disgrace."[2] The defensive character of the war *(Verteidigungskrieg)* on the usual Nazi lines was stressed in Article 3: "It has been imposed upon us by our enemies in order to cut off any national chances of living and developing."[3] A lost war would mean that the present generation of Germans had gambled away the achievements of innumerable preceding generations. With increased grimness Goebbels appealed once more to the people to integrate themselves and to let their deeds and thoughts be fed by the deepest sense of community from which the duties of the individual German in wartime derive. Because it appears that only this "community-fixation" (a term, of course, not used by Goebbels) can induce the individual to observe the required taboos and to trust the Government even when it is silent.

The growing impact of enemy propaganda can be detected between the lines of Article 11, which speaks of "an old trick of political warfare to separate a people from its Government, in order to deprive it of its leadership and to make it defenceless." The possible success of this trick would be the only means by which the enemy could overcome Germany.[4] Those who fell prey to this ruse were branded blockheads or traitors and severe penalties were threatened against them. Other types denounced in more or less strong terms were the "know-alls" *("Sie sind zwar Besserwisser, aber keineswegs Besserkönner"*—Article 12), the thoughtless or irritated talkers (Article 13), who forgot, in annoyance, that the enemy was often listening, the war parasites who took no interest in the war effort (Article 19) and the amusement mob, who thought only of their creature comforts and lacked all historical sense (Article 29). Significantly, Goebbels also attacked "the stupid phrase" that the Leaders *(Leitung)* led a better life than the people. However heavy the material losses of some individuals might be, they could not be compared with the very heavy burden of responsibility carried by the leadership and involving never-ending worries (Article 18).

[1] Diary entry of 9 September 1943 (02645).
[2] *Der steile Aufstieg,* p. 464.
[3] Op. cit., p. 465.
[4] Op. cit., p. 467.

Goebbels tried to justify his sharp attacks on non-conformists at home with the need to be worthy of the soldiers at the front. Those who died at the front fulfilling their hard duties could "demand that persons who sabotage or endanger the war at home should suffer death" (Article 21).

The sacrifices demanded are to be made for Freedom. As was seen earlier, it was not individual freedom, but national freedom which Goebbels propagated with rationalizations of the existing situation such as "It is better for a nation to come out of a war very poor but free than seemingly in full control of its property but unfree" (Article 25).

A further rationalization put forward was more Utopian. Like other revolutionary movements National Socialism tended to stress the necessity of bearing the hardships of the present for the sake of a better life to be enjoyed by future generations. Goebbels used this argument by contrasting the contemptible attitude of the materialists ("after us the deluge") with the stoicism of the true patriots. "If we have to renounce happiness for many years, at least our children and grandchildren will have a better life" (Article 29).

Fanatical belief and an unbridled pride in the nation which culminated in a secularized teleology on the lines of *per aspera ad astra,* of passing through hardship to reach for the stars. "In everything you do and omit to do, you say and keep silent about, bear in mind that you are a German. Believe loyally and unshakably in the Führer and in victory! Remember always that you are a child of the bravest and most industrious people on earth, a people that has to bear much adversity and suffering to reach its goal. . . . in order to safeguard its freedom and its future" (Article 30).[1] This, the climax of the manifesto, was a skilful exploitation of a dictum by the Great Elector ("Remember that you are a German!") with the addition of the usual demand for loyalty to the Führer. It further relied on the appeal to national arrogance, to the superior qualities of the nation. What was novel was the insistence on a national Golgotha which had to be passed by all on the road to ultimate freedom and self-fulfilment of a chosen people.

[1] Op. cit., p. 474.

CHAPTER 13

The B.B.C. Hits Back
(1942-1944)

1. DIFFICULT DAYS

IT MAKES all the difference whether war-time propaganda is backed by military successes and coups or whether it has to operate in the dark days of reverses and defeats on the battlefield. As we saw, during the first half of the war Goebbels could point with arrogant ease to the extraordinary succession of victories scored by the German *Wehrmacht*. He could talk proudly of this phase as a *Zeit ohne Beispiel*, a matchless time, and indulge in the idea of Greater Germany as a *Führungsmacht* in a German-controlled Europe. The German victories advertised themselves, so to speak, and were more impressive or frightening than the most skilfully conducted propaganda could ever have been. It is true, propaganda could and did supplement them, but in the last instance it played only second fiddle. There were other drawbacks for Germany from controlled propaganda. It would probably have been more effective had it been something quite new, had its machinery not been in existence for six long years before the war began. In other words, its war effect was a continuation and intensification of its efforts in the previous warless phase. People outside the Axis countries were therefore more conscious of the "propaganda character" of German broadcasts and newspaper articles and more sceptical towards them than they might otherwise have been.

British propaganda was in a quite different position. It had both the disadvantage and the advantage of a late-comer in the field. Perhaps the first propaganda broadcasts put out by the B.B.C. for countries outside the Commonwealth were those in Arabic. They started at the beginning of 1938 as a counter-weapon to sharp attacks on Britain which Mussolini's régime had sponsored for some years in the Arabic transmissions to the peoples of the Near East and North Africa from Radio Bari. But it was only some months later, in September 1938, in the turmoil of the world crisis before the Munich Conference, that the B.B.C. decided to establish special services for listeners in Europe, in French, German and Italian.[1]

This indicates clearly the slowness of advance in a hitherto unexploited field and proved a handicap to a Western democracy in competition with the ruthless speed of totalitarian states. But it was only after the beginning of the Second World War that "the task of building up a comprehensive and adequate propaganda service to Europe and to the world overseas was taken seriously in hand. Then admittedly progress was rapid and by 1941 or 1942 British foreign radio services represented a force which the enemy found more and more formidable both at home and in the conquered territories." [2]

Nevertheless in those early war-years British counter-propaganda was in a difficult position. It could not boast of any major military victories at a time when successes, such as the Battle of Britain in the autumn of 1940 or the reverses of Rommel's troops in Libya, were largely defensive. It could only emphasize the undaunted morale of the English people and promise that the days of retaliation and of an offensive would come. Its main chance was to prove the accuracy and reliability of its news service in German and in other foreign languages. When you are in the weaker position you cannot afford to lie, and to send out inaccurate news reports might well prove a boomerang which injures the thrower. It is perhaps an exaggeration to assert that the B.B.C. news service in German was "throughout the war more objective and sober than any British or American newspapers," [3] but the man responsible for it certainly realized the indispensable advantage of objective and sober reporting.

One of the difficulties encountered by the B.B.C. reporting in its European service was the sometimes faulty intelligence about British air attacks on Germany. In 1940 and 1941 some serious inaccuracies occurred in R.A.F. communiqués on bomb damage claimed to have been inflicted on German towns. It was alleged that important targets had been badly hit, when in fact the bombs had been dropped many miles away. It is unlikely that there was any intention to lie behind these communiqués: [4] it was a question of misinformation received from the returning pilots,

---

[1] The first B.B.C. broadcast in German was a translation of Neville Chamberlain's radio talk on the Czechoslovakian crisis on Tuesday, 27 September 1938.

[2] Lindley Fraser, *Propaganda*, London 1957, p. 88.

[3] R. H. S. Crossman, "Supplementary Essay" in Daniel Lerner (ed.) *Sykewar, Psychological Warfare against Germany, D-Day to VE-Day*, New York, 1949, p. 333.

[4] R. H. S. Crossman, at the time head of the German Section of the Political Intelligence Division of the Foreign Office, wrote after the war: "I have no doubt that the German propagandists were sincere enough accusing us of lying when we published these communiqués, but, in reality, we just did not know the truth": R. H. S. Crossman, op. cit., p. 333.

but, of course these mistakes gave a good inning to German propaganda.[1] Even a pro-British American journalist then stationed in Germany expressed his surprise about the discrepancy between B.B.C. claims regarding British air raids on Western Germany and the little damage he had found.[2]

To create the impression of truthfulness in war-time propaganda, there should be no exaggeration of military successes and no silence on, or denial of, serious setbacks and defeats. In 1940 and 1941 the second aspect was more important. A power involved in war can hardly be expected to draw attention to the weaknesses of its position, though it may be able to exploit the heroic or stoical attitude of its people during dark days. This was largely the attitude of the British propaganda services to enemy countries during the first two or three years of the war. It was not only the conviction that in competition with an authoritarian system honesty was the best policy, but also the awareness that even a certain dissatisfaction and criticism voiced in Britain during times of adversity could be turned to advantage by adroit propaganda.

When early in January 1942 the Japanese had made astounding progress in the Far Eastern war and the Philippines and Singapore were gravely threatened, Lindley Fraser, a prominent commentator of the B.B.C.'s German service admitted in a talk to Germany that: "Many of us in Great Britain are not satisfied about the way in which our strategy in the Far East has been conducted. . . . In Australia, too, there is open criticism of the weakness of the Allied defences against the Japanese attack. Some Australians believe that we have grossly underestimated the relative importance of the Far East as compared with the other main theatres of war." [3] A similar critical spirit had shown itself in the United States after Pearl Harbour. Fraser went on to say that there would shortly be a lengthy debate in the House of Commons in which the members could speak out. "It may well be," he declared, "that by the end of the debate, they will prove to have influenced the Government's policy— perhaps even its structure."

Although British propaganda to Germany made little effort to minimize the strategic significance of lost bastions, it is understandable that the Propaganda Ministry was quick to exploit Fraser's candid admission of a possible loss of Singapore, which he had already made in earlier broadcasts. At a press conference on 17 December 1941 German editors

[1] See for instance Goebbels' sneering remarks on the English "propaganda successes" in bombing German towns in his article "Aus Churchills Lügenfabrik", in *Das Reich* on 12 January 1941: "The Royal Air Force has pulverized Hamburg, as is well known, as well as every railway station in Berlin, reduced the German war materials factories to ashes and rubble, but has been scrupulously careful never to hit any infirmaries, hospitals, or even any civilian targets" (reprinted in *Die Zeit ohne Beispiel*, p. 365).

[2] W. Shirer, *Berlin Diary*, London, 1941, p. 273 ff., entry of 19 May 1940.

[3] *Sonderbericht*, "The Right to Criticize", by Lindley Fraser, B.B.C. German Service, 26 January 1942.

were advised to keep in their files Fraser's admission of the adverse effects the possible fall of Singapore would mean for the overall Allied position. It could be utilized when this event happened and the English tried to belittle the actual significance of their Far Eastern stronghold.[1] However, when the dreaded event did occur, Fraser, doubtlessly following an official P.W.E. directive, was as frank as before. After the fall of Singapore there was in England, he declared in a broadcast, "no disposition whatsoever on the part of the people" . . . to minimize the strategic significance of the news. As one man had said to him: " 'Singapore has been like a dam checking the Japanese advance towards India and Australia. Now the dam has burst and the Japs can pour into the Indian Ocean. We'll have a job to stop them and to hold them back.' The man was right and we know it." [2]

It is doubtful if many Germans listened to that broadcast. Those who did were unlikely to be impressed by Fraser's confidence that one day the British and Americans would drive the Japanese back. "We know that the worst is still to come—for our enemies and for ourselves," he declared, "and we also know that in due course, as the United Nations gather their overwhelming strength, we shall convert defence into attack and carry forward attack into crashing victory." [3] In the long run such a sober and yet confident attitude was likely to be wise, provided the tide turned. As we now know, behind the candour, there was a "calculated policy of admitting defeats," [4] which was to pay dividends in the end, for it established the confidence of the listeners in the objectivity and the integrity of the B.B.C. broadcasts.

In this context some observations on the set-up of the British machinery for political warfare should be made as it ultimately directed the policy for B.B.C. programmes to German listeners. The Political Warfare Executive in London (P.W.E.) was the highest authority on all matters of propaganda to enemy countries as part of the British war effort. Its head, Sir Robert Bruce Lockhart, was directly responsible to the Prime Minister. In origin a small policy-making committee it had to co-ordinate and to some extent to supervise the propaganda activities of the three main bodies conducting propaganda: The Political Intelligence Department (P.I.D.), the British Broadcasting Corporation

---

[1] ZSg 102/35, "Aus der Pressekonferenz das Propaganda Ministeriums", 17 December 1941.

[2] B.B.C. *Sonderbericht,* "Darkest Lindley", by Lindley Fraser, 16 February 1942. Churchill called the fall of Singapore "the greatest disaster to British arms which our history affords": Arthur Bryant, *The Turn of the Tide 1939-1943,* London, 1957, p. 305.

[3] Ibid. A month later Fraser ventured to forecast the events in the Far East during the coming months and years, predicting that the tide would turn against Japan in the South Pacific, dependent as she was on sea routes for supplies and reinforcements, once the United Nations brought "their overwhelming sea force into action against her, as one day they will." B.B.C. *Sonderbericht,* "Twilight of the Rising Sun", by Lindley Fraser, 5 March 1943.

[4] R.H.S. Crossman, "Supplementary Essay", in D. Lerner, *Skyewar,* p. 335.

(B.B.C.), and the Ministry of Information (M.o.I.). Of these only the B.B.C. was a permanent institution, the others had been born on the eve of the Second World War. P.I.D. had originated from the pre-war Research Department of the Foreign Office and since 1940 had attracted a number of university dons, journalists, lawyers, etc., who were soon assisted by a number of intellectuals of foreign origin.

While P.W.E. issued regular directives which guided the B.B.C. output to enemy and enemy-controlled countries, the B.B.C. never lost its identity and independence. On the basis of the overall policy directives the brilliant Director of the B.B.C. European Services, Noel Newsome, issued daily directives to his staff, which kept in mind the different requirements of broadcasts to Germany, Austria, France, Holland, Norway and a number of other European countries. His comments and admonitions were particularly impressive and helpful in days of adversity. The B.B.C., in its turn, furnished much ammunition for P.W.E. policy makers and for its own broadcasts through the daily B.B.C. Monitoring Digests which came out every morning in two bulky volumes; they covered all important broadcasts transmitted abroad the day before and provided a particularly useful guide to the content and trends of Nazi broadcasts in the Reich and the occupied territories.[1]

The work of P.W.E. had both positive and negative aims. "It tried to destroy the morale of the enemy, on the home as well as on the battle fronts, by destroying his faith in his ability to win. At the same time it sought to raise the morale of all those hostile to the enemy—the peoples of the occupied countries, and even anti-Nazi and anti-Fascist elements in the enemy homelands."[2]

P.W.E. as the leading body formulated policy, P.I.D. gathered intelligence from many sources, while the B.B.C. carried out the policy through the medium of broadcasting. But despite its apparent monopoly the B.B.C. was not the only channel available for broadcasting propaganda. One has to keep in mind that during the last war there was "Black" as well as "White" propaganda. "White" broadcasts explicitly stated their source, whereas "Black" ones deliberately tried to mislead their public by masquerading under a false label and by claiming to be something different from what they were.[3]

---

[1] P.I.D. published its own *News Digest* every day, which also furnished valuable intelligence background for programmes to Europe.

[2] John Baker-White, *The Big Lie*, London, 1955, p. 64. See also Hugh Dalton, *The Fateful Years, Memoirs 1931-1945*, London, 1957, chapter XXVI, pp. 366-384. Minister of Economic Warfare and a member of the Cabinet, Mr. Dalton was in charge of "Special Operations Executive" (S.O.E.) from 1940-1942. S.O.E. was divided into two branches. The name of S.O.E.1 which was concerned with propaganda to enemy and enemy-occupied territories was later changed to P.W.E. (Political Warfare Executive).

[3] D. Lerner, *Sykewar*, pp. 262-272, on "covert" and "overt" methods of psychological warfare. For an authoritative account of the operations of "Black" propaganda originating from Britain see Sefton Delmer, *Black Boomerang*, London, 1962.

No mystery existed about the origin of the B.B.C. news service in German, but there was a descrepancy not easily detected by listeners between the claim of the black *Soldatensender Calais* to be a radio station of the German Forces and its actual sponsors. "'Black" propaganda was what purported to come from within enemy territory—broadcasts from clandestine stations, leaflets printed on illegal presses, forged ration cards and money, and rumours.[1] It was largely bogus and deliberately deceptive.

B.B.C. broadcasts in German were "overt" and most of the men who gave talks or took part in discussions in this service did not conceal their identity. Among its star performers were its director, Hugh Carlton Greene, before the war Berlin Correspondent of *The Daily Telegraph* (London), Patrick Gordon-Walker, a prominent member of the Labour Party, who ran the B.B.C. programme for German workers, Mrs. Gibson, in charge of broadcasts to German women, and Lindley Fraser, a regular commentator, whose distinctive voice and lively manner had become familiar to hundreds of thousands of German listeners by the end of the war.

It is no state secret that there was often marked disagreement between the policy makers of P.W.E. and the executives of the B.B.C.'s European Service "with P.W.E. trying to increase the propaganda content of programmes and the B.B.C. determined to maintain a proper proportion of hard facts and straight news."[2] Usually a compromise was reached.

Fraser, who before the war had been a Professor of Economics at Aberdeen, developed into a first-rate political radio commentator, sensible, sober, and preserving a sense of proportion. This very quality made him particularly suited for the fight against Goebbels. For in the field of white propaganda an imitation of Goebbels' tricks and methods would have been disastrous. Either the B.B.C. was able and willing to establish a reasonable reputation for objectivity and straight news or it could never hope to combat Goebbels' propaganda machinery with much chance of success.

2. WHEN THE TIDE TURNED

After the battle of El Alamein and the disasters of the German Sixth Army at Stalingrad, the Germans were suddenly faced with serious defeats, whilst both the Western Allies and the Russians could point to undeniable successes. This development made the task of British and American propaganda considerably easier. By then the aim of allied propaganda was not only to play up these successes as an assurance of the certainty of final victory, but also to discredit faith in German official statements and promises. This was done by contrasting former utterances of Hitler, Goebbels and other Nazi leaders with the grim reality of the

---

1 Baker-White, op. cit., p. 64.
2 J. Baker-White, op. cit., p. 65.

present. The technique of contrasts was employed with increasing intensity in 1943 and 1944.[1]

To illustrate this technique of deliberate contrasts, only a limited number of typical examples can be given here. On the one hand significant omissions and changes in the German propaganda machine were explained by the London counter-propagandists; on the other, former claims and promises put forward by German leaders were confronted with the harsh reality of the present day. Examples of the first aspect were the omission of the "Fanfares of Victory" *(Siegesfanfaren)* in German radio transmissions and the growing silence of Hitler.

In the summers of 1940 and 1941 the special announcements or *Sondermeldungen* had abounded on the German side. How often had the fanfares of victory proudly announced German victories, first in the West, and later in the East. However, in July 1943 no such fanfares were heard over the air. The B.B.C. commentators in German were not slow in pointing this out. "There is something curious about these fanfares," said a broadcaster from London in German on 21 July 1943.[2] ". . . Goebbels' strongest arm has struck back at him; the silence of the drums and fifes today sounds almost louder and more impressive than the fanfares themselves used to do. July was always the month of fanfares. Do you remember? July 1940: fanfares after the collapse of France: Germans on the Channel, ready to jump off for the invasion of England, and then Hitler's triumphal entry into Berlin." Then followed a recital of the romantic phrases used by German radio announcers at the time of Hitler's triumphant return to Berlin after the fall of France, and again after the first big successes in Russia a year later. In the first week of the German invasion of Russia no less than twelve "Special Announcements" for the German people had been broadcast. Quotations from the German press of that date created the impression that the war in the East was as good as over.[3] By July, 1942 the German fanfares had sounded more sparingly, having lost a good deal of their romantic aura. Nevertheless there were still occasions for some *Sondermeldungen*, e.g. the capture of Sevastopol or the fall of Voroshilov. But the curve of decreasing *Sondermeldungen* was very telling: "1941—65 *Sondermeldungen;* 1942—19 *Sondermeldungen;*

[1] This technique was pursued *faute de mieux,* as, tied to the official policy of "unconditional surrender," Political Warfare or, as the Americans called it, "Psychological Warfare" could promise nothing. It was compelled to rely exclusively on two themes: a) the inevitability of Allied victory and b) the integrity and decency of the democratic world. But it was helped in this effort considerably "by selecting and repeating *ad nauseam* German boasts which had not come true and German promises which had not been fulfilled". See R. H. S. Crossman, op. cit., pp. 332-333.

[2] See the B.B.C. feature "The Month of Fanfares", written and produced by H. Fischer, 21 July 1943.

[3] e.g. "Today the war in the east is as much a lost cause for the Englishman as once the war in the west was" *(Das Reich,* 20 July 1941).

1943—2 *Sondermeldungen*. Could there be any clearer evidence that Hitler's defeat was sealed in the East too?" [1]

The silence of Hitler was another target of British propaganda in this category. On 30 January 1943, the date of the 10th anniversary of the Third Reich, Hitler only sent a long proclamation to Berlin, but decided not to speak himself at the mass meeting at the Sport Palace. Goebbels told the masses assembled there, that Hitler was too deeply absorbed by the business of directing the war to be able to come all the way from his Headquarters to the capital.[2] However, Lindley Fraser ventured to give the real reasons for the Führer's silence.[3] Firstly, Hitler had not turned up "because he does not feel cheerful himself, because he knows that some of his anxiety might have reflected itself in his voice and manner." Secondly, had Hitler spoken, his message would have been the same which in fact Goebbels and Göring had conveyed to the German people, the message that the war situation was extremely serious and that "only by complete unity and superhuman effort" could they have "a glimmer of hope of winning through." The day would come when the Führer himself would have to tell the masses: "It's a case of backs to the wall now, the situation is almost desperate." [4]

When Hitler did speak in the autumn of that year, his words were contrasted by the B.B.C. with some of his much more optimistic earlier addresses. Here is a typical example of this second aspect of the technique of confrontation in British propaganda.

In his speech of 10 September 1943, delivered from his headquarters, Hitler "explained" that Italy's leaving the German camp would have no effect on Germany's chances of winning. In a symposium by three speakers of the B.B.C.'s German service on the same day, one of them drew this comparison: "What struck me most in Hitler's speech today was its difference from the speech he made a year ago. Today, a talk no longer than fifteen minutes, hastily rattled off, without modulation of the voice, without any climax, without an introduction by Goebbels—who only spoke a couple of words at the end, serving as announcer—perhaps Hitler can no longer stand to have a stranger around him, even as an announcer. In addition, this speech was read in the quiet of his own quarters, at a desk. In September 1942 a gigantic crowd had gathered in the gigantic Sport Palace in Berlin, shouting, applauding, laughing, rejoicing as Hitler gave them the cue." [5]

---

[1] "The Month of Fanfares" by H. Fischer.

[2] See Goebbels' address at the Sport Palace reported in the *Frankfurter Zeitung*, 31 January 1943.

[3] Fraser's view was put forward very tentatively. "I know that it is only my opinion and that you may have better opinions to offer": Lindley Fraser, "Is Silence Golden?", B.B.C. German Women's Programme, 1 February 1943.

[4] Ibid.

[5] B.B.C. *Sonderbericht*, "Hitler's Musings" II, by M. Goring, 10 September 1943, 9 p.m.

In September, 1942 Hitler could still boast confidently of his aims in Russia:—

"The goal was first: to deprive the enemy of his last great wheat-growing region. Second: to take away his last reserve of coal. Third: to advance to his sources of oil." By contrast, in September 1943, Russia was hardly mentioned in his speech, and the commentator in London could cuttingly ask:—

"Where has it gone, the spirit of last year? Where are the ambitious plans that, only a year ago, Hitler announced to the German people for this year of 1943?"

Hitler's contempt for the leaders in the enemy camp expressed on that earlier occasion of 30 September 1942, was highlighted in another B.B.C. broadcast in the same month (on 30 September 1943). Hitler had then declared arrogantly: "If I had an enemy of calibre—an enemy of military calibre—I could almost predict where he would strike. But when you are faced with military idiots . . ." [1] It was now gratifying to nail down this ill-placed derision: "Military idiots. How does that sound today? It has a different meaning from a year ago. Today, when Italy has collapsed, today, when British and American troops stand on the mainland of Fortress Europe." In the same speech Hitler had confidently predicted that the German troops would take Stalingrad and that no one would be able to dislodge them from that town. The high hopes then raised by Hitler had been utterly frustrated by the course of events, at Stalingrad and in Tunisia, in Sicily and at Salerno, in Charkov and in the Battle of the Atlantic. "Hitler has miscalculated. Hundreds of thousands of German troops have paid for his mistakes with their lives." [2]

3. TECHNIQUES OF CONTRAST

The "Then and Now" contrast formed one of the major lines in German broadcasts from London since the summer of 1943. Skilful use was made, for instance, of the melancholy reflections in the oration Goebbels delivered at the funeral of the leader of the Stormtroopers, Lutze, who had died after a car accident in May, 1943. [1] This recorded passage from Goebbels' address on 7 May was played back in a B.B.C. feature: "One must say farewell to a much-loved man, and—what is almost as sad— to a whole period of one's own life. He sinks away, slowly fading to a memory. You try with both hands to hold onto him, but the noisy rush of the present day surges over him and away." [2]

The nostalgia for "the good old days," which no totalitarian power

[1] "Boomerang Boasts", script by J. Preszlenyi, produced by J. Gellner, 30 September 1943.

[2] Ibid.

[3] Goebbels' funeral oration is to be found in *Völkischer Beobachter* (Berlin edition), 8 May 1943.

[4] B.B.C. feature: "All Their Yesterdays", 20 May 1943.

could bring back, formed an attractive theme for comment: ". . . the high priests of the Nazis *(Nazibonzen)* have become sad, they long for the good old days . . . when there were still cheap successes, easy victories, victories over divided enemies, victories over the good sense of the German people. But where are those days. . . ." There followed quotations from utterances by Hitler and Goebbels during the peak days of their rule, from the *"Tag der Machtergréifung,"* from the days of the *Anschluss* and from the victories in the summer of 1940 when England seemed doomed. "They want to hold onto the good old days," ran the refrain of this broadcast, "because they know that only one road lies before them: the way downhill, defeat." [1]

Goebbels' denunciation of British "terror bombing" of German towns provided another topic for the technique of contrast. When on 28 November 1943 he had talked of the methods of the R.A.F. as of "this base and cynically barbaric method of making war, which for this reason is so typically English," the B.B.C. played back Hitler's boast of 1940: "We are going to eradicate your cities." It reiterated what the Luftwaffe had done to Polish towns and villages, to the open towns of Rotterdam and Belgrade, to Coventry and London.[2] The liberation of Paris in August 1944 was a welcome opportunity for flashbacks to the German march into the French capital four years earlier.[3] Listeners heard the lively narrative of a German war correspondent reporting the triumphant entry of German troops at the *Place de l'Étoile* on 14 June 1940 and ending with the words: "All of them, the soldiers who are crossing the square, all of them are aware that this is a historical moment—the hour for which they have fought for weeks—the hour for which many a comrade died a hero's death. It has not been in vain. From the Arc de Triomphe the flag of the German Reich utters its song of victory." [4]

There followed extracts from the German press on Paris of the summer of 1941 and 1942, which illustrated poignantly the change in the situation: "For four years the swastika hung from the Eiffel Tower. For four years the streets of the city that had first proclaimed the Rights of Man rang with the jackboots of the Nazi soldiers. But all this belongs to the past. Today the boulevards ring with the celebration of the liberated French people and with the tune of the Marseillaise." [5] The French National Anthem followed.

Even more dramatic and serious for the Germans was the historic moment in the middle of September 1944 when Allied troops stood on German soil. The event spoke for itself. The war had reached parts of the

[1] Ibid.

[2] B.B.C. German feature: "Guilty Goebbels", 29 November 1943.

[3] See the two features in German: "Paris Free Again", script by R. Ehrenzweig, and "When Paris Fell", script by J. Preszlenyi, both broadcast on 23 August 1944.

[4] "When Paris Fell", 23 August 1944.

[5] "Paris Free Again", 23 August 1944. The broadcast ended with the confident words: "Und die Panzer der allierten Armeen rollen weiter Richtung Berlin".

Reich and this in spite of Hitler's frequent boasts, now liberally quoted by the B.B.C., that he had succeeded in keeping the fighting away from Germany. Listeners were reminded of a relevant passage in *Mein Kampf,* written as early as 1924:—

"Imagine that the bloody battles of the World War took place not on the Somme, in Flanders and Artois, before Warsaw, Ivangorod, Kaunas, Riga, and the like, but in Germany, in the Ruhr, on the Main and the Elbe, before Hanover, Leipzig, Nürnberg, and so on. And you will have to agree that there would have been the possibility of Germany's destruction." [1]

The dreaded event had now become a close possibility, the London commentary emphasized, and if it came, it would be entirely due to the "Scorched Earth Policy" proclaimed by Hitler. It was for the German people to decide if Germany would be destroyed, or if this war would cease before it was too late.[2] The passage from *Mein Kampf* was also quoted in a fictitious weekly B.B.C. feature, "Briefe des Gefreiten Hirnschal," by Robert Lucas, broadcast three weeks before the end of the war." [3] Modelled on Jaroslav Hašek's famous figure of the soldier Schweijk in World War I, Corporal Hirnschal writes on his experiences in the Russian campaign with an unforgettable mixture of cunning, robust common sense and droll humour, which by implication exposes the boasts, high-faluting phrases and promises of the official propaganda more effectively than could any direct counter-argument. His amusing letters reveal a sharp discrepancy between the reality which he and his comrades are facing in the endless hostile steppes of Russia and the official speeches and pep slogans. Once his company is halted on the roadside to enable everyone to listen to a speech by the Führer. The men use the time to hunt the lice in their shirts. Another episode shows them in a bitter struggle in the trenches against superior Russian forces. One of Hirnschal's comrades receives a letter from an SS leader safely at home who, having read in the Party paper that mighty Germany was now transforming the Russian steppe into a paradise of fertility, wants to secure a profitable post for himself out there and is willing to invest a large sum of money in the promising enterprise. Indeed, Robert Lucas developed the art of persiflage and exposure by contrast to a remarkable degree.[4]

Another trick of this contrast technique was to confront the different versions of a speech by a leading National Socialist, as broadcast and as published in the German press. It was a way of exposing the arbitrary censorship exercised by the Propaganda Ministry. A case in point was a

---

[1] Adolf Hitler, *Mein Kampf,* Munich, 1943, p. 763 f.

[2] B.B.C. German feature: "The Battle of Germany", 12 September 1944.

[3] On 18 April 1945. See the selection of these broadcasts, published after the War: R. Lucas, *Teure Amalia, vielgeliebtes Weib! Briefe des Gefreiten Hirnschal an seine Frau in Zwieselsdorf,* Zürich, n.d. pp. 145-146.

[4] So did Bruno Adler in another comic B.B.C. feature in German, "Kurt und Willi", a weekly conversation between a cynical official in the Propaganda Ministry and a more honest but bewildered German *Studienrat,* or Secondary School Teacher.

speech delivered by Reich Marshal Göring, early in February 1943. The version broadcast by the German radio had been monitored in England and the original passages later cut or changed in the German press were played back by the B.B.C.[1] They included Göring's realistic remark that the average soldier had to take for granted the expectation that he would not return from the war. His admission that some Germans had questioned the wisdom of sacrificing the Sixth Army at Stalingrad also found no favour with Goebbels and his men. When Göring spoke with remarkable frankness of the weakness of some German army leaders in Russia in the previous year, and referred to "the severity of war, as well as the weakness of certain leaders," the final words were changed by the censor to "weaknesses that crop up here and there." It was funny enough, each time Göring talked of "the Russians," Goebbels' office replaced the term by "Bolshevists" or "Sowjets," apparently, the English commentator suggested, because they wanted the Germans to think of the Russians in terms of "evil Bolshevists" rather than of "Russian people."

The B.B.C. in any case could not be misled, as its speaker explained: "Yes, we can learn a lot by following with open eyes the maneuvering of the Propaganda Ministry. Whatever Goebbels may change with his blue pencil, we have the words of Göring, Goebbels and Hitler in our record collection. And we shall see to it that the German people hear them when the time comes." [2]

4. DIRECT ANSWERS TO GOEBBELS

In political warfare it is by no means always wise to answer the arguments and tricks of your opponent directly. It has been aptly remarked that to be effective, such direct answers are advisable under two circumstances only: the one is "from strength"—when the possible risk of providing your adversary with a free advertisement is outweighed by the damage your crushing reply is likely to inflict on him; the other is "from weakness," when the opponent has already attracted so much attention with his telling arguments, that it would be more detrimental to you to ignore them than to attempt to hit back.[3]

In 1943 and 1944 the B.B.C. German service often answered Goebbels' arguments and tricks. It did so "from strength" and with much skill. These answers fell under three categories. They were: direct refutations of Goebbels' claims, or interpretations of them, or exposures of his statements by confronting them with the reality of the war situation. The first method of reply had primarily a political motive, the second and third a propaganda motive, though both motives were often closely allied. A good example of the method of "direct refutation" is provided by a broadcast on "Peace Feelers" by Lindley Fraser.[4] It replied to a wireless

---

[1] B.B.C. German feature: "Censored *Reichsmarschall*", 5 February 1943.
[2] Ibid.
[3] Lindley Fraser, *Propaganda*, London, 1957, p. 99.
[4] B.B.C. *Sonderbericht*, "Peace Feelers", by Lindley Fraser, 25 April 1942.

talk on the German *Reichsprogramm* by Admiral Lützow a few days earlier, in which the speaker had bemoaned "the forthcoming collapse of the British Empire" as "one of the greatest catastrophes of world history" and declared it "unseemly if we were to feel nothing but *Schadenfreude* at such an occurrence." Dr. Goebbels had taken a similar though less sympathetic line by talking of the "melancholy chaos which had descended on the British Empire." [1] The B.B.C. speaker refused to argue with Lützow and Goebbels about the state of the British Empire. Undoubtedly following an official directive, he told his audience that the British "were not interested in German peace-feelers." They had held out against Hitler in the dark days, when Britain had been without allies or supporters. It remained the same now with the growing strength of the Royal Air Force.

Some statements by Goebbels and his broadcasters were not refuted, but re-interpreted, put into a perspective that was detrimental to the German war effort. When the Minister of Propaganda sometimes raised delicate points of German morale, which obviously worried him and other National Socialist leaders, British counter-propaganda put them into their "proper" setting and showed them up in all their hollowness. A case in point was Goebbels' mournful article *"Warum wird es uns so schwer gemacht?"* (Why are things made so difficult for us?) [2], painting a sombre picture of Germany's plight in history, at a moment when the fortunes of war were turning increasingly against her. Germany's long history was interpreted as *"ein einziger grosser Leidensweg,"* one long road to Golgotha. Other nations had found it much easier to become great powers. They possessed such rich resources that the length of the war hardly seemed to affect them. "We on the other hand must labor and wear ourselves out in the sweat of our brows," lamented Goebbels, "and the little that we call our own, even that little our enemies begrudge us." [3]

It was a line similar to some extent to that taken by Goebbels in 1938–1939, when he used to contrast the plight of the "Have-Nots" with the easy surplus of those who had. Yet the arrogant self-confidence of those pre-war years had now given way to a gloomy self-pity, though his claims for Germany could not be accused of undue modesty. He maintained "that for centuries Germany has been the leaven not only of Europe but of the whole world." He also argued regretfully that Germany's fate and geopolitical position forced the Germans to make greater efforts to shape their national life than were necessary for her few friends and many foes.[4]

How did Goebbels account then for the unpopularity of the Germans?

[1] See article "Schwarze Wolken über England", *Das Reich*, 26 April 1942; reprinted in *Das eherne Herz*, p. 301.
[2] *Das Reich*, 9 April 1944.
[3] Ibid.
[4] *Das Reich*, 9 April 1944.

By alleging their superiority, their greater efficiency, and a more marked quality of their cultural achievements. A different explanation, however, was offered by Lindley Fraser in his comment on this Goebbels article. First, he explained, the Germans were disliked, because others could not trust them. For instance, they had invaded Norway and Denmark in direct contravention of promises and guarantees, previously given by Hitler to the Governments of these countries. Secondly, they were hated because of their principles: "If you won't be my brother, I will knock your skull in!" a motto worthy of German behaviour in all occupied countries, which was one of brutal recourse to physical force. Thirdly, "when Germany thought she was going to win, she released her plans for a German-controlled post-war Europe, making it perfectly clear that she was to be the dominant nation of Europe and of the whole world." The answer to Goebbels' question, the British broadcaster suggested, was in reality quite simple: "If a country wants to obtain continental and world domination, it must expect to be hated and resisted and, in the end, to be beaten on the field of battle." [1]

In this article Goebbels had tackled a theme on which Allied propaganda had harped for several years, the unpopularity of the Germans in occupied countries. For instance, this had been discussed in a B.B.C. broadcast from London in May 1941.[2] In it, Fraser cited a long list of the shootings of civilians and hostages by the German conquerors in Holland, France, Czechoslovakia, Poland and Greece. He argued somewhat vaguely that the Germans were hated, but not feared, in these countries.[3] The terroristic methods of the Gestapo had transformed a state of former apathy and passive opposition there to one of active sabotage, incendiarism and violence. The oppressed people therefore no longer distinguished between Nazis and other Germans. For them the Gestapo men and the SS were the representatives of Germany and of the German Reich.

While the *Herrenvolk* idea was a major feature of the National Socialist ideology, there is little evidence to indicate that Goebbels himself boosted it much—at least not in public.[4] For some years Allied propa-

[1] B.B.C. *Sonderbericht,* "Germany, the Ugly Duckling", by Lindley Fraser, 10 April 1944.

[2] B.B.C. *Sonderbericht,* "Hate Without Fear", by Lindley Fraser, 12 May 1942.

[3] Germans might defend these atrocities, Fraser argued, in the same manner as they used to justify the treatment of their own fellow-countrymen in concentration camps, by appealing to an imaginary supreme self-interest of the German people or by saying defiantly: "Let them hate us, as long as they fear us".

[4] Even before the war Goebbels had, however, expressed himself in favour of the incorporation of Italy and parts of Western Europe in the Reich. According to a report to his government by the French Ambassador Robert Coulondre, Goebbels had said in a speech in June 1939, that Germany intended to regain all the countries which she had lost in the course of her history. This sentence had, however, been omitted from the official report. See Report to Paris, 22 June 1939, *French Yellow Book,* doc. no. 143, p. 194.

ganda could do little more than to attack the *Herrenvolk* idea as arrogant and conceited and to expose the danger of this pathological superiority feeling. But when Hitler's regime proclaimed a "New Order in Europe," it provided Western counter-propaganda with one of its most telling arguments. The glaring discrepancy between this European ideology and the German *Herrenvolk* practice could easily be exploited. Apart from native Fascists, few people in German-controlled Europe were attracted by the vague talk of a Germany which, as one writer in a German newspaper put it, was now "taking its place as a super-national *Ordnungsmacht*, assuming a responsibility beyond that of a National State." [1] There was to be a marriage of the German *Herrenvolk* theory with the Führer principle and the Germans would be the *Führungsvolk,* or Leader Nation, which "welded the *Grossraum* into one unity" and which created the *Grossraum Ordnung* (Order for the greater area). [2] As another German writer put it brutally: "The small states have become the prey of an inexorable course of history, and the only question is, whether they will give in without hope or full of hope." [3]

But when by the end of 1942 the Germans were facing a difficult situation both in North Africa and at Stalingrad, their European ideology took on a defensive tinge. Ever since the invasion of Russia, Germany had been presented as the bulwark of Europe against Bolshevism, as committed to a holy war of defence for the whole continent of Europe. But by November 1942 Goebbels positively wooed the peoples of Europe. "If Europe can't exist without us," he wrote in *Das Reich*, "neither can we survive without Europe." "Germany's one object." he explained, was "to set up a Europe united in the spirit of comradeship and mutual self-respect.' " [4]

In fact, Goebbels' feelings towards Europe were far less amiable. What he and other Nazi leaders had in mind was a policy towards the people of the occupied countries of *Zuckerbrot und Peitsche,* of the carrot and the stick. In Goebbels' eyes, the treatment meted out by Seyss-Inquart to the Dutch in the Netherlands was exemplary. He regarded Seyss-Inquart as "a master in the art of alternating gingerbread with whippings, and of putting severe measures through with a light touch." [5]

The Goebbels line that Germany had friendly and even brotherly feelings towards the non-German Europeans was promptly attacked as sham by British counter-propaganda. It invited Goebbels to preach his gospel

[1] Heinrich Scharp in *Frankfurter Zeitung,* 1 March 1942.

[2] Werner Best in *Zeitschrift für Politik,* June 1942, quoted in *Hitler's Europe,* edited by Arnold Toynbee and Veronica Toynbee, London, 1955, pp. 240-275.

[3] Dr. E. H. Bockhoff in *Brüsseler Zeitung,* 6, 7 and 16 August 1942, quoted in *Hitler's Europe,* p. 53.

[4] J. Goebbels, "Die Vision eines neuen Europa", *Das Reich,* 11 November 1942; reprinted in *Der steile Aufstieg,* Munich, 1944, pp. 67-68.

[5] *The Goebbels Diaries,* entry of 8 September 1943, p. 339. See also *Hitler's Europe,* p. 125.

to the "Poles and Czechs, who today are being treated as worse than cattle," as well as to the Norwegians and Dutch, to the Greeks and Yugoslavs, "you have been breaking their skulls—and now you say you 'only want to be their brother.' " [1]

5. ANSWERING GOEBBELS IN ADVANCE

Before publication in Germany, the text of Goebbels' weekly article in *Das Reich* was conveyed by teleprinter to some overseas countries. In 1944 the English authorities managed by a technical device regularly to obtain the text of these articles. This enabled the B.B.C. commentators to comment critically on them one or two days before the articles became available to the German public. German blacklisteners who listened to the B.B.C. previews of these articles would thus have an advance knowledge of them and of their "faulty" reasoning some hours before their publication.

A good example is the handling of Goebbels' piece on "The Party in Wartime" which appeared on 14 May 1944.[2] It was read by an announcer over the German radio stations two days earlier, on 12 May, but the B.B.C. could offer its preview even one day before that date, on 11 May.[3]

In this article Goebbels praised at length the great achievements of the Party in the war and spoke of its function as that of a representative minority. The B.B.C. preview, in its turn, concentrated on the items which Goebbels, it suggested, would not care to mention: that leading Party officials had been exempted from active service after three months service at the front and that the Party brass-hats *(Parteibonzen)* had managed to send vast sums for themselves out of the country. When found guilty of fraud or corruption they were only given a nominal fine, while ordinary Germans were sentenced to death for the smallest offence. Above all, Goebbels had conveniently forgotten to mention, "that the NSDP had since its founding been a war party. . . . And that if the NSDP had not come to power there would have been no war, no bombs, no casualties at the front, and no party corruption." [4] This treatment illustrates the aim of counter-indoctrination" in Allied propaganda of shaking the confidence of the German people in the proper leadership of the Party.[5]

As the war situation became progressively worse for the Germans, the

[1] B.B.C. *Sonderbericht,* "Herrenvolk über Alles", by Lindley Fraser, 8 December 1942.

[2] Joseph Goebbels, "Die Partei im Kriege", *Das Reich,* 14 May 1944.

[3] B.B.C. German feature: "Goebbels Preview" (3), 11 May 1944.

[4] Ibid.

[5] The same Goebbels article was again commented upon on these lines ten days later, when it had become clear to the counter-propagandists that it formed part of a new Goebbels propaganda campaign to advertise the Party and to rehabilitate its shaken prestige. See the B.B.C. *Sonderbericht,* "Boosting the Party", by Lindley Fraser, 22 May 1944.

British intensified their technique of propaganda by contrast. More and more emphasis was put on the false and misleading prognoses which Goebbels and other top leaders had made. In war both sides are tempted to soothe themselves by rash and over-confident predictions, but after the early lesson of Dunkirk the British war leaders were perhaps less inclined to be sanguine and over-optimistic than their enemies. Further they did not make the mistake of claiming to be infallible. Goebbels, on the other hand, came out as late as April 1944 with the unsubstantiated boast: "Our predictions for the course of this war have been fulfilled with an almost sinister exactitude. We have not deceived ourselves in the past and do not intend to do so in the future." [1]

This bold assurance was duly exposed by three short B.B.C. features entitled "Nazi Prognosen" and broadcast on 6, 7, and 8 April 1944. They reminded listeners of such statements as Göring's prediction on 9 August 1940: "We shall not allow a single enemy bomb to fall on the Ruhr," or Hitler's prognosis in his New Year's Message of 1941 that the year would bring final victory. The frivolity of Goebbels' predictions was further illustrated by quotations from his earlier forecasts on the impending doom of England (25 October and 22 December 1940), and on the hopelessness of British air raids on German towns (18 November 1940 and 25 June 1943).

By an earlier exposure of such false Goebbels forecasts listeners interested in "hundreds of similar prophecies which had proved abortive" were even advised by the British speaker to get hold of the collections of some of Goebbels' earlier wartime articles, such as *Die Zeit ohne Beispiel* and *Das eherne Herz*. [2] Using the same trick on another occasion, Lindley Fraser warmly recommended one of Goebbels' articles after publication as "quite the most interesting and significant he had ever written." [3] The article, he suggested, should be "widely studied and read . . . not for the sake of the arguments it contains, but in order to picture the state of mind of a man who can produce such arguments." [4]

With the long delayed establishing of the "Second Front" in France, Allied propaganda could hit back with greater punch. Before the invasion

---

[1] In *Das Reich,* 2 April 1944. Goebbels had made a similar statement a year earlier, on 15 March 1943, when he wrote in the same periodical: "We do not prophesy lightly, and take pride in the fact that during the whole war we have not once made a pronouncement that was not borne out by developments." This pronunciamento was less comprehensive than the later one as it only referred to his articles in *Das Reich*.

[2] B.B.C. feature in German, "Goebbels' Garland", 16 December 1943.

[3] Lindley Fraser, B.B.C. broadcast in German, English script, 30 October 1943.

[4] The Goebbels' article referred to had appeared in *Das Reich* on 31 October 1943, under the title "Der Stichtag" and had been broadcast in the *Reichsprogramm* two days earlier. In it Goebbels had admitted: "It cannot be contested that the fifth year of the war confronts us with enormous difficulties, which sometimes seem almost insurmountable. The war, in its long drawn-out course, has not taken the direction that many of us would have wished."

Goebbels had coolly assured his public that the German leaders had taken into account the material superiority of the Allies. After D-Day he naturally belittled the Allied advance in Normandy and a month later predicted that the decisive battle of the West was still to come. Frantically demanding the total mobilization of every German for the war effort *(totaler Kriegseinsatz)*, Goebbels appealed both to fear and to hope. On the one hand he predicted that should the Allies win, they would destroy the German way of life. Moreover, there would be no chance for the Germans to fight again in ten, twenty or fifty years. On the other hand he made much of the success of V.1, which had become for England "a permanent and very serious problem." But the highest guarantee of victory was still the existence of the Führer.[1]

In his brief but caustic comment Lindley Fraser pointed to the many weak spots and veiled admissions in these arguments.[2] Goebbels had not only admitted the material superiority of the Allies, but had called upon the German people to cut down their standard of life still further. He had in vain offered the flying bomb as the one positive hope which—as Fraser put it—was to "convert England's certainty of victory into a willingness to make a compromise peace." As to Goebbels' point that Germany would have no other chance of making war in years to come, for once Fraser agreed. To Germans, who were still Nazis at heart, he would say: "listen to your Propaganda Minister—he is quite right—this war *is* going to be the final one." [3]

By then British propaganda was trying to drive a wedge between the Nazi leaders losing ground and "those Germans who want an end of war and aggression and world conquest." The latter were advised to realize that the Nazi bosses knew the defeat of Germany would be *their* end. "They have every interest in persuading you to go on fighting. When Germany's defeat is certain, *of course* they try to persuade you to continue as long as you will. They have their own lives to think of. But you— you have not merely to think of yourselves, you have to think of Germany after the war is over." [4]

In the earlier days of the war, personal attacks by the B.B.C. on Goebbels were rare, though sometimes his opportunism, his indulgence in half-truths, his selfishness were branded. But by May 1944 the belief among Germans in the magic of his propaganda was shaken, a fact which played into the hands of the Allied counter-propagandists. Their comments became more biting and aggressive. Their aim was to disillusion and "counter-indoctrinate" the German public. The B.B.C. commentary on a remarkable Goebbels article, addressed to soldiers at the front in mid-May 1944, can illustrate this approach. Goebbels had attacked soldiers who

[1] Speech by Goebbels in an unnamed town in East Germany, reported in the *Hamburger Fremdenblatt* under the caption "Totaler Kriegseinsatz jedes einzelnen", 8 July 1944.
[2] B.B.C. *Sonderbericht*, "Anti-Goebbels," 8 July 1944.
[3] Ibid.
[4] Ibid.

did not fight but managed to secure comfortable jobs in the *Etappe*, in the rear of the front line. They were denounced by him as drones who, by their parasitic existence, had become real traitors.[1]

This debunking of the *Etappenschweine* (Base-pigs)—a slang term of German soldier-language carefully avoided by Goebbels—provided excellent copy for exposure as well as ridicule of the Nazi system. It was well suited for facetious treatment in the weekly B.B.C. serial "Die Briefe des Gefreiten Adolf Hirnschal an seine Frau."[2] Half naive, half shrewd, Corporal Hirnschal expressed pity for the shirkers in the Party now even attacked by "our dear Minister of Propaganda." With fun and irony he listed the many worries which plagued the parasitical darlings of the régime, who were leading a comfortable life, leaving the fighting to their less fortunate countrymen. Such laughing exposure was likely to appeal to German listeners, for by then the higher Party functionaries, often nicknamed *Goldfasanen* (Gold pheasants) and *Bonzen* (Bigshots), had become widely unpopular and their privileges, such as exemption from military service or better air raid shelters, were resented.[3]

In another, more serious, B.B.C. broadcast Goebbels' article was caustically described as a trick, "a transparent device for deflecting the indignation of the Germans away from those who deserved it—the men who prepared for the war, started it, have drawn profit from it and have consistently avoided sharing in its dangers and hardships."[4] Taking a leaf out of the Propaganda Minister's book, Fraser used Goebbels' latest manoeuvre for an all-out attack on him, describing him as an *Etappenschwein*, "the man who above all others believes in fighting from a comfortable armchair with a typewriter, the man who stays in his bomb-proof shelter during raids and then with such great bravery drives round the streets afterwards and condoles with the victims of his and Hitler's war."[5] While the cowardice of Goebbels "who, having never in his life visited the front line," exhorted "soldiers to fight to the last round" was one leitmotif of this onslaught, his selfishness formed another. Goebbels was depicted as calling upon "the German people to sacrifice its existence and happiness in order that he and his friends may enjoy a few months longer the delights of power and comfort." They hoped to postpone for a few months the fate which they knew they could not escape in the long run.

Four months later, when Allied troops were fighting on German soil in the west of the Reich, Allied propaganda insisted more and more on

[1] Reichminister Dr. Goebbels, "Ein Wort zum Thelma Etappe", Schreibfunk "Front und Heimat", 15 May 1944 (text monitored by the B.B.C.).

[2] B.B.C. Broadcast in German on 22 May 1944. The text has been reprinted in Robert Lucas, *Teure Amalia, Vielgeliebtes Weib! Die Briefe des Gefreiten Adolf Hirnschal and seine Frau in Zwieselsdorf*, pp. 143-146.

[3] See the study by Guenther Roth and Kurt H. Wolff *The American Denazification of Germany, A Historical Survey and Appraisal* (mimeographed), Ohio State University, Columbus, September 1954.

[4] B.B.C. *Sonderbericht*, "Goebbels' New Scapegoat", by Lindley Fraser, 16 May 1944.

[5] Ibid.

the different interests of the German masses and of the small clique of Party bosses. At that time, when Goebbels and Himmler made desperate efforts to push the masses into a fanatical participation in a *"guerre à outrance,"* the B.B.C. spotlighted the desperate recourse of Goebbels' propaganda machine to mere myth and faith, to a trusting in the irrational factors in history. The increased use of words like "fanatical," "fanatic" and "fanaticism" in the language of Party leaders was said to be significant and so was a characteristic headline of 11 November 1944 in the leading Party newspaper *"Das Weltgeschehen lässt sich nicht errechnen"* ("World events cannot be calculated").[1] In that article it was admitted that from the point of view of rational analysis, the war could not be won by Germany because of the numerical superiority of the Allied troops and armament production, the destruction of German industrial plants, the loss of France, Rumania and Poland and of food exports from territories formerly occupied and now no longer under German control. But such rational observations were declared by the writer to be irrelevant. As he put it grimly: "In time of peace, such calculations may be admissible, but in war destiny can only be mastered through iron determination. Only in this way can an apparently unavoidable fate be altered, against all the rules of reason." [2]

Closely allied with this belief in the triumph of national will power over the promptings of reason was Goebbels' odd argument that, as this time the Germans "had deserved victory, the Goddess of History could not deprive" them of it.[3] The absurdity of this line was exposed by Fraser. If Goebbels argued that the Germans had earned victory because they had put up with immense hardships, the Russians, the English and the French could argue the same way. The only purpose of such obscure and emotional propaganda phrases was to try to persuade the German people to commit suicide. It was true, Fraser remarked, the Party had always appealed to emotion, to enthusiasm and faith, and not to reason. But behind this obscure appeal there had then been the full might of German armaments and the immense superiority of the German *Wehrmacht* over unprepared opponents. But now that had gone and what remained was nothing but the fading appeal to irrationality and the rejection of common sense.[4]

6. No Blue-prints for Post-war Germany

In the final phases of the war Allied propaganda to Germany differed from its forerunner in 1918 in one important point. It had to operate without any attractive blueprint of the post-war world. For better or for

[1] *Völkischer Beobachter* (Viennese edition), 11 November 1944.
[2] Ibid.
[3] See Goebbels' radio address on the eve of Hitler's birthday on 19 April 1944.
[4] B.B.C. German feature, "Fanatic Fraser", script by R. Ehrenzweig, 19 November 1944.

worse there existed no successor to President Wilson's "Fourteen Points" of January 1918. Any declaration of that type was ruled out after the policy of "Unconditional Surrender" had been agreed upon by President Roosevelt and Mr. Churchill at the Conference of Casablanca in January, 1943.[1] Seen in the light of the history since 1945 one can deplore this policy for a number of reasons as being shortsighted, but it is doubtful if it ever was a serious handicap from the viewpoint of Allied propaganda. For Goebbels had constantly decried the "Fourteen Points" as a test case of Allied dishonesty and trickery.[2] In this he had been undeniably successful. In castigating the "Atlantic Charter" of August 1941 he simply pointed to the aftermath of the "Fourteen Points." As a result, long before D-Day the Western propagandists had "discovered, while trying to 'sell' the Atlantic Charter how effective this German counter-propaganda had been." [3]

Could an approach to the German problem less uncompromising than the Unconditional Surrender Policy have paid better dividends to the propaganda effort? Indeed, it is doubtful whether an appeal to the German people would have been greatly strengthened by the Allied propaganda being able "to make use of precise promises about the treatment to be accorded to Germany if Nazism were overthrown." [4]

In the First World War Allied propaganda had promised the Germans a "Brave New World," once they had dethroned the Kaiser and established a democracy. No similar promises were possible in the Second World War. The rigidity of the "Unconditional Surrender" policy prevented any serious attempt at dividing the sheep from the goats, of hoping to rouse the "Good Germans" to end the misrule of the "Bad Germans" by the *fata morgana* of a post-war Utopia. With this policy only indirect en-

[1] "A main reason for this was that Roosevelt could never forget President Wilson's troubles; he thought that the production of the "Fourteen Points" as a basis for honourable surrender had plagued the post-war world by controversy as to whether they had been violated": M. Balfour and J. Maier, *Four Power Control in Germany and Austria 1945-1946*, London, 1956, p. 15. See also Robert E. Sherwood, *Roosevelt and Hopkins: an Intimate History*, New York, 1948, p. 227.

[2] Compare for instance Goebbels' venomous article, written after the "Atlantic Charter" had been issued. "Ein Attentat auf den gesunden Menschenverstand", *Das Reich*, 17 August 1941; reprinted in *Die Zeit ohne Beispiel*, pp. 549-551. See also Goebbels' address at the Sport Palace in Berlin on 18 February 1943, in which he said of the English: "They offer us sanctimonious advice about what to do and what not to do, always making the erroneous assumption that today's German people is like the German people of November 1918, who were taken in by their tricks. I do not think it necessary to offer counter-evidence against these fantasies. The counter-evidence is daily produced by the fighters and the workers among the German people." J. Goebbels, *Der steile Aufstieg*, Munich, 1944, p. 198.

[3] R.H.S. Crossman, *Sykewar*, p. 331.

[4] Crossman, op. cit., p. 332. But there is much truth in the view of a German historian that through the slogan of "Unconditional Surrender", "Roosevelt presented Goebbels with the best of all his propaganda slogans"; G. Ritter, *The German Resistance*, London, 1958, p. 219.

couragement could be given to oppositional groups in Germany and no promises could be made to them. But any reported attempts of resistance and opposition inside Germany were utilized by Western propaganda to weaken the Hitler regime. Critical statements on some aspects of official policy by leading clergymen like the Protestant bishop Dr. Wurm or the Catholic bishop of Münster, Count Galen, were quoted by the B.B.C. and so was one of the leaflets originating from the rebellious students Hans and Sophie Scholl.[1] About the same time Fraser did make the point that the action of Hans and Sophie Scholl in Munich and of all the others who were actively taking part in the revolt against National Socialism represented "the one great hope for the Germany of the future." Their work and their bravery would not be forgotten.[2]

Even by September, 1944 a B.B.C. German feature on "The Good Germans" did not go much beyond quoting from Pastoral Letters of Catholic Bishops such as Galen and Preysing and from Hans Scholl's manifesto. However, a German prisoner of war in England, formerly a student in Munich, came to the microphone to praise Scholl as the man who had opened the eyes of many of his fellow-countrymen. The B.B.C. speaker confined himself to reiterating the earlier promise: "We shall not forget the few courageous Germans who were filled with a real love of their country." [3]

How then did Western propaganda picture a defeated Germany after the war? It has to be remembered that there had been a significant shift of opinion in the attitude of the British authorities during the early years of the war. At first the official British attitude was inclined to make a distinction between the National Socialists and the Military in Germany on the one hand and the millions of mere subjects of the Third Reich on the other. At the beginning of the war "the B.B.C. . . . reflecting perhaps the general trend of British public opinion, felt not merely that there was no need for bitterness towards Germans as such, but also that by stressing this point it might persuade some of them at least to join in the struggle against the common enemy. Hence the often repeated slogan in the first year of the war: 'Peace with the German people, certainly, peace with the Nazis, never.' " [4] It was only after the bitter and dramatic events in the summer and autumn of 1940, when British public opinion had hardened, that British propaganda took a more drastic line. Though it was not denied that some Germans were opposed to the National Socialist régime, they were now regarded as ineffectual and of little importance compared with the backing, active or passive, which the bulk of the

[1] See for instance the B.B.C. German feature, "The Objective Opposition", broadcast on 7 June 1943.

[2] B.B.C. *Sonderbericht,* "Schollplatte" by Lindley Fraser, German Women's Programme, 16 June 1943. On the resistance activities of the Scholl group in Munich, see Inge Scholl, *Die weisse Rose,* Frankfurt/M, 1953. English edition, *Six Against Tyranny,* London, 1955.

[3] B.B.C. German feature, "The Good Germans", 24 September 1944.

[4] Lindley Fraser, *Propaganda,* p. 95 f.

Germans gave to Hitler. Later it was frequently stressed by the B.B.C. that the acquiescence of so many Germans in the regime meant that in the occupied countries no distinction was drawn any longer between Nazis and other Germans. "Don't forget this one vital point"—a broadcast from London in German in May 1942 emphasized [1]—"many Germans hate the Gestapo and are disgusted with their way of behaviour;" they did not think of the Gestapo as representative of the true Germany—they thought perhaps that behind all the terror and sadism and corruption of National Socialism, there could still survive "the soul of Germany with its traditions of culture and decency." But the peoples of Occupied Countries did not make this distinction: "for them the Gestapo Men and the SS" were "the representatives of *Germany*—of the German Reich."

A year later German listeners to the B.B.C. were told there existed a considerable difference of opinion in Britain on the question of whether a distinction could be made "between the Germans as a whole, and the Nazis." It was not denied that some Englishmen favoured such a distinction; they argued: "We are fighting the *Nazis* . . . the German *people* we regard as the victims and dupes of the Nazis rather than their partners." [2] But the B.B.C. spokesman made it quite clear that the British authorities did not share this view. "The German people," he said, had—with a few courageous exceptions—"backed and supported the Nazis from the time of their seizure of power onwards. To that extent it *must* bear some of the responsibility for what the Nazis had done, and were still doing, in their name." [3]

The official British view, as put forward by Fraser, did however distinguish between two types of Germans likely to be found after the collapse of the Nazi regime. It was expected that some Germans would "genuinely be anxious to work for peace and a lasting understanding between Germany and her neighbours." Others would retain their old warlike ambitions and would try "behind the scenes to organize and prepare for a second National Socialism, the third World War." These people had to be rendered powerless. Therefore it would be absolutely essential "to see to it that Germany was disarmed and that the secret rearmament and warlike preparations of the nineteen-twenties could not be repeated."

Whether Goebbels called this "a devil's plan" or not, Germany would *not* be given a chance of rearming and "a great many Germans," Fraser believed, would be "pleased and relieved" that this was so. The reassurance was given that the German people as different from such warmongers would be "treated with complete fairness after the war." As the Lord Chancellor had declared on behalf of the British Government, they could not and would not indulge in mass reprisals against a whole people.[4]

[1] B.B.C. *Sonderbericht*, "Hate without Fear" by Lindley Fraser, 12 May 1942.
[2] B.B.C. *Sonderbericht*, "Germany After the War", 28 June 1943.
[3] Ibid.
[4] B.B.C. *Sonderbericht*, "Germany after the War", 28 June 1943. For the statement by the Lord Chancellor (Viscount Simon) of 10 March 1943, see *The Times,* 11 March 1943.

Penal measures against the bulk of the population, Fraser explained, were out of the question, for they would prove a boomerang by producing a burning sense of hatred and resentment in the Germans, the effects of which would prevent a lasting peace. Moreover, such penal treatment would offend "the sense of justice of the British people," who looked at this problem neither sentimentally nor in terms of hatred and passion, but realistically as aiming at the best method of keeping the peace of the world. This meant that Germany had to be "on the one hand completely and permanently disarmed, and on the other hand itself peaceful and stable and prosperous." [1]

Five months afterwards, when large slices of Italy were in Allied hands and the Russians had pushed the German armies out of the Crimea and Kiev, Fraser returned to the theme, probably following, as usual, the line of the valid P.W.E. directive.[2] Again his message did not contain any substantial promises; if it was not without a ray of hope, it was certainly outspoken and drastic in parts. Conditions of life would be hard in Germany for everyone and for many years to come. The standard of life was bound to be low for a considerable time. Though the German people would share in the help to be given to Europe by the "United Nations"— a term that then meant the combination of Russia, the United States, Great Britain and their minor Allies [3]—the countries which had been ravaged and plundered by the armies of the Third Reich would have first claim on the Allied resources. Yet there would certainly be no unemployment. In the long run Germany's major contribution to the work of rebuilding Europe must take the form of supplying her products, such as machinery, to the now occupied countries. This meant, as Fraser explained somewhat ingeniously, that Germany's own industries would have to be set on their feet again for this purpose. After occupation, steps would be taken to place Germany under strict discipline designed to prevent lawlessness or civil war.[4] Not only would the whole Nazi apparatus with its brutality and corruption, its spying and terror, disappear, but also the German military machine would be utterly destroyed. How tentative and reserved the official Allied attitude towards the "good" Germans still

[1] Ibid.

[2] B.B.C. *Sonderbericht*, "Post War Balance Sheet", by Lindley Fraser, 22 November 1943.

[3] For this earlier concept of the "United Nations" as the Grand Alliance of 26 free nations determined to achieve victory in what Cordell Hull called "the greatest war effort of history", see the text of the United Nations Declaration issued at the Arcadia Conference in Washington on 1 January 1942, in *Documents on American Foreign Relations 1941-1942*, pp. 203-208; and in Great Britain, Foreign Office: *Declaration by United Nations, Washington, 1 January 1942*, Cmd. 6388, London, 1942.

[4] The speaker visualized, however, an interim period between the capitulation of the German Army and the establishment of this discipline. During this interval many Nazi criminals would have reason to fear the wrath of their infuriated fellow citizens. If they survived this period, they would have to stand trial for their misdeeds.

was, becomes evident from Fraser's remark that he left it to his listeners to decide whether the ordinary German regarded this as a credit or a debit. By way of these measures the stage would be set "for the slow and painful process of rebuilding a Germany" freed from the Nazi pest and "able to take its place among the free peoples of the world." [1] A few weeks later the Declaration of Teheran issued by Roosevelt, Stalin, and Churchill at their conference in December 1943 gave the B.B.C. spokesman occasion for comment on the brighter aspects of life in store for a post-Nazi Germany. Though the Allied leaders had proclaimed short-term ruthless warfare, in the long run they had also promised co-operation with the vanquished.[2] Six months later, after the success of the Allied landings in Normandy had swelled the ranks of the black listeners in Germany, a special B.B.C. feature programme was arranged for the benefit of the new listeners. It was anticipated that they wished to know not only the truth about the war situation on all the fronts, but also to learn about the war aims of the United Nations. For this purpose significant extracts from speeches by President Roosevelt, Stalin and Churchill and the British Lord Chancellor were given.

In looking back on these official pronunciamentos it becomes clear that the two statements cited by Viscount Simon and by Stalin on the post-war treatment of the Germans differed to some extent. The view expressed by the Lord Chancellor in March 1943 that the British could not and would not indulge in mass reprisals against a whole people was reticent and negative compared with Stalin's statement of 23 February 1943. Stalin predicted that the war for the liberation of the Soviet land would very likely result in "ousting or destroying the Hitler clique"; but, he insisted, "it would be ridiculous to identify Hitler's clique with the German people and the German state. History shows that Hitlers come and go, but the German people and the German state remain." [3]

Western policy did not allow such a clear distinction, but the broadcasters from London were at least able to quote some hopeful words by Mr. Churchill, made at a press conference in Washington in May 1943.

[1] Ibid.

[2] B.B.C. *Sonderbericht,* "Teheran Talk", by Lindley Fraser, 6 December 1943. "We shall smash your war machine," the commentator explained, "and the longer that takes, the greater will be your sufferings and losses. But when that has been done, we look forward to the time when you, with all other peoples in the world—in the words of the Declaration—'may live free lives, untouched by tyranny'."

[3] In his May Day speech of 1942, Stalin took the line: "It is becoming increasingly clear to the German people that the only way out of the present situation is the liberation of Germany from the Hitler-Göring adventurist clique." Whatever the motive, this statement clearly indicated that Stalin was not identifying the German people with the Nazi regime, a fact which helped the propaganda of the Russian sponsored National Committee "Freies Deutschland". See W. H. McNeill, *America, Britain and Russia—Their Cooperation and Conflict, 1941-1946*, London, 1953, pp. 164-170. The quotation is on p. 169.

He had then outlined the idea of a new World Order and of a Supreme World Council, to be composed of the biggest victor states. In an effort to make an impression on the Italians, Churchill had said that in this new and great world body there should be space for the happiness and the welfare of all; eventually it should be able to bring these even to the guilty and vanquished peoples.[1]

If the criticism can be made of British propaganda in World War I that it promised the German man in the street a democratic panacea in a brotherhood of nations, which did not materialize, a similar reproach cannot be levelled at the B.B.C. transmissions to Germany during the Second World War. The policy of "Unconditional Surrender" and the meagre blue-print offered for a post-Nazi Germany at least made it impossible for the Germans to accuse the British authorities of unkept promises. But they also narrowed the scope of British propaganda.

It is an established fact that the numbers of listeners to the B.B.C. grew in spite of the heavy jamming arranged by order of the Propaganda Ministry, and the severe punishment black listeners had to face. No exact figures are available, but there is reason to believe that there were millions of Germans and other Continentals listening to the B.B.C. transmissions in German in the last year of the war.[2] How far were they affected by their occasional or regular listening? All we can say with a reasonable degree of certainty is that the impact of the broadcasts became stronger with the growth of Allied military strength and success. The B.B.C. transmissions were unlikely to stimulate the growing number of black listeners into action against the Hitler régime, but they could, and did, make an impact in two ways: they projected and explained the increasing might and efficiency of the Allied war machine, and they exposed and ridiculed the contradictions and falsehoods of Goebbels' propaganda. A facetious but astute feature of the "Kurt and Willi" type probably paid more dividends than many a serious talk as, with the chain-reactions of German military defeats, countless Germans became more disposed to realize the absurdities and untruths of National Socialist propaganda. In such a situation debunking, if done cleverly and with a knowledge of local conditions and jargon, would have at least as much (if not more) value as a passionate appeal to their national honour.

It is probably true that the long-term propaganda of the B.B.C. broadcasts in German "did much to affect the mood of the average German listener but relatively little to affect his behaviour." [3] However, an attitude of growing apathy and fatalism was in the long run bound to harm

---

[1] See B.B.C. *Sonderbericht,* "Teheran Talk", 6 December 1943. The press conference in Washington at which Churchill made these remarks was held on 24 May 1943. Cf. also the leader "Concurrent Action", in *The Times* (London) of 27 May 1943.

[2] Lindley Fraser, *Propaganda,* p. 97.

[3] Op. cit., p. 100.

the Nazi attempts at a desperate resistance and to play into the hands of their opponents.

As early as September 1942 a B.B.C. observer reported after a visit to Sweden: "The speakers in our transmissions who are best known in Germany seem to be Kurt and Willi, Hirnschal, Lindley Fraser, Sefton Delmer and Adolf Hitler. A Swedish correspondent in Berlin was told by an official in the German Foreign Office, an enthusiastic Kurt and Willi fan, that Willi was a perfect characterization of a Propaganda Ministry official." [1]

[1] B.B.C. Listening Intelligence Report, September 1942, p. 3.

CHAPTER 14

Promises of Revenge and Appeals To Fear (1943-1945)

AS THE WAR advanced and the expected German victory appeared more and more remote Goebbels' propaganda faced new problems and developed new slogans. Few Germans had expected the heavy round-the-clock enemy air raids which commenced in the second half of May 1943— with the R.A.F. attacking during the night and the U.S. Eighth Air Force by day. Only a few experts knew then of the secret work being carried out at that time on the Baltic Coast, work which aimed at a German production of long range rocket weapons. But at least it enabled Goebbels to throw out strong hints that a terrible retaliation against English towns and lives was only a question of time. As we shall see this theme of revenge to come was handled with different emphasis at different times, but its target always remained the same: to strengthen and reassure home morale by the promise of a devastating crescendo of destruction in enemy lands through some unheard of miracle weapons. Implied in such a bold conjuring up of forthcoming annihilation was the assurance that the war would still be won and the foes, in spite of all appearances to the contrary, be decisively defeated.

Another propaganda line pursued in this period did not dwell upon victory but rather on the sinister spectre of defeat. "Strength through Fear" could only be gained by producing a nightmarish image of the deeds the enemy would commit should Germany be defeated. Fear of this dreadful possibility was to make the last German man and woman prefer to die stoically than to live as a slave under the foreign yoke. Fear of Bolshevism was to spread to all European nations. Both these avenues of propaganda, one aggressive and boastful, the other defensive and heroic, were of considerable significance during the last two years of the war; they were also more complex than one might suppose. They therefore deserve some special consideration here.

1. V FOR VERGELTUNG

Goebbels and Hitler began to allude to a forthcoming retaliation against the enemy air terror through new and secret weapons in the

summer of 1943. At a mass meeting in the Sport Palace in Berlin on 5
June Goebbels declared amid the stormy applause of his audience: "The
entire German people is only filled with one idea, to retaliate in an
equal fashion *(Gleiches mit Gleichem zu vergelten)*. It is far from us
to boast or to threaten. We only register facts. . . . The British nation
has no reason for triumph. It will have to foot the bill, which its responsible men have incurred here by their guilt of blood, by order of their
Jewish whips and instigators." [1] A fortnight later, at a memorial meeting
for the victims of the air war in Elberfeld, Goebbels was more explicit:
"The hour will come one day", he predicted, "when we shall break
terror by counter-terror. The enemy is piling up one crime of violence
upon the other, and by doing so incurs a bill of blood, which will have
to be paid one day." Goebbels asserted that innumerable labourers,
engineers and constructors were at work to speed up the arrival of that
day. He knew that the German people expected it and were burning
with impatience. In their hearts the enemy had "inscribed a confession
of guilt in indelible letters" during the grievous weeks through which
they had passed. This guilt would be presented to him one day as a
counter-bill and as a justification for their action.[2]

This theme of retaliation was continued during the following months
with varying emphasis. On 14 August Goebbels wrote: "Against the
enemy air attacks we possess for the time being the means of military
and civil defence, but at a later date we shall have in addition the means
of massive counter-attack. Until then we shall have to put up with them,
and there is no one in Germany who regards this as impossible." [3] Hitler
took the same line in a radio speech on 10 September: "The technical
and organizational conditions are in process of being created, not only
to break his (the enemy's) terror for good, but also to pay him back
by other and more effective means." [4] Retribution was only hinted at in
Hitler's speech before the old Guard of the Party in Munich at the
traditional occasion of the 8th November anniversary. "Thank God,
though at the moment we cannot get at America"—he said—"one state
is near enough for us to touch and on that state we shall concentrate." [5]
In his New Year's Manifesto to the German People in 1944 Hitler
admitted that the year 1943 had brought the most severe setbacks for
them, but added after expressing sympathy with the plight of the people
in bombed areas that "the hour of retribution will come." [6] Goebbels

[1] Article "Überwundene Winterkrise", *Der steile Aufstieg*, p. 293.
[2] Address "In vorderster Reihe", Elberfeld, 18 June 1943; *Der steile
Aufstieg*, p. 329. See also the report on a similar speech delivered at another
memorial meeting at Wuppertal by Goebbels in the *Hamburger Fremdenblatt*,
19 June 1943, under the heading "Vergeltung für den Tod an der Ruhr".
[3] *Der steile Aufstieg*, p. 417.
[4] Quoted in W. Carroll, *Persuade or Perish*, Boston, 1948, p. 153.
[5] Text of speech relayed by *Reichsprogramm*, 8 November 1943, B.B.C.
Monitoring.
[6] "Neujahrsaufruf des Führers an das Deutsche Volk", *Reichsprogramm*, 1
January 1944, B.B.C. Monitoring.

had first learned of the Führer's plans for building guided missiles and rockets on 23 March, 1943. At his special request, Speer had sent him regular information about the progress made with them in Peenemünde. Several times between that date and June 1944, when the first of these weapons went into operation against Britain, Goebbels received scientists from Peenemünde working on the project.[1]

Realizing that the idea of retaliation was popular with the masses,[2] Hitler had insisted on the term *Vergeltung* (retaliation) against the advice of the military. It did not matter to him in the least that von Braun and Dornberger, the men responsible for the development and production of the new weapons, were worried and annoyed by his propaganda. They deplored the exaggerated hopes it was bound to create.[3]

According to Dornberger's version he had, during an interview at the Führer's Headquarters on 7 July 1943, implored Hitler to discourage the propaganda about the decisive effect these "all-annihilating wonder-weapons" were claimed to have. Hitler had simply cut him short and faced by one of his outbursts Dornberger, the mere expert, had felt that it would be risky for him to pursue the matter any further.[4] In any case there was considerable delay in the production of these weapons particularly after a successful air raid by the R.A.F. on the *Wunderwaffen* workshop at Peenemünde in August 1943.[5]

When Western Allied Intelligence had come to the conclusion that some new weapon was in preparation and that the threat was more than bluff, Allied propaganda pointed to the discrepancy between Nazi promises and deeds. This was the reason why in a speech in the Sport Palace in Berlin, early in October 1943, Goebbels declared: "As regards the theme of '*Vergeltung*' discussed by the entire German people with such hot passion, I can for obvious reasons only say that the English commit an extraordinarily fateful error if they believe it was a mere rhetorical or propagandist slogan without any reality behind it. England will come to know this reality one day." [6] After this Goebbels became more cau-

[1] R. Semmler, op. cit., 17 June 1944, p. 131.

[2] See O. Dietrich, *12 Jahre mit Hitler*, p. 119.

[3] Major-General Walter Dornberger, *V2*, London, 1954, pp. 107-108.

[4] Op. cit., pp. 104-105.

[5] Dornberger claims that the raid which killed 735 people only delayed the work on the V2 by four to six weeks (op. cit., p. 164). But there seems reason to doubt this estimate. According to the British Air Marshal Joubert six months is the more likely figure. He comes to the conclusion that the "V1 programme was not seriously affected by the bombardment of Peenemünde. Other causes conspired to hold it back. V2 was delayed directly by the attack and about this there is no question." Sir Philip Jourbert de la Forte, *Rocket*, London, 1957, pp. 76-77. On the other hand it has been asserted by two English historians in this field that "the effect of the attacks on Peenemünde and other sites may well have caused a delay of two months in the V2 offensive". (Sir Charles Webster and Noble Frankland, *The Strategic Air Offensive against Germany, 1939-1945*, London, 1961, vol. II, p. 285).

[6] *Hamburger Fremdenblatt*, 5 October 1943.

tious in his predictions, temporarily pinning his hopes on some minor retaliation measures.[1] In his address on New Year's Eve he confined himself to vague hints: Under the impact of events they had become accustomed to some extent to the horrors of modern war. The English people, however, would have to get used to it once more. "The war in the air only gives pleasure to the enemy, so long as it is one-sided; when it becomes bilateral the outbursts of joy about it will soon cease in the London press." [2]

At the beginning of 1944 Goebbels issued a directive that the term "retaliation" should for the time being not be used in press and radio. In fact the more the population talked of it, the more devastating and frequent the enemy air raids became. "Retaliation" now headed the list of subjects declared taboo, because Goebbels "did not wish to intensify the great expectations by discussing the issue in public." [3] The continuous delay in the appearance of the *Wunderwaffen* made him feel uneasy. As his adjutant recorded, since Goebbels' first speeches on the subject "the responsibility for retaliation or rather for its failure to appear weighed like a nightmare on the mind of the Minister." True, he had no influence on the acceleration or the delay of the action, being neither the Reich Marshal (Göring) nor Speer. "But he is, so to speak, responsible for the *Vergeltung*, because he announced it, and because he has also taken before the public the responsibility for the entire war in the air or at least for the civil defence against it." [4] So Goebbels felt much relieved and encouraged when on his visit to the Führer's Headquarters at the beginning of 1944 Hitler gave him details of the progress made in the development of the new weapons. "The weapons of attack," Goebbels told von Oven, "are entirely novel [he apparently had V2 in mind]; no anti-aircraft measures and no alarm signals can help against them . . . the English believe now that they have the victory in their pocket. The greater a shock must our retaliation mean to them." Perhaps after it the English might be more inclined to conclude a compromise peace. "Who knows? There might perhaps result some far-reaching political effects from it." [5]

But alas there were considerable snags. The enemy air attacks were slowing down production. "Half a year ago the drawings for the con-

---

[1] "Göring travelled west, on the Führer's orders," Goebbels wrote in his diary on 7 December, "to prepare a retaliatory blow against England. We need about 200 heavy four-motored planes for it. They are to fly to England twice in the course of one night and strike a heavy blow against the British capital. Naturally we cannot repeat such an assault as often as we would like, but it will give the English something to think about. I expect great psychological results from it." *The Goebbels Diaries*, pp. 446-447.

[2] Goebbels' "Sylvester-Ansprache an das Deutsche Volk", *Reichsprogramm, 31 December 1943.

[3] W. von Oven, op. cit., I, p. 169, entry of 5 January 1944.

[4] Op. cit., pp. 169-170.

[5] Ibid.

struction of the weapons of retaliation were completely finished and in the hands of the Führer," Goebbels confessed, "and even today we are not in a position that would enable us to fix the date of their first use with any certainty." [1] All he could promise was some "normal" air raids on London and other English towns. During one of the previous air raids on Berlin Goebbels had given his personal word of honour to the people that retaliation would come.

Nevertheless, Goebbels was now very guarded in references to *Vergeltung*. He avoided the term and confined himself to vague generalities. "In a not too distant time the initiative would be in the hands of the Germans again," he said, "and they would not only match the temporary technical superiority of the enemy, but gain it for themselves." [2] A few weeks afterwards, he boasted in *Das Reich* of "the more drastic measures" by which the enemy would have to realize that the war in the air paid neither from a material nor from a moral point of view. "This can only be partly discussed", Goebbels went on, "but it will not be long before the proof of this argument, which we are forced to apply to the enemy, will be very much more convincing. Above all, the British people will then have to show that they possess the same stoicism *(Standhaftigkeit)* as the Germans. We have the hardest part of the war behind us, England has it still in front of her. We have not been broken by it, the English people will still have to pass this severe test." [3]

After V1 had at last gone into operation in mid-June 1944 he confessed to von Oven that he had felt very anxious over the continuous delay in the completion of the first of these new weapons. This date had been first fixed for December 1943, then for New Year's Day 1944; then technical difficulties had necessitated a further postponement of two months. But neither March nor the Führer's birthday in April had brought the expected news. "May passed in an intolerable tension. The retaliation is to be coupled with the beginning of the invasion, the Führer replied to my constant anxious enquiries. In June the enemy was ready for his invasion while they were still busy with changes in our weapon." [4] Goebbels' reaction to the final news of the first V1 in operation was a mixture of relief and caution. The long non-fulfilment of the promises contained

[1] Op. cit., pp. 170-171.

[2] *Hamburger Fremdenblatt,* 16 March 1944.

[3] Article "Das Leben geht weiter", *Das Reich,* 16 April 1944.

[4] W. von Oven, op. cit., II, p. 22, Diary entry, 20 June 1944. The first V1 fell on Southern England during the evening of 15 June, ten days after D-Day. It is interesting that as early as November 1943 British experts of the Political Warfare Executive were able to make a prediction as to the date of the new German weapon, which they were convinced was being prepared. On the basis of the German statements available up to that time, they deduced that the German leaders expected to use the new offensive weapon some time between the middle of January and the middle of April. They allowed for a margin of error in both dates and estimated that D-Day for the weapon might be as late as mid-June. The sustained use of rocket bombs against England began during the night of 13 to 14 June (W. Carroll, *Persuade or Perish,* p. 154).

in his earlier articles and addresses had proved to be a boomerang, damaging his prestige. When one month after another passed without the weapon appearing Goebbels' prestige fell lower and lower. "He knew that the promised retaliation could not be delayed much longer without becoming a public joke." [1] Now Schwarz van Berk, a well known journalist on Goebbels' staff, had suggested that the new missile should be known as "V weapon" (V for *Vergeltung*). To cause a sensation and hint at further development, he proposed "that they should be called V1, V2, V3, etc." [2] This proposal seems to have been submitted to Hitler by Goebbels as coming from himself.[3] The Führer accepted it.

The Propaganda Minister was satisfied and relieved. "I believe", he confessed to von Oven, "that among all Germans I feel perhaps the greatest satisfaction that *Vergeltung* (retaliation) has at last become a fact. For it was I who promised it to the German people. And I would have been made responsible if it had not come. You know the hundreds of letters which often contained the one question only: Where is the retaliation?" He admitted now the uneasiness he had felt at the thought that "the silk cord to which retaliation was attached up to the last moment, might break." [4] Goebbels was, however, shrewd enough to insist on a cautious propaganda line. He persuaded the Führer that the daily Bulletin of the Supreme Command of the *Wehrmacht* should only contain one factual sentence on the event and that the word *Vergeltung* should be avoided.[5] At his daily Ministerial Conference on 16 June Goebbels also insisted that radio and press should not talk of *Vergeltung*. "The mere fact", he insisted, "in its very sobriety as it is contained in the Bulletin of the Supreme Command of the Armed Forces is going to create an extraordinary effect on the German people. It must be our task

[1] R. Semmler, op. cit., entry of 17 June 1944, p. 131.
[2] Ibid.
[3] See O. Dietrich, *12 Jahre mit Hitler*, p. 119.
[4] W. von Oven, op. cit., II, p. 21 f. Diary entry of 20 June 1944. The various reactions to the propaganda of the V-weapons before they could be used have been neatly described in the diary of Ruth Andreas-Friedrich: "Sunday, June 18th 1944. . . . The use of the long-promised, too-often-threatened first German secret weapon. After the preceding months of whispered propaganda, there was hardly any doubt that it would come. How it would come, though, was a puzzle, even to the wisest. Everyone had good authority for a different version of what it would do. 'You press a button. The thing scoots off. The upper half of the British Isles flies sky high, the lower half sinks into the ocean, and the missile comes back with fifty thousand prisoners', the doubters jeer. 'Our secret weapon is frightful', say the believers earnestly, 'twenty-four hours of bombardment, and England will be whining for mercy, for armistice and peace terms. You know . . . splitting the atom. Rearranging electrons. . . . A German invention. The effect will be world shaking'. . . . Ten days after the invasion started, Hitler launched his counterblow. 'Against London and southern England', yesterday's papers reported, 'explosives of a new type and of the heaviest calibre' ". Ruth Andreas-Friedrich, *Berlin Underground, 1939-1945*, pp. 114-115.
[5] W. von Oven, op. cit., II, p. 18, entry of 16 June 1944.

not to incite but to calm down the excitement which can be expected." [1]
He was afraid the German masses might entertain false hopes that the
end of the war was in sight. Small wonder Goebbels was very annoyed
when he discovered that his old rival Otto Dietrich in his *Tagesparole*
(daily directive to the press) had disregarded the line desired by the
Minister. This led a well known Berlin journalist, Otto Kriegk, to write
a leader in a Berlin evening paper, the *Berliner Nachtausgabe*, which
began with the chiliastic sentence: "The day for which 80 million Germans have waited has come. . . ." Goebbels was so furious that he
threatened to have the unfortunate leader-writer shot, until he realized
that the whole thing was actually Otto Dietrich's fault.[2]

Nevertheless, the German press soon indulged in wild accounts of
the damage done by V1. A war reporter's account of life in London,
dated 6 July 1944, described the city as burning. "A fiery circle has
been drawn round the town, which has been fighting for days for its life
against a terrible weapon of attack. In the centre of the town at the
bend of the Thames fierce fires must be raging. A thin veil of clouds
over London is coloured dark red . . . in London the fires will never be
extinguished." [3]

How did Goebbels treat the V1 and V2 theme in his own articles after
these weapons had made their appearance? Addressing a mass meeting
in the capital of a Gau in East Germany on 7 July 1944 he declared
amid the stormy applause of his audience, that "without wanting to
indulge in exaggerated illusions on its immediate effects, in the long run
it (V1) cannot remain without far-reaching influence on the entire public
life [in England]." [4]

In an article on "The Question of Retaliation",[5] broadcast on 21 July,
Goebbels spoke of the "paralysing feeling of horror" V1 caused and
claimed that none of the British defence measures against the pilotless
guided missile were able to prevent "our V1 missiles flying in a mass
stream without interference over the Channel into England." He alleged

---

[1] Op. cit., II, p. 19.

[2] Op. cit., II, p. 20. In his memoirs Otto Dietrich does not mention the incident or his rivalry and clashes with Goebbels. He asserts, however, that after
V1 had been in operation for a week, Hitler had felt very disappointed with its
results and had ordered that press and radio should avoid any exaggerations in
their reporting of the effects of the new weapon, though he had started them
himself. The press should not go further than the description published abroad
(O. Dietrich, *12 Jahre mit Hitler*, Munich, 1954, p. 119).

The discrepancies between Goebbels' directive and Dietrich's *Tagesparole*
for the press increased Goebbels' desire to undermine Dietrich's position with
the Führer. He seems to have succeeded in obtaining a decision from Hitler
that Dietrich's *Tagesparole* was in future to be submitted to the Propaganda
Minister for his approval before distribution. See also W. von Oven, op. cit.,
II, pp. 23–26.

[3] W. Hagemann, *Publizistik in Dritten Reich*, p. 478.

[4] *Hamburger Fremdenblatt*, 8 July 1944.

[5] "Die Frage der Vergeltung" in *Das Reich*, broadcast by the *Reichsprogramm* on 21 July and published on 23 July 1944.

that the British Government had now given up all attempts to deceive the world about the extent of the damage done. On the contrary, it now went to the other extreme "dramatizing things in a sentimental manner in order to evoke pity from the world and trying its best to pose as the personification of an insulted and tortured innocence."

At a time when the invasion was making headway in France Goebbels clung to the success of the V1 weapon, and took credit for his hints during the long months of waiting. "When we drew attention in all modesty to the fact that we had also a little word to say on this matter, that we were preparing a corresponding retaliation (*Vergeltung*) with new weapons and these would burst on England one day, then they laughed uproariously in London and asked the witty question, if these new weapons had perhaps been invented by propagandists instead of by inventors and technicians!" "But by now they have lost the urge to laugh in England. . . . In the first few days the English papers called our V1 missiles 'troublesome beetles', today they are named 'robot bombs'. That shows the difference in their judgment on them yesterday and today." [1]

Some of the arguments in defence of the right to use the V-weapons undoubtedly appealed to a good many of the heavily bombed Germans. They were thrilled and felt encouraged now that the long promised *Wunderwaffe* had at last come off.[2] Goebbels refuted the English criticism that V1 lacked precision in hitting a definite target and therefore had not the military value of the British air raids on German towns during nights of the last winter. The Germans had only to view their bombed towns in order to observe easily that the exact opposite was true. In order to justify V1 as a military weapon Goebbels produced one of his smartest and most ingenious arguments: the London newspapers clamoured for retaliation, only in order to make the world forget that the German V1 action was already a retaliation. If the English could carry out retaliation they would hardly have any repressions about it. For this they and their American allies had sufficient aeroplanes at their disposal, but these were now required for the Allied invasion bridgehead. Should they be taken from there, a considerable operative advantage would result for Germany. This alone proved, said Goebbels, that, in spite of the assertions of some critics to the contrary, the German V1 weapon had definitely military aims and objectives. The English did not want to admit this because they wished to appeal to the pity of the public all over the world.[3]

[1] Ibid.

[2] "V1 is king—not indeed in London, where one is said to be hitting every fifteen minutes, but in Berlin, where Dr. Goebbels is brandishing it in practised propaganda hands. Perhaps it was invented solely to keep the German people in a war mood; for judging by the look of things at the moment, its propaganda effect in Germany is considerably greater than its explosive effect in England" (Ruth Andreas-Friedrich, op. cit., p. 115).

[3] Article "Die Frage der Vergeltung", in *Das Reich*, 21 July 1944.

It is understandable that the British and American counter-propagandists, realizing Goebbels had scored a considerable success, issued
instructions that the military value of the *Wunderwaffe* should be belittled.
An American propaganda planner suggested as a possible line of argument that no military results were visible. The Allied troops in Normandy
were able to continue their advance and military supplies were flown in
without interruption. Allied leaders were a little puzzled as to why the
Germans put so much time and effort into the *Wunderwaffe*. A British
directive to propagandists at the time recommended emphasis on the
military futility of the flying bombs.[1]

But there is evidence that Goebbels' propaganda exploitation of the
V-weapons raised the morale of the German troops. In looking back on
the early phases of the invasion struggle in Normandy General Eisenhower reported to the Combined Chiefs of Staff: "It cannot be doubted
that the (German) Governmental propaganda on V-weapons had a considerable effect in strengthening morale in these early stages of the campaign." It also affected General Eisenhower's decision to attack the
Pas-de-Calais area in September 1944: "There was the great desirability
of capturing the flying bomb, not only to remove this menace to England, but also to deny to the enemy the propaganda value which he
enjoyed on the home front and in the army from the attacks on London
and talk of new weapons which would 'decide the war'." [2] Goebbels
rejected the English argument that the German V1 weapon was particularly mean and unfair because although not guided by human beings
it destroyed human beings. The same applied "almost exactly and equally
to British night attacks"—he retaliated—"then the sky is completely
clouded over and on the ground the weather is so unfavourable that
our fighters cannot go up." [3]

Goebbels assured his readers in Germany and abroad that he did not
indulge in *Schadenfreude* "over the desolate conditions created by our
fires of retaliation in London." No, the Propaganda Minister was sensitive: "We even recoil with some horror when we think what the British
capital has to expect from the application of our further and heavier
weapons of retaliation. For our acts of retaliation are not at their end,
but at their beginning!" Everywhere the military critics were agreed that
the German V1 weapon was the beginning of a revolution in the technology of weapons. "What will they say once our most novel weapons
have appeared which cannot in any way be compared with this?" Goebbels ended on a comforting note: "We do not belong to those who see
in technology the only decisive factor in modern warfare; but it undoubtedly belongs to it in a decisive manner. Morale and technology lead to
victory. Until now the enemy was superior to us in technology, as we

[1] W. Carroll, *Persuade or Perish,* p. 258.
[2] W. Carroll, op. cit., p. 259.
[3] Article "Die Frage der Vergeltung", loc. cit.

were to him in morale. We can and shall become his equal in technology, but he never ours in morale. This is the decisive plus on which we have to rely. Here it will show whose breath lasts longest in spite of everything." While Goebbels continued to pursue a restrained propaganda line on the impact of the *Wunderwaffen,* he was deeply impressed when he saw a coloured film on the V2 which was shown to him, to Minister Speer and to Field Marshal Milch in great secrecy two months before the weapon was ready to go into operation. Afterwards he expressed privately his belief "that this weapon will bring England to her knees. Could we show this film in all German cinemas, I need not make any more speeches nor write any more articles; even the most hard-boiled pessimist could no longer doubt our victory." [1]

The first appearance of the V1 caused little surprise in British Government circles. But the official optimism was rudely shaken when the first V2 fell on Chiswick, a suburb of London, on 7 September 1944. For only the day before, Duncan Sandys, the Minister of Supply, had predicted that the second "Battle of Britain" had come to a close, "except for possibly a last few shots." His optimism had been fed by British Intelligence reports on the destruction of the German launching sites of the *Wunderwaffen.* In fact, "the last few shots" which were to explode over England during the next six months amounted to a total of 1,000 V2's and nearly 500 V1's.[2] Nevertheless they did not bring England to her knees.

2. "STRENGTH THROUGH FEAR" (1943-1944)

The term "strength through fear" as a device of propaganda is not a German invention. It was coined by British counter-propagandists at the end of 1942 in order to describe and expose an important trend in the output of German propaganda at a time when German troops in Russia were on the eve of their first major disaster. "The English" observed Goebbels in his diary in December 1942, a few weeks before the German debacle at Stalingrad, "are organizing a great propaganda campaign against our propaganda, which they refer to as Strength through Fear." [3]

In fact during the second half of the war, with the German armies forced more and more on to the defensive, the German propagandists pursued a line of creating strength through fear at home and of weakening through fear in the enemy camp. The first was employed to reinforce the flagging morale of the German soldiers and civilians and to bolster the wavering confidence of Germany's allies and friends. The second aimed at weakening the enemy coalition, at paralysing the war effort of

---

[1] W. von Oven, op. cit., II, p. 54, Diary entry of 11 July 1944.
[2] John Baker White, *The Big Lie,* pp. 188 f.
[3] Goebbels Diary, entry of 12 December 1942 (01559)

the Western powers by conjuring up for them a grisly picture of their Bolshevist ally. Through skilful manipulation the same stereotype of annihilation, disaster and death could be employed as a tonic for reinforcing the morale of the Axis and as a poison intended to disintegrate the united front of its opponents. After Stalingrad the terrible fate said to be in store for every German man, woman and child should the impossible happen and Germany lose the war, remained a constant theme in the German press and radio. Obviously the top Nazi leaders had a vested interest in this approach as they were well aware that there was no future for them in a post-Nazi Germany.

"Strength through fear" aimed at imbuing the German masses and Germany's allies with the determination to bear the harshness and the inconveniences of war rather than face an infinitely worse situation in a crushed fatherland. "Weakening through fear," on the other hand, signified a Macchiavellian effort to drive a wedge between the partners of the enemy coalition by trying to persuade the West that a Bolshevik victory would be more dangerous than a German victory or a compromise peace with the Third Reich.

The technique of fostering "strength through fear" was largely based on the alleged evil plans of Germany's foes to make life in a beaten Germany hard and intolerable. Any intransigent utterance in Britain or America, any harsh comment on the future of a conquered Germany was eagerly exploited for this purpose by the Propaganda Ministry. Sir Robert Vansittart's condemnation of all Germans without exception was therefore a gift from the gods for the German propaganda machine.[1] For instance a directive to German editors in December 1943 ran: "Our enemies' wishdreams of annihilation, which find expression in the practical commentaries of Vansittart and in the announcement of the Conservative Member of Parliament Lloyd that he hopes Stalin will frustrate any attempt to lighten Germany's fate, deserve special attention. We shall remember any such statements, made just at a time when it has become clear that Germany is also stronger in its defensive operations than its enemies, as an outburst of madness." [2]

A clue to this directive can be found in some remarks of Goebbels in his diary a few days earlier, which indicate his concern about the intensified propaganda campaign of the other side:

"To put it short and sweet, there is developing a drama of a war of nerves that puts anything in the past in the shade. It reaches its climax in the threat: 'Surrender or die.' In any case it must be remarked, on the other side, that this campaign has no effect on us. The German people know their enemies very well, and are aware of what they could expect if they should put themselves in their enemies' hands." [3]

Partly as a result of the intense anti-Bolshevist indoctrination between

[1] See below, Chapter 18, pp. 425-426.
[2] V.I. No. 310/43, 16 December 1943, *Tagesparole des Reichspressechefs.*
[3] Goebbels diary, entry of 5 December 1943 (03397)

1933 and 1939, and again after Hitler's invasion of Soviet Russia in June 1941, the average German was probably much more frightened of a Russian than of a Western occupation. When in November 1943 foreign newspapers carried reports of Soviet Russia's demand that after the war ten million German workers should be put at her disposal for five years to help rebuild the country, Goebbels rubbed his hands delightedly.

"Such demands are the best thing imaginable for our propaganda," he wrote in his diary; "they make a very deep impression on German public opinion. The idea that our soldiers would not come home at all, but must remain as forced laborers in the Soviet Union, is anathema to every wife and every mother. To avoid this the German people prefer to fight to the last breath." [1]

After the invasion of the Continent by Allied troops had begun in June 1944 there was a special need to spread fear of the Anglo-Saxon troops among the German masses, and the German press and radio duly painted a grim picture of their behaviour. A directive of the Reich Press Chief Dietrich alleged that:

"Countless letters to English newspapers and other periodicals demand over and over the murder of all Germans, wives and children not excepted—even infants in their cradles." [2]

With the advance of the Allied armies in France and Belgium and the growing threat to the German *Heimat* this line was intensified. On 12 September 1944 German editors were advised that they would receive archive material on significant slogans for the annihilation of Germany *(Vernichtungsparolen)* devised by the enemy during the war. "These slogans make clear the real dangers faced by the whole German people." [3] Emphasis on the determination of the enemies to destroy the German nation was to form part of a regular press campaign. For German newspapers this was to become in the immediate future "a sort of continuous feature which will remind the reader daily of the dangers that threaten him unless he exerts all his energies against his enemies." [4]

It was not an easy matter to persuade the hard pressed but disciplined German masses that they had to fear the Western armies on German soil as much as they feared the Soviet troops. The official view was that anyone, who felt occupation by Western troops to be a minor evil, badly deceived himself. He who supped with the devil was bound to perish. The situation in France now occupied by Anglo-Saxon troops was a pointer and the German press was instructed to explain, "that there, as in all other countries where there are English and American troops, hunger, anarchy and disorganization rule." [5]

When in October Anglo-American troops occupied some territory in

[1] *Goebbels Tagbücher,* p. 485, entry of 21 November 1943.
[2] V.I. No. 122/44, 16 June 1944.
[3] V.I. No. 200/44, 12 September 1944. *Tagesparole.*
[4] *Ibid.*
[5] V.I. No. 189/44, 1 September 1944.

the Rhineland east of Aachen their behaviour towards German civilians was severely denounced in the German press. The editors were obliged to publish sharp commentaries on "the first Anglo-American decrees issued in the small strip of occupied German territory:"

"The brutal régime of the bayonet and hunger proclaimed there, together with the steps taken to take away the German labor force and to bring in Jews as slave-drivers, show in a new light the inner affinity of plutocracy and bolshevism. The gangsters of the West are no less brutal vandals than the hordes of the East." [1]

However, privately Goebbels was little afraid of these Western "gangster methods" for a few months afterwards he suggested to his wife that she should move westward with their children, anywhere where they might meet the British. "They would do nothing to you," he said.[2] The Propaganda Minister did believe that a Soviet occupation of the Reich would mean a harsh fate for the German people. He was in fact afraid of the Russian troops on German soil, which did not prevent him from amplifying and distorting this fear in the service of propaganda. In November 1943, after Berlin had suffered severe air-raids, Goebbels was shocked by the sight of certain once fashionable districts in the West of the capital. "How beautiful it used to be in Berlin," he sighed, "and how wretched and ruined it looks now. But what good is it to grieve and suffer, we cannot change this state of affairs. This war has to be fought out. It is better that our workers crawl into their cellars than that they be carried off to Siberia as slaves." [3] Goebbels could perhaps use the sinister image of a Bolshevist enslavement of the German people all the more effectively as he himself dreaded it:

"There is no more frightful prospect for the German people than to come under the hand of Bolshevism." [4]

To drive home the terrifying prospect of such an event every suitable device was welcome and permissible. It was in this context that Goebbels introduced a new concept into the vocabulary of his propaganda, a term destined for internal use only among his staff. The new phrase was "'poetic truth,' in contrast to—or rather in amplification of—'the concrete truth.' " [5] Different from the 'concrete truth' of established fact, 'poetic truth' meant an embroidering of facts on which there was only scanty information. Whenever the propagandists knew a little about an event or plan or operation of the enemies they would in Goebbels' view "not be violating the truth" if they added "something to the story to fill in the gaps." They should "describe things as they might well have happened or as they probably did happen." Goebbels argued that such a procedure of *corriger la vérité* was all to the benefit of the public. "We

---

[1] V.I. No. 224/44, 11 October 1944 *Tagesparole des Reichspressechefs.*
[2] R. Semmler, op. cit., p. 186, diary entry of 25 February 1945.
[3] *Goebbels Tagebücher*, p. 484, diary entry of 25 November 1943.
[4] Op. cit., p. 479, diary entry of 14 November 1943.
[5] R. Semmler, op. cit., p. 163, diary entry of 2 November 1944.

are only helping the public when we call imagination to our aid in certain cases where the record of the facts is for some reason incomplete!" he remarked. 'Poetic truth' had a didactic function, as, Goebbels asserted, "many events in international politics . . . could not be understood unless one embroidered them a little with the 'poetic truth' and so made them understandable to the German public." [1]

The example by which Goebbels illustrated his idea shows that his concept of 'poetic truth' served him as a means of evoking "strength through fear" in the people. He pointed out how inadequate were the details they "were getting about atrocities and cruelties perpetrated in the East on German women and children." It was "the task of German propaganda to make powerful indictments out of these stories by embroidering them with suitable details." 'Poetic truth' was a corollary of fear: "what happened in reality would be so much worse," Goebbels explained, "than anything we could imagine." For that reason they should add 'poetic truth' "which would generally be reasonably accurate." [2]

It was on this basis that a simultaneous press directive on the treatment of the "atrocious Bolshevist crimes against German men, women and children left behind" in East Prussia, requested the use of the most drastic language in comments and headlines. Moreover these 'poetical' news items were to serve as an eye-opener to all who had so far disbelieved German propaganda.

"If there have been up till now only a few harmless commentators, not only in Germany but in the rest of Europe," explained a *Tagesparole* at the end of October 1944, "who had believed that the reports we published of the inhuman horrors committed by the Bolshevists were merely a device of our propaganda, now even these naive views should have been emphatically refuted by the events in East Prussia that have become known. Here for everybody to see is the very dreadful truth about what will become of us if Bolshevism penetrates further into the Reich. . . . A cruel, systematic murder of every single German would take place, and Germany would be turned into a single great cemetery." [3]

A ghoulish prospect intended to call forth a maximum of defiance and inner resistance from every German. A wave of sullen rage (*verbissener Ingrimm*) was needed to throw "the Bolshevist monster" back from Germany's frontiers. In Germans the fear of the Bolshevist soldiery, played up by Goebbels propaganda, was intended to produce a galvanising rather than a paralysing effect and to spur them on to even bigger sacrifices and efforts to stem the tide. However, a different motive was behind the exploitation of the same stories of atrocities, said to have been committed by the advancing Russian soldiers, in German propaganda directed to the countries of the West, both enemy and neutral.

[1] Ibid.
[2] R. Semmler, op. cit., p. 164.
[3] V.I. No. 237/44, 26 October 1944, *Tagesparole des Reichspressechefs und Erläuterungen.*

There the overall aim was not to strengthen, but to weaken the enemy coalition and to frighten the people of neutral countries.

The greatest success Goebbels ever scored with the technique of weakening through instilling fear was the effect of the Katyn story which he released in April 1943. Its repercussions led to the breaking off of diplomatic relations between two members of the Allied coalition, the Soviet Union and the Polish Government in exile in London. On 13 April 1943 the German radio stations announced the discovery of a mass grave in Katyn forest near Smolensk containing over 10,000 bodies of Polish officers who had been methodically killed by a pistol shot in the back of the head.[1] Describing the ghastly deed as a typical example of 'Jewish-Bolshevik bestiality' the murders were alleged to have been carried out by the N.K.V.D., the Soviet secret police, in the spring of 1940. This sensational news was bound to cause uneasiness among the many Poles in exile, as in fact large numbers of Polish officers were missing who had been taken prisoner by the Russians after their occupation of Eastern Poland in 1939. These officers had not reappeared when following the German invasion of Russia the Polish prisoners in Russian hands were released to form a special Polish army on Russian soil.

From the beginning Goebbels regarded the discovery of the bodies—the number of which was much exaggerated in the German accounts [2]—as first-class material for anti-Bolshevist propaganda, likely to weaken the Russian prestige in the eyes of her Western allies and of the neutral states. "The discovery of 12,000 Polish officers murdered by the GPU will now be given a leading place in the anti-Bolshevist propaganda," he wrote in his diary.[3] "We took neutral reporters and Polish intellectuals to see the place where they were found. The news stories that are appearing in the foreign press are hair-raising. Now the Führer has given us permission to release a dramatic account to the German press ourselves.[4] I am giving instructions to use this propaganda material to the fullest. *This will give us several weeks' lease on life.*" [5]

This joy of having hit the jackpot increased when Goebbels was able to observe "the very deep impression" the Katyn revelations were making everywhere, even in enemy countries. "The whole subject of Katyn is becoming a tremendous political event, which might have far-reaching repercussions," Goebbels remarked triumphantly on 17 April. "So we are exploiting the story with all the means at our command. Since the ten to twelve thousand Polish victims have already given their lives—perhaps

---

[1] For the wide repercussions of the Katyn story see the account in *The Realignment of Europe*, edited by Arnold Toynbee and Veronica M. Toynbee, London, 1955, pp. 138-147.

[2] In fact there were not more than 4,500 bodies. See J. Mackiewicz, *The Katyn Wood Murders*, London, 1951, p. 206.

[3] *Goebbels Tagebücher*, p. 298, diary entry of 14 April 1943.

[4] See for instance the *Völkischer Beobachter* of 15 and 16 April 1943.

[5] The italics are mine (E.B.).

not altogether without guilt, for were they not really the ones who brought on the war?—now they too shall serve to open the eyes of the peoples of Europe to Bolshevism." [1]

Foreign journalists who had visited the scenes of the massacre and published their impressions in the neutral and satellite press were inclined to accept the German story as substantially true.[2] For their part, the Russians retaliated by accusing the Germans of "vile fabrications" and attributing the massacre to them. According to an official Russian communiqué of 15 April the Polish officers had been engaged in construction work west of Smolensk in 1941 and had fallen into German hands after the Russian troops had withdrawn in the summer of that year. More surprising was the attitude of the Polish Government which, after some initial restraint, on 17 April issued a communiqué through its Minister of National Defence, Kukiel. It drew attention to the long and unsuccessful efforts made by the Polish authorities to obtain information about the missing officers. No answer to their inquiries had been received from the Soviet authorities. Though the Poles were by no means unaware of the frequent lies of German propaganda on the basis of information received by the Polish Government in this case it had approached the International Red Cross with a request that the charges should be "verified by a competent international body" and that a delegation should be sent to Katyn.[3] It so happened that on the same day (17 April) the International Red Cross received a similar request from the German Government.

But there the matter did not rest. The Soviet Government took exception to the step taken by the Polish authorities who were bitterly attacked in an article in *Pravda* on 19 April under the caption "Hitler's Polish Collaborators" and described as playing the Nazi game. Little wonder that Goebbels followed the course of events with much satisfaction. "It is true, here and there you can find the opinion in England," he jotted down in his diary, "that we hoped, by this barrage of propaganda, to poison the relations between the Allies. But this argument is no longer effective for the affair has already gone too far. Our enemies have made a mistake in the first place in discussing the matter. If I had been on the other side, I would probably have kept completely silent." [4] Hitler and Goebbels who had agreed to make a *cause célèbre* of it [5] were richly rewarded. There was no exaggeration in Goebbels' comment on 21 April: "The goal of our propaganda, to fill the European public with horror at

---

[1] Goebbels Diary, entry of 17 April 1943 (02055).

[2] See for instance the article by Robert Broess published in *El Pampero* (Buenos Aires), 13 April 1943.

[3] See *Polish-Soviet Relations 1918-1943, Official Documents,* issued by the Polish Embassy in Washington in 1945, document 39, p. 119.

[4] Goebbels Diary, entry of 18 April 1944 (02070-1).

[5] Goebbels Diary, entry of 17 April 1943 (02062). In the same entry Goebbels paid tribute to the merit of one of his officials, A.O. Berndt, who "with immense and sometimes even excessive zeal" saw to it that the propaganda offices intensified their efforts in the Katyn affair.

Bolshevism, has now been completely achieved."[1] but things were to move even more dramatically and profitably for the Germans. On 26 April the Soviet Government took action. In a note handed to the Polish Ambassador to the U.S.S.R. by Molotov the Polish Government was severely reprimanded for having acted simultaneously with the Germans in asking for a Red Cross investigation "behind the back of the Soviet Government" and for carrying out a press campaign "along the same lines." As the Polish Government had "sunk so low as to enter the path of accord with the Hitlerite Government" and had displayed a hostile attitude towards the Soviet Union, the Soviet Government had "decided to interrupt relations with the Polish Government."[2]

British and American circles were alarmed over this dangerous rift between the Allies. The actions of the Polish Government came in for a good deal of criticism in the British, and to a lesser extent in the American press. The London *Times* of 28 April blamed the Poles for contributing to this triumph of Goebbels, while the *New York Times* regretted "that both the Russians and the Poles had fallen into a Nazi trap. The Poles were criticized for raising the issue and the Russians for abruptly breaking off relations."[3]

Goebbels had good reason for rejoicing. He felt flattered to have been able to engineer a break between two Allied governments. "All enemy broadcasts and newspapers agree that this break represents a 100 per cent victory for German propaganda and especially for me personally," he wrote. "The commentators marvel at the extraordinary cleverness with which we have been able to convert the Katyn incident into a highly political question. There is grave apprehension in London about this success of German propaganda. Suddenly all sorts of rifts are noticed in the allied camp the existence of which nobody had hitherto admitted. There is talk of a total victory by Goebbels!"[4] Yet, anxious to avoid a false step and not to be carried away by this considerable success, the Propaganda Minister issued strict orders to the German propaganda services "under no circumstances to make a public show of having triumphed." Though the break between Moscow and the Polish Government in exile could be regarded as a major success of Germany's mental warfare, it would be unwise to say so in public.[5]

[1] Goebbels Diary, entry of 21 April 1943 (02112).
[2] *Soviet Foreign Policy During the Patriotic War: Documents and Materials*, translated by A. Rothstein, London, n.d. (1946), vol. I, p. 202.
[3] *The Realignment of Europe*, p. 143, quoting the *New York Times* of 27 April 1943.
[4] *The Goebbels Diaries*, p. 270, entry of 28 April 1943.
[5] Goebbels Diary, entry of 27 April 1943 (02171-2). Goebbels admitted to himself that in occupied Poland the German Katyn story had not done the trick. "Obviously our propaganda has clearly failed there, for in the end the Polish resistance has managed to make full use of the matter against us, even though it humiliates and hits the Poles very deeply." Goebbels felt that there were some very skilful propagandists in the Polish resistance movement.

Goebbels was hardly exaggerating when he felt that "a complete triumph of German propaganda" had been achieved, and that during the whole war they had rarely been able to register such a success.[1] With his tongue in his cheek he observed that on all sides German propaganda was suspected of having made so much of the Katyn incident in order to obtain a separate peace for Germany either with the English or the Soviet Union. This, he told himself dryly, was not their intention, although such a possibility would indeed be very attractive to them.[2]

In retrospect both the extent and the limitation of Goebbels' success with the Katyn affair can be discerned. As a result of his adroit propaganda coup a quarrel between the Poles in London and the Soviet Union had broken out which proved irreparable. But if the Poles and the Russians fell out with each other, the British and the Soviet Governments did not follow suit, and Goebbels' constant hopes that a permanent rift between them might develop proved futile. His tactics of weakening the enemy coalition by instilling fear of the Russian partner worked in the case of the exiled Poles, whose relations with Moscow had in any case been precarious for a long time, but it did not pay any dividends in the case of the major Allied powers. The master-stroke of Katyn could never be repeated. There is reason to believe that the unfortunate Polish officers had lost their lives not later than the spring of 1940 while prisoners of the Russians.[3] But that was not then established and counted for little during the war years in the Western camp. Many were inclined to dismiss the story as German propaganda. The relative indifference was partly due to the desire of the British and American Governments to maintain the coalition with the Soviet Union, and partly to the awareness of Western public opinion that mass murder was taking place all the time on a gigantic scale in German concentration camps.

To the end Goebbels believed that England might dissociate herself from her Soviet partner. Among his intimates he later even described the rapid westward advance of Russian troops as advantageous for the tottering Reich, because this event would bring about a political change in England in Germany's favour. According to Werner Stephan, Goebbels assured his close associates well up to 1945, that the day would come "when they will have to free themselves in England from their propaganda, from their pacts, from all hindrances, because they will be forced to act on the basis of their real interest." At the decisive moment the true

---

[1] Diary entry of 28 April 1943 (02180).

[2] Diary entry of 30 April 1943 (02197).

[3] See G.F. Hudson, "A Polish Challenge", *International Affairs*, April 1950 Vol. XXVI, pp. 309-310, and the reports of the Select Committee of Congress set up in Washington in September 1951. The first paragraph of its findings says: "This Committee unanimously agrees that evidence . . . proves conclusively and irrevocably the Soviet NKVD (People's Commissariat of Internal Affairs) committed the massacre of Polish Army Officers in the Katyn Forest near Smolensk, Russia, not later than the spring of 1940". Quoted in *The Realignment of Europe*, p. 147 fn. 3.

insights would mature there quickly. That is, he said, "how things occur in the life of the nations." [1] With such vain hopes the propagandist Goebbels scored over Goebbels the realist. He continued to underestimate the immense dislike of Hitler and of himself which existed on the other side of the Channel and the determination of the Churchill Cabinet to see the war through to the final fall of the Nazi régime.

[1] W. Stephan, *Joseph Goebbels*, p. 285.

CHAPTER 15

Goebbels and The Revolt of 20 July, 1944

1. "An acute case of historical idealism"

WHAT has become known as the 20th July, was a daring attempt by military and civilian opponents of the Nazi régime to assassinate Hitler, to remove his associates and to overthrow the entire existing order. It is not intended here to tell the complete story of the 20th July 1944 but to consider Goebbels' behaviour on that fateful day and the impact its events had on his propaganda tactics. It is true, Berlin was only one of the centres in which the drama unfolded itself, but there Goebbels played an important role in paralyzing the actions of the conspirators. With his remarkable *sangfroid* he helped to stem the tide and to enforce the continuation of the régime on which his own survival depended. Although the events around him were as confused and complicated as elsewhere in the capital, it is now possible to reconstruct them with a fair amount of accuracy even if the evidence is conflicting on some points.[1]

Goebbels spent the morning of that day at work in his official residence at No. 20 Hermann Göring Strasse. In the early afternoon, when he had retired for his usual nap, a telephone call came through to the office from Hitler's headquarters at the *Wolfsschanze* [2] (near Rastenburg in East Prussia). A junior member of the staff of the Reich Press Chief

[1] The best critical survey of the events which has so far appeared is Eberhard Zeller, *Geist der Freiheit, Der Zwanzigste Juli*, 3rd edition, Munich, 1956; it has a valuable bibliography. See also Constantine FitzGibbon, *The Shirt of Nessus*, London, 1957. For documentary material compiled from the Gestapo point of view, see *Spiegelbild einer Verschwörung*, edited by Archiv Peter, Stuttgart, 1961, which reproduces the reports by Kaltenbrunner to Bormann and Hitler on the coup of July 20. Some relevant documents in an English translation are to be found in *Germans against Hitler, July 20, 1944*, published by the Press and Information Office of the Federal German Government, Bonn, 1960.

[2] There is a marked discrepancy between various accounts of the events of July 20th about the time when this telephone call from Hitler's headquarters came through. Von Oven times it between 2 and 3 p.m. (*Mit Goebbels bis zum Ende*, II, p. 59), while Semmler gives the time as "one o'clock or shortly afterwards" (op. cit., p. 132). There seems little reason for accepting FitzGibbon's version that it happened as late as "a little before half past 5" (op. cit., p. 183).

Dietrich, named Lorenz, wished to speak to the Reich Minister urgently. Von Oven, Goebbels' personal Press Secretary, regretted that he could not be reached at that moment. Lorenz agitatedly declared it to be a matter of the greatest national importance and then explained that an attempt had been made on the life of the Führer who had, however, miraculously escaped. On Hitler's orders a suitable news item was to be broadcast over all radio stations. Lorenz then dictated to von Oven the text of the bulletin as drafted by the Führer. The alarmed adjutant hastened to awaken his master, who ordered Secretary of State Naumann to see him at once. Goebbels talked to Lorenz, but was unable to obtain any further information on the events at the *Wolfsschanze*. Once more Lorenz urged speed in the release of the news which was regarded by the Führer as of the greatest importance. The Minister directed Hans Fritzsche, the man in charge of the Radio Division of the Propaganda Ministry and a prominent political commentator, to write a short piece explaining what had happened. A bare account of the facts might stun the public, so that Goebbels was not in a hurry to release the big news, particularly as he had no idea of the extent of the plot, being blissfully unaware of its dangerous ramifications in Berlin. He thought they should mitigate the shock to the people which the admission of an attempt on the Führer's life would mean. "The present situation," he explained to his entourage, was "so delicate that one has somehow to tone down such psychological drum beats." The early or late release of this news mattered less than the manner in which it was conveyed. "We cannot afford any propagandist extravaganzas," declared Goebbels, "considering the psychological tension under which the German people are living to-day. The news has to be commented upon carefully, its shock effect has to be minimized, and the entire programme of to-day's broadcasts has to be orientated round it." [1] Fritzsche was instructed accordingly.

About 5:30 p.m. Hitler spoke to Goebbels on the telephone and ordered him to have the news broadcast without delay. The people should be told that an attempt had been made on the life of the Führer. He was safe, however, and had even been able to receive the Duce as planned.[2] After some time Hitler again rang the Propaganda Minister reproaching him bitterly because the radio announcement had not yet been released. Suffering from the after effects of his narrow escape Hitler and some of the men around him at the *Wolfsschanze* seem to have become suspicious even of Goebbels himself, who in his turn, passed the buck to Fritzsche accusing him suddenly of "irresponsible" negligence and "sabotage of orders." [3] At last, at about 6:30 p.m. a voice could be heard on the radio. "Attention, attention, we are broadcasting a particularly important news item." [4] Then came the *Sondermeldung* of the *Deutschlandsender*: an attempt had been made to assassinate the Führer by a bomb, but he had

---

[1] Von Oven, op. cit., II, p. 60; entry of 23 July 1944.
[2] Zeller, op. cit., pp. 278-279.
[3] Von Oven, op. cit., II, p. 76.
[4] Ibid.

only been slightly hurt. Some members of his entourage had been severely wounded, others only slightly.[1]

Meanwhile a message from the *Wolfsschanze* was received in the Propaganda Ministry that the Führer wished to give a brief radio address himself. Considerable technical difficulties had to be overcome. There was no recording van at the *Wolfsschanze*, the nearest was in Königsberg the capital of East Prussia. This meant that some hours had to pass before the Führer's broadcast could be recorded and relayed. In fact, it was not heard until 1 a.m. the next morning.[2]

In the meantime a number of people had gone to Goebbels' house with an urgent request to see the Minister. First came the fat Schach, Goebbels' chief assistant in running the Gau Berlin. He had received in his office a teleprinted message from Bormann, the head of the Party Chancellery, to all Gauleiters, informing them of the attempt on the life of the Führer and hinting at the possibility of a military *coup d'état*. Schach, rather bewildered, arrived accompanied by the burgomaster of Berlin, Steeg, and by the City Councillor Petzke. A less excited visitor was Dr. Speer, the Reich Minister of Armaments, who simply wanted to know what was going on.

And then appeared one of those minor figures in history who, though unimportant in themselves, assume a momentary importance as a link in the chain of events. Dr. Hans Hagen was a pre-war official *(Referent)* in the Propaganda Ministry. After being seriously wounded during the campaign in France in 1940 and subsequently declared unfit for further active service, he had returned to the Ministry and was attached to the branch concerned with propaganda to the Russians.[3] In addition, he then contributed regular articles on music to Goebbels' weekly *Das Reich*. Hagen has been called by a fellow German "a radical champion of integral National Socialism, as represented by the ideology of the S.S." [4] However, in 1943 he seems to have attracted the attention of the Gestapo for being "too sympathetic towards the Russians." He asked for and obtained a transfer from the Ministry to the army, then less susceptible to Gestapo control, and was given the position of National Socialist Guidance Officer with the Guards Battalion of the *Grossdeutschland* division in Berlin.

In July, 1944 Hagen lived at Bayreuth working on a "National Socialist history of culture" [5] which Bormann had commissioned him to write. On July 20th he happened to be in Berlin to attend a memorial meeting for a German writer (Trüstedt) who had died in Russia. He was also to give one of his routine lectures as National Socialist Guidance Officer to the

[1] Zeller, op. cit., p. 250.

[2] The *Deutschlandsendehr* had already announced after 9 p.m. that the Führer would soon speak over the radio.

[3] Fitz Gibbon, op. cit., pp. 167-168 and pp. 182-184.

[4] Jochen Klepper, *Unter dem Schatten Deiner Flügel: Aus den Tagebüchern der Jahre 1932-1942*, Stuttgart, 1955, p. 1154; see also R. Manvell and H. Fraenkel, *Doctor Goebbels*, p. 310.

[5] Zeller, op. cit., p. 291.

officers of the *Wachbataillon Grossdeutschland* in Döberitz on the out-
skirts of the capital. On the way to Döberitz Lieutenant Hagen saw a
General Staff car pass in which was an officer whom he took to be Field
Marshal Walther von Brauchitsch, the former Commander-in-Chief of the
Army. This was a fallacy, as Brauchitsch was not in Berlin on that day;
but as Hagen may have heard rumours of hostility to Hitler in the army
his suspicions were aroused. The Commander of the *Wachbataillon
Grossdeutschland* was a young major, Otto Ernst Remer, who had recently received the Knight's Cross from the hands of the Führer for his
valour on the Eastern front. Having attended Hagen's lecture, Major
Remer was, shortly after 4 o'clock, suddenly summoned to the office of
his superior, Lieutenant-General Paul von Hase, Commandant of Berlin
and one of the conspirators. He was asked to place his troops in a state of
immediate alert and was told that there had been an SS *Putsch* in the
Wolfsschanze and that the Führer was dead. His, Remer's task was to
completely seal off the governmental quarters in the *Wilhelmstrasse*. No
one, including ministers and high-ranking officers, was allowed to leave.[1]

Remer returned to Döberitz before carrying out these instructions and
ordered his troops to leave for Berlin. It was then that Hagen told him
he had seen von Brauchitsch in a staff car and thought there might have
been a military *coup*. He also suggested that immediate contact should be
made with Goebbels, the Gauleiter of Berlin. "Remer, who though at that
time not essentially a Nazi supporter, was yet very conscious of the
necessity of being on the winning side in any military revolt, at once
provided Hagen with a motor-cycle and ordered him to reconnoitre the
position, to visit the Gestapo headquarters and the Ministry of Propaganda and to meet him, Remer, at a given place and time." [2]

Lieutenant Hagen arrived at 20, Hermann Göring Strasse, wearing the
golden Party badge on his uniform. He was very excited, breathing heavily and insisted that he had to see Minister Goebbels on a matter of the
greatest importance to the State. Hagen's credentials were thoroughly
checked and it seems he had to force his way through to Goebbels' office.[3]
The Minister still had no idea of the revolt at the War Ministry in the

[1] J.W. Wheeler-Bennett, *The Nemesis of Power*, p. 655.

[2] J.W. Wheeler-Bennett, op. cit., p. 656. "With this motorcycle and the cry
of 'A military coup by Brauchitsch,' Goebbels' official whirled through the
city to the Ministry of Propaganda, into Goebbels' private house, to the Brandenburg Gate, to the City Headquarters (*Stadtkommandatur*), back to the
Ministry, and in the end brought Remer over to Goebbels' side and through
Goebbels got Remer to talk to Hitler on the telephone." Zeller, op. cit., p. 291.

[3] According to Semmler, op. cit., p. 133, who was, however, not at 20
Hermann Göring Strasse that afternoon, Hagen contacted Goebbels by telephone after 4 p.m. "Goebbels at first refused to speak to a complete stranger
claiming to be an official of the Ministry." At last he listened to him and then
saw from his room the guards surrounding his house. Von Oven, on the other
hand, who was working with Goebbels at the time, says that Hagen was
admitted to Goebbels' room and convinced him of the truth of his story
(op. cit., II, p. 75).

Bendlerstrasse, although he knew that the leading men there were under the misapprehension that the Führer was dead. When Hagen was announced Goebbels was busy making arrangements for the news broadcast requested by Hitler and disliked being interrupted. The Minister was first sceptical of Hagen's report that the *Wachbataillon* had been given orders to occupy the Government quarters and that there was a revolt in Berlin. But he quickly realized the truth of the story when he saw from the window of his room that soldiers were actually surrounding the house. Goebbels then ordered Hagen who vouchsafed for Remer's reliability and loyalty to the Führer, to ask him to come at once to 20, Hermann Göring Strasse. "Were Remer not there within a specified time, twenty minutes or half an hour, Goebbels would assume that he was either disloyal or held by force and would order SS troops to attack and capture the headquarters of the Berlin Commandant at No. 11 Unter den Linden." [1]

Being in uniform Hagen was able to leave the building, though the civilians Naumann and von Oven were not allowed by the troops outside to pass.[2] By that time all those in Goebbels' house were forced to realize that they were trapped. But oddly enough, the rebels had omitted to cut the vital telephone wires, thus enabling Goebbels and his staff to telephone all the time safely with the *Wolfsschanze* and various offices in Berlin.[3]

Meanwhile Hagen tried to deliver Goebbels' message to Remer. After some search he found out that Remer was with his superior, General von Hase, at his headquarters at No. 11 Unter den Linden. He tried in vain to reach him there, the orderlies and clerks preventing him from entering the General's office, where Hase was conferring with Remer. But he at least managed to pass on Goebbels' urgent message to two lieutenants of Remer's battalion who were waiting for their commanding officer.

The delay in Remer's appearance alarmed Goebbels who had made fruitless efforts to contact him by telephone. At two minutes before 7 o'clock, the time limit set by Goebbels, Major Remer appeared, tall, slim, sun-tanned, wearing the *Ritterkreuz* with oak leaves on the collar of his uniform. He had received Hagen's message, realised the seriousness of his own position and suspected a trap. He came therefore accompanied by twenty armed soldiers whom he placed in front of the house and in the hall and whom he ordered to fetch him out of the Minister's room by force if he had not appeared within an arranged time. Perhaps the exact course of this historic interview and the words exchanged by the two

[1] Fitz Gibbon, op. cit., p. 184.

[2] Von Oven claims that it was he who had drawn Goebbels' attention to the soldiers with hand grenades and machine guns roping off his house. Impressed by the seriousness of the situation, Goebbels then fetched a revolver from the drawer of his desk and asked his entourage to be prepared if necessary to sell their lives at the highest possible price (von Oven, op. cit., II, p. 78).

[3] Von Oven, op. cit., II, p. 78 f., and Semmler, op. cit., p. 133.

men will never be fully known.[1] (Major Remer's account of it, written several years afterwards, can hardly be called reliable).[2]

Remer informed Goebbels that he had come to arrest him. Goebbels, far from losing his self-control, inquired into the reasons: who had authorized this step? Remer replied that as the Führer was dead he was following an order from his military superiors. Goebbels told Remer that the position was different: Hitler had been only slightly wounded and would broadcast later that evening. Well aware of Goebbels' reputation as an arch manipulator of news, Remer accused him of lying. Then Goebbels had a brain-wave. Noticing Remer's Knight's Cross he asked him if this high decoration had been bestowed on him by the Führer. When Remer affirmed this, Goebbels asked him if he would recognize Hitler's voice if he heard it. Remer said he would. "However, with a last attempt at bluster, he threatened Goebbels that he would have no hesitation in shooting him were this a trap." [3]

In a few minutes, the connection with the Führer's headquarters was established. First Goebbels spoke to the Führer "explaining" the situation. Then Remer came to the telephone. Hitler asked him if he recognized his voice. "Yes, my Führer," came the delighted answer. "Do you believe that I am alive?" came the second question. "Yes, my Führer." Hitler ordered Remer to crush the revolt in Berlin with every means in his power in the shortest possible time.[4] He was to take orders only from Goebbels, from Himmler, whom Hitler had now appointed Commander-in-Chief of the Home Army, and from General Reinicke, a Nazi general then in Berlin. He also promoted Remer on the spot to the rank of Colonel. Afterwards Party writers endeavoured to romanticize this episode in order to "prove" the comparative insignificance of the plot, which they described, in line with the opening sentence of Hitler's broadcast, as the work of "a very small clique of ambitious irresponsible and at the same time senseless and criminally stupid officers." [5] Official propagandists were eager "to pretend that this Lilliputian rebellion had been crushed by a single officer with a handful of troops who were conscious of their duty." [6]

Certainly, the new Colonel had no doubts about where his duty lay. He did not lose any time, but acted with lightning speed. Making Goebbels' residence his headquarters, he lifted the blockade of the Government

---

[1] There are conflicting statements on the time of this important encounter. Semmler (op. cit., p. 134) talks of "five o'clock," but Remer in his later account, gives the time of the completion of the cordoning off of the Government quarters as six-thirty. Fitz Gibbon (op. cit., p. 184) dates it "a little after six o'clock" whilst according to Wheeler-Bennett, it took place "about seven o'clock" (op. cit., p. 656).

[2] Otto Ernst Remer, 20. Juli 1944, Hamburg, 1951.

[3] Fitz Gibbon, op. cit., p. 190.

[4] Zeller, op. cit., p. 280, and Fitz Gibbon, op. cit., p. 190.

[5] For the text of Hitler's broadcast, see Hamburger Fremdenblatt, 21 July 1944, and The Times, 22 July 1944.

[6] Fitz Gibbon, op. cit., p. 191.

quarter at once. Instead his troops occupied the office of the Commandant of Berlin at No. 11, Unter den Linden. He also contacted all the commanding officers of army units then in Berlin and put them under his control. Meanwhile, the company of the *Wachbataillon* was addressed passionately by Goebbels in the garden of his house and the "true facts" of the situation and of their obligation to the Führer were explained to them. Goebbels ended his piece with a *Sieg Heil* to the living Führer. Considerable time passed, however, before action was taken against the centre of the plot in the Bendlerstrasse. Remer maintained in his postwar account of the event "that it was only three or four hours later that he realized where this centre was." [1] According to one report, Remer wanted to attack the rebels at the War Ministry immediately, but Goebbels advised him against it, as the forces at the disposal of the plotters were still an unknown quantity. Kaltenbrunner, the Head of the Gestapo, who had come to Goebbels to seek advice, agreed with him that sufficiently strong forces should first be found to crush the rebels in the Bendlerstrasse. Moreover, Goebbels was anxious not to risk the life of Remer in such an enterprise, "who for the time being was irreplaceable from his point of view." [2] Eventually, reinforcements arrived from Rangsdorf and Döberitz. By about half-past-eight the tanks of the Krampnitz tank school, which for a time had been at the disposal of the rebels, were again under Nazi control. By nine o'clock Field-Marshal Erwin von Witzleben realized that the cause of the plotters was lost because its leaders, Generaloberst Ludwig Beck and Colonel Claus Schenk von Stauffenberg, were not in control of Berlin. The radio announcement at 9 o'clock, that Hitler was to make a broadcast later, had its effect. Soon afterwards, some junior officers at the War Ministry turned against their superiors whose revolt had proved abortive. Shots were fired, but apparently the crippled Colonel Stauffenberg was the only one wounded.

When at about 11 p.m. Oberleutnant Schlee and a detachment of Remer's *Wachbataillon* appeared at the War Ministry, there was no resistance. They were met by Generaloberst Friedrich Fromm, perhaps the most doubtful figure of that dramatic day, an opportunist who had risen on the crest of the Nazi wave but had lately realized that the tide was turning against the Hitler régime. In the early afternoon he had hesitated to back the plot hatched by his subordinates until its success was assured. When the coup in Berlin failed he set up a court-martial to try the major plotters. Four of them were executed at once in the courtyard, including Colonel Stauffenberg [3] and General Friedrich Olbricht. Beck, the former Chief of the General Staff, was allowed to put an end to his life himself.[4]

By midnight, a group of Gestapo officials with Kaltenbrunner and

[1] Op. cit., p. 190.

[2] Von Oven, op. cit., II, p. 80.

[3] Stauffenberg died shouting *"Es lebe unser heiliges Deutschland"* (Long live our sacred Germany): Zeller, op. cit., p. 259.

[4] When two attempts to kill himself were unsuccessful, an N.C.O. had to give him the *coup de grâce*: Zeller, op. cit., pp. 257-259.

Skorzeny entered the Supreme Command of the Army and stopped any further summary executions. A more terrible death awaited the surviving conspirators of the Bendlerstrasse now under arrest. This step was the logical result of the arrival of Heinrich Himmler in Berlin from Rastenburg at 8 p.m. with express orders and full powers from the Führer to crush the rebellion mercilessly. He may or may not have been disappointed to have found on arrival that Goebbels had taken charge of this task. In any case, Himmler went at once to 20 Hermann Göring Strasse, where he, jointly with Goebbels, set up an enquiry into the rebellion. They began at once with the interrogation of the arrested officers. Himmler, who was accompanied by his elderly Chief of Staff, SS *Obergruppenführer* Jüttner,[1] asked Kaltenbrunner to round up the conspirators and to conduct the investigation, whilst Skorzeny was to make the actual arrests.

That night Goebbels' house became a mixture of military camp and prison, in which quite a number of suspected officers were detained. The room of Goebbels' press secretary was crowded with generals, ministers, adjutants and other officers, most of whom were only too glad to discover that the *Putsch* was over and that anyway they had remained on the right side of the fence.[2]

During the night General von Hase, Generaloberst Hoepner, Police President Count Helldorf, Generaloberst Fromm, General von Kortzfleisch and others were taken by Skorzeny to Goebbels' house and appeared before the enquiry commission with Goebbels acting as unofficial chairman. Most of them were kept apart under guard in different rooms. They were treated well, even given wine and cigars, as long as their guilt was not yet established. Some of them left the house as free men, for instance General von Kortzfleisch, the superior of General von Hase, who was able to prove that he had not been involved in the plot. Generaloberst Fromm, the Commander-in-Chief of the Home Army, entered von Oven's office during the night giving the Hitler salute. We know little about his interrogation after midnight by Himmler and Goebbels, but his eagerness to explain his loyal attitude during the last twelve hours did not convince them and he was arrested by the Gestapo the next day.[3]

The interrogations provided many important clues and so did the massive documentary evidence discovered by Skorzeny in the offices of Olbricht and Stauffenberg. At one o'clock a.m. Hitler's speech was at last relayed over all stations. Though muddled it must have destroyed the last shadow of doubt in the minds of millions of listeners that the plot

[1] Von Oven, op. cit., II, p. 82.

[2] Among them were General Reinecke, a "political general" charged by the Führer with the indoctrination of the Wehrmacht and Generaloberst Stumpf, commander of the air force inside the Reich.

[3] See von Oven, op. cit., II, p. 83. Fromm appeared before the People's Court as late as February 1945 on a charge of "Cowardice". He was accused of having been afraid to inform the authorities of his previous knowledge of the plot. He was sentenced to death and shot in Brandenburg prison on 19 March 1945.

had miscarried. The fact that Goebbels felt unhappy and angry about the speech, as the Führer had in his opinion "struck quite the wrong note" was of little importance.[1]

The investigations in Goebbels' house went on until dawn. By then the excitement had died down and only a few guards remained in the hall. Colonel Remer and his staff had left. When at 4 a.m. the doors of Goebbels working room opened, the Minister and Himmler appeared still surrounded by adjutants and officers. Dr. Goebbels smiled radiantly. "Gentlemen," he explained, "the *Putsch* is over." He accompanied Himmler to his car and took leave of him with a long handshake. These two men, often rivals, may well have reflected how different their position might have been, had the *coup d'état* succeeded. Even at that late hour Goebbels was alert, talkative and pleased. He eagerly outlined what had happened to his closest subordinates, Werner Naumann, the *Staatssekretär*, von Oven and Schwäger, his adjutant. Placing himself on a little table in the corridor outside his office, a table adorned with a bronze bust of the Führer, he told them: "This was a purifying thunderstorm. Who would have dared to hope when the horrible news arrived early this afternoon that all this would end so quickly and so well. At times the situation looked more than threatening. This is now the sixth *Putsch* against the Führer which I have experienced. None has been so dangerous, but none has also been overcome so quickly as this one. Had the attempt on the Führer's life succeeded we would not be sitting here. I realize this completely. The fact that it did not succeed is nothing short of a miracle." [2] He went on to discuss the fortunate circumstances which had doomed the assassination to failure: the fact that Hitler had changed his place just before the bomb exploded; the circumstance that, as the Führer's Bunker was being repaired, the daily conference with Hitler had taken place in the guests' barracks. The same explosion in the Bunker would have destroyed the lives of all persons in it, and so on.

Seen from the plotters' point of view, the survival of Goebbels was most unfortunate and unlike the accidental circumstances at the Führer's headquarters, an event which could have been avoided. The arrest of Goebbels was quite possible in the early hours of the afternoon and, whilst it would not have decided the outcome of the *Putsch*, it probably would have had a tonic effect on the overt and latent anti-Nazi elements.

The plotters in the Bendlerstrasse were altogether too lenient in their treatment of their enemies; they detained them but did not shoot them. They were far from judicious in their choice of the officers whom they entrusted with important tasks, such as the arrest of Goebbels. General von Hase should have asked a more senior officer to carry out this job. "Since Goebbels was undoubtedly the most dangerous man in Berlin and was recognized as such, it would only have been sensible to send a platoon, composed of officers, if need be, to seize him between four and

[1] Von Oven, op. cit., II, pp. 85-86.
[2] Von Oven, op. cit., II, p. 86.

five o'clock." [1] As a German public prosecutor remarked some years later: "In the decisive phase of active resistance no mercy must be shown to those who hold leading positions in the régime and thus are defending their own crimes. For instance, as things were in Berlin on July 20th, short shrift should have been given to Goebbels instead of merely arresting him. . . . If Goebbels remained alive on July 20th, this was not due to weakness or lack of determination of the resistance fighters, but resulted from their inner decency." [2]

One may agree or disagree with this view, the fact is that in fighting a ruthless dictatorship one cannot be too particular in one's methods. Actually in the case of the conspiracy of the 20th July, it was much less a question of ethical, but of practical behaviour. Not only should a superior officer, fully *au fait* with the aims of the plot, have been sent to get hold of Goebbels instead of the politically inexperienced and untested Major Remer, but the conspirators should have seen to it that the telephone communications between Hitler and the outside world were destroyed at the earliest possible moment. But General Fellgiebel had in the first instance failed to blow up the communication centre at the Führer's headquarters,[3] and Goebbels could comment coldly afterwards: "It was a revolution on the telephone which we crushed with a few rifle shots. But just a little bit more skill behind it and the rifle shots would not have done the trick." [4] At least von Hase could have easily given orders to Major Remer to destroy the telephone lines at 20, Hermann Göring Strasse before tackling Goebbels himself. Allowing Goebbels and Hitler to converse by telephone was one of the fateful flaws in the preparation and execution of the plot. "Indeed, unrestricted undamaged communications were a vital factor in quelling the revolt." [5]

Once the nocturnal "inquisition" in his house was over Goebbels thought in professional terms, in terms of propaganda. Although he had been unhappy over Hitler's broadcast that night, he took over two points from it for all the subsequent propaganda interpretations of July 20th: first, the legend that only a very small clique of treacherous officers was involved and, secondly, the idea that the hand of Providence had miraculously protected the Führer. When Goebbels explained the events to his immediate subordinates at dawn on 21 July he may have believed his own peculiar theology. Though he described himself as "a sober and clear-

[1] Fitz Gibbon, op. cit., pp. 191-192.

[2] *Oberstaatsanwalt* Hölper in a discussion on "high treason" printed in *Die Vollmacht des Gewissens*, edited by Europäische Publikation E.V., Munich, 1956, p. 38.

[3] "One thing is certain", noted Semmler in his diary, "the group of generals and their helpers had carried out their plan and above all their preparations with astonishing carelessness and lack of foresight. Few telephone lines had been cut and they had made no provision against the possibility that Hitler might survive the explosion." (op. cit., p. 138).

[4] Ibid.

[5] J.W. Wheeler-Bennett, *The Nemesis of Power*, p. 643.

thinking man averse to all exaggeration," in this case he could only say: "This is a visible expression of Divine intervention. *Even the most hard-boiled realist must feel the touch of a supernatural fate. I am convinced we have indeed an acute case of historical idealism."* [1] God was visibly protecting Hitler. "An historical development which small-minded men try to interrupt, is being continued against all probability and human calculations through the intervention of a Higher Power." [2] God and Fate were identical for Goebbels' theory of the miracle that had happened. "Fate has apparently chosen him to bring our cause to a good end." Every revolt in the history of the Nazi Movement had in the past increased its strength and led to new successes. Therefore, rationalized the propagandist, "this *Putsch* too, the climax of a severe crisis would very soon be followed by a final victory." [3]

From giving thanks to Providence to deriding the unsuccessful conspirators was only a small step. Like Hitler before him Goebbels scoffed at "the unlimited stupidity" and "the crude dilettantism" of the insurgents. While Goebbels despised the hesitant bunglers, men like Beck, Olbricht and von Witzleben, for Count Stauffenberg he seems to have felt a grudging respect. "That Stauffenberg, it must be admitted, there's a fellow for you! One might almost feel sorry for his fate. What coldbloodedness, what intelligence, what an iron will! Incomprehensible that he surrounded himself with such a troop of blockheads. Had the attempted assassination succeeded, Stauffenberg alone could have been dangerous to us." [4] In spite of his excursion into theological mysticism, Goebbels was well aware of the consequences of a successful *coup*: "Not only the plotters on their part," he declared, "but also the people would have believed in a kind of Judgment of God. The consequences would have been incalculable. For in history only facts speak as evidence. And they are this time on our side." [5] The instructions to the press on how to treat the dramatic and dangerous events reflect the same attitude, only in a more simplified and crude manner. The editors had to play down the conspiracy and to invigorate German morale by making the most of its failure.

The *Tagesparole* (daily slogan) for the press of 21 July contained these points: "Out of the outraged and clamoring feeling of the German people and its embattled soldiers toward the criminal plot of a little clique in league with the enemy and toward the almost miraculous escape of the Führer, there must and will come a blessing on our battle and a greater strength for it. It is the job of the German press to give a great emphasis to these thoughts and feelings, through a full-fledged publicity campaign. With the lightning-quick and relentless breaking-up of the criminal intrigues, whose source in and close ties with an enemy power are

[1] The italics are mine. E.B.
[2] Von Oven, op. cit., II, pp. 86-87.
[3] Ibid.
[4] Ibid.
[5] Op. cit., pp. 87-88.

proven by conclusive evidence, a new wave of resolve and of inner confidence will seize the German people." [1]

The endeavour to utilize the failure of the *coup* for a bigger war effort and for greater national integration is well expressed in a supplementary press directive of the same day: "The answer to the frustrated attempt to deliver a stab-in-the-back to the fighting front must be the inner exaltation of the nation." [2]

In his first public comment on the events of July 20th, an address broadcast over all German stations on 26 July, Goebbels showed much of his skill in dramatic moralizing and in emotional appeal. He painted with a thick brush in black and white. That there was no acknowledgement of von Stauffenberg's qualities is not surprising. Instead, the attempt to remove the Führer was presented as a satanic plot foiled by a divine miracle. [3] The salient points in Goebbels' address were these:

(I) *What might have been: relief after the crisis.* When Goebbels had received the first news from the Führer's headquarters on July 20th of "the horrible crime," he confessed now that he had for a moment felt as though the ground were shaking under him. "In my mind I saw apocalyptic images of an historical possibility which would have resulted for our people, even for the whole of Europe, from a success of that cowardly and callous *coup*. Countless millions of decent German labourers, peasants, soldiers and brain workers would under those circumstances have met with a disaster which we cannot imagine to-day. A disaster let loose by the hand of a common criminal who, by order of an ambitious and unscrupulous little clique of adventurers and gamblers, had raised his hand to put an end to the life which is the dearest on earth to all of us."

(II) *The Miracle: God is with us!* Then, however, "an almost religious and reverent gratitude" had filled his heart. He had felt often before, but never so visibly and unequivocally as this time, that the Führer was fulfilling his work "under the protection of PROVIDENCE," that "no low conduct or baseness" was able "to prevent him from doing it or to delay him in it," that a Divine Fate ruling over all human events had given them this sign that his work could and would be completed, "however great the difficulties might be."

(III) *Character assassination of the plotters.* As was to be expected, Goebbels denounced the unlucky opponents in the sharpest terms, without even mentioning their names, apart from Count Stauffenberg. The

---

[1] Vertrauliche Informationen (V.I.), Nr. 150/44, 21 July 1944, 1. Tagesparole (Oberheitmann). The appointment of Himmler as Commander-in-Chief of the Home Forces had also to be duly emphasized by the newspapers. On the other hand, they were warned not to go beyond the factual account of the events as given in the Führer's broadcast. Any insults to the German Army or its officers in commentaries should be avoided.

[2] V.I., Nr. 151/44, 1. Erg. (first supplement) (Oberheitmann).

[3] For the text of Goebbels' speech, see *Hamburger Fremdenblatt*, 27 July 1944. An English translation is to be found in the Appendix to Semmler, op. cit., pp. 199–210.

plotters were presented not only as unmasked criminals, but what is perhaps worse, as incompetent officers. "A general, who only distinguished himself in warfare by his habit of sabotaging every great decision, is the head (Field Marshal von Witzleben). A Colonel-General who had to be replaced and pensioned off years ago, because he suffered from nervous breakdowns and weeping fits at the slightest burden, was intended to take over the civilian leadership. So he arrived in civilian's clothes, the only qualifications he had for his new office. (Colonel-General Beck). Another Colonel-General, who had been thrown out of the *Wehrmacht* quite a while ago on account of a cowardly retreat on the Eastern Front and had been sentenced to forfeit the right to wear uniform, had been chosen to lead the German Army (Colonel-General Hoepner). The criminal would-be murderer Count Stauffenberg played the role of political adviser.[1]

(IV) *No reflection on the army as a whole.* On 24 July Martin Bormann issued a directive to all Reichsleiter, Gauleiter and Kreisleiter which said: "It is the Führer's wish that in the treatment of the events of 20th July 1944, no one should allow himself to attack the Officer's Corps, the Generals, the nobility, or the armed forces as a body or to offer them insults. On the contrary, it must always be emphasized that those who took part in the *Putsch* were a definite and relatively small officer's clique." [2] One of the reasons for this order was a fumbling address given by Robert Ley at 7 a.m. on 21 July before a specially called meeting of the workers at the Siemens Works in Berlin. In this speech, which was subsequently broadcast with the "crassest idiocies" cut out by the angry men of the Propaganda Ministry,[3] he made the aristocracy responsible for the events of July 20th, calling them "dirty dogs of blue blood." Ley also talked of "the international ties" of that class. Alluding to Count Stauffenberg, without mentioning his name, Ley rattled on: "His wife was born in Poland, his sister-in-law is a Russian Bolshevik. There is the international plot. These are the 'liberators' of Germany. . . . These creatures must be destroyed."

In his broadcast Goebbels did not refer to the nobility, but took pains to say that there was no reflection on the army or on the profession of the soldier. "What appears material to me is that an attempted *coup* by a number of criminally ambitious climbers, who wanted to drag the memory of their fallen comrades into the mud and to stab the fighting front in the back, has been smashed by the Army itself. No soldier and no officer need feel ashamed to wear the same uniform as was worn by those

[1] For an objective account of the role, history and personality of these men, see J.W. Wheeler-Bennett, *The Nemesis of Power,* Part III, and the contributions by H. Krausnick and K. Sendtner in *Die Vollmacht des Gewissens.*

[2] For the text of Bormann's directive, see J.W. Wheeler-Bennett, op. cit., pp. 677-678.

[3] See the remarks in R. Semmler's diary, p. 140, and the text of the broadcast version of Ley's speech in the Appendix to it, pp. 212-213.

gamblers unfit to wear it. A profession is not discredited by harbouring some criminals in its ranks." [1]

(V) *Conspiracy with the enemy.* Like Ley, however, Goebbels attempted to expose the plot as a conspiracy with the enemy. The proof of this he claimed was fourfold:

(a) Constant references in the enemy press during the months preceding the *coup* that there existed opposition in Germany amongst certain generals; certain names had been mentioned, and these had now come to the fore in the *Putsch.* (b) An English bomb had been used in the attempt on Hitler's life. (c) The murderer (i.e. von Stauffenberg) was related to the English higher aristocracy. (d) After the first news of the attempt the English press had expressed the hope that the collapse of the Reich would result from it very soon. All in all, Goebbels declared, "it was indeed a plot from the camp of our enemy, though creatures with German names were prepared to carry it out."

2. MORE POWER FOR GOEBBELS

On the evening of 21 July Goebbels set out for the Führer's headquarters accompanied by some members of his staff and arrived there next morning. One of the proposals he put forward to Hitler was a change in the oath of the troops. The new oath should extend the loyalty from Hitler to his successor should he die. Another suggestion with which Goebbels seems to have had more success was that all soldiers cease giving the specifically military salute and replace it with the Hitler greeting. They were to stretch out their right arm instead of touching their cap. Hitler accepted this idea at once and Himmler issued an order.[2] According to Semmler, "Goebbels remarked that this was a first-rate move and rubbed his hands with satisfaction, a typical gesture whenever he feels triumphant." [3]

But these were trifles compared with the re-integration of the régime and of the war effort which Goebbels had in mind. He pressed for an

---

[1] Behind the scene Goebbels suggested that a reckoning with the nobility or the officer class, if at all necessary should be postponed until after the war. He took a similar line as regards the Churches. In both cases it did not seem expedient to him to act against groups or institutions at once. In an address to the Gauleiters at Posen in August, Goebbels declared it was not Hitler's intention at that time to launch a general attack upon the German army, upon the officers of the army, or upon the German nobility. In so far as it would prove necessary to attack the members of a class or of a profession, such action would be postponed "until the times were more suitable". (Fitz Gibbon, op. cit., pp. 219-220).

[2] Semmler, op. cit., p. 140 and p. 144.

[3] In the official DNB bulletin of July 24th no mention was made of Goebbels in connection with this order. It was said to have originated from the *Reichsmarschall* of the Greater German Reich, as Senior Officer of the German Armed Forces, (Göring) who had followed a request by all divisions of the Armed Forces.

intensification of total war and saw golden opportunities for himself. Far from well and suffering from mental blackouts, Hitler was probably only too willing to accept the ideas of Himmler and Goebbels. The Propaganda Minister took the view that "faults of leadership" were partly responsible for the attempt on the Führer's life. As Goebbels saw it, "there were two possibilities: one was to put an end to it all, but as this was a war to the finish," there was now "little chance of a successful approach to either of the principal enemies. The other alternative was to make a mighty effort to regain the military and political initiative. The last opportunity had now come to wage total war". Although its organization "at this late date would be a thankless and gigantic task, he would take the responsibility for it and guarantee to raise within three months a new army of about a million men." Though even the optimistic Dr. Naumann regarded that figure as humbug, Hitler was immensely impressed by it.[1]

This time, Goebbels declared confidently on his way home, Hitler had no choice but to grant him the far-reaching powers he had clamoured for ever since the spring of 1943. As he put it with scant reverence for the Führer: "If I had received these powers when I wanted them so badly, victory would be in our pockets to-day, and the war would probably be over. But it takes a bomb under his arse to make Hitler see reason."

The appointment of Goebbels as "Reich Plenipotentiary for the Total War Effort" on 25 July meant indeed a considerable triumph for him. Though he now exaggerated and glorified his earlier efforts to obtain such powers, it may be advisable in this context to consider them briefly. Goebbels had long felt frustrated by what he now called "the bureaucratic methods of Lammers, Bormann and Keitel."

After Stalingrad, Goebbels looking back alleged that he had received verbal orders from the Führer to take over the organizing of the war effort at home, but these had never been confirmed in writing. Soon after his famous Sport Palace speech of 18 February 1943 Bormann, on leave from the Führer's headquarters had visited him and congratulated him on it. Calling him "the herald of the war" he had stressed the Führer's confidence in Goebbels to carry out this important task. But weeks had passed by and nothing happened. When Goebbels enquired, he was at last told by Lammers that for the practical execution of the idea of total war some experienced experts were required who would form a committee with Goebbels on it. After a further few weeks, Himmler had issued a decree on the formation of a Committee of Three, but Goebbels was not included. Its members, the "Three Magi from the East," as Göring dubbed them ironically, belonged to different sectors of the regime: Martin Bormann was something of a super-clerk to the Party; Field Marshal Wilhelm Keitel, Chief of the High Command of the Armed Forces, and Hans Lammers, Head of the Reich Chancellery. Their backgrounds, too,

[1] Semmler, op. cit., p. 146.
[2] Op. cit., pp. 146-147.

were widely different: the ambitious Bormann had achieved his appointment as personal secretary to Hitler in April 1943; Keitel, nicknamed by some of his military colleagues "Lakeitel," was utterly servile and Lammers was a colourless career bureaucrat. All three, however, had one thing in common: they were all inclined to translate any mere passing phrase which the Führer might make into a decree.

They were further united by their wish to "manage" Hitler and keep undesirable competitors out of the field, Bormann, the most pushing of the three, was tenacious and possibly jealous of Goebbels' superior intellect. It was probably Bormann who carefully instilled into Hitler's mind the idea that Goebbels wanted to leave the execution of total warfare on the home front to the practical experts.[1] The Propaganda Minister alleged later that, when he had drawn Hitler's attention to this flagrant misrepresentation of his (Goebbels') aims, the Führer had been aghast, but this seems doubtful. In any case, in spite of his complaints Goebbels remained excluded from the committee. However much Hitler appreciated Goebbels' mental powers and agility, it is likely that, deeply immersed in his strategic problems, he was quite content to leave affairs on the home front to the willing tools of the "Committee of Three." Though Goebbels was not cut out for teamwork, in the spring of 1943 he seems to have joined in a counter-intrigue with Funk, Speer, Ley, and even with his old rival Göring, in order to reduce the power of the "Three Magi."

As early as 2 March 1943, Goebbels quoted in his diary Göring's description to him of Lammers as "a super-bureaucrat" and of Bormann as a person "pursuing ambitious aims."[2] A week later he complained of "Bormann's unduly bureaucratic conduct of Party affairs," adding with an eye on himself: "Bormann is not a man of the people. He has always been engaged in administrative work and therefore has not the proper qualifications for the real tasks of leadership."[3] Further talks with Speer, Ley, Funk and Göring followed. Göring discussed the existing division of power and gave them the benefit of his psychological reading of the Führer's mind by "pointing out that it is all-important to handle him the right way and at the right time to support one's proposals with the right arguments." "Unfortunately," commented Goebbels, "we were distinctly negligent in this respect whereas Bormann, Lammers and Keitel proceeded much more cleverly. That must be changed."[4]

Goebbels fumed, at least in his diary, against the machinations of Messrs. Bormann, Lammers and Keitel, of whom he regarded Bormann as the most authoritative and powerful and Keitel as "an absolute nonentity." "Unquestionably," he lamented in March, "these three intend to establish a sort of kitchen cabinet and to erect a wall between the Führer and his ministers. The Committee of Three is to be the instru-

---

[1] Von Oven, op. cit., II, pp. 90-91, entry of 25 July 1944.
[2] *The Goebbels Diaries*, p. 198.
[3] Op. cit., pp. 209-210, entry of 6 March 1943.
[4] Op. cit., p. 235, entry of 18 March 1943.

ment for putting this scheme into effect. Tis is simply intolerable." [1]

But as so often, Goebbels changed his mind quickly if expediency demanded it. Only two months later he criticized Göring and *nolens volens,* praised Bormann. After Hitler had discussed some necessary Party appointments jointly with Bormann, Ley and himself, Goebbels suddenly observed that "Bormann acted exceedingly loyally," and found that "the criticism levelled at him is mostly unjustified. When you think how many promises he keeps compared with Göring, the latter is undoubtedly at a disadvantage." Now Göring was declared to be no longer dependable.[2] As a German proverb has it, "When the rabble fight they soon make up." By the end of 1943 Goebbels seems to have realized that Bormann was in a strong position. Talking to him he found with great satisfaction that Bormann, too, was worried about German foreign policy and seemed to share Goebbels' criticism of Ribbentrop's rigidity.[3] Bormann's complaint that it was "so hard to get the Führer to make decisions" also found a sympathetic echo in the Propaganda Minister.

About that time Rudolf Semmler noticed "that Goebbels now admits to his intimates his weakness in his relations with Bormann. He will not allow the slightest ill-feeling to arise between himself and the head of the Party Chancellery. How inconsistent Goebbels can be! The day before yesterday he referred disparagingly to Bormann's moderate intellectual ability. He called him a 'primitive Ogpu type.' To-day he shows that he is frightened of him." [4]

After July 20th Goebbels was confident that his frustrations were at an end. He argued that until then the energies which he had awakened in the people since Stalingrad had been allowed to evaporate unused. Now he would no longer receive sneering letters asking: "What has become of your total war which you announced with a big mouth?" Now he would act and the mighty *Reichsleiter* would be subordinated to him. He felt invigorated and intoxicated by his new powers. Only a few days before the plot he had told Dr. Naumann that a combination of Himmler controlling the army with himself (Goebbels) in charge of civilian warfare might offer a last chance to turn the tide. But this would probably remain a dream. Now the dream had become a reality. Himmler had received the additional post of Commander-in-Chief of the Home Army and he himself had been given, as he expressed it, "dictatorial powers on the home front." Goebbels was jubilant and determined: "Now we shall get down to work. Now the opportunity will be ruthlessly seized. All the abuses and all the corruption that have embittered the German people for years will now be rooted out in their entirety." [5]

What were the tasks and the powers of the new Reich Plenipotentiary

1 Ibid.

2 Op. cit., p. 285, entry of 9 May 1943.

3 Op. cit., p. 442, entry of 30 November 1943.

4 R. Semmler, op. cit., p. 107, entry of 20 November 1943.

5 Von Oven, op. cit., II, p. 94, entry of 25 July 1944.

for the Total War Effort? The Führer's decree of 25 July on total mobilization, valid for the territory of the Greater German Reich and the annexed and occupied territories, described his task as "to see to it that all public activities are in line with the aim of total mobilization and do not take away any forces from the *Wehrmacht* or the armament industry." He would have "to re-examine the whole State administration, including the railways, postal services and all public establishments, institutions and undertakings with the purpose of freeing a maximum of manpower. To do this, men and material must be used rationally and to the last, tasks of lesser importance stopped or reduced, organization and procedure must be simplified." [1]

What was Goebbels' position with regard to the "Committee of Three"? The decree seemed to subordinate the competency of Lammers and Bormann to that of the new Reich Plenipotentiary, at least to force them to take orders from him. "Legal decrees and administrative orders" it declared will subsequently be issued by the responsible highest authorities of the Reich in agreement with the Reich Minister and Chief of the Reich Chancellery, Dr. Heinrich Lammers, and the head of the Party Chancellery, Martin Bormann. The latter will energetically support the measures which I have ordered by mobilizing the Party in accordance with the full powers he (Goebbels) has been given." [2]

As the future was to show, even such a definite order did not prevent Bormann from putting spokes in Goebbels' wheel and sometimes side-tracking memoranda to the Führer. But for the time being some co-operation was forthcoming. Goebbels threw himself into the new task with feverish activity, worked far into the night and even cut down the time for his meals to a minimum.[3] At once he created three new agencies: (1) a planning committee headed by Under-Secretary of State Dr. Naumann, to cope with all ideas and plans for the totalisation of war; (2) an executive committee under Gauleiter Wegener, to be responsible for carrying out the approved plans through decrees, orders and directives; and (3) a General Secretariat which was to coordinate the work of the two committees and to provide liaison between them and the Reich Plenipotentiary.[4]

In his important radio address of 26 July Goebbels assured the German public that he would carry out his new task without favour to any person or class. He hoped that he would bring to it the necessary imagination and art of improvisation, being extremely confident, however, that "there are so many possibilities for saving manpower that I am not worried about the success of my work." He pointed to his achievements in Berlin, which under his leadership had adopted a much simplified standard of living after the heavy air attacks had begun, "without having

[1] DNB text of the Führer decree, 25 July 1944.
[2] Ibid.
[3] Von Oven, op. cit., II, p. 97, entry of 27 July 1944.
[4] *Ibid.*

lost in energy, zest for work, belligerent spirit and even in a sense of humour." He flattered himself to have carried out "this comprehensive process of simplification without any dangerous friction." His experience in Berlin had shown to him "that we can be much simpler in our way of life if we want to be—and particularly if we have to be." [1] In other words, the living standard and distribution of manpower in the German regions especially exposed to enemy air raids were now to become the normal standard for the entire nation.

Goebbels did not hesitate to make capital out of his strengthened position and increased importance through his propaganda machine. The directive of 26 July interpreting the order of the Führer on the intensification of the war effort formulated the new task of the press as follows: "The press will present the Reichminister's address with great emphasis. The German people must gain the impression and the conviction that the great national effort which is the order of the day is bringing about a turning point in the war." [2]

An explanation of this directive made the revealing point: "Dr. Goebbels is to be presented as the champion of the total war effort. In this connection the memorable speech at the Sport Palace last year, in which he proclaimed the total war effort of the German people, should be recalled.[3] What he then demanded unstintingly has now gained the force of law. The personal achievements of Dr. Goebbels, as Reichminister, Reichsleiter, Defense Commissioner for Berlin, etc., guarantee that through the concentration of all the means at our disposal the greatest possible success will be achieved. Dr. Goebbels is laying the groundwork of a rational administration. A centralization and tight concentration of the executive machinery is essential for leadership as Dr. Goebbels understands it. This principle has been realized in his ministry and in his office as President of the City of Berlin." [4]

Soon the first measures under Goebbels' new powers were proclaimed. On 30 July the age of women liable for war work was raised to 50 years. On 10 August Goebbels issued five decrees, which he explained in a statement issued by the press and radio on the following day. Their aim was "to distribute the burdens as justly as possible" and "to make available manpower for armaments and war production and soldiers for the front." [5]

Six main measures would now have to be enforced:

1. All foreign domestic servants would be drafted into the armament industry, while German domestic helps were either to be employed in

[1] *Hamburger Fremdenblatt,* 27 July 1944.

[2] V.I. Nr. 154/44, 26 July 1944, Tagesparole (Oberheitmann).

[3] This refers to Goebbels' major address at the Sport Palace in Berlin on 18 February 1943. See above ch. 11, pp. 262-268.

[4] V.I. Nr 154/44, 26 July 1944, Erläuterung zu Punkt 1 der Tagesparole (Oberheitmann).

[5] *Völkischer Beobachter,* 12 August 1944.

war industry or sent to households in which they were urgently needed, particularly those with many children.

2. A goodly number of age groups of employees so far exempted from military service as "indispensable" in their jobs would be transferred to the front at once, or in the case of war workers, as soon as replacements had been trained.

3. Elements of the population which hitherto had little opportunity of taking part in the common war effort were to be used for work on war production in their homes.

4. Cultural life in all its branches was to be limited to essentials.

5. Further major measures to husband labour in the fields of administration, railways, postal services, and cultural life were in progress or in preparation.

6. All public functions unconnected with the war effort were to be cancelled. Those still indispensable should be carried out with a minimum display and be strictly confined to their purpose.[1]

Two weeks later, on 24 August, Goebbels gave details of the extent of these new measures and the sectors of the national economy affected by them. All theatres, music halls, cabarets and dramatic schools were to be closed by 1 September. The closing of all orchestras, music schools and conservatoria, except a few leading ones, would follow and in both cases the artists would either be called up to the armed forces or be transferred to armament work. Similar restrictive practices would be applied to the fine arts. In literature no further works of fiction or *belles lettres* were to be published, and many publishing firms were to be closed down. The number of newspapers would be reduced and some of them combined. All illustrated papers except two had to cease publication. There would be also considerable reductions in the number of schools, certain types would be closed altogether, while at the universities far-reaching measures would cut down the number of courses available and thus release a good many thousand students for armament work. Finally office hours in public administration and business were now uniformly fixed at a minimum of 60 per week, which would enable heads of departments and firms to release many members of their staff to war work. Apart from exceptional cases all annual leave would be cancelled until further notice. Any infringement of the new regulations would be regarded as sabotage and severely punished, in particularly serious cases with hard labour or death. When the whole German people devoted its full strength to final victory, pronounced Goebbels, then it was "entitled to demand that the law proceed with its full weight against elements sabotaging the measures for the totalisation of the war effort by indifference, slackness, lack of a sense of responsibility or even with intent." [2]

Nevertheless Goebbels was so fully aware of the hardships which these measures would impose on the people that he thought it expedient

[1] Ibid.
[2] *Völkischer Beobachter,* 26 August 1944.

to warn the press not to over-advertise them. "It is understood," declared a directive of 7 September, "that the expedients necessary for the total war effort are the most important internal political subject, which must be dealt with in editorials and commentaries. It should generally suffice for the newspapers to limit themselves to commentaries on these measures on the day they are announced, and in the issue for the following Sunday. In any case, editors must be sure not to let certain measures— namely, the ones that impose a heavy burden on the population—crop up again and again in their pages." [1]

Goebbels was too realistic to overlook the growing obstacles to a full acceptance of the idea of total war. At the beginning of September, when German troops had suffered heavy defeats in the West as well as in the East, Goebbels had to admit in an article that not the *Wunderwaffen,* but only the transfer of the last men and women to war work could change the precarious situation in favour of Germany. "In spite of all the progress made by modern war technology, this war is nevertheless a contest of nations in their totality. The idea that weapons will replace manpower more and more can perhaps claim the appearance of authenticity here and there in individual cases, but otherwise it belongs to the realm of fiction." Goebbels felt the concept of "total war" was "already so outworn that one almost has misgivings about using it any longer"—an odd confession from the man who had propagated this term for many months. Yet it still had "a categorical meaning." To Goebbels it was imperative to drive home to the people that the fate of the nation was at stake and that it was only logical to employ the total national manpower for this gigantic struggle. The question was simply how to achieve this in the most practical manner.[2] Hitler hoped to use these last reserves of manpower to replace the heavy losses of the old divisions at the fronts in the East and the West. In addition he intended "to create twenty to twenty-five new *Volksgrenadier* divisions, each eight to ten thousand men strong under Himmler's direction." [3] These infantry divisions were made up largely of office workers sent after a few weeks of intensive military training to the Siegfried Line.[4] Field Marshal von Rundstedt who had taken over command in the West from von Kluge after July 20th was determined to hold that line. As he said after the war: "I knew there was no winning the war, but I hoped that if I held

---

[1] V.I. Nr. 195/44, erste Ergängzung, 7 September 1944 (Oberheitmann).
[2] Article "Die Festigkeit unseres Vertraunes," *Das Reich,* 3 September 1944.
[3] A. Bullock, *Hitler, A Study in Tyranny,* p. 694.
[4] G. Blond, *The Death of Hitler's Germany,* New York, 1954, p. 79. The *Volksgrenadiere* who were proper soldiers, even if they had only a brief training, should not be confused with the People's Army (*Volkssturm*), a kind of Home Guard which wore no uniform, but only a special badge. They were only formed during the last months of the war and organized on the basis of the Party Gaue. For the text of Hitler's decree on the formation of the German *Volkssturm* of 25 September 1944, see *Dokumente zur Deutschen Politik und Geschichte,* vol. V, ii, pp. 504-505.

on long enough, a shift in political events might save Germany from complete collapse." It might be possible to negotiate with the Anglo-Americans, if they were delayed in their advance and worried by the Soviet descent upon Europe.[1] Goebbels entertained even more sanguine hopes in mid-December after the start of von Rundstedt's bold and desperate counter offensive in the Ardennes. He confidently expected that before the end of the year one and a half American armies in the field would be surrounded or driven into the sea.[2]

Goebbels furnished the necessary arguments. "More soldiers and more weapons," he declared in a radio talk on 27 October 1944, "this is our slogan. While the barracks are being filled with the young soldiers of the *Volksgrenadier* divisions, the German worker must show his most sacred zeal by putting sufficient quantities of the best weapons in the world into their hands." What the German armament industry was achieving, he described as almost a miracle. In spite of the uninterrupted enemy air terror against the homeland, the curve of production of weapons and munitions was constantly rising. In the factories and mines the hopes of the enemy were daily frustrated by the diligence and devotion of the German workers. They were producing good and solid weapons of a quality admired by the whole world, and in addition entirely novel weapons in all fields of warfare. "We can put great and greatest hopes in them for the more immediate and for the more distant future." A romantic promise which Goebbels hastened to water down by warning his listeners not to expect miracles from technological developments.[3]

During this final phase of the war Goebbels co-operated closely, though not always harmoniously, with Albert Speer, the able Minister for War Production. If we can believe his statement at the Nuremberg Trial, Speer had succeeded up to the autumn of 1944 in increasing the figures of armament production. He claimed that Germany had reached the highest figures of the war for munitions in August 1944, for planes in September, and for U-boats in December of that year. New weapons such as planes directed by beams, new types of U-boats, new anti-aircraft defences were expected to be finishd in a few months time, by February or March 1945, but the efforts in that direction failed. Fuel for all weapons had been reduced by 90% since the systematic attacks on centres of fuel production by enemy planes on and after 12 May 1944. The success of these air raids meant that the war was lost for Germany as far as war production was concerned, for even the best new types of tanks and fighters directed by beam were useless without fuel.[4]

---

[1] G. Blond, op. cit., p. 77 f.

[2] See R. Semmler, op. cit., pp. 168-169, entry of 16 December 1944.

[3] Speech by Goebbels, *Grossdeutscher Rundfunk*, 27 October 1944, B.B.C. Monitoring.

[4] IMT, vol. XVI, pp. 532-533. For Speer's position and attitudes during the last phase of the war see Webster and Frankland, *The Strategic Air Offensive against Germany, 1939-1945*, Vol. III, pp. 217-224.

Compared with the superiority of the United States war potential, completely unimpaired by air attacks, all the far-reaching measures for total war proclaimed by Goebbels were palliatives unable to affect the issue. Yet his efforts were not entirely in vain. After the war one of Goebbels' shrewdest critics, a member of his staff until the spring of 1945, said of his campaign for total mobilization: "How far did it succeed? Very far! It sounds hardly credible, but Goebbels' propaganda did keep the munition workers in the factories. In spite of the immense difficulties brought about by the air attacks, the intensity of the work still increased. The Gestapo terror would never have succeeded by itself in obtaining record figures just when the external ties of discipline began to loosen." [1] Indeed, it must be reckoned as a considerable success for Goebbels, but a success that came too late to reverse the overall trend of events.

Looking back to the dramatic events of July 20th six months later, Otto Dietrich blamed the abortive rebellion for the desperate military situation in which the German leaders found themselves by then. With this he conceded that its impact had been more far-reaching and fateful than had been officially admitted. In a confidential address to representatives of the German press in Berlin on 22 January 1945 Dietrich is reported to have said: "The most important event of the last year was the twentieth of July, which has had a very strong impact on happenings since then—perhaps stronger than people are ready to admit. Fortunately, no member of the press was involved. The connections between this twentieth of July and the military events that followed were frightening to think of. Even though much remained obscure, still the conspiracy had harmed the war effort immeasurably. Even the collapse of our invasion defenses was both directly and indirectly connected with the plot." [2]

This interpretation tending to prepare the way for a new "stab in the back" legend was at most a half-truth; however it throws significant light on the long-term shock effect the attempt of July 20th had on Hitler and his entourage, an effect which even Goebbels' plucky and determined efforts towards total integration could not eradicate altogether.

[1] W. Stephan, *Joseph Goebbels*, pp. 271-272.
[2] *Sonder-Informationen* (Oberheitmann). The information was conveyed in the form of a letter to his press colleagues by Dr. Metger and dated "Berlin, 22 January 1945". It was marked "Strictly confidential. For information only! Must be kept secret!"

CHAPTER 16

The Strategy of Consolation (1943-1945)

1. THE "HIGHER PERSPECTIVE"

DURING the last year of the war and of the Third Reich, Goebbels intensified the strategy of consolation he had developed since Stalingrad. He admitted some disagreeable facts and situations, but discovered others alleged to be favourable, which he suggested would obviously balance the former if not dwarf them.

As early as June 1943 Goebbels used the trick of "balancing" to the advantage of the German cause. Instead of talking of the recent defeats of German armies at Stalingrad and in Tunisia, he discussed the advantages and disadvantages of their earlier *Blitz* victories. He argued that the military victories of the Axis had produced only one disadvantage, namely that they had "followed each other too quickly and had thus become a matter of routine." Only since December 1941 had the Germans waged war in what Goebbels called the proper sense of the word, i.e. "with changing chances, the highest stakes and the possibility of temporary crises." Before that date they had not been threatened by any immediate war perils. They had been accustomed to begin a campaign as well as to end it in a relatively short time. This very fact had proved unfortunate, it had not only spoiled German but also non-German public opinion. From it resulted "the psychological difficulties" which they were encountering more frequently now.[1]

But this psychological (*not* military!) handicap was largely outweighed by another fact. It was, claimed Goebbels, "of immense material advantage" that the Germans had gained those early successes, because they gave them a chance of enlarging their war potential in time and through this of facing the forthcoming onslaught of weapons (*Materialsturm*) with quiet equanimity. For such a far-reaching *material advantage* in war one can put up with a *psychological disadvantage*. "Viewed in its entirety, in this respect, too, we are the absolute winners. Only that many do not know this or do not want to believe it." [2] Later, with a good deal

[1] Goebbels' article "Vom Reden und Schweigen", *Das Reich*, 20 June 1943; see *Der steile Aufstieg*, p. 334.
[2] Ibid.

of sophistry Goebbels 'discovered' some advantage even in the most desperate military situation. Towards the end of 1944, when the actual fighting had shifted to Western and Eastern provinces of the Reich, he admitted, "We are fighting with our backs to the wall," adding "this is, of course, very dangerous, but offers also a number of advantages. Our defence on inner lines saves us from almost insoluble difficulties which in their turn allow activities of our enemies only on a limited scale and only for a limited period." [1]

A few days after the publication of that article there began the last German counter-offensive in the West under General von Rundstedt. Its initial success delighted Goebbels. He was sufficiently optimistic to express the view to his staff that "before the end of the year one and a half American armies" would "be surrounded or driven into the sea. The rest of the British and American forces would then have to retreat, might even take flight to France." [2] In an article composed in the second part of December Goebbels felt justified in talking of "the slow, but definite restoration of German military power of defence and attack". Promptly a new aspect of "balancing" appeared. "The others," wrote Goebbels, "are superior through the wealth of their supplies, we through our national character and morale, toughness and power of resistance which makes us the first people of the world, and with it quite invincible." [3]

Two months later, at the end of March 1945, when neither Goebbels nor the man in the bombed street had much hope left, Goebbels drew a subtle distinction between the military and the political situation. He admitted freely that "there was no point in talking around the danger in which we find ourselves at the moment . . . We do not conceal that his [the enemy's] blows have hit us hard. Who would wish to deny it? But they have only wounded and not killed us. We are not beaten as he thinks." [4] The war, he admitted, had reached the peak of its crisis, both politically and militarily. But then he made up an ingenious balance sheet: "As far as its political aspects are concerned, they can be entered nearly exclusively to our credit and on the enemy's debit side. Its military aspects, however, operate almost equally exclusively in favour of our

[1] Article "Die entscheidende Runde", *Das Reich*, 10 December 1944.

[2] R. Semmler, op. cit., p. 168, entry of 16 December 1944. Goebbels felt flattered by praise from the Führer, who, if we can believe Goebbels, attributed half of the military success to him. His total war measures, Hitler declared, "had made possible the raising of the *Volksgrenadier* (People's Infantry) divisions and now it had been possible to surprise the enemy by throwing in fresh troops." (op. cit., p. 169). But most of them had not even machine guns. By Christmas the offensive had been stopped and early in January the German troops were thrown back to their starting point.

[3] Article "Kraft und Einsicht des Volkes", *Das Reich*, 7 January 1945. In this context Goebbels thought it expedient to amend a saying by his idol Frederick the Great that "God is marching with the stronger battalions" to "God will help us, if we help ourselves. He does not take the side of the strongest, but that of the bravest battalions".

[4] Article "An die Arbeit und zu den Waffen", *Das Reich*, 25 March 1945.

enemies and in our own disfavour. The one conditions the other. The enemies have no joint war-aims in common and the greater their military success, the more they will realize their lack and the artificiality of their unnatural coalition."

From this aspect Goebbels boldly deduced the existence of a political crisis in the enemy camp. The position seemed quite clear: "Whilst we have to cope with the effects of the *military* crisis, our enemies are fully occupied with keeping the effects of their *political* crisis under control. The decision of this war depends on nothing else but which side will lose the ground from under its feet first. That side will also lose the war and forfeit victory. This is the crux of the present war situation." [1]

A related line, often pursued by Goebbels during this period, was the argument that "the enemy is in the same boat". "The enemy, too," Goebbels pointed out, "is tired and exhausted. Therefore we are not worse off than he is." "The enemy, too," Goebbels wrote in September 1944, "has his worries. He has been waging this war for over five years and knows as well as we do what this means." [2] This comparison was more the expression of wishful thinking than of any concrete evidence and particularly so as regards the Soviet Union. At the end of October 1944 Goebbels remarked somewhat obscurely: "Though one should not praise the day before the evening, it seems to us as if the nearly inexhaustible manpower of the Soviet Union would become exhausted one day in the future." [3] Even as late as the end of February 1945, with the battle line coming closer and closer to Berlin, Goebbels still clung to this argument with considerable audacity: "Is the position of our enemies better than ours? By no means! The Soviet Union estimates its own losses as over fifteen million men. A military reverse will awaken her from her boldest dreams." On that scanty basis of fact Goebbels built a lofty structure of high moral symbolism: "Certainly Bolshevism carries the true work of Satan into this world, but in the end Lucifer, who has so often wanted to subject the earth to himself, is always thrown into the darkest abyss." [4] A more spirited argument of consolation was: "What the enemy did in the past, we can do now." And conversely: "Our former dangers are theirs today."

As Goebbels explained to the readers of *Das Reich* in September 1944, there were three nations who had to pass through a profound crisis in the war. [5] The crisis was a test of character, first for the British, then for the Soviet Russians and now, last but not least, for the Germans. "When we conquered the Atlantic coast in the summer of 1940 and

---

[1] Ibid.

[2] Article "Das höhere Gesetz", *Das Reich,* 24 September 1944.

[3] Radio address by Goebbels, 27 October 1944, see *Hamburger Fremdenblatt,* 28 October 1944.

[4] Radio address by Goebbels, "Die Bewährung in der Krise", 28 February 1945, B.B.C. Monitoring.

[5] Article "Unser Wille und unser Entschluss", *Das Reich,* 14 September 1944.

England lay open to the attack of our Luftwaffe, the testing time (*die Stunde der Erprobung*) had come for the British people. When we encircled Moscow in the autumn of 1941, the Soviet Union had to arouse herself to a last effort. Today, when our enemies throw themselves against our fronts with their wealth of men and material, fate is knocking at our own door." Strength through trial by ordeal, this is the common denominator in all these cases. "Even the lessons of this war prove that a danger overcome means additional strength and this will be the greater the greater the danger that has been overcome." "There is perhaps a deep historical symbolism"—speculated Goebbels—"in the fact that the decisive crises of the war do not stop short of any nation and that the war only gets its historical face according to which nations master them and which do not." A similar pattern of thought ran through an article, written five months later with the desperate leitmotif: "Nothing is irreparable, as long as the war is still on." [1] That the war was being fought on German soil Goebbels dismissed with one of his most far-fetched parallels. "It is not alone decisive," he assured his readers, "at what place the fighting takes place at this moment. We stood once at the coast of the Atlantic, before Moscow and Leningrad, but nevertheless, the enemy did not capitulate. He stands today at the Rhine and the Oder. Why should we therefore do at this stage what they refused to do then?" Of course, some Germans might point to the greater material resources of the enemy which enabled him to hope now for a complete change in the war-situation. But this argument was rejected by Goebbels. "Having no true ideals and a lower morale the enemy will fail. . . ."

The more hopeless the German situation became, the bolder and more artful were the images and metaphors which Goebbels employed to convince his dwindling public of the contrary. There was his famous comparison of the German people with the Marathon runner, conjured up two months before the end of the war. The runner had traversed 35 of the 42 km to be covered. "He has to continue to run at any cost, even if he should pass the post first fainting and with the applause of the crowd as a mere distant rustling in his ears. He is the victor, to him the laurel wreath will go." [2]

The image of the "Marathon runner" was part of a desperate attempt to persuade the people to see things in their "proper perspective". To restore a "sense of proportion" and to make people view the situation under a "higher" historical perspective is the thread which runs through Goebbels' propaganda efforts during the last few months of the war. At the end of February 1945, when Goebbels himself had long lost all hope,

[1] Article "Unsere Chance", *Das Reich*, 18 February 1945.
[2] Radio address "Die Bewährung in der Krise", 28 February 1945, B.B.C. Monitoring. Goebbels tried to substantiate this positive image by predicting in the same address that the enemies would have to face a revival of the German U-boat warfare "the extent of which they cannot really imagine" and also an intensification of the V-weapons, which they were already finding intolerable.

he declared it the purpose of his radio address to present to his listeners "an overall picture of affairs which during the last few weeks have developed so deplorably for us and to do so by viewing them from a due distance." [1]

Goebbels, the restless fanatic, now became the high priest of contemplative calm. It was an ideology of camouflaged despair, for off the stage he had long been convinced, as he told von Oven, that "the war cannot be brought either politically or militarily to a favourable, or even a tolerable end."[2] Was this "higher perspective" *faute de mieux* a deliberate device of Goebbels to mislead the masses? There is evidence that in the final months of the war Goebbels himself toyed with the idea of seeing things from a dispassionate height, *sub specie historiae*. In January 1945 he tried to "sell" this "higher perspective" to his wife who found it hard to acquiesce in the plans for a joint death for her children, her husband and herself. "In desperate situations like this," Goebbels advised her, "one has to take the standpoint of Frederick the Great who transferred himself in his thoughts to a distant star from which the events on our little planet look quite insignificant, however immensely important they appear to us." "You may be right," Frau Goebbels is said to have replied softly, "but Frederick the Great had no children." [3]

2. "PROVIDENCE IS ON OUR SIDE"

The "higher perspective", as propagated by Goebbels, implied at first a semi-religious and later a fatalistic belief in Providence. His "historical theology", with its emphasis on a specific mission of the German nation underwent considerable changes during the last sixteen months of the war. At the turn of 1943-1944 it had still sounded optimistic, more like a fanfare for a crusade than the measured rhythm of wise acquiescence in the decrees of Fate. "We are true fighters of God," Goebbels had announced then, "who have to carry out a high historical mission. . . . It has to be fulfilled in our time and through us, or mankind will perish." [4]

There was still the quasi-religious zeal of a Messianic mission which ignored all inconvenient facts; "To us look all the suppressed and tortured nations today, because they expect from us a New Order and the salvation of the world." [5]

Contemporary developments were presented as far as possible on the line of "Providence is with us". After the astonishing escape of Hitler on 20 July 1944, Goebbels had expressed his belief that the Führer was working under "the protection of Providence".[6] From the events of that day he had drawn the conclusion that "there is no misfortune and danger

[1] Ibid.
[2] W. von Oven, op. cit., II, entry of 7 February 1945, p. 236.
[3] W. von Oven, op. cit., II, entry of 21 January 1945, pp. 212-213.
[4] Article "Vor einem Neuen Jahre", *Das Reich,* No. 1, 2 January 1944.
[5] Ibid.
[6] See above ch. 15, pp. 344-346.

which in the end would not be overcome to our advantage".[1] "My belief
in the deep meaning of history," Goebbels had pronounced, "has found
a renewed confirmation on 20 July, materialist interpreters of history
may smile about it. . . . Fate has taken the Führer under its gracious
protection because it wants to keep him still ready for a great future. . . ."
It will be noted that the Providence of Fate rather than the Providence
of God is referred to.

At that time Goebbels, with the keenly desired appointment as Reich
Plenipotentiary for total warfare in his pocket, still hoped that the Nazi
régime might survive and conclude a compromise peace. By March 1945
these hopes to all intents and purposes ceased to exist. And yet the old
gramophone record of "Providence is on our side" continued to be
played. Goebbels wrote at the beginning of March 1945: "History does
not furnish any example where the courage of a people remaining unbroken to the last hour could in the end be overcome by crude force.
At the decisive moment that power of Providence which remains inex-
plicable to man interferes in time. It does not permit the suspension of
the eternal laws of history." [2]

Wishful thinking . . . Goebbels must have felt this himself, for he
added: "Such an argument is not as abortive as it might seem at first
glance." By then he no longer believed in the potency of the ideological
cocktail which he still presented to his public: "When the decision is
ripe, it will take place. In the last clash between spirit and crude force,
the spirit will be victorious." [3]

There was, however, one last occasion for his claim that he could
detect the Finger of Providence moving in favour of Nazi Germany.
It came with the unexpected news of the death of President Franklin D.
Roosevelt, on 12 April 1945. For a day or so Goebbels thought the tide
had turned. "My Führer," he remarked excitedly to Hitler over the
telephone, "I congratulate you, Fate has laid low your greatest enemy.
God has not abandoned us. Twice he saved you from savage assassins.
Death, which the enemy aimed at you in 1939 and 1944, has now struck
down our most dangerous enemy. A miracle has happened." And Goebbels added: "This is like the death of the Empress Elizabeth in the
Seven Years' War." [4] He really believed in the parallel with Frederick's
fate he had drawn so often. As an Austrian cook employed in a Berlin
household put it neatly, the same day, while crossing herself: "This is
the miracle that Dr. Goebbels has been promising us so long." [5]

Though he was exhilarated for a short time by the news, Goebbels
was soon forced to realize that the parallel with the death of the Russian
Empress Elizabeth in 1761 was faulty. Whereas then the event had indeed

---

[1] Goebbels' radio address on 26 July; see *Hamburger Fremdenblatt,* no.
205, 27 July 1944.
[2] Article "Der Zeitpunkt, der die Wende bringt", *Das Reich,* 11 March 1945.
[3] Ibid.
[4] R. Semmler, op. cit., entry of 13 April 1945, p. 192.
[5] Op. cit., p. 191.

proved a turning point in the fate of Frederick the Great and his Prussia, the death of the American President was making no difference to the final defeat of Nazi Germany. But for a moment Goebbels' propaganda could exploit an event certainly unwelcome to the Allies. "The War is approaching its end," Goebbels asserted in his radio address on 19 April, the eve of Hitler's last birthday, "the perverted coalition between plutocracy and Bolshevism is breaking up. The head of the enemy conspiracy has been smashed by Fate. . . . the same Fate which allowed the Führer to survive a July 20th upright and unhurt in the midst of the killed and badly wounded and the ruins, in order that he should complete his work, with pain and burdened it is true, but in the manner desired by Providence." Goebbels' fervent secularized theology knew no bounds: "As often before, God will throw Lucifer back into the abyss, when he stands at the very gates of power over all nations. Hitler, a man of truly secular greatness, will be his tool in this." [1] However, off stage Goebbels' impressions of the Führer in those days were definitely less romantic. "I regard it very likely for instance," Goebbels confessed to von Oven on 16 April 1945, "that at the moment the Führer is under a very unfavourable star. A person who has not seen him for two or three years would be shocked to meet him today." Not only had he aged a great deal but also his initiative, his ability to make blitz-like decisions with an intuitive certainty had gone. "Now he hedges and hesitates and postpones decisions which are disagreeable to him." The spell of Hitler's magic was breaking. The Führer himself had lamented to Goebbels several times: "It is as if things were bewitched. I have no more luck with anything." [2] A gigantic *va banque* game was approaching its close.

3. Utopia round the Corner

When the military situation deteriorates, the propagandist of any country faces a difficult situation. He should, on the one hand, radiate confidence in final victory and in a better world thereafter, but on the other he must make some concessions to the present "temporary" setbacks. He has to argue that capitulation is out of the question, but he has to create 'strength through fear' to avoid it. He may draw a rosy picture of the post-war world after a victory, but he will be inclined to supplement it by a grim survey of that world in case his side should be defeated.

In the last two years of the war Goebbels' propaganda oscillated between consolation through the conjuring up of a post-war elysium and an appeal to fear by way of grim descriptions of life in Germany and Europe under the enemy's yoke. Both images, that of the "Utopia round the corner" and that of "Europe as a slave camp" in the event of a

[1] Radio address by Goebbels "Unser Hitler", 19 April 1945.
[2] W. von Oven, op. cit., II, p. 296.

German defeat can often be traced together, but in the last few months the negative image prevailed.

To the very last Goebbels was a juggler with words, trying to intoxicate the masses by his vision of a happier, peaceful, attractive post-war world. Frequently he attempted to compensate for the bad news of today with the good news of a post-war life tomorrow. In a Sport Palace address in Berlin in October 1943, for instance, in which he discussed the "betrayal" of the Badoglio clique in Italy, declaring with grim determination "there is no going back for us, only a marching forward," he ended by building up a post-war *fata morgana*: "But one day it (the war) will come to an end with a last test of nerves and of strength. Then suddenly the curtain that is in front of the enigma of our time will be torn asunder, and the picture of a new world will open up before us. It will be the world of an august and fine peace into which we shall step from the bloody world of war." [1] This picture was further developed three months later, in Goebbels' radio address on New Year's Eve 1944. Victory, he declared, will open "the gate to the final liberty and independence of our nation. Ahead of us then there lies a road of peace and of free work, of rebuilding of our homeland and of a deep social happiness, based on the community of all. Indeed a goal which makes the burdens, sufferings and efforts of this war well worth-while." [2]

In July 1944, a few days before the anti-Hitler plot, Goebbels had devoted an entire article in *Das Reich* to his enticing post-war idyll, perhaps in order to divert attention from the invasion in the West.[3] A kind of verbal euphoria was displayed in his references to a better world: "For after the war all the nations wish themselves a state of calm and relaxation, of national progress, of a far-reaching social renewal, of economic prosperity and a secure happiness of the nations, and all this not at the expense of the happiness of other nations, but from their own strength."

As late as February 1945, when Russian troops stood at the Oder, the Americans at the Rhine and the turmoil of war hit Germany more than ever, Goebbels tried to soothe the nerves of his shocked and rather dwindling public by the sweet song of the garden of Eden in better days to come. "The furies of war rush above our heads in a wild frenzy. Some will look up to them frightened; they should know that one day the hour will come when their (the furies') hoarse shouts will be silent and once more the lovely tunes of a beautiful and happy peace will sound." [4]

When the Russian troops knocked at the gates of Berlin and plans for the suicide of Hitler and the entire Goebbels family were well advanced, Goebbels played the melody of sweeter days of peace to come on his battered flute for the last time. Now the familiar eulogy of the Führer

[1] See *Hamburger Fremdenblatt,* 5 October 1943.
[2] Radio address by Goebbels, 31 December 1943, B.B.C. Monitoring.
[3] Article "Was alle Völker sich wünschen", *Das Reich,* 16 July 1944.
[4] Article "Die politische Bourgeoisie vor der Entscheidung", *Das Reich,* 4 February 1945.

was related to the vision of a better tomorrow. The grimmer and more hopeless the reality of the present appeared, the more eloquence was devoted by Goebbels to the shape of the wonderful things to come both for Germany and for the rest of Europe. "After this war," he predicted, "Germany will blossom once more as never before. Her destroyed landscapes and provinces will be rebuilt with new and more beautiful towns and villages in which happy people will live. The whole of Europe will participate in this upsurge. Once more we shall be friends with all nations who are of good will. Together with them we shall let the deep wounds heal which disfigure the noble face of our Continent. In rich cornfields the daily bread will grow banishing the hunger of the millions who are needy and suffering today. There will be plenty of work and out of it as the deepest spring of human happiness there will come bliss and strength for all."[1] It was the wish-dream of a disappointed cynic, prepared to face the final consequences of the defeat of his cause. . . .

The Iron Curtain Predicted. Towards the end the glowing Utopia was more and more interspersed with sinister forebodings of the twilight of the Gods, the Nazi-Gods whose fall, it was suggested, Germany and Europe were unlikely to survive. For some time Goebbels harped much on the disaster in store for Europe should Germany be defeated. Following the significant Russian success near the Baranov bridgehead on 12 January 1945 which opened the road to the invasion of Eastern Germany, Goebbels made much of the allegedly worried voices of the Neutrals in Madrid, Lisbon, Stockholm and Berne. He painted a tragic picture of the German nation at its lonely post deserted by nearly all its allies in Europe, heroically defending its life and that of the whole civilized world. Germany and Europe, or Germany and the West, remained identical with Germany as the spearhead of true civilization: "Our success," pronounced Goebbels, "would mean a new beginning for mankind, our failure the end of the Occident."

The cold war of the post-1945 years was clearly anticipated by Goebbels, though in fact it did not become the hot war he wishfully predicted. Woe to a Continent at the mercy of the Bolshevist Hordes!

It is not generally recognized that it was Goebbels who first, in February 1945, coined the term of "the Iron Curtain", which he said was about to be clamped down on Russian-occupied Europe by the Soviet Forces.[2] This he did in one of his last articles designed to put the fear of Bolshevism into the minds of the Germans and the Western Allies. "Should the German people lay down their arms," predicted Goebbels, "according to Yalta the Soviets would occupy the whole of Eastern and South Eastern Europe, plus the largest part of the Reich. In front of these territories which, if one includes the Soviet Union, are gigantic, an iron curtain would come down at once behind which the mass-slaughter of the people would take place, probably amidst the applause of the Jewish

[1] *Ibid.*
[2] Article "Das Jahr 2000", *Das Reich,* 25 February 1945.

Press in London and New York." What remained would be only a certain "robot-type of man" *(Rohstoffmensch),* "a dull seething mass of millions of pauperized and desperate working animals who only come to know that news of the outside world which the Kremlin regards useful for its purposes." [1] It was the case of the Chief Propagandist of one totalitarian system denouncing another or of the pot calling the kettle black!

But what would be the position of the Western European countries? Goebbels predicted England's national potential would shrink and a British Labour Government would turn its back on Europe. In the U.S.A. Roosevelt's regime would come to an end by the defeat of his Party at the Presidential election of 1948 and a Republican, i.e. Isolationist, President would then quietly withdraw all American troops from Europe. A Third World War would lead to the Bolshevization of England and the Iron Curtain would come down on her, too. Even the silhouette of World War IV could be seen on the distant horizon. After having built up armaments with the sweat of millions of labour camp slaves in five years, Soviet Russia would begin to attack the U.S.A. But whatever happened, Stalin (secretly admired by both Hitler and Goebbels) would be the winner and Roosevelt and Churchill the losers.

The prophecy of the Iron Curtain was the climax of a propaganda trend pursued for some years intended to frighten the Western powers and to drive a wedge between Moscow on the one hand and London and Washington on the other. But at the beginning of that line stood Goebbels' stereotype of the "Trojan Horse". In November 1943 Goebbels had ordered his Propaganda Services at home and abroad to start an intensified new anti-Bolshevik campaign. It was to be "based on the military success of the Soviets" and was "to give Europe and our enemies the creeps". As Goebbels coldly remarked in his diary: "I hope especially to stir up Anglo-American public opinion against the war with this campaign." [2] He hoped against hope for a change of mind or a change of Government in the Western countries which would help to break up their alliance with Soviet Russia and thus lead to a compromise peace with Germany.

Much as Goebbels scoffed at the Western bourgeoisie he still wanted to imbue it with suspicion of Bolshevist aims and with fear of Communist actions. [3] He did this, or had it done by others, through the media of the radio and the press, but perhaps one of his most significant attempts to "enlighten" the West on these lines deserves special analysis. In the articles in question Goebbels continued his old technique of

[1] Ibid.

[2] *The Goebbels Diaries,* entry of 16 November 1943, p. 419.

[3] The German propaganda machine exploited to the full any criticism of Soviet Russian and Communist intentions and methods raised in neutral or Anglo-American countries, particularly the articles by Arthur Voigt in *The Nineteenth Century* (London) published in the spring of 1944. See W. von Oven, op. cit., entry of 3 June 1944, I, p. 276, and entry of 15 July 1944, II, p. 56.

"unmasking".[1] Just as he had previously "unmasked" the sinister mimicry of World Jewry or the intrigues of the treacherous clique "of the plotters of July 20th", so he now proceeded to expose the various devices used by the Kremlin and by Communism to hoodwink its short-sighted democratic allies in general and the Western bourgeoisie in particular. Bolshevism, Goebbels maintained, operated abroad with the tactics of a Trojan Horse. It undertook to achieve its aims outside the Soviet Union by adopting slogans of "a typical bourgeois democratic phraseology". Its tactics in countries like Finland, Rumania, Bulgaria were identical. First the Communists acquiesced in democratic governments with a few Communist members only. Gradually under the pressure of the mob this middle-of-the-road government changed its complexion to that of a left-wing government with the Communists in it in the ascendancy. Finally all non-Communist members were eliminated.

Though this analysis proved wrong in the case of Finland, altogether it revealed a shrewd insight into the Kremlin's *modus operandi*. Had he lived longer, Goebbels could have triumphantly pointed to the successful Communist manoeuvres in Poland and Hungary from 1945 to 1947 and in Czechoslovakia in February 1948. As it was, he made much of the precedent set by the Kerenski episode in Russia in 1917 from which, he lamented, the bourgeoisie in other countries had learned nothing. The bourgeois politicians, he argued, were too stupid to see through the Bolshevist tricks. Not only did they lack completely the intellectual weapons of defence with which to refute the Bolshevist ideology, but in Eastern Europe they had even entered into a relationship of military dependence on the Soviet Union which made it impossible for them to stop the rapid expansion of Bolshevism. There is sarcasm in Goebbels' angry voice: "It does no good to the leading political bourgeois strata, which a few months ago had reported with deep satisfaction the Soviet success against the German *Wehrmacht*, to try today to ingratiate themselves with the Red Tsars by declarations of loyalty. King Michael of Rumania has to bow before the mob of the Bukarest streets incited by the Soviets and surrender one part of his crown after the other until one day he will be a king without a country, just as Marshal Mannerheim of Finland is forced to extradite brave generals filled with the glory of the Finnish army to the Soviets as so-called 'war-criminals'." [2]

[1] See Goebbels' articles "Das Trojanische Pferd", *Das Reich,* 19 November 1944, and "Das politische Bürgertum vor der Entscheidung", *Das Reich,* 4 February 1945.

[2] While in the case of King Michael Goebbels' predictions were to prove more or less correct, this was not so in the case of Finnish "war-criminals". The "Finish War Guilt Trials" ended with sentences for all accused ranging from two to ten years, but though the Allied Control Commission, which had a Soviet Chairman, made its influence felt during the trials, there was no question of extradition of Finnish civilians or generals to Russia: See *The Realignment of Europe,* ed. by Arnold Toynbee and Veronica M. Toynbee, London, 1955, pp. 280-284.

The leading political strata of the countries "liberated" or overrun by the Russian armies, argued Goebbels, were struck with blindness, with a lack of political acumen. They foolishly let in the Trojan Horse, unaware that the Russians had hidden men and weapons in it, which would bring to an end the existing non-Communist regimes. Their leaders lacked not only intelligence, but also conscience. They were "weather-cocks" who "think they serve their own purposes and yet are heading for an inevitable downfall sooner or later." The German leadership, on the other hand, had nothing to learn in that field. On the contrary, as Goebbels puts it still in a semi-religious language: "Tortured Europe is waiting for the saving deed. This can only be carried out by us." [1]

In a subsequent article "The Political Bourgeoisie before a Decision" [2] this line was further pursued. The hint to Britain became distinct for, as Goebbels explained, the threatened annihilation of Europe by Bolshevism will extend to the British Isles. Goebbels painted black in black: "It is true that the cries of pain and misery of millions of tortured people in the countries now under the Kremlin's tyranny are gone with the wind, but the closer the monster of Bolshevism pushes itself to the heart of Europe the more threatening the accusations wil be against the instigators of this immense calamity." [3] It was not Germany, argued Goebbels, which was endangered in the first instance, for she knew how to defend herself. But what would happen to the nations that are facing the threatening peril without a defence? They cannot rely on England, for she is unable and unwilling to help. And as regards America, Europe did not matter, anyway, to her. There was only one conclusion to be drawn, Europe would be at the mercy of her henchmen, if she did not help herself. [4]

The further the Russian armies advanced towards and into Germany, the more acute, in Goebbels' shrill tones, became the danger—to the Western Allies. As he expressed it after the dramatic Russian breakthrough from the bridge-head across the Vistula near Baranov on 12 January 1945, which smashed the middle part of the German front and led to the quick occupation of Warsaw, Lodz and Cracow and to the invasion of Upper Silesia: "The English and American newspapers have all reason to put a few drops of bitterness into the cup of joy. Things are not as simple as if victory would be equal to defeat and defeat equal to victory. According to British accounts the Soviets have thrown 200 divisions into the mass attack in the East. The largest part of our armed forces is at the Eastern front. . . . According to reliable reports they themselves [the Anglo-American forces] have about eighty divisions for the fight in the West. What would happen to them if the German divisions in the East should suddenly cease to exist? If the two hundred attacking

[1] Ibid.
[2] *Das Reich,* 4 February 1945.
[3] Ibid.
[4] Ibid.

divisions of the Soviets would in a relatively short time face the eighty British and American divisions in the West? If the Kremlin would suddenly—and this possibility cannot be entirely dismissed—remember its old aim of the Bolshevization of Europe as a preliminary step to the Bolshevization of the world, and if Stalin would throw the tatters of the Atlantic Charter at the feet of Messrs. Churchill and Roosevelt?" [1] Goebbels denied, of course, the anticipated allegations of enemy propaganda that he "tried to fish in troubled waters and to sow discord between the partners of the enemy coalition".[2] He also refuted the idea, that he was "begging the enemies for an understanding" (of the hard-pressed German situation). In fact, he seems to have hoped sometimes even then that the Hitler régime could still profit from the rifts and stresses in the enemy coalition. His moods and hopes varied a good deal. . . . "The quarrel in the enemy coalition," he remarked privately on 30 January 1945, "forces us to continue the fight until there is a break in the camp of our enemies and we yet get off with a black eye, or until. . . ." He did not finish the depressing part of the sentence.[3]

4. "To set an example for Posterity"

Only a week later he gave up all hope. "The Minister," noted W. von Oven on 7 February 1945, "has in these days come to the conclusion that it is now definitely too late to exploit a discord between the Allies to our advantage. For that we are already too close to the abyss. Things should never have gone as far as this." He was convinced that "no favourable or even tolerable end of the War" could be achieved. "We have no other alternative but to perish decently, in order to give posterity an example and prove that nothing has been left untried to save Germany, and with it Europe, from Bolshevization." [4] Perhaps the last sentence gives us a clue to the continuing of the "Fear of Bolshevization" motto in German propaganda during the remaining three months of the war. Probably Goebbels felt he had to adhere to it as long as he was at liberty to write and speak, and perhaps he also did it with a view to the post-Nazi situation in Europe.

On 23 February, in an article "The Year 2000"—based on alleged American reports that the Big Three had accepted a motion by President Roosevelt at Yalta that Germany should be occupied until that year [5]—he admitted that nobody could predict the distant future. He proceeded, however, to reveal the near future as determined by Stalin's ruthless

[1] Article "Unausgesprochene Perspektiven", Das Reich, 29 January 1945.
[2] Ibid.
[3] W. von Oven, op. cit., II, entry of 30 January 1945, p. 227.
[4] W. von Oven, op. cit., II, p. 236.
[5] There is no evidence to this effect. See W.H. McNeill, America, Britain and Russia, Their co-operation and conflict 1941-1946, London, 1954, pp. 547-551.

plans. "Though his dream of power is fantastic and absurd, if we Germans should not cross it, he would undoubtedly make it come true".[1] Goebbels used this as a peg for a grim description of the "Iron Curtain" in Europe in the case of an Allied victory. He still asserted with undeterred bluff and as a matter of course that this would not happen. "We carry the world on our shoulders and we do not despair. In the year 2000 Germany will not be occupied by her enemies, but the German nation will be the spiritual leader of civilized mankind." [2]

Thus Goebbels with despair in his heart continued to pursue the old theme of Allied disunity, playing the same gramophone record over and over again. The steadily advancing Allies were depicted as disunited and confused. "There is not a single world problem," he declared contemptuously early in April 1945, "in which they have been able to establish unity of their views. Their programmes only agree in their wish to annihilate the German Reich and to extinguish the German people. But even as far as this problem is concerned they are pursuing fundamentally different views and methods. Each of them would like to snatch from the others as much as possible of the hoped for booty." [3] But by then Goebbels' voice was hardly listened to any longer. He had to admit that "many a heart begins to waver and to tremble" and that there was "a kind of lethargy with slack and weak characters, fatigue and apathy with people particularly hard hit by the war, doubt and hopelessness with faithless hearts worn out and made spineless by the hard times." Germans were now disinclined to believe Goebbels' blood-curdling descriptions of the revengeful, devilish enemies. "The one side will decimate and destroy the German people by shots through our necks and mass deportations, the other by terror and famine." For the Propaganda Minister had now to warn his public: "It would require more than a good-natured [German] *Michel* to believe that things would be only half as bad. It would be worse than bad, for us, if we should put the matter to a test." [4]

To the very end Goebbels stuck to his anti-Bolshevist propaganda guns. This was natural, particularly as it was the Russian troops who approached Berlin first and fought for its conquest. Goebbels issued his last public statement not as Propaganda Minister (whose Ministry lay in ruins), but as Gauleiter and Town President of Berlin. The incessant concoctor of facile but clever perspectives had then a very concrete problem on the door-step of his city. In his last two proclamations to the Berliners of 22 and 24 April 1945 the old feverish and dramatic note of "unheard-of events", of decisions of world-wide importance can once more be detected. Theory and practice, realistic private insight and desperate public bravado clashed now more than ever in the mind

[1] Article "Das Jahr 2000," *Das Reich*, 25 February 1945.
[2] Ibid.
[3] Article "Kämpfer für das Ewige Reich", *Das Reich*, 8 April 1945.
[4] Ibid.

of the Minister of Propaganda. On 21 April Goebbels held his last Minister Conference with his staff. Although only twenty to thirty people had gathered in the badly damaged film hall of Goebbels' villa in the Herman Göring Strasse that morning, the Minister addressed them as if it were a mass meeting in the Sport Palace. He was in a bitter mood and attacked and attacked—first the old German officers and "reaction" and later the entire German people. He accused them of cowardice: "What shall I do with a nation whose men do not fight any longer even when their wives are being raped?" The German nation had failed. "In the East they run away, in the West they prevent the soldiers from fighting and receive the enemy with white flags." [1]

But these galling words, which implied also a failure of the Goebbels propaganda machine, were of course not included in the last two proclamations to the Berliners by Gauleiter Goebbels of 22 and 24 April. In the first he admitted that the Bolshevists had reached the exterior defence lines of the capital: "Through this Berlin has become a frontier-town." After giving detailed emergency instructions to the people for the defence by barricades, etc., Goebbels declared it as a matter of course that he and his collaborators, his wife and his children would remain in the besieged city. He once more struck his anti-Bolshevist note, and made a strong appeal to the fear motive. "The Soviets wish to establish a régime of terror in Germany which is beyond our imagination. They are without any restraint in their fury of annihilation against everything that is German. There must be no weakness and no softness against this onslaught of the Mongols. We are now waging a war without any mercy against those who rape German women or want to send them into the brothels of the Soviet front, who torture and want to murder our children, liquidate millions of men by shooting them in the neck and to drag the remainder as working slaves into the Concentration Camps of Siberia." [2]

The second and final proclamation stressed even more the desperate but holy crusade of defence against the Bolshevist hordes, la guerre à outrance: "The fights in the outer districts are swaying to and fro. They are fought by attackers and defenders with the greatest bitterness. The losses of the Bolshevists in men and material are exceedingly high. Even the Moscow press must admit today that the resistance met by the Soviets in Berlin is unrivalled in history." Echoes of Stalingrad, a last flicker of the heroic and historically unique resistance theme!

It was only fitting that Goebbels' last Proclamation of 24 April should end on the note struck by Nazi propaganda ever since the invasion of Russia by Germany had begun at dawn on 22 June 1941: " I need not stress particularly that it is and will remain our ardently desired aim to free Berlin from the Bolshevik enemy of the world and to preserve it

[1] Hier spricht Hans Fritzsche, Zürich, 1948, pp. 28-29.
[2] DNB Presseschreibfunk (Inland) and Reichsprogramm (Nord), 22 April 1945, B.B.C. Monitoring.

from annihilation. Bolshevism in the Reich capital—this would mean a terror without end. I am convinced that the leadership and the people of the Reich capital will succeed in their common efforts to throw back the new onslaught of the Mongols. Important forces for the support of the defenders of Berlin are about to be led against it. Until they arrive, we will have to pull together all our strength and courage, in order to resist the enemy. Our hearts must not waver and not tremble. It must be our pride and our ambition to break the Bolshevist mass onslaught which is surging from the East against the heart-land of Europe at the walls of the Reich Capital".[1]

False promises and futile admonitions! A week later Russian troops entered the ruins of the Reich Chancellery and discovered in the garden the bodies of Joseph Goebbels, his wife and their six children.

In his "Political Testament", signed in the Bunker on 29 April, Hitler had designated Goebbels Reich Chancellor under Grand Admiral Doenitz as Reich President. But in an "Appendix to the Führer's Political Testament", written on the same day, Goebbels felt obliged to explain to the world and to posterity why he could not accept. "For the first time in my life I must categorically refuse to obey an order of the Führer. My wife and children join me in this refusal. Otherwise—quite apart from the fact that feelings of humanity and loyalty forbid us to abandon the Führer in his hour of greatest need—I should appear for the rest of my life as a dishonourable traitor and common scoundrel, and should lose my own self-respect with the respect of my fellow citizens; a respect I should need in any further attempt to shape the future of the German nation and State.

"In the delirium of treachery which surrounds the Führer in these most critical days of the war, there must be someone at least who will stay with him unconditionally until death. . . .

"In doing this, I believe that I am doing the best service I can to the future of the German people. In the hard times to come, examples will be more important than men." [2]

As Goebbels, propagandist to the last, could no longer influence the hopeless present, he was determined to remain at least a symbol and an exemplar for a future nationalist Germany. Undeniable courage, cynical realism and cool calculation led to the decision to follow his Führer in death.

[1] *Drahtloser Dienst* (*Nord*), 24 April 1945, B.B.C. Monitoring.

[2] Goebbels "Appendix to the Führer's Political Testament", was made available at the Nuremberg trial. For an English translation see H.R. Trevor-Roper, *The Last Days of Hitler*, London, 1947, pp. 202-203. This remarkable book also covers the last days of Goebbels and his family in Hitler's Bunker.

PART V

Aspects and Attitudes

CHAPTER 17

Denouncing The Jews

WITH Goebbels anti-Semitism was both an obsession and a target of adroit and ruthless propaganda ever since he had become a rabid nationalist in the early nineteen-twenties.[1] There existed much traditional latent anti-Semitic prejudice in the circles of the German bourgeoisie from which Goebbels sprang, while at the universities many student groups and associations excluded Jews from membership and some subscribed to a definite anti-Semitic doctrine.[2] But though some German students looked down on Jews their anti-Semitism had not yet taken on the aggressive and absolute forms of the later National Socialists. Goebbels' anti-Jewish attitude began as the hatred of an outsider and as a self-appointed spokesman of the dispossessed towards a prosperous minority. The Jews were physically repugnant to the hero of *Michael*, Goebbels' one and only novel, who observed, "when I see one of them I feel like vomiting". Goebbels' cold contempt for the Jews might well have been rooted in a feeling of inferiority towards a group which he regarded as both uncannily successful and utterly alien. It ended with the fanaticism of a man who told himself and millions of others daily that the Jews were a pest which had to be eliminated. But personal feelings were of secondary importance to Goebbels compared with the calculated drives of the propagandist who saw in the constant spreading of an anti-attitude the guarantee of more and more power for the Nazi *élite*. As was shown earlier,[3] Goebbels had developed the technique of anti-Semitic imagery to an effective art during the years of opposition. He had transformed a harmless Jewish police chief into the half sinister, half ludicrous figure of the eternal Jew.

[1] See above, ch. 1, pp. 9 ff.
[2] From the extensive analytical literature on modern anti-Semitism two books should be mentioned here as they throw considerable light on the historic roots of pre-Nazi anti-Semitism in Germany: Eva G. Reichmann, *Hostages of Civilisation*, London, 1950 (German edition: *Flucht in den Hass*, Frankfurt a.M., 1956) and Adolf Leschnitzer, *The Magic Background of Modern Antisemitism. An Analysis of the German-Jewish Relationship*, New York, 1956.
[3] See above, ch. 2, pp. 34-39.

If one considers, even briefly, the phases and methods of Goebbels' anti-Semitic propaganda in the years of his Ministry, the continuity of his anti-Jewish attitude should be kept in mind; it grew in intensity but never changed basically. "I took up the war against Jewry in Berlin in 1926," Goebbels wrote in his diary at the end of August 1941, "and it will be my ambition never to rest or stop until the last Jew has left Berlin." The elimination of the Jews not only from Berlin, but from the whole of Germany, nay, from most of Europe was an aim towards which Goebbels and Hitler worked during the entire span of the Third Reich with the certainty of somnambulists and the resourcefulness of demonic tacticians who often varied the means but never lost sight of their ultimate goal of mass destruction.

On 1 April 1933 the Hitler Government organized a boycott of Jewish shops, doctors and lawyers by the SA in protest against the "atrocity and boycott campaign" which Jewish organizations in London and New York were said to have carried out against the new régime in Germany. This first official anti-Jewish measure of the Hitler Government came only a few days after the grandiose "Day of Potsdam" on 21 March where the joint presence of President von Hindenburg and of Chancellor Hitler was presented to the nation as a symbol of the alliance between the old Prussia and modern National Socialism. As Hindenburg disliked the anti-Jewish campaign Hitler and Goebbels had to be wary and to move slowly. Yet Goebbels' address in Berlin on the day of the boycott, though relatively moderate in tone, already contained many of his later more violently expressed anti-Jewish arguments.

First there was the idea of the international power of Jewry which had turned against the Third Reich. To this was added the slogan of collective responsibility, the argument that the German Jews were held responsible for what the Jews abroad had done: "If they announce to-day" pronounced Goebbels, "that they could do nothing when their kin in England and America dragged the German national régime in the mud, then we can do nothing when the German people takes it out of them." [1] This threat of "taking it out" of the Jews for what they were alleged to have done, became a recurring theme in Goebbels' anti-Semitic articles and broadcasts. It is significant that nine years later, when Goebbels ordered the mass arrests and shootings of Berlin Jews as a precautionary measure after the assassination of Heydrich in Prague, he used exactly the same phrase of "taking it out of them" (*sich an hinen schadlos halten*). The Jews in Germany, Goebbels insisted, could thank their odious co-religionists abroad and such fugitives from Germany as Einstein for being called to account by Germany on "a strictly legal basis".

A third point made by Goebbels on this occasion, and on many others

[1] Address by Goebbels in Berlin, 1 April 1933, *Frankfurter Zeitung*, 2 April 1933. Reprinted under the heading "Wider die Greuelhetze" in his *Revolution der Deutschen*, pp. 154-161. The quotation is on p. 157.

to come, was his attempt to present the National Socialist anti-Jewish measures as nothing but the result of sharp unjustified Jewish provocation.[1] A fourth feature in Goebbels' speech to recur frequently in later years was the element of threat. If during the next three days the Jewish atrocity campaign abroad ceased, he declared, the Government would be prepared to restore normal conditions of life to the Jews, but if not, the boycott would be renewed "in such a way that it would destroy German Jewry". It was for the Jews to take heed.[2]

Then, and many times later, Goebbels took great pains to assure his listeners that the anti-Jewish boycott was the will of the people. Although the Government was demanding restraint and discipline from them, in carrying out the boycott it was following the people's own wishes. "The people will stick with us through thick and thin!" Goebbels asserted. "The people understand us. If the leadership of the National Socialist Party had not organized the boycott, it would have arisen from the people themselves." [3]

1. WORLD JEWRY OR "COMMUNISM WITH THE MASK OFF"

Between 1935 and 1938 Goebbels' anti-Semitic campaign became more and more identified with his anti-Bolshevist drive. In fact, in many of his speeches and articles the two were practically identical. This was the period in which the Russian show trials, the sensational purges of Soviet Generals and prominent Communists like Zinoviev, Kamenev, Bukharin, Rykov, Yagoda caused a world wide sensation and, at least in the eyes of the West, seriously weakened the Soviet régime.

To many liberal observers in Western countries the Bolshevik and National Socialist systems were both totalitarian and therefore had many features in common. In August 1935 the London *Times* made this point in a leader entitled "Two Dictatorships".[4] It emphasized that the recent developments in Russia with their trend towards a system based on nationalism, State capitalism and partnership between peasants and urban workers bore a marked resemblance to many features of the Third Reich. In both countries propaganda and secret police, whether GPU or Gestapo, ensured "that no heretical discussion openly takes place, that there shall be no opposition party". Both countries had "the same censorship on art, literature and, of course the press, the same

---

[1] "We haven't curled a hair on their heads, nor done them any wrong. In return, they kindle boycotts against us in London and New York and incite the world press against Germany. We were far too easy-going, far too soft-hearted. Now they challenge us to battle, well then, we shall pick up this gauntlet." *Revolution der Deutschen*, pp. 158-159.

[2] Op. cit., p. 160. "Jews are now in a position to think better of it."

[3] Ibid.

[4] *The Times,* 7 August 1933.

war on the intelligentsia and the massed display of arms, whether in the Red Square or the *Tempelhofer Feld*." [1]

This outspoken article provoked Goebbels to a reply in his address before the Party Congress in Nuremberg in September 1935 on "Communism with the mask off". Goebbels found the *Times* writer "naive and misdirected" and complained that his mistaken judgments were the result of "the profound hatred in literary circles throughout the world of National Socialism and its practical constructive work in Germany". [2] The Minister then proceeded to offer a "true" picture of Bolshevism as a "grandiose attempt to overthrow civilization". Its theory was attractive but its practice was poisonous. In fact, its reality was "terrible and forbidding". If it takes a thief to catch a thief,—reasoned Goebbels—it also needs a propagandist to expose the tricks of the trade employed by a rival propagandist. [3] Bolshevism was based on the principle that the end justified the means and did "not stop at anything or anybody."

Goebbels painted a grim and frightening picture of execution and starvation, of persecution and godlessness in Soviet Russia. He also "revealed" the sinister machinations of the Comintern in many countries and finally asked who were the men "behind the scenes of this virulent world movement . . . the inventors of all this madness?" The answer was, of course, the Jews. It was they who had discovered Marxism and who were now at the head of Marxist movements everywhere. He insisted that "only in the brain of a nomad could this satanism have been hatched." With vehement denunciation Goebbels provided a long list of German and other Jewish Communists and Socialists ranging from Ferdinand Lassalle to Rosa Luxemburg and Bela Kun. By amassing names and alleged atrocities of countless Jews Goebbels hoped to unmask Communism and to impress on the world that it was the Führer who had rendered it a signal service by setting up "a barrier to halt world Bolshevism against which the waves of this vile Asiatic-Jewish flood break in vain". [4]

By identifying the Jews with Bolshevism Goebbels attacked two targets of Nazi aversion simultaneously. In doing this he hoped to justify the ever increasing anti-Semitic measures of the régime in the eyes of many Germans not previously anti-Semitic, and also to influence Western public opinion which did not share the hatred of the Jews, but was frightened by the spread of Bolshevism. Goebbels posed as the master

[1] Ibid.

[2] Joseph Goebbels, "Communism with the Mask off", speech delivered in Nuremberg on 13 September 1935 at the Seventh National Socialist Party Congress, Berlin, n.d., p. 8, (text in English).

[3] "The fact that, in order to carry out its aims, Bolshevism uses propagandist methods which are perceptible only to those who have experience in such things and are entirely accepted in good faith by the average citizen make this Terror International extraordinarily dangerous for other states and peoples." Op. cit., p. 11.

[4] Op. cit., p. 33.

detective who with passionate skill unmasked the hidden hand of Jewish Bolshevism.

A year later with the outbreak of the Civil War in Spain and the intervention of both the Fascist Powers and Soviet Russia, "Jewish Bolshevism" had become even more the main bogey of National Socialist propaganda, its World Enemy No. 1. Again it furnished the topic of Goebbels' address at the following Party Congress in September 1936. Once more satanic Bolshevism was assailed as "the dictatorship of inferiors. It reaches power through lies, and maintains power by force." [1] Goebbels argued that bourgeois Europe did not understand the clever and calculating propaganda methods of Bolshevism. It was blissfully unaware of the fact that the question of Bolshevism was one of the survival of Europe itself.

Again Goebbels devoted many words to the role of the Jews in Bolshevism. He claimed that it could be discussed frankly only in the Third Reich for in other countries it was as dangerous to call Jewry by its name as it had once been in Germany. [2] Alleging that the Jews were the only leading stratum of the Soviet Union Goebbels employed an ingenious argument in order to parry a possible objection. At the sensational trials in Russia a number of Jews had, in fact, been involved who, like others, confessed their counter-revolutionary designs and were sentenced to death and executed. Goebbels must have reasoned that Western democrats could argue this proved a lack of homogeneity, of a solid front among the Jews, that it showed Jew devouring Jew. To this argument Goebbels had a smart answer by describing every discord inside Bolshevism as "more or less a family quarrel among Jews". The recent executions in Moscow meant simply "that Jews had shot dead Jews from a greed for power and a will to annihilation". [3] It was Germany's mission, he insisted, first to expose the danger of Jewry inside the country and then to the whole world. [4] Presenting Stalin's purges as essentially a Jewish affair and without mentioning Stalin's name, he claimed that the triumvirate which had carried victory in "the quarrel of the Jews" and now ruled over the Soviet Union, consisted of the three "ghetto Jews" Yagoda, Kaganovich and Litvinov. [5]

Piling quotation upon quotation Goebbels highlighted licentiousness and exploitation rife in Soviet Russia and the aggressive militarism of

---

[1] *Der Bolschewismus in Theorie und Praxis,* Rede von Reichsleiter Reichsminister Dr. Goebbels auf dem Parteikongress in Nürnberg 1936, Berlin, p. 5.

[2] Op. cit., p. 8.

[3] Goebbels declared it a mistake to think of the Jews as being always united. Their unity only lasted while they were a threatened minority inside a different racial majority. When all powerful, as in Soviet Russia, "the old rifts in the Jewish camp" became apparent—an argument in flat contradiction to his usual claim of the conspiratorial oneness of all Jews in all countries. Op. cit., pp. 8-9.

[4] Op. cit., p. 9.

[5] Op. cit., p. 14.

the Bolshevist system. Atrocities and cruelties perpetrated in the Spanish Civil War were described as the exclusive work of the agents of the Comintern. A long list of shocking cases of murder and the savage fury of the Red mob in Spain was cited partly from foreign right wing newspapers and partly from special reports Goebbels claimed to have received from Germans living in that unhappy country. There was no mention of the misdeeds committed by the Nationalists. Details which had reached him on the murder of priests and the rape of nuns were beyond imagination, declared Goebbels. He showed equal concern over the role of children participating in Red massacres and over the destruction of famous monasteries. Invaluable treasures of art, he lamented, had been destroyed and the intellectual *élite* of the country had been annihilated. Against this sinister background the merits of National Socialism shone in all their purity, with even a tinge of the miraculous.[1] Adolf Hitler came forth like Dürer's Knight, *sans peur et sans reproche,* his head erect, carrying the great banner of European civilization in his strong hands and calmly facing all the threats and attacks of world revolution.[2]

Goebbels returned to his main theme in 1937. The Jew was the incarnation of everything evil in Bolshevism, he explained to the thousands assembled at the Party Congress in Nuremberg.[3] The Propaganda Minister concentrated all his energy on unmasking the dark machinations of Bolshevism, he indulged in such trick phrases as "in a democracy, the heads are outvoted by weight of numbers, in a dictatorship heads are cut off with the blade of the guillotine! The result is the same here and there: the heads are lacking, and the Jews are able to establish the dictatorship of terror and money over the leaderless masses."[4] Goebbels now visualized contemporary history as a clash between two worldwide forces. There was going on "a crude cheeky attempt at establishing Jewish world domination" against which, however, a healthy reaction was taking place in some countries. By 1937 the issue of the holy crusade against the enemy of mankind was no longer only one of "Germany awake!" It had taken on European proportions.[5] On this occasion Goebbels' fanatic obsession reached a new peak of intensity as with all the power of his lungs he pronounced parasitic Jewry a world enemy and the main carrier of the Bolshevist disease.[6]

[1] Op. cit., p. 35.

[2] Op. cit., p. 36.

[3] *Völkischer Beobachter,* 10 September 1937, "Dr. Goebbels enthüllt die dunklen Pläne des Bolschewismus".

[4] Ibid.

[5] *Völkischer Beobachter,* 12 September 1938, "Die grosse Kongressrede des Reichspropagandaministers".

[6] "But Europe must see this danger and realize that we shall not be slow to point it out. Unfrightened, we will point to the Jew as the inspiration, originator, and the one who profits from these frightful catastrophes." "Look, there is the world's enemy, the destroyer of cultures, the parasite on the peoples, the son of Chaos, the incarnation of evil, the stew of corruption, the shapeless demon who brought about the decay of mankind." Ibid.

At the following Party Congress in September 1938 when everything was overshadowed by the German-Czech crisis, Goebbels attacked the Western democracies more bitterly than Bolshevism. Nevertheless in exposing the mendacity of world democracy he denounced a fictitious unity front of Democracy and Bolshevism against the authoritarian national states. Alleging wilfully that Bolshevism and Western Democracy had the same military organization and even the same economic system he went on to explain that they shared the same negative views on "Germany's defensive measures against the Jews". The Propaganda Minister also poked fun at untrue reports in the foreign press that many Jews had recently died in German concentration camps.

In the twelve months between the Party Congress of 1938 and the outbreak of the Second World War Goebbels made much of the International of the enemies of the Reich with world Jewry as its most vicious partner, though using the word Bolshevism less and less. It was this International, he declared, that incited the world to war. In an article "War in Sight", published in February 1939,[1] he asserted that wire-pullers behind a world-wide campaign of incitement against peaceful Germany were "the circles of international Jewry, international Free-masonry and of international Marxism". While this denunciation of a tripartite secret force can hardly be called original—already under the Second Empire and during the Weimar Republic German Nationalists had decried "the black, red and golden International", the sinister hand of Catholicism, Socialism and Jewry—the constant repetition of Goebbels' formula was bound to have its effect. There were no Freemasons left in Germany in 1939 and only a few camouflaged Marxists, but there still existed thousands of Jews in the Reich, a displaced and persecuted minority. Every anti-Semitic word coming from Goebbels' whiplike tongue was a further step towards their moral assassination and final elimination from the Third Reich.

2. GOEBBELS AND THE POGROMS OF 10 NOVEMBER 1938.

As we have seen, Goebbels used the trick of presenting anti-Semitic measures he wanted to see implemented as a request from the people, as genuinely desired by the *furor teutonicus*. This technique of justifying sharp anti-Jewish measures as the result of a spontaneous outburst of the masses can be detected in his ambiguous and dishonest attitude during and after the anti-Semitic excesses in November 1938. On the morning of 7 November 1938, Ernst von Rath, Third Secretary at the German Embassy in Paris was seriously wounded by five shots from the pistol of a seventeen year old Polish Jew, Herschel Grynszpan (Grünspan). Von Rath, a career diplomat from a well known German family, died two days later. When interviewed by the French police, Grünspan said he

[1] Ibid.

had wanted to avenge his parents who had been persecuted in Germany.[1]

Hitler and Goebbels were determined to exploit this dramatic incident to oust the Jews from the German economy and to make life as hard as possible for them. A few hours after the shots had been fired in Paris "spontaneous" acts of violence were already foreshadowed in a DNB statement issued to the German papers. The editors were instructed to give fullest prominence to the news item on the front page. "In your own commentaries you will point out that the Jewish plot must have the most unfortunate results for the Jews as well as for the foreign Jews in Germany. In a language that makes clear the outrage of the German people it can be stated that the clique of Jewish emigrants who formerly put the revolver in Frankfurter's hand are also responsible for this crime."[2] The newspapers were not slow in carrying out these instructions.[3]

It so happened that on 9 November, the day on which von Rath succumbed to his wounds, the traditional anniversary reunion of the Party leaders in honour of the abortive Hitler *Putsch* of November 1923 took place in Munich. All the Party organizations were represented. In the evening the Party veterans assembled in the Old Town Hall. Hitler was present, but contrary to his usual custom, did not address the comrades. It seems that before or during the dinner Hitler gave orders to Goebbels that severe repressive measures should at once be carried out against the Jews. After Hitler had left, Goebbels made a speech. The exact words are not available, but indirect evidence points to its having been "calculatedly ambiguous. It followed the same lines as had the press campaign of the previous few days. It was an invitation to anti-Jewish violence, but not explicitly so. It came from the highest Party level, but somehow left the initiative with the lower Party echelons. It asked for action, but did not specify what kind of action, or who was to carry it out."[4] A confidential report issued later by the Supreme Judge of the Party on the drastic events which followed the anti-Semitic demonstrations during the early hours of 10 November, clearly shows that Goebbels' deliberate vagueness was interpreted by the Party leaders present in the Munich Town Hall in one way only.

The report declared that "the oral instructions of the Reich propaganda leader were understood by the whole party leadership to mean

---

[1] Helmut Heiber, "Der Fall Grünspan", *Vierteljahrshefte für Zeitgeschichte*, vol. V, no. 2, April 1957, pp. 134-172, and Lionel Kochan, *Pogrom, 10 November 1938*, London, 1957, pp. 40-47.

[2] ZSg. 102/13, DNB Rundruf, 7 November 1938; David Frankfurter, a German émigré, had shot and killed Wilhelm Gustloff, the leader of the German National Socialist organization in Switzerland in 1936.

[3] The *Deutsche Allgemeine Zeitung* wrote of the "most severe consequences that must be expected to follow for the Jews in Germany", while the *Völkischer Beobachter* asserted that "the German people" were "entitled to identify the Jews in Germany with this crime". Jewry could be certain that the shots fired in Paris would not go unpunished. See L. Kochan, op. cit., pp. 41-42.

[4] Op. cit., p. 52.

that outwardly the party was not to give the appearance of having elicited the demonstrations, while in reality it was to organize and carry them out. The instructions so interpreted were thus immediately passed on— a long time before their release by teleprinter [1]—by most of the party comrades present, who telephoned them to their local groups." [2] The result of Goebbels' grape-vine instructions was a haphazard wave of looting, robbery and burning of Jewish property. Up to 11 November 191 synagogues were set on fire and 76 others completely demolished. The number of destroyed Jewish shops exceeded one thousand. About 20,000 Jews were arrested and most of them taken to Concentration Camps. The number of these killed given in Heydrich's report to Göring of 11 November as 36 with another 36 badly injured was very likely a crude understatement.[3] Goebbels did his utmost to present the sordid events as a result of popular fury. The next morning the *Völkischer Beobachter* reported that "in the entire Reich spontaneous anti-Semitic demonstrations" had developed and that "the deep indignation of the German people had also expressed itself in strong anti-Jewish actions".[4]

Goebbels himself wrote on 12 November in the same vein, but definitely denied that the Government had had anything to do with it: "They announce that the spontaneous reactions of the German people have been carried out by organized groups. How little these scribblers know about Germany! Think of how the demonstrations would have looked if they had been organized!" Goebbels insisted that this reaction to the cowardly murder of von Rath had neither been organized nor prepared, but had erupted spontaneously from the nation.[5] In fact, crimes committed during the action such as looting and rape were at once put outside the jurisdiction of the ordinary courts and transferred to the Supreme Party Court. Its findings three months later, which were made accessible to the higher Party circles only, contained implied criticism of Goebbels' ambiguous instructions to Party leaders. "Even the public knows, to the last man, that political actions such as that of November ninth are either organized or carried out by the party, whether or not this fact is admitted. When several synagogues burn down in the same night the affair must be organized somehow, and only the party could organize it." [6]

There is a sharp discrepancy between Goebbels' malevolent glee in the ransacking of Jewish shops during the *Kristallnacht* and his brazen denials of them in public. "One of the most outstanding features of the

[1] This took place after midnight between 12:30 a.m. and 1:40 a.m.

[2] International Military Tribunal, vol. XXXII, p. 21, 3063-PS.

[3] Report by Heydrich, Chief of the Security Police to the Prussian Ministerpräsident Göring of 11 November 1938: IMT, vol. XXXII, pp. 1-2, 3658-PS.

[4] *Völkischer Beobachter,* 11 November 1938.

[5] "Der Fall Grünspan" by Reichminister Dr. Goebbels, *Völkischer Beobachter,* 12 November 1938.

[6] Report of the Supreme Party Court to Göring of 13 February 1939: IMT, vol. XXXII, p. 27 (3063-PS).

anti-Jewish actions which took place in the last few days," Goebbels wrote on 12 November,[1] "is the fact that, although it is true that demolitions did occur, nowhere was there any plundering."

This denial was in glaring contrast to what he said to his officials off the record about the same time: "There the man in the street in Berlin was at least able to equip himself nicely. You should have seen how they enjoyed it—ladies' furs, carpets, valuable material, everything was to be had free of charge. The people were enthusiastic—a great success for the Party." [2]

Foreign correspondents who had witnessed the attacks on Jewish temples and shops had immediately despatched to their papers lengthy "stories" of burning synagogues, demolished shop windows, beaten Jews and Nazi gangsters moving through the streets and shouting *"Juda verrecke!"* ("Wipe out the Jews!")[3] Yet on the next day, 10 November, Goebbels unexpectedly appeared at the daily conference for foreign correspondents in his Ministry and told them that all the accounts that had come to his ears about alleged looting and destruction of Jewish property were "a stinking lie. Not a hair of a Jew had been disturbed": a story impossible to swallow for a prominent foreign journalist like Louis Lochner, who with his wife had "spent hours the night before watching frenzied Nazis at their work of destruction." [4]

The "indignation of the people over the campaign of incitement *(Hetze)* of International Jewry against national Germany" was used as a pretext for introducing further severe anti-Semitic measures. Goebbels proved one of the most eager and cynical participants in a conference on these measures which was convened by Göring and took place in Berlin on 12 November.[5] When Göring announced that a special fine of one billion Marks would be imposed on the German Jews, Goebbels urged him to make sure that none of them could escape from it. He also wanted to do away with synagogues altogether. All those damaged or partly burned should be demolished by the Jews themselves, who should be made to pay for this. Jews must also be forbidden to visit German theatres, cinemas and circuses.[6] Goebbels at once issued a decree to that effect in his

---

[1] "Der Fall Grünspan", *Völkischer Beobachter,* 12 November 1938.

[2] W. Stephan, op. cit., p. 182. See also Heydrich's report to Göring of 11 November: "In many cities looting of Jewish stores and business offices took place. In order to prevent further looting, in all cases drastic measures were taken. As a result 174 people were arrested": IMT, vol. XXXII, p. 1.

[3] L. Lochner in his Introduction to *The Goebbels Diaries,* p. XXVI.

[4] Op. cit., pp. XXV-XXVI.

[5] IMT Document PS 1816; see Leon Poliakov and Josef Wulf, *Das Dritte Reich und die Juden,* Berlin, 1955, pp. 75-80 and pp. 346-348. Some directives then issued to the press on the preparation of the public for these forthcoming anti-Jewish measures have been discussed above, ch. 4.

[6] *Das Dritte Reich und die Juden,* pp. 346-347. At the conference Goebbels declared it no longer possible for Jews to sit beside Germans in shows, cinemas and theatres.

capacity as President of the Reich Chamber of Culture.[1] He insisted on racial segregation and barriers everywhere. There should also be special compartments for Jews in trains. Once these were occupied they would not be entitled to any seats but would have to stand in the corridors. Jews should be banned from German spas, sea-resorts and convalescent homes and also confined to special benches in parks, labelled "for Jews only." [2]

While such vindictive measures appealed to Goebbels' blind hatred and sadistic instincts, he constantly described them as a natural outcome of the people's fury. Addressing the personnel of the Winter Help organization in Berlin on 13 November he praised the anti-Semitic steps which had been taken "for according to the conception of the National-Socialist state, the actions of the government must be in direct accord with the will of the people." The official report of the German News Agency alleged that "the stormy applause that rose over and over showed how well the measures described in detail by the Minister correspond to the unanimous will of the German people." [3] In other words, the will of the more active and fanatic members of the Party was simply identified with that of the voice of the people. The National Socialist audience applauded the ruthless Propaganda Minister when he summed up the position as he wanted the masses to see it: "The Jew Grünspan has announced that he wanted to strike a blow at the German people. This people has now, through its government, made a worthy reply." [4] The medieval crusaders had claimed it was God's will which they followed. Goebbels substituted the people for God. "The Jewish question," he predicted, "will in a short time find a solution satisfying the sentiment of the German people. *The people want it this way, and we only carry out the people's will.*" [5]

3. ANTI-SEMITISM ABROAD—A PROFITABLE INVESTMENT

Goebbels was always convinced that the spreading of anti-Semitism abroad would be very much in the German interest. He was confident that the German model would foster in each of the Western nations a big

---

[1] It was dated 12 November 1938. See *Völkischer Beobachter,* 14 November 1938.

[2] Such restrictions were legalized by the *Polizeiverordnung über das Auftreten der Juden in der Öffentlichkeit,* of 28 November 1938. *Reichsgesetzblatt* 1938, part I, no. 189, p. 1579.

[3] See *Frankfurter Zeitung,* 14 November 1938, Report "Die Massnahmen gegen das Judentum."

[4] Grünspan did not make such a statement.

[5] Ibid. The italics are mine. E.B. Not all the prominent Nazi leaders agreed with Goebbels. When Rudolf Hess visited the Munich publisher Hugo Bruckmann and his wife on 23 December, "he left no doubt that he thoroughly disapproved of the action against the Jews". He claimed that he "had implored" the Führer "to stop the pogrom. Unfortunately his efforts had been in vain. Hess pointed to Goebbels as the real instigator." *The von Hassel Diaries, 1938-1944,* p. 32.

anti-Jewish movement which would prevent their governments from waging war against National Socialist Germany.[1] Moreover, those groups might obtain power themselves and put an end once and for all to the "decadent" democratic system. Top boots, shirt, uniform colours and swastika were adopted by most of the fascist groups going abroad. "In Sweden the *Svenska Nationalsocialistika Partiet* demonstrated under flags adorned with the swastika just as fervently as, in Denmark, the *Danmarks National Socialistika Arbeyder Parti,* in France the Breton fascists, in England the "Imperial Fascist League," in Latvia the "Thundercrosses," in Hungary the *Magyar Nemzeti Szocialists Part* (Hungarian National Socialist Party), in Rumania the "Iron Guard." [2] There were other groups such as the *Action française* in France which, while not actually pro-German or Swastika-minded, favoured an anti-democratic, authoritarian and anti-Semitic régime.

When Léon Blum, a Jew, became French Prime Minister in June, 1936, Goebbels hoped not unrealistically for a new anti-Semitic wave in France. Though he had no first-hand knowledge of that country, he was aware that its various extreme right wing organizations from the older *Action française* to the younger *Croix de Feu* of Colonel de la Rocque, to Pierre Taittinger's *Jeunesses Patriotes* and Coty's *Solidarité française,* taken together "provided all the elements of propaganda, private army and mystique which in Germany, Italy and elsewhere produced Fascist revolutions." [3] Goebbels instinctively realized what was to become more obvious later, that, "between 1934 and 1936, all the circumstances favourable to a Fascist revolution co-existed in France." [4] The fact that Blum was a Jew would, in Goebbels' view, automatically strengthen the French anti-Semitic forces. He gave orders that the German press should not abuse Blum, in order not to weaken the effect of French anti-Semitic attacks on him.[5] Goebbels was happy to let rightist Frenchmen do the work for him, such as Léon Daudet, "the last great pamphleteer of the French Right," who ridiculed Blum as *"l'hermaphrodite circoncise."*

Goebbels believed that "anti-Semitism would split the democratic nations of the West and thus enable Germany to secure a free hand 'in her unavoidable fight with Bolshevism.' " [6] During the war the hope that anti-Semitism would weaken the régimes of the West and would play into the hands of Germany was persistently cherished by Goebbels and Hitler. In 1943 when the "final solution" of the Jewish problem in German-controlled Europe was well under way, Hitler and Goebbels were confident that their fanatic hatred of the Jews would catch on in enemy coun-

---

[1] W. Stephan, op. cit., pp. 183-184.

[2] Louis de Jong, *The German Fifth Column in the Second World War,* London, 1956, p. 8.

[3] D. Thomson, *Democracy in France, The Third Republic,* London, 1949, p. 196.

[4] Ibid.

[5] W. Stephan, op. cit., p. 184.

[6] Ibid.

tries. They gloated over any report on the alleged growth of anti-Semitic attitudes abroad, particularly in England and the United States. When in April 1943 the Führer issued orders that the Jewish problem should be raised again, Goebbels hailed this as an "exceptionally good idea" and commented in his diary: "anti-Semitism is growing rapidly even in the enemy states. Reports to that effect reach us, especially from England. If we continue to stress the anti-Semitic questions, the Jews, in the long run, will be much discredited. All one needs is to be tough and determined, for the Jewish problem has now been frozen so tight that it will be difficult to thaw it out again." [1]

The fact that Goebbels' merciless press campaign against the Jews together with reports of their mass-annihilation in Poland and Russia were widely commented upon in countries outside German control was misinterpreted by the Propaganda Minister. He obviously thought the seeds of his persistent propaganda were bearing fruit abroad, an impression which flattered both his vanity and his calculated anti-Jewish venom. "My article against the Jews is still a much-discussed topic." [2] he remarked in his diary.[3] "It is quoted everywhere, even in London. In my opinion the Jewish question is the next-best propaganda horse in the stall, after Bolshevism." Goebbels had drawn the attention of all the mass media at his disposal to "the extraordinary chances" offered by the anti-Semitic theme. "The press is called in for a special conference, where it is made clear that there is no question of writing an anti-Semitic article every second day; the point is that all our newspapers are to take on an anti-Jewish slant." [4]

Goebbels jumped at the slightest evidence of growing Jewish influence, or of increased anti-Semitic feeling abroad. After the publication of American statistics, according to which there were 5,000,000 orthodox Jews in the United States, he held that "the United States can certainly be described as a Class I Jew State. We are going to step up our anti-Semitic propaganda so much that the word 'Jew' will again be pronounced in the derisive manner that it deserves, just as it was in the time of our struggle for power. It must come to pass that even an enemy statesman won't dare to be seen in the company of a Jew without immediately being suspected by his own people of being a stooge of the Jews." [5]

In his astonishing ignorance of life in England and of the liberal English background Goebbels predicted that what he regarded as a rising tide of British anti-Semitism would succeed along the pattern of the Nazi hatred of the Jews. The comparison clearly indicated how much Goebbels believed in the recurrence of the same development elsewhere: "The Jews

[1] *The Goebbels Diaries*, entry of 18 April 1943, p. 259.
[2] This remark obviously refers to Goebbels' article published a few days earlier under the caption "Der Krieg und die Juden", *Das Reich*, 9 May 1943; reprinted in *Der Steile Aufstieg*, pp. 263-270.
[3] Diary entry of 10 May 1943 (02278).
[4] Ibid.
[5] *The Goebbels Diaries*, entry of 17 April 1943, p. 257.

in England are now demanding laws to protect them against anti-Semitism. We know these tactics from our own past when we were struggling for power. It didn't help much. We were always able to find loopholes in the law. Besides, anti-Semitism cannot be eradicated by law once it has taken root among a people. A law against hating Jews is usually the beginning of the end for the Jews." [1]

When in May 1943 the English journalist Hannan Swaffer received some letters critical of the Jews in reply to an article in which he had expressed his sympathy with the plight of the Jews in Europe, Goebbels rejoiced and somewhat uncritically regarded this as a success of German propaganda. He alleged that the English anti-Semites were using the same arguments which were continuously employed in German radio transmission to foreign countries. [2] "From this it is obvious," Goebbels wrote in his diary, "that our foreign radio propaganda is most likely to succeed if it is skilfully presented and if it takes the form rather of factual bulletins than of commentaries." [3]

To make the whole world anti-Semitic was to Goebbels only a question of very adroit manipulation, of cleverly conducted and, if necessary, camouflaged propaganda. "The Jewish question, as the Führer hopes, will prove to be of decisive significance in England. We have only to keep our propaganda skillful and directed to this goal, must not lay it on too thick, and must give more news talks." [4] Once more German propaganda was faced with "an extraordinary task." "But in this connection we must not forget that the English public is not so clear on the Jewish question as is the German. For this reason we must never let our intention be discovered, in order not to create resentment." [5] While still clinging to his old cliché that the English were "in general the Aryan nation who had most picked up Jewish ways," Goebbels added hopefully: "But the English people will nevertheless experience a great awakening about the Jewish question. On our side, we must help and hasten this awakening in every way possible through our propaganda." [6]

Hitler's and Goebbels' belief in the creating of a world-wide anti-Semitic wave was also shared by Heinrich Himmler. In a letter to the Chief of the Security Police and of the Security Service (SD), Dr. Kaltenbrunner, in May, 1943, Himmler suggested unofficial purely anti-Semitic broadcasts in English to Britain and the United States. They should contain sensational material of the sort Der Stürmer had offered in Germany. A special staff should look out for police and court news on

[1] Op. cit., entry of 19 April 1943, p. 261.
[2] See also the Diary entry of 23 May 1943 (02472): "Even the leader of the Communist Party in England laments the extraordinary growth of hatred of the Jews and demands protective racial laws as do the bourgeois newspapers. We use this as a welcome opportunity to continue our anti-Semitic propaganda."
[3] Diary entry of 13 May 1943 (02342).
[4] Ibid. (02344-5).
[5] Ibid.
[6] Ibid. (02348).

missing children in England. Such news items should then be broadcast over the "black" station with the suggestion that what had occurred were probably cases of Jewish ritual murder. Himmler held the view that a strong anti-Semitic propaganda in English, perhaps also in Russian, on those lines could do immense service in promoting anti-Semitism.[1] It is also significant that the German authorities had faked English stamps with the imprint "This war is a Jewish war." They were produced in a special workshop of the Concentration Camp Sachsenhausen.[2]

Although Goebbels occasionally expressed doubts about the existence of a Jewish world plot in the terms of the "Protocols of Zion," [3] he did, in fact, constantly think in such categories. To him, it is true, the concept of a united international Jewish front was good propaganda, but it was more than this, it was real. Indeed, he often interpreted the moves of Germany's enemies in terms of Jewish machinations. For instance he regarded the dissolution of the Comintern by Stalin in May, 1943 not as a Communist but as a Jewish trick. "The Soviet Jews are breaking up, and the Anglo-Saxon Jews applaud the break-up," Goebbels noted in his diary. "It is clear that we must respond to this camouflage trick with all the power of the greatest German propaganda campaign. . . . We will spoil the picnic of the Jews in Moscow, London, and Washington." [4]

The alleged world-wide Jewish conspiracy was an obsession with Goebbels as it was with Hitler. Time and again it forced them to view the World War, so to speak, through anti-Semitic spectacles and it spurred on their pathological hatred to the pitch of arriving at a merciless "final solution" of the Jewish problem.

4. PROPAGANDA FOR MASS-ANNIHILATION

During the war the constant anti-Semitic note in Goebbels' articles clearly served a double purpose. First it pinned on the Jews the responsibility for the war—"the great conspiracy" theme; secondly it should make the people approve of, or at least acquiesce in, the anti-Jewish

[1] Himmler to Kaltenbrunner, Feld-Kommandostelle, Mai 1943. Geheim: Document no. 2527; see *Das Dritte Reich und die Juden*, pp. 359-360.

[2] Op. cit., p. 372.

[3] Goebbels regarded the "Protocols of Zion" as a very suitable instrument of propaganda though in 1943 he seems to have somewhat doubted their authenticity. "The Protocols of Zion," he observed in his Diary, "are just as modern today as the day on which they were first made public. It is astounding with what extraordinary logic the Jewish movement for world rule is formulated. If the Protocols of Zion are not genuine, they are the work of a man of genius who is critical of our times." The Führer regarded the "Protocols" as "absolutely authentic"; Goebbels, however, was more cautious, admitting that "we cannot speak flatly of a conspiracy of the Jewish race against western man; this conspiracy is more a matter of race than of thought-out intentions. Jews will always act the way their Jewish instinct tells them to." Diary entry of 13 May 1943 (02344-345). See also below ch. 18, p. 416, footnote 4.

[4] Diary entry of 23 May 1943 (02475).

measures of defamation and deportation which the Nazi authorities carried out ruthlessly between 1941 and 1944. As we have seen nearly all the aggressive war-time speeches or articles contained some abuse of the "Jewish plutocrats" or "Jewish Bolsheviks" in the camp of the enemy. The slogan of the "great conspiracy" said to involve Jews inside as well as outside Germany was meant to prepare the people for the successive steps towards the "final solution" of the Jewish problem.

Frequently Goebbels referred to a prediction the Führer had made in a speech on 30 January, 1939: "Today I will once more be a prophet: if the international Jewish financiers in and outside Europe should succeed in plunging the nation once more into a world war, then the result will not be the bolshevization of the earth, and thus the victory of Jewry, but the annihilation of the Jewish race in Europe!" [1]

During the war Goebbels had not only direct access to the Führer for talks on anti-Semitic measures but he also backed Hitler in his fervid desire to make them ever more complete and effective.[2] It was Goebbels who in September, 1942 proposed to Otto Thierack, the Reich Minister of Justice, that Jews and gipsies should be "unconditionally exterminable" and that "the idea of extermination through labour was best." [3] There may have been a grain of truth in the claims made by Himmler to his Finnish therapist Felix Kersten in November, 1942 and to Count Berna-dotte in April, 1945 that "his persecution of the Jews had been forced on him by Goebbels' superior influence on Hitler." [4] "Goebbels' attitude was," Himmler asserted, "that the Jewish question could only be solved by the total extermination of the Jews." Against this Himmler claimed as his view that "it would be enough to expel the Jews." [5] "Ach, Kersten," he sighed, "I never wanted to destroy the Jews. I had quite a different idea. But Goebbels has it all on his conscience." It was actually a question of the pot calling the kettle black. But it is worth noting that according to Himmler, "up to the spring of 1940, Jews could still leave Germany without any trouble—then Goebbels got the upper hand." [6]

However it was only in July, 1941, a few weeks after the German invasion of Soviet Russia had begun, that Goebbels devoted an entire article to the Jewish impertinence (Chuzbe) in using socialism as an instrument for Jewish world domination. Here was at last the squaring of Goebbels' circle. "The crudest plutocracy," he maintained, "made use of

---

[1] The Speeches of Adolf Hitler, edited by Norman H. Baynes, vol. I, p. 741. For references to that "prophecy", by Goebbels see his article "Die Juden sind schuld!", in Das Reich, 16 November 1941, reprinted in Das eherne Herz, p. 85; and The Goebbels Diaries, p. 183, entry of 14 December 1942.

[2] See the entries in The Goebbels Diaries, pp. 220, 257, 259 and 160.

[3] IMT 687, PS, and IMT, IV, 389; quoted in G. Reitlinger, The Final Solution, London, 1953, p. 158.

[4] See G. Reitlinger, op. cit., p. 158 and The Kersten Memoirs 1940-1945, by Felix Kersten, London, 1956, pp. 161-162.

[5] The Kersten Memoirs, p. 162.

[6] Op. cit., p. 161.

socialism in order to establish the most drastic dictatorship of money."
Although the Jews camouflaged their aims, they were the same in London and in Moscow. They would not escape their Day of Judgment.
"Today we can already hear the cry that will come from the desperate
and misled peoples all over the world: 'The Jews are guilty! The Jews
are guilty!' " The punishment that would befall them would be terrible.
"We have nothing to contribute to it, it will come by itself, because it
has to come." Goebbels concluded this sinister article with the assurance
that the forthcoming actions would be carried out "without pity and
without mercy." [1] In a significant conversation between Goebbels and
the Führer in the middle of August, 1941, Hitler claimed with satisfaction that his prophecy about the annihilation of the Jews in the war was
coming true: "It is coming true in these weeks and months with an almost
uncanny accuracy. In the East the Jews must pay the bill; in Germany
they have paid up in part, and in the future they will have more to pay." [2]
Hitler felt that there was a united front in Europe against Jewry today,
and added "but I shall not rest or be satisfied until we have exacted the
last consequence from Jewry."

Goebbels certainly did his best to push the Führer on this dismal path.
His ice-cold hatred of the Jews found ever new reasons for squeezing
them out of existence. "On the Jewish question the Führer fully accepts
my views," he jotted down in his diary.[3] "He agrees that we should introduce a large, clear symbol for the Jews, which the Jews must wear in
public, so that we may avoid the danger that the Jews may act as alarm-
ists and pessimists without being recognized. We shall also in the future
limit those Jews who do not work to smaller rations than Germans get.
This is no more than just and right. If a person doesn't work he shouldn't
eat. What is more, in Berlin for example only 26,000 out of 76,000 Jews
work, while the rest live not only off the work but off the rations of the
people of Berlin! The Führer tells me, moreover, to get the Berlin Jews
out of Berlin as quickly as possible, as soon as any transportation becomes
available, and send them to the East. There they will be taken in hand in
a severe climate."

"Berlin," Goebbels insisted, "must become a city without Jews. It is an
outrage and a scandal that in the capital city of the German Reich 76,000
Jews can walk around, most of them parasites. They spoil not only the
looks of the streets, but the atmosphere. Things will be improved when
they have to wear an insignia, but we can only make a real improvement
by getting rid of them. We must go about this matter without any sentimentality. You only need to consider what the Jews would do to us if
they were in power to realize what we must do to them since we have the

[1] Article "Mimicry", in *Das Reich,* 20 July 1941; see *Die Ziet ohne Beispiel,*
p. 530f.
[2] Goebbels' diary entry, middle of August 1941.
[3] This entry in Goebbels' diary was written in August 1941, one or two
days after the one quoted above.

power. For the rest, I am still alert to the Jewish problem. Although there are still powerful bureaucratic and in part even sentimental objections to overcome in the Reich civil service, I am not letting them bluff me or throw me off my stride."[1] Soon afterwards, in September, 1941, the wearing of the yellow Star of David was made compulsory for all Jews in Germany and a little later the deportation to the East began. In Berlin these deportations had a very practical aspect. "It was said quite openly, in fact," observed a Swedish journalist then in the capital, "that the mounting shortage of housing facilities was sufficient justification for the transfer of the Jewish population to territories in the East."[2] The Jewish homes were quickly made available for the families of Party members. One of the reasons why Goebbels stepped up his anti-Semitic propaganda was the unfavourable reaction of some Germans to these measures. Many realized the absurdity of the official claim that the Jews still left in the Reich by the autumn of 1941, "mostly old people who kept themselves alive with the greatest difficulty," meant a danger to the German people.[3] When Ulrich von Hassell visited Berlin in October of that year he found "revulsion on the part of all decent people towards the shameless measures taken against the Jews in Berlin and other large cities."[4] It is difficult to assess the percentage of people who were upset by these measures, but they at least made it necessary for the Party authorities "to distribute handbills saying the Jews were to blame for everything, and anybody who sympathized with them was a traitor to his people."[5] It happened sometimes that Jews, after they had been forced to wear the yellow star, were molested in the street by Nazi fanatics. But "people in Berlin and in Hamburg treated the Jews much more decently than those in smaller towns which were more affected by National Socialism."[6]

It was in any case telling that Goebbels found it necessary to defend the branding Jewish badge as a hygienic preventative measure which would make it impossible for the Jews to creep into the ranks of the Germans in order to sow discord. He wrote an article to "prove" with ferocious venom that the Jews were guilty.[7] Ignoring the sympathy shown to them by some people, Goebbels alleged that most Germans had only noticed that there were still so many Jews left in Berlin after the introduction of the badge. "Who of us," he asked fervently, "had realized that the enemy was standing directly at his side, that he was a silent or a skilfully inciting listener in the street, in the underground, in the queues

[1] Ibid.
[2] A. Fredborg, *Behind the Steel Wall*, p. 54f.
[3] Ibid.
[4] *The von Hassell Diaries, 1938-1944*, London, 1948, p. 201.
[5] Op. cit., p. 202.
[6] Rabbi Leo Baeck in *We Survived* by Eric Boehm (New Haven, 1949), quoted in *Das Dritte Reich und die Juden*, p. 439.
[7] Article "Die Juden sind schuld!" *Das Reich*, 16 November 1941, reprinted in *Das eherne Herz*, pp. 85-91.

outside tobacco shops?" [1] Not the persecutor but the persecuted was declared guilty. Any humanitarian defence of them was sharply rejected. Goebbels claimed that the Jews, forced into the open, tried to appeal to the sentimental feelings of the good-natured Germans. They attempted to arouse pity for their charming babies or frail old women. They might confuse some harmless souls for a moment, but not the determined Germans who saw through them. "There is a world of difference between human beings just as between animals. We are aware of good and bad human beings, just as we know good and bad animals. The fact that the Jew is still living among us proves as little that he belongs to us as a flea becomes a domesticated animal by being in our home." [2] The official policy of annihilation was justified with simple logic. "Every German soldier who falls in this war," Goebbels explained, "is to be debited to the account of the Jews. They are responsible for it and they must therefore pay for it." It was all a question of the security of the State and not of any humanitarian ethics—a line of argument not very different from that used after the Night of the Broken Glass of 9 to 10 November, 1938.[3] The good citizen had to acquiesce in and to appreciate the measures of the Government as being inevitable.[4]

By May, 1942 the evacuation of Jews from Berlin was in full swing though many of them did useful work for the German war effort. "We are trying now to evacuate the Jews remaining in Berlin in greater numbers to the East," Goebbels observed in his diary. "A third of all the Jews living in Germany are in the capital. Obviously, in the long run this is an intolerable state of affairs. But one must remember that a relatively large number of the Berlin Jews are employed in the war industries, and by law their families cannot even be evacuated. I am trying to have the ordinance lifted, so that we can deport all the Jews who are not directly engaged in essential war production." [5] Goebbels did not allow any considerations of the war economy to interfere with the aim of "the final solution."

By that time, the mass extinction of Jews in Auschwitz and in other concentration camps in the East was proceeding according to plan. Goebbels knew and approved. Already on 27 March, 1942 he had noted in his diary: "Beginning with Lublin, the Jews controlled by the *General Government*, are now being evacuated eastward. The procedure is pretty barbaric. It is not to be described here more definitely. Not much will remain of the Jews. About 60 per cent of them will have to be liquidated; only about 40 per cent can be used for forced labour." [6]

[1] Op. cit., p. 86.
[2] In an address at a Berlin mass meeting in June 1943 Goebbels compared the Jews with the potato beetle. As it destroyed entire potato fields, so the Jews destroyed states and nations. See *Der steile Aufstieg*, p. 301.
[3] See above, p. 105.
[4] Op. cit., pp. 90-91.
[5] Diary entry of 17 May 1942 (01432).
[6] *The Goebbels Diaries*, pp. 102-103.

5. CLIMAX OF A DEADLY HATRED

For once Goebbels was not telling stories to others which he did not believe himself. He hated the Jews and wanted their mass destruction. Anything Jewish was "to him like a red rag to a bull." [1] In this respect there was no descrepancy between his convictions and his propaganda message, they coincided. "One must not be sentimental in these matters," he taught himself with a mixture of fanatic belief and ruthless opportunism, "If we did not fight the Jews, they would destroy us. It's a life and death struggle between the Aryan race and the Jewish bacillus. No other Government and no other régime would have the strength for such a global solution as this. . . . Fortunately a whole series of possibilities presents itself to us in war time which would be denied to us in peace. We shall have to profit by this." [2]

Those were ominous hints which Goebbels even in the privacy of his diary thought it wise not to elaborate upon. But two months later after a talk with the Führer Goebbels expressed himself more clearly. "The Germans," the Führer had told him at the end of May, 1942, "take part in subversive movements only when Jews have tricked them into it. For this reason the Jewish danger must be liquidated, cost what it may. How little the Jews can integrate themselves into West European life becomes obvious when they are returned to the ghetto and are so quickly reassimilated. West European civilization only gives them an external coat of paint." [3]

It would therefore seem logical to settle them in Eastern Europe. But Hitler and Goebbels were obviously afraid of the Jews: "There are always elements among the Jews who set to work with a dangerous brutality and vengeance. For this reason the Führer does not want to send the Jews to Siberia. There, in the most severe living conditions, they would certainly produce another hardy element. He would prefer to send them to colonize Central Africa. There they would live in a climate that would surely not make them strong and resistant. In any case, it is the Führer's goal to free Western Europe completely of Jews. They must no longer find a homestead here." [4]

It appears that both Hitler and Goebbels were at that time rather affected by the attempt, a few days earlier, on the life of Reinhardt Heydrich, the Reich Protector of Bohemia-Moravia and former head of the Security Office (SD) of the Gestapo, by Czech partisans. Goebbels used this event to initiate further persecution of the Berlin Jews: "An alarming news item has come from Prague. In the suburbs of Prague an attempt has been made to assassinate Heydrich with a bomb. . . . We must be clear about this, such an assassination would become a model for others

[1] R. Semmler, op. cit., entry of 16 August 1943, p. 98.
[2] The Goebbels Diaries, entry of 27 March 1942, p. 103.
[3] Diary entry of 30 May 1942.
[4] Diary entry of 30 May 1942.

unless we proceeded to take the most brutal measures. But no such danger exists: we shall definitely put down this attempt to bring chaos to the Protectorate and the occupied territories." [1]

Though even Goebbels did not suggest that the Jews were responsible for the bomb thrown at Heydrich, he eagerly picked them as a scapegoat: "I shall now likewise complete my war against the Berlin Jews. At the moment I am having a list drawn up of the Jewish hostages to be followed by many arrests. I have no desire to put myself into a position to be shot in the belly by a 22 year old Jew from the East—such types are to be found among the assassins at the Anti-Soviet Exhibition. Ten Jews in a concentration camp or under the earth are better than one going free. We are engaged today in a fight for life and death and he will win who most energetically defends his political existence. Surely we are the one." [2] A few days later Goebbels jotted down further details of the new anti-Jewish drive after noticing that Heydrich's condition was very disquieting.[3] "We still don't know the background of the plot. . . . In any case, we are making the Jews pay. I am having my planned arrest of 500 Jews in Berlin carried out, and am informing the leaders of the Jewish community that for every Jewish plot or attempt at revolt 100 or 150 Jews whom we are holding are to be shot. As a consequence of the attempt on Heydrich a whole group of Jews, against whom we had evidence, were shot in Sachsenhausen. The more of this rubbish we get rid of, the better for the security of the Reich." [4]

By the spring of 1943 the elimination of Jews from Berlin had made considerable progress, but not without running into some unexpected obstacles: "We are now definitely pushing the Jews out of Berlin," Goebbels observed in his diary early in March.[5] "They were suddenly rounded up last Saturday, and are to be carted off to the East as quickly as possible. Unfortunately our better circles, especially the intellectuals have once again failed to understand our policy about the Jews and in some cases have even taken their part. As a result our plans were disclosed prematurely, and a lot of Jews slipped through our hands. But we will still catch them."

A week later he complained that:[6] "the scheduled arrest of all Jews on one day failed because of the shortsighted behaviour of industrialists who warned the Jews in time. We therefore failed to lay our hands on about 4,000. They are now wandering about Berlin without homes, are not registered with the police and are naturally quite a public danger. I ordered the police, the *Wehrmacht,* and the Party to do everything pos-

[1] Diary entry of 27 May 1942.
[2] Ibid. An Anti-Soviet Exhibition in Berlin had been arranged by the Propaganda Ministry.
[3] Heydrich died from his wounds on 4 June 1942.
[4] Diary entry end of May 1942.
[5] *The Goebbels Diaries,* diary entry of 2 March 1943, p. 196.
[6] Op. cit., entry of 11 March 1943, p. 225.

sible to round these Jews up as quickly as practicable." Goebbels also lamented that a number of Jews and Jewesses from "privileged marriages" had been arrested and these arrests had "caused a terrific commotion, especially in artistic circles." [1]

The problem of these marginal Jews continued to trouble the authorities for some time. In the middle of April Goebbels ordered a renewed examination of all Jews left in Berlin. He did not want to see Jews with the "Jewish Star" running about in the capital. "Either they must be classed as privileged, and the Star taken from them, or they must be evacuated altogether from the capital of the Reich." [2] Goebbels was convinced he had completed "one of the greatest political achievements" of his career with the liberation of Berlin from the Jews. "When I consider how Berlin looked in 1926 when I came here," he claimed proudly, "and how it looks now in 1943 when the Jews are being evacuated completely, only then can I see what has been achieved in this sector." [3]

At the end of May, 1943 the Greater German Reich was officially declared *"Judenfrei"* (free from Jews), though in fact this claim was not completely correct.[4] At this time the Führer ordered the Jewish question to be given prominence in German propaganda. Goebbels wholeheartedly agreed, but complained that the German press did not fully carry out his instructions on this point.[5] At a press conference on 16 April, 1943 editors were therefore told: "The press must accustom itself to acting vigorously when it deals with Jews. From now on it must be taboo for any newspaper to mention, for example, the Jew Ehrenberg in connection with the Katyn massacre, without adding the word "Jew." Any newspaper that failed to do so would not go unpunished. Anti-Semitism is the most pointed weapon we have. It must be used with great vigor." [6]

More than ever before Goebbels presented the whole war, the full cruel impact of which was now felt by the German people, as being a racial issue, as a struggle of survival between the Jews and their opponents. The Jews who started the war, he asserted, aimed at the extermination *(Ausrottung)* of the German people. They were the cement that kept the enemy coalition together. "Although Jewry uses all possible devices against the growing anti-Semitism in the camp of the enemies—the word "Jew" can hardly ever be traced in the English and U.S.A. papers, otherwise so talkative, let alone in the Bolshevist press—the anti-Semitic mood

---

[1] The Nazis regarded as "privileged marriages" certain categories of marriages in which the one partner was Jewish and the other a Gentile. Originally the Jewish partner was protected from deportation and liquidation, but during the last months of the war the Nazis began to arrest such Jews too.

[2] *The Goebbels Diaries*, entry of 18 April 1943, p. 260.

[3] Ibid.

[4] For data on Jews who nevertheless had managed to remain in the Reich, see G. Reitlinger, *The Final Solution*, p. 155.

[5] Diary entry of 17 April 1943 (02054). He added that the Katyn story was very suitable for anti-Semitic propaganda.

[6] Zsg. 102/33, "Aus der Pressekonferenz", *Tagesparole*, 16 April 1943.

in the public life of our adversaries is continually growing." [1] National Socialism not only had a world mission but was to carry it out ruthlessly. They would finish off the most dangerous enemy who has ever threatened the life, liberty and dignity of mankind. Mercy was out of place. "We pity only the countless millions of our own and other European nations who would be a defenceless prey of the hatred and will for destruction of this devilish race if we should weaken and in the end fail in this struggle." [2]

Behind such articles was Hitler's definite wish to see the anti-Jewish campaign intensified all over Europe. "The Führer attaches great importance to powerful anti-Semitic propaganda," Goebbels noted on 10 May, 1943. "He agrees that success depends upon constant repetition. He is immensely pleased with the way in which we have sharpened up anti-Semitic propaganda in the press and on the air. I informed him about the extent to which this anti-Semitic propaganda was being pushed in our foreign broadcasts. At present about 70-80 per cent of our broadcasts are devoted to it. The anti-Semitic bacilli naturally exist everywhere in all Europe; we must merely make them virulent." [3]

By then Goebbels seems to have been aware that at least a section of the German population disliked the idea of transporting the Jews to an unknown destination from which they might never return. In June, 1943 at a mass meeting at the Sport Palace in Berlin he thought it necessary to "explain" the harsh measures: "In face of world danger there is no room for sentimentalities. Though some people may not understand the profundity of the Jewish problem, this should not confuse us. The complete elimination of the Jews from Europe is not a question of ethics, but a question of State security. . . . Just as the potato beetle destroys the potato fields, yes, is bound to destroy them, the Jew destroys states and nations. There is only one remedy for this: radical elimination of the danger." [4]

Like the newspapers, many periodicals echoed their master's voice. It was about this time that the campaign of hatred and defamation of the Jews was intensified in German propaganda, if this was still possible. It has been rightly observed that hatred and brutality have never been so much glorified as by National Socialism.[5] A typical and illuminating

[1] Article "Der Krieg und die Juden", *Das Reich*, 9 May 1943; reprinted in *Der steile Aufstieg*, pp. 263-270; the quotation is on p. 265.

[2] Ibid., p. 269f.

[3] *The Goebbels Diaries*, p. 287. As Goebbels felt there were too few journalists for carrying out this intensified anti-Semitic propaganda, he received permission from the Führer to call back a considerable number of young journalists from the "Propaganda Companies" attached to the army, and to distribute them throughout the German press.

[4] "Uberwundene Wirtschaftskrise", address in the Berlin Sport Palace, 5 June 1943; reprinted in *Der steile Aufstieg*, p. 301.

[5] Eva G. Reichmann, *Die Flucht in den Hass, Die Ursachen der deutschen Judenkatastrophe*, p. 242.

example of the intensified incitement against the Jews is a special anti-Semitic issue of the *Deutscher Wochendienst* of May, 1943. This was an official agency under Otto Dietrich feeding periodicals with propaganda material.[1] Continuous anti-Semitic propaganda was declared indispensable both for domestic and for foreign consumption.[2] However, at that time editors of journals apparently felt satiated with anti-Jewish material, for the *Wochendienst* thought it necessary to reject the argument that "the German people were sufficiently well informed about the Jews and did not need further enlightenment." How tepid was the interest of the hard-pressed journalists in the eternal anti-Jewish topic can be judged by the solemn warning that: "The current special number of the *Deutscher Wochendienst* must not be read quickly through once and then filed away for good; every chief editor must review it daily for the next few months, and use its ideas constantly in the planning of his forthcoming issues."[3]

To the propagandists the impact of their anti-Jewish campaign on foreign countries was more important than that made on Germany. Particular effort was made to imbue foreign workers in the Reich with the spirit of anti-Semitism. They in their turn could influence by letter their families at home in France, Belgium, Denmark and Norway. German anti-Jewish arguments had, it was claimed, even found their way into the enemy press and anti-Semitic discussions going on in Britain were obviously the result of the German propaganda effort.

In conformity with the usual Nazi technique editors were strictly advised what to emphasize and what to avoid in their articles which had to explain the progressive elimination of the Jews from the political economic and cultural life of Europe.[4] The emphasis was on strength through creating fear, by forming an image of the acute danger of complete annihilation of all Germans. Here is a typical directive:

"*Line to be taken.*

"*Emphasize:* If we should lose this war, we should not fall into the hands of some other nation; but all nations will be destroyed by world Jewry. The Jews are resolved to eradicate all Germans. International law and national custom will give no protection from the Jews' desire to de-

---

[1] *Deutscher Wochendienst* 211/80. Ausgabe, 21 May 1943, nos. 8838-8846. "Anti-Juden-Sondernummer. Das Ziel: Eine antijüdische Zeitschriften-presse." IMT document NG-4716.

[2] Op. cit., p. 8838. The directive stressed significantly that "only by continuous emphasis on a recognized truth can you get all the people to embrace this truth and act accordingly."

[3] Ibid.

[4] *Deutscher Wochendienst*, 65. Ausgabe, 5 February 1943, no. 8312-8337. "When the Jew is in control . . ." IMT document NG-4714. The theme was said to be topical, for "the measures taken to eliminate Jewry from the political, economic, and cultural life of the European nations, which will be fully realized as a result of further arrangements, offer an opportunity to the journals in articles of their own to throw light on some parts of this trend in the context of the anti-Jewish measures."

stroy everything. Thus we must under all circumstances be victorious, and weather our reverses."

At the same time the powers-that-be were very anxious that no reference whatsoever to the actual transportation of European Jews to the East should be made. Therefore the negative advice:

"Avoid: Criticism of the actions taken by individual countries (much better to mention any action that demonstrates the joint European war against the Jews)—questions about how far existing legal measures are being put into practice." [1]

The "evoking of hatred" *(Weckung von Hassgefühlen)* was explicitly described as desirable.[2] An image of the colossal collective guilt of the Jews was to be impressed on the millions. It might help to justify the elimination of all Jews, although the actual mass slaughter was never directly mentioned. The target set to the editors was not only the total denunciation of the Jews but also the removal of "the last remnants of a bourgeois sentimental attitude towards the poor Jews." [3] Obviously many Germans seemed to have felt that not all Jews were bad, but that some of them were quite "decent." This can be clearly discerned from the following directive:

"Line to be taken.

"Emphasize: Every single Jew, wherever he is and whatever he is doing, shares the guilt. There is no such thing as a 'good Jew,' but only degrees of skill and camouflage. The Jew is a notorious criminal." [4]

Among the points of discussion to be avoided at all costs were such religious controversies as "Was Christ a Jew?"

Though the actual mass murder and gassing of several millions of Jews which was then taking place in Auschwitz and other concentration camps in Eastern Europe was nowhere mentioned, the wholesale destruction of human beings was "justified" by crude arguments, for instance: "The destruction of Jewry is not a loss to mankind, but for the peoples of the world just as useful as capital punishment or penitentiaries for criminals. Nor do we make any distinction between the Biblical people of Israel and the Jews of today, for both are criminal. We do not refer to the ethically valuable parts of the Jewish tradition, for these were borrowed from the Egyptian and Babylonian cultures." [5]

There is little doubt that in his fanaticism Goebbels believed such nonsense. According to Rudolf Semmler, his hatred of the Jews was so intense that "he becomes incapable of even recognizing facts when he has to deal with them." [6] Semmler had a significant experience with Goebbels

[1] Ibid.

[2] *Zeitschriften-Dienst* 204/73, Ausgabe, 2 April 1943, no. 8613-8647.

[3] *Deutscher Wochendienst,* 21 May 1943, no. 8838-8846.

[4] Op. cit., no. 8839.

[5] *Zeitschriften-Dienst,* 2 April 1943, no. 8615.

[6] R. Semmler, *Goebbels—The Man next to Hitler,* entry of 16 August 1943, p. 98.

in this respect. In August, 1943 he reported to his chief that the writers of sixteen out of 150 letters from the public received in the Ministry in one week had protested against the reappearance of the Jewish question in the press and in broadcasts. Some were of the opinion, that the Germans had other things to worry about than a campaign of anti-Semitic abuse. Other letter-writers emphasized that what the Germans were suffering now was the price they were paying for their extremist attitude towards the Jews which had made the whole world their enemy. When Semmler summed up his impressions with the words "Anti-Semitism is as unpopular as ever among the mass of the people and causes distrust or definite opposition," Goebbels became angry, accused him of giving merely his own point of view and asked to see the original letters.[1]

This pathological hatred even extended to those 'Aryans' who had married a Jewish partner and who refused to agree to the divorce suggested by the Nazi authorities. For the tragedies which occurred in some of these mixed marriages Goebbels had only a contemptuous sneer. A case in point was the fate of the renowned actor Joachim Gottschalk who had been particularly successful in a number of films. When he insisted on standing by his Jewish wife, Goebbels simply declared: "I can bear this face no longer." His subordinates understood, and Gottschalk was banned from performing on the stage, in films or in broadcasts. There seemed only one way out: to put an end to this "privileged marriage" by the joint suicide of husband and wife and their eight-year-old son. In a farewell letter Gottschalk quoted the melancholy words of the playwright Heinrich von Kleist, who had also put an end to his life over a century earlier: "The truth is that nothing on this earth could help me." When Goebbels heard of the tragedy, he commented on it in terms "of diabolical cynicism."[2] Small wonder, for the life of an individual meant little to him, especially when it did not conform to the official line.

[1] Op. cit., p. 99.
[2] W. Stephan, op. cit., p. 181; see also the article on Joachim Gottschalk in *Das Gewissen steht auf*, edited by Annedore Leber, Berlin, 1956, pp. 72-75.

CHAPTER 18

British Attitudes In National Socialist Eyes

GOEBBELS, THE ENGLISH AND
WINSTON CHURCHILL, 1939-1945.

1. "PERFIDIOUS ALBION"

GOEBBELS has been described as "a peculiar mixture of realist and wishful thinker." [1] One should add that his inventiveness in thinking out ever new propaganda slogans and tricks in the service of the National Socialist movement went hand in hand with his use of traditional clichés, many of them much older than National Socialism. This combination of a reliance on traditional formulas with his quick adaptability to the needs of the hour becomes particularly evident if we examine Goebbels' attitude to Britain. The Reich Minister of Propaganda had scant personal knowledge of foreign countries and none of the Anglo-Saxon world. As he possessed little command of the English language,[2] his impressions of Britain and of the United States of America remained throughout secondhand. This seems to have made him all the more inclined to follow and to reformulate traditional German clichés of the British national character and particularly of British weaknesses and vices. The picture of the character of one nation in the mind of another is rarely flattering and such stereotypes often stick a long time.

Images of England and English policy, fed by anglophilia as well as by anglophobia, existed in German minds long before 1918 or 1933. Among the liberals of the 19th century there was widespread admiration for the English constitutional monarchy and for the English Parliament. Freiherr von Stein was impressed by English self-government and Niebuhr declared England the pride and envy of mankind. Dahlmann and other moderate liberals of the Frankfurt Parliament of 1848 quoted Burke, Macauley and Cobden in support of their demands for free self-government both on the municipal and the state levels and were inclined to idealize and exaggerate the role of the English masses in politics. To

---

[1] Louis Lochner in his Introduction to *The Goebbels Diaries*, p. XXXVI.
[2] W. Stephan, *Joseph Goebbels—Dämon einer Diktatur*, p. 189 f. See also Goebbels' own statement on his inconvenient lack of knowledge of English in W. von Oven, *Mit Goebbels bis zum Ende*, vol. I, p. 182 f.

the more radical liberals England was the citadel of Manchesterdom, the Eldorado of a sensible commercial policy.[1]

This type of anglophilia was still strong in the sixties and seventies but had lost its grip by the end of the century through the growing economic competition with English commerce, the subsequent propaganda for a strong German navy and the gradual growth of the "encirclement" theory. It was under William II that the tradition of anglophobia which went back to the 18th century revived and developed. Since the days of Frederick the Great, Wieland and Schiller, there had been a strong current of criticism and dislike of the envied nation ruling the seven seas. In particular, three features in the English national character were singled out as abhorrent and pernicious. Firstly, there was Britain's alleged perfidy in political dealings with other nations. Secondly, there was the hypocrisy of the English who were said to hide very real commercial interests behind the camouflage of high-sounding moral and religious phrases. This was strikingly summed up in a saying ascribed to Theodor Fontane: "They say Christ and they mean cotton." Thirdly, the British were held to desire control of the whole world, to aim at *Weltherrschaft*.[2]

In the second Empire this negative picture of the English found its passionate champion in the historian Heinrich von Treitschke. He indulged in emotional statements such as "We must get so far that not a German dog will accept a piece of bread from an Englishman" (1882) or, "Why have we to throw ourselves without dignity on the neck of the Grandmother (Queen Victoria), when in England every baby is determined to deceive us" (1891). As a young man Admiral von Tirpitz, deeply convinced of British perfidy, had listened reverently to Treitschke as the oracle of German nationalism.[3] It is true that the cliché of "perfidious Albion" dates back as far as the Hundred Years' War, and is of French origin; Frenchmen like Robespierre and Napoleon revived it later for purposes of propaganda.[4] In Germany Frederick the Great in his *Political Testament* of 1768 wrote of the habit of the "haughty" and "arrogant" British of sacrificing their allies at the first moment they no longer needed them. A hundred years later Treitschke revived for the general German public the story of *"les faux Anglais."* In his main work, the *German History in the Nineteenth Century,* he wrote that the world regarded it "as a political law of nature that all the allies of perfidious Albion had been unfailingly betrayed." [5]

Before the first world war this view became part of the German theory

---

[1] Hermann Kantorowicz, *Der Geist der englischen Politik und das Gespenst der Einkreisung,* Berlin, 1929, pp. 22-27. (There is also a rather modified English edition: *The Spirit of British Policy and the Myth of the Encirclement in Germany,* London, 1931.)

[2] Hermann Kantorowicz, op. cit., pp. 28-38.

[3] Op. cit., pp. 37-38.

[4] See H.D. Schmidt, "The Idea and Slogan of 'Perfidious Albion' ", *Journal of the History of Ideas,* October 1953, vol. XIV, no. 4, pp. 604-616.

[5] H. von Treitschke, *Deutsche Geschichte im neunzehnten Jahrhundert,* Berlin, 1885, vol. iii, pp. 145-146.

of the British policy of encirclement, an allegation revived and even intensified by German right-wing organizations and publicists during the period of the Weimar Republic.[1]

The fear of "encirclement" and of perfidy and possible betrayal by other nations points to a collective German complex which needs mentioning here if we want to understand the half Quixotic, half aggressive attitude of National Socialist propaganda. Recently a Swiss historian has drawn attention to the basic roots of this traditional German attitude: "The dissatisfaction of German thought with destiny," says Walther Hofer,[2] "extends (however) not only to historical development, to the dimension of historic *time,* but also to the geographic situation, and therefore to the dimension of historic *space.* If the first notion is illuminated by the refrain 'We came too late in history,' then the second notion can be expressed in the words 'We have an unfavourable position in the historical world.' Both thoughts, however, justify the conviction that the extraordinary, that is, what cannot be justified by European standards, is permitted or rather, even more required for Germany. . . ."

Seen in this perspective, it is somewhat surprising that in his early days Hitler did not accept the traditional cliché of "perfidious and hypocritical Albion." In *Mein Kampf* he even criticized the wrong conceptions of the English so widespread among Germans before World War I and described it then as an error to think the English were personally too cowardly to risk their own blood for their economic policy. "England always possessed the armaments she needed. She always fought with mercenaries as long as mercenaries sufficed; but she also made deep inroads into the valuable blood of her entire nation, if victory could only be assured by such a sacrifice. There always remained the determination to wage the war and the tough and ruthless leadership required for it." [3] Hitler argued that it had been a German misconception before 1914 to regard the Englishman as a "businessman as artful as he was incredibly cowardly." Unfortunately such professorial wisdom overlooked the fact "that it was hardly possible to acquire an Empire of the size of the English one merely by intrigues and swindle." [4]

At that time Hitler had not yet become convinced that the British Empire was disintegrating and that its ruling class was weak, and even decadent. But by 1934 he told Hermann Rauschning that the British Empire showed

"all the marks of decay and inexorable breakdown because there is nowhere in it the courage of firm leadership. If you no longer have the strength to rule by means of force, and are too humane to give orders then it's time to resign. Britain will yet regret her softness. It will cost

[1] See H. Kantorowicz, op. cit., ch. VI.

[2] Walther Hofer, "Toward a Revision of the German Concept of History", in *German History. Some New German Views.* Ed. H. Kohn, London, 1954, p. 202.

[3] Adolf Hitler, *Mein Kampf,* Munich, 1943, p. 158.

[4] Op. cit., p. 159.

her her Empire. Even if an old ruling class may be able to vegetate for another decade or so without any real leadership, a new Empire can never rise otherwise than by blood and iron, by a firm will and brutal force." [1]

It was this new feature, the Nazi belief in the fatal decadent softness of British rule, together with the negative traditional cliché of the English national character which were to determine the core of Goebbels' propaganda in years of peace and more intensely in years of war.

After Munich, Goebbels' articles on England oscillated between contempt for English decadence and hope that England would see the light before it was too late, would realize where her true interest lay and abstain from any interference with the German *"Drang nach Osten."* With the stiffening of the British attitude towards Nazi Germany after the German occupation of Prague and the British guarantee to Poland on 31 March, 1939, Goebbels fell back more and more on the old slogan of a vicious encirclement of Germany by England and France. By May, 1939 the slogan of *Einkreisung* (Encirclement) was a top-line in German propaganda. The headings of the following Goebbels' articles speak for themselves: "Die Einkreiser" (20 May, 1939), "Nochmals: Die Einkreiser" (27 May, 1939), and "Das Schreckliche Wort von der Einkreisung" (1 May, 1939).[2] Now the cliché of the wicked war-mongers who attempt to put an iron ring round peace-loving Germany received a new tinge, a distinctly anti-capitalist emphasis. The decadent "Haves" wished to encircle the healthy "Have-Nots" whose strength was growing day by day. There was a secret conspiracy against the Führer's Germany: "Look at them closely," exclaims Dr. Goebbels, "as they squat in their clubs, masonic lodges and Jewish banks and hatch the catastrophe which they want to come down on Europe."[3] Their acquisitive, exploiting and hypocritical attitude was described as identical with that of 1914, but they overlooked the fact that the Germany of 1939 was different from that of 1914. Germany was now much more alive to the danger. "Today the English encirclers are no longer facing bourgeois Germany as in 1913 and 1914 . . . we all know that the London encirclers would bite on granite if they would attack us. And it is to be hoped that they know this themselves, too." [4]

The master's voice was echoed a hundredfold in the German press, crudely in the Party papers and in a more refined fashion in the *Frankfurter Zeitung*. The case of the latter is more interesting in this context as by its rather academic style and literary tradition its articles were calcu-

[1] Hermann Rauschning, *Hitler Speaks,* London, 1940, p. 127 f. There is some truth in the theory that Hitler was obsessed by a peculiar love-hate attitude to England. See Fritz Hesse, *Hitler and the English,* London, 1954, p. 112 f. and also John W. Wheeler-Bennett, *The Nemesis of Power,* p. 499.

[2] These articles are reprinted in J. Goebbels, *Die Zeit ohne Beispiel,* Munich, 1941.

[3] Article, "Die Einkreiser," *Völkischer Beobachter,* 20 May, 1939. See also *Die Zeit ohne Beispiel,* pp. 144-149.

[4] Article, "Die Einkreiser", *Die Zeit ohne Beispiel,* p. 148.

lated to influence foreign readers. At the beginning of June the *Frank-furter Zeitung* alleged that British foreign policy had lost itself in a cul-de-sac.

"It has, in a way, encircled itself, in an attempt to increase and complete the policy of encirclement. It gets further and further en-tangled in alliances which its best interests required it to avoid." [1]

The Berlin politicians would have liked to see England withdraw into splendid isolation. That Britain instead was now looking for allies on the Continent was unforgivable. In spite of her denials England was strongly suspected of planning encirclement as she was trying to come to an arrangement with Soviet Russia.

"It is true they talk of a Peace Front. But it is easy to point out that no encirclement has taken place because nothing has been intended against Germany and Italy. But why all these hopeless efforts to bring the most heterogeneous interests together under one hat?" [2]

Either, the writer argued, England was so weak that she needed such an unusual ally as Soviet Russia in order to defend her own in-terests or England was bent on encirclement. Two months later when Hitler's rapprochement with Moscow was well advanced, the *Frank-furter Zeitung* still continued to harp on the encirclement theme. It maintained that England did nothing,

"to limit the dangerous results of its attempted encirclement and of its policy of guarantees. On the contrary, the English act as if the Poles were acting in complete accord with British ideas." [3]

A week afterwards the paper denounced the policy of encirclement of the Western powers as being

"not conservative, but reactionary. . . . The conservative always looks to the positive task; the reactionary is blind . . . he is 'simply *against*.'" [4]

The makers of encirclement were sharply accused of "plotting against the spirit of History." Goebbels now declared it the continuous ten-dency of English politics "to let other nations protect the interests of the British Empire as much as possible. England dislikes sacrificing her own blood for her Empire and does so only under the strongest pressure." The ring which England tried to lay round Germany had "no other task but to suppress the rise of the Reich and thus to restore that notorious 'balance of power' on which England believes she must base her security in the motherland as well as in her Empire." [5]

[1] Article, "Was ist das: Einkreisung-", *Frankfurter Zeitung*, nos. 279-80, 4 June 1939.

[2] Ibid.

[3] Article, "Sind die Polen blind?", *Frankfurter Zeitung*, nos. 409-410, 13 August 1939.

[4] Article, "Die Reaktionäre", *Frankfurter Zeitung*, nos. 409-410, 20 August 1939.

[5] Article, "Nochmals die Einkreiser", *Völkischer Beobachter*, 27 May 1939; *Die Zeit ohne Beispiel*, p. 151.

Goebbels' pseudo-socialist criticism of England went so far as to talk of a "class struggle between the nations" and to confront the Western "plutocracies" with the (Fascist) "proletarian nations." [1] After all, was not Hitler's Party called "National Socialist Party"? While inside their own nation class struggle was taboo to the Nazis and was denounced as a "Jewish" device of disintegration, the phrase *Völkerklassenkampf* (class struggle between the nations) proved a new slogan of propaganda destined particularly for consumption by the German workers, many of whom had been Communists and Socialists before 1933.[2]

By describing the mentality of the victors of Versailles and of their followers as "capitalist" Goebbels managed to exploit jointly the two components of National Socialist ideo' ry, i.e. "nationalism" and "socialism." He came out with one of his inge. ous parallels, this time between developments inside Germany and those in European affairs. Just as before 1914 the bourgeois parties in Germany had no understanding for the justified demands of the workers, so since 1918 the capitalist victorious powers had not any proper appreciation of the underdog nations, of the "Have-nots" who do not wish to remain under-privileged any longer.[3] There were countries like England living on the fat of the land, who did not know what to do with their supplies of raw materials and gold, whilst other nations like Germany and Italy were reduced to a bare minimum, owing their existence solely to their intelligence, industry and gifts of organization.[4] The English were not interested, alleged Goebbels, in doing justice to the "Have-Nots", for such a step would imperil the most fundamental concept of British foreign policy, "the balance of power in Europe", a concept declared by him to be "an impudence." [5] There is an obvious dualism in Goebbels' propaganda picture of the English: on the one hand he alleged that these arrogant "Haves" had tried to repeat their old game of *Einkreisung*, remaining superior and tactless, on the other hand he insisted that they were gradually losing their former world prestige and their position of unchallenged hegemony.[6]

With a good deal of *Schadenfreude* Goebbels made much of press

[1] See the article "Klassenkampf der Völker", 3 June 1939; reprinted in *Die Zeit ohne Beispiel*, pp. 157-163.

[2] Same article, *Die Zeit ohne Beispiel*, p. 157 f.

[3] Op. cit., p. 159 f.

[4] Article, "Ein paar Worte über politischen Takt", 27 April 1939; *Die Zeit ohne Beispiel*, p. 111 f.

[5] Op. cit., p. 112.

[6] The Berlin correspondent of the London *Times* in May 1939 summed up the attitude of German propaganda in the critical months prior to the war neatly: "At present, however, Great Britain is the chief target for abuse, and no opportunity is lost to depict the English as a wealthy people over-burdened by their own riches and laughably ineffective in political and military matters" (*The Times*, 11 May 1939).

reports on an incident in Tienstin in June 1939 when the Japanese forced some Englishmen to strip in public.[1] He drew the conclusion somewhat sneeringly that "the power of the Empire is no longer what it was about twenty years ago when a small English fleet used to sail at once, if only a hair on the head of one son of Albion was hurt somewhere in the world, let alone if his trousers were taken off." [2]

Oddly enough, this argument regarding the visible decrease of British world prestige and world power was used to defend both the Nazi "encirclement" theory against its English critics and to put Britain under pressure with a view to wringing further concessions from her. "What should London do?", asked Goebbels in the same article, two months before the outbreak of the war, "Quite simple; turn round the wheel of her policy; not make speeches but show deeds! What do we actually want from her? Nothing more simple than that the wrong done to us is made good!" [3]

Goebbels versus King-Hall.

This is perhaps the place to mention Goebbels' remarkable clash with an English counter-propagandist just before the war. The episode is of interest, not only because we know that the *News-Letters* by Stephen King-Hall in German, first posted and later smuggled into Germany in the summer of 1939, worried the leading men in Berlin, but also because it offers us a convenient insight into Goebbels Macchiavellian tactics. The author of the *News-Letters,* published in London, was a retired naval commander, well-known in England for his broadcasts. During a visit to Berlin in May 1939 he had formed the impression that the new encirclement theory of the National Socialists was proving increasingly successful with the German public. He discovered that it served the régime well to allay the anxieties felt by Germans over Hitler's annexation of Czecho-Slovakia [4] and he recognized the nec-

---

[1] For the stripping and other indignities inflicted upon British subjects in Tientsin, see *The Times* (London), June 23, 26 and 28, 1939. The British Government took a cautious view on this matter, regarding the act rather as an outburst of extremists in the Japanese army in Tientsin than as the outcome of a deliberate policy of the Tokio Cabinet. See Mr. Chamberlain's statement in the House of Commons on 27 June 1939. Quoting it in a leader "Japanese Threats" on 28 June, *The Times* declared: "The Prime Minister seems to have been justified in his confidence at all events in regard to the local indignities imposed on British subjects."

[2] Article "Das schreckliche Wort von der Einkreisung", 1 July 1939, in *Die Zeit ohne Beispiel*, p. 189.

[3] *Die Zeit ohne Beispiel*, p. 191.

[4] "The Nazis were getting away with it by explaining to the German people that this extension of Hitler's policy of bringing 'all Germans' inside the Reich frontier had been made necessary, because the democracies—linked with Russia—had intended to use Czecho-Slovakia as part of an encirclement plan": Stephen King-Hall, *Total Victory*, London, 1941, appendix 3, *The German News-Letters*, p. 283.

essity of trying to project the British point of view among Germans in spite of the totalitarian screen surrounding them.

As the British Foreign Office showed nothing but a polite indifference to his misgivings and plans he decided to start with a few friends "a private war on Goebbels." Raising private funds they began "to write News-Letters in German and to send them through the post to private citizens." [1] Altogether five such *News-Letters* were despatched by the King-Hall organization. Their author seems to have been surprised by the extensive publicity given to them at first in the Nazi press, which published large extracts with sarcastic comments. Goebbels himself "honoured" the first letter with a vituperative reply, and there is irony in the fact that while Mr. King-Hall had tried in vain to interest H.M. Government in his bold enterprise, Goebbels lost no time in what he called "unmasking" the English author as an organ and tool of Lord Halifax and the Foreign Office.[2]

Though it is difficult to agree with Mr. King-Hall's later description of the official German publicity given to his *News-Letters*, as an "enormous blunder on Goebbels' part",[3] there is evidence that the successful despatch of his first attempt to offer an English point of view to a number of Germans in all walks of life, considerably annoyed and troubled Hitler and Goebbels. Some years later Goebbels admitted to a member of his personal staff, that King-Hall's pamphlets had been "so good and effective that we could not ignore them in silence." Hitler and Goebbels had therefore discussed how to take the most suitable steps against them. They decided to beat the English newsletter by a faked King-Hall leaflet which was to be so bad and stupid that it would shatter any German's faith in the authenticity of the English publication. "We both," explained Goebbels in February 1944, "made drafts. When we read them to each other, we realized that this was not the right method. My draft was so bad that the people would have seen through our swindle, while the Führer's draft was so good that through this leaflet an effect might have been brought about contrary to that which we had intended. We had chosen a method too subtle and intellectual. Later I dealt with King-Hall in a leader which ended with the words which have since become proverbial: "You good old honest sea-dog!" In it I finished him so completely with the sledge-hammer method that afterwards we had not to fear him any longer." [4]

With a peculiar mixture of shrewdness and naivety this public-spirited Englishman had tried to persuade the German public that there was a real danger of war and had suggested that ordinary German citizens

[1] Stephen King-Hall, op. cit., p. 210.

[2] Article "Antwort an England", *Völkischer Beobachter*, 14 July 1939; reprinted in *Die Zeit ohne Beispiel*, pp. 193-204.

[3] Stephen King-Hall, op. cit., p. 284.

[4] W. von Oven, *Mit Goebbels bis zum Ende*, vol. I, p. 205; diary entry of 27 February 1944.

should work for the preservation of peace. In the first letter from the British crusader [1] addressed to "Dear German Reader" (*Lieber Deutscher Leser*) he introduces himself as a retired British naval officer, with experience in research, journalism and broadcasting. He explains that he is writing to Germans, because, like them, he wants peace. He knows what war is like as he had commanded the cruiser Southampton in the Battle of Skagerrak (Jutland). "Your night action," he tells the Germans, "was a good deal better than ours, and if my ship had not sunk the German cruiser *Frauenlob* I should not be writing to you today!" As a middle-aged man and father of three children, he told his German readers, "I want Peace if I can have it on honourable terms, I imagine you feel the same." But will there be peace? The writer was doubtful and explained why. Ribbentrop seemed to tell the Führer that the British would not keep their promises to the Poles and that Hitler could safely solve the Danzig problem by force without British interference. But warned King-Hall, "Ribbentrop must be off his head, or he is deliberately misleading the Führer." For the man in the street in Britain, indignant "at what seems to him to be the disgraceful manner in which the German Government tore up the Munich agreement" was inclined to view Ribbentrop, Goebbels and Himmler as "quite impossible people with whom one can never make any agreements which will be kept." Moreover, "shocking as it might sound to German ears, the value of Herr Hitler's word in England today is pretty low." What would be Germany's chance in a war against Britain? Even if "you did beat us," the Commander predicted, "I doubt if you would gain much. The German air force might indeed kill 3,000,000 civilians in London, but this would make the name of Germany 'stink from the North to the South Pole' ", would bring the Americans into the fight in a week, and would thus eventually result in a German defeat.

King-Hall used both the carrot and the stick in his arguments. He was not always adroit in doing so. He predicted that after a war deliberately engineered by their Government the Germans must expect "a peace treaty compared with which the Treaty of Versailles will be like the cooing of doves"; on the other hand when a defeated Germany had purged the country of "the gangsters of the Nazi Party", Germany would be given credits, raw materials as gifts and be invited to take over a mandate for a colony. The first *News-Letter* ended with the suggestion that the final decision over war or peace lay with the German masses. Though the theory "what the Führer thinks *you* [Germans] think" seemed often true, the English writer regarded it as equally evident "that the German nation had just as high a proportion of intelligent men and women in it as any nation (and more than some), so perhaps one can say that to some extent, 'What *you* think the Führer

---

[1] An English translation of this letter is to be found in S. King-Hall, op. cit., appendix 3, pp. 285-289. All quotations here are taken from this translation.

thinks.' " Finally the German reader was advised to ponder the *News-Letter*, show it to some good friends and talk it over with them, also to send his frank comments to the author in England.[1] The piece was written altogether in a conversational vein with some sly asides; as for example when the author, referring to a performance of *Der Ring der Nibelungen* which he saw in London, drew a comparison between Wotan's and Hitler's outlook on life: "Loge is Dr. Goebbels and, I think you will agree, Mr. Chamberlain fills Fricka's role."

In Goebbels' reply by way of an article in the German press, five aspects of his propaganda technique can be traced,[2] all of them closely interrelated. The first is the *tendency to unmask*, to expose the hidden "true" face of the opponent. Significantly Goebbels' article was not headed "Answer to an Englishman" but "Answer to England." Mr. King-Hall was denounced as a propagandist in the pay of the British Foreign Office, as a tool of "the Propaganda workshop in Downing Street." The assumption that the English author had the blessings and support of Lord Halifax made it imperative to "unmask" his "entire clap-trap."

We can here see the second aspect of Goebbels' technique in the fact that to unmask meant to him *to belittle and to ridicule*. As Mr. King-Hall had mentioned his nomination as candidate for Parliament, Goebbels referred to him often as "Herr Kandidat" or "Herr Propaganda-kandidat", implying that he had still to learn his job. Goebbels added sneeringly: "At that time [in 1918] unfortunately propaganda was made by candidates [in Germany]. Today candidates make propaganda in England and masters make politics in Germany."

In order to discredit the views of his opponent, Goebbels developed a *method of distortion* which forms the third aspect of his technique. He took up a number of his sentences either verbatim or with small readjustments, deliberately ignoring the context which gave them their proper meaning. For instance the fact that during the First World War King-Hall had been an officer in the Royal Navy served merely as material for a diatribe. The British Navy had then, according to Goebbels, carried out a food blockade against Germany that led to the death by starvation of hundreds of thousands of defenceless German women and children. Or Goebbels used King-Hall's remark that he

---

[1] Perhaps the most striking feature in the *News-Letter* to a reader in an authoritarian state was the author's admission that he did not suggest that English opinions in politics were "bound to be right". "We may be wrong, but it really is important that you should know what we believe to be right." The suggestion that there may be right and wrong on either side, so typical of a pluralistic parliamentary society was bound to appear odd to people under a dictatorship. "Don't mince matters when you write back," Mr. King-Hall told them, "I want to know where you think I'm all wrong, as well as where you agree."

[2] Article "Antwort an England", 14 July 1939; reprinted in *Die Zeit ohne Beispiel*, pp. 193-204.

had worked for seven years at the Research Department of the Royal Institute of International Affairs (Chatham House) to point out that the Commander must have a wide knowledge of the atrocities committed by the British against defenceless nations in the Empire, and to present a long list of them. This ranged from the slave-trade in Liverpool in 1771 and the "ruthless" English bombardment of Zanzibar and the conquest of Burma in 1890 [sic] to the blood bath of Amritsar in 1919 and the suppression of the riot in Waziristan in 1937. Gladstone's condemnation of the Opium War in 1840 and J.A. Froude's criticism, in his work *Oceana,* of English methods employed in Afghanistan and Turkestan in the 1880's were strung together with quotations from George Lansbury's book *My England* and from Edith Sitwell's *Victoria of England* to prove the predatory attitude of the English in India and their hypocritical interference in the affairs of foreign nations.

The fourth aspect of Goebbels' riposte is his tendency to ignore facts and statements put forward by his opponents which might disturb the picture of the world as presented by Nazi propaganda, in other words *the fine art of keeping silent.* King-Hall had slyly thrown doubts on the reliability of the Italians as allies: "we had them last time, so we know all about them", and had pointed to the plight of the German minority in South Tyrol oppressed by the Fascist régime. He had asked his German readers: "why do you not agitate about those unfortunate Germans?" Goebbels by-passed this dangerous point entirely, but hit back on a different issue: "You say that the Italians are short in raw materials and have no great power of resistance. Why did you then not attack them in the Abyssinian conflict? You always threatened it. You wanted to do it! Or were you perhaps incapable of doing it?"

Finally, Goebbels was perhaps at his most effective in the *reply to some of the more insular arguments* of the former British naval commander. The British pamphleteer claimed that each of the two countries could learn from the other and each was in certain fields superior, in others inferior. "I often think you ought to let us run your foreign policy for you, and you could come and organize some of our muddles, such as road transports." Goebbles declined the offer with a neat mixture of realism and sarcasm: "As far as the 'superior' British handling of foreign policy is concerned," he replied, "you have taught us little, e.g. in the settlement of the Abyssinian conflict, on the occasion of the Rhineland occupation, the solution of the Austrian problem and of the Sudeten German problem, etc." In answer to the somewhat odd invitation to take over the control of English street traffic, Goebbels simply became abusive: "We thank you for so much kindness. But you had better restore order in your chaos yourself. We are not world traffic policemen. Morover, the greatest chaos seems to prevail in the brains of English propagandists at the moment. In any case, your letter suggests this idea to us."

But these were side issues. The political significance of this prop-
aganda-controversy centred around two main points: the Nazi doctrine of
"encirclement" and the position of both nations in and after a future
war. "Your leaders say you are being encircled," Mr. King-Hall had
explained, "so you are, if you want to settle problems by force and
seize other races' territory, but otherwise why on earth should we
wish to encircle you? . . . a prosperous Germany is a world asset in
world trade." Goebbels for his part declared the Englishman's question
to be hypocritical. "The answer is only too close at hand: in order to
finish us! Because we are troublesome to England with our demands for
our rights to live. . . . Because they begrudge us our life, because we
are "Have-Nots" in their eyes and shall remain so." [1] The alleged
English interest in a prosperous Germany as an asset in world trade is
sheer humbug, Goebbels went on, as "it is most effectively supported
by a large-scale boycott of goods against Germany all over the world."

Goebbels also ignored King-Hall's prediction of developments in the
next war and of the elimination of the Nazi Party in a defeated Germany.
Instead he concentrated on the threatened Super-Versailles after a German defeat. This gauche forecast suited his propaganda line very well,
as it helped him to exploit the negative German memories of the Treaty
of Versailles. "With that," he answered back, "you let the cat out of
the bag. We know where we stand. You say frankly what we have sur-
mised and supposed for a long time. Therefore we have to be prepared
for an attack and this time it will not find the nation economically helpless and militarily badly prepared." This time, too, Germany possessed
a superior propaganda machine, a fact of which Goebbels seems to have
been genuinely proud: "We have become a political people. We know
what is at stake. With little tricks like your letters the German people
can no longer be befogged, you good old English sea-dog, you." And
on that graphic sarcastic note Goebbels ended his reply to the embarrassing letter from a freelance opponent in London.

2. Years of Attack

In the months prior to the war, when Hitler still had some hopes of
the British Government acquiescing in the German drive against Poland,
German propaganda sometimes made a distinction between the British
Government and "the warmonger clique" in London, said to consist of
men like Eden, Churchill, Duff Cooper. "This clique," wrote Goebbels

[1] The argument that Britain was jealous of Germany's growing prosperity
which was only a new version of the pre-1914 cliché of England's *Handelsneid,*
seems to have impressed a good many Germans. In his third *News-Letter* Mr.
King-Hall remarks that as a result of his earlier letters many Germans had
written to him "explaining that Great Britain wishes to destroy Germany
because Germany is becoming rich". They "do not believe me when I say
that we want a prosperous Germany." (S. King-Hall, *Total Victory,* p. 295).

at the end of April 1939, "does not yet sit in the Government, it is true, but it is close to it." [1] By June 1939 Goebbels attacked and abused the English in general, indulging in explanations of the odd phenomenon of English hypocrisy: "They do not admit their hypocrisy amongst themselves. . . . They not only pretend that they have taken up piety and morals for good, no, they even believe it themselves. This is on the one hand the amusing, but on the other hand the dangerous aspect of the matter." [2] But as long as the road to peace and another Munich remained open, Goebbels refrained from abusive personal attacks on the leading members of the British Cabinet, the Prime Minister, Mr. Chamberlain, or the Foreign Secretary, Lord Halifax, however severely he criticized their policies.

During the Polish campaign Hitler hoped for an early peace with England and France on his terms and on 5 October Goebbels warned the press not to commit itself irrevocably against the Western powers: a door should be kept open for sensible Englishmen to come to an understanding with the Reich.[3] On 6 October in the Reichstag Hitler appealed for an Anglo-German understanding, protesting that he had "regarded it as nothing less than the goal of my life to bring about a rapprochement between the two peoples not by way of reason only, but also by way of feeling", and he spoke of "the hostility of some of the British statesmen and journalists".[4] When Chamberlain reacted negatively to this olive branch, Goebbels, though insisting on a sharper tone against England in his directive to the press, still advised it to make a distinction: "Lies, perfidy (*Wortbruch*), rape [of other nations] are the three themes with which England has now to be attacked continuously. It shall be demonstrated from English history that these have always been the fundamentals of British policy. But a distinction shall also further be drawn between people, Government and war-mongers, without making it too distinct." [5]

Meanwhile the term "British plutocracy" with its anti-capitalistic tinge was used by the German propaganda machine to indict not the English, but "only" their ruling class. After the fall of France Hitler's statement before the Reichstag on 19 July 1940 carefully distinguished between the irresponsible war-mongers and plutocrats on the one hand and the English people on the other.[6] He demanded that Mr. Churchill should be dropped, German colonies be returned and his own new position as Master of Europe be recognized. Otherwise there would be unimagin-

---

[1] Article "Lord Halifax macht Witze", 22 April 1939, *Die Zeit ohne Beispiel*, p. 104.

[2] Article "Die abgehackten Kinderhände", 24 June 1939, *Die Zeit ohne Beispiel*, p. 181.

[3] W. Hagemann, *Publizistik im Dritten Reich*, p. 276.

[4] Ibid.

[5] Ibid. (Press Directive of 13 October 1939).

[6] For an English translation of this speech by Hitler, see *My New Order*, ed. Count Raoul de Ronsey de Sales, New York, 1941, pp. 809-838.

able misery for millions of Englishmen, but not for Churchill and his clique of war-mongers who were already escaping to Canada.

When in a broadcast on 22 July Lord Halifax as Foreign Secretary gave a sharp answer to that clumsy approach by the Führer,[1] Goebbels' instructions to the press did not divert from his previous line to any great extent: "The slogan (*Stichwort*) is: the die is cast. The calling to account in the German press-commentaries shall be very earnest and dignified and shall, above all, be directed against the British plutocracy. They have taken their property, their families and their racehorses to America and left the people in the lurch. It should no longer be stressed that the English people have been unable to express their opinion. We do not want to excuse the people nor to make them jointly responsible."[2]

By then the term "plutocracy" in German propaganda meant the sinister rule of the few, deceiving and exploiting the many who were a defenceless prey to the machinations of the ruling clique.[3] The concept of the few who had "become a European, even a world danger" was obviously modelled on the idea of a Jewish conspiracy as expressed in the faked "Protocols of Zion" which Hitler regarded as genuine.[4]

These plutocrats, Goebbels told his public, tried to keep down both the young rising nations abroad and their own lower classes at home.[5]

[1] See Winston S. Churchill, *The Second World War*, vol. 2, Edition of the Reprint Society, London, 1951, p. 218.

[2] Hagemann, op. cit., 277. Two very different foreign observers agreed in their comments on the disappointment felt by the German people when their hopes of an early peace had been dashed. Count Ciano noted in his diary that "Late in the evening of the 19th, when the first cold British reaction to the speech arrived, a sense of ill-concealed disappointment spread among the Germans." William Shirer, the American journalist in Berlin observed: "The Germans I talk to simply cannot understand it. They want peace. They don't want another winter like the last one. They have nothing against Britain despite all the provocative propaganda. (Like a drug too often given, it is losing what little force it had.) They think they are on top. They think they can lick Britain too, if it comes to a showdown. But they would prefer peace." See *Ciano's Diary, 1939-1943*, London, 1947, pp. 277-278, and William L. Shirer, *Berlin Diary*, London, 1941, p. 359, entry for 20 July 1940.

[3] In a speech at Münster on 28 February 1940 Goebbels defined plutocracy as "a kind of political and economic leadership, in which a few hundred families rule the world". These families had "anything but a moral justification for doing so". *Die Zeit ohne Beispiel*, p. 248.

[4] See H. Rauschning, *Hitler Speaks*, p. 235. *The Protocols of Zion* were a fabrication by the Tsarist police. Their most effective passages were taken over verbatim from an anonymous book by Maurice Joly *Dialogue aux enfers entre Macchiavel et Montesquieu ou la politique de Macchiavel au XIXe siècle*. This anonymous work by a Belgian author which appeared during the days of Napoleon III's Second Empire discusses the chances of a Machiavellian dictatorship with the help of the modern Government machinery and the control of public opinion. The evolution of this falsification has been analysed by the American historian John S. Curtiss, in his book *An Appraisal of the Protocols of Zion*, New York, 1942. See also E. Faul, "Hitler's Übermacchiavellismus," *Vierteljahrshefte für Zeitgeschichte*, 1954, vol. II, no. 4, p. 369 and above, Ch. 17, p. 39, footnote 3.

[5] *Die Zeit ohne Beispiel*, p. 249 f.

The men who still punished offenders in their own country with the barbarous "cat o' nine tails", would like to reintroduce the slave trade in the whole civilized world were they only able to do so.[1] In his denunciation of the English plutocracy which, he claimed would not hesitate "to annihilate the entire German people",[2] Goebbels made much capital out of a contemporary British satire, A.G. Macdonnell's *Autobiography of a Cad,* published in London in 1938. Soon after the outbreak of the war a German translation, probably under the auspices of the Propaganda Ministry, appeared under the distorted title *Selbstbildnis eines Gentleman* (Self-Portrait of a Gentleman). It was the story of a clever rogue in the English ruling class without any moral sense. Educated at Eton and Oxford, he became a Tory M.P. and finally even a Minister of the Crown. He prospered by lying and cheating, through fornication and by a cynical hypocrisy which made him cover up his most caddish and immoral deeds with an insidious self-righteousness.[3] Such a book was a great find for Goebbels. He boldly praised it as a key to an understanding of the English ruling class and suggested it should have been called "Self-unmasking of the British plutocracy". What was a playful satire with Macdonnell became a factual report in the hands of the German propagandist. "It is simply horrible," Goebbels declared in great indignation: "A worse moral barbarism (*Verwilderung*) in social, business and political life cannot be imagined." [4]

But it was only after the fall of France and the unexpected resolve of the British to continue the war, *Blitz* or no *Blitz,* that the Propaganda Minister attacked the English with his full blast of vituperation. All the lines of "unmasking" and "debunking" a perfidious, hypocritical and definitely finished Albion now reached a new peak of ferocity. Goebbels' article *Von der Gottähnlichkeit der Engländer* (On the Similarity of the English to God) is a case in point.[5] It has all the ingredients of a strong Goebbels cocktail. There is the Fontane quotation, though cited as a proverb and this incorrectly. There is also the usual attack on the nasty English plutocracy, said to have exploited colonial peoples over the centuries. At the very moment when all the world expected an imminent invasion of England, Goebbels offered a catalogue of the vices of the English plutocrat; "His limitless stupid arrogance, his inertia in thinking, his irritating phlegmatic attitude towards the worries and interests of other nations, his hypocritical and deceitful morals, his half silly, half cheeky

---

[1] Op. cit., p. 250.

[2] Op. cit., p. 253. The same argument was used by Goebbels in his address for the Führer's birthday broadcast on 19 April 1940. See *Die Zeit ohne Beispiel,* p. 282.

[3] This "cynical hypocrisy" of the English is also pictured in many other articles by Goebbels. See for instance "Von der Gottähnlichkeit der Engländer," *Das Reich,* 16 June 1940.

[4] Article "Was denkt sich Churchill eigentlich?" *Das Reich,* 28 December 1940. *Die Zeit ohne Beispiel,* p. 346.

[5] Reprinted in *Die Zeit ohne Beispiel,* pp. 301-304.

naivety in the propagation of lies and slanders which has been developed, so to speak, to a kind of political art." [1]

This enigmatic caste was described as "the Jews among the Aryans" who belong to the sort of people "whose teeth one has first to knock out before one can talk to them sensibly".[2] A somewhat vainglorious abuse of an opponent who was expected soon to be as soundly beaten as his already crushed allies. And yet in this rhapsody of character assassination an undertone of respect is unmistakable, "there is something magnificent," admitted Goebbels, "in the manner they (the English) face the world after a defeat which would shake up any other nation profoundly, at least in its morale. With a most hypocritical air they proceed to transform the catastrophe by lying into a glorious victory." [3]

Six months later, when heavy German air attacks on British towns had followed the unsuccessful German onslaught of the Battle of Britain, Goebbels still pursued the same line.[4]

The *Blitz* of the Luftwaffe on British towns evoked a new variety of his old theme from the versatile Propaganda Minister. With sensational description he depicted the plight of the British masses, a plight they owed entirely to the heartless arrogance of their own misguided ruling class. Goebbels indulged in an almost Dickensian pity for the helpless man in the street, whose ordeal in the bombed towns he painted in the darkest colours.[5]

Yet the enemy did not give in. Shortly before Christmas 1940 Goebbels assured the German public who had by then expected England to be on her knees, that there was no point in measuring "this strange and evil world according to our criteria or habits." One day it would collapse for it is overripe for a fall, for the end of a rotten system. Had not every German learned in school Schiller's famous dictum: *"Die Weltgeschichte ist das Weltgericht"* (World History is World Judgment). At this moment Goebbels felt it appropriate to lay on a thick coat of Schillerian moralism. When the second year of the war passed and the English still held out, the Propaganda Minister somewhat readjusted his old line in order to "explain" the puzzling fact of the continued British resistance.[6] Early in 1941 he wrote that the English "were not at all the highly developed, politically mature people such as the people on the Continent

---

[1] *Die Zeit ohne Beispiel,* p. 301.

[2] Op. cit., p. 304.

[3] Op. cit., p. 302.

[4] Article "Eine andere Welt", *Das Reich,* 22 December 1940. *Die Zeit ohne Beispiel,* pp. 336-341.

[5] "The people descend afternoon after afternoon into the pits of the underground, are sitting fourteen hours in pain, misery, filth and epidemics and wait for the miracle promised them by Churchill. Or they stray weepingly in the ruins of Bristol, Birmingham or Sheffield, only filled with the one thought how to obtain a piece of bread and a roof over their heads." Op. cit., p. 340.

[6] See his article, "England und seine Plutokraten", *Das Reich,* 5 January 1941, reprinted in *Die Zeit ohne Beispiel,* pp. 359-363. The quotation is on p. 359.

like to see them." Only in the critical moments of their history did they display "a certain instinct for what is necessary and real" but otherwise they had "not the slightest idea of the problems which move the world." [1]

It was all very well to debunk, ridicule and belittle Mr. Churchill, but Goebbels had now also to account for the fact that he was still head of the British Cabinet and that he had not escaped to Canada after Dunkirk, as predicted by Hitler and himself. Whilst presenting the picture of a heartless cynic, ruthlessly gambling away the happiness and fortune of his nation, Goebbels was prepared to concede his obstinacy at one moment and to dismiss it as sign of an arrested development at the next. Mr. Churchill, he declared, had his roots in the First World War, he was simply out of touch with the great changes that had taken place in the European situation since then and with the moving forces which now determined it. "His stiff-necked obstinacy forbids him admitting that an action which succeeded in November 1918, was entirely hopeless in the spring of 1941." He only thought in terms of the First World War and his leadership in the present struggle was nothing but a "stupid repetition of it." [2] Churchill was like the unfortunate *émigrés* of the French Revolution, who had neither forgotten anything nor learned anything: "a voice from the tomb of the past", a man without imagination, without any constructive thought and national *élan*. Seeing only his own milieu, he presented "a typical insular figure without any width of vision and intellectual boldness." The trouble with Mr. Churchill, one might paraphrase Goebbels' line of propaganda, was that he was a gambler instead of being a good business man who knows when to come to an arrangement with his rivals. "You cannot make it clear to gambler-types like Mr. Churchill", lamented Goebbels, "that it is better to go home with the remaining part of one's fortune than to risk it and lose it in a last wild gamble for a hopeless cause. Thus Mr. Churchill will gamble and England will pay for it." [3]

Goebbels' techniques in anti-British propaganda. To an effective propagandist the "how" matters as much as the "what", the language and form of argument as much as the subject matter. He knows that his speeches or articles, are "reacted to in terms of the style, structure, emotional appeal, and so on, in some degree of independence of its propaganda content;" [4] vivid language, bold similes, phrases which stick are preferable to factual information, let alone to quiet reasoning. Goebbels' approach was not so much emotional, but graphic and drastic, he had often a shrewd intuitive insight into what might appeal to the masses and

---

[1] Op. cit., p. 360.

[2] Article "Über die geistige Kriegführung," *Das Reich,* 2 March 1941; *Die Zeit ohne Beispiel,* pp. 401-405. The quotation is on p. 404.

[3] Op. cit., p. 405.

[4] H. D. Lasswell and A. Kaplan, *Power and Society,* New Haven, 1950, p. 113.

influence them. If propaganda was to him an art, and therefore subject to ever new tricks and devices, there were, nevertheless, certain techniques which recurred. The same theme had to be approached from various angles, but if there were different verses, they all had, explicitly or implicitly, the same propagandist refrain. The task was one of polarity,[1] on the one hand one had to belittle, debunk, expose and ridicule the enemy, on the other, to demonstrate the greatness, the success of one's own cause and the certainty of its final victory. To unmask and expose, to contrast the enemy's large claims with his pitifully small achievements was the same as to propagate German superiority and certainty of victory. You have only to realize the absurd *impasse* in which the English find themselves, suggested Goebbels, to realize that their defeat is inevitable.[2]

Obviously Goebbels was aware that in the past British prestige had affected many Germans. After all, England had been a world power for centuries. And thus the master propagandist thought it prudent to play off the present versus the past, to belittle the importance of history and to stress what he called a nation's "revolutionary will to live." Revolutionary dynamics were what mattered, not reliance on a weakening tradition. There the Germans were "superior to England, quite apart from the better organization of our state and nation, the greater numbers, the better weapons and military training, and the more favourable positions and chances on all the fronts." [3] Using his favourite technique of contrasting symbols, Goebbels could then argue with considerable plausibility: "We possess a Führer who has so far always drawn a winner. Why should he now pick the wrong card? England has a Prime Minister, who has had so far to put up with nothing but defeats. Why should he lead his nation to victory at the very moment when the position of Great Britain is hopeless?" [4]

Churchill was the stumbling block. He was constantly presented as the archetype of the shameless cynic, as a frivolous old sinner who "will figure in history as the grave-digger of the English Empire, a role which none of his fellow countrymen will envy." He must go, if the world wants to have peace. The image of the death of that arch-enemy—so pleasing to the German mind at that time—was evoked by Goebbels in a playful, but calculated return to the *leitmotif* of the article: "What the English people will do with him [after their defeat] is their business. Perhaps he will be forced after the war to re-read aloud all the speeches which he made during the war. He would then enjoy the most original way of death ever granted to a mortal: he would be drowned in the laughter of the world." [5] A clever way of suggesting that your obstinate

---

[1] For the role of 'polarization' in National Socialist propaganda see the article by Henry M. Pachter, "National-Socialist and Fascist Propaganda for the Conquest of Power" mentioned above p. 34, footnote 4.

[2] See the article "Im Gelächter der Welt", *Das Reich*, 16 February 1941; *Die Zeit ohne Beispiel*, pp. 391-395.

[3] Op. cit., p. 395.   [4] Ibid.   [5] Ibid.

enemy No. 1 was after all nothing but the personification of humbug, to be unmasked finally for all the world to see.[1] Goebbels' constant abuse of Mr. Churchill seems to have been to some extent a device to compensate the German public for the frustration resulting from the abandonment of the major campaign against England. A press directive of 7 February 1941 is revealing: "As there was much talk of an invasion last year, they [the public] felt disappointed at the end when it did not take place. This must not happen again." [2]

Yet Goebbels did not always stick to this line himself. In an article published early in March 1941 he threw out strong hints: "England will soon have other worries. Forthcoming events throw their shadows ahead. In our radio stations the fanfares for the special announcements [*Sondermeldungen*] are being polished up. Front and home fronts are set for action. All are waiting for the order of the Führer." [3] As by then the Führer had long called off "Operation Sea Lion" and was in fact set instead on the invasion of Soviet Russia,[4] this pronouncement of Goebbels was probably a deliberate manoeuvre to mislead the world and camouflage the forthcoming attack in the East, a trick similar to that which Goebbels was to employ three months later. On 13 June 1941 the first edition of the *Völkischer Beobachter,* which contained an article by Goebbels, "The Example of Crete", was confiscated by Gestapo officials. The article, which was omitted from subsequent editions, gave strong hints that an invasion of England would be forthcoming during the next two months and would be as successful as the recent German parachutist invasion of Crete. The incident caused a minor sensation abroad.[5] In any case it was not until the end of that year that Goebbels would admit in public the hopelessness of an invasion of the British Isles. In an article then published in *Das Reich* he remarked that "from a purely

[1] Next to Mr. Churchill, Lord Halifax, then British Ambassador to the United States, was Goebbels' *bête noire;* he presented him as the embodiment of the religious hypocrisy, typical of his class. See particularly the articles in *Das Reich,* "Der Frömmste unter uns allen," 23 March 1941, and "Lord Halifax als Bankettredner," 6 April 1941; both were reprinted in Goebbels' book, *Die Zeit ohne Beispiel,* pp. 434-439, and pp. 446-451, respectively.

[2] W. Hagemann, *Publizistik im Dritten Reich,* p. 250.

[3] Article "Wenn der Frühling auf die Berge steigt", *Das Reich,* 9 March 1941, reprinted in *Die Zeit ohne Beispiel,* pp. 415-419. The quotation is on p. 419.

[4] On Hitler's reasons for the final rejection of an invasion of England, see the authoritative account by Ronald Wheatley, *Operation Sea Lion, German Plans for the Invasion of England 1939-1942,* Oxford, 1958, pp. 144-149.

[5] See *The Times* (London), 14 June 1941, reporting from Stockholm on the confiscation under the heading "Goebbels Censored." An interesting account of this deliberate manoeuvre of which, besides Hitler and Goebbels, only Dr. Naumann from the Propaganda Ministry and the Editor-in-Chief of the *Völkischer Beobachter* were aware at the time, was given later by Goebbels to Wilfred von Oven. See the latter's book, *Mit Goebbels bis zum Ende,* vol. II, pp. 172-174. The incident had its farcical aspects, as it caused a rumour that Goebbels had fallen into disgrace whereupon some of his colleagues promptly thought it wiser not to contact him.

military point of view an invasion of Great Britain is, of course, difficult, but an invasion of Europe by England is certainly equally difficult, probably much more so." [2]

3. ON THE DEFENSIVE

It was the attack on Soviet Russia which forced Goebbels to modify his technique of deriding and unmasking the English ruling class. The fact that plutocratic Britain and Communist Russia were now both in the enemy camp necessitated some readjustment in German propaganda. No longer was Britain the isolated chief target of Goebbels' attacks. Now a new avenue opened, which led to the debunking of a world conspiracy, of piercing the facade of the strange bedfellows in the new anti-Nazi alliance. Goebbels was quick to expose the common denominator in their attitudes. The Jews, he declared emphatically, were as active and dominant in Downing Street as they were in the Kremlin. It only needed a political master detective to see through their camouflage. "The Veil has fallen" and "Mimicry" were significant headings of articles, in which Goebbels pursued this line in July 1941.[2] As we saw, the idea of a Jewish world conspiracy had been a standard stereotype before, but now it was resuscitated with a fresh and even more fantastic angle. At the same time the idea of encirclement was revived. Until the Führer's decision to attack Soviet Russia, argued Goebbels, the Jewish heads of Bolshevism had been cleverly kept in the background, probably on the erroneous assumption that they would thus deceive the Germans. The Litvinovs and Kaganovitches hardly appeared in public. But all the more sinister were their activities behind the curtain. They tried to create the false impression in Germany that the Jewish Bolsheviks in Moscow and the Jewish Plutocrats in London and Washington were deadly enemies. In fact in secret they had worked together all the more closely to further the encirclement which was to crush Germany.[3]

When in 1941 the German troops in Russia first piled success upon success and Rommel's armies in Africa reconquered Cyrenaica, with Britain remaining on the defensive, Goebbels found it easy to deride British propaganda as a mere "offensive of the mouth" which would turn out "as much a failure as all previous Churchillian offensives, both in the military and the propagandist fields." [4]

As he expressed it in a venomous attack in September 1941: "In war not wishdreams decide, but facts. And they speak without exception for

[1] Article "Verändertes Weltbild", *Das Reich*, 21 December 1941; reprinted in *Das eherne Herz*, Munich, 1943, p. 128.

[2] Articles "Der Schleier fällt", *Das Reich*, 6 July 1941 and "Mimikry", *Das Reich*, 20 July 1941, reprinted in *Die Zeit ohne Beispiel*, pp. 520-525, and pp. 526-531 respectively.

[3] *Die Zeit ohne Beispiel*, p. 528.

[4] Op. cit., p. 548, article "Die britische Mauloffensive", *Das Reich*, 10 August 1941. *Die Zeit ohne Beispiel*, pp. 543-548.

us. London has no further possibility of intervening decisively in the course of events. Grinding her teeth, she must look on and see how the European continent develops a New Order, even if with pain and hard birth-pangs. England talks, the Reich acts. That is the difference." [1]

The high German hopes of a speedy victory over Russia were, however, disappointed by the autumn of 1941, just as their hopes for a quick knockout of England had been frustrated a year earlier. As it has been shown in an earlier chapter,[2] after Otto Dietrich's serious blunder of pronouncing the war as practically ended, Goebbels did his best to damp down such exaggerated hopes and to induce the man in the street to take a less sanguine view.

As far as Britain was concerned, it is true throughout 1941 Goebbels went on to predict the eventual collapse of the British Empire and to abuse Churchill.[3] But in an article published on 9 November 1941,[4] the suggestion of an early collapse of the British Empire was rejected for the first time. Goebbels now claimed that he did "not belong to those fantasts and illusionists who predict a collapse of the British Empire for tomorrow or the day after tomorrow. A good thing takes time, and what had been built in centuries, does not fall in a few months." He viewed the situation soberly, knowing very well that many a push would be required "in order to make the colossus of clay totter". This was, however, by no means decisive. What appeared to him essential was the fact that England had "no longer any chance of winning" finding herself "already on the road to defeat".[5]

By 1942 Goebbels' image of Churchill had become more complex. Though the severe blows Britain suffered in the Far East early in that year allowed him triumphantly to proclaim "a Prime Minister who exposes a world Empire to such dangers, is an unfathomable gain to his adversar es, we can congratulate ourselves on this Churchill",[6] yet he admitted at the same time that Churchill was an extraordinarily skilful tactician, who mastered "the ABC of democratic party and press control

[1] Article "Die Angeber", *Das Reich*, 14 September 1941; *Die Zeit ohne Beispiel*, p. 577 f.

[2] See above Chapter 11, pp. 246 f.

[3] See e.g. Goebbels' article "Der tönerne Koloss", *Das Reich*, 23 November 1941, reprinted in *Das eherne Herz*, pp. 92-98. Churchill is described as belonging "to the most widely known liars in the world".

[4] "Wann oder Wie?" *Das Reich*, 9 November 1941. See above chapter 11, p. 247.

[5] *Das eherne Herz*, p. 95 f.

[6] Article by Goebbels "Churchill's Trick", *Das Reich*, 1 March 1942, reprinted in *Das eherne Herz*, pp. 222-228. See also a further article by him on the same lines, "Das Gesetz der neuen Welt", *Das Reich*, 12 July 1942. Goebbels wrote: "A man like Churchill would not be acceptable in Germany. Though according to the view of the English we live in Germany under a dictatorship, this alleged dictatorship yet has so much self-control that it would drive a failure of his calibre out of office disgraced within 24 hours." See *Das eherne Herz*, p. 393.

with a certain virtuosity". He called him "a white raven amongst the present British politicians who do not strike the eye with their outstanding intelligence".[1] The time of the lightning successes having past, Goebbels changed his similes and metaphors accordingly. He now compared the war with a drawn-out boxing match which had not ended in the first round with a sudden knock-out blow; it had to be fought through several rounds. "What matters most is to beat the opponent by dangerous blows slowly, but surely. Sometimes when about to sink down he is once more saved by the gong, and then a new round must be started. The decisive second will come when he falls to the ground as though struck by lightning. We do not know when that will be, but we know that it will come." [2]

The growing number of British air raids on German towns in 1942 was bound to persuade many Germans that Britain was far from being beaten, and that the entry of the U.S.A. into the war had increased her striking power. The fact that, for example, on 11 September Düsseldorf was subjected to its fiftieth air raid made it inadvisable for Goebbels to present the English as cowards or nitwits. Goebbels had his ear sufficiently close to the ground to realize that it might be wise to admit a point or two in favour of the enemy, "We know, of course," he wrote in September 1942, "that the English, too, are not a nation of devils. They, too, have qualities which deserve admiration. But we shall not talk of them, as long as they do not admit any redeeming features in us. And besides we are at war." [3]

In 1942 much of Goebbels' propaganda was still directed against England in such telling headlines over his articles as "Smoke from London", "Shadows over the Empire" and "Black Clouds over England". By comparison it is indicative that none of the headings of the thirty-nine articles and speeches written and delivered by the Reich Propaganda Minister between January and September 1943 and reprinted in his book *Der steile Aufstieg*, bears any reference to England and the English. Instead the growing anxiety on the home front and Goebbels' systematic efforts to allay it are reflected in such headlines as "The Winter Crisis and Total War", "Does the Government actually know this?", "Morale as a Factor Decisive in War", "The Realities of War", "A Word on the War in the Air", "Indomitable Berlin", "The Great Drama", "Of the National Duties in War Time", etc., etc. But if England and the English were now of secondary importance to Goebbels' attempts to galvanize and integrate the masses in a total war effort, they were by no means absent from his calculated perorations. His famous address before a mass meeting at the Berlin Sport Palace on 18 February 1943, two weeks after the Stalingrad disaster had reached its climax, is a case in point.

As has been shown, Goebbels concluded his powerful and lengthy

[1] Op. cit., p. 222.

[2] Article "Churchill's Trick", *Das eherne Herz*, pp. 227-228.

[3] Article "Seid nicht allzu gerecht!" *Das Reich*, 16 September 1942, (*Das eherne Herz*, p. 456.)

speech with an effective trick by putting ten questions to his well-selected audience to which they duly reacted with frenzied waves of shouting and enthusiasm.[1] The first five of these suggestive questions referred to alleged British lies. His approach clearly indicated a change of position from his high-handed arrogance of 1940 to a stubborn and hard pressed fight on the defensive. It also reveals that by then he apparently regarded the impact of British propaganda as more serious than that coming from Moscow.

During the first half of the war Goebbels had been busy pronouncing the impending doom of England and boosting the *furor teutonicus* as an aggressive force. After Stalingrad he appealed to fear among his fellow countrymen, fear of what the Russians and the English would do to them should they win. The line of the international Jewish conspiracy with its two wings, Plutocracy in London and Washington and Bolshevism in Russia, was kept up right to the end of the war. After June 1941 Churchill was therefore depicted as "the prisoner of the Kremlin", who had to carry out Stalin's orders, a puppet in the hands of Moscow.[2] While the obstinate cynic Churchill now appeared as a figurehead or puppet, it was Lord Vansittart, who, according to Goebbels, had let the cat of true and sinister British war aims out of the bag. Lord Vansittart, that die-hard of "Unconditional Surrender" had refused to make a distinction between Nazis and Germans and in his writings and speeches in the House of Lords had demanded harsh treatment of a defeated Germany. To Goebbels this was manna from heaven. "This fellow Vansittart", he jotted down in his diary on 24 April 1943, "is really worth his weight in gold to our propaganda. After the war a monument ought to be erected to him somewhere in Germany with the inscription: 'To the Englishman who rendered the greatest service to the German cause during the war!' "[3]

Goebbels made much of Vansittart's thesis that Germany had been treated far too mildly at Versailles and had to be crushed after the war. Fearing that the Atlantic Charter, proclaimed by Mr. Churchill and

[1] See the analysis of Goebbels' address at this meeting, above ch. 11, pp. 261-268.

[2] See Goebbels' article "Der Gefangene des Kremlin", *Das Reich*, 24 August 1942, reprinted in *Das eherne Herz*, pp. 443-450.

[3] *The Goebbels Diaries*, p. 267. For Sir Robert Vansittart's "total" anti-German views see his pamphlet *Black Record: German Past and Present*, London, 1941. The pamphlet contains the text of seven broadcasts delivered by the author in the Overseas Programme of the B.B.C. The following passage is typical: "The bird of prey is no sudden apparition. It is a species. Hitler is no accident. He is the natural and continuous product of a breed which from the dawn of history has been predatory and bellicose. It has thriven on indulgence, which has always been in favour of giving the aggressor another chance. And the aggressor has always taken it." (p. 16) Other wartime publications by Vansittart in the same vein are: *Roots of the Trouble*, London, 1941; *The Greatest Swindle in the World, the Story of the German Reparations*, London, 1942; *Lessons of my Life*, London, 1943 and *Bones of Contention*, New York, 1945.

President Roosevelt in August 1941, might appeal to some Germans just as President Wilson's Fourteen Points had done in 1918, Goebbels declared: "We have more confidence in the German weapons than in the British promises. We are convinced that Lord Vansittart and not Mr. Churchill speaks the truth." [1]

In 1943-44 Goebbels hoped to be able to drive a wedge between the Allies. Recognizing that Germany could not win the war against the strong enemy coalition, he pondered the chances of an understanding with either Churchill or Stalin, and felt the necessity of coming to an arrangement with one side or the other. "The Reich has never won a two-front war," he wrote in his diary on 23 September, 1943, "we must therefore see how we can somehow or other get out of a two-front war." [2] With his Macchiavellian opportunism, he thought it safer and "much more agreeable" to come to terms with London than with Moscow. "One can always make a better deal with a democratic state and once peace has been concluded, such a state will not seize the sword for at least twenty years to come." [3] A totalitarian system, on the other hand, could embark on another war at any time.

Already six months earlier, Goebbels had publicly indulged in some wishful thinking on these lines. The English, he asserted then, had begun to recognize that Bolshevism meant a danger to the West. "It is true," Goebbels wrote, "they sing the International in London, but they do not sing 'God Save the King' in Moscow. It is true that over England the flags of Bolshevism fly, but have you ever heard that the flags of the British Empire fly over the Soviet Union? . . ." [4] If a more or less healthy person lay down in the same bed with a man suffering from typhoid he would not infect the typhoid case with his health, but instead would catch typhoid from the sufferer. In the co-operation between radicalism and conservatism, radicalism always has the better chance.

When the wave of heavy air raids on German towns brought home to the civilians the full grimness of war and the deadly weapons in the hands of the Anglo-Saxon powers,[5] Goebbels came out with a new line of comparison between the Germans and the English. To make admissions three or four years after the event seemed safe enough. Now he simply argued that if the English could take it in 1940, so could the Germans in 1943 or 1944. A well devised argument, for the Propaganda Minister was aware of what was then in the mind of the Berliners. As one of his assistants noted in his diary on 3 March 1943: "The Berliner is a steady, objective kind of fellow. That is why he admires the stoical

[1] Goebbels' article "Was auf dem Spiele steht", *Das Reich,* 27 September 1942. *Der steile Aufstieg,* p. 7.

[2] *The Goebbels Diaries,* p. 386.

[3] Op. cit., p. 387.

[4] Goebbels' article "Damals und Heute", in *Das Reich,* 7 March 1943; see *Der steile Aufstieg,* p. 217.

[5] See above, ch. 12, pp. 269-271.

calm with which the British stand up to air raids. One hears it said that
the British take them better than we do. Many people think that the
Berliners would have collapsed long ago under such raids. Goebbels gets
very angry at such a low estimate of "his Berliners", for whose political
morale he feels responsible. He does not believe the British are tougher
than the Germans." [1]

At that time Goebbels told a German journalist in a confidential talk
that he regarded it his task "to train the people in the coming months
to be tough. To applaud a Blitz campaign needs no toughness. But I
have a feeling that this war will not end quickly." [2]

A few months afterwards when as Gauleiter of Berlin Goebbels had
to organize the mass evacuation of children from the Reich capital, he
mentioned the stoicism the Londoners had shown earlier in the war.
"What the English stuck out in the autumn of 1940 and for which a
few of us admired them," he told the Berliners, "that we have to stick
out now. I reject indignantly the enemy allegation that the Berliners have
weaker nerves than the Londoners. This is out of the question. Just as
for the English a turn for the better has come in the field of air warfare
since 1940, so things will also turn round for us. The English waited two
years for this; our waiting period will be a much shorter one than the
English." [3]

Soon Goebbels widened the parallel between Berliners and Londoners
to one between the Germans and the English. It was a variation of the
same theme which he developed in an article headed "Morale as the
Decisive Factor in War": The English, he argued, "had endured this test
of nerves under much more unfavourable political and military conditions in 1940; we have to endure it in 1943." But the comparison did
not end there, it extended even to the uncertain field of 'Miracle Weapons'. "Just as then the British Government decided to bring about a
fundamental change in the air war by a radical solution, i.e. the development of a new weapon of attack," [4] Goebbels darkly hinted, "so we took
such a definite decision some time ago"—an oblique reference to the
Wunderwaffen then still in the making.[5] Another parallel between the
situations in England in 1940 and in Germany in 1943 presented itself
by the organized mass evacuation of people from the big cities into less
endangered reception areas. Goebbels did not deny the difficulties arising
from evacuation on a large scale, but he was confident that they would
be overcome in the same way that the English had mastered their
emergency in 1940. "If the English press makes its readers believe that

[1] R. Semmler, *Goebbels—The Man next to Hitler*, p. 72.
[2] Op. cit., p. 73.
[3] Article "Ein Wort zum Luftkrieg", *Völkischer Beobachter* (Berlin edition),
4 August 1943; see *Der steile Aufstieg*, p. 403.
[4] Article "Die Moral als kriegsentscheidender Faktor", *Völkischer Beobachter*, 7 August 1943; see *Der steile Aufstieg*, p. 408.
[5] See above ch. 14.

such and similar measures could cause a panic in the German war effort, then its readers will one day have to pay dearly for this error." Why? Because as Goebbels was now prepared to concede, "we, too, made a similar mistake when, in 1940, the British Government sent the children of London to the country. Hardly any of our hopes then were fulfilled. We therefore do not mind discussing these problems quite openly." [1] A mixture of studied frankness and an agreeable belief that a past error now admitted by the Germans was about to be repeated by their enemy.

5. The Other Side of the Medal

It is perhaps in the nature of a totalitarian régime that its rulers better than those of democracies can afford to speak with two voices, one in public and one in private. Power-politicians and power-fans are only impressed by power, both military and psychological, and by resistance to it. Apart from his fanatical attachment to the Führer and his fixed hatred of the Jews, Goebbels was able and to some extent willing, to learn from experience. And while, as we have seen, he attacked the British and Churchill incessantly and viciously in public, his traditionally negative picture of them gradually underwent a certain change after the "Battle of Britain" and the Blitz on the English towns had proved inconclusive and thus a failure. Goebbels may have hated Churchill, but as time went on and the British continued to resist and even to hit back in air-warfare, he learned more and more to respect him.

Like many other Germans, Goebbels had anticipated in the summer of 1940 that England would throw in the sponge. In September of that year he had expected her capitulation any day. According to Werner Stephan, then in his entourage, Goebbels did not believe in the success of an invasion because he was aware that the German naval units were inadequate for such an enterprise, but he thought that Britain would collapse under the pressure of an encirclement stretching from the North Cape to Spain and through the terrific bombardment by the *Luftwaffe*.[2] When the British army escaped from Dunkirk in June 1940, Goebbels saw in the British soldiers only "propagandists in defeat",[3] and in the autumn he expected that the British masses, probably made decadent by democracy, would no longer tolerate Mr. Churchill's weighty leadership. How could they be strong enough, he argued, to accept the British Prime Minister's famous prophecy of "blood, sweat and tears" which was all he had to offer them? Gradually, however, he realized that Churchill was not only obstinate but also a skilful propagandist or, as Goebbels dubbed him, "a demagogue of a high calibre".[4] Both contradictory and single-

---

[1] *Der steile Aufstieg*, p. 409.
[2] W. Stephan, op. cit., p. 219 f.
[3] Op. cit., p. 221.
[4] Cf. W. Stephan, *Joseph Goebbels*, p. 222. See also Goebbels' earlier acknowledgement of Churchill as "an extraordinary skilful tactician", quoted above, p. 423.

minded, Goebbels liked to embarrass people. He surprised and even shocked many members of his staff and some big Party bosses by telling them after 1940 that "what the British Prime Minister had made of the events of Dunkirk, deserved the highest respect".[1]

It was characteristic of Goebbels' inclination to contrariness that he liked to praise one person at the expense of another. There is evidence that as early as the beginning of 1941 the Propaganda Minister ventilated his intense dislike of his rival von Ribbentrop by praising Churchill whenever people in his entourage talked of the German Foreign Minister. Perhaps he was not insincere when he contrasted Ribbentrop with the British Prime Minister lamenting it as "a tragedy that Hitler had such a dilettante as adviser on foreign policy".[2] Apart from practical considerations dictated by the necessities of the war effort the Führer did little to make Goebbels and Ribbentrop friends, probably because he felt that there was strength in a leadership based on the principle of "divide and rule".[3] The grudging respect Goebbels had for Churchill, and his tendency to blame his rival Ribbentrop and the Ministry of Foreign Affairs for the Nazi failure to combat Churchill's adroit global foreign policy effectively, grew as the war went on.

An example from the last quarter of 1944 can illustrate this. In October 1944 Churchill and Eden had flown from Quebec to Moscow. In Germany the Propaganda Ministry and the Reich Press Chief, Dr. Dietrich, who was then in league with Ribbentrop, issued divergent directives on that event to the German press. Goebbels regarded this trip as an indication that Churchill wanted to re-cement a coalition which was disintegrating and as he pinned great hopes on a possible rift in it, he gave orders for the greatest reserve to be exercised in the comments by press and radio. Neverthless, the German newspapers published front page reports on the matter and indulged in long and sarcastic comments on the event. In other words, the press had followed the Ribbentrop-Dietrich line instead of the Goebbels directive.

This resulted in a sharp clash between Dr. Goebbels and the representative of the Foreign Ministry at the daily conference of the Propaganda Ministry: "One makes oneself ridiculous before the whole world," Goebbels thundered, "by trying, as was unfortunately done, to treat the

---

[1] W. Stephan, op. cit., pp. 221-222. Apparently he was also impressed by the official British statement issued during the German invasion of France that the R.A.F. could not be spared for war activities in France, as it was required for the defence of the British Isles. He used to recommend Churchill's tough realism, telling his ministerial staff "that was the right thing to do, so ruthless had a true statesman to be". Goebbels probably had in mind the statement made by Churchill to General Weygand during the last stage of the Battle of France on 11 June 1940. See W. S. Churchill, *The Second World War*, vol. II, *Their Finest Hour;* Reprint Society Edition, London, 1951, p. 137.

[2] Cf. R. Semmler, *Goebbels—The Man Next to Hitler,* p. 18, diary entry of 16 January 1941.

[3] See the Führer's order to Ribbentrop and Goebbels of 8 September 1939 mentioned above in ch. 3, p. 52, fn. 1.

journey of the British Prime Minister ironically in our press as his 'taking orders' (from Moscow). There I have a view and our public opinion shares it, which differs from that of the Foreign Ministry. I have thorough respect for this seventy year old man who flies round half the globe, from London to Quebec, from Canada to London, from London to Moscow in order to re-cement a coalition, which has become fragile and on which his entire concept of the war depends. This evokes respect even from the simplest of our fellow countrymen, all the more so as he must realize that by the same toughness and energy we could have prevented one after another of our allies from deserting us." [1] When two months later Churchill had set off again with Eden, this time to Athens, to deal with the complicated internal situation in Greece, the Propaganda Minister told his intimates that the German press would "be making fun of the two travelling diplomatists. But I feel only respect for this man for whom no humiliation is too base and no trouble too great when the victory of the Allies is at stake". How different was Ribbentrop, who during the last four years "had not once visited a Balkan capital".[2]

There is historical irony in the reflection that Goebbels employed the same brush of abuse against Ribbentrop behind the curtain that he used against Churchill in front of it. In any case, by then Goebbels was, to quote a witness, "deeply impressed by Churchill".[3]

Goebbels was much more realistic in his appraisal of Churchill than was Hitler who seems to have largely accepted the official Nazi propaganda cartoon of the English Prime Minister. Whereas Goebbels in private compared Churchill favourably with Axis personalities like Ribbentrop and Badoglio,[4] Hitler contrasted him with Lloyd George or even with Lord Runciman to the disadvantage of his most formidable opponent in Britain. Hitler was unwilling and perhaps constitutionally unable to see Churchill in a more detached light, at least to judge by what he said in one of his table talks in May 1942: "The English regarded Churchill as the only man suitable for their political leadership. They were quite aware of his negative side, but considered him apparently as the prototype of their own character. If one compared the leader of the English in the First World War, the fanatic Lloyd George, with Churchill

---

[1] W. von Oven, *Mit Goebbels bis zum Ende*, II, p. 157. Diary entry 11 October 1944.

[2] R. Semmler, op. cit., p. 172 f. Diary entry of 15 December 1944.

[3] Ibid.

[4] "You have to have the courage to face destruction," Goebbels observed to his entourage after Mussolini's fall in August 1943. "That the Italians gave up the war and with it freedom and greatness as a sovereign nation, to which the Duce had led them, only because a few bombs fell on their cities will be regarded by history as a miserable weakness. On the other hand, it constitutes the historical greatness of Churchill—whatever may be said against him in other respects—that he did not allow the *Blitz* on London to discourage him, but that he led his nation through this moment of an understandable weakness and beyond it." W. von Oven, op. cit., I, p. 88; diary entry of 10 August 1943.

one cannot escape the observation that the calibre of leadership was appalling in England. From an objective point of view Churchill was nothing but a typical big mouth (*ausgemachte Quadratgoschen*), unscrupulous, a man whose self-confidence cannot be impaired by anything and in his private life, not a gentleman either." [1]

On the other hand Goebbels did not allow his hatred of the enemy to interfere with a cool appraisal of him. During the last two years of the war the Propaganda Minister oscillated in his hopes for a *rapprochement* with either Russia or England. In September 1943 Hitler told him he thought it would be easier to come to an arrangement with England than with Soviet Russia. Goebbels held a different view. "I am rather inclined," he wrote in his diary on 10 September, "to regard Stalin as more approachable, for Stalin is more of a practical politician than Churchill. Churchill is a romantic adventurer, with whom you can't talk sensibly." [2] At the same time, Goebbels was fully aware that Churchill remained opposed to Bolshevism. The Propaganda Minister commented that from the German point of view he was "not even sure that it would be a good thing for Churchill to be ousted in England". "His successor would no doubt be Eden," but Eden was "more contaminated by Bolshevik ideology than Churchill," who was in fact "an old anti-Bolshevik and his collaboration with Moscow today" was "only a matter of expediency".[3]

It throws light on the dialectics of warfare that during the winter 1943-1944 with its devastating air attacks on German towns, including Berlin, some people of Goebbels' staff drew a parallel between him and Churchill. Commenting on Goebbels' "come-back" into Hitler's favour, Wilfred von Oven noted in his diary on 16 March 1944: "The air war and its mastery by him have provided an essential impetus to this rise. Particularly what Berlin and its inhabitants achieved under Goebbels' leadership during the last few weeks and months, has rightly evoked general admiration. Just as Churchill in England created an immense fund of confidence on

---

[1] Dr. Henry Picker, *Hitler's Tischgespräche im Führerhauptquartier 1941-1942*, Bonn, 1951, p. 90, entry for 20 May 1942. The different English edition, *Hitler's Table Talk, 1941-1944*, London, 1953, which is based on another source, does not contain this passage. Cf. also Dr. Otto Dietrich, *12 Jahre mit Hitler*, pp. 260 ff. In October 1942 Goebbels told Fritzsche that Hitler was prepared to make great concessions to the West in order to end the war. If this did not prove possible it was due only to personalities like Churchill and Roosevelt. But there existed circles in England and U.S.A. who recognized the false position of their countries in this struggle. According to Fritzsche, Goebbels mentioned "well-known names in the Anglo-Saxon countries" and showed him some evidence for this view. *Hier spricht Hans Fritzsche*, p. 221.

[2] *The Goebbels Diaries*, pp. 347-349.

[3] Goebbels' hatred of Anthony Eden was probably more intense than that of Churchill. "The English, anyway," he wrote in his diary on 19 December 1942, "are the Jews among the Aryans. The perfumed British Foreign Minister, Eden, cuts a good figure among these characters from the synagogue. His whole education and his entire bearing can be characterised as thoroughly Jewish." *The Goebbels Diaries*, p. 190.

which he is still drawing by taking on the sole responsibility in the hardest hour of his country . . . in the same way Goebbels has inspired confidence because he did not hesitate to take on the responsibility for such a hopeless affair as the air war, a responsibility dodged by the person actually responsible," [1] an obvious allusion to Göring.

During 1944-1945 Goebbels' attitude to Britain and particularly to Churchill was one of resignation mingled with admiration and minor abuse. In February 1944 he declared privately that Churchill's continued hatred of Nazi Germany was the reason why he, "an artful old fox and an opponent not to be underestimated, will never reach as a statesman the outstanding calibre of a Stalin but will always remain a juggler in politics, a charlatan".[2] One month later, after one of his rare visits to the Führer at the Berghof, Goebbels deplored that Churchill was an American in race and feelings ("*blut-und-gefühlmässig*") and thus unable to act in the true interests of Britain. As long as Churchill is at the helm, he lamented, a "reasonable solution from the English and German points of view is out of the question. In this the Führer and I are completely of the same opinion." [3] At that time Goebbels discovered that "apparently the only way out of our dilemma which the Führer can still see is Churchill's fall." However, the ambitious Reich Minister seems to have been none too happy about the task Hitler had allotted him, then three months before the beginning of the Allied invasion in the West. It was "to drive a wedge between Churchill and his party, between Churchill and the English people, between Churchill and the members of his own class (*Standesgenossen.*)"[4]

Goebbels probably realized that such an effort was practically hopeless, because in private his attitude became increasingly what one might describe as a mournful "*If only. . . .*" Three examples of this line relevant to our theme may be given here. In retrospect the change on the British throne at the end of 1936 now seemed to Goebbels a tragedy.[5] "*If only* Edward Windsor were on the English throne today," he said to von Oven, "provided that it would have come to a war at all under his rule—he would have long ago taken the decisive step, and our two nations would now fight side by side against the Bolshevist world enemy instead

---

[1] W. von Oven, *Mit Goebbels bis zum Ende,* I, p. 215 f.

[2] W. von Oven, op. cit., I, p. 202; diary entry of 19 February 1944.

[3] W. von Oven, op. cit., I, p. 220; diary entry of 16 March 1944.

[4] Ibid. According to Fritz Hesse, Hitler and Ribbentrop believed all through the war that German anti-Churchill propaganda would effectively undermine Churchill's position and would succeed in making the English realize that Churchill was responsible for all their sufferings. (Fritz Hesse, *Hitler and the English,* London, 1954, p. 114).

[5] It seems that from the beginning of the reign of Edward VIII the National Socialists had great expectations of his pro-German attitude. See the memorandum for Hitler by the Duke of Coburg after his visit to London in January 1936, *Documents on German Foreign Policy,* series C, vol. IV, no. 531.

of tearing each other to pieces. . . . Edward would never have let this cruel spectacle materialize." [1]

Goebbels' memory went back to his meeting with the Duke in Berlin in October 1937, which the Minister described now as one of "the great impressions of my life". The Duke of Windsor had impressed him as "a far-sighted, clever and yet modern man". Above all, he had recognized the paramount importance of the social problem. He was forced to go, Goebbels lamented, because "he was too clever, too progressive, too appreciative of the problem of the under-privileged and too pro-German." "This tragic figure could have saved Europe from her doom, but instead, as Governor of the Bahamas, has to witness the disintegration of the British Empire and perhaps of Europe and the West altogether." [2]

The second example of the "*If only* . . ." attitude is more grotesque. To understand it, we have to consider Goebbels' odd reactions to a radio speech delivered by Churchill on 26 March 1944.[3] In it he reviewed the war position, hinted at the approaching invasion, and discussed some aspects of the Government's planned post-war policy, particularly in the fields of education and health. There was also, for a war-time address, some surprisingly drastic criticism of people at home who criticized the Government. Churchill condemned particularly the unprofitable inclination of these critics to produce blue-prints, "fool-proof solutions for the whole future of the world".[4]

It is understandable that Goebbels was struck by such passages and was inclined to exaggerate their importance. The fact that this was Churchill's first radio speech for nearly a year meant to him that the British Prime Minister was afraid of criticism and had therefore eschewed a speech in the House of Commons where he would have been exposed to hecklers. Goebbels talked to his staff of the bitter disappointment evoked by this speech in England. In his opinion the vital questions avoided in it were those resulting from the growing danger of the Bol-

[1] W. von Oven, op. cit., I, p. 220 ff. In this context a report of 2 August 1940 from Huene, the German Minister in Lisbon, to the German Foreign Ministry is of interest. On the basis of information said to have been received from the Portuguese host of the Duke of Windsor, a Lisbon banker, it claims that the Duke was then "firmly convinced that if he had been king it would never have come to war". *Documents on German Foreign Policy*, series D, vol. X, no. 276, p. 398.

[2] W. von Oven, op. cit., I, p. 221. Hitler shared this view. Cf. *Hitler's Table Talk, 1941-1944*, p. 678. (Entry for the evening of 3 August 1942). In July 1940 German secret agents in Lisbon did their best to prevent the Duke and the Duchess of Windsor from leaving Europe for the Bahamas. See *Documents on German Foreign Policy*, series D, vol. X, particularly docs. no. 264, 265, 276 and 277. For Schellenberg's story of a German attempt then to kidnap the Duke at the request of Hitler and Ribbentrop see *The Schellenberg Memoirs*, London, 1956, pp. 127-143.

[3] For the text, see *The Times*, 27 March 1944. Also *The Dawn of Liberation, War Speeches by the Right Hon. Winston S. Churchill, C.H., M.P., 1944*, compiled by Charles Eade, London, 1945, pp. 36-47.

[4] Ibid.

shevist colossus for England and Europe. Churchill was a disaster both for his own country and for Germany. *"If only"* Goebbels were Churchill's opponent in the House of Commons! "If, on the other side of the Channel, Churchill had only the right opponent (*Gegenspieler*) he would be finished in a few weeks." "Were I sitting in the British House of Commons instead of in the German Propaganda Ministry," Goebbels boasted, "I guarantee that if he (Churchill) were not brought down within four weeks, he would at least be ripe for his fall." [1] Certainly a striking display of Goebbels' unimpaired self-confidence and of his ignorance of parliamentary procedure in Westminster.

How would Goebbels have operated in such a case? To judge from his words to von Oven, by asking searching questions in the press, in Parliament, at mass meetings and in leaflets. Following an old Nazi device Goebbels would have raised these questions again and again. It would be admittedly a hard task, for Churchill was "not a tree which can be brought down by one stroke. One has to hit into the same cut persistently. . . . But you know my persistence. With a sullen rage I would take on this job." [2] This wishful brooding soon ceased and Goebbels returned to earth on a note of realistic resignation. He lamented that he was unable to sit in the House of Commons and that he had no other weapon at his disposal but his articles in *Das Reich*.

There is a third example of Goebbels' half self-pitying, half playful *"If only"* line during that last year of the war. Goebbels was torn. While his hopes made him look for a German *rapprochement* with either the West or Soviet Russia, his realistic astuteness told him to discard this as a wishdream. The fact that he sometimes toyed with the idea of an Anglo-German understanding and sometimes with a Russo-German understanding led to some odd mental associations, to an imaginary changing round of the main figures on the political chessboard. Goebbels revealed these ideas only to a few subordinates; he had no friend.

After the invasion of Western Europe had begun he still speculated on the chances of a crisis in Britain, provided the German troops managed to hold their own and eliminated the invaders. Then he hoped the English would realize the folly of their effort and of spending the last ounce of their blood for Stalin. He regarded Churchill as the biggest obstacle to an Anglo-German understanding, as the British Prime Minister was more motivated by personal feelings such as hatred and vanity than by the necessities of *raison d'état*. *"If only"*, Goebbels told von Oven on 11 June 1944, "if only Stalin sat in Churchill's place in No. 10 Downing Street," for he was "of a different calibre, clear, sober, ice-cold, unaffected by personal emotions, keeping only his aim in mind." [3] If Stalin were leading England, a reasonable agreement be-

[1] W. von Oven, op. cit., I, p. 229, diary entry of 2 April 1944.
[2] Op. cit., I, p. 230.
[3] W. von Oven, op. cit., II, p. 11.

tween "his" England and Nazi Germany would have been concluded long ago. He would have been aware that the only chance of saving the British Empire would be by an understanding with Germany and he would have backed up his insight by action.[1]

In a memorandum on foreign policy for Hitler written in September 1944, in which Goebbels criticized the flabbiness of Ribbentrop's foreign policy in the hope of replacing him, the Minister of Propaganda toyed with the idea of a separate peace with Russia.[2] But by then the writing on the wall had become more visible and the German position had much deteriorated from what it was at the beginning of that year, when Goebbels still thought that Germany possessed the chance of an understanding with one side or the other. "In fact, we have become the tongue of the balance," Goebbels had remarked privately and with some confidence in January 1944, "for the favour of which both sides are making efforts while at the same time they are still fighting us with extreme bitterness." [3]

By the end of January 1945, when the Russian armies had occupied Upper Silesia and crossed the Oder, Goebbels had shed all such illusions. "What a world! What chaos! Where is there still a way out?", he lamented to one of his assistants, "Either Western man comes to his senses very soon or he can lie down in the grave which he has dug for himself most successfully during the last five years. The Mongols are at the gates of the capital of Europe. *'Stalin ante portas!'* " [4] But "Western man" was not prepared to come to the rescue of the desperate Nazi leaders who had misjudged him so long and with such devastating results.

[1] Ibid.

[2] W. Stephan, op. cit., p. 290; see also R. Semmler, op. cit., p. 148, diary entry of 20 September 1944.

[3] W. von Oven, op. cit., I, p. 180; diary entry of 27 January 1944.

[4] W. von Oven, op. cit., II, p. 229; diary entry of 30 January 1945.

CHAPTER 19

The Lure of Historical Parallels (1939-1945)

1. AGAIN THROUGH STRUGGLE TO VICTORY

IN HIS LATER years Goebbels made striking use of historical parallels in propaganda. Not only did he look at them as an effective device, but he sometimes believed in them himself. Though they primarily served for the indoctrination of the masses, they were also occasionally an instrument of auto-suggestion.

After the Munich Agreement and particularly during the Second World War Goebbels was fond of drawing comparisons with earlier critical or dramatic situations in the history of the National Socialist Party or of the German nation. In doing so his aim was either to prove that this time, too, the dawn of victory would follow the long night of struggle, or conversely, to dismiss any parallels unfavourable to the aspirations and claims of National Socialism and damaging to the cause of the Third Reich. The parallels he put forward were thus either positive or negative, calculated to instil hope and confidence, or to dismiss fears and uneasy memories. Goebbels based his positive parallels on the Party's earlier history, or on the shining example set by Frederick the Great when Prussia's very existence was at stake. On the other hand, his negative parallels usually referred to the developments in the two world wars, the one decided over twenty years ago, the other still in the balance.

Like Hitler, Goebbels was fond of recalling the good and sometimes bad old days of the Party before it had come to power. He never tired of reminding his listeners and readers of the hard struggle the Nazi Party had been forced to live through. What had then happened in internal German politics, was now, he suggested, about to be repeated in the wider setting of world affairs. The reason for this repetition: the Führer had remained the same. For instance, on the occasion of the Führer's birthday, in April 1939, Goebbels declared:

"Then, too, there were doubters who, concerning the big and bold decisions of the Führer in his struggle for power, regarded as proper and expedient that false cleverness which Clausewitz had already said was only the wish to avoid danger. We cannot therefore be taken by surprise or be frightened when we see events happening around the Reich in

436

international politics that are identical with, or similar to, those which then took place in German domestic politics around the National Socialist Movement . . . In the course of the years only the dimensions of the political actions of the Führer have changed; their ways and aims have remained the same." [1]

A few months afterwards, in June 1939, Goebbels described the Western democracies as "quite as trivial and ineffective as were the bourgeois parties in the Weimar Republic". They "have not the strength to organize the masses and to impose a uniform will on them. Though they always refer to the masses, secretly they are afraid of them . . . That was the way the bourgeois parties used to handle the people in the former days of the [old] system. They only approached the broad masses, the millions of people, when they were in a tight corner. To them they were only a jumping-board to the power they wished to obtain or a support for the power they had gained". "Are not the democracies of Western Europe today in a position similar to that of the bourgeois parties then?" asked Goebbels boldly. "Their political arguments abound in thoughtless commonplaces. They talk of something they do not know at all and claim something they do not possess. The phrases with which they oppose us are hackneyed and worn out. Their venerable age proves less their wisdom than the fact that they are out of date." [2]

After the outbreak of the Second World War the comparison between the former opponents at home and the present enemies abroad became a favourite point in Goebbels' repertory. In drawing this parallel he would occasionally startle his public by a touch of cynical frankness. In June 1940 Goebbels argued that both the German anti-Nazi forces before 1933 and the western European plutocracies afterwards had let decisive chances slip by. "Whom God wishes to punish, He first smites with blindness. As regards our enemies this is shown by the entire history of the National Socialist Movement." [3] The Weimar Republic had missed a big chance, he suggested, after the first great Nazi success in the elections of 14 September 1930. It could have either recognized the Führer or have tried to destroy him. "The former would have been logical and sensible, the latter difficult, but not impossible. The Republic did not choose either alternative." [4] The Republic had been equally blind to its final chance on 13 August 1932, when Reich President Hindenburg had offered Hitler the Vice-Chancellorship in von Pappen's Cabinet. Hitler, who wished to become Chancellor, had refused. By the obstinate attitude of the highest authorities of the Republic, Goebbels now suggested, the Führer had been given time for the preparation of the final piercing of

[1] "Führergeburtstag 1939, Rundfunkrede zum 50. Geburtstag des Führers, 19 April 1939", printed in *Die Zeit ohne Beispiel*, pp. 99-100.
[2] Article "Der neue Stil", 10 June 1939, *Die Zeit ohne Beispiel*, p. 168.
[3] Article "Die verpassten Gelegenheiten", 2 June 1940, *Die Zeit ohne Beispiel*, pp. 296-304.
[4] Op. cit., p. 296.

the front of parliamentary resistance by the National Socialist movement.[1]

In Goebbels' eyes the same phenomenon had repeated itself in the field of foreign policy after the Nazis had obtained control of the Reich. The Western plutocracies then proved no less shortsighted than the men behind the Republic. On 30 January or at the latest on 31 January 1933, the Western powers had had the choice of either destroying the new Germany at once, completely, or of arranging for a definite peace with her. The former had been perhaps still possible, the latter would have involved some sacrifices, but would have been sensible and not too expensive. Yet the Western powers had done neither. Again the enemy had waited, indulged in illusions and missed a truly common-sense approach. When Germany left the League of Nations in October 1933, the other side still had a further, though a more difficult chance. They could then either have declared war on Germany or concluded a true peace with her. Again neither of these possibilities was seized. When later the Germans proclaimed their freedom to rearm, when German troops reoccupied the Rhineland, the West scoffed and threatened but did not act. Schuschnigg in Austria, Beneš in Czechoslovakia, Beck and Rydz-Smigly in Poland, all had let their chances of coming to a peaceful arrangement with Hitler pass by. These statesmen were now (in 1940) forgotten but, Goebbels suggested, the present leaders of Germany's enemies in the West had proved no less clumsy. On the one hand they had refused the generous offer of the Führer to conclude peace with their countries after the brief Polish campaign, on the other hand they had not made use of the lull of the "phoney" war period for an energetic preparation leading to victory. "The question has often been asked: what do they really think, Churchill and Chamberlain and Reynaud and Daladier? I answer, nothing at all. They think as little as Scheidemann and Braun and Brüning did. They are of such a boastful and arrogant conceit that they believe they can afford not to think." [2]

That confident parallel was drawn when the German armies triumphed in Belgium and France, breaking all resistance with incredible speed. Eighteen months later, when German soldiers had penetrated far into Russia, Goebbels felt no less sure of victory. This time he used a parallel of contrast with the pre-1933 days from a different angle. Then, under the Republic, it had been necessary for the National Socialist opposition to have faith in a German victory—

"when Jewry still entirely controlled public opinion, parliament, the

[1] On 13 August 1932 Hitler had conversations with the Reich Chancellor, von Papen, who offered him the post of Vice-Chancellor in his Cabinet. Hitler indignantly rejected this, insisting, as the leader of the largest party, on the Chancellorship. Later that day Hitler was received by President von Hindenburg who refused to take the responsibility for giving exclusive power to him and was in favour of a coalition Cabinet. The result of these abortive talks was "Hitler's humiliation in the eyes of the world and of his own Party". Cf. A. Bullock, *Hitler, A Study in Tyranny*, pp. 199-201.

[2] Op. cit., p. 299.

stock exchange, the administration, the government, the film and the theatre, and we had only twelve modest seats in the *Reichstag* and did not know how to proceed from one day to the next. Then we had to believe in a victory. But today we have it before our eyes and within our grasp. Today we have the strongest armed forces of the world at our disposal. The most gigantic machinery of rearmament ever seen in history forges their arms, a whole continent with all its inexhaustible resources is on our side or works for us. Yes, we do not only believe in victory, but we are sure of it. We would be ready to hold our hands into the flames for it." [1]

There is another aspect of Goebbels' parallels between the incompetent German Republicans of yesterday and the hated Western democracies of the day. Goebbels liked his public to think that the latter lacked any bold or original ideas and that their feeble efforts at reforming their obsolete régimes were nothing but imitations of the National Socialist model. In the summer of 1939 Goebbels chided the Western democracies for their lack of political style. The same defect had been observed in the Weimar Republic, no feeling for and understanding of the masses. Similar types, Goebbels asserted, ruled in the Western democracies today. "If one reads of their political actions in the press," he remarked contemptuously, "one is tempted to believe in the big words used. But if one watches these political actions in photographs or in sound films, one is repelled with a shock by the chasm which opens up between reality and appearance. One sees fat and jovial elderly gentlemen, who have all sorts of characteristics except the daemonic ability to move and lead the masses . . . and these very democracies sit in judgment on us." [2]

During the war Goebbels fell back on the line that the paucity of war aims and propaganda methods on the side of the Western democracies forced them to follow the Nazi lead. In May 1942 Goebbels alleged that "the longer the war lasts the stronger is the endeavour on the side of our enemies to approximate their war aims and to equate them with those of the Axis powers, if not in fact, at least in their propaganda". As proof of this assertion Goebbels referred to the "well-known English author Bernard Shaw", who had allegedly declared in a recent interview that no nation would probably emerge from the war without a strong Nazi infection, and that even the Soviet Union had only gained successes when imitating the Nazi way of leadership and government.[3] Goebbels poked fun at the pleas in the English and American press at the time (May 1942) "for a more reasonable world order, for a just distribution of raw materials, for the freedom of the seas and of other channels of

[1] Article "Eine notwendige Klarstellung", *Das Reich*, 7 December 1941; reprinted in *Das eherne Herz*, p. 116.

[2] Article "Der neue Stil", 10 June 1939, *Die Zeit ohne Beispiel*, p. 165.

[3] Article "Wofür?", *Das Reich*, 31 May 1942; reprinted in *Das eherne Herz*, pp. 330-336. The present writer has been unable to trace the text of this alleged Shaw interview.

transport, for a new social structure of the peoples as well as against capitalist and plutocratic exploitation, imperialist greed for power and egotistic hunt for profits". According to Goebbels the enemy had simply taken a large leaf out of the Nazi book. "If this goes on then presumably the man in the street in England and in the U.S.A. will soon ask in surprise, why he should continue to fight, as what Churchill and Roosevelt were trying to achieve through war had already been desired and aimed at by Hitler in days of peace."

It is at this point that Goebbels brought in his favourite trick of drawing a historical parallel with the German domestic situation in 1931-1932. At that time, he alleged, National Socialism had begun to move the masses and its enemies. The parliamentary parties could only hope to survive by proving they had borrowed National Socialist ideas. "None wanted to have anything to do with the democracy they had until then praised so highly. All turned against the corrupt party system (die Parteienmisswirtschaft) which had been unable to produce any national leadership.[1] Suddenly all the parties gave the idea of a national community (Volksgemeinschaft) first place in their programme and from the Communists to the German National Party the idea of reconciliation between the classes became the declared aim of all."

Where is the tertium comparationis, one is inclined to ask, between the attitude of the enemy governments in 1942 and that of the German parties of 1932 in this highly coloured version of the party situation prior to the Hitler régime? Propagandist Goebbels finds it in the alleged plagiarism in both cases. "You have to admit," he says cheekily, "that if one wants to have a new suit made, it would be at least unwise to go to a shoemaker. It was then as equally unwise to combat the parliamentary system through the parliamentary parties as it is unwise today to crusade with Churchill and Roosevelt against imperialism and plutocracy and for a new order on the Continent. They and their systems are the profiteers of the evil in question." What is then the conclusion reached by this propaganda tour de force? "The Allies," declared Goebbels, "attempt plagiarism on a large scale, they live only on intellectual theft, and their real war aims are so discredited that they do not dare to mention them in public." [2]

Perhaps the most astonishing parallel between the struggle for power by National Socialism in 1932-1933 at home and its bid for world supremacy in the Second World War was drawn by Goebbels in a con-

[1] Op. cit., p. 332.
[2] Op. cit., pp. 331-332. An interesting point is Goebbels' ambiguous use of the adjective 'daemonic'. In his article "Der neue Stil" of 10 June 1939, Die Zeit ohne Beispiel, pp. 164-168, 'daemonic' has a laudatory meaning. The "daemonic ability to move and lead the masses" is regarded as something positive. In the war-time article referred to above, however, Goebbels ridicules the reproach hurled by Churchill and Roosevelt against the Führer, that he wanted to conquer the world "in order to satisfy his daemonic ambition". It becomes evident from the context that here 'daemonic' is given a negative meaning.

versation with Hitler in September 1943. It reveals to what lengths his
wishful thinking in parallels went, how it could almost become an
obsession. By that time the war situation had deteriorated considerably
from the German point of view and the necessity of coming to terms
with one or the other of the enemy powers impressed itself on the minds
of Hitler and Goebbels. As the Propaganda Minister formulated it now
with a somewhat belated insight: "Germany has never yet had luck with
a two-front war in the long run; she won't be able to stand this one."
Again consolation was to be found in a parallel with the position of
the Nazi Movement ten years earlier: "I pointed out to the Führer,"
Goebbels recorded in his diary, "that in 1933, too, we did not attain
power by absolute demands. We presented absolute demands on 13
August 1932, but failed for that reason. After that, we had to suffer a
whole series of defeats, before we came into power on 30 January 1933
with more modest demands. Very soon thereafter, however, we forced
all our demands through. In all probability similar circumstances prevail
today." [1]

At the same time this argument was also employed by Goebbels in
an article in a more dramatic fashion:

"When we came to power on 30 January 1933, we had behind us a few
victories, but also a chain of defeats. The victories had been a test for
our equanimity, the defeats for our steadfastness. Those who still remember the decisive hour of our revolution know that the news of our taking
over the State appeared at first quite incredible to most people. The
outsiders had expected anything but this. Today we know why this was
so. The great test had come to an end. We had passed it. Victories and
defeats were counted together and the scales of Fate moved in our
favour. When everything was over, we realized that triumph and adversity both had a meaning. Only we did not always want to understand
it in this way." [2] Obviously the parallel helped Goebbels to provide his
readers with the consolations of a "higher" philosophy or semi-religion,
lending meaning to what seemed meaningless:

"The same will be the case in this war. One day the last battle will be
waged. Fortunate the nations who are then among the winners. We do
not doubt for a moment that we shall take first place among them. . . .
Even if the wildest storms are sweeping over Europe today and are

[1] *The Goebbels Diaries*, pp. 348-349; entry dated 10 September 1943. There
is a striking difference in the interpretation of the events of 13 August 1932 in
this article from that in the earlier one, referred to on p. 437. In the earlier
case it served only as an argument for mass propaganda, while in the case
referred to on this page, it was used by Hitler and Goebbels to persuade themselves that there was still a way out of a very sticky situation.

[2] Article "Von den nationalen Pflichten im Kriege", *Das Reich*, 12 September
1943; reprinted in *Der steile Aufstieg*, pp. 448-455. The quotations are on pp.
454-455.

shaking our Continent to its very depth: the world does not perish, it is only being reborn. This we know and this we believe." [1]

The flaw in this parallel is easily seen. The setbacks of the Nazi movement in 1932-1933 were not as formidable as those of Nazi Germany in 1943, when an agreement of the Third Reich with either the Western powers or the Soviet Union was much less likely than had been the Hitler-Hugenberg coalition of January 1933. Then the National Socialists had been the strongest party, whereas in September 1943 Germany's military and political strength was clearly on the decline, although the Nazis still controlled large areas of Europe.

2. No Repetition of the First World War

With the largely negative memories of the outcome of the First World War still in the minds of the older German generation, Goebbels took great trouble in emphasizing the differences rather than the parallels in the position of Germany during the two wars. Already in May 1940 he had been at pains to explain: "History does not repeat itself. It is therefore quite unhistorical to compare the war of today with the world war or to draw parallels with it and its various phases. The times through which we live today are unique and their structure and execution are entirely without example in history. He who tries to analyse them according to the former criteria runs the risk of committing the worst political and military errors." [2] The situation, Goebbels argued, was profoundly different in the military, political, economic, and propaganda fields. In 1914 Germany had been completely encircled and had to wage war on two fronts, a fact "which made the military burden nearly intolerable". From the beginning the German Government had then missed every big diplomatic chance. It had played its trump-cards into the enemy's hands. Today any false neutrality which was only intended to serve as a platform for marching against Germany had been destroyed and the extraordinary dangers of the war on two fronts had been avoided. In the economic field, too, present-day Germany was much better prepared than she had been in 1914. Then the enemy blockade had found Germany defenceless while today the same weapon proved ineffective; "The Reich has such stocks of raw materials that it can stand the war in the economic field for an unlimited time." [3] Although in 1914 Germany had the strongest military forces, only today did she also possess the most modern technical equipment imaginable for them, and careful planning had contributed much to the recent great German successes in the West, admired by the whole world.

In the field of psychological warfare, too, Goebbels argued that Ger-

[1] Ibid.
[2] Article "Die Zeit ohne Beispiel", 26 May 1940; reprinted in the book with the same title, *Die Zeit ohne Beispiel*, pp. 289-295. The quotation is on p. 289.
[3] Op. cit., p. 291.

many had been entirely on the defensive in 1914. Then German leadership had been completely ignorant of the art of influencing public opinion and had not the faintest idea of "the dynamics of the people themselves". Yet their enemies were trained in cunning and slander and knew how to put the German Government in the wrong in any question of importance. Today this had completely changed; in this field too Germany was well prepared and on the offensive. "She knows how to handle the weapon of Truth with sovereign certainty. Her news policy is quick, experienced, clear and effective. She has formed a very detailed system of the highest perfection in the treatment of the opinion of the people and of the public opinion of the world." [1] Goebbels could indeed then, in May 1940, talk plausibly of "the charm of invincibility and the magic of a glorious revolution", which, he said, had accompanied the advancing German armies:

"The comparison with 1914 is entirely wrong. If then the German people held out for four years, it was only because their inner strength compensated for the mistakes and weaknesses of their leadership. Today the position is quite different . . . What achieves victory today is a system that had been prepared in fights for fourteen years and had been practised for seven. It has been inspired by the creative breath of a political and military genius and now lives and becomes effective through its own strength." [2]

Twenty months afterwards, in January 1942, the German position looked less glamorous. By then Germany was fighting on two fronts and the German hopes of a decisive victory in the campaign in Russia had proved futile. Goebbels, who as usual had his finger well on the pulse of the masses at home, felt bound to acknowledge that "the third winter of war finds the German people in a condition (*Verfassung*) different from that of the first." The war had taken on much vaster proportions, compared with which "the worries, which occupied us mainly two years ago, shrink to nothing". "The soldiers have become more serious, more conscious of the issues involved and more determined. Formerly victory was a large brilliant wish; today it is a hard and tough necessity to them." At home the position was similar. Goebbels conjured up an impressive picture: "Big and small people, the rich and the poor compete with each other to devote themselves completely to the task of enabling the nation to fight out its gigantic struggle for survival (*Lebenskampf*) victoriously. In two and a half years we have become a nation of warriors (*Kriegsvolk*)." [3]

The dreaded fight on two fronts, which the Minister of Propaganda had boasted of avoiding in 1940, had now become a grim reality. Goebbels was anxious to discourage and to brand as false all ominous paral-

[1] Op. cit., p. 292.
[2] Op. cit., p. 293.
[3] Article "Wandlung der Seelen", *Das Reich*, 25 January 1942; see also *Das eherne Herz*, pp. 187-193. The quotations are on pp. 188-189.

lels with the second half of the First World War. "One has only to compare the attitude of the German people during the First World War in 1917 with that of the Second World War," he declared in 1942, "in order to know what profound psychological changes all of us have experienced. While then new difficulties only weakened and discouraged us, today they are more prone to harden us and to strengthen our resistance. People debate less about the war and its possibilities, but fight and work all the tougher and more determinedly for it." [1]

As is well known, in 1917 the question of an annexationist or a moderate peace had divided the German *Reichstag* and German public opinion and the famous resolution for a peace without annexations and conquests accepted by a majority in the *Reichstag* had reflected the widespread longing for peace. Small wonder that in 1942 Goebbels was at pains to suggest the complete difference in the German attitude:

"Ask a thousand Germans, if they prefer peace to war and they will give you the unanimous answer, peace. Ask them further if they would prefer to wage war or to give in and the answer will be equally unanimous, to wage war as long as it might last. This is the difference from 1917. Then large sections of the German people wanted peace at any price. Today the entire German people want peace only and exclusively through victory. . . . To wage war successfully it is not the love of war by the people that is required, but their belief in victory. And we Germans possess the latter fully. It is completely unshakable." [2]

After Stalingrad and the turn of the tide in Africa and the Mediterranean, Goebbels dropped his comparisons with the First World War. Instead he fell back on parallels with a situation some two hundred years earlier, the position of Prussia during the Seven Years War. Frederick the Great's dogged stoicism in adversity became the lodestar to which the master propagandist pointed in order to sustain the morale of the German civilians and soldiers in their ever-increasing plight.

3. Frederick the Great as a Model in Harsh Times

Since his early days as a Party agitator in opposition, Goebbels had evoked again and again the image of Frederick the Great as a symbol of national greatness, of heroism in difficulties, of indifference to the changing tides of fortune. As has been shown above, in 1929 he had tried to ridicule Gustav Stresemann, the Foreign Minister, by contrasting his allegedly prosaic figure with the impressive death-mask of the great Prussian king. [3] During the war this cult of Frederick expanded. Six portraits of his hero adorned the walls of the Minister's house in

[1] Op. cit., p. 189.
[2] Article "Vom Vertrauen in die eigene Kraft", *Das Reich*, 8 February 1942; cf. *Das eherne Herz*, p. 207.
[3] See above ch. 2, pp. 35-36.

Berlin in 1943.[1] However much Goebbels played up the figure of Frederick the Great deliberately as a national model in times of hardship and calamity, appealing to the Prussian tradition with all the propaganda methods at his disposal, he had a genuine admiration for the Macchiavellian author of *l'Anti-machiavel*. In February 1940 he described Hitler as the *Vollender* of a heroic tradition of the German idea of Reich, which Frederick the Great had begun and Bismarck had continued.[2]

Frederick had always been a positive symbol in the National Socialist ideology and interpretation of German history. But it was only during the second half of the war that he attained a new significance as a fighter against heavy odds, one who had never allowed grave defeats and misfortunes to wrest ultimate victory from him. In a speech before the German Academy at the University of Berlin on 1 December 1941, Goebbels had quoted a saying by Frederick the Great that in times of emergency one had to provide oneself "with the entrails of iron and an iron heart in order to dispose of all sensitiveness". It was that phrase *Das eherne Herz* which provided the title for one of Goebbels' war-time books.[3] As has been seen earlier in this book, in the spring of 1942, Goebbels expected a great upsurge of home morale from the showing of a revised film on Frederick and his stoicism during the vicissitudes of war.[4]

After the fall of Stalingrad Goebbels' resuscitation of Frederick the Great took on a new and dramatic accent. In his passionate address at the Sport Palace in Berlin on 18 February 1943, he declared:
"In the past years we have often referred to the Frederician example in our newspapers and speeches. We had no right to do so. According to Schlieffen, Frederick had to face ninety million Europeans with five million Prussians during the Third Silesian War. Already in the second of the seven years of hell, he suffered a defeat which shook the entire Prussian State. He never had sufficient soldiers and weapons to wage his battles without the greatest risks. He always carried out his strategy as a system of improvisations. . . . It was not decisive that he suffered defeats, but that the great king remained unbroken under all the blows of fate, that he faced the vacillating fortunes of war and his iron heart overcame every danger. And yet at the end of seven years he stood on the devastated battlefield as a victor, 51 years old, a toothless old man, troubled by gout and a thousand pains. What have we to show com-

---

[1] W. von Oven, *Mit Goebbels bis zum Ende*, vol. I, p. 27. In Goebbels' working room were pictures both of the Führer and of Frederick the Great. When first observing the wealth of portraits of the Prussian king, von Oven remarked: "It seems that old Fritz is the protector of Goebbels' intellectual world altogether."

[2] Address at a mass meeting at Münster, "Gelobt sei, was hart macht", 28 February 1940; see *Die Zeit ohne Beispiel*, p. 247.

[3] Cf. the foreword by M. A. v. Schirmeister, in *Das eherne Herz*, p. 9.

[4] See above ch. 12, pp. 278–279.

pared with this? At the utmost only the will and the determination to equal him if the hour demands this, to remain unshakable in all the vicissitudes of fate, to force victory even under the most unfavourable circumstances, and never to despair of the great cause for which we fight." [1] In this way Goebbels provided a new angle to the story of the Seven Years' War, a theme familiar to every German schoolboy. He could fall back on a tradition and let it appear in a completely fresh light.

Two months later Goebbels admitted in an article, "The Eternal Law", that "this war is the enigma of all enigmas for all involved and even for those not involved in it". He further declared for the first time that "it was demanding too much of a Government that it should prove right in every case". In history great deeds were only to be achieved through suffering and pain. This argument was once more reinforced by a parallel with Frederick and the Seven Years' War:

"The Prussians in the fifth and sixth years of the Third Silesian War may have thought and felt as we think and feel sometimes today. They would certainly have collapsed under the weight of the misfortune which befell them, had not the masterful mind of the great king raised them again and again. History tells us that he was sometimes the only one to encounter the vicissitudes of fate with a firm and manly attitude and by it to overcome every crisis, even the hardest. Without him Prussia would undoubtedly have remained a small German buffer state (Zwischenstaat); through him it became the great and leading power of the Reich. It had to traverse a deep vale of suffering and trouble until it could rise to the heights. What we admire as the sum of heroism and strength of character was then only the sum of tragic sacrifices, sufferings and privations. History does not give away something for nothing, and certainly not its most precious gifts. As the mother has to risk her own life when she wants to give birth to a new life, so the peoples have to risk their existence in order to mould their life and even to preserve it." [2]

Goebbels inclined to such comparisons with the ruthless efficiency of Frederick the Great in private as much as in public. When in March 1944 the Russian steamroller had broken through the German lines, particularly near Leningrad, Goebbels had nothing but contempt for the self-indulgent and ineffective attitude of some German generals, who, he said, thought of their comforts while their privates froze to death in the grim Russian winter. "I feel disgusted by such wretchedness," he told von Oven. "I should be the Führer! I would clear out that miserable gang! How did Frederick the Great deal with his generals? When they had committed only the smallest mistakes, he personally tore their epaulettes off, broke their swords, took their flags from them. When he thought that the Bernburg regiment had not fought in the manner it

[1] Address "Nun, Volk, Steh auf, und Sturm brich los!" delivered at the Berlin Sport Palace on 18 February 1943, *Der steile Aufstieg*, p. 197.

[2] Article "Das ewige Gesetz", *Das Reich*, April 1943; see *Der steile Aufstieg*, p. 250.

was its duty to fight, the officers were deprived of their epaulettes; these with the flag were withdrawn from the regiment and were only returned to it after it had stood the test of many battles so bravely that it was reduced to one-tenth of its strength." [1]

In March 1945, six weeks before his suicide, Goebbels was alarmed by the failure of Göring to prevent the immense enemy air attacks on German towns. He then drew a parallel with the failure of Frederick's brother, Prince August William, who had lost an army during the Seven Years' War, and the way he had been punished for it by the King. Goebbels read the relevant chapter from Carlyle's *History of Frederick the Great* to his entourage, emphasizing that even the subsequent death of his brother from a broken heart a year after he had been dismissed from the army, had evoked sadness but no regrets from Frederick. The demands of *raison d'état* had come first. [2]

As we saw, when Goebbels realized that the game was up and that all hopes of avoiding the collapse of the Third Reich would be frustrated, he recommended the attitude of Frederick to his wife, who by then (January 1945) knew that final defeat would mean suicide and death for her husband, herself and even her small children. [3]

It is not surprising that, in his public utterances during those last months of the régime, Goebbels clung to parallels not only with the era of the great Prussian king but also with desperate episodes and situations in the present war experienced and mastered by the enemies of Germany. In a radio address at the end of February 1945, the plight of Britain in the summer of 1940 and the desperate threat to Moscow and Leningrad through the advancing German armies in the late autumn of 1941 furnished Goebbels with as much "evidence" for the survival of a determined nation in days of adversity, as did the grim position in which Frederick the Great had found himself during the Seven Years' War. All of them, Frederick the Great and his troops, the English and even the Soviet armies, Goebbels now insisted kept up their fighting spirit and had managed to extricate themselves from a seemingly hopeless situation by self-reliance and *sang froid*. What then had held good for the enemy, *must* now be true for the Germans:

"We find ourselves in a military crisis similar in many respects to that experienced by the Soviet Union in the late autumn of 1941 during the threatened encirclement of Moscow and Leningrad, and successfully overcome by her. Then, too, the entire world regarded her cause as lost

[1] W. von Oven, *Mit Goebbels bis zum Ende*, vol. I, p. 224; diary entry of 24 March 1944.

[2] Cf. W. von Oven, II, p. 278; diary entry of 21 March 1945. For Carlyle's account of the removal of Prince August William from his army command by his enraged brother in July 1757, see T. Carlyle, *History of Frederick II of Prussia, called Frederick the Great*, vol. vi (Centenary edition, London, 1898), Book xvii, Ch. V. The correspondence between the brothers is on pp. 213-214. Goebbels read it aloud "with a strong emphasis and visibly moved by it".

[3] See above, ch. 16, p. 362.

with the exception of the Soviet leaders themselves. Everyone will remember that, when our armies stood threateningly on the shore of the Atlantic in the late summer of 1940 and the German air and U-boat forces smashed the British armament potential and sea transport system, England had to stand up to a similar crisis which she finally overcame, though only after efforts lasting several years." [1]

The address which hinted at the suicide then planned by Goebbels and Hitler concluded significantly with a long quotation from a letter by Frederick the Great to his sister Amelia, written in March 1757, as Goebbels put it, "in one of the critical peak situations of his great war". These words, Goebbels suggested, should become "our companions in these days and weeks":

"Put yourself, I implore you, above the events; think of the Fatherland and remember that its defence is our first duty. If you hear that one of us has met with misfortune, ask if he died fighting. And if he did so, thank God for it. There is only death or victory for us. One of them is required. Everybody here thinks so. What, would you want everyone to sacrifice his life for the State, but not that your brothers should set an example? Oh, my dear sister, at this moment there is nothing to be spared. To be either at the zenith of fame or to be annihilated! Before this decision one must expose oneself to terrible incidents; but afterwards the sky clears up and brightens. This is our position. One must not despair about anything, but one has to anticipate every event and has to accept what Providence allocates to us, with a quiet faith, without any pride in successes, and without being humiliated by failures." [2]

For Goebbels, as once for Frederick, patriotism had become a kind of religion; but to the German masses this pseudo-religion had long lost its appeal, as the facts of the progressive destruction of their country and of Allied military superiority in all spheres spoke their own grim language. Less than a fortnight before the Führer and Goebbels were to take their lives amidst the ruins of Berlin, the desperate Propaganda Minister offered to the stunned people one last pep-talk, one last historical perspective, from which to view the present drama, culminating in a *Götterdämmerung*, in the utter collapse of the Third Reich. In his radio tribute to the Führer on what was to be Hitler's last birthday Goebbels tried to interpret that gigantic drama as having been continuous ever since 1914. The first act of it had ended in November 1918, he argued; the second was not yet finished:

"What we experience today is the last act of a tremendous tragic drama, which began with 1 August 1914 and was interrupted by us Germans on 9 November 1918, at the very moment when it was about to be decided. This is the reason why we had to begin it once more and from

[1] Goebbels' radio address appeared under the heading "Deutschlands Kraft im Daseinskampf, Der Lagebericht von Dr. Goebbels", in the *Hamburger Fremdenblatt*, 1 March 1945.

[2] Ibid.

scratch on 1 September 1939. For what we wanted to spare ourselves in November 1918 we have to make up today two- or threefold. There is no escape from it, unless the German nation forsakes a life of human dignity and is ready to lead for ever an existence of which the most primitive African tribes would have to be ashamed." [1]

By then Joseph Goebbels was well aware that the curtain was about to come down with a crash on the Third Reich, and that no historical parallels, contrasts or perspectives, however ingenious and cunning could prevent this end of the drama.

[1] *"Unser Hitler! Die Rundfunkansprache von Reichsminister Dr. Goebbels zum Führergeburtstag 1945", Grossdeutscher Rundfunk,* 19 April 1945 (B.B.C. Monitoring Report).

Conclusion

OUR SURVEY of Goebbels' role as a propagandist and of the techniques which he and his ministry employed would be incomplete without further reflection on some of the main points which emerged. Any study of the propaganda methods and output of a totalitarian country runs the risk of isolating its theme. To be valid it must clearly see propaganda and its machinery as an integral part of the entire system. Although in the case of the National Socialist state this system was manipulated by opportunists and was subject to frequent readjustments, it represented throughout an authoritarian rule in which the will of the leader and to a lesser degree of his lieutenants backed by a mass party was decisive. Propaganda in the Third Reich was an instrument and channel of a specific power constellation, of a state based on the concentrated power of a dynamic minority which continuously endeavoured to enlarge, to strengthen and to accentuate this power.

One of the characteristic features of the propaganda system in Nazi Germany was its monopoly, the other its character as an important by-product of an uninterrupted display of force. While it had no serious competitors, it was all the time *Machtpropaganda*, that is propaganda which would have been pointless without concentration and accent on Power. In this as in other totalitarian régimes propaganda would have been largely ineffective without the pressure of overt and hidden force behind it. Force (or terror) without propaganda would have been too inarticulate and blunt, while propaganda without force (or terror) would have been deprived of much of its appeal and impetus.

Goebbels was fully aware that propaganda had to be accompanied by coercion to make it effective. In November 1943 he noted in his diary that German home morale was excellent and explained that this was so "partly owing to our good propaganda but partly also to the severe measures which we have taken against defeatists".[1] On another occasion he remarked that "a sharp sword must always stand behind propaganda, if it is to be really effective".[2]

As early as 1933 one of Goebbels' young Party ideologues in the Ministry commented with remarkable candour on the relationship between propaganda and national power. In an unemotional and somewhat Mac-

[1] *The Goebbels Diaries*, p. 419, entry of 26 November 1943.
[2] *The Goebbels Diaries* (American edition), p. 460.

450

chiavellian pamphlet Eugen Hadamovsky not only called ridicule and fear "two factors in propaganda indispensable for its success", but also discussed the various links between propaganda and the display of force. "Propaganda and force are never absolutely opposed to each other", he declared. "The use of force can be part of the propaganda. Between them lie different degrees of effective influence over people and masses: from the sudden exciting of attention or the friendly persuasion of the individual to incessant mass propaganda; from the loose organizing of the proselytes to the creation of semi-state or state institutions, from individual terror to mass terror; from the authorized use of the might of the stronger to the military enforcement of obedience and discipline by means of the death penalty." [1]

The importance of the visible display of power as an intermediary between the persuasiveness of rational and emotional appeals and pressure through the evoking of fear is here clearly recognized. For in a totalitarian state it is not enough to have power, it has also to be advertised continuously. In other words, the possession of power is nothing without its display. "All the power one has, even more than one has, has to be displayed and demonstrated. One hundred speeches, five hundred newspaper articles, radio talks, films and plays are unable to produce the same effect as a procession of gigantic masses of people taking place with discipline and active participation or a demonstration of the means of power and the weapons of the state as expressed in its military, its police and its political cadres." [2]

However to this frank assertion of *Machtpolitik* the corollary must be added that all propaganda speeches, articles, radio talks, films and plays acquire a specific instrumentality under a system in which a concentration of power is regarded as of primary importance. They have in part at least the function of advertising and highlighting power, of conveying a feeling of its comforting strength and of its uncomfortable and dangerous threat.

A display of propaganda and a display of the cadres of power can coincide as they did annually at the Party Congresses in Nuremberg. Propaganda is able to advertise military victories and indirectly help to prepare the atmosphere for new ones as did the frightening and impressive films Goebbels' ministry ordered on the campaigns against Poland and France. The Power continuously advertised in the Third Reich was fourfold: it meant firstly the charismatic powers of the unique, the incomparable Führer, secondly the massed power of the Party and its affiliated organization; thirdly the disciplined strength of the Wehrmacht, of the armed forces, systematically built up after 1933 and last but not least the furtive power of the political police, the Gestapo. We have seen that the part played by Goebbels in building up and advertising the

[1] E. Hadamovsky, *Propaganda und Nationale Macht, Die Organisation der öffenlichen Meinung,* Oldenburg, 1933, p. 2.
[2] Op. cit., p. 48.

personality power of the Führer both as a super-man and as a human being can hardly be overestimated. Of an equally determined and confident kind were his incessant efforts to propagate and stress the strength and grandeur of the Party. Goebbels was also an advocate of the growing might and efficiency of the Wehrmacht, though, as a civilian and conscious of this limitation, perhaps less so than in the case of the Party. On the other hand the Secret Police needed little publicity, as it operated best in the twilight. A mere mention that XY had been sent to a concentration camp was all the more effective as rumours and hints made these places of unrestricted violence appear sinister enough in a vague way. It was only in the early days of the régime that the public was given strong hints of the brutality practised in the concentration camps. "To conceal that in the meantime some of those arrested had experienced a not too gentle treatment, would be foolish and altogether inconceivable. Inconceivable, as such a treatment met an urgent necessity," declared the *Kommandant* of the concentration camp of Oranienburg near Berlin in a published statement in March 1934. And he added with uninhibited candour: "I have seldom seen such admirable educators as my old SA men, who being partly an offspring of the proletarian *milieu* themselves, attended to these particularly provocative Communist rowdies with extraordinary devotion." [1]

Goebbels himself rarely referred to the concentration camps, but there was a threatening note in many of his speeches and articles, a deliberate hint that non-conforming elements, let alone opponents of the régime, would be ruthlessly dealt with. Though Goebbels once described grumbling as "the digestive process of the soul," [2] he was far from allowing his readers and listeners to indulge in it. Idlers, pessimists, rumourmongers and at times intellectuals were attacked by him with a venom and an intensity behind which the dark shadow of the Gestapo and of the perversities of the concentration camps was lurking. He frequently declared it imperative "to talk drastically" with such recalcitrant fellows or suggested that "they should have their ears boxed by everyone at the proper moment." For obvious reasons the outburst of a leading minister against a section of the populace is more significant and more serious in a totalitarian state than is some well-tempered criticism of it by a functionary of a parliamentary system. However there were degrees of relevance in Goebbels' well-calculated outbursts. When in September, 1943, for instance, he decried "the thin layer of opportunists" whom he called "as vain and arrogant in days of good fortune as they are cowardly and spineless in times of ill luck," his remarks were relatively vague and harmless, but when he denounced the Jews after July 20th as a clique

[1] SA Sturmführer Schäfer, *Kommandant* of the Concentration Camp Oranienburg, *Hamburger Nachrichten*, 24 March 1934 (evening edition).
[2] Article "Der Papierkrieg" in *Das Reich*, 12 April 1942. See *Das eherne Herz*, p. 278.

of plotters his words were accompanied by drastic action taken against these hunted people by the SS or the Gestapo.

Today, nearly twenty years after the collapse of the Third Reich, Himmler and the Gestapo have few defenders even among veteran Nazis who still cling to some of their original views. It is now argued among them that in a free election in the Third Reich, "Hess, at times Göring, perhaps even Goebbels, but never Himmler would have had a chance of being chosen by the people against rival candidates." [1] It is also admitted that "Himmler's secret mass murders belong to the darkest chapters in the history of the twentieth century." [2] But what is not conceded by the survivors and heirs of the National Socialists is that before the bar of history Goebbels bears his full share of responsibility for these "darkest chapters"; for not only were the executioners of mass murder on an unprecedented scale involved, but also its advocates and champions. As has been documented in this book during the war Goebbels was aware of and constantly supported Hitler's policy for the elimination of the Jews. Even a recent apologist of the Third Reich refers to "the mad planned setting on fire of the synagogues during the night of the 9th to the 10th November 1938, resulting from a spontaneous brainwave of the very Minister of Propaganda" and calls it "the incident for which admittedly no word of criticism is harsh enough." [3]

But the overall murderous impact of Goebbels' propaganda over the years is not realized or admitted by such writers. There can be no doubt that Goebbels' half pathologically genuine and half calculated anti-Semitism gave to his propaganda campaigns a severity and a force which imbued millions with dislike and hatred of the Jews. Coupled with the fear of the Gestapo it also blunted the conscience of innumerable others causing them to acquiesce in mass persecution and indirectly—though often without a real knowledge of what was going on behind the scenes —in mass murder.

Looking back it is safe to argue that the omnipresence of propaganda and the constant repetition of its slogans was its strength as well as its weakness. Had the Third Reich lasted forty years instead of twelve, those features might have been accepted by practically everyone; but probably a dozen years was too short a time to obliterate entirely in the older generation the memories of the freedom of thought and of the plurality of opinions which had existed in Germany before 1933. Nor did this span suffice for a younger generation to reach maturity and to take over leading national positions.

It is noteworthy that National Socialist terminology did not make the difference between agitation and propaganda which has been a distinct feature of the Soviet Russian régime. There agitation has the task of in-

[1] H. Sündermann, *Das Dritte Reich, Eine Richtigstellung in Umrissen*, Leoni, 1959, p. 68.
[2] Ibid.
[3] Op. cit., p. 51.

fluencing the mind and the moods of the masses through ideas and slogans, while propaganda serves to spread the Communist ideology, the doctrines of Marxism and Leninism. What the Nazis called propaganda campaigns, in Soviet Russia comes under the category of agitation, whereas propaganda there busies itself with the political training, the indoctrination of the Party and Soviet functionaries and of the intellectuals.[1] This dualism dates back to Plephanov's famous definition: "A propagandist presents many ideas to one or few persons, an agitator presents only one or a few ideas, but presents them to a mass of people." [2] According to *The Political Dictionary,* an official Soviet publication issued first in 1940 and re-issued in 1956, propaganda is "the intensive elucidation of the writings of Marx, Engels, Lenin and Stalin, and of the history of the Bolshevik Party and its tasks." [3] It is equivalent to the indoctrination of Soviet citizens, particularly of Party members, for whom a knowledge of Marxism-Leninism is essential. Lenin himself had laid down the maxim that a revolutionary movement had to be carried out "by a party guided by the most advanced theory."

The National Socialists, on the other hand, did not regard propaganda merely as an instrument for reaching the leading minority, the Party élite, but rather as a means for the persuasion and indoctrination of all Germans. With them it had not a specific, but a total validity. Their propaganda concept covered both agitation and propaganda as understood in Soviet Russia. It was simply a convenient instrument for maintaining power, a tactical weapon to achieve short-term rather than long-term goals. The varnish of *Weltanschauung* was in fact much thinner in National Socialist than in Communist propaganda; blood and soil, Rosenberg's myth of the twentieth century, were much less significant for making political decisions in Germany than the tenets of Marxism-Leninism proved to be for the Soviet Russian rulers. In Soviet Russia propaganda aimed at creating in the people "an absolute devotion to communist principles and an implacable hostility to all others." [4]

Though in both cases the aim was total indoctrination, with National Socialism principles were much less defined and only "the implacable hostility" towards all outside the National Socialist camp was as intense as it was towards non-Communists in Stalinist Russia. In Germany propaganda served to strengthen an opportunist cult of power, power for the nation, for its leaders, above all for the charismatic Führer. After 1933 National Socialist propaganda as a weapon of control developed into something that existed for its own sake quite apart from its ideological aims. "The Leninist slogans have a rational basis, even if they definitely appeal to instincts and fundamental myths. But when Hitler threw his

[1] See Bruno Kalmins, *Der Sowjetische Propagandastaat,* Stockholm, 1956, p. 22.
[2] R. N. Carew-Hunt, *A Guide to Communist Jargon,* London, 1958, p. 3.
[3] Op. cit., p. 132.
[4] Carew-Hunt, op. cit., p. 134.

invocations of blood and race to a fanatic crowd which answered him with 'Sieg Heil' he was only concerned with whipping up hatred and with the desire for power by this means." [1]

In the National Socialist context propaganda was primarily an instrument of tactics which, by its drive, its colourful pictures, its promises and threats aimed at conditioning the public in such a way that it responded more or less automatically to the changing appeals and directives. Here as in other totalitarian systems the continuous use of propaganda without competition both presupposed and created a gullibility which is less likely to flourish under a multi-party system, where it is possible to listen to competitive views. Only so could the National Socialists "sell" their glaring *volte face* in August 1939 when, by concluding a Non-Aggression Pact with Stalin, Hitler put the anti-Bolshevist line into cold storage, and again in June 1941 when Soviet Russia, the friendly power of yesterday, was once more presented as the arch-enemy of mankind. In the German bookshops literature hostile to the Soviet régime was simply removed from the shelves in the first case and put back in the second. While confidence in the Führer and his coups was high, the contradictions of propaganda mattered little. Attitudes were easily exchangeable as long as the régime exuded strength. On the eve of another world war the surprise of an understanding with Soviet Russia was undoubtedly welcome to many Germans, as it would obviously remove the danger of having to fight on two major fronts. It is true that the change over from friendship with to war against the Soviet Union in June 1941 stunned many Germans but, remembering the recent chain of startling military successes, they were confident that the Führer's intuition would prove "right" once more. Moreover, long years of propaganda had sufficed to condition most people to accept the official line.

In Soviet Russia both agitation and propaganda are a matter for the Party; there exists no dual control by Party and State over these functions and no Ministry of Propaganda enables its head to speak with a one-man authority. Agitation and propaganda are entirely in the hands of special central and regional agencies of the Party.[2] No single man has ever become the symbol of the propaganda system as was Goebbels during the entire duration of the Third Reich.

A man seldom loved (except perhaps after air-raids when he knew how to strike the right note in talking to the people), often feared but always taken seriously, Goebbels, with his agile and fertile mind, was much more than a top executive, he was the alpha and omega of his propaganda system. He also became to some extent its prisoner. It is ironic how at the end this ruthless uniformist had to confide to Semmler that "he personally would find it intolerable, and for any person with intellectual power undignified, to attend daily at the official press conference to have ten

[1] Jean-Marie Domenach, *La Propagande Politique*, Paris, 1944, p. 34.
[2] B. Kalmins, op. cit., p. 21.

commandments all beginning "Thou shalt not" handed out by Hans Fritzsche,"[1] who after all was merely carrying out his Minister's instructions. Goebbels deplored that the journalists were getting lost in a thicket of instructions and taboos and conveniently put the blame for this decay of journalism on others, particularly on his rival Otto Dietrich. For in April 1943 he complained that no decent journalist could stand the treatment meted out to him by the Press Department of the Reich Government, which dealt with the members of the press as if they were schoolboys.[2] But such lament remained purely academic, for Goebbels would and could do nothing to change this regimentation, at least so long as the war lasted.

As far as his own prestige was involved, Goebbels was always eager to push himself as much as his propaganda. He was well aware that in times of war the civilian, however skilful and authoritative, counted far less than the soldier. He was sensitive to the fact that "generally speaking, war brings only the fighting men and their deeds into the foreground and they steal the limelight from other groups."[3] One of the reasons why Goebbels began in May 1940 to write regular leaders for his new periodical *Das Reich* was the desire to put himself more prominently before the public. Particularly during the war years he was anxious "to conduct skilfully thought-out publicity." Conscious of the need for keeping his name constantly before the public he saw to it that it appeared "in cautious doses several times a week in the press." He broadcast regularly every Friday in 1943. Any minor reception at which Goebbels appeared was mentioned in the press to create the impression that he was "nearly snowed under with work."[4]

Most politicians try to serve their cause and their own ends simultaneously. Goebbels certainly was as much concerned with furthering his own prestige as that of the Movement or the State. In fact to him both largely coincided. According to Semmler his frequent speeches in Berlin and other towns during the war had three purposes: "to satisfy his new urge for work; to help the war [effort]; and to recall himself to people's memories in new and interesting ways, to make himself a centre of conversation, and to command the headlines in the newspapers."[5] Thus Goebbels was able to employ for his own purposes the immense machinery at his disposal to influence the public mind. Lack of popularity with some of his colleagues in the top layer of the hierarchy, especially with Martin Bormann in later years, prevented him from obtaining a decisive say in foreign affairs. In the end, Goebbels did not succeed in his ambition to replace Ribbentrop in the Foreign Ministry in 1943–44. In spite of his continual efforts to extend his sphere of power, his main significance lay

---

[1] R. Semmler, op. cit., p. 22, entry of 6 March 1941.
[2] *The Goebbels Diaries,* p. 253, entry of 14 March 1943.
[3] R. Semmler, op. cit., pp. 74-75, entry of 13 March 1943.
[4] Op. cit., p. 75.
[5] Ibid.

in his extraordinary skill as a manipulator of words. By and large his role remained confined to that of chief propagandist, moulder of public opinion and prop of public morale. As has been shown, Goebbels was indefatigable in projecting the myth of the Führer both as a superman and a human being. It should be added that during the last years of the war Goebbels' prestige and influence increased in the proportion that Hitler himself became less and less visible to the masses and only a shadow of his former self to his entourage. It can be said that at a time when German towns were in ruins and the war was grim indeed for the civilians Goebbels managed to raise people's morale by his personal appearances and the example of his *sang froid* in a way only comparable with that of Winston Churchill in the summer of 1940. Although the Propaganda Minister could never inspire the same enthusiasm as did the British Prime Minister, he was yet able to profit from the declining health and strength of purpose of the Führer after the 20th July and to rally support for the crumbling régime through his fortitude and undiminished persuasiveness. It is true that its magic was gradually obliterated by the irresistible might of the Allied forces, but Goebbels played his role *nolens volens* to the very end of the régime. His final exit at least saved him from Allied retribution and from the hangman's rope.

Joseph Goebbels was neither the first nor the last practitioner in the art of political propaganda, though perhaps the most brilliant and malignant this century has known so far. The story of his field of operation and his techniques belongs as much to history as to the psychopathology of mankind. Significant in itself it may serve as a permanent warning of the dangerous implications the magic of persuasion can have if and when it becomes a calculated Macchiavellian instrument for establishing and maintaining monopolistic power.

Appendix
What Goebbels Left Out

SOME SIGNIFICANT OMISSIONS IN HIS WARTIME BOOKS

I

DURING the last war three collections of speeches and articles by Dr. Joseph Goebbels were published: *Die Zeit ohne Beispiel (The Time without Comparison)* (Munich, Eher, 1942), *Das eherne Herz (The Iron Heart)* (Munich, Eher, 1943), and *Der steile Aufstieg (The Steep Ascent)* (Munich, Eher, 1944). All three were compiled and introduced, not by the Reich Minister of Propaganda himself, but by a member of his ministerial and literary entourage, who evidently did the work under his chief's direction. The first collection, covering the period from the beginning of 1939 to September 1941, was put together by Hans Schwarz van Berk, a well-known Nazi journalist and one time editor-in-chief of *Das Schwarze Korps,* the official organ of the SS. The second and third collections both contain selections from one year only of Goebbels' output: *Das eherne Herz* from the period September 1941 to September 1942 and *Der steile Aufstieg* for that from September 1942 to September 1943. The sub-editor of both was M. A. von Schirmeister, *Oberregierungsrat* in the Propaganda Ministry, and Goebbels' personal press assistant, a devoted servant of his exacting master.[1]

How were the contents of these books selected? Only in the foreword to one of them is an explanation given and are the reasons for omitting some articles and speeches discussed:

> "It must be admitted," says von Schirmeister in the introduction to *The Steep Ascent,* "that the impending birth of a new epoch of German history led to such an amplification of his [Goebbels'] activities as a publicist that it has not been possible this time to press all the speeches and articles of the last twelve months into the narrow compass of this book. A work in two volumes would have been required to fulfill the duty of the chronicler precisely. Instead, all speeches had to be ignored which were not directly connected with the war events, e.g. the obituary speeches for the deceased Reich Sport Leader [Hans von Tschammer und Osten] and for the Chief of Staff of the SA [Victor

[1] For Schirmeister's personality and background, see Wilfred von Oven, *Mit Goebbels bis zum Ende,* Vol. I, p. 14.

458

Lutze], who lost his life by a tragic accident. Other speeches held annually as a regular occurrence were cut down to their essentials or omitted altogether, e.g. the speech at the opening of the Reich Winter Relief." [1]

As far as Goebbels' articles were concerned a different reason for exclusion from the book is put forward: "From the articles published weekly in *Das Reich* or the *Völkischer Beobachter* some had to be dropped on account of the fixed size of this volume. They commented on the burning questions of the day, but not so much on the principles governing our warfare." But there was consolation for the Goebbels' fans: "It may be left to a later collection of the entire writings [of Goebbels] to offer this all-including survey. Only by compression of the materials is it possible to give at least a complete survey of the course of the events of the year, a mirror of the time with its strong ups and downs, with its fevers and crises. As previously, not a single line or syllable has been changed in the articles collected in this volume." [2] At the time few readers were inclined to reflect on the reasons for these omissions. But Goebbels himself confided to his diary a different and more adequate explanation: "My new book, *The Steep Ascent*," he wrote on 25 September 1943, "is being put together by Schirmeister. A number of articles and speeches of last year cannot be used because they contain wrong forecasts. I don't want to edit them, but prefer simply to omit them. There is enough unchallengeable material available to fill more than a book." [3]

It is therefore rewarding to examine a number of major omissions in the last two Goebbels books published when the war no longer meant to Germans an uninterrupted chain of victories and when obviously the task of reassuring propaganda had become more difficult.

The first of these volumes, *Das eherne Herz*, takes its title from a sentence of Frederick the Great who, as has been shown, was a lodestar for Goebbels in times of peace and war alike.[4] In an address before Party functionaries at the University of Berlin on December 1, 1941, Goebbels made the point that Frederick the Great had demanded two things as indispensable in hard but also great times: "Entrails of iron and an iron heart" (*Eingeweide aus Eisen und ein ehernes Herz*).[5] Yet the address with this significant quotation is not to be found in the book. In its foreword von Schirmeister explained that "it summed up an idea which had already been discussed in other works and publications or was further developed in later articles." [6] Though Goebbels was fond of repeating

---

[1] *Der steile Aufstieg*. Second edition, Munich, 1944, pp. viii-ix
[2] Op. cit., p. ix.
[3] *The Goebbels Diaries*, p. 393.
[4] See above ch. 19, pp. 444-448.
[5] Cf. *Das eherne Herz*, p. 9. Goebbels frequently repeated this phrase, for instance, in a speech before Party functionaries of the Gau Berlin on 24 March 1942, reported in the *Hamburger Fremdenblatt*, 25 March 1942 (not reprinted).
[6] *Völkischer Beobachter*, 21 December 1941, reprinted in *Das eherne Herz*, pp. 131-137. The quotation is on p. 132.

ideas, metaphors and arguments, his brain was sufficiently fertile to invent new slogans at any moment. It seems therefore, the true reason for this omission lies elsewhere. One has to keep in mind the situation when the address was delivered. By that time, Hitler's high hopes that Russia would be defeated without a severe winter campaign had proved futile. In his appeal to the home population for warm clothing and underwear for the soldiers in the East on 21 December 1941, Goebbels admitted that "this winter has arrived in the regions of the wide East, the South East, Norway and Finland early and with an intensity unusual until now in normal years."

Nevertheless, at the time the full extent of the German military advance had not yet reached its maximum; this only materialized in summer 1942 when "the area dominated by the armed forces of the Third Reich stretched from the Continental European shore of the Atlantic to the North-Western end of the Caucasus, and from the North Cape to the Libyan desert." [1] But by the beginning of 1943, when *Das eherne Herz* appeared, some grim shadows marred this impressive picture. After the fall of Stalingrad and the capitulation of the remnants of the Sixth German Army, after the German defeat at El-Alamein and the successful occupation of vast stretches of North Africa by an Anglo-American force under General Eisenhower, the chances of an early German victory appeared remote. Thus there was little point and even some danger in reprinting this passage from Goebbels' speech of 1 December 1941: "Never in our history were the national chances so favourable and with them did the effort promise so much success as today. The great hour demands the last ounce from all of us, but also offers the nation the maximum. Never were we so armed as now. Never had we such a comprehensive strength, never did we possess such decisive positions of military power as at present and never did we possess such a heroic *Wehrmacht* and brilliant leadership as in this fateful struggle." [2]

Although early in 1943 the confidence of the German masses in Hitler's military genius was by no means shattered, Goebbels may well have felt that by then the following sentences of unmitigated Führer-worship in the same address would have cut less ice than at the time they were originally pronounced: "If he who carries the responsibility is silent, then the nation shall stand still before it in shy awe; for that which will one day be history is not seldom born in silence. And history is now being made." [2] History was indeed made when the volume reached its readers, but at least some of them must have asked themselves if it were not moving in a hostile direction.

This speech of Goebbels was one out of at least ten excluded from *Das eherne Herz*. Not all of them seem to have been left out for reasons of political expediency. Some were probably dropped because they had

[1] *Hitler's Europe*. Edited by A. and V. M. Toynbee. London, 1954. p. 6.
[2] *Hamburger Fremdenblatt*, 2 December 1941.

been delivered before a specialised audience or because they had no direct bearing on the war effort. Two addresses given by Goebbels in Vienna are cases in point. The one eulogised the genius of Mozart during a Mozart Festival,[1] the other celebrated the fourth anniversary of the *Anschluss*.[2] Of merely regional interest was also a speech delivered at mass meetings of the Gau Westmark in Metz and Saarbrücken, in which the people of Metz in Lorraine were told that "their town was filled with the best German military tradition and had never been anything but German."[3]

Other speeches were by their very nature not destined for general consumption and had at the time of delivery only been given brief mention in the press. This applies to two addresses delivered at the Propaganda Ministry to war reporters from Propaganda Companies (PK) at the Eastern Front who had come to the capital for a training course,[4] and to district and local branch Party leaders of the Gau Berlin.[5] In a talk to and with soldiers from the army in Sebastopol, Goebbels only put forward arguments he had used elsewhere.[6] Moreover, the form of this piece, half conversation, half address, made it hardly suitable for inclusion in a book. Similarly Goebbels' speech at the distribution to Berliners of prizes in a politeness campaign was too specialised and perhaps also too irrelevant to be worthy of inclusion.[7] Finally, a special interview the Minister had granted to the editor-in-chief of *Der Angriff* [8] on the occasion of the 15th anniversary of the paper discussed and praised Nazi propaganda in such general terms that it might have bored and annoyed later readers of the book.

On the other hand, the omission of a Goebbels speech before student soldiers from nine European nations, who fought in the East as volunteers in the Army and the Waffen-SS, on 14 April 1942,[9] had probably a political reason. In it the idea of the New Europe had been stressed and the present fight described as the last war in Europe, which would end for ever the dismemberment of the Continent. Later there came a change in emphasis. Whilst that address had declared that Europe was now experiencing a period of continental development which could be regarded as one of the most magnificent epochs in her history, three months later Goebbels rather stressed the line that "Europe would be

[1] *Hamburger Fremdenblatt*, 5 December 1941, where the speech is reported under the caption "Mozart's music is also defended by our Soldiers".
[2] *Münchner Neueste Nachrichten*, 16 March 1942.
[3] *Strassburger Neueste Nachrichten*, 6 October 1941.
[4] *Hamburger Fremdenblatt*, 4 April 1942. A similar news item was included in the Reichsprogramm of Radio Frankfurt on 2 April 1942, the actual date of the address.
[5] *Völkischer Beobachter*, 17 June 1942.
[6] Reported in Reichsprogramm Radio Zeesen, "Zeitspiegel", 22 August 1942.
[7] Reported by Radio Zeesen, 15 June 1942.
[8] Quoted in *Hamburger Fremdenblatt*, 6 July 1942.
[9] *Hamburger Fremdenblatt*, 15 April 1942.

lost if the Axis Powers did not protect her." [1] Soon afterwards the idea
of a New Order was put into cold storage altogether. As an historian has
recently said: "From the date of the German capitulation at Stalingrad
until the end of the war the New Order was seldom discussed except in
relation to the Russian danger." [2]

The necessity of priming the masses for a long war gathered momentum as the first war winter in the East proceeded. On 24 February 1942
Goebbels noted in his diary: "We shall have to change our propaganda
and our politics in the East, as already arranged with the Führer. These
were hitherto based on the assumption that we would take possession of
the East very quickly. This hope, however, has not been realized. We
must therefore envisage operations of longer duration and are accordingly compelled to change our slogans and our policies fundamentally." [3]
This far-reaching change of propaganda line made it impossible for Goebbels to reprint his article "The End of the Illusions" which had appeared
on 17 October 1941. The "illusions" reviewed were, of course, those of
the British, not of the Germans. Quoting a *Daily Mail* despatch on the
serious position of the Russian armies, Goebbels triumphantly alleged
even Germany's enemies were now confirming that "the Soviet Union
was in deadly peril, and there is hardly a way out for her, that the war
in the East has to be regarded as decided, if not as ended." [4] It means,
Goebbels argued, that England has no chances whatsoever. "How will
England manage to win the war, serious critics in U.S.A. are asking. How
will she manage not to be beaten, we ask. Just as her illusions of the day
before yesterday fluttered away, so will her illusions of yesterday and
tomorrow be scattered." [4] In a later speech in Berlin (27 March 1942)
on the "Agony of the British Empire," also not reprinted, Goebbels was
more cautious. Though predicting the death of the Empire, he compared
it with a moribund human being who need not die at once today or tomorrow. "Sometimes this process could take weeks or months, and the
observer could witness the most varied periods of ups and downs in this
agony. But then one day the moment comes in which this life is extinguished instantaneously" *(blitzartig)*.[5] Words which probably sounded
quite plausible when they were spoken, but which would have looked
rather unconvincing in print a year later with Rommel defeated and the
German troops pushed out of North Africa.

Being remarkably alert in readjusting his ideology and slogans to the
changing military and political situations, Goebbels tried to "prove" his
veracity by admitting a wrong forecast, but only when the error stood out
a mile. "We admit," he declared in an article, "The Law of the New

---

[1] Article "Die Sogenannte russische Seele": *Das Reich,* 19 June 1942, reprinted in *Das eherne Herz,* pp. 398-405. The quotation is on p. 404.

[2] C. J. Child in *Hitler's Europe,* p. 54.

[3] *The Goebbels Diaries,* p. 61.

[4] Article "Das Ende der Illusionen"; *Völkischer Beobachter,* 17 October
1941.

[5] *Hamburger Fremdenblatt,* 25 March 1942.

World," published on 12 July 1942 in *Das Reich*, "that during the entire war we once issued a wrong prognosis and that referred to the powers of resistance still at the disposal of the Soviets in the late autumn of last year [1941]. Even this forecast was correct at the time it was made," he went on, "but was wiped out later by a winter which began abnormally early. At the end of the winter we were not ashamed to point out ruthlessly to our people the critical consequences of this change in the winter campaign." [1]

In fact, Goebbels had confined himself to a diversion in the form of his appeal for the collection of clothing and furs for the troops in Russia— a smart showpiece on his part. For as Professor Hagemann has aptly remarked, this collection was "much too late and too badly prepared to bring real help to the troops, but very useful from a propaganda point of view as a substitute for a people's plebiscite." [2] In the same article Goebbels posed as a cautious publicist averse to all daring forecasts. Apart from the mistake over Soviet Russia, he asserted, "usually we wisely refrained from predicting any forthcoming developments and confined ourselves to describing and explaining those which have come to a close. We left it to the public to ponder the date and the development of an offensive, and our estimates were mostly very agreeably undercut by the facts." [3]

II

Compared with the omissions in *Das eherne Herz* those in the subsequent volume *Der steile Aufstieg* are more significant. Whilst they apply again to both Goebbels' speeches and articles, it is the growing number of the omitted speeches which is of interest to the historical inquiry.

Before we deal with the articles, a few words are needed about the omitted speeches. Again, it is likely that, as Schirmeister indicates in his foreword, quoted above, some of them were too ephemeral or too irrelevant from a war-propaganda point of view to be included. Others, though relevant to the war effort, like Goebbels' account of the third year of the activities of the Winter Help, were too crammed with facts and figures to hold the attention of most readers. [4] The Minister's congratulatory words on the 25th anniversary of the UFA film company in which he bestowed honours on prominent men of the film industry, including Dr. Hugenberg and Dr. L. Klitsch, and on leading film producers such as Veit Harlan and Wolfgang Liebeneiner, were of interest to few people outside the limited world of the German film. [5] Orations on the funeral of prominent Party bosses were soon forgotten at a time when

[1] Article "Das Gesetz der Neuen Welt": *Das Reich*, 12 July 1942, reprinted in *Das eherne Herz*, pp. 390-397.
[2] W. Hagemann, *Publizistik im Dritten Reich*, p. 254.
[3] *Das eherne Herz*, pp. 392-393.
[4] *Hamburger Fremdenblatt*, 2 October 1942.
[5] *Reichsprogramm*, Radio Frankfurt, 4 March 1943.

death reaped its harvest in hundreds of thousands.[1] Other speeches, mainly before local and Gau Party functionaries, had at the time been so briefly reported in the press that there was no point in including them in the book. With two of his pep talks even the extracts published in the press contained sentences uncomfortably dated when *Der steile Aufstieg* left the hands of the printers. "From the extraordinarily limited and narrow operational basis we had in 1939," Goebbels told the Party leaders of the Gau Party on 5 December 1942, "we have penetrated so far, particularly in the East, that its fertile fields and its regions rich in raw materials are at our disposal. This is the decisive factor." [2]

That line of daring sanguine prose was repeated and even intensified in a speech in Munich a fortnight later in which Goebbels predicted: "Today we possess the control over the Dnieper, the Don and, when after a hard struggle Stalingrad will be in our hands, also over the Volga for good. When at the right moment the drive into the Caucasus will have been completed, then the richest soil areas will be in our hands. He who possesses wheat, oil, iron and coal, and in addition the strongest armed forces, will win the war. What the enemy lost, we have today." [3] Considering the changed situations in the East a year afterwards, Goebbels had no intention of looking foolish and therefore eliminated these speeches from his book.

To turn from the omitted speeches to the articles not reprinted. As far as has been possible to ascertain, at least fourteen of Goebbels' celebrated weekly articles in *Das Reich* during the period September 1942 to September 1943 did not find a place in *Der steile Aufstieg*. Of them, one each had appeared in October 1942, in January, March and June 1943 and two each in November and December 1942, in February, April and May 1943. When the first article in the volume had originally been published (27 September 1942) the German armies had not yet suffered any major defeat either in Russia or in North Africa. But by the time the last article included in *Der steile Aufstieg* had first appeared in print (26 September 1943), the situation had much deteriorated from the German point of view. In Russia the catastrophe of Stalingrad had been followed by the collapse of the Don front. By September the Germans had been pressed back beyond the Dnieper and the Desna and by November Kiev was again in Russian hands. In the Mediterranean theatre the Anglo-American landings in North Africa in November 1942 and the British victory at El Alamein had by May 1943 led to the elimination of all German and Italian forces from Africa. The overthrow of Mussolini and the Fascist regime in Italy had been followed in September 1943 by an armistice between Badoglio and the Allies who by then were well established on the Italian mainland. By the end of the year the German armies

---

[1] For the oration at the funeral of Viktor Lutze, see *The Goebbels Diaries*, pp. 276-277.

[2] *Hamburger Fremdenblatt*, 6 December 1942.

[3] *Hamburger Fremdenblatt*, 20 October 1942.

at the Eastern and Southern fronts were everywhere on the defensive, and at home the enemy air raids had increased their ferocious intensity since the spring.

It is therefore significant that the first Goebbels article omitted from this volume had, in October 1942, posed the question: "For Whom does Time Work?" The answer given was: "For him who has the space *(Raum)*." Goebbels had then proudly argued: "In the course of this summer we have again acquired territories which the Soviet Union, to put it mildly, cannot spare for her warfare. Our warfare is, on the other hand, profiting from them already to some extent and will do so completely sooner or later." [1]

Only six weeks afterwards Goebbels' tenor was much sobered by Montgomery's vital success at El Alamein, which is reflected in the article "The Fortitude of the Heart." [2] Why was this also not reprinted? Probably because a year later it would have made some readers realise, looking back, that El Alamein had been the beginning of the turning of the tide and the end of all German hopes to wrest victory by attack in land warfare. "It cannot be doubted," Goebbels had then, in November 1942, admitted for the first time, "that the present war has undergone enormous developments during the last two months. It shows a face different from the one it had only a short time ago. New perspectives have become visible in it. New dangers have turned up and new possibilities have come close. It would, of course, be exceedingly foolish to expect that they had to be favourable for our side without exception. There is no war in which the positive chances exist only for the one side and the negative factors only for the other. . . ." [3]

A closer analysis of the omitted articles in that volume points to three different propaganda devices or tricks employed by the master juggler. All of them could possibly have been discerned at a later date when the position of the German armies and of the home front had progressively deteriorated. The first trick was not very original, for the attempt to minimise the seriousness of the situation and the successes of the enemy is a device favoured in times of adversity by many belligerents. Goebbels tried to increase its effect by coupling it with a pose of frankness, by purporting to tell the people the full harsh truth. In his masterly speech in the Sport Palace in Berlin on 18 February 1943 [4]—when the cloud of the Stalingrad defeat lay heavily on the German masses—Goebbels declared: "I shall furnish my words with the full sacred seriousness and the open frankness the hour demands of us. The German nation educated,

[1] Article "Für wen arbeitet die Zeit?" *Das Reich,* 25 October 1943, not reprinted.
[2] Article "Die Tapferkeit des Herzens", *Das Reich,* 22 November 1942, not reprinted.
[3] Article "Die Tapferkeit des Herzens", *Das Reich,* 22 November 1942, not reprinted.
[4] See above ch. 11, pp. 264-268.

trained and disciplined by National Socialism can stand the full truth." [1] Though Goebbels could not deny the serious challenge evoked by the adverse development in the East, he had no intention whatsoever of revealing the "full truth." Goebbels simply transformed a major blow into a simple setback. Thus he wrote at the same time in *Das Reich* [2]: "We have suffered a setback in the East; this is indisputable and shall also not be disputed. We have apparently somewhat underestimated the force of the enemy and for the reason that we could not imagine what can be extracted from a people, if total war is waged without any consideration for comfort and the standards of a social and civilised life." A year later he did not dare to reprint this article.

All propaganda in wartime is inclined to overplay the military successes and to play down the defeats of its own side. When in May 1943 the Allies had rounded up the last German and Italian troops, Goebbels tried to minimise the loss of Africa: "Europe is the centre of our warfare, Africa its periphery. Of course, the black Continent is of vital value for the national future of the Axis nations. But for the further continuation of the war they can do without it. Through it we do not lose any position which we would have to hold in order to win the war." [3] A month afterwards, when the Allied occupation of Sicily was imminent, Goebbels reverted to the same line: "That the fight for North Africa or for Pantellaria or Lampedusa cannot be compared with the fight for Europe stands to reason. . . . The fight for Europe has to be waged in Europe herself." [4]

More original, but also more risky, was the second trick Goebbels employed in many articles discarded later. It was the device to embellish the stormy present by contrasting it with the allegedly more sinister, or at least more unfavourable, past. He suggested that a year ago or three years ago at the beginning of the war, the German position had been much more threatened and uncertain. The present should appear in a rosier light at the expense of a manipulated past. "When we entered the war last year," Goebbels wrote in November 1942, "we faced by far more dangerous possibilities than we do this winter. . . . The front with which we embrace the European Continent is unbreakable." [5]

A fortnight later he played an even bolder variation of the same theme in a speech at a mass meeting in Berlin: "Had it been foretold to us in September 1939 that in December 1942 we would fight for the Volga, at Stalingrad and for Tunis and Biserta, then we would have been relieved of many worries. For at that time we did not look towards the

[1] The speech is reprinted in *Der steile Aufstieg*, pp. 167-204, under the heading "Nun, Volk, steh auf und Sturm brich los!" The quotation referred to is on p. 168.

[2] Article "Unser Wille und Unser Weg": *Das Reich*, 14 February 1943, not reprinted.

[3] Article "Mit souveräner Ruhe"; *Das Reich*, 23 May 1943, not reprinted.

[4] Article "Der Krieg im Zweilicht"; *Das Reich*, 27 June 1943, not reprinted.

[5] Article "Die Tapferkeit des Herzens", *Das Reich*, 22 November 1942, not reprinted.

Volga, but towards the Rhine and we did not fight for Biserta but for Saarbrücken. By this you can best realise the difference of our positions now and then." [1] Though at the time there had occurred, according to the press reports, "strong applause by his audience," when Goebbels read this passage, in the light of subsequent developments it is not surprising that he excluded the speech from *The Steep Ascent*. For early in 1944 this would have made ironic reading, at least to Germans who felt that the day might not be very far off when the nation would look once more to the Rhine, but this time much more anxiously.

Even after the disastrous winter of 1942-3 Goebbels stuck to this line, though with a slightly different emphasis. At the beginning of May, 1943, he wrote: "One should, for example, not compare our most favourable position in the autumn of 1942 with our most unfavourable position in the winter of 1943. One has to compare the beginning of the war with its present stage and one will arrive at the convincing conclusion that the Axis Powers have won by far more military successes in over 3½ years than they would have ever dared to imagine in September 1939." [2] Shortly before he had tried to reassure worried Party leaders in the heavily bombed town of Essen by reminding them that "none of us had dared to hope in his wildest dreams in December 1939 that our heroic *Wehrmacht* would ever be able to push the German defence lines as far into enemy territories as has actually happened." [3]

If the second trick played off the present against the past, Goebbels' third trick presented the German people with a blank cheque for a more cheerful future free from all the troubles of the present. The dreaded Anglo-American air raids on German towns for instance would soon fade away once the effect of the ruthless German U-boat war on England would make itself felt. In an article in April 1943 Goebbels argued: "Just as they [the English] have the instrument of air warfare at their disposal, so do we possess the instrument of the U-boat war which is by far more dangerous for England. Against it England has no counter-weapon, while we shall have one at our disposal against their air attacks to a sufficient degree very soon." [4] The same theme is embroidered with such sophistry in another article, also not reprinted. [5] For the time being the English are superior to us in this field of [air] warfare only from a psychological point of view; for the impact of the war in the air can be observed immediately by everybody whereas the effects of the U-boat war waged by us against the British Empire are noticed by the masses of the English people only after a certain lapse of time. But by then they will have already become inevitable."

Hints, sometimes distinct and sometimes vague, of future miracle

---

[1] *Hamburger Fremdenblatt,* 8 December 1942.
[2] Article "Wo stehen wir?"; *Das Reich,* 2 May 1943, not reprinted.
[3] Extracts from the speech were broadcast in the *Reichsprogramm* Radio Allouis, 10 April 1943.
[4] Article "Ceterum Censeo", *Das Reich,* 21 March 1943, not reprinted.
[5] Article "Stimmung und Haltung", *Das Reich,* 11 April 1943, not reprinted.

weapons with which to end or at least to weaken the enemy raids formed another means of diversion from the unpleasant present. As has been analysed above,[1] the idea of future retaliation on the English people for the present sufferings of the hard-pressed civilians in Western and Northern Germany would act as a tonic. An article on the regions particularly exposed to and harassed by enemy bombers makes this point: "If Churchill and his henchmen believe we had to face them defenceless and that they could play about with our innocent population without any danger and risk, then they have miscalculated. The fury and resentment which has piled up in the German people and in their leaders will explode at a given date. Our Days of Judgment (*Strafgerichte*) have, it is true, sometimes kept the world waiting a very long time, but they have always come. Until they come again, we have to fortify ourselves with patience and rigour." [2] When giving these hints, Goebbels may or may not have had the V-weapons in mind, which were then being developed.

A similar line, though less direct, was used in another article two months later. It attacked the erroneous English thesis that the Axis Powers could be forced to their knees by air warfare only. "The air war," wrote Goebbels on 27 June 1943, "is an extraordinarily effective additional means of military warfare in land operations. But it cannot bring about the decision by itself alone. Moreover, the losses suffered by the enemy in his day and night attacks during the last few weeks have been so high that he will soon have to face the question of whether they are still worth his while—quite apart from the fact that one day he will be given a reply which will make the expediency of his present air warfare highly problematical." [3]

As Goebbels excluded these articles from his book *Der steile Aufstieg* he must have felt that their arguments and devices were unlikely to assist in propping up civilian morale. With the endless and intensified activities of enemy bombers, Goebbels, who usually had nothing but contempt for the fleeting memory and the low intelligence of the masses, seems to have come to the conclusion that the sufferings and misery of the bereaved and dispossessed were likely to sharpen their minds and to render the tricks he had conjured with in these articles more transparent and discernible. It is perhaps significant that the austere tone of "The Thirty Articles of War for the German People," first published in September 1943, which later filled the last pages in Goebbels' final book,[4] concentrated on a rigid *levée en masse* of the Home Front. Whilst emphasising the Prussian virtues of a high sense of duty and of self-discipline in a besieged fortress, it no longer tried to console the readers through twisted parallels with the past or sanguine promises for the future.

[1] See above ch. 14, pp. 316-325.
[2] Article "Luftkriegsgebiete", *Das Reich*, 25 April 1943, not reprinted.
[3] Article "Der Krieg im Zwielicht", *Das Reich*, 27 June 1943, not reprinted.
[4] Article "Die 30 Kriegsartikel für das deutsche Volk", *Das Reich*, 26 September 1943, reprinted in *Der steile Aufstieg*, pp. 464-74. See also above ch. 12, pp. 286-287.

Bibliography

The following list includes only primary and secondary source material used for this study and with few exceptions referred to in the text or in footnotes. It does not aim at completeness.

(1) Unpublished Source Material

I. *Goebbels Tagebücher* (diaries) for the period 21st January, 1942, to 9th December, 1943 (incomplete). Photo copy Institut für Zeitgeschichte, Munich. (The original is with the Hoover Institution on War, Revolution and Peace, Stanford University).

II. The following collections of press directives and reports on the daily conferences at the Reich Ministry of Propaganda:

    (a) The Brammer collection: 1933-1936. Bundesarchiv Koblenz.

    (b) The Sänger collection: 1934-1943, Bundesarchiv Koblenz.

    (c) The Oberheitmann collection: 1939-1945, Institut für Publizistik, University of Münster. This includes "Vertrauliche Informationen," the "Tagesparole des Reichspressechefs" and "Sonder-Informationen."

(2) Collection of Documents

The Trial of the Major War Criminals before the International Military Tribunal (I.M.T.), 42 vols., Nuremberg, 1947-1949.

The Trial of German Major War Criminals, H.M.S.O., 22 parts, London, 1946-1950.

Proceedings of the 'Ministries Case', No. 11 (von Weizsäcker and 20 others) before U.S. Military Tribunal IV at Nuremberg, November 1947–April 1949.

Documents on International Affairs, 1933-1938 (R.I.I.A.), Oxford, 1934-1943.

Documents on International Affairs, 1939-1946 (R.I.I.A.), Oxford, 1951, Vol. I, March–September 1939.

Documents on German Foreign Policy, 1918-1945, Series C, vols., I-IV; Series D, vols. I-X, London, 1949-1962.

Documents on British Foreign Policy, 1919-1939, Third Series, vol. IV, 1939, London, 1951.

Dokumente der Deutschen Politik und Geschichte von 1848 bis zur Gegenwart, vols. IV and V, Berlin, n.d.

Le livre jaune français: documents diplomatiques 1938-1939, Paris, 1939.

The French Yellow Book. Diplomatic Documents 1938-1939, London, 1939.
Documents on American Foreign Relations 1941-42, Boston, 1942.
Soviet Foreign Policy during the Patriotic War. Documents and Materials, translated by A. Rothstein, London, n.d. [1946].
Polish-Soviet Relations 1918-1943. Official Documents issued by the Polish Embassy in Washington, 1945.
Declaration by the United Nations, Washington, January 1942. Cmd. 6388, London, 1942.
Der Nationalsozialismus: Dokumente 1933-1945. Herausgegeben und kommentiert von Walther Hofer, Frankfurt am Main, 1959.
20. Juli 1944. Herausgegeben von der Bundeszentrale für Heimatdienst. Third edition, Bonn, 1960.

(3) *Diaries*, etc.

Das Tagebuch von Joseph Goebbels 1925/26. Mit weiteren Dokumenten herausgegeben von Helmut Heiber. Schriftenreihe der *Vierteljahrshefte für Zeitgeschichte*, Munich, n.d. [1960].
Goebbels Tagebücher aus den Jahren 1942-43. Herausgegeben von Louis P. Lochner, Zürich, 1948.
The Goebbels Diaries, translated and edited by Louis P. Lochner, London, 1948. American edition, New York, 1948.

Ruth Andreas-Friedrich, *Der Schattenmann, Tagebuchaufzeichnungen 1938-1945*, Berlin, 1947. English edition: *Berlin Underground 1939-1945*, London, 1948.
Ciano's Diary 1939-1943, London, 1947.
Ambassador Dodd's Diary 1933-1938, London, 1941.
The von Hassel Diaries 1938-1944, London, 1948.
Hitlers Tischgespräche im Führerhauptquartier 1941-42, recorded by Dr. Hary Picker and edited by Gerhard Ritter, Bonn, 1951.
Hitler's Table Talk, with an Introductory Essay on The Mind of Adolf Hitler by H.R. Trevor-Roper, London, 1953.
Jochen Klepper, *Unter dem Schatten deiner Flügel. Aus den Tagebüchern der Jahre 1932-1942*, Stuttgart, 1957.
Wilfred von Oven, *Mit Goebbels bis zum Ende*, two vols., Buenos Aires, 1949-1950.
Das politische Tagebuch Alfred Rosenbergs 1933/34 und 1939/40, edited by Dr. Hans-Günther Seraphim, Quellensammlung zur Kulturgeschichte, vol. 8, Göttingen, 1958.
Alfred Rosenberg, *Letzte Aufzeichnungen*, Göttingen, 1955.
Robert Semmler, *Goebbels—The Man next to Hitler*, London, 1947.
William Shirer, *Berlin Diary. The Journal of a Foreign Correspondent 1934-41*, London, 1941.

Winston S. Churchill, *The Dawn of Liberation. War Speeches*. Compiled by Charles Eade, London, 1945.

(4) *Books and Collections of Speeches by Joseph Goebbels*

Lenin oder Hitler? Zwickau, 1926.
Die Zweite Revolution. Briefe an Zeitgenossen. Zwickau, n.d. [1926].
Das Buch Isidor. Ein Zeitbild von Lachen und Hass. By Mjoelnir and Dr. Goebbels, Munich, n.d. [1928].
Michael. Ein Deutsches Schicksal in Tagebuchblättern. Munich, 1929.
Kampf um Berlin. Der Anfang. Munich, 1932.
Wesen und Gestalt des Nationalsozialismus. Berlin, 1933.
Rede bei der Eröffnung der Reichskulturkammer. Frankfurt, 1933.
Revolution der Deutschen: 14 Jahre Nationalsozialismus, Goebbelsreden mit einleitenden Zeitbildern von Hein Schlecht. Oldenburg, 1933.
Signale der Neuen Zeit: 25 ausgewählte Reden. Munich, 1934.
Vom Kaiserhof zur Reichskanzlei. Eine historische Darstellung in Tagebuchblättern (vom 1. January 1932 bis zum 1. Mai 1933). Munich, 1934. English translation by Kurt Fiedler: *My Part in Germany's Fight*, London, 1935.
Der Angriff. Aufsätze aus der Kampfzeit. Munich, 1935.
Wetterleuchten. Aufsätze aus der Kampfzeit. Herausgegeben von Georg-Wilhelm Müller. Munich, 1939.
Kommunismus Ohne Maske. Munich, 1935.
English edition: *Communism with the Mask Off*, Berlin, 1935.
Der Bolschewismus in Theorie und Praxis. Rede von Reichsleiter Reichsminister Dr. Goebbels auf dem Parteikongress in Nürnberg 1936. Berlin [1936].
Die Zeit ohne Beispiel. Reden und Aufsätze aus den Jahren 1939/40/41. Munich, 1941.
Das Eherne Herz. Reden und Aufsätze aus den Jahren 1941/42. Munich, 1943.
Der Geistige Arbeiter im Schicksalskampf des Reiches. Munich, 1943.
Der Steile Aufstieg. Reden und Aufsätze aus den Jahren 1942/43. Munich, 1944.

(5) *Publications—Speeches—Table Talk by Adolf Hitler*

Mein Kampf. German editions: (a) Jubiläumsausgabe, Munich, 1939; (b) edition, Munich, 1943. Unabridged English translation, New York, 1939.
Adolf Hitlers Reden, ed. Dr. Ernst Boepple, Munich, 1933.
Der grossdeutsche Freiheitskampf, vol. III. Reden Adolf Hitlers vom 16. März 1941 bis 15. März 1942. Munich, 1943.
The Speeches of Adolf Hitler, April 1922–August 1939, ed. Norman H. Baynes, Oxford, 1942. 2 vols.
"Rede Hitlers vor der deutschen Presse" in *Vierteljahrshefte für Zeitgeschichte*, vol. VI, no. 2, April 1958.
Gerhard Ritter (ed.), *Hitlers Tischgespräche im Führerhauptquartier 1941-42*, Bonn, 1951.
Hitler's Table Talk 1914-1944. With an introductory essay on the Mind of Adolf Hitler by H.R. Trevor-Roper. London, 1953.

(6) *Newspapers and Periodicals,* etc.

Frankfurter Zeitung, 1933-1942.
Völkischer Beobachter (Berlin edition) 1933-1943.
                  (Vienna edition) 1944.
Hamburger Fremdenblatt, 1942-1944.
Das Reich, vol. 1-5, 1940-1944.
Süddeutsche Monatshefte, vols. 16-30, 1918-1933.
Deutscher Wochendienst, Munich, 1943.
Zeitschriften-Dienst, Munich, 1943.
Der Angriff, 1927-1933.
Neue Züricher Zeitung, 1943.
The Times, London, 1933-1941.

(7) *British Broadcasting Material (B.B.C.)*

B.B.C., German Service. Selected Scripts of Broadcasts to Germany,
    1941-1944.
Robert Lucas, *Teure Amalia vielgeliebter Weib! Briefe des gefreiten*
    Hirnschal an seine Frau in Zwieselsdorf, Zürich, n.d. (A selection
    of the B.B.C. feature in German broadcast under this title, 1940-
    1945).
B.B.C. Monitoring Reports on broadcasts from Germany 1941-1945.

(8) *Handbooks*

Organisationsbuch der NSDAP, third edition, Munich, 1937.
Führer durch die Behörden und Organisationen, ed. L. Münz, fourth edi-
    tion, Munich, 1939.
Handbuch des deutschen Rundfunk 1939-40, ed. Hans-Joachim Wein-
    brenner, Heidelberg, 1939.
Handbuch der Weltpresse: Eine Darstellung des Zeitungswesens aller
    Länder, ed. Professor Karl Bömer, third edition, Leipzig, 1937.
Germany: Basic Handbook, London, July 1944.
Who's Who in Germany and Austria, London, n.d. [April 1945].

(9) *Memoirs and Autobiographies*

Erwin von Aretin, *Krone und Kerker. Erinnerungen eines bayrischen*
    Edelmanns, Munich, 1955.
Winston S. Churchill, *The Second World War,* vol. II, *Their Finest Hour.*
    London, 1949. (Reprint Society ed. London, 1951).
Hugh Dalton, *The Fateful Years: Memoirs 1931-1945,* London, 1957.
Otto Dietrich, *12 Jahre mit Hitler,* Munich, 1955.
    English edition: *The Hitler I Knew,* London, 1957.
Hier Spricht Hans Fritzsche, Zürich, 1948.
Putzi Hanfstaengl, *Hitler: The Missing Years,* London, 1957.
Hansi et E. Tonnelet, *A travers les lignes ennemies. Trois années d'offen-*
    sive contre le moral allemand, Paris, 1922.
Field Marshal von Hindenburg, *Out of My Life,* London, 1920.

Heinrich Hoffmann, *Hitler was my Friend*, London, 1955.
Felix Kersten, *The Kersten Memoirs, 1940-1945*, London, 1956.
Albert Krebs, *Tendenzen und Gestalten der NSDAP*, Stuttgart, 1959.
Lutz Schwerin von Krosigk, *Es geschah in Deutschland*, Tübingen, 1951.
General Ludendorff, *My War Memoirs 1914-1918*, London, 1919.
Field Marshal Erich von Manstein, *Lost Victories*, London, 1958. Ed.
and trans. by Anthony G. Powell, London, 1958.
Otto Meissner, *Staatsekretär unter Ebert-Hindenburg-Hitler*, Hamburg,
1950.
Wolfgang von Putlitz, *The Putlitz Dossier*, London, 1957.
Otto Ernst Remer, *20. Juli 1944*, Hamburg, 1951.
Paul Reynaud, *In the Thick of the Fight 1930-1949*, London, 1955.
Friedrich Christian zu Schaumburg-Lippe, *Zwischen Krone und Kerker*,
Wiesbaden, 1952.
Walter Schellenberg, *The Schellenberg Memoirs*, London, 1956.
Otto Strasser, *Hitler and I*, London, 1940.
Viscount Templewood (Sir Samuel Hoare), *Nine Troubled Years*, Lon-
don, 1954.
H.G. Wells, *Experiment in Autobiography*, 2 vols., London, 1934.
A. Zoller, *Hitler Privat. Erlebnisbericht seiner Geheimsekretärin*, Düssel-
dorf, 1949.

(10) *Secondary Works*

Michael Balfour and John Maier, *Four Power Control in Germany and
Austria, 1945-1946*, London, 1956.
Lord Beaverbrook, *Men and Power, 1917-1918*, London, 1956.
Max Beloff (ed.), *On the Track of Tyranny. Essays presented by the
Wiener Library to Leonard G. Montefiore, O.B.E., on the Occasion
of his Seventieth Birthday*, London, 1960.
George Blond, *The Death of Hitler's Germany*, New York, 1954.
Professor Dr. F. Böhm, *Antisemitism*, Munich, 1958.
D. Bracher, *Die Auflösung der Weimarer Republik*, Second edition, Stutt-
gart, 1957.
G. Bruntz, *Allied Propaganda and the Collapse of the German Empire
in 1918*, London, 1938.
Arthur Bryant, *The Turn of the Tide, 1939-1945*, London, 1957.
Alan Bullock, *Hitler: A Study in Tyranny*, London, 1952.
J.R.M. Butler, *Lord Lothian (Philip Ker), 1882-1940*, London, 1960.
Borris von Borresholm (ed.), *Dr. Goebbels. Nach Aufzeichnungen aus
seiner Umgebung*, Berlin, 1949.
R.N. Carew-Hunt, *A Guide to Communist Jargon*, London, 1958.
Thomas Carlyle, *History of Frederick II of Prussia, called Frederick the
Great*. (centenary edition), London, 1898.
William Carroll, *Persuade or Perish*, Boston, 1948.
Gordon Alexander Craig, *The Politics of the Prussian Army 1640-1945*,
Oxford, 1955.
John S. Curtiss, *An Appraisal of the Protocol of Zion*, New York, 1942.
Sefton Delmer, *Black Boomerang*, London, 1962.
T.K. Derry, *The Campaign in Norway*, London, 1952.

Die Vollmacht des Gewissens. Herausgegeben von der Europäischen Publication e.V., Munich, 1956.

Rudolf Diels, *Luzifer Ante Portas: Zwischen Severing und Heidrich,* Zürich, n.d.

Jean-Marie Domenach, *La propagande politique,* Paris, 1955.

Leonard W. Doob, "Goebbels' Principles of Propaganda", in *Public Opinion and Propaganda,* ed. by D. Katz, D. Cartwright, S. Eldersveld and A. McGlunglee, New York, 1954.

Major-General Walker Dornberger, *V2,* London, 1954.

Erich Ebermayer und Hans Roos, *Gefährten des Teufels,* Hamburg, 1952.

Constantine FitzGibbon, *The Shirt of Nesus,* London, 1957.

Lindley Fraser, *Propaganda,* London, 1959.

A. Fredborg, *The Steel Wall: A Swedish Journalist in Berlin, 1941-1943,* New York, 1944.

Erich Fromm, *The Fear of Freedom,* London, 1942.

H.H. Fyfe, *Northcliffe. An Intimate Biography,* London, 1930.

H. Gunther-Roth and Kurt Wolff, *The American Denazification of Germany. A Historical Survey and Appraisal,* Ohio State University, Columbus, 1954.

Eugen Hadamovsky, *Der Rundfunk im Dienste der Volksführung,* Leipzig, n.d. [1934].

Eugen Hadamovsky, *Propaganda und Nationale Macht,* Oldenburg, 1933.

Walter Hagemann, *Publizistik im Dritten Reich,* Hamburg, 1948.

Walter Hagemann, *Vom Mythos der Masse,* Heidelberg, 1957.

Joseph Harsh, *Pattern of Conquest,* London, 1942.

Wolf Heinrichsdorff, *Die liberale Opposition in Deutschland seit den 30. Januar 1933* (dargestellt an der Entwicklung der "Frankfurter Zeitung"), Hamburg, 1937.

Fritz Hesse, *Hitler and the English,* London, 1954.

Theodor Heuss, *Hitlers Weg,* Stuttgart, 1932.

F.H. Hinsley, *Hitler's Strategy,* Cambridge, 1951.

Ein Jahrhundert Frankfurter Zeitung 1856-1956. Gegenwart Sonderheft, Frankfurt am Main 1956.

Louis de Jong, *The German Fifth Column in the Second World War,* London, 1956.

Sir Philip Joubert de la Forte, *Rocket,* London, 1957.

Bruno Kalmins, *Der Sowjetische Propagandastaat,* Stockholm, 1956.

Ursula von Kardorff, *Berliner Aufzeichnungen. Aus den Jahren 1942-45,* Munich, 1962.

Erich Kästner, *Bei Durchsicht meiner Bücher,* Zürich, n.d.

Walter Kaufmann, *Monarchism in the Weimar Republic,* New York, 1943.

Douglas M. Kelley, *22 Cells in Nuremberg,* New York, 1947.

Stephen King-Hall, *Total Victory,* London, 1941.

Ludwig Klages, *Der Geist als Widersacher der Seele,* 2 vols., Leipzig, 1929.

K. von Klemperer, *Germany's new Conservatism. Its History and its Dilemma in the Twentieth Century,* Princeton, 1957.

G.W. Klimsch, *Die Entwicklung des national-sozialistischen Film-Monopols von 1933-1940,* Munich, 1954.

Lionel Kochan, *Pogrom. 10 November 1938*, London, 1957.

R.R. Koerner, *So haben sie es damals gemacht. Die Propagandavorbereitungen zum Österreichanschluss durch das Hitlerregime 1933-1938*, Vienna, 1938.

Hans Kohn (ed.), *German History. Some new German Views*, London, 1954.

Ernst Kris and Hans Speyer, *German Radio Propaganda. Report on Home Broadcasts during the War*, New York, 1944.

Harold D. Lasswell and A. Kaplan, *Power and Society*, New Haven, 1950.

Harold D. Lasswell, *Propaganda Techniques in the World War*, London, 1927.

Annelore Leber (ed.), *Das Gewissen steht auf*, Berlin, 1956.

H. Lehmann-Haupt, *Art under Dictatorship*, New York, 1954.

Daniel Lerner (ed.), *Sykewar. Psychological Warfare against Germany. D-Day to VE-Day*, New York, 1949.

Daniel Lerner, *The Nazi Elite*, Hoover Institute Studies, Stanford, 1951.

Adolf Leschnitzer, *The Magic Background of Modern Antisemitism. An Analysis of the German Jewish Relationship*, New York, 1956.

P.M.A. Linebarger, *Psychological Warfare*, second edition, Washington, 1954.

Mathilde Ludendorff, *Deutscher Gottglaube*, Munich, 1927.

Vernon McKenzie, *Here lies Goebbels!* London, 1940.

J. Mackiewicz, *The Katyn Wood Murders*, London, 1957.

William Hardy McNeill, *America, Britain and Russia. Their Co-operation and Conflict, 1941-1946* (R.I.I.A.), London, 1953.

Roger Manvell and Heinrich Fraenkel, *Dr. Goebbels. His Life and Death*, London, 1960.

Charles Maurras, *Mes idées politiques*, Paris, 1937.

Hans Otto Meissner und Harry Wilde, *Die Machtgreifung*, Munich, 1958.

H.C. Meyer, *Mitteleuropa in German Thought and Action, 1815-1945*, The Hague, 1955.

Georg Wilhelm Müller, *Das Reichministerium für Volksaufklärung und Propaganda*, Berlin, 1940.

L.B. Namier, *1848. The Revolution of the Intellectuals*, London, 1944.

Heinz Pohle, *Der Rundfunk als Instrument der Politik*, Hamburg, 1955.

Leon Poliakov and Josef Wulf, *Das Dritte Reich und die Juden. Dokumente und Aufsätze*, Berlin, 1955.

Sir Arthur Ponsonby, *Falsehoods in Wartime*, London, 1928.

R. Pound and G. Harmsworth, *Northcliffe*, London, 1959.

Presse in Fesseln, Berlin, 1947.

Hans Georg Rahn, *Der nationalsozialistische Typ der Kampfzeitung*, Berlin, 1959.

Hermann Rauschning, *Hitler Speaks*, London, 1940.

Paul Otto Rave, *Kunst Diktatur im Dritten Reich*, Hamburg, 1949.

Eva G. Reichmann, *Die Flucht in den Hass. Die Ursachen der deutschen Judenkatastrophe*, Frankfurt a.M., n.d. [1956]

Eva G. Reichmann, *Hostages of Civilisation. The Social Sources of National Socialist Anti-Semitism*, London, 1950.

Curt Reiss, *Furtwüngler*, London, 1955.

Curt Reiss, *Joseph Goebbels,* London, 1948.
Gerhard Reitlinger, *The Final Solution,* London, 1953.
Gerhard Ritter, *The German Resistance,* London, 1958.
Stephen H. Roberts, *The House that Hitler Built,* eleventh edition, London, 1939.
Sydney Rogerson, *Propaganda in the Next War,* London, 1938.
Hans Rothfels, *The German Opposition to Hitler,* London, 1961.
Paul Seabury, *The Wilhelmstrasse,* Berkeley, 1954.
Karlheinz Schmeer, *Die Regie des öffentlichen Lebens im Dritten Reich,* Munich, 1956.
Inge Scholl, *Six against Tyranny,* London, 1955.
Karl Schwend, *Bayern zwischen Monarchie und Diktatur,* Munich, 1954.
William Shirer, *The Rise and Fall of the Third Reich. The History of Nazi Germany,* London, 1960.
Derrick Sington and Arthur Weidenfeld, *The Goebbels Experiment, A Study of the Nazi Propaganda Machine,* London, 1942.
Howard K. Smith, *Last Train from Berlin,* London and Sydney, 1943.
Werner Stephan, *Joseph Goebbels: Dämon einer Diktatur,* Stuttgart, 1949.
Edgar Stern-Rubarth, "The Methods of Political Propaganda" in *Public Opinion and World Politics,* ed. G. Wright, Chicago, 1933.
Dietrich Strothmann, *Nationalsozialistische Literaturpolitik,* Bonn, 1960.
Sir Campbell Stuart, *Opportunity Knocks Once,* London, 1952.
Sir Campbell Stuart, *Secrets of Crewe House. The Story of a Famous Campaign,* London, 1920.
Hermann Sündermann, *Das Dritte Reich. Eine Richtigstellung,* Leoni, 1959.
The History of The Times, vol. IV, London, 1952.
Hans Thimme, *Weltkrieg ohne Waffen,* Stuttgart, 1936.
Arnold Toynbee and Veronica M. Toynbee, *Hitler's Europe,* (R.I.I.A.), London, 1955.
Arnold Toynbee and others (eds.), *Survey of International Affairs, 1936, 1937, 1938* (R.I.I.A.), London, 1937-1951.
Arnold Toynbee and Veronica M. Toynbee, *The Eve of the War, 1939,* London, 1958.
Arnold Toynbee and Veronica M. Toynbee, *The Realignment of Europe,* (R.I.I.A.), London, 1955.
Arnold Toynbee and Frank T. G. Ashton-Gwatkin (eds.), *The World in March 1939,* (R.I.I.A.) London, 1952.
David Thomson, *Democracy in France. The Third Republic,* London, 1949.
H. R. Trevor-Roper, *The Last Days of Hitler,* London, 1947.
Heinrich von Treitschke, *Deutsche Geschichte im neunzehnten Jahrhundert,* London, 1885.
Ernst Troeltsch, *Spektatorbriefe. Aufsätze aus der deutschen Revolution und Weltpolitik 1918-1922,* Tübingen, 1924.
(U.N.E.S.C.O.), *The Third Reich,* London, 1955.
Sir Robert Vansittart, *Black Record. German Past and Present,* London, 1941.
H. Wanderscheck, *Weltkrieg und Propaganda,* Berlin, 1936.

Sir Charles Webster and Noble Frankland, *The Strategic Air Offensive against Germany 1939-1945*, 3 vols., London, 1961.

Günther Weissenborn (ed.), *Der lautlose Widerstand. Bericht über die Widerstandsbewegung des Deutschen Volkes 1933-1945*, Hamburg, 1953.

Ronald Wheatley, *Occupation Sea Lion. German Plans for the Invasion of England 1939-1942*. London, 1955.

J.W. Wheeler-Bennett, *Munich. Prologue to Tragedy*, London, 1948

J.W. Wheeler-Bennett, *Nemesis of Power. The German Army in Politics, 1918-1945*, London, 1953.

J. Baker White, *The Big Lie*, London, 1955.

J.K. Zawodny, *Death in the Forest. The Story of the Katyn Forest Massacre*, Notre Dame, Indiana, 1962.

Eberhard Zeller, *Geist der Freiheit. Der zwanzigste Juli 1944*, Third edition, Munich, 1956.

Index

DATE DUE